The Editor

PAUL B. ARMSTRONG is Professor of English and former Dean of the College at Brown University. He was previously Dean of the College of Arts and Sciences and Professor of English at the State University of New York at Stony Brook. He has also taught at the University of Oregon, the University of Copenhagen, Georgia Institute of Technology, the Free University of Berlin, and the University of Virginia. He is the author of *Play and the Politics of Reading: The Social Uses of Modernist Form, Conflicting Readings: Variety and Validity in Interpretation, The Challenge of Bewilderment: Understanding and Representation in James, Conrad, and Ford*, and *The Phenomenology of Henry James*. He is editor of the Norton Critical Edition of E. M. Forster's *Howards End*.

W. W. NORTON & COMPANY, INC.
Also Publishes

A NORTON CRITICAL EDITION

Joseph Conrad

HEART OF DARKNESS

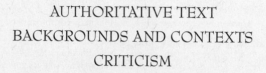

AUTHORITATIVE TEXT
BACKGROUNDS AND CONTEXTS
CRITICISM

FOURTH EDITION

Edited by

PAUL B. ARMSTRONG

BROWN UNIVERSITY

Previous Editions Edited by

ROBERT KIMBROUGH

UNIVERSITY OF WISCONSIN

W. W. NORTON & COMPANY

New York • London

W. W. Norton & Company has been independent since its founding in 1923, when William Warder Norton and Mary D. Herter Norton first published lectures delivered at the People's Institute, the adult education division of New York City's Cooper Union. The Nortons soon expanded their program beyond the Institute, publishing books by celebrated academics from America and abroad. By mid-century, the two major pillars of Norton's publishing program—trade books and college texts—were firmly established. In the 1950s, the Norton family transferred control of the company to its employees, and today—with a staff of four hundred and a comparable number of trade, college, and professional titles published each year—W. W. Norton & Company stands as the largest and oldest publishing house owned wholly by its employees.

The text of this book is composed in Fairfield Medium
with the display set in Bernhard Modern.
Composition by PennSet, Inc.
Manufacturing by the Courier Companies—Westford Division.
Production manager: Benjamin Reynolds.
Drawn art by John McAusland.

Library of Congress Cataloging-in-Publication Data
Conrad, Joseph, 1857–1924.
    Heart of darkness : an authoritative text, backgrounds and contexts, criticism / Joseph Conrad ; edited by Paul B. Armstrong.— 4th ed.
        p. cm. — (A Norton critical edition)
    Includes bibliographical references (p.   ).

ISBN 0–393–92636–2 (pbk.)

    1. Europeans—Africa—Fiction. 2. Conrad, Joseph, 1857–1924.
Heart of darkness. 3. Trading posts—Fiction. 4. Degeneration—Fiction.
5. Imperialism—Fiction. 6. Africa—Fiction. I. Armstrong, Paul B., 1949–
II. Title. III. Series.

PR6005.O4H4 2005
823'.912—dc22

2005052325

W. W. Norton & Company, Inc., 500 Fifth Avenue, New York, N.Y. 10110-0017
www.wwnorton.com

W. W. Norton & Company Ltd., Castle House,
75/76 Wells Street, London W1T 3QT

8 9 0

Contents

Criticism

Introduction

By now, more than a century after its first publication in 1899, *Heart of Darkness* is indisputably a "classic" text. This is both good and bad. The advantages are clear: a "classic" continues to be read, if only because it has already been read again and again and has thereby become part of the cultural air we breathe. If authors generally intend anything, it is that their works survive beyond their passing. Demonstrating a capacity to be interpreted in many different ways (some of these perhaps not imaginable at the time of writing) is how a text lives on. *Heart of Darkness* is a "classic" not because it has an immutable meaning that has endured for several generations but because readers have been able to attribute so many different meanings to it. The disadvantages of "classic" status may be less obvious but are nevertheless real and demonstrable, and *Heart of Darkness* has suffered from them as well. A text that has been read and analyzed and discussed as thoroughly as has Conrad's short novel runs the risk of becoming so familiar that it grows tired, losing its ability to surprise, please, or give rise to thought. A classic text also sets itself up as a target to be shot down—to be demystified for its complicity with prevailing ideologies whose interests are served by its preservation (and may, in the view of suspicious-minded critics, be the reason for its veneration). Especially after Marlon Brando's performance as Kurtz in *Apocalypse Now*, the once resounding words "the horror, the horror" have become a cliché. For that very reason (and perhaps ironically), some of the scathing attacks that have recently been directed at *Heart of Darkness*—exposing it as a racist, sexist, or imperialist text—have made it more interesting by showing new and unexpected ways of reading it and by revivifying the critical debates through which it is preserved. Attacking and demystifying a classic text can, paradoxically, give it a new lease on life.

The critical conversation about *Heart of Darkness* over the last two decades has been spirited and diverse. This is in no small measure because readers are still responding to Chinua Achebe's charge in a 1975 address that Conrad was "a bloody racist" and that his novel purveyed colonial stereotypes about Africans. These charges came at a time when literary criticism had begun to be

more deeply engaged with questions of social and political history
and when the role of imperialism in British and European literature
had emerged as a topic of particular importance. For critics with
such interests, the colonial subject matter of *Heart of Darkness* and
its status as an exemplar of modernist form provided compelling
reasons to return to it with new questions and fresh eyes.

They did not always agree, however, about what they saw there.
Does Conrad's text reflect the late nineteenth-century prejudices
of Europeans about Africa and the "civilizing mission" of imperialism, or is he a pioneering early critic of the blindness and cruelty
of colonial practices? Does his portrayal of Africans reinforce
nineteenth-century racial attitudes, or is the text critical of European claims to racial superiority and mindful of the humanity of
Africans and the suffering that imperialism caused? Is the novel's
formal experimentation a tool for critical inquiry that questions
dominant ideologies and challenges conventional assumptions, or
is Conrad's preoccupation with innovations in narrative form a de-
flection from political questioning and historical analysis—an attempt to cover up real atrocities with fanciful artistic structures?
Did Conrad's brief but intense experience in Africa open his eyes to
Europe's crimes, or did he visit and return with the same blinders
worn by others at his time?

As the selections in this Norton Critical Edition demonstrate, no
critical consensus has emerged around these questions. I have attempted to collect materials that demonstrate how they have been
debated and explored, with special emphasis on the years since
1988, when the last Norton *Heart of Darkness* appeared, so as to
enable students and teachers to participate in the inquiries and
controversies that this text still inspires. The novel's attitudes toward race and imperialism seem more complex now than they did
when Achebe first issued his blast, not only because critical discourse about these matters has become significantly more sophisticated in the last two decades, but also because his critique of
Conrad has prompted closer investigation and more rigorous analysis of these issues.

What can we learn from studying the history of the Congo and
European reactions to King Leopold's abuses there that would
shed light on Conrad's attitudes toward colonialism, Africa, and
Africans? The controversies spawned by Achebe's charges have
brought renewed interest and attention to the historical backgrounds out of which the novel arose, especially Conrad's journey
to the Congo in 1890 and his experience traveling upriver on the
steamer named in Leopold's honor, the *Roi des Belges* ("the King of
the Belgians"). This Norton Critical Edition includes new materials
about the Congo Free State that explain the history of its founding

before Conrad's visit and describe the abuses that led to its disman-
tlement a decade after *Heart of Darkness* was written. Two articles
from different editions of the *Encyclopædia Britannica* at the turn
of the century show how Conrad's contemporaries viewed the state
that Leopold administered as his private domain. The first article,
which appeared in 1902, the same year that *Heart of Darkness* was
published in book form, gives an account of the diplomatic maneu-
vering that led European nations to grant Leopold control of the
Congo and describes its geography and natural resources (especially the ivory and rubber that Europeans coveted). The second
article, a supplement added just eight years later, records how
growing public criticism throughout Europe of his brutal exploitation of the Congo compelled Belgium to end his regime. Leopold's
statement of his "sacred mission" to "civilize" the Congo stands in
stark contrast to two reports from eyewitnesses who traveled exten-
sively there. George Washington Williams, an African American
minister and lawyer, wrote Leopold a long letter after visiting the
Congo in 1890 in which he describes "the deceit, fraud, robberies,
arson, murder, slave-raiding, and general policy of cruelty . . . to the
natives" that he observed and that he appeals to the king to remedy.[1] Conrad apparently never met Williams, although they were in
the Congo at the same time, but he did know Sir Roger Casement,
whose 1904 "Congo Report" to the British Parliament was pivotal
in turning British public opinion against Leopold. Conrad wrote to
Casement in December 1903 as Casement was finishing his report:
"You cannot doubt that I form the warmest wishes for your success.
. . . It is an extraordinary thing that the conscience of Europe
which seventy years ago has put down the slave trade on humanitarian grounds tolerates the Congo State today. It is as if the moral
clock had been put back many hours."[2] Excerpts from Casement's
report, reprinted below, give graphic evidence of the brutality and
suffering that were endemic in Leopold's Congo.
    The leader of the Congo Reform Association in Britain, Edmund
D. Morel, used Casement's report and Conrad's letter of support in
his campaign against Leopold's atrocities. As the excerpt below
from his influential book *King Leopold's Rule in Africa* shows, however, Morel was opposed only to the techniques of "forced production" that Leopold's representatives employed and not to the
transformation of Africa into a market for European trade. One of
the best histories of the Congo Free State and the protest Morel or-

---

1. George Washington Williams, "An Open Letter to His Serene Majesty Leopold II, King
   of the Belgians and Sovereign of the Independent State of the Congo," reprinted in this
   Norton Critical Edition.
2. Joseph Conrad, letter to Roger Casement, 21 December 1903, reprinted in this Norton
   Critical Edition.

ganized against it is *King Leopold's Ghost: A Story of Greed, Terror, and Heroism in Colonial Africa* (1998) by Adam Hochschild. An excerpt from this book describes Conrad's six-month journey to Stanley Falls and speculates on a possible model for the figure of Kurtz. As Alan Simmons suggests in his account of Conrad's and Casement's friendship and their different experiences in Africa, criticism of *Heart of Darkness* has generally paid insufficient attention to the role of this text in shaping British public opinion about Leopold's exploitative reign. *Heart of Darkness* is not only a text about the history of imperialism but was itself a participant in that history through its effects on the Congo reform movement. Morel called it "the most powerful thing ever written on the subject."[3] Casement's report is very different from Conrad's novel, however, and Simmons analyzes the contrasts between them to ask about the capacity of language, whether a governmental document or a work of fiction, to adequately represent unspeakable atrocities.

In order to understand Conrad's attitude toward Africans and to evaluate the charge that he is "racist," it is important to situate *Heart of Darkness* in the discourse about race characteristic of his time. A new section of this Norton Critical Edition is consequently devoted to documents that represent a range of nineteenth-century attitudes toward race in general and the relation of Europeans to Africans in particular. As with the atrocities recounted by Williams and Casement, some of these materials may make for distasteful reading, but they should aid an understanding of Conrad's complicated, sometimes contradictory depictions of Africans that is informed by historical differences. One of the most influential nineteenth-century philosophers, the German idealist G. W. F. Hegel, made extraordinary generalizations about the supposed lack of a history or a fully developed moral or spiritual consciousness among Africans, claims that seemed so self-evident to him as to require little proof or argumentation. Charles Darwin, the founder of modern evolutionary theory, gave rise to a tradition of speculation about the role of different races in human evolution that sometimes had unfortunate manifestations in the eugenics movement and in Social Darwinism. (A useful history of Darwinism and race theory is Joseph L. Graves, *The Emperor's New Clothes: Biological Theories of Race at the Millennium* [New Brunswick: Rutgers UP, 2001].) As the excerpt reprinted below from *The Descent of Man* suggests, however, Darwin himself was more struck by the similarity of people from different races that to him proved that humans originated from a common ancestor than he was by dissimilari-

3. From a letter to Sir Arthur Conan Doyle, 7 October 1909, quoted in Alan Simmons, "The Language of Atrocity: Representing the Congo of Conrad and Casement," reprinted in this Norton Critical Edition.

ties that led other thinkers to treat races as if they were different species. By contrast, his contemporary Alfred Russel Wallace, a naturalist who independently developed a similar theory of evolution, argued that humans may have been at one time, long ago, "a homogeneous race" with a common origin, but that subsequent differential development of the "higher faculties" had resulted in the formation of distinctly different races.

Such reasoning prompted Francis Galton to speculate about the "comparative worth of different races" and to construct elaborate scales to measure relative intelligence that will strike a reader today as absurd and pseudo-scientific but that were regarded in the late nineteenth and early twentieth century as rigorous, objective analysis. Darwin viewed evolution as morally neutral and not necessarily progressive (a variant with adaptive advantages in a particular environment may help a species survive and propagate, but its value is entirely relative to its circumstances). Under the sway of Victorian convictions about moral progress, however, Social Darwinists equated the "survival of the fittest" with the constant improvement of a species. The prominent and influential Social Darwinist Benjamin Kidd, for example, regarded differences between races as an evolutionary progression in which, not surprisingly, European peoples epitomize the pinnacle of evolutionary success, with non-European peoples ranked as more or less "backward." By analyzing different contemporary uses of the term *race*, Peter Edgerly Firchow shows how the positions of thinkers like these were reflected in language and attitudes common among Conrad's audience. In the late nineteenth century, the semantic ground covered by *race*, he shows, also included territory that we would separate into the categories *ethnicity* and *nationality*. Such distinctions neither exonerate Conrad nor condemn him, but they may help the reader begin to delineate where his depictions of Africans reinforce assumptions characteristic of his period and where they challenge or depart from prevailing prejudices.

Conrad's own journey to the Congo in June–December 1890 began with high hopes and great expectations but ended in illness, exhaustion, and disillusionment. His autobiography *A Personal Record* recalls the youthful spirit of adventure with which he pointed to a map of Africa and declared, "When I grow up I shall go *there*."[4] He eventually did, and his letters document how his eager, naive sense of anticipation gave way to the sobering realization that he had not understood what he was getting himself into, as well as disappointment and anger at the failure of promises and expectations as he endured what turned out to be a life-threatening ordeal.

4. Joseph Conrad, *A Personal Record* (1912), reprinted in this Norton Critical Edition.

"Everything here is repellent to me," he wrote to his aunt from the Congo. "Men and things, but men above all. And I am repellent to them, also."[5] His diary is a particularly fascinating document, not only for the hints it gives of the observations and experiences that he drew on in composing *Heart of Darkness*, but also for all it does not say about what he must have been thinking, feeling, and enduring that eventually found expression in his novel. The short excerpt from his "Up-river Book" of detailed navigational notations shows the professional consciousness of a steamship officer at work, blocking out all of the emotions and reflections that the future author of *Heart of Darkness* must have been experiencing in order to focus single-mindedly on the task at hand. The retrospective reflections of the older and wiser Conrad in "Geography and Some Explorers" (written the year before he died in 1924 at age 66) provide a revealing summary of his African adventure. He recalls how he felt at Stanley Falls when he remembered his "boyish boast" that he had so inauspiciously fulfilled: "A great melancholy descended on me. Yes, this was the very spot. But there was no shadowy friend to stand by my side in the night of the enormous wilderness, no great haunting memory, but only . . . the distasteful knowledge of the vilest scramble for loot that ever disfigured the history of human conscience and geographical exploration. What an end to the idealized realities of a boy's daydreams!"[6]

Conrad was not as insightful or prolific a critic as, say, Henry James or Virginia Woolf, but his writings about art and literature are often eloquent and profound, and they offer interesting perspectives on his fictions, even if they are often more suggestive than conclusive. Such is the case with his most important declaration of his artistic intentions, his preface to *The Nigger of the "Narcissus,"* in which he famously says that he intends above all "to make you *see*." What kind of "vision" Conrad means to impart, however, has occasioned no end of critical commentary and illuminating disagreement. Other selections from his essays and prefaces reveal as much about Conrad's own art as they do about their putative topic. For example, when he defends a novelist's "freedom" in the essay "Books" and then worries lest this descend into "moral Nihilism," he expresses his own lifelong struggle between a desire to believe in what he called "a few very simple ideas" like "the idea of Fidelity"[7] and his sometimes corrosive skepticism that no conviction could withstand sustained critical scrutiny. When he calls Henry James

---

5. Joseph Conrad, letter to Marguerite Poradowska, 26 September 1890, reprinted in this Norton Critical Edition.
6. Joseph Conrad, "Geography and Some Explorers," *Last Essays* (1926), reprinted in this Norton Critical Edition.
7. Joseph Conrad, "A Familiar Preface" (1912), from *Conrad's Prefaces*, ed. Edward Garnett (London: J. M. Dent, 1937), p. 208.

"the historian of fine consciences," the double meaning of the French "conscience" suggests Conrad's own double fascination with the workings of consciousness and the morality of conduct.[8] Conrad's prefaces are not, however, always informative or reliable keys to his intentions, as is seen with the brevity and tantalizing elusiveness of his remarks on *Heart of Darkness* in the introduction to the volume *Youth*. The preface to *A Personal Record* gives revealing if perhaps somewhat disingenuous testimony to the deep affinity this Polish writer felt for the English language: "The truth of the matter is that my faculty to write in English is as natural as any other aptitude with which I might have been born."[9] Some of the letters I have reprinted have to do with the writing of *Heart of Darkness*, and others are important because of their more general observations about the art of the novel. This is true, for example, of his late letter to his disciple Richard Curle, in which Conrad declares: "Didn't it ever occur to you . . . that I knew what I was doing in leaving the facts of my life and even of my tales in the background? Explicitness, my dear fellow, is fatal to the glamour of all artistic work, robbing it of all suggestiveness, destroying all illusion."[1] This is a useful reminder that backgrounds and contexts, although revealing, invariably leave crucial matters unexplained.

As the selections of contemporary responses reprinted below suggest, Conrad's reviewers recognized almost immediately that *Heart of Darkness* was an unusual work that did not fit their customary categories. The reviews are interesting for what they suggest about his audience's attitudes toward the generic conventions of adventure- and travel-writing that Conrad invokes but overturns, as well as for the evidence they give of somewhat puzzled but admiring readers attempting to assimilate literary novelty. As the perceptive anonymous critic of the review in the *Athenaeum* notes, for example, Conrad has "made his own class of work as he has made his own methods," and "the reader is warned that this book cannot be read understandingly—as evening newspapers and railway novels are perused—with one mental eye closed and the other roving."[2] The selections I have reprinted from his fellow modern writers attempt to characterize Conrad's methods in ways that are relevant to *Heart of Darkness* even if their remarks were occasioned by other works. Henry James's wonderful description of Marlow's manner of

8. Joseph Conrad, "Henry James: An Appreciation" (1905), reprinted in this Norton Critical Edition.
9. Joseph Conrad, "Preface" to *A Personal Record* (1912), reprinted in this Norton Critical Edition.
1. Joseph Conrad, letter to Richard Curle, 24 April 1922, reprinted in this Norton Critical Edition.
2. Unsigned review, *Athenaeum* (20 December 1902), reprinted in this Norton Critical Edition.

rumination as "a prolonged hovering flight of the subjective over the outstretched ground of the case exposed" pertains to many of Conrad's works (and to James's own as well).[3] Virginia Woolf's 1924 literary obituary of Conrad similarly singles out Marlow's persona for praise, commenting perceptively on his double role as a memorable character and an extraordinary narrative device. By contrast, E. M. Forster is not so sure that the effort Conrad's works require is repaid, because "the secret casket of his genius contains a vapour rather than a jewel," a famous (or infamous) criticism that raises important questions about the effectiveness of his deliberate ambiguity.[4] Ford Madox Ford, a disciple and sometime collaborator, is more fulsome and unqualified in his praise of Conrad's methods. I have reprinted extensive selections from his entertaining and provocative memoir, with the caveat that his observations, although often extremely insightful, sometimes say more about Ford's techniques and aims than Conrad's (but it is also true that a reader can learn more about the methods of *Heart of Darkness* from Ford's masterpiece *The Good Soldier* than from any number of critical essays).

Choosing a representative selection of the criticism that has been generated by *Heart of Darkness* is a daunting challenge. I have reprinted selections from several classic treatments of the novel but have then devoted most of the section of critical essays to the debates and controversies since the last Norton Critical Edition of this text appeared. The most important and perceptive analysis of *Heart of Darkness* as a psychological journey is still Albert J. Guerard's 1958 study, which combines an unusual range of reference to the historical and autobiographical contexts of the novel with a writer's appreciation of a fellow novelist's craft. What it means for Conrad to make us "see" is elucidated with exemplary thoroughness and precision by Ian Watt, whose distinction between "impressionism" and "symbolism" as different modes of vision is important and useful. The selection by Peter Brooks demonstrates how a narratological and linguistic analysis of Conrad's narrative techniques can illuminate the novel's exploration of the inability of language to deliver the "truth" a reader may expect and desire. Although recent criticism has emphasized political and social issues, the psychological, existential, and linguistic concerns that have long interested readers of *Heart of Darkness* still resonate in the critical conversation, as can be seen in Daphna Erdinast-Vulcan's analysis of the modernity of Conrad's exploration of ethical responsibility and metaphysical desire. The final classic statement is, of course,

3. Henry James, "The New Novel" (1914), reprinted in this Norton Critical Edition.
4. E. M. Forster, "Joseph Conrad: A Note" (1921), reprinted in this Norton Critical Edition.

Achebe's essay, which is reprinted as he revised it for the 1988 Norton Critical Edition, with excerpts from the original version given in the notes when the revision is significant (for example, the earlier much-quoted phrase "bloody racist" which he later changed to the still pointed but less inflammatory "thoroughgoing racist").

The selections from recent criticism attempt to suggest the considerable range of disagreement, sometimes stark and sometimes subtle, that exists about Conrad's attitudes toward race and imperialism as well as the differing assessments of his art to which these conflicting interpretations give rise. Critics like Patrick Brantlinger, Marianna Torgovnick, and Edward Said develop Achebe's charges into a fuller critique of Conrad's complicity with the imperialist project. Said and Brantlinger disagree, however, over whether Conrad's narrative innovations allow him to express a critical perspective on the limitations of his era even though he cannot escape them (the "two visions" Said finds in the novel) or are evidence of a will to power through the domination of language that carries on the politics of imperial domination in another realm (Brantlinger's claim about Conrad's "will-to-style"). Hunt Hawkins offers a careful, detailed assessment of the ways in which the depictions of Africans in *Heart of Darkness* sometimes support Achebe's charges and sometimes call them into question. He and Anthony Fothergill find significant differences between Conrad's depiction of European exploitation of the Congo and late Victorian attitudes toward Africa and Africans, and their historical analyses portray Conrad as more a critic of imperial politics than a tacit defender of them. My own essay's interpretation of Conrad's narrative experiments in *Heart of Darkness* attempts to work from style to politics by suggesting that contradictions in the text demonstrate the limits of his period's ways of knowing Africans even as he tries to get beyond them by transforming problems he cannot resolve into challenges for the reader. When J. Hillis Miller asks if we should still read *Heart of Darkness*, he answers in the affirmative because he believes that studying Conrad's stylistic innovations and verbal strategies can be a way of rigorously exploring ethical and political dilemmas that defy easy, univocal resolution. For Miller and myself, Conrad's art is a critical instrument that exposes dominant ideologies of race and empire and points beyond them, whereas for Brantlinger and Torgovnick, the aesthetic dimension of the text is part of the deception that must be unmasked.

As the discussion of race and imperialism in *Heart of Darkness* has become more complicated and diverse, gender has also emerged as an interesting and complex topic. This is perhaps surprising because Conrad the novelist of the sea, adventure, and exploration has seemed to many readers to be a man's writer with a peculiar blindness to women and their concerns. For some critics, however, this very blindness offers revealing insights about dominant sexual and cultural attitudes. Torgovnick focuses on the portrayal of the African woman in *Heart of Darkness* to demystify a fascination with "primitivism" and the "savage" body that in her view says much about European fantasies about masculinity, desire, and power and their role in forming the sensibility of avant-garde art. Jeremy Hawthorn argues, however, that the novel's portrayal of gender divisions reinforces its critique of imperialism and that Conrad is skeptical of the illusions of ineffectual, hypocritical idealists in their claims not only about women but also about the European mission in Africa. Andrew M. Roberts explores the male homosocial bonds that are forged in the construction of women as an "other" and that are also at work in the pursuit of empire as well as in the narrative relation between Marlow and his audience on the *Nellie*—homologous forms of male-male relationship and desire in the novel's representations of gender, imperialism, and the narrative contract. Lissa Schneider shows that the iconography of the novel's depiction of the feminine both replicates and criticizes idealizations that pervade European art and literature, exposing the masculine vanity and will-to-power that Conrad nevertheless participates in and carries on. Whether Conrad purveys illusions or debunks them is once again open to dispute, and this ambiguity has continued to inspire commentary not only about his politics but also about his art and his moral vision.

A film based on a novel often provides illuminating perspectives on the source-text, if only because the differences between them typically help to foreground characteristics of the literary work that are lost or transformed in the translation from one genre to another. The relation between *Heart of Darkness* and Francis Ford Coppola's 1979 movie *Apocalypse Now*, a masterpiece and a "classic" in its own right, is much more intimate and profound, however, than the typical case of the conversion of a novel to film. The two works are inextricably linked in the cultural imagination and are frequently taught together, and a wealth of serious scholarship about their relationship now exists. I have selected examples that provide a close reading of the parallels between them (Louis Grieff's careful interpretation of their similarities and differences), that study their different originating contexts (Margot Norris's analysis of modernism and Vietnam), and that explore how both works have acquired iconic status in popular culture (Linda Dryden's analysis of Conrad's relation to Coppola, *The Simpsons*, and *Star Trek*).

The text of *Heart of Darkness* reprinted here is the version masterfully prepared by Robert Kimbrough for previous Norton editions of the novel. The "Textual Appendix" includes Kimbrough's helpful history of the text and an explanation of the editorial principles he followed in revising the 1921 Heinemann edition based on evidence from other editions, the surviving partial typescript, and the manuscript. I have collected variants from the typescript and the manuscript in the appendix, where they are readily available but will not distract the general reader, and I have added materials from both sources based on my own inspection of them. The footnotes to the text have been entirely revised with an eye to the needs of students today.

I am glad to acknowledge the assistance I have received in assembling this edition. I owe a special debt to Hunt Hawkins, eminent Conradian and good friend from graduate school, where I learned from him what a firsthand appreciation of Africa and a detailed understanding of its history could reveal about *Heart of Darkness*. He graciously availed me of his expertise on Conrad and the Congo, the Achebe debate, and nineteenth-century race-theory with a thoroughness and a generosity for which I am deeply grateful. I also benefited from the wisdom and wide knowledge of Jeremy Hawthorn, who provided prompt and thoughtful criticisms of my plans at various stages. The ever-generous Keith Carabine was typically helpful and encouraging as well. He and Owen Knowles offered good advice at an early stage. Brown colleagues Jonathan Waage and Lundy Braun gave me guidance about evolutionary theory and current biological thinking about race. I am also glad to thank my longtime mentor, teacher, and friend Tom Moser, whose unfailing support and guidance have meant more to me over the years than he probably realizes or than I can easily express. I received gracious and professional help from the staffs of the Berg Collection at the New York Public Library, the Beinecke Library at Yale, the Houghton Library at Harvard, and the John Hay and Rockefeller libraries at Brown. I could also not have managed without the cheerful and ready assistance of the staff in the office of the Dean of the College, including especially Barbara Sardy, Ivone Aubin, and Betsy Valle.

As always, I am grateful to my children, Tim, Maggie, and Jack, for the example of their independent spirit and for making sure that I would not "go through life with eyes half shut, with dull ears, with dormant thoughts" (the everyday complacency Marlow warns against in *Lord Jim*). As for Beverly, a complacent life was never what we bargained for—and it is not what we have—and this is only a small part of my ever-growing debt to her.

The Text of
HEART OF DARKNESS

Heart of Darkness

I

The *Nellie*, a cruising yawl, swung to her anchor without a flutter of the sails and was at rest. The flood had made, the wind was nearly calm, and being bound down the river the only thing for it was to come to and wait for the turn of the tide.

The Sea-reach of the Thames stretched before us like the beginning of an interminable waterway. In the offing[1] the sea and the sky were welded together without a joint and in the luminous space the tanned sails of the barges drifting up with the tide seemed to stand still in red clusters of canvas, sharply peaked with gleams of varnished sprits. A haze rested on the low shores that ran out to sea in vanishing flatness. The air was dark above Gravesend,[2] and farther back still seemed condensed into a mournful gloom brooding motionless over the biggest, and the greatest, town on earth.

The Director of Companies was our Captain and our host. We four affectionately watched his back as he stood in the bows looking to seaward. On the whole river there was nothing that looked half so nautical. He resembled a pilot which to a seaman is trustworthiness personified. It was difficult to realise his work was not out there in the luminous estuary, but behind him, within the brooding gloom.

Between us there was as I have already said somewhere,[3] the bond of the sea. Besides holding our hearts together through long periods of separation it had the effect of making us tolerant of each other's yarns—and even convictions. The Lawyer—the best of old fellows—had, because of his many years and many virtues, the only cushion on deck and was lying on the only rug. The Accountant had brought out already a box of dominoes and was toying architecturally with the bones. Marlow sat cross-legged right aft, leaning against the mizzen-mast. He had sunken cheeks, a yellow complexion, a straight back, an ascetic aspect, and with his arms dropped, the palms of hands outwards, resembled an idol. The Director sat-

1. The more distant part of the sea.
2. The last major town in the Thames estuary, twenty-six miles east of London.
3. In "Youth" (1898), the first story to use Marlow as narrator, reprinted with "Heart of Darkness" in *Youth* (1902).

isfied the anchor had good hold made his way aft and sat down amongst us. We exchanged a few words lazily. Afterwards there was silence on board the yacht. For some reason or other we did not begin that game of dominoes. We felt meditative and fit for nothing but placid staring. The day was ending in a serenity of still and exquisite brilliance. The water shone pacifically, the sky without a speck was a benign immensity of unstained light, the very mist on the Essex marshes was like a gauzy and radiant fabric hung from the wooded rises inland and draping the low shores in diaphanous folds. Only the gloom to the west brooding over the upper reaches became more sombre every minute as if angered by the approach of the sun.

And at last in its curved and imperceptible fall the sun sank low, and from glowing white changed to a dull red without rays and without heat, as if about to go out suddenly, stricken to death by the touch of that gloom brooding over a crowd of men.

Forthwith a change came over the waters, and the serenity became less brilliant but more profound. The old river in its broad reach rested unruffled at the decline of day after ages of good service done to the race that peopled its banks, spread out in the tranquil dignity of a waterway leading to the uttermost ends of the earth. We looked at the venerable stream not in the vivid flush of a short day that comes and departs for ever but in the august light of abiding memories. And indeed nothing is easier for a man who has, as the phrase goes, "followed the sea" with reverence and affection, than to evoke the great spirit of the past upon the lower reaches of the Thames. The tidal current runs to and fro in its unceasing service crowded with memories of men and ships it has borne to the rest of home or to the battles of the sea. It had known and served all the men of whom the nation is proud, from Sir Francis Drake to Sir John Franklin, knights all, titled and untitled— the great knights-errant of the sea.[4] It had borne all the ships whose names are like jewels flashing in the night of time, from the *Golden Hind* returning with her round flanks full of treasure, to be visited by the Queen's Highness and thus pass out of the gigantic tale, to the *Erebus* and *Terror*, bound on other conquests— and that never returned. It had known the ships and the men. They had sailed from Deptford, from Greenwich, from Erith—the adventurers and the settlers; kings' ships and the ships of men on Change; Captains, Admirals, the dark "interlopers" of the Eastern trade, and the commissioned "Generals" of East India

4. Drake was the first Englishman to circumnavigate the globe (1577–88), sailing in the *Golden Hind*, and was knighted by Queen Elizabeth I; Franklin led an ill-fated expedition (1845–48) in search of the Northwest Passage in the ships *Erebus* and *Terror*, which became stuck in the Arctic ice.

fleets.[5] Hunters for gold or pursuers of fame they all had gone out on that stream, bearing the sword, and often the torch, messengers of the might within the land, bearers of a spark from the sacred fire. What greatness had not floated on the ebb of that river into the mystery of an unknown earth? . . . The dreams of men, the seed of commonwealths, the germs of empires.

The sun set; the dusk fell on the stream and lights began to appear along the shore. The Chapman lighthouse, a three-legged thing erect on a mud-flat, shone strongly. Lights of ships moved in the fairway—a great stir of lights going up and going down. And farther west on the upper reaches the place of the monstrous town was still marked ominously on the sky, a brooding gloom in sunshine, a lurid glare under the stars.

"And this also," said Marlow suddenly, "has been one of the dark places of the earth."

He was the only man of us who still "followed the sea." The worst that could be said of him was that he did not represent his class. He was a seaman, but he was a wanderer too, while most seamen lead, if one may so express it, a sedentary life. Their minds are of the stay-at-home order, and their home is always with them—the ship—and so is their country—the sea. One ship is very much like another and the sea is always the same. In the immutability of their surroundings the foreign shores, the foreign faces, the changing immensity of life glide past, veiled not by a sense of mystery but by a slightly disdainful ignorance, for there is nothing mysterious to a seaman unless it be the sea itself which is the mistress of his existence and as inscrutable as Destiny. For the rest, after his hours of work, a casual stroll or a casual spree on shore suffices to unfold for him the secret of a whole continent, and generally he finds the secret not worth knowing. The yarns of seamen have a direct simplicity, the whole meaning of which lies within the shell of a cracked nut. But Marlow was not typical (if his propensity to spin yarns be excepted) and to him the meaning of an episode was not inside like a kernel but outside, enveloping the tale which brought it out only as a glow brings out a haze, in the likeness of one of these misty halos that, sometimes, are made visible by the spectral illumination of moonshine.

His remark did not seem at all surprising. It was just like Marlow. It was accepted in silence. No one took the trouble to grunt even, and presently he said very slow:

"I was thinking of very old times, when the Romans first came here, nineteen hundred years ago—the other day. . . . Light came out of this river since—you say Knights? Yes, but it is like a running blaze

5. Deptford, Greenwich, and Erith are ports on the Thames; the Exchange is the financial and trading center of London; "interlopers" trespassed on the rights of the trade monopoly held by the East India Company.

on a plain, like a flash of lightning in the clouds. We live in the flicker—may it last as long as the old earth keeps rolling! But darkness was here yesterday. Imagine the feelings of a commander of a fine—what d'ye call 'em—trireme in the Mediterranean, ordered suddenly to the north; run overland across the Gauls in a hurry; put in charge of one of these craft the legionaries—a wonderful lot of handy men they must have been too—used to build, apparently by the hundred, in a month or two, if we may believe what we read.[6] Imagine him here—the very end of the world, a sea the colour of lead, a sky the colour of smoke, a kind of ship about as rigid as a concertina— and going up this river with stores, or orders, or what you like. Sandbanks, marshes, forests, savages, precious little to eat fit for a civilised man, nothing but Thames water to drink. No Falernian wine here, no going ashore. Here and there a military camp lost in a wilderness like a needle in a bundle of hay—cold, fog, tempests, disease, exile, and death—death skulking in the air, in the water, in the bush. They must have been dying like flies here. Oh yes—he did it. Did it very well too, no doubt, and without thinking much about it either, except afterwards to brag of what he had gone through in his time, perhaps. They were men enough to face the darkness. And perhaps he was cheered by keeping his eye on a chance of promotion to the fleet at Ravenna,[7] by and by, if he had good friends in Rome and survived the awful climate. Or think of a decent young citizen in a toga—perhaps too much dice, you know—coming out here in the train of some prefect, or tax-gatherer, or trader even—to mend his fortunes. Land in a swamp, march through the woods, and in some inland post feel the savagery. The utter savagery had closed round him—all that mysterious life of the wilderness that stirs in the forest, in the jungles, in the hearts of wild men. There's no initiation either into such mysteries. He has to live in the midst of the incomprehensible which is also detestable. And it has a fascination too, that goes to work upon him. The fascination of the abomination—you know. Imagine the growing regrets, the longing to escape, the powerless disgust, the surrender—the hate."

He paused.

"Mind," he began again, lifting one arm from the elbow, the palm of the hand outwards, so that with his legs folded before him he had the pose of a Buddha preaching in European clothes and without a lotus-flower—"Mind, none of us would feel exactly like this. What saves us is efficiency—the devotion to efficiency. But these chaps were not much account really. They were no colonists, their adminis-

6. Roman legions conquered Britain in the first century C.E. Trireme: galley with three banks of oars. Gaul: roughly the equivalent of modern France, conquered by Julius Caesar in 58–51 B.C.E.
7. The chief Roman naval base on the Adriatic Sea.

tration was merely a squeeze, and nothing more, I suspect. They were conquerors, and for that you want only brute force—nothing to boast of, when you have it, since your strength is just an accident arising from the weakness of others. They grabbed what they could get for the sake of what was to be got. It was just robbery with violence, aggravated murder on a great scale, and men going at it blind—as is very proper for those who tackle a darkness. The conquest of the earth, which mostly means the taking it away from those who have a different complexion or slightly flatter noses than ourselves, is not a pretty thing when you look into it too much. What redeems it is the idea only. An idea at the back of it, not a sentimental pretence but an idea; and an unselfish belief in the idea—something you can set up, and bow down before, and offer a sacrifice to. . . ."

He broke off. Flames glided on the river, small green flames, red flames, white flames, pursuing, overtaking, joining, crossing each other—then separating slowly or hastily. The traffic of the great city went on in the deepening night upon the sleepless river. We looked on, waiting patiently—there was nothing else to do till the end of the flood; but it was only after a long silence, when he said in a hesitating voice, "I suppose you fellows remember I did once turn fresh-water sailor for a bit," that we knew we were fated, before the ebb began to run,[8] to hear about one of Marlow's inconclusive experiences.

"I don't want to bother you much with what happened to me personally," he began, showing in this remark the weakness of many tellers of tales who seem so often unaware of what their audience would best like to hear; "yet to understand the effect of it on me you ought to know how I got out there, what I saw, how I went up that river to the place where I first met the poor chap. It was the farthest point of navigation and the culminating point of my experience. It seemed somehow to throw a kind of light on everything about me—and into my thoughts. It was sombre enough too—and pitiful—not extraordinary in any way—not very clear either. No. Not very clear. And yet it seemed to throw a kind of light.

"I had then, as you remember, just returned to London after a lot of Indian Ocean, Pacific, China Seas—a regular dose of the East—six years or so, and I was loafing about, hindering you fellows in your work and invading your homes, just as though I had got a heavenly mission to civilise you. It was very fine for a time, but after a bit I did get tired of resting. Then I began to look for a ship— I should think the hardest work on earth. But the ships wouldn't even look at me. And I got tired of that game too.

"Now when I was a little chap I had a passion for maps. I would

8. The "flood" is the flowing in of the tide, and the "ebb" is its return to sea.

look for hours at South America, or Africa, or Australia and lose myself in all the glories of exploration. At that time there were many blank spaces on the earth and when I saw one that looked particularly inviting on a map (but they all look that) I would put my finger on it and say: When I grow up I will go there. The North Pole was one of these places I remember. Well, I haven't been there yet and shall not try now. The glamour's off. Other places were scattered about the Equator and in every sort of latitude all over the two hemispheres. I have been in some of them and . . . well, we won't talk about that. But there was one yet—the biggest—the most blank, so to speak—that I had a hankering after.

"True, by this time it was not a blank space any more. It had got filled since my boyhood with rivers and lakes and names. It had ceased to be a blank space of delightful mystery—a white patch for a boy to dream gloriously over. It had become a place of darkness. But there was in it one river especially, a mighty big river that you could see on the map, resembling an immense snake uncoiled, with its head in the sea, its body at rest curving afar over a vast country and its tail lost in the depths of the land. And as I looked at the map of it in a shop-window it fascinated me as a snake would a bird—a silly little bird. Then I remembered there was a big concern, a Company for trade on that river. Dash it all, I thought to myself, they can't trade without using some kind of craft on that lot of fresh water—steamboats! Why shouldn't I try to get charge of one. I went on along Fleet Street,[9] but could not shake off the idea. The snake had charmed me.

"You understand it was a Continental concern, that Trading Society; but I have a lot of relations living on the Continent, because it's cheap and not so nasty as it looks—they say.

"I am sorry to own I began to worry them. This was already a fresh departure for me. I was not used to get things that way, you know. I always went my own road and on my own legs where I had a mind to go. I wouldn't have believed it of myself, but then—you see—I felt somehow I must get there by hook or by crook. So I worried them. The men said, 'My dear fellow,' and did nothing. Then—would you believe it—I tried the women. I, Charlie Marlow, set the women to work—to get a job! Heavens! Well, you see, the notion drove me. I had an aunt, a dear enthusiastic soul. She wrote: 'It will be delightful. I am ready to do anything, anything for you. It is a glorious idea. I know the wife of a very high personage in the Administration and also a man who has lots of influence with,' etc. etc. She was determined to make no end of fuss to get me appointed skipper of a river steamboat, if such was my fancy.

9. A central business street in London, location of many newspaper offices.

"I got my appointment—of course; and I got it very quick. It appears the Company had received news that one of their Captains had been killed in a scuffle with the natives. This was my chance and it made me the more anxious to go. It was only months and months afterwards, when I made the attempt to recover what was left of the body, that I heard the original quarrel arose from a misunderstanding about some hens. Yes, two black hens. Fresleven—that was the fellow's name, a Dane—thought himself wronged somehow in the bargain, so he went ashore and started to hammer the chief of the village with a stick. Oh, it didn't surprise me in the least to hear this and at the same time to be told that Fresleven was the gentlest, quietest creature that ever walked on two legs. No doubt he was, but he had been a couple of years already out there engaged in the noble cause, you know, and he probably felt the need at last of asserting his self-respect in some way. Therefore he whacked the old nigger mercilessly while a big crowd of his people watched him, thunderstruck, till some man—I was told the chief's son—in desperation at hearing the old chap yell, made a tentative jab with a spear at the white man—and of course it went quite easy between the shoulder-blades. Then the whole population cleared into the forest expecting all kinds of calamities to happen, while, on the other hand, the steamer Fresleven commanded left also in a bad panic, in charge of the engineer, I believe. Afterwards nobody seemed to trouble much about Fresleven's remains till I got out and stepped into his shoes. I couldn't let it rest, though, but when an opportunity offered at last to meet my predecessor, the grass growing through his ribs was tall enough to hide his bones. They were all there. The supernatural being had not been touched after he fell. And the village was deserted, the huts gaped black, rotting, all askew within the fallen enclosures. A calamity had come to it, sure enough. The people had vanished. Mad terror had scattered them, men, women, and children, through the bush and they had never returned. What became of the hens I don't know either. I should think the cause of progress got them, anyhow. However, through this glorious affair I got my appointment before I had fairly begun to hope for it.

"I flew around like mad to get ready and before forty-eight hours I was crossing the Channel to show myself to my employers and sign the contract. In a very few hours I arrived in a city that always makes me think of a whited sepulchre.[1] Prejudice no doubt. I had no difficulty in finding the Company's offices. It was the biggest thing in the town and everybody I met was full of it. They were going to run an oversea empire and make no end of coin by trade.

---

1. Tomb, grave.

"A narrow and deserted street in deep shadow, high houses, innumerable windows with venetian blinds, a dead silence, grass sprouting between the stones, imposing carriage archways right and left, immense double doors standing ponderously ajar. I slipped through one of these cracks, went up a swept and ungarnished staircase, as arid as a desert, and opened the first door I came to. Two women, one fat and the other slim, sat on straw-bottomed chairs knitting black wool. The slim one got up and walked straight at me—still knitting with downcast eyes—and only just as I began to think of getting out of her way, as you would for a somnambulist, stood still, and looked up. Her dress was as plain as an umbrella cover, and she turned round without a word and preceded me into a waiting-room. I gave my name, and looked about. Deal table in the middle, plain chairs all round the walls, on one end a large shining map marked with all the colours of a rainbow. There was a vast amount of red[2]—good to see at any time because one knows that some real work is done in there—a deuce of a lot of blue, a little green, smears of orange, and, on the East Coast, a purple patch, to show where the jolly pioneers of progress drink the jolly lager-beer. However, I wasn't going into any of these. I was going into the yellow. Dead in the centre. And the river was there—fascinating—deadly—like a snake. Ough. A door opened, a white-haired secretarial head, but wearing a compassionate expression, appeared, and a skinny forefinger beckoned me into the sanctuary. Its light was dim and a heavy writing-desk squatted in the middle. From behind that structure came out an impression of pale plumpness in a frock-coat. The great man himself. He was five feet six, I should judge, and had his grip on the handle-end of ever so many millions. He shook hands, I fancy, murmured vaguely, was satisfied with my French. *Bon voyage.*

"In about forty-five seconds I found myself again in the waiting-room with the compassionate secretary who full of desolation and sympathy made me sign some document. I believe I undertook amongst other things not to disclose any trade secrets. Well, I am not going to.

"I began to feel slightly uneasy. You know I am not used to such ceremonies and there was something ominous in the atmosphere. It was just as though I had been let into some conspiracy—I don't know—something not quite right, and I was glad to get out. In the outer room the two women knitted black wool feverishly. People were arriving and the younger one was walking back and forth introducing them. The old one sat on her chair. Her flat cloth slippers were propped up on a foot-warmer and a cat reposed on her

---

2. The color typically used to mark the territories of the British Empire.

lap. She wore a starched white affair on her head, had a wart on one cheek, and silver-rimmed spectacles hung on the tip of her nose. She glanced at me above the glasses. The swift and indifferent placidity of that look troubled me. Two youths with foolish and cheery countenances were being piloted over and she threw at them the same quick glance of unconcerned wisdom. She seemed to know all about them and about me too. An eerie feeling came over me. She seemed uncanny and fateful. Often far away there I thought of these two, guarding the door of Darkness, knitting black wool as for a warm pall, one introducing, introducing continuously to the unknown, the other scrutinising the cheery and foolish faces with unconcerned old eyes. '*Ave!* Old knitter of black wool. *Morituri te salutant.*'[3] Not many of those she looked at ever saw her again—not half—by a long way.

"There was yet a visit to the Doctor. 'A simple formality,' assured me the secretary with an air of taking an immense part in all my sorrows. Accordingly a young chap wearing his hat over the left eyebrow, some clerk I suppose—there must have been clerks in the business, though the house was as still as a house in a city of the dead—came from somewhere upstairs, and led me forth. He was shabby and careless, with ink-stains on the sleeves of his jacket, and his cravat was large and billowy under a chin shaped like the toe of an old boot. It was a little too early for the Doctor, so I proposed a drink and thereupon he developed a vein of joviality. As we sat over our vermuths he glorified the Company's business and by and by I expressed casually my surprise at him not going out there. He became very cool and collected all at once. 'I am not such a fool as I look, quoth Plato to his disciples,' he said sententiously,[4] emptied his glass with great resolution, and we rose.

"The old doctor felt my pulse, evidently thinking of something else the while. 'Good! Good for there,' he mumbled, and then with a certain eagerness asked me whether I would let him measure my head. Rather surprised, I said Yes, when he produced a thing like callipers and got the dimensions back and front and every way, taking notes carefully. He was an unshaven little man in a thread-bare coat like a gaberdine with his feet in slippers, and I thought him a harmless fool. 'I always ask leave, in the interests of science, to measure the crania of those going out there,' he said. 'And when they come back too?' I asked. 'Oh, I never see them,' he remarked, 'and, moreover the changes take place inside, you know.' He smiled as if at some quiet joke. 'So you are going out there. Famous. Interesting too.' He gave me a searching glance and made another note.

3. "Hail! . . . We who are about to die salute you." Proclaimed by Roman gladiators as they marched past the emperor.
4. Pithily; not, however, a maxim of Plato's.

'Ever any madness in your family?' he asked in a matter-of-fact tone. I felt very annoyed. 'Is that question in the interests of science too?' 'It would be,' he said without taking notice of my irritation, 'interesting for science to watch the mental changes of individuals on the spot, but . . .' 'Are you an alienist?'[5] I interrupted. 'Every doctor should be—a little,' answered that original imperturbably. 'I have a little theory which you Messieurs who go out there must help me to prove. This is my share in the advantages my country shall reap from the possession of such a magnificent dependency. The mere wealth I leave to others. Pardon my questions, but you are the first Englishman coming under my observation. . . .' I hastened to assure him I was not in the least typical. 'If I were,' said I, 'I wouldn't be talking like this with you.' 'What you say is rather profound and probably erroneous,' he said with a laugh. 'Avoid irritation more than exposure to the sun. Adieu. How do you English say, eh? Good-bye. Ah! Good-bye. Adieu. In the tropics one must before everything keep calm.' . . . He lifted a warning forefinger. . . . 'Du calme, du calme. Adieu.'

"One thing more remained to do—say good-bye to my excellent aunt. I found her triumphant. I had a cup of tea—the last decent cup of tea for many days—and in a room that most soothingly looked just as you would expect a lady's drawing-room to look, we had a long quiet chat by the fireside. In the course of these confidences it became quite plain to me I had been represented to the wife of the high dignitary and goodness knows to how many more people besides as an exceptional and gifted creature—a piece of good fortune for the Company—a man you don't get hold of every day. Good Heavens! And I was going to take charge of a two-penny-half-penny river-steamboat with a penny whistle attached! It appears however I was also one of the Workers, with a capital—you know. Something like an emissary of light, something like a lower sort of apostle. There had been a lot of such rot let loose in print and talk just about that time, and the excellent woman living right in the rush of all that humbug got carried off her feet. She talked about 'weaning those ignorant millions from their horrid ways,' till, upon my word, she made me quite uncomfortable. I ventured to hint that the Company was run for profit.

" 'You forget, dear Charlie, that the labourer is worthy of his hire,' she said brightly. It's queer how out of touch with truth women are! They live in a world of their own and there had never been anything like it and never can be. It is too beautiful altogether, and if they were to set it up it would go to pieces before the first sunset. Some confounded fact we men have been living con-

5. Psychiatrist.

tentedly with ever since the day of creation would start up and knock the whole thing over.

"After this I got embraced, told to wear flannel, be sure to write often and so on—and I left. In the street—I don't know why—a queer feeling came to me that I was an impostor. Odd thing, that I, who used to clear out for any part of the world at twenty-four hours' notice with less thought than most men give to the crossing of a street, had a moment—I won't say of hesitation, but of startled pause before this commonplace affair. The best way I can explain it to you is by saying that for a second or two I felt as though instead of going to the centre of a continent I were about to set off for the centre of the earth.

"I left in a French steamer and she called in every blamed port they have out there, for as far as I could see the sole purpose of landing soldiers and custom-house officers. I watched the coast. Watching a coast as it slips by the ship is like thinking about an enigma. There it is before you—smiling, frowning, inviting, grand, mean, insipid, or savage, and always mute with an air of whispering—Come and find out. This one was almost featureless, as if still in the making, with an aspect of monotonous grimness. The edge of a colossal jungle so dark green as to be almost black, fringed with white surf, ran straight, like a ruled line, far far away along a blue sea whose glitter was blurred by a creeping mist. The sun was fierce, the land seemed to glisten and drip with steam. Here and there greyish, whitish specks showed up, clustered inside the white surf, with a flag flying above them perhaps—settlements, some centuries old, and still no bigger than pin-heads on the untouched expanse of their background. We pounded along, stopped, landed soldiers, went on, landed custom-house clerks to levy toll in what looked like a God-forsaken wilderness with a tin shed and a flagpole lost in it, landed more soldiers—to take care of the custom-house clerks—presumably. Some I heard got drowned in the surf, but whether they did or not nobody seemed particularly to care. They were just flung out there, and on we went. Every day the coast looked the same, as though we had not moved, but we passed various places—trading places—with names like Gran' Bassam, Little Popo, names that seemed to belong to some sordid farce acted in front of a sinister back-cloth. The idleness of a passenger, my isolation amongst all these men with whom I had no point of contact, the oily and languid sea, the uniform sombreness of the coast, seemed to keep me away from the truth of things, within the toil of a mournful and senseless delusion. The voice of the surf heard now and then was a positive pleasure, like the speech of a brother. It was something natural, that had its reason, that had a meaning. Now and then a boat from the shore gave one a momentary contact with reality. It was paddled by black fellows. You could see from afar the white of their eyeballs glistening. They shouted, sang; their bodies streamed with perspiration; they had faces like grotesque masks—these chaps; but they had bone, muscle, a wild vitality, an intense energy of movement that was as natural and true as the surf along their coast. They wanted no excuse for being there. They were a great comfort to look at. For a time I would feel I belonged still to a world of straightforward facts; but the feeling would not last long. Something would turn up to scare it away. Once, I remember, we came upon a man-of-war anchored off the coast. There wasn't even a shed there and she was shelling the bush. It appears the French had one of their wars going on thereabouts. Her ensign drooped limp like a rag, the muzzles of the long six-inch guns stuck out all over the low hull, the greasy, slimy swell swung her up lazily and let her down, swaying her thin masts. In the empty immensity of earth, sky, and water, there she was, incomprehensible, firing into a continent. Pop, would go one of the six-inch guns; a small flame would dart and vanish, a little white smoke would disappear, a tiny projectile would give a feeble screech—and nothing happened. Nothing could happen. There was a touch of insanity in the proceeding, a sense of lugubrious drollery in the sight; and it was not dissipated by somebody on board assuring me earnestly there was a camp of natives—he called them enemies—hidden out of sight somewhere.

"We gave her her letters (I heard the men in that lonely ship were dying of fever at the rate of three a day) and went on. We called at some more places with farcical names where the merry dance of death and trade goes on in a still and earthy atmosphere as of an overheated catacomb; all along the formless coast bordered by dangerous surf, as if Nature herself had tried to ward off intruders; in and out of rivers, streams of death in life, whose banks were rotting into mud, whose waters, thickened into slime, invaded the contorted mangroves that seemed to writhe at us in the extremity of an impotent despair. Nowhere did we stop long enough to get a particularised impression, but the general sense of vague and oppressive wonder grew upon me. It was like a weary pilgrimage amongst hints for nightmares.

"It was upward of thirty days before I saw the mouth of the big river. We anchored off the seat of the government. But my work would not begin till some two hundred miles farther on. So as soon as I could I made a start for a place thirty miles higher up.

"I had my passage on a little sea-going steamer. Her captain was a Swede and knowing me for a seaman invited me on the bridge. He was a young man, lean, fair, and morose, with lanky hair and a shuffling gait. As we left the miserable little wharf he tossed his

head contemptuously at the shore. 'Been living there?' he asked. I
said, 'Yes.' 'Fine lot these government chaps—are they not?' he went
on speaking English with great precision and considerable bitterness. 'It is funny what some people will do for a few francs a
month. I wonder what becomes of that kind when it goes up country?' I said to him I expected to see that soon. 'So-o-o!' he exclaimed. He shuffled athwart keeping one eye ahead vigilantly.
'Don't be too sure,' he continued. 'The other day I took up a man
who hanged himself on the road. He was a Swede too.' 'Hanged
himself! Why, in God's name!' I cried. He kept on looking out
watchfully. 'Who knows! The sun too much for him, or the country
perhaps.'

"At last we opened a reach.[6] A rocky cliff appeared, mounds of
turned-up earth by the shore, houses on a hill, others with iron
roofs amongst a waste of excavations hanging to the declivity. A
continuous noise of the rapids above hovered over this scene of inhabited devastation. A lot of people, mostly black and naked, moved
about like ants. A jetty projected into the river. A blinding sunlight
drowned all this at times in a sudden recrudescence of glare.
'There's your Company's station,' said the Swede pointing to three
wooden barrack-like structures on the rocky slope. 'I will send your
things up. Four boxes did you say? So. Farewell.'

"I came upon a boiler wallowing in the grass, then found a path
leading up the hill. It turned aside for the boulders and also for an
undersized railway truck lying there on its back with its wheels in
the air. One was off. The thing looked as dead as the carcass of
some animal. I came upon more pieces of decaying machinery, a
stack of rusty rails. To the left a clump of trees made a shady spot
where dark things seemed to stir feebly. I blinked, the path was
steep. A horn tooted to the right and I saw the black people run. A
heavy and dull detonation shook the ground, a puff of smoke came
out of the cliff, and that was all. No change appeared on the face of
the rock. They were building a railway. The cliff was not in the way
of anything, but this objectless blasting was all the work going on.

"A slight clinking behind me made me turn my head. Six black
men advanced in a file toiling up the path. They walked erect and
slow, balancing small baskets full of earth on their heads, and the
clink kept time with their footsteps. Black rags were wound round
their loins and the short ends behind waggled to and fro like tails. I
could see every rib, the joints of their limbs were like knots in a
rope, each had an iron collar on his neck and all were connected
together with a chain whose bights swung between them, rhythmically clinking. Another report from the cliff made me think sud-

6. A straight section of a river.

denly of that ship of war I had seen firing into a continent. It was
the same kind of ominous voice; but these men could by no stretch
of imagination be called enemies. They were called criminals and
the outraged law like the bursting shells had come to them, an insoluble mystery from the sea. All their meagre breasts panted together, the violently dilated nostrils quivered, the eyes stared stonily
uphill. They passed me within six inches, without a glance, with
that complete, deathlike indifference of unhappy savages. Behind
this raw matter one of the reclaimed, the product of the new forces
at work, strolled despondently carrying a rifle by its middle. He had
a uniform jacket with one button off and seeing a white man on the
path hoisted his weapon to his shoulder with alacrity. This was simple prudence, white men being so much alike at a distance that he
could not tell who I might be. He was speedily reassured and with
a large, white, rascally grin, and a glance at his charge, seemed to
take me into partnership in his exalted trust. After all, I also was a
part of the great cause of these high and just proceedings.

"Instead of going up I turned and descended to the left. My idea
was to let that chain-gang get out of sight before I climbed the hill.
You know I am not particularly tender; I've had to strike and to fend
off. I've had to resist and to attack sometimes—that's only one way
of resisting—without counting the exact cost—according to the demands of such sort of life as I had blundered into. I've seen the
devil of violence, and the devil of greed, and the devil of hot desire;
but by all the stars these were strong, lusty, red-eyed devils that
swayed and drove men—men, I tell you. But as I stood on this hillside I foresaw that in the blinding sunshine of that land I would become acquainted with a flabby, pretending, weak-eyed devil of a
rapacious and pitiless folly. How insidious he could be too I was
only to find out several months later and a thousand miles farther.
For a moment I stood appalled, as though by a warning. Finally I
descended the hill, obliquely, towards the trees I had seen.

"I avoided a vast, artificial hole somebody had been digging on
the slope, the purpose of which I found it impossible to divine. It
wasn't a quarry or a sandpit, anyhow. It was just a hole. It might
have been connected with the philanthropic desire of giving the
criminals something to do. I don't know. Then I nearly fell into a
very narrow ravine, almost no more than a scar in the hillside. I discovered that a lot of important drainage-pipes for the settlement
had been tumbled in there. There wasn't one that was not broken.
It was a wanton smash-up. At last I got under the trees. My purpose
was to stroll into the shade for a moment, but no sooner within
than it seemed to me I had stepped into the gloomy circle of some
Inferno. The rapids were near and an uninterrupted, uniform,
headlong rushing noise filled the mournful stillness of the grove

where not a breath stirred, not a leaf moved, with a mysterious
sound, as though the tearing pace of the launched earth had suddenly become audible.

"Black shapes crouched, lay, sat between the trees, leaning
against the trunks, clinging to the earth, half coming out, half ef-
faced within the dim light, in all the attitudes of pain, abandonment, and despair. Another mine[7] on the cliff went off followed by
a slight shudder of the soil under my feet. The work was going on.
The work! And this was the place where some of the helpers had
withdrawn to die.

"They were dying slowly—it was very clear. They were not enemies, they were not criminals, they were nothing earthly now, nothing but black shadows of disease and starvation lying confusedly in
the greenish gloom. Brought from all the recesses of the coast in all
the legality of time contracts, lost in uncongenial surroundings, fed
on unfamiliar food, they sickened, became inefficient, and were
then allowed to crawl away and rest. These moribund shapes were
free as air—and nearly as thin. I began to distinguish the gleam of
the eyes under the trees. Then glancing down I saw a face near my
hand. The black bones reclined at full length with one shoulder
against the tree, and slowly the eyelids rose and the sunken eyes
looked up at me, enormous and vacant, a kind of blind, white
flicker in the depths of the orbs which died out slowly. The man
seemed young—almost a boy—but you know with them it's hard to
tell. I found nothing else to do but to offer him one of my good
Swede's ship's biscuits I had in my pocket. The fingers closed
slowly on it and held—there was no other movement and no other
glance. He had tied a bit of white worsted round his neck—Why?
Where did he get it? Was it a badge—an ornament—a charm—a
propitiatory act? Was there any idea at all connected with it. It
looked startling round his black neck this bit of white thread from
beyond the seas.

"Near the same tree two more bundles of acute angles sat with
their legs drawn up. One, with his chin propped on his knees,
stared at nothing in an intolerable and appalling manner. His
brother phantom rested its forehead as if overcome with a great
weariness; and all about others were scattered in every pose of contorted collapse, as in some picture of a massacre or a pestilence.
While I stood horror-struck one of these creatures rose to his hands
and knees and went off on all-fours towards the river to drink. He
lapped out of his hand, then sat up in the sunlight crossing his
shins in front of him, and after a time let his woolly head fall on his
breastbone.

7. A subterranean explosive charge.

"I didn't want any more loitering in the shade and I made haste towards the station. When near the buildings I met a white man in such an unexpected elegance of get-up that in the first moment I took him for a sort of vision. I saw a high, starched collar, white cuffs, a light alpaca jacket, snowy trousers, a clean necktie, and varnished boots. No hat. Hair parted, brushed, oiled, under a green-lined parasol held in a big white hand. He was amazing and had a pen-holder behind his ear.

"I shook hands with this miracle and I learned he was the Company's chief accountant and that all the book-keeping was done at this station. He had come out for a moment, he said, 'to get a breath of fresh air.' The expression sounded wonderfully odd with its suggestion of sedentary desk-life. I wouldn't have mentioned the fellow to you at all only it was from his lips that I first heard the name of the man who is so indissolubly connected with the memories of that time. Moreover I respected the fellow. Yes. I respected his collars, his vast cuffs, his brushed hair. His appearance was certainly that of a hairdresser's dummy, but in the great demoralisation of the land he kept up his appearance. That's backbone. His starched collars and got-up shirt-fronts were achievements of character. He had been out nearly three years and, later on, I could not help asking him how he managed to sport such linen. He had just the faintest blush and said modestly, 'I've been teaching one of the native women about the station. It was difficult. She had a distaste for the work.' Thus this man had verily accomplished something. And he was devoted to his books, which were in apple-pie order.

"Everything else in the Station was in a muddle—heads, things, buildings. Caravans. Strings of dusty niggers with splay feet arrived and departed; a stream of manufactured goods, rubbishy cottons, beads, and brass-wire set into the depths of darkness and in return came a precious trickle of ivory.

"I had to wait in the station for ten days—an eternity. I lived in a hut in the yard, but to be out of the chaos I would sometimes get into the accountant's office. It was built of horizontal planks and so badly put together that as he bent over his high desk he was barred from neck to heels with narrow strips of sunlight. There was no need to open the big shutter to see. It was hot there too; big flies buzzed fiendishly and did not sting but stabbed. I sat generally on the floor, while of faultless appearance (and even slightly scented) perching on a high stool he wrote, he wrote. Sometimes he stood up for exercise. When a truckle-bed with a sick man (some invalided agent from up-country) was put in there, he exhibited a gentle annoyance. 'The groans of this sick person,' he said, 'distract my attention. And without that it is extremely difficult to guard against clerical errors in this climate.'

"One day he remarked without lifting his head, 'In the interior you will no doubt meet Mr. Kurtz.' On my asking who Mr. Kurtz was he said he was a first-class agent, and seeing my disappointment at this information he added slowly, laying down his pen, 'He is a very remarkable person.' Further questions elicited from him that Mr. Kurtz was at present in charge of a trading-post, a very important one, in the true ivory-country, at 'the very bottom of there. Sends in as much ivory as all the others put together. . . .' He began to write again. The sick man was too ill to groan. The flies buzzed in a great peace.

"Suddenly there was a growing murmur of voices and a great tramping of feet. A caravan had come in. A violent babble of uncouth sounds burst out on the other side of the planks. All the carriers were speaking together, and in the midst of the uproar the lamentable voice of the chief agent was heard 'giving it up' tearfully for the twentieth time that day. . . . He rose slowly. 'What a frightful row,' he said. He crossed the room gently to look at the sick man and returning said to me, 'He does not hear.' 'What! Dead?' I asked, startled. 'No. Not yet,' he answered, with great composure. Then alluding with a toss of the head to the tumult in the station-yard, 'When one has got to make correct entries one comes to hate those savages—hate them to the death.' He remained thoughtful for a moment. 'When you see Mr. Kurtz,' he went on, 'tell him from me that everything here'—he glanced at the desk—'is very satisfactory. I don't like to write to him—with those messengers of ours you never know who may get hold of your letter—at that Central Station.' He stared at me for a moment with his mild, bulging eyes. 'Oh, he will go far, very far,' he began again. 'He will be a somebody in the Administration before long. They, above—the Council in Europe, you know—mean him to be.'

"He turned to his work. The noise outside had ceased, and presently in going out I stopped at the door. In the steady buzz of flies the homeward-bound agent was lying flushed and insensible; the other bent over his books was making correct entries of perfectly correct transactions; and fifty feet below the doorstep I could see the still tree-tops of the grove of death.

"Next day I left that station at last, with a caravan of sixty men, for a two-hundred-mile tramp.

"No use telling you much about that. Paths, paths, everywhere; a stamped-in network of paths spreading over the empty land, through long grass, through burnt grass, through thickets, down and up chilly ravines, up and down stony hills ablaze with heat; and a solitude, a solitude, nobody, not a hut. The population had cleared out a long time ago. Well if a lot of mysterious niggers armed with all kinds of fearful weapons suddenly took to travelling

on the road between Deal[8] and Gravesend catching the yokels right
and left to carry heavy loads for them, I fancy every farm and cottage thereabouts would get empty very soon. Only here the
dwellings were gone too. Still I passed through several abandoned
villages. There's something pathetically childish in the ruins of
grass walls. Day after day with the stamp and shuffle of sixty pair of
bare feet behind me, each pair under a 60-lb. load. Camp, cook,
sleep, strike camp, march. Now and then a carrier dead in harness,
at rest in the long grass near the path, with an empty water-gourd
and his long staff lying by his side. A great silence around and
above. Perhaps on some quiet night the tremor of far-off drums,
sinking, swelling, a tremor vast, faint; a sound weird, appealing,
suggestive, and wild—and perhaps with as profound a meaning as
the sound of bells in a Christian country. Once a white man in an
unbuttoned uniform, camping on the path with an armed escort of
lank Zanzibaris,[9] very hospitable and festive—not to say drunk. Was
looking after the upkeep of the road, he declared. Can't say I saw
any road or any upkeep, unless the body of a middle-aged negro,
with a bullet-hole in the forehead upon which I absolutely stum-
bled three miles farther on may be considered as a permanent improvement. I had a white companion too, not a bad chap, but
rather too fleshy and with the exasperating habit of fainting on the
hot hillsides miles away from the least bit of shade and water. Annoying, you know, to hold your own coat like a parasol over a man's
head while he is coming to. I couldn't help asking him once what
he meant by coming there at all. 'To make money, of course. What
do you think?' he said scornfully. Then he got fever and had to be
carried in a hammock slung under a pole. As he weighed sixteen
stone[1] I had no end of rows with the carriers. They jibbed, ran
away, sneaked off with their loads in the night—quite a mutiny. So,
one evening I made a speech in English with gestures, not one of
which was lost to the sixty pairs of eyes before me, and the next
morning I started the hammock off in front all right. An hour afterwards I came upon the whole concern wrecked in a bush—man,
hammock, groans, blankets, horrors. The heavy pole had skinned
his poor nose. He was very anxious for me to kill somebody, but
there wasn't the shadow of a carrier near. I remembered the old
doctor—'It would be interesting for science to watch the mental
changes of individuals on the spot.' I felt I was becoming scientifi-
cally interesting. However, all that is to no purpose. On the fif-
teenth day, I came in sight of the big river again and hobbled into

8. A port on the English Channel near Dover, about forty-five miles east of Gravesend.
9. Natives of an island off the east coast of Africa who were often used as porters or mer-
　　cenaries in European expeditions.
1. 224 pounds (1 stone = 14 pounds).

the Central Station. It was on a back water surrounded by scrub and forest, with a pretty border of smelly mud on one side and on the three others enclosed by a crazy fence of rushes. A neglected gap was all the gate it had, and the first glance at the place was enough to let you see the flabby devil was running that show. White men with long staves in their hands appeared languidly from amongst the buildings strolling up to take a look at me and then retired out of sight somewhere. One of them, a stout, excitable chap with black moustaches informed me with great volubility and many digressions, as soon as I told him who I was, that my steamer was at the bottom of the river. I was thunderstruck. What, how, why? Oh it was 'all right.' The 'Manager himself' was there. 'All quite correct.' Everybody had behaved splendidly! splendidly! 'You must,' he said in agitation, 'go and see the General Manager at once. He is waiting.'

"I did not see the real significance of that wreck at once. I fancy I see it now—but I am not sure—not at all. Certainly the affair was too stupid—when I think of it—to be altogether natural. Still. . . . But at the moment it presented itself simply as a confounded nuisance. The steamer was sunk. They had started two days before in a sudden hurry up the river with the Manager on board, in charge of some volunteer skipper, and before they had been out three hours they tore the bottom out of her on stones and she sank near the south bank. I asked myself what I was to do there—now my boat was lost. As a matter of fact I had plenty to do in fishing my command out of the river. I had to set about it the very next day. That and the repairs when I brought the pieces to the station took some months.

"My first interview with the Manager was curious. He did not ask me to sit down after my twenty-mile walk that morning. He was commonplace in complexion, in feature, in manners, and in voice. He was of middle size and of ordinary build. His eyes of the usual blue were perhaps remarkably cold and he certainly could make his glance fall on one as trenchant and heavy as an axe. But even at these times the rest of his person seemed to disclaim the intention. Otherwise there was only an indefinable, faint expression of his lips, something stealthy—a smile—not a smile—I remember it, but I can't explain. It was unconscious, this smile was, though just after he had said something it got intensified for an instant. It came at the end of his speeches like a seal applied on the words to make the meaning of the commonest phrase appear absolutely inscrutable. He was a common trader, from his youth up employed in these parts—nothing more. He was obeyed, yet he inspired neither love nor fear, nor even respect. He inspired uneasiness—that was it. Uneasiness. Not a definite mistrust—just uneasiness—nothing

more. You have no idea how effective such a . . . a . . . faculty can
be. He had no genius for organising, for initiative, or for order
even. That was evident in such things as the deplorable state of the
station. He had no learning, and no intelligence. His position had
come to him—why? Perhaps because he was never ill. He had
served three terms of three years out there. Triumphant health in
the general rout of constitutions is a kind of power in itself. When
he went home on leave he rioted on a large scale—pompously. Jack
ashore—with a difference in externals only. This, one could gather
from his casual talk. He originated nothing, he could keep the routine going—that's all. But he was great. He was great by this little
thing that it was impossible to tell what could control such a man.
He never gave that secret away. Perhaps there was nothing within
him. Such a suspicion made one pause—for out there there were
no external checks. Once when various tropical diseases had laid
low almost every 'agent' in the station he was heard to say, 'Men
who come out here should have no entrails.' He sealed the utterance with that smile of his as though it had been a door opening
into a darkness he had in his keeping. You fancied you had seen
things—but the seal was on. When annoyed at meal-times by the
constant quarrels of the white men about precedence he ordered
an immense round table to be made for which a special house had
to be built. This was the station's mess-room. Where he sat was the
first place—the rest were nowhere. One felt this to be his unalterable conviction. He was neither civil nor uncivil. He was quiet. He
allowed his 'boy'—an overfed young negro from the coast—to treat
the white men, under his very eyes, with provoking insolence.

"He began to speak as soon as he saw me. I had been very long
on the road. He could not wait. Had to start without me. The up-
river stations had to be relieved. There had been so many delays already that he did not know who was dead and who was alive and
how they got on—and so on, and so on. He paid no attention to my
explanations and, playing with a stick of sealing-wax, repeated several times that the situation was 'very grave, very grave.' There were
rumours that a very important station was in jeopardy and its chief,
Mr. Kurtz, was ill. Hoped it was not true. Mr. Kurtz was. . . . I felt
weary and irritable. Hang Kurtz, I thought. I interrupted him by
saying I had heard of Mr. Kurtz on the coast. 'Ah! So they talk of
him down there,' he murmured to himself. Then he began again assuring me Mr. Kurtz was the best agent he had, an exceptional
man, of the greatest importance to the Company; therefore I could
understand his anxiety. He was, he said, 'very, very uneasy.' Certainly he fidgeted on his chair a good deal, exclaimed, 'Ah! Mr.
Kurtz,' broke the stick of sealing-wax and seemed dumbfounded by
the accident. Next thing he wanted to know 'how long it would take

to'. . . . I interrupted him again. Being hungry, you know, and kept on my feet too, I was getting savage. 'How can I tell,' I said. 'I haven't even seen the wreck yet. Some months, no doubt.' All this talk seemed to me so futile. 'Some months,' he said. 'Well. Let us say three months before we can make a start. Yes. That ought to do the affair.' I flung out of his hut (he lived all alone in a clay hut with a sort of verandah) muttering to myself my opinion of him. He was a chattering idiot. Afterwards I took it back when it was borne in upon me startlingly with what extreme nicety he had estimated the time requisite for the 'affair.'

"I went to work the next day, turning, so to speak, my back on that station. In that way only it seemed to me I could keep my hold on the redeeming facts of life. Still, one must look about sometimes; and then I saw this station, these men strolling aimlessly about in the sunshine of the yard. I asked myself sometimes what it all meant. They wandered here and there with their absurd long staves in their hands like a lot of faithless pilgrims bewitched inside a rotten fence. The word 'ivory' rang in the air, was whispered, was sighed. You would think they were praying to it. A taint of imbecile rapacity blew through it all like a whiff from some corpse. By Jove! I've never seen anything so unreal in my life. And outside, the silent wilderness surrounding this cleared speck on the earth struck me as something great and invincible, like evil or truth, waiting patiently for the passing away of this fantastic invasion.

"Oh, those months! Well, never mind. Various things happened. One evening a grass shed full of calico, cotton prints, beads, and I don't know what else, burst into a blaze so suddenly that you would have thought the earth had opened to let an avenging fire consume all that trash. I was smoking my pipe quietly by my dismantled steamer and saw them all cutting capers in the light with their arms lifted high when the stout man with moustaches came tearing down to the river, a tin pail in his hand, assured me that everybody was 'behaving splendidly, splendidly,' dipped about a quart of water, and tore back again. I noticed there was a hole in the bottom of his pail.

"I strolled up. There was no hurry. You see the thing had gone off like a box of matches. It had been hopeless from the very first. The flame had leaped high, driven everybody back, lighted up everything—and collapsed. The shed was already a heap of embers glowing fiercely. A nigger was being beaten near by. They said he had caused the fire in some way; be that as it may, he was screeching most horribly. I saw him later on for several days sitting in a bit of shade looking very sick and trying to recover himself. Afterwards he arose and went out—and the wilderness without a sound took him into its bosom again. As I approached the glow from the dark I found myself at the back of two men, talking. I heard the name of Kurtz pronounced, then the words, 'take advantage of this unfortunate accident.' One of the men was the Manager. I wished him a good evening. 'Did you ever see anything like it—eh? it is incredible,' he said, and walked off. The other man remained. He was a first-class agent, young, gentlemanly, a bit reserved, with a forked little beard and a hooked nose. He was stand-offish with the other agents and they on their side said he was the Manager's spy upon them. As to me, I had hardly ever spoken to him before. We got into talk and by and by we strolled away from the hissing ruins. Then he asked me to his room, which was in the main building of the station. He struck a match and I perceived that this young aristocrat had not only a silver-mounted dressing-case but also a whole candle all to himself. Just at that time the Manager was the only man supposed to have any right to candles. Native mats covered the clay walls; a collection of spears, assegais,[2] shields, knives, was hung up in trophies. The business entrusted to this fellow was the making of bricks—so I had been informed; but there wasn't a fragment of a brick anywhere in the station, and he had been there more than a year—waiting. It seems he could not make bricks without something, I don't know what—straw maybe. Anyway it could not be found there, and as it was not likely to be sent from Europe it did not appear clear to me what he was waiting for. An act of special creation perhaps. However, they were all waiting—all the sixteen or twenty pilgrims of them—for something; and upon my word it did not seem an uncongenial occupation, from the way they took it, though the only thing that ever came to them was disease—as far as I could see. They beguiled the time by backbiting and intriguing against each other in a foolish kind of way. There was an air of plotting about that station, but nothing came of it, of course. It was as unreal as everything else—as the philanthropic pretence of the whole concern, as their talk, as their government, as their show of work. The only real feeling was a desire to get appointed to a trading-post where ivory was to be had, so that they could earn percentages. They intrigued and slandered and hated each other only on that account—but as to effectually lifting a little finger—oh no. By Heavens! There is something after all in the world allowing one man to steal a horse while another must not look at a halter. Steal a horse straight out. Very well. He has done it. Perhaps he can ride. But there is a way of looking at a halter that would provoke the most charitable of saints into a kick.

"I had no idea why he wanted to be sociable, but as we chatted in there it suddenly occurred to me the fellow was trying to get at

---

2. Slender, javelinlike spears.

something—in fact, pumping me. He alluded constantly to Europe, to the people I was supposed to know there—putting leading questions as to my acquaintances in the sepulchral city, and so on. His little eyes glittered like mica discs—with curiosity—though he tried to keep up a bit of superciliousness. At first I was astonished, but very soon I became awfully curious to see what he would find out from me. I couldn't possibly imagine what I had in me to make it worth his while. It was very pretty to see how he baffled himself, for in truth my body was full only of chills and my head had nothing in it but that wretched steamboat business. It was evident he took me for a perfectly shameless prevaricator. At last he got angry and to conceal a movement of furious annoyance he yawned. I rose. Then I noticed a small sketch in oils, on a panel, representing a woman draped and blindfolded carrying a lighted torch. The background was sombre—almost black. The movement of the woman was stately, and the effect of the torchlight on the face was sinister.

"It arrested me and he stood by civilly holding an empty half-pint champagne bottle (medical comforts) with the candle stuck in it. To my question he said Mr. Kurtz had painted this—in this very station more than a year ago—while waiting for means to go to his trading-post. 'Tell me, pray,' said I, 'who is this Mr. Kurtz?'

" 'The chief of the Inner Station,' he answered in a short tone, looking away. 'Much obliged,' I said laughing. 'And you are the brickmaker of the Central Station. Every one knows that.' He was silent for a while. 'He is a prodigy,' he said at last. 'He is an emissary of pity, and science, and progress, and devil knows what else. We want,' he began to declaim suddenly, 'for the guidance of the cause entrusted to us by Europe, so to speak, higher intelligence, wide sympathies, a singleness of purpose.' 'Who says that?' I asked. 'Lots of them,' he replied. 'Some even write that; and so *he* comes here, a special being, as you ought to know.' 'Why ought I to know?' I interrupted really surprised. He paid no attention. 'Yes. To-day he is chief of the best station, next year he will be Assistant-Manager, two years more and . . . but I dare say you know what he will be in two years' time. You are of the new gang—the gang of virtue. The same people who sent him specially also recommended you. Oh, don't say no. I've my own eyes to trust.' Light dawned upon me. My dear aunt's influential acquaintances were producing an unexpected effect upon that young man. I nearly burst into a laugh. 'Do you read the Company's confidential correspondence?' I asked. He hadn't a word to say. It was great fun. 'When Mr. Kurtz,' I continued severely, 'is General Manager, you won't have the opportunity.'

"He blew the candle out suddenly and we went outside. The moon had risen. Black figures strolled about listlessly, pouring water on the glow, whence proceeded a sound of hissing; steam ascended in the moonlight; the beaten nigger groaned somewhere. 'What a row the brute makes!' said the indefatigable man with the moustaches appearing near us. 'Serve him right. Transgression—punishment—bang! Pitiless, pitiless. That's the only way. This will prevent all conflagrations for the future. I was just telling the Manager. . . .' He noticed my companion and became crestfallen all at once. 'Not in bed yet,' he said with a kind of servile heartiness; 'it's so natural. Ha! Danger—agitation.' He vanished. I went on to the river-side, and the other followed me. I heard a scathing murmur at my ear, 'Heaps of muffs[3]—go to.' The pilgrims could be seen in knots gesticulating, discussing. Several had still their staves in their hands. I verily believe they took these sticks to bed with them. Beyond the fence the forest stood up spectrally in the moonlight and through the dim stir, through the faint sounds of that lamentable courtyard, the silence of the land went home to one's very heart—its mystery, its greatness, the amazing reality of its concealed life. The hurt nigger moaned feebly somewhere near by and then fetched a deep sigh that made me mend my pace away from there. I felt a hand introducing itself under my arm. 'My dear sir,' said the fellow, 'I don't want to be misunderstood and especially by you who will see Mr. Kurtz long before I can have that pleasure. I wouldn't like him to get a false idea of my disposition. . . .'

"I let him run on, this papier-mâché Mephistopheles,[4] and it seemed to me that if I tried I could poke my forefinger through him and would find nothing inside but a little loose dirt, maybe. He, don't you see, had been planning to be Assistant-Manager by and by under the present man, and I could see that the coming of that Kurtz had upset them both not a little. He talked precipitately and I did not try to stop him. I had my shoulders against the wreck of my steamer hauled up on the slope like a carcass of some big river animal. The smell of mud, of primeval mud by Jove, was in my nostrils, the high stillness of primeval forest was before my eyes; there were shiny patches on the black creek. The moon had spread over everything a thin layer of silver—over the rank grass, over the mud, upon the wall of matted vegetation standing higher than the wall of a temple, over the great river I could see through a sombre gap glittering, glittering as it flowed broadly by without a murmur. All this was great, expectant, mute, while the man jabbered about himself. I wondered whether the stillness on the face of the immensity looking at us two were meant as an appeal or as a menace. What were we who had strayed in here? Could we handle that dumb thing, or would it handle us? I felt how big, how confoundedly big, was that thing that couldn't talk and perhaps was deaf as well. What was in

3. Failures, bunglers.
4. Devil.

there? I could see a little ivory coming out from there and I had heard Mr. Kurtz was in there. I had heard enough about it too—God knows! Yet somehow it didn't bring any image with it—no more than if I had been told an angel or a fiend was in there. I believed it in the same way one of you might believe there are inhabitants in the planet Mars. I knew once a Scotch sailmaker who was certain, dead sure, there were people in Mars. If you asked him for some idea how they looked and behaved he would get shy and mutter something about 'walking on all-fours.' If you as much as smiled he would—though a man of sixty—offer to fight you. I would not have gone so far as to fight for Kurtz, but I went for him near enough to a lie. You know I hate, detest, and can't bear a lie, not because I am straighter than the rest of us, but simply because it appals me. There is a taint of death, a flavour of mortality in lies—which is exactly what I hate and detest in the world—what I want to forget. It makes me miserable and sick like biting something rotten would do. Temperament, I suppose. Well, I went near enough to it by letting the young fool there believe anything he liked to imagine as to my influence in Europe. I became in an instant as much of a pretence as the rest of the bewitched pilgrims. This simply because I had a notion it somehow would be of help to that Kurtz whom at the time I did not see—you understand. He was just a word for me. I did not see the man in the name any more than you do. Do you see him? Do you see the story? Do you see anything? It seems to me I am trying to tell you a dream—making a vain attempt, because no relation of a dream can convey the dream-sensation, that commingling of absurdity, surprise, and bewilderment in a tremor of struggling revolt, that notion of being captured by the incredible which is the very essence of dreams. . . ."

He was silent for a while.

". . . No, it is impossible; it is impossible to convey the life-sensation of any given epoch of one's existence—that which makes its truth, its meaning—its subtle and penetrating essence. It is impossible. We live, as we dream—alone. . . ."

He paused again as if reflecting, then added:

"Of course in this you fellows see more than I could then. You see me, whom you know. . . ."

It had become so pitch dark that we listeners could hardly see one another. For a long time already he, sitting apart, had been no more to us than a voice. There was not a word from anybody. The others might have been asleep, but I was awake. I listened, I listened on the watch for the sentence, for the word that would give me the clue to the faint uneasiness inspired by this narrative that seemed to shape itself without human lips in the heavy night-air of the river.

". . . Yes—I let him run on," Marlow began again, "and think what he pleased about the powers that were behind me. I did! And there was nothing behind me! There was nothing but that wretched old mangled steamboat I was leaning against while he talked fluently about 'the necessity for every man to get on.' 'And when one comes out here, you conceive, it is not to gaze at the moon.' Mr. Kurtz was a 'universal genius,' but even a genius would find it easier to work with 'adequate tools—intelligent men.' He did not make bricks—why, there was a physical impossibility in the way—as I was well aware; and if he did secretarial work for the Manager, it was because 'no sensible man rejects wantonly the confidence of his superiors.' Did I see it? I saw it. What more did I want? What I really wanted was rivets, by Heaven! Rivets. To get on with the work—to stop the hole. Rivets I wanted. There were cases of them down at the coast—cases—piled up—burst—split! You kicked a loose rivet at every second step in that station yard on the hillside. Rivets had rolled into the grove of death. You could fill your pockets with rivets for the trouble of stooping down—and there wasn't one rivet to be found where it was wanted. We had plates that would do but nothing to fasten them with. And every week the messenger, a lone negro, letter-bag on shoulder and staff in hand, left our station for the coast. And several times a week a coast caravan came in with trade goods—ghastly glazed calico that made you shudder only to look at it, glass beads value about a penny a quart, confounded spotted cotton handkerchiefs. And no rivets. Three carriers could have brought all that was wanted to set that steamboat afloat.

"He was becoming confidential now, but I fancy my unresponsive attitude must have exasperated him at last, for he judged it necessary to inform me he feared neither God nor devil, let alone any mere man. I said I could see that very well, but what I wanted was a certain quantity of rivets—and rivets were what really Mr. Kurtz wanted—if he had only known it. Now letters went to the coast every week. . . . 'My dear sir,' he cried, 'I write from dictation.' I demanded rivets. There was a way—for an intelligent man. He changed his manner; became very cold and suddenly began to talk about a hippopotamus; wondered whether sleeping on board the steamer (I stuck to my salvage night and day) I wasn't disturbed. There was an old hippo that had the bad habit of getting out on the bank and roaming at night over the station grounds. The pilgrims used to turn out in a body and empty every rifle they could lay hands on at him. Some even had sat up o' nights for him. All this energy was wasted though. 'That animal has a charmed life,' he said, 'but you can say this only of brutes in this country. No man— you apprehend me?—no man here bears a charmed life.' He stood there for a moment in the moonlight with his delicate hooked nose

set a little askew and his mica eyes glittering without a wink, then
with a curt Good-night, he strode off. I could see he was disturbed
and considerably puzzled, which made me feel more hopeful than I
had been for days. It was a great comfort to turn from that chap to
my influential friend, the battered, twisted, ruined tin-pot steamboat. I clambered on board. She rang under my feet like an empty
Huntley & Palmer biscuit-tin kicked along a gutter; she was nothing so solid in make, and rather less pretty in shape, but I had
expended enough hard work on her to make me love her. No influential friend would have served me better. She had given me a
chance to come out a bit—to find out what I could do. No. I don't
like work. I had rather laze about and think of all the fine things
that can be done. I don't like work—no man does—but I like what
is in the work—the chance to find yourself. Your own reality—for
yourself—not for others—what no other man can ever know. They
can only see the mere show, and never can tell what it really means.

"I was not surprised to see somebody sitting aft on the deck with
his legs dangling over the mud. You see I rather chummed with the
few mechanics there were in that station, whom the other pilgrims
naturally despised—on account of their imperfect manners, I suppose. This was the foreman—a boiler-maker by trade—a good
worker. He was a lank bony yellow-faced man with big intense eyes.
His aspect was worried and his head was as bald as the palm of my
hand; but his hair in falling seemed to have stuck to his chin and
had prospered in the new locality, for his beard hung down to his
waist. He was a widower with six young children (he had left them
in charge of a sister of his to come out there), and the passion of
his life was pigeon-flying. He was an enthusiast and a connoisseur.
He would rave about pigeons. After work hours he used sometimes
to come over from his hut for a talk about his children and his pigeons; at work when he had to crawl in the mud under the bottom
of the steamboat he would tie up that beard of his in a kind of
white serviette[5] he brought for the purpose. It had loops to go over
his ears. In the evening he could be seen squatted on the bank rins-
ing that wrapper in the creek with great care, then spreading it
solemnly on a bush to dry.

"I slapped him on the back and shouted 'We shall have rivets!' He
scrambled to his feet exclaiming 'No! Rivets!' as though he couldn't
believe his ears. Then in a low voice, 'You . . . eh?' I don't know why
we behaved like lunatics. I put my finger to the side of my nose and
nodded mysteriously. 'Good for you!' he cried, snapped his fingers
above his head, lifting one foot. I tried a jig. We capered on the iron
deck. A frightful clatter came out of that hulk and the virgin forest

5. Napkin.

on the other bank of the creek sent it back in a thundering roll
upon the sleeping station. It must have made some of the pilgrims
sit up in their hovels. A dark figure obscured the lighted doorway of
the Manager's hut, vanished, then a second or so after the doorway
itself vanished too. We stopped and the silence driven away by the
stamping of our feet flowed back again from the recesses of the
land. The great wall of vegetation, an exuberant and entangled
mass of trunks, branches, leaves, boughs, festoons motionless in
the moonlight, was like a rioting invasion of soundless life, a rolling
wave of plants piled up, crested, ready to topple over the creek to
sweep every little man of us out of his little existence. And it moved
not. A deadened burst of mighty splashes and snorts reached us
from afar as though an ichthyosaurus[6] had been taking a bath of
glitter in the great river. 'After all,' said the boiler-maker in a reasonable tone, 'why shouldn't we get the rivets?' Why not, indeed! I
did not know of any reason why we shouldn't. 'They'll come in
three weeks,' I said confidently.

"But they didn't. Instead of rivets there came an invasion, an infliction, a visitation. It came in sections during the next three
weeks, each section headed by a donkey carrying a white man in
new clothes and tan shoes bowing from that elevation right and left
to the impressed pilgrims. A quarrelsome band of footsore sulky
niggers trod on the heels of the donkey; a lot of tents, camp-stools,
tin boxes, white cases, brown bales would be shot down in the
courtyard and the air of mystery would deepen a little over the
muddle of the station. Five such instalments came, with their absurd air of disorderly flight with the loot of innumerable outfit
shops and provision stores that, one would think, they were lugging, after a raid, into the wilderness for equitable division. It was
an inextricable mess of things decent in themselves but that human
folly made look like the spoils of thieving.

"This devoted band called itself the Eldorado[7] Exploring Expedition and I believe they were sworn to secrecy. Their talk however
was the talk of sordid buccaneers. It was reckless without hardihood, greedy without audacity, and cruel without courage. There
was not an atom of foresight or of serious intention in the whole
batch of them, and they did not seem aware these things are
wanted for the work of the world. To tear treasure out of the bow-
els of the land was their desire, with no more moral purpose at the
back of it than there is in burglars breaking into a safe. Who paid
the expenses of the noble enterprise I don't know; but the uncle of
our Manager was leader of that lot.

6. An extinct fishlike reptile.
7. Fabled South American land of gold and treasure sought in vain by Sir Walter Raleigh
   and various Spanish adventurers.

"In exterior he resembled a butcher in a poor neighbourhood and his eyes had a look of sleepy cunning. He carried his fat paunch with ostentation on his short legs and during the time his gang infested the station spoke to no one but his nephew. You could see these two roaming about all day long with their heads close together in an everlasting confab.

"I had given up worrying myself about the rivets. One's capacity for that kind of folly is more limited than you would suppose. I said Hang!—and let things slide. I had plenty of time for meditation and now and then I would give some thought to Kurtz. I wasn't very interested in him. No. Still, I was curious to see whether this man who had come out equipped with moral ideas of some sort would climb to the top after all and how he would set about his work when there."

II

"One evening as I was lying flat on the deck of my steamboat I heard voices approaching—and there were the nephew and the uncle strolling along the bank. I laid my head on my arm again and had nearly lost myself in a doze when somebody said—in my ear as it were—'I am as harmless as a little child, but I don't like to be dictated to. Am I the Manager—or am I not? I was ordered to send him there. It's incredible.' . . . I became aware that the two were standing on the shore alongside the forepart of the steamboat just below my head. I did not move. It did not occur to me to move. I was sleepy. 'It *is* unpleasant,' grunted the uncle. 'He had asked the Administration to be sent there,' said the other, 'with the idea of showing what he could do; and I was instructed accordingly. Look at the influence that man must have. It is not frightful?' They both agreed it was frightful, then made several bizarre remarks: 'Make rain and fine weather—one man—the Council—by the nose'—bits of absurd sentences that got the better of my drowsiness, so that I had pretty near the whole of my wits about me when the uncle said, 'The climate may do away with this difficulty for you. Is he alone there?' 'Yes,' answered the Manager; 'he sent his assistant down the river with a note to me in these terms: "Clear this poor devil out of the country and don't bother sending more of that sort. I had rather be alone than have the kind of men you can dispose of with me." It was more than a year ago. Can you imagine such impudence?' 'Anything since then?' asked the other hoarsely. 'Ivory,' jerked the nephew; 'lots of it—prime sort—lots—most annoying, from him.' 'And with that?' questioned the heavy rumble. 'Invoice,' was the reply fired out, so to speak. Then silence. They had been talking about Kurtz.

"I was broad awake by this time but, lying perfectly at ease, remained still, having no inducement to change my position. 'How did that ivory come all this way?' growled the elder man who seemed very vexed. The other explained that it had come with a fleet of canoes in charge of an English half-caste clerk Kurtz had with him; that Kurtz had apparently intended to return himself, the station being by that time bare of goods and stores, but after coming three hundred miles had suddenly decided to go back, which he started to do alone in a small dugout with four paddlers, leaving the half-caste to continue down the river with the ivory. The two fellows there seemed astounded at anybody attempting such a thing. They were at a loss for an adequate motive. As for me, I seemed to see Kurtz for the first time. It was a distinct glimpse: the dugout, four paddling savages, and the lone white man turning his back suddenly on the headquarters, on relief, on thoughts of home perhaps, setting his face towards the depths of the wilderness, towards his empty and desolate station. I did not know the motive. Perhaps he was just simply a fine fellow who stuck to his work for its own sake. His name, you understand, had not been pronounced once. He was: 'that man.' The half-caste who as far as I could see had conducted a difficult trip with great prudence and pluck was invariably alluded to as: 'that scoundrel.' The 'scoundrel' had reported that the 'man' had been very ill—had recovered imperfectly. . . . The two below me moved away then, a few paces, and strolled back and forth at some little distance. I heard: 'Military post—doctor—two hundred miles—quite alone now—unavoidable delays—nine months—no news—strange rumours.' They approached again just as the Manager was saying, 'No one, as far as I know, unless a species of wandering trader—a pestilential fellow snapping ivory from the natives.' Who was it they were talking about now? I gathered in snatches that this was some man supposed to be in Kurtz's district, and of whom the Manager, did not approve. 'We will not be free from unfair competition till one of these fellows is hanged for an example,' he said. 'Certainly,' grunted the other; 'get him hanged! Why not? Anything—anything can be done in this country. That's what I say; nobody, here, you understand *here*, can endanger your position. And why? You stand the climate—you outlast them all. The danger is in Europe, but there before I left I took care to. . . .' They moved off and whispered, then their voices rose again. 'The extraordinary series of delays is not my fault. I did my possible.' The fat man sighed, 'Very sad.' 'And the pestiferous absurdity of his talk,' continued the other; 'he bothered me enough when he was here. "Each station should be like a beacon on the road towards better things, a centre for trade of course but also for humanising, improving, instructing." Conceive you—that ass! And he wants to

be Manager! No, it's. . . .' Here he got choked by excessive indignation, and I lifted my head the least bit. I was surprised to see how
near they were—right under me. I could have spat upon their hats.
They were looking on the ground absorbed in thought. The Manager was switching his leg with a slender twig; his sagacious relative
lifted his head. 'You have been well since you came out this time?'
he asked. The other gave a start. 'Who? I? Oh! Like a charm—like
a charm. But the rest—oh, my goodness! All sick. They die so
quick, too, that I haven't the time to send them out of the country—it's incredible!' 'H'm. Just so,' grunted the uncle. 'Ah! my boy,
trust to this—I say trust to this.' I saw him extend his short flipper
of an arm for a gesture that took in the forest, the creek, the mud,
the river—seemed to beckon with a dishonouring flourish before
the sunlit face of the land a treacherous appeal to the lurking
death, to the hidden evil, to the profound darkness of its heart. It
was so startling that I leaped to my feet and looked back at the edge
of the forest, as though I had expected an answer of some sort to
that black display of confidence. You know the foolish notions that
come to one sometimes. The high stillness confronted these two
figures with its ominous patience, waiting for the passing away of a
fantastic invasion.

"They swore aloud together—out of sheer fright, I believe—then,
pretending not to know anything of my existence, turned back to
the station. The sun was low; and leaning forward side by side, they
seemed to be tugging painfully uphill their two ridiculous shadows
of unequal length, that trailed behind them slowly over the tall
grass without bending a single blade.

"In a few days the Eldorado Expedition went into the patient
wilderness, that closed upon it as the sea closes over a diver. Long
afterwards the news came that all the donkeys were dead. I know
nothing as to the fate of the less valuable animals. They no doubt,
like the rest of us, found what they deserved. I did not inquire. I
was then rather excited at the prospect of meeting Kurtz very soon.
When I say very soon I mean it comparatively. It was just two
months from the day we left the creek when we came to the bank
below Kurtz's station.

"Going up that river was like travelling back to the earliest beginnings of the world, when vegetation rioted on the earth and the big
trees were kings. An empty stream, a great silence, an impenetrable
forest. The air was warm, thick, heavy, sluggish. There was no joy in
the brilliance of sunshine. The long stretches of the waterway ran
on, deserted, into the gloom of overshadowed distances. On silvery
sandbanks hippos and alligators sunned themselves side by side.
The broadening waters flowed through a mob of wooded islands.
You lost your way on that river as you would in a desert and butted

all day long against shoals trying to find the channel till you thought yourself bewitched and cut off for ever from everything you had known once—somewhere—far away—in another existence perhaps. There were moments when one's past came back to one, as it will sometimes when you have not a moment to spare to yourself; but it came in the shape of an unrestful and noisy dream remembered with wonder amongst the overwhelming realities of this strange world of plants and water and silence. And this stillness of life did not in the least resemble a peace. It was the stillness of an implacable force brooding over an inscrutable intention. It looked at you with a vengeful aspect. I got used to it afterwards. I did not see it any more. I had no time. I had to keep guessing at the channel; I had to discern, mostly by inspiration, the signs of hidden banks; I watched for sunken stones; I was learning to clap my teeth smartly before my heart flew out when I shaved by a fluke some infernal sly old snag[8] that would have ripped the life out of the tinpot steamboat and drowned all the pilgrims; I had to keep a look-out for the signs of dead wood we could cut up in the night for next day's steaming. When you have to attend to things of that sort, to the mere incidents of the surface, the reality—the reality I tell you—fades. The inner truth is hidden—luckily, luckily. But I felt it all the same; I felt often its mysterious stillness watching me at my monkey tricks, just as it watches you fellows performing on your respective tight-ropes for—what is it? half a crown a tumble. . . ."

"Try to be civil, Marlow," growled a voice, and I knew there was at least one listener awake besides myself.

"I beg your pardon. I forgot the heartache which makes up the rest of the price. And indeed what does the price matter if the trick be well done? You do your tricks very well. And I didn't do badly either since I managed not to sink that steamboat on my first trip. It's a wonder to me yet. Imagine a blindfolded man set to drive a van over a bad road. I sweated and shivered over that business considerably, I can tell you. After all, for a seaman, to scrape the bottom of the thing that's supposed to float all the time under his care is the unpardonable sin. No one may know of it, but you never forget the thump—eh? A blow on the very heart. You remember it, you dream of it, you wake up at night and think of it—years after—and go hot and cold all over. I don't pretend to say that steamboat floated all the time. More than once she had to wade for a bit, with twenty cannibals splashing around and pushing. We had enlisted some of these chaps on the way for a crew. Fine fellows—cannibals—in their place. They were men one could work with, and I am grateful to them. And, after all, they did not eat each other before

8. Submerged tree, stump, or branch.

my face: they had brought along a provision of hippo-meat which went rotten and made the mystery of the wilderness stink in my nostrils. Phoo! I can sniff it now. I had the Manager on board and three or four pilgrims with their staves—all complete. Sometimes we came upon a station close by the bank clinging to the skirts of the unknown, and the white men rushing out of a tumble-down hovel with great gestures of joy and surprise and welcome seemed very strange, had the appearance of being held there captive by a spell. The word 'ivory' would ring in the air for a while—and on we went again into the silence, along empty reaches, round the still bends, between the high walls of our winding way, reverberating in hollow claps the ponderous beat of the stern-wheel. Trees, trees, millions of trees, massive, immense, running up high, and at their foot, hugging the bank against the stream, crept the little begrimed steamboat like a sluggish beetle crawling on the floor of a lofty portico. It made you feel very small, very lost, and yet it was not altogether depressing, that feeling. After all, if you were small, the grimy beetle crawled on—which was just what you wanted it to do. Where the pilgrims imagined it crawled to I don't know. To some place where they expected to get something, I bet! For me it crawled towards Kurtz—exclusively; but when the steam-pipes started leaking we crawled very slow. The reaches opened before us and closed behind, as if the forest had stepped leisurely across the water to bar the way for our return. We penetrated deeper and deeper into the heart of darkness. It was very quiet there. At night sometimes the roll of drums behind the curtain of trees would run up the river and remain sustained faintly, as if hovering in the air high over our heads till the first break of day. Whether it meant war, peace, or prayer we could not tell. The dawns were heralded by the descent of a chill stillness. The woodcutters slept, their fires burned low, the snapping of a twig would make you start. We were wanderers on a prehistoric earth, on an earth that wore the aspect of an unknown planet. We could have fancied ourselves the first of men taking possession of an accursed inheritance, to be subdued at the cost of profound anguish and of excessive toil. But suddenly as we struggled round a bend there would be a glimpse of rush walls, of peaked grass-roofs, a burst of yells, a whirl of black limbs, a mass of hands clapping, of feet stamping, of bodies swaying, of eyes rolling under the droop of heavy and motionless foliage. The steamer toiled along slowly on the edge of a black and incomprehensible frenzy. The prehistoric man was cursing us, praying to us, welcoming us—who could tell? We were cut off from the comprehension of our surroundings; we glided past like phantoms, wondering and secretly appalled, as sane men would be before an enthusiastic outbreak in a madhouse. We could not understand because we were too far and could not remember because we were travelling in the night of first ages, of those ages that are gone, leaving hardly a sign—and no memories.

"The earth seemed unearthly. We are accustomed to look upon the shackled form of a conquered monster, but there—there you could look at a thing monstrous and free. It was unearthly and the men were. . . . No they were not inhuman. Well, you know that was the worst of it—this suspicion of their not being inhuman. It would come slowly to one. They howled and leaped and spun and made horrid faces, but what thrilled you was just the thought of their humanity—like yours—the thought of your remote kinship with this wild and passionate uproar. Ugly. Yes, it was ugly enough, but if you were man enough you would admit to yourself that there was in you just the faintest trace of a response to the terrible frankness of that noise, a dim suspicion of there being a meaning in it which you—you so remote from the night of first ages—could comprehend. And why not? The mind of man is capable of anything—because everything is in it, all the past as well as all the future. What was there after all? Joy, fear, sorrow, devotion, valour, rage—who can tell?—but truth—truth stripped of its cloak of time. Let the fool gape and shudder—the man knows and can look on without a wink. But he must at least be as much of a man as these on the shore. He must meet that truth with his own true stuff—with his own inborn strength. Principles? Principles won't do. Acquisitions, clothes, pretty rags—rags that would fly off at the first good shake. No. You want a deliberate belief. An appeal to me in this fiendish row—is there? Very well. I hear, I admit, but I have a voice too, and for good or evil mine is the speech that cannot be silenced. Of course, a fool, what with sheer fright and fine sentiments, is always safe. Who's that grunting? You wonder I didn't go ashore for a howl and a dance? Well, no—I didn't. Fine sentiments, you say? Fine sentiments be hanged! I had no time. I had to mess about with white-lead and strips of woollen blanket helping to put bandages on those leaky steam-pipes—I tell you. I had to watch the steering and circumvent those snags and get the tin-pot along by hook or by crook. There was surface-truth enough in these things to save a wiser man. And between whiles I had to look after the savage who was fireman. He was an improved specimen; he could fire up a vertical boiler.[9] He was there below me and, upon my word, to look at him was as edifying as seeing a dog in a parody of breeches and a feather hat walking on his hind legs. A few months of training had done for that really fine chap. He squinted at the steam-gauge and at the water-gauge with an evident effort of intrepidity—and he had

9. Closed tank heated by a furnace to generate the steam that drives a ship's turbine.

filed teeth too, the poor devil, and the wool of his pate shaved into
queer patterns, and three ornamental scars on each of his cheeks.
He ought to have been clapping his hands and stamping his feet on
the bank, instead of which he was hard at work, a thrall to strange
witchcraft, full of improving knowledge. He was useful because he
had been instructed; and what he knew was this—that should
the water in that transparent thing disappear the evil spirit inside
the boiler would get angry through the greatness of his thirst and
take a terrible vengeance. So he sweated and fired up and watched
the glass fearfully (with an impromptu charm, made of rags, tied to
his arm and a piece of polished bone as big as a watch stuck flat-
ways through his lower lip) while the wooded banks slipped past us
slowly, the shore noise was left behind, the interminable miles of silence—and we crept on, towards Kurtz. But the snags were thick,
the water was treacherous and shallow, the boiler seemed indeed to
have a sulky devil in it, and thus neither that fireman nor I had any
time to peer into our creepy thoughts.

"Some fifty miles below the Inner Station we came upon a hut of
reeds, an inclined and melancholy pole with the unrecognisable
tatters of what had been a flag of some sort flying from it and a
neatly stacked wood-pile. This was unexpected. We came to the
bank and on the stack of firewood found a flat piece of board with
some faded pencil-writing on it. When deciphered it said: 'Wood
for you. Hurry up. Approach cautiously.' There was a signature, but
it was illegible—not Kurtz—a much longer word. 'Hurry up!'
Where? Up the river? 'Approach cautiously.' We had not done so.
But the warning could not have been meant for the place where it
could be only found after approach. Something was wrong above.
But what—and how much? That was the question. We commented
adversely upon the imbecility of that telegraphic style. The bush
around said nothing and would not let us look very far, either. A
torn curtain of red twill hung in the doorway of the hut and flapped
sadly in our faces. The dwelling was dismantled, but we could see a
white man had lived there not very long ago. There remained
a rude table—a plank on two posts; a heap of rubbish reposed in a
dark corner, and by the door I picked up a book. It had lost its covers, and the pages had been thumbed into a state of extremely dirty
softness, but the back had been lovingly stitched afresh with white
cotton thread, which looked clean yet. It was an extraordinary find.
Its title was *An Inquiry into some Points of Seamanship* by a man
Towser, Towson—some such name—Master in His Majesty's Navy.
The matter looked dreary reading enough with illustrative diagrams
and repulsive tables of figures and the copy was sixty years old. I
handled this amazing antiquity with the greatest possible tenderness lest it should dissolve in my hands. Within, Towson or Towser

was inquiring earnestly into the breaking strain of ships' chains and tackle, and other such matters. Not a very enthralling book, but at the first glance you could see there a singleness of intention, an honest concern for the right way of going to work which made these humble pages thought out so many years ago luminous with another than a professional light. The simple old sailor with his talk of chains and purchases[1] made me forget the jungle and the pilgrims in a delicious sensation of having come upon something unmistakably real. Such a book being there was wonderful enough, but still more astounding were the notes penciled in the margin, and plainly referring to the text. I couldn't believe my eyes! They were in cipher! Yes, it looked like cipher. Fancy a man lugging with him a book of that description into this nowhere and studying it— and making notes—in cipher at that! It was an extravagant mystery.

"I had been dimly aware for some time of a worrying noise and when I lifted my eyes I saw the wood-pile was gone and the Manager aided by all the pilgrims was shouting at me from the riverside. I slipped the book into my pocket. I assure you to leave off reading was like tearing myself away from the shelter of an old and solid friendship.

"I started the lame engine ahead. 'It must be this miserable trader—this intruder,' exclaimed the Manager looking back malevolently at the place we had left. 'He must be English,' I said. 'It will not save him from getting into trouble if he is not careful,' muttered the Manager darkly. I observed with assumed innocence that no man was safe from trouble in this world.

"The current was more rapid now, the steamer seemed at her last gasp, the stern-wheel flopped languidly and I caught myself listening on tiptoe for the next beat of the float,[2] for in sober truth I expected the wretched thing to give up every moment. It was like watching the last flickers of a life. But still we crawled. Sometimes I would pick out a tree a little way ahead to measure our progress towards Kurtz by, but I lost it invariably before we got abreast. To keep the eyes so long on one thing was too much for human patience. The Manager displayed a beautiful resignation. I fretted and fumed and took to arguing with myself whether or no I would talk openly with Kurtz, but before I could come to any conclusion it occurred to me that my speech or my silence, indeed any action of mine, would be a mere futility. What did it matter what any one knew or ignored? What did it matter who was Manager? One gets sometimes such a flash of insight. The essentials of this affair lay deep under the surface, beyond my reach and beyond my power of meddling.

1. Levers or pulleys.
2. Blade of a paddle wheel.

"Towards the evening of the second day we judged ourselves about eight miles from Kurtz's station. I wanted to push on, but the Manager looked grave and told me the navigation up there was so dangerous that it would be advisable, the sun being very low already, to wait where we were till next morning. Moreover, he pointed out that if the warning to approach cautiously were to be followed we must approach in daylight—not at dusk or in the dark. This was sensible enough. Eight miles meant nearly three hours' steaming for us and I could also see suspicious ripples at the upper end of the reach. Nevertheless, I was annoyed beyond expression at the delay, and most unreasonably too, since one night more could not matter much after so many months. As we had plenty of wood and caution was the word, I brought up in the middle of the stream. The reach was narrow, straight, with high sides like a railway cutting. The dusk came gliding into it long before the sun had set. The current ran smooth and swift, but a dumb immobility sat on the banks. The living trees, lashed together by the creepers and every living bush of the undergrowth, might have been changed into stone, even to the slenderest twig, to the lightest leaf. It was not sleep—it seemed unnatural, like a state of trance. Not the faintest sound of any kind could be heard. You looked on amazed and began to suspect yourself of being deaf—then the night came suddenly and struck you blind as well. About three in the morning some large fish leaped and the loud splash made me jump as though a gun had been fired. When the sun rose there was a white fog, very warm and clammy, and more blinding than the night. It did not shift or drive, it was just there standing all round you like something solid. At eight or nine perhaps, it lifted, as a shutter lifts. We had a glimpse of the towering multitude of trees, of the immense matted jungle, with the blazing little ball of the sun hanging over it—all perfectly still—and then the white shutter came down again smoothly as if sliding in greased grooves. I ordered the chain which we had begun to heave in to be paid out again. Before it stopped running with a muffled rattle, a cry, a very loud cry as of infinite desolation, soared slowly in the opaque air. It ceased. A complaining clamour, modulated in savage discords, filled our ears. The sheer unexpectedness of it made my hair stir under my cap. I don't know how it struck the others; to me it seemed as though the mist itself had screamed, so suddenly and apparently from all sides at once did this tumultuous and mournful uproar arise. It culminated in a hurried outbreak of almost intolerably excessive shrieking which stopped short, leaving us stiffened in a variety of silly attitudes and obstinately listening to the nearly as appalling and excessive silence. 'Good God! What is the meaning . . .' stammered at my elbow one of the pilgrims, a little fat man with sandy hair and red whiskers, who wore side-spring boots, and pink pyjamas tucked into his socks. Two others remained open-mouthed a whole minute, then dashed into the little cabin, to rush out incontinently and stand darting scared glances, with Winchesters at 'ready' in their hands. What we could see was just the steamer we were on, her outlines blurred as though she had been on the point of dissolving and a misty strip of water perhaps two feet broad around her—and that was all. The rest of the world was nowhere as far as our eyes and ears were concerned. Just nowhere. Gone, disappeared, swept off without leaving a whisper or a shadow behind.

"I went forward and ordered the chain to be hauled in short, so as to be ready to trip the anchor and move the steamboat at once if necessary. 'Will they attack?' whispered an awed voice. 'We will all be butchered in this fog,' murmured another. The faces twitched with the strain, the hands trembled, slightly, the eyes forgot to wink. It was very curious to see the contrast of expressions of the white men and of the black fellows of our crew, who were as much strangers to that part of the river as we, though their homes were only eight hundred miles away. The whites, of course greatly dis-composed, had besides a curious look of being painfully shocked by such an outrageous row. The others had an alert, naturally inter-ested expression, but their faces were essentially quiet, even those of the one or two who grinned as they hauled at the chain. Several exchanged short grunting phrases which seemed to settle the mat-ter to their satisfaction. Their head-man, a young broad-chested black, severely draped in dark-blue fringed cloths, with fierce nos-trils and his hair all done up artfully in oily ringlets, stood near me. 'Aha!' I said, just for good fellowship's sake. 'Catch 'im,' he snapped with a bloodshot widening of his eyes and a flash of sharp teeth— 'catch 'im. Give 'im to us.' 'To you, eh?' I asked; 'what would you do with them?' 'Eat 'im!' he said curtly, and leaning his elbow on the rail looked out into the fog in a dignified and profoundly pensive at-titude. I would no doubt have been properly horrified had it not oc-curred to me that he and his chaps must be very hungry, that they must have been growing increasingly hungry for at least this month past. They had been engaged for six months (I don't think a single one of them had any clear idea of time as we at the end of count-less ages have. They still belonged to the beginnings of time—had no inherited experience to teach them, as it were) and of course, as long as there was a piece of paper written over in accordance with some farcical law or other made down the river, it didn't enter any-body's head to trouble how they would live. Certainly they had brought with them some rotten hippo-meat which couldn't have lasted very long anyway, even if the pilgrims hadn't, in the midst of a shocking hullabaloo, thrown a considerable quantity of it over-

board. It looked like a high-handed proceeding, but it was really a
case of legitimate self-defence. You can't breathe dead hippo waking, sleeping, and eating and at the same time keep your precarious
grip on existence. Besides that, they had given them every week
three pieces of brass wire each about nine inches long, and the theory was they were to buy their provisions with that currency in
river-side villages. You can see how *that* worked. There were either
no villages, or the people were hostile, or the director, who like the
rest of us fed out of tins with an occasional old he-goat thrown in,
didn't want to stop the steamer for some more or less recondite reason. So, unless they swallowed the wire itself or made loops of it to
snare the fishes with, I don't see what good their extravagant salary
could be to them. I must say it was paid with a regularity worthy of
a large and honourable trading company. For the rest, the only
thing to eat—though it didn't look eatable in the least—I saw in
their possession was a few lumps of some stuff like half-cooked
dough of a dirty lavender colour, they kept wrapped in leaves and
now and then swallowed a piece of, but so small that it seemed
done more for the look of the thing than for any serious purpose of
sustenance. Why in the name of all the gnawing devils of hunger
they didn't go for us—they were thirty to five—and have a good
tuck-in for once amazes me now when I think of it. They were big
powerful men with not much capacity to weigh the consequences,
with courage, with strength, even yet, though their skins were no
longer glossy and their muscles no longer hard. And I saw that
something restraining, one of those human secrets that baffle prob-
ability, had come into play there. I looked at them with a swift
quickening of interest—not because it occurred to me I might be
eaten by them before very long, though I own to you that just then
I perceived—in a new light, as it were—how unwholesome the pilgrims looked, and I hoped, yes I positively hoped, that my aspect
was not so—what shall I say?—so—unappetising: a touch of fantastic vanity which fitted well with the dream-sensation that per-
vaded all my days at that time. Perhaps I had a little fever too. One
can't live with one's finger everlastingly on one's pulse. I had often
'a little fever,' or a little touch of other things—the playful paw-
strokes of the wilderness, the preliminary trifling before the more
serious onslaught which came in due course. Yes—I looked at them
as you would on any human being with a curiosity of their impulses, motives, capacities, weaknesses, when brought to the test of
an inexorable physical necessity. Restraint! What possible restraint?
Was it superstition, disgust, patience, fear—or some kind of primitive honour? No fear can stand up to hunger, no patience can wear
it out, disgust simply does not exist where hunger is, and as to superstition, beliefs, and what you may call principles, they are less

than chaff in a breeze. Don't you know the devilry of lingering starvation, its exasperating torment, its black thoughts, its sombre and
brooding ferocity? Well, I do. It takes a man all his inborn strength
to fight hunger properly. It's really easier to face bereavement, dis-
honour, and the perdition of one's soul—than this kind of prolonged hunger. Sad, but true. And these chaps too had no earthly
reason for any kind of scruple. Restraint! I would just as soon have
expected restraint from a hyena prowling amongst the corpses of a
battlefield. But there was the fact facing me—the fact, dazzling, to
be seen, like the foam on the depths of the sea, like a ripple on an
unfathomable enigma, a mystery greater—when I thought of it—
than the curious, inexplicable note of desperate grief in this savage
clamour that had swept by us on the river-bank behind the blind
whiteness of the fog.

"Two pilgrims were quarrelling in hurried whispers as to which
bank. 'Left.' 'No, no, how can you? Right, right, of course.' 'It is very
serious,' said the Manager's voice behind me; 'I would be desolated
if anything should happen to Mr. Kurtz before we came up.' I
looked at him and had not the slightest doubt he was sincere. He
was just the kind of man who would wish to preserve appearances.
That was his restraint. But when he muttered something about going on at once I did not even take the trouble to answer him. I
knew, and he knew, that it was impossible. Were we to let go our
hold of the bottom, we would be absolutely in the air—in space.
We wouldn't be able to tell where we were going to—whether up or
down stream or across—till we fetched against one bank or the
other—and then we wouldn't know at first which it was. Of course
I made no move. I had no mind for a smash-up. You couldn't imagine a more deadly place for a shipwreck. Whether drowned at once
or not, we were sure to perish speedily in one way or another. 'I au-
thorise you to take all the risks,' he said after a short silence. 'I refuse to take any,' I said shortly, which was just the answer he
expected, though its tone might have surprised him. 'Well, I must
defer to your judgment. You are Captain,' he said with marked civil-
ity. I turned my shoulder to him in sign of my appreciation and
looked into the fog. How long would it last? It was the most hopeless look-out. The approach to this Kurtz grubbing for ivory in the
wretched bush was beset by as many dangers as though he had
been an enchanted princess sleeping in a fabulous castle. 'Will they
attack, do you think?' asked the Manager in a confidential tone.

"I did not think they would attack, for several obvious reasons.
The thick fog was one. If they left the bank in their canoes they
would get lost in it as we would be if we attempted to move. Still I
had also judged the jungle of both banks quite impenetrable—and
yet eyes were in it, eyes that had seen us. The river-side bushes

were certainly very thick, but the undergrowth behind was evidently penetrable. However, during the short lift I had seen no canoes anywhere in the reach—certainly not abreast of the steamer. But what made the idea of attack inconceivable to me was the nature of the noise—of the cries we had heard. They had not the fierce character boding of immediate hostile intention. Unexpected, wild, and violent as they had been they had given me an irresistible impression of sorrow. The glimpse of the steamboat had for some reason filled those savages with unrestrained grief. The danger if any, I expounded, was from our proximity to a great human passion let loose. Even extreme grief may ultimately vent itself in violence—but more generally takes the form of apathy. . . .

"You should have seen the pilgrims stare! They had no heart to grin or even to revile me, but I believe they thought me gone mad—with fright maybe. I delivered a regular lecture. My dear boys, it was no good bothering. Keep a look-out? Well, you may guess I watched the fog for the signs of lifting as a cat watches a mouse, but for anything else our eyes were of no more use to us than if we had been buried miles deep in a heap of cotton-wool. It felt like it too—choking, warm, stifling. Besides, all I said, though it sounded extravagant, was absolutely true to fact. What we afterwards alluded to as an attack was really an attempt at repulse. The action was very far from being aggressive; it was not even defensive in the usual sense; it was undertaken under the stress of desperation and in its essence was purely protective.

"It developed itself, I should say, two hours after the fog lifted, and its commencement was at a spot, roughly speaking, about a mile and a half below Kurtz's station. We had just floundered and flopped round a bend when I saw an islet, a mere grassy hummock of bright green in the middle of the stream. It was the only thing of the kind, but as we opened the reach more I perceived it was the head of a long sandbank or rather of a chain of shallow patches stretching down the middle of the river. They were discoloured, just awash, and the whole lot was seen just under the water exactly as a man's backbone is seen running down the middle of his back under the skin. Now, as far as I did see, I could go to the right or to the left of this. I didn't know either channel, of course. The banks looked pretty well alike, the depth appeared the same, but as I had been informed the station was on the west side I naturally headed for the western passage.

"No sooner had we fairly entered it than I became aware it was much narrower than I had supposed. To the left of us there was the long uninterrupted shoal and to the right a high steep bank heavily overgrown with bushes. Above the bush the trees stood in serried ranks. The twigs overhung the current thickly, and from distance to distance a large limb of some tree projected rigidly over the stream. It was then well on in the afternoon, the face of the forest was gloomy, and a broad strip of shadow had already fallen on the water. In this shadow we steamed up, very slowly as you may imagine. I sheered her well inshore, the water being deepest near the bank as the sounding-pole informed me.

"One of my hungry and forbearing friends was sounding in the bows just below me. This steamboat was exactly like a decked scow.[3] On the deck there were two little teak-wood houses with doors and windows. The boiler was in the fore-end and the machinery right astern. Over the whole there was a light roof supported on stanchions. The funnel projected through that roof and in front of the funnel a small cabin built of light planks served for a pilot-house. It contained a couch, two campstools, a loaded Martini-Henry[4] leaning in one corner, a tiny table, and the steering-wheel. It had a wide door in front and a broad shutter at each side. All these were always thrown open, of course. I spent my days perched up there on the extreme fore-end of that roof, before the door. At night I slept, or tried to, on the couch. An athletic black belonging to some coast tribe and educated by my poor predecessor was the helmsman. He sported a pair of brass earrings, wore a blue cloth wrapper from the waist to the ankles, and thought all the world of himself. He was the most unstable kind of fool I had ever seen. He steered with no end of a swagger while you were by, but if he lost sight of you he became instantly the prey of an abject funk and would let that cripple of a steamboat get the upper hand of him in a minute.

"I was looking down at the sounding-pole and feeling much annoyed to see at each try a little more of it stick out of that river when I saw my poleman give up the business suddenly and stretch himself flat on the deck without even taking the trouble to haul his pole in. He kept hold on it though, and it trailed in the water. At the same time the fireman, whom I could also see below me, sat down abruptly before his furnace and ducked his head. I was amazed. Then I had to look at the river mighty quick because there was a snag in the fairway. Sticks, little sticks, were flying about, thick; they were whizzing before my nose, dropping below me, striking behind me against my pilot-house. All this time the river, the shore, the woods were very quiet—perfectly quiet. I could only hear the heavy splashing thump of the stern-wheel and the patter of these things. We cleared the snag clumsily. Arrows, by Jove! We were being shot at! I stepped in quickly to close the shutter on the

3. Barge with flat-bottomed rectangular hull and sloping ends.
4. Military rifle widely used in the British Empire.

land-side. That fool-helmsman, his hands on the spokes, was lifting his knees high, stamping his feet, champing his mouth, like a reined-in horse. Confound him! And we were staggering within ten feet of the bank. I had to lean right out to swing the heavy shutter and I saw a face amongst the leaves on the level with my own looking at me very fierce and steady, and then suddenly, as though a veil had been removed from my eyes, I made out deep in the tangled gloom, naked breasts, arms, legs, glaring eyes—the bush was swarming with human limbs in movement, glistening, of bronze colour. The twigs shook, swayed, and rustled, the arrows flew out of them, and then the shutter came to. 'Steer her straight,' I said to the helmsman. He held his head rigid, face forward, but his eyes rolled, he kept on lifting and setting down his feet gently, his mouth foamed a little. 'Keep quiet!' I said in a fury. I might just as well have ordered a tree not to sway in the wind. I darted out. Below me there was a great scuffle of feet on the iron deck; confused exclamations; a voice screamed, 'Can you turn back?' I caught sight of a V-shaped ripple on the water ahead. What? Another snag! A fusillade burst out under my feet. The pilgrims had opened with their Winchesters and were simply squirting lead into that bush. A deuce of a lot of smoke came up and drove slowly forward. I swore at it. Now I couldn't see the ripple or the snag either. I stood in the doorway, peering, and the arrows came in swarms. They might have been poisoned, but they looked as though they wouldn't kill a cat. The bush began to howl. Our wood-cutters raised a warlike whoop; the report of a rifle just at my back deafened me. I glanced over my shoulder and the pilot-house was yet full of noise and smoke when I made a dash at the wheel. The fool-nigger had dropped everything to throw the shutter open and let off that Martini-Henry. He stood before the wide opening, glaring, and I yelled at him to come back, while I straightened the sudden twist out of that steamboat. There was no room to turn even if I had wanted to, the snag was somewhere very near ahead in that confounded smoke, there was no time to lose, so I just crowded her into the bank, right into the bank where I knew the water was deep.

"We tore slowly along the overhanging bushes in a whirl of broken twigs and flying leaves. The fusillade below stopped short as I had foreseen it would when the squirts got empty. I threw my head back to a glinting whiz that traversed the pilot-house in at one shutter-hole and out at the other. Looking past that mad helmsman who was shaking the empty rifle and yelling at the shore, I saw vague forms of men running bent double, leaping, gliding, distinct, incomplete, evanescent. Something big appeared in the air before the shutter, the rifle went overboard, and the man stepped back swiftly, looked at me over his shoulder in an extraordinary, profound, familiar manner, and fell upon my feet. The side of his head hit the wheel twice and the end of what appeared a long cane clattered round and knocked over a little camp-stool. It looked as though after wrenching that thing from somebody ashore he had lost his balance in the effort. The thin smoke had blown away, we were clear of the snag, and looking ahead I could see that in another hundred yards or so I would be free to sheer off away from the bank, but my feet felt so very warm and wet that I had to look down. The man had rolled on his back and stared straight up at me; both his hands clutched that cane. It was the shaft of a spear that, either thrown or lunged through the opening, had caught him in the side just below the ribs; the blade has gone in out of sight after making a frightful gash; my shoes were full; a pool of blood lay very still gleaming dark-red under the wheel; his eyes shone with an amazing lustre. The fusillade burst out again. He looked at me anxiously, gripping the spear like something precious, with an air of being afraid I would try to take it away from him. I had to make an effort to free my eyes from his gaze and attend to the steering. With one hand I felt above my head for the line of the steam whistle and jerked out screech after screech hurriedly. The tumult of angry and warlike yells was checked instantly and then from the depths of the woods went out such a tremulous and prolonged wail of mournful fear and utter despair as may be imagined to follow the flight of the last hope from the earth. There was a great commotion in the bush; the shower of arrows stopped; a few dropping shots rang out sharply—then silence, in which the languid beat of the stern-wheel came plainly to my ears. I put the helm hard a-starboard at the moment when the pilgrim in pink pyjamas, very hot and agitated, appeared in the doorway. 'The Manager sends me. . . . ' he began in an official tone and stopped short. 'Good God!' he said glaring at the wounded man.

"We two whites stood over him and his lustrous and inquiring glance enveloped us both. I declare it looked as though he would presently put to us some question in an understandable language, but he died without uttering a sound, without moving a limb, without twitching a muscle. Only in the very last moment as though in response to some sign we could not see, to some whisper we could not hear, he frowned heavily, and that frown gave to his black death-mask an inconceivably sombre, brooding, and menacing expression. The lustre of inquiring glance faded swiftly into vacant glassiness. 'Can you steer?' I asked the agent eagerly. He looked very dubious, but I made a grab at his arm and he understood at once I meant him to steer whether or no. To tell you the truth, I was morbidly anxious to change my shoes and socks. 'He is dead,' murmured the fellow immensely impressed. 'No doubt about it,' said I tugging like mad at the shoe-laces. 'And by the way, I suppose Mr. Kurtz is dead as well by this time.'

"For the moment that was the dominant thought. There was a sense of extreme disappointment as though I had found out I had been striving after something altogether without a substance. I couldn't have been more disgusted if I had travelled all this way for the sole purpose of talking with Mr. Kurtz. Talking with . . . I flung one shoe overboard and became aware that that was exactly what I had been looking forward to—a talk with Kurtz. I made the strange discovery that I had never imagined him as doing, you know, but as discoursing. I didn't say to myself, 'Now I will never see him,' or 'Now I will never shake him by the hand,' but, 'Now I will never hear him.' The man presented himself as a voice. Not of course that I did not connect him with some sort of action. Hadn't I been told in all the tones of jealousy and admiration that he had collected, bartered, swindled, or stolen more ivory than all the other agents together. That was not the point. The point was in his being a gifted creature and that of all his gifts the one that stood out pre-eminently, that carried with it a sense of real presence, was his ability to talk, his words—the gift of expression, the bewildering, the illuminating, the most exalted and the most contemptible, the pulsating stream of light or the deceitful flow from the heart of an impenetrable darkness.

"The other shoe went flying unto the devil-god of that river. I thought, By Jove! it's all over. We are too late; he has vanished—the gift has vanished by means of some spear, arrow, or club. I will never hear that chap speak after all—and my sorrow had a startling extravagance of emotion, even such as I had noticed in the howling sorrow of these savages in the bush. I couldn't have felt more of lonely desolation somehow had I been robbed of a belief or had missed my destiny in life. . . . Why do you sigh in this beastly way, somebody? Absurd? Well, absurd. Good Lord! mustn't a man ever. . . . Here, give me some tobacco." . . .

There was a pause of profound stillness, then a match flared, and Marlow's lean face appeared worn, hollow, with downward folds and dropped eyelids with an aspect of concentrated attention; and as he took vigorous draws at his pipe it seemed to retreat and advance out of the night in the regular flicker of the tiny flame. The match went out.

"Absurd!" he cried. "This is the worst of trying to tell. . . . Here you all are each moored with two good addresses like a hulk with two anchors, a butcher round one corner, a policeman round another, excellent appetites, and temperature normal—you hear—normal from year's end to year's end. And you say, Absurd! Absurd be—exploded! Absurd! My dear boys, what can you expect from a man who out of sheer nervousness had just flung overboard a pair of new shoes? Now I think of it, it is amazing I did not shed tears. I am, upon the whole, proud of my fortitude. I was cut to the quick at the idea of having lost the inestimable privilege of listening to the gifted Kurtz. Of course I was wrong. The privilege was waiting for me. Oh yes, I heard more than enough. And I was right, too. A voice. He was very little more than a voice. And I heard—him—it— this voice—other voices—all of them were so little more than voices—and the memory of that time itself lingers around me, impalpable, like a dying vibration of one immense jabber, silly, atrocious, sordid, savage, or simply mean without any kind of sense. Voices, voices—even the girl herself—now. . . ."

He was silent for a long time.

"I laid the ghost of his gifts at last with a lie," he began suddenly. "Girl! What? Did I mention a girl? Oh, she is out of it—completely. They—the women I mean—are out of it—should be out of it. We must help them to stay in that beautiful world of their own lest ours gets worse. Oh, she had to be out of it. You should have heard the disinterred body of Mr. Kurtz saying, 'My Intended.' You would have perceived directly then how completely she was out of it. And the lofty frontal bone of Mr. Kurtz! They say the hair goes on growing sometimes, but this—ah—specimen was impressively bald. The wilderness had patted him on the head, and behold, it was like a ball—an ivory ball; it had caressed him and—lo!—he had withered; it had taken him, loved him, embraced him, got into his veins, consumed his flesh, and sealed his soul to its own by the inconceivable ceremonies of some devilish initiation. He was its spoiled and pampered favourite. Ivory! I should think so. Heaps of it, stacks of it. The old mud shanty was bursting with it. You would think there was not a single tusk left either above or below the ground in the whole country. 'Mostly fossil,' the Manager had remarked disparagingly. It was no more fossil than I am, but they call it fossil when it is dug up. It appears these niggers do bury the tusks sometimes— but evidently they couldn't bury this parcel deep enough to save the gifted Mr. Kurtz from his fate. We filled the steamboat with it and had to pile a lot on the deck. Thus he could see and enjoy as long as he could see because the appreciation of this favour had remained with him to the last. You should have heard him say, 'My ivory.' Oh yes, I heard him. 'My Intended, my ivory, my station, my river, my . . .' everything belonged to him. It made me hold my breath in expectation of hearing the wilderness burst into a prodigious peal of laughter that would shake the fixed stars in their places. Everything belonged to him—but that was a trifle. The thing was to know what he belonged to, how many powers of darkness claimed him for their own. That was the reflection that made

you creepy all over. It was impossible—it was not good for one either—trying to imagine. He had taken a high seat amongst the devils of the land—I mean literally. You can't understand? How could
you—with solid pavement under your feet, surrounded by kind
neighbours ready to cheer you or to fall on you, stepping delicately
between the butcher and the policeman, in the holy terror of scan-
dal and gallows and lunatic asylums—how can you imagine what
particular region of the first ages a man's untrammelled feet may
take him into by the way of solitude—utter solitude without a policeman—by the way of silence—utter silence, where no warning
voice of a kind neighbour can be heard whispering of public opinion. These little things make all the great difference. When they are
gone you must fall back upon your own innate strength, upon your
own capacity for faithfulness. Of course you may be too much of a
fool to go wrong—too dull even to know you are being assaulted by
the powers of darkness. I take it no fool ever made a bargain for his
soul with the devil. The fool is too much of a fool or the devil too
much of a devil—I don't know which. Or you may be such a thun-
deringly exalted creature as to be altogether deaf and blind to anything but heavenly sights and sounds. Then the earth for you is
only a standing place—and whether to be like this is your loss or
your gain I won't pretend to say. But most of us are neither one nor
the other. The earth for us is a place to live in, where we must put
up with sights, with sounds, with smells too, by Jove!—breathe
dead hippo so to speak and not be contaminated. And there, don't
you see, your strength comes in, the faith in your ability for the digging of unostentatious holes to bury the stuff in—your power of devotion not to yourself but to an obscure, back-breaking business.
And that's difficult enough. Mind, I am not trying to excuse or even
explain—I am trying to account to myself for—for—Mr. Kurtz—for
the shade of Mr. Kurtz. This initiated wraith[5] from the back of
Nowhere honoured me with its amazing confidence before it vanished altogether. This was because it could speak English to me.
The original Kurtz had been educated partly in England and—as he
was good enough to say himself—his sympathies were in the right
place. His mother was half-English, his father was half-French. All
Europe contributed to the making of Kurtz, and by and by I learned
that most appropriately the International Society for the Suppression of Savage Customs had entrusted him with the making of a report for its future guidance. And he had written it too. I've seen it.
I've read it. It was eloquent, vibrating with eloquence, but too high-
strung I think. Seventeen pages of close writing. He had found time
for it. But this must have been before his—let us say—nerves went

5. Apparition, spirit.

wrong and caused him to preside at certain midnight dances ending with unspeakable rites, which—as far as I reluctantly gathered from what I heard at various times—were offered up to him—do you understand—to Mr. Kurtz himself. But it was a beautiful piece of writing. The opening paragraph, however, in the light of later information, strikes me now as ominous. He began with the argument that we whites, from the point of development we had arrived at, 'must necessarily appear to them [savages] in the nature of supernatural beings—we approach them with the might as of a deity,' and so on, and so on. 'By the simple exercise of our will we can exert a power for good practically unbounded,' etc. etc. From that point he soared and took me with him. The peroration was magnificent, though difficult to remember, you know. It gave me the notion of an exotic Immensity ruled by an august Benevolence. It made me tingle with enthusiasm. This was the unbounded power of eloquence—of words—of burning noble words. There were no practical hints to interrupt the magic current of phrases, unless a kind of note at the foot of the last page, scrawled evidently much later in an unsteady hand, may be regarded as the exposition of a method. It was very simple and at the end of that moving appeal to every altruistic sentiment it blazed at you luminous and terrifying like a flash of lightning in a serene sky: 'Exterminate all the brutes!' The curious part was that he had apparently forgotten all about that valuable postscriptum because later on when he in a sense came to himself, he repeatedly entreated me to take good care of 'my pamphlet' (he called it) as it was sure to have in the future a good influence upon his career. I had full information about all these things, and besides, as it turned out I was to have the care of his memory. I've done enough for it to give me the indisputable right to lay it, if I choose, for an everlasting rest in the dustbin of progress, amongst all the sweepings and, figuratively speaking, all the dead cats of civilisation. But then, you see, I can't choose. He won't be forgotten. Whatever he was he was not common. He had the power to charm or frighten rudimentary souls into an aggravated witch-dance in his honour, he could also fill the small souls of the pilgrims with bitter misgivings—he had one devoted friend at least, and he had conquered one soul in the world that was neither rudimentary nor tainted with self-seeking. No, I can't forget him, though I am not prepared to affirm the fellow was exactly worth the life we lost in getting to him. I missed my late helmsman awfully—I missed him even while his body was still lying in the pilot-house. Perhaps you will think it passing strange this regret for a savage who was no more account than a grain of sand in a black Sahara. Well, don't you see, he had done something, he had steered; for months I had him at my back—a help—an instrument. It was a kind of partnership. He steered for me—I had to look after him, I worried about his deficiencies, and thus a subtle bond had been created of which I only became aware when it was suddenly broken. And the intimate profundity of that look he gave me when he received his hurt remains to this day in my memory—like a claim of distant kinship affirmed in a supreme moment.

"Poor fool! If he had only left that shutter alone. He had no restraint, no restraint—just like Kurtz—a tree swayed by the wind. As soon as I had put on a dry pair of slippers I dragged him out, after first jerking the spear out of his side, which operation I confess I performed with my eyes shut tight. His heels leaped together over the little door-step; his shoulders were pressed to my breast; I hugged him from behind desperately. Oh! he was heavy, heavy; heavier than any man on earth, I should imagine. Then without more ado I tipped him overboard. The current snatched him as though he had been a wisp of grass and I saw the body roll over twice before I lost sight of it for ever. All the pilgrims and the Manager were then congregated on the awning-deck about the pilot-house chattering at each other like a flock of excited magpies, and there was a scandalised murmur at my heartless promptitude. What they wanted to keep that body hanging about for I can't guess. Embalm it, maybe. But I had also heard another and a very ominous murmur on the deck below. My friends the wood-cutters were likewise scandalised, and with a better show of reason—though I admit that the reason itself was quite inadmissible. Oh, quite! I had made up my mind that if my late helmsman was to be eaten, the fishes alone should have him. He had been a very second-rate helmsman while alive, but now he was dead he might have become a first-class temptation and possibly cause some startling trouble. Besides, I was anxious to take the wheel, the man in pink pyjamas showing himself a hopeless duffer at the business.

"This I did directly the simple funeral was over. We were going half-speed, keeping right in the middle of the stream, and I listened to the talk about me. They had given up Kurtz, they had given up the station; Kurtz was dead and the station had been burnt—and so on, and so on. The red-haired pilgrim was beside himself with the thought that at least this poor Kurtz had been properly revenged. 'Say! We must have made a glorious slaughter of them in the bush. Eh? What do you think? Say?' He positively danced, the blood-thirsty little gingery[6] beggar. And he had nearly fainted when he saw the wounded man! I could not help saying, 'You made a glorious lot of smoke, anyhow.' I had seen from the way the tops of the bushes rustled and flew that almost all the shots had gone too high.

6. Ruddy-complexioned.

You can't hit anything unless you take aim and fire from the shoulder, but these chaps fired from the hip with their eyes shut. The retreat, I maintained—and I was right—was caused by the screeching of the steam-whistle. Upon this they forgot Kurtz, and began to howl at me with indignant protests.

"The Manager stood by the wheel murmuring confidentially about the necessity of getting well away down the river before dark at all events, when I saw in the distance a clearing on the river-side and the outlines of some sort of building. 'What's this?' I asked. He clapped his hands in wonder. 'The station!' he cried. I edged in at once, still going half-speed.

"Through my glasses I saw the slope of a hill interspersed with rare trees and perfectly free from undergrowth. A long decaying building on the summit was half buried in the high grass; the large holes in the peaked roof gaped black from afar; the jungle and the woods made a background. There was no enclosure or fence of any kind, but there had been one apparently, for near the house half a dozen slim posts remained in a row, roughly trimmed, and with their upper ends ornamented with round carved balls. The rails or whatever there had been between had disappeared. Of course the forest surrounded all that. The river-bank was clear and on the water side I saw a white man under a hat like a cart-wheel beckoning persistently with his whole arm. Examining the edge of the forest above and below, I was almost certain I could see movements—human forms gliding here and there. I steamed past prudently, then stopped the engines and let her drift down. The man on the shore began to shout, urging us to land. 'We have been attacked,' screamed the Manager. 'I know—I know. It's all right,' yelled back the other, as cheerful as you please. 'Come along. It's all right. I am glad.'

"His aspect reminded me of something I had seen—something funny I had seen somewhere. As I manoeuvred to get alongside I was asking myself, 'What does this fellow look like?' Suddenly I got it. He looked like a harlequin. His clothes had been made of some stuff that was brown holland[7] probably, but it was covered with patches all over, with bright patches, blue, red, and yellow—patches on the back, patches on the front, patches on elbows, on knees, coloured binding round his jacket, scarlet edging at the bottom of his trousers, and the sunshine made him look extremely gay and wonderfully neat withal because you could see how beautifully all this patching had been done. A beardless boyish face, very fair, no features to speak of, nose peeling, little blue eyes, smiles and frowns chasing each other over that open countenance like sun-

7. Sturdy cotton cloth.

shine and shadow on a wind-swept plain. 'Look out, Captain!' he cried; 'there's a snag lodged in here last night.' What! Another snag? I confess I swore shamefully. I had nearly holed my cripple, to finish off that charming trip. The harlequin on the bank turned his little pug-nose up to me. 'You English?' he asked all smiles. 'Are you?' I shouted from the wheel. The smiles vanished and he shook his head as if sorry for my disappointment. Then he brightened up. 'Never mind!' he cried encouragingly. 'Are we in time?' I asked. 'He is up there,' he replied with a toss of the head up the hill and becoming gloomy all of a sudden. His face was like the autumn sky, overcast one moment and bright the next.

"When the Manager, escorted by the pilgrims, all of them armed to the teeth, had gone to the house, this chap came on board. 'I say, I don't like this. These natives are in the bush,' I said. He assured me earnestly it was all right. 'They are simple people,' he added; 'well, I am glad you came. It took me all my time to keep them off.' But you said it was all right,' I cried. 'Oh, they meant no harm,' he said and as I stared he corrected himself, 'Not exactly.' Then vivaciously, 'My faith, your pilot-house wants a clean-up!' In the next breath he advised me to keep enough steam on the boiler to blow the whistle in case of any trouble. 'One good screech will do more for you than all your rifles. They are simple people,' he repeated. He rattled away at such a rate he quite overwhelmed me. He seemed to be trying to make up for lots of silence and actually hinted, laughing, that such was the case. 'Don't you talk with Mr. Kurtz?' I said. 'You don't talk with that man—you listen to him,' he exclaimed with severe exaltation. 'But now . . .' He waved his arm and in the twinkling of an eye was in the uttermost depths of despondency. In a moment he came up again with a jump, possessed himself of both my hands, shook them continuously while he gabbled: 'Brother sailor . . . honour . . . pleasure . . . delight . . . introduce myself . . . Russian . . . son of an Arch-Priest . . . Government of Tambov . . . What! Tobacco! English tobacco; the excellent English tobacco! Now, that's brotherly. Smoke! Where's a sailor that does not smoke.'

"The pipe soothed him and gradually I made out he had run away from school, had gone to sea in a Russian ship; ran away again; served some time in English ships; was now reconciled with the Arch-Priest. He made a point of that. 'But when one is young one must see things, gather experience, ideas, enlarge the mind.' 'Here!' I interrupted. 'You can never tell! Here I met Mr. Kurtz,' he said, youthfully solemn and reproachful. I held my tongue after that. It appears he had persuaded a Dutch trading-house on the coast to fit him out with stores and goods and had started for the interior with a light heart and no more idea of what would happen to him than a baby. He had been wandering about that river for nearly two years alone, cut off from everybody and everything. 'I am not so young as I look. I am twenty-five,' he said. 'At first old Van Shuyten would tell me to go to the devil,' he narrated with keen enjoyment; 'but I stuck to him, and talked and talked till at last he got afraid I would talk the hind-leg off his favourite dog, so he gave me some cheap things and a few guns and told me he hoped he would never see my face again. Good old Dutchman, Van Shuyten. I sent him one small lot of ivory a year ago so that he can't call me a little thief when I get back. I hope he got it. And for the rest, I don't care. I had some wood stacked for you. That was my old house. Did you see?'

"I gave him Towson's book. He made as though he would kiss me, but restrained himself. 'The only book I had left and I thought I had lost it,' he said, looking at it ecstatically. 'So many accidents happen to a man going about alone, you know. Canoes get upset sometimes—and sometimes you've got to clear out so quick when the people get angry.' He thumbed the pages. 'You made notes in Russian?' I asked. He nodded. 'I thought they were written in cipher,' I said. He laughed, then became serious. 'I had lots of trouble to keep these people off,' he said. 'Did they want to kill you?' I asked. 'Oh no!' he cried, and checked himself. 'Why did they attack us?' I pursued. He hesitated, then said shamefacedly, 'They don't want him to go.' 'Don't they?' I said curiously. He nodded a nod full of mystery and wisdom. 'I tell you,' he cried, 'this man has enlarged my mind.' He opened his arms wide, staring at me with his little blue eyes that were perfectly round."

III

"I looked at him, lost in astonishment. There he was before me in motley as though he had absconded from a troupe of mimes, enthusiastic, fabulous. His very existence was improbable, inexplicable, and altogether bewildering. He was an insoluble problem. It was inconceivable how he had existed, how he had succeeded in getting so far, how he had managed to remain—why he did not instantly disappear. 'I went a little farther,' he said, 'then still a little farther—till I had gone so far that I don't know how I'll ever get back. Never mind. Plenty time! I can manage. You take Kurtz away quick—quick—I tell you.' The glamour of youth enveloped his parti-coloured rags, his destitution, his loneliness, the essential desolation of his futile wanderings. For months—for years—his life hadn't been worth a day's purchase—and there he was gallantly, thoughtlessly alive, to all appearance indestructible solely by the virtue of his few years and of his unreflecting audacity. I was seduced into something like admiration—like envy. Glamour urged him on, glamour kept him unscathed. He surely wanted nothing from the wilderness but space to breathe in and to push on through. His need was to exist and to move onwards at the greatest possible risk and with a maximum of privation. If the absolutely pure, uncalculating, unpractical spirit of adventure had ever ruled a human being, it ruled this be-patched youth. I almost envied him the possession of this modest and clear flame. It seemed to have consumed all thought of self so completely that even while he was talking to you, you forgot that it was he—the man before your eyes—who had gone through these things. I did not envy him his devotion to Kurtz, though. He had not meditated over it. It came to him and he accepted it with a sort of eager fatalism. I must say that to me it appeared about the most dangerous thing in every way he had come upon so far.

"They had come together unavoidably, like two ships becalmed near each other, and lay rubbing sides at last. I suppose Kurtz wanted an audience because on a certain occasion, when encamped in the forest, they had talked all night, or more probably Kurtz had talked. 'We talked of everything,' he said quite transported at the recollection. 'I forgot there was such a thing as sleep. The night did not seem to last an hour. Everything! Everything! . . . Of love too.' 'Ah, he talked to you of love!' I said much amused. 'It isn't what you think,' he cried almost passionately. 'It was in general. He made me see things—things.'

"He threw his arms up. We were on deck at the time, and the headman of my wood-cutters lounging near by turned upon him his heavy and glittering eyes. I looked around, and I don't know why, but I assure you that never, never before did this land, this river, this jungle, the very arch of this blazing sky appear to me so hopeless and so dark, so impenetrable to human thought, so pitiless to human weakness. 'And ever since you have been with him, of course?' I said.

"On the contrary. It appears their intercourse had been very much broken by various causes. He had, as he informed me proudly, managed to nurse Kurtz through two illnesses (he alluded to it as you would to some risky feat) but as a rule Kurtz wandered alone far in the depths of the forest. 'Very often coming to this station, I had to wait days and days before he would turn up,' he said. 'Ah! it was worth waiting for—sometimes.' 'What was he doing? exploring or what?' I asked. Oh! Yes. Of course he had discovered lots of villages, a lake too—he did not know exactly in what direction; it was dangerous to inquire too much—but mostly his expeditions had been for ivory. 'But he had no goods to trade with by that time,' I objected. 'There's a good lot of cartridges left even yet,' he answered, looking away. 'To speak plainly, he raided the country,' I said. He nodded. 'Not alone, surely!' He muttered something about the villages round that lake. 'Kurtz got the tribe to follow him, did he?' I suggested. He fidgeted a little. 'They adored him,' he said. The tone of these words was so extraordinary that I looked at him searchingly. It was curious to see his mingled eagerness and reluctance to speak of Kurtz. The man filled his life, occupied his thoughts, swayed his emotions. 'What can you expect!' he burst out; 'he came to them with thunder and lightning, you know—and they had never seen anything like it—and very terrible. He could be very terrible. You can't judge Mr. Kurtz as you would an ordinary man. No, no, no! Now—just to give you an idea—I don't mind telling you, he wanted to shoot me too one day—but I don't judge him.' 'Shoot you!' I cried. 'What for?' 'Well, I had a small lot of ivory the chief of that village near my house gave me. You see I used to shoot game for them. Well, he wanted it and wouldn't hear reason. He declared he would shoot me unless I gave him the ivory and then cleared out of the country because he could do so, and had a fancy for it, and there was nothing on earth to prevent him killing whom he jolly well pleased. And it was true too. I gave him the ivory. What did I care! But I didn't clear out. No, no. I couldn't leave him. I had to be careful, of course, till we got friendly again for a time. He had his second illness then. Afterwards I had to keep out of the way, but I didn't mind. He was living for the most part in those villages on the lake. When he came down to the river, sometimes he would take to me and sometimes it was better for me to be careful. This man suffered too much. He hated all this and somehow he couldn't get away. When I had a chance I begged him to try and leave while there was time; I offered to go back with him. And he would say yes—and then he would remain—go off on another ivory hunt—disappear for weeks—forget himself amongst these people—forget himself—you know.' 'Why! he's mad,' I said. He protested indignantly. Mr. Kurtz couldn't be mad. If I had heard him talk only two days ago I wouldn't dare hint at such a thing. . . . I had taken up my binoculars while we talked and was looking at the shore, sweeping the limit of the forest at each side and at the back of the house. The consciousness of there being people in that bush, so silent, so quiet—as silent and quiet as the ruined house on the hill—made me uneasy. There was no sign on the face of nature of this amazing tale that was not so much told as suggested to me in desolate exclamations, completed by shrugs, in interrupted phrases, in hints ending in deep sighs. The woods were unmoved like a mask—heavy like the closed door of a prison—they looked with their air of hidden knowledge, of patient expectation, of unapproachable silence. The Russian was explaining to me that it was only lately that Mr. Kurtz had come down to the river, bringing along with him all the fighting men of that lake tribe. He had been absent for several months—getting himself adored, I suppose—and had come down unexpectedly, with the intention to all appearance of making a raid either across the river or down stream. Evidently the appetite for more ivory had got the better of the—what shall I say—less material aspirations. However, he had got much worse suddenly. 'I heard he was lying helpless, and so I came up—took my chance,' said the Russian. 'Oh, he is bad, very bad.' I directed my glass to the house. There were no signs of life, but there were the ruined roof, the long mud wall peeping above the grass, with three little square window-holes no two of the same size, all this brought within reach of my hand, as it were. And then I made a brusque movement and one of the remaining posts of that vanished fence leaped up in the field of my glass. You remember I told you I had been struck at the distance by certain attempts at ornamentation, rather remarkable in the ruinous aspect of the place. Now I had suddenly a nearer view and its first result was to make me throw my head back as if before a blow. Then I went carefully from post to post with my glass, and I saw my mistake. These round knobs were not ornamental but symbolic; they were expressive and puzzling, striking and disturbing—food for thought and also for vultures if there had been any looking down from the sky; but at all events for such ants as were industrious enough to ascend the pole. They would have been even more impressive, those heads on the stakes, if their faces had not been turned to the house. Only one, the first I had made out, was facing my way. I was not so shocked as you may think. The start back I had given was really nothing but a movement of surprise. I had expected to see a knob of wood there, you know. I returned deliberately to the first I had seen—and there it was black, dried, sunken, with closed eyelids—a head that seemed to sleep at the top of that pole, and with the shrunken dry lips showing a narrow white line of the teeth, was smiling too, smiling continuously at some endless and jocose dream of that eternal slumber.

"I am not disclosing any trade secrets. In fact the Manager said afterwards that Mr. Kurtz's methods had ruined the district. I have no opinion on that point, but I want you clearly to understand that there was nothing exactly profitable in these heads being there. They only showed that Mr. Kurtz lacked restraint in the gratification of his various lusts, that there was something wanting in him—some small matter which when the pressing need arose could not be found under his magnificent eloquence. Whether he knew of this deficiency himself I can't say. I think the knowledge came to him at last—only at the very last. But the wilderness had found him out early, and had taken on him a terrible vengeance for the fantastic invasion. I think it had whispered to him things about himself which he did not know, things of which he had no conception till he took counsel with this great solitude—and the whisper had proved irresistibly fascinating. It echoed loudly within him because he was hollow at the core. . . . I put down the glass, and the head that had appeared near enough to be spoken to seemed at once to have leaped away from me into inaccessible distance.

"The admirer of Mr. Kurtz was a bit crestfallen. In a hurried, indistinct voice he began to assure me he had not dared to take these—say, symbols—down. He was not afraid of the natives; they would not stir till Mr. Kurtz gave the word. His ascendancy was extraordinary. The camps of these people surrounded the place and the chiefs came every day to see him. They would crawl. . . . 'I don't want to know anything of the ceremonies used when approaching Mr. Kurtz,' I shouted. Curious, this feeling that came over me that such details would be more intolerable than those heads drying on the stakes under Mr. Kurtz's windows. After all, that was only a savage sight while I seemed at one bound to have been transported into some lightless region of subtle horrors, where pure, uncomplicated savagery was a positive relief, being something that had a right to exist—obviously—in the sunshine. The young man looked at me with surprise. I suppose it did not occur to him that Mr. Kurtz was no idol of mine. He forgot I hadn't heard any of these splendid monologues on, what was it? on love, justice, conduct of life—or what not. If it had come to crawling before Mr. Kurtz, he crawled as much as the veriest savage of them all. I had no idea of the conditions, he said: these heads were the heads of rebels. I shocked him excessively by laughing. Rebels! What would be the next definition I was to hear. There had been enemies, criminals, workers—and these were—rebels. Those rebellious heads looked very subdued to me on their sticks. 'You don't know how such a life tries a man like Kurtz,' cried Kurtz's last disciple. 'Well, and you?' I said. 'I! I! I am a simple man. I have no great thoughts. I want nothing from anybody. How can you compare me to . . .?' His feelings were too much for speech and suddenly he broke down. 'I don't understand,' he groaned. 'I've been doing my best to keep him alive and that's enough. I had no hand in all this. I have no abilities. There hasn't been a drop of medicine or a mouthful of invalid food for months here. He was shamefully abandoned. A man like this, with such ideas. Shamefully! Shamefully! I—I—haven't slept for the last ten nights. . . .'

"His voice lost itself in the calm of the evening. The long shadow of the forest had slipped downhill while we talked, had gone far beyond the ruined hovel, beyond the symbolic row of stakes. All this was in the gloom while we down there were yet in the sunshine, and the stretch of the river abreast of the clearing glittered in a still and dazzling splendour with a murky and over-shadowed bend above and below. Not a living soul was seen on the shore. The bushes did not rustle.

"Suddenly round the corner of the house a group of men appeared, as though they had come up from the ground. They waded waist-deep in the grass in a compact body bearing an improvised stretcher in their midst. Instantly in the emptiness of the landscape a cry arose whose shrillness pierced the still air like a sharp arrow flying straight to the very heart of the land. And as if by enchantment streams of human beings—of naked human beings—with spears in their hands, with bows, with shields, with wild glances and savage movements, were poured into the clearing by the dark-faced and pensive forest. The bushes shook, the grass swayed for a time, and then everything stood still in attentive immobility.

" 'Now, if he does not say the right thing to them we are all done for,' said the Russian at my elbow. The knot of men with the stretcher had stopped too, half-way to the steamer, as if petrified. I saw the man on the stretcher sit up, lank and with an uplifted arm, above the shoulders of the bearers. 'Let us hope that the man who can talk so well of love in general will find some particular reason to spare us this time,' I said. I resented bitterly the absurd danger of our situation, as if to be at the mercy of that atrocious phantom had been a dishonouring necessity. I could not hear a sound, but through my glasses I saw the thin arm extended commandingly, the lower jaw moving, the eyes of that apparition shining darkly far in its bony head that nodded with grotesque jerks. Kurtz—Kurtz—that means 'short' in German—don't it? Well, the name was as true as everything else in his life—and death. He looked at least seven feet long. His covering had fallen off and his body emerged from it pitiful and appalling as from a winding-sheet. I could see the cage of his ribs all astir, the bones of his arm waving. It was as though an animated image of death carved out of old ivory had been shaking its hand with menaces at a motionless crowd of men made of dark and glittering bronze. I saw him open his mouth wide—it gave him a weirdly voracious aspect as though he had wanted to swallow all the air, all the earth, all the men before him. A deep voice reached me faintly. He must have been shouting. He fell back suddenly. The stretcher shook as the bearers staggered forward again, and almost at the same time I noticed that the crowd of savages was vanishing without any perceptible movement of retreat, as if the forest that had ejected these beings so suddenly had drawn them in again as the breath is drawn in a long aspiration.

"Some of the pilgrims behind the stretcher carried his arms—two shotguns, a heavy rifle, and a light revolver-carbine—the thunderbolts of that pitiful Jupiter. The Manager bent over him murmuring

as he walked beside his head. They laid him down in one of the little cabins—just a room for a bed-place and a camp-stool or two,
you know. We had brought his belated correspondence, and a lot of
torn envelopes and open letters littered his bed. His hand roamed
feebly amongst these papers. I was struck by the fire of his eyes and
the composed languor of his expression. It was not so much the exhaustion of disease. He did not seem in pain. This shadow looked
satiated and calm as though for the moment it had had its fill of all
the emotions.

"He rustled one of the letters, and looking straight in my face
said, 'I am glad.' Somebody had been writing to him about me.
These special recommendations were turning up again. The volume
of tone he emitted without effort, almost without the trouble of
moving his lips, amazed me. A voice! a voice! It was grave, profound, vibrating, while the man did not seem capable of a whisper.
However, he had enough strength in him—factitious no doubt—to
very nearly make an end of us, as you shall hear directly.

"The Manager appeared silently in the doorway; I stepped out at
once and he drew the curtain after me. The Russian, eyed curiously
by the pilgrims, was staring at the shore. I followed the direction of
his glance.

"Dark human shapes could be made out in the distance, flitting
indistinctly against the gloomy border of the forest, and near the
river two bronze figures leaning on tall spears stood in the sunlight
under fantastic head-dresses of spotted skins, warlike and still in
statuesque repose. And from right to left along the lighted shore
moved a wild and gorgeous apparition of a woman.

"She walked with measured steps, draped in striped and fringed
cloths, treading the earth proudly with a slight jingle and flash of
barbarous ornaments. She carried her head high, her hair was done
in the shape of a helmet, she had brass leggings to the knees, brass
wire gauntlets to the elbow, a crimson spot on her tawny cheek, innumerable necklaces of glass beads on her neck, bizarre things,
charms, gifts of witch-men, that hung about her, glittered and
trembled at every step. She must have had the value of several elephant tusks upon her. She was savage and superb, wild-eyed and
magnificent; there was something ominous and stately in her deliberate progress. And in the hush that had fallen suddenly upon the
whole sorrowful land, the immense wilderness, the colossal body of
the fecund and mysterious life seemed to look at her, pensive, as
though it had been looking at the image of its own tenebrous[8] and
passionate soul.

"She came abreast of the steamer, stood still, and faced us. Her

8. Dark.

long shadow fell to the water's edge. Her face had a tragic and fierce aspect of wild sorrow and of dumb pain mingled with the fear of some struggling, half-shaped resolve. She stood looking at us without a stir and like the wilderness itself, with an air of brooding over an inscrutable purpose. A whole minute passed and then she made a step forward. There was a low jingle, a glint of yellow metal, a sway of fringed draperies, and she stopped as if her heart had failed her. The young fellow by my side growled. The pilgrims murmured at my back. She looked at us all as if her life had depended upon the unswerving steadiness of her glance. Suddenly she opened her bared arms and threw them up rigid above her head as though in an uncontrollable desire to touch the sky, and at the same time the swift shadows darted out on the earth, swept around on the river, gathering the steamer in a shadowy embrace. A formidable silence hung over the scene.

"She turned away slowly, walked on following the bank and passed into the bushes to the left. Once only her eyes gleamed back at us in the dusk of the thickets before she disappeared.

" 'If she offered to come aboard I really think I would have tried to shoot her,' said the man of patches nervously. 'I had been risking my life every day for the last fortnight to keep her out of the house. She got in one day and kicked up a row about those miserable rags I picked up in the storeroom to mend my clothes with. I wasn't decent. At least it must have been that, for she talked like a fury to Kurtz for an hour pointing at me now and then. I don't understand the dialect of this tribe. Luckily for me, I fancy Kurtz felt too ill that day to care, or there would have been mischief. I don't understand. . . . No—it's too much for me. Ah, well, it's all over now.'

"At this moment I heard Kurtz's deep voice behind the curtain: 'Save me—save the ivory, you mean. Don't tell me! Save *me!* Why, I've had to save you. You are interrupting my plans now. Sick. Sick. Not so sick as you would like to believe. Never mind. I'll carry my ideas out yet—I will return. I'll show you what can be done. You with your little peddling notions—you are interfering with me. I will return. I . . .'

"The Manager came out. He did me the honour to take me under the arm and lead me aside. 'He is very low, very low,' he said. He considered it necessary to sigh, but neglected to be consistently sorrowful. 'We have done all we could for him—haven't we. But there is no disguising the fact, Mr. Kurtz has done more harm than good to the Company. He did not see the time was not ripe for vigorous action. Cautiously. Cautiously. That's my principle. We must be cautious yet. The district is closed to us for a time. Deplorable. Upon the whole, the trade will suffer. I don't deny there is a remarkable quantity of ivory—mostly fossil. We must save it, at all events—but look how precarious the position is—and why? Because the method is unsound.' 'Do you,' said I, looking at the shore, 'call it "unsound method"?' 'Without doubt,' he exclaimed hotly. 'Don't you?' . . . 'No method at all,' I murmured after a while. 'Exactly,' he exulted. 'I anticipated this. Shows a complete want of judgment. It is my duty to point it out in the proper quarter.' 'Oh,' said I, 'that fellow—what's his name—the brickmaker will make a readable report for you.' He appeared confounded for a moment. It seemed to me I had never breathed an atmosphere so vile, and I turned mentally to Kurtz for relief—positively for relief. 'Nevertheless, I think Mr. Kurtz is a remarkable man,' I said with emphasis. He started, dropped on me a cold heavy glance, said very quietly, 'He *was*,' and turned his back on me. My hour of favour was over; I found myself lumped along with Kurtz as a partisan of methods for which the time was not ripe. I was unsound. Ah, but it was something to have at least a choice of nightmares.

"I had turned to the wilderness really, not to Mr. Kurtz who, I was ready to admit, was as good as buried. And for a moment it seemed to me as if I also were buried in a vast grave full of unspeakable secrets. I felt an intolerable weight oppressing my breast, the smell of the damp earth, the unseen presence of victorious corruption, the darkness of an impenetrable night. . . . The Russian tapped me on the shoulder. I heard him mumbling and stammering something about 'brother seaman—couldn't conceal—knowledge of matters that would affect Mr. Kurtz's reputation.' I waited. For him evidently Mr. Kurtz was not in his grave; I suspect that for him Mr. Kurtz was one of the immortals. 'Well,' said I at last, 'speak out. As it happens, I am Mr. Kurtz's friend—in a way.'

"He stated with a good deal of formality that had we not been 'of the same profession' he would have kept the matter to himself without regard to consequences. He suspected 'there was an active ill-will towards him on the part of these white men that . . .' 'You are right,' I said, remembering a certain conversation I had overhead. 'The Manager thinks you ought to be hanged.' He showed a concern at this intelligence which amused me at first. 'I had better get out of the way quietly,' he said earnestly. 'I can do no more for Kurtz now and they would soon find some excuse. What's to stop them. There's a military post three hundred miles from here.' 'Well, upon my word,' said I, 'perhaps you had better go if you have any friends amongst the savages near by.' 'Plenty,' he said. 'They are simple people—and I want nothing, you know.' He stood biting his lip, then: 'I don't want any harm to happen to these whites here, but of course I was thinking of Mr. Kurtz's reputation—but you are a brother seaman and . . .' 'All right,' said I after a time. 'Mr. Kurtz's reputation is safe with me.' I did not know how truly I spoke.

"He informed me, lowering his voice, that it was Kurtz who had ordered the attack to be made on the steamer. 'He hated sometimes the idea of being taken away—and then again . . . But I don't understand these matters. I am a simple man. He thought it would scare you away—that you would give it up, thinking him dead. I could not stop him. Oh I had an awful time of it this last month.' 'Very well,' I said. 'He is all right now.' 'Ye-e-es,' he muttered not very convinced apparently. 'Thanks,' said I, 'I shall keep my eyes open.' 'But quiet—eh?' he urged anxiously. 'It would be awful for his reputation if anybody here . . .' I promised a complete discretion with great gravity. 'I have a canoe and three black fellows waiting not very far. I am off. Could you give me a few Martini-Henry cartridges?' I could and did with proper secrecy. He helped himself with a wink at me to a handful of my tobacco. 'Between sailors—you know—good English tobacco.' At the door of the pilot-house he turned round—'I say, haven't you a pair of shoes you could spare?' He raised one leg. 'Look.' The soles were tied with knotted strings sandal-wise under his bare feet. I rooted out an old pair at which he looked with admiration before tucking it under his left arm. One of his pockets (bright red) was bulging with cartridges, from the other (dark blue) peeped 'Towson's Inquiry,' etc. etc. He seemed to think himself excellently well equipped for a renewed encounter with the wilderness. 'Ah! I'll never, never meet such a man again. You ought to have heard him recite poetry—his own too it was, he told me. Poetry!' He rolled his eyes at the recollection of these delights. 'Oh, he enlarged my mind!' 'Good-bye,' said I. He shook hands and vanished in the night. Sometimes I ask myself whether I had ever really seen him—whether it was possible to meet such a phenomenon! . . .

"When I woke up shortly after midnight his warning came to my mind with its hint of danger that seemed in the starred darkness real enough to make me get up for the purpose of having a look round. On the hill a big fire burned, illuminating fitfully a crooked corner of the station-house. One of the agents with a picket of a few of our blacks armed for the purpose was keeping guard over the ivory, but deep within the forest red gleams that wavered, that seemed to sink and rise from the ground amongst confused columnar shapes of intense blackness, showed the exact position of the camp where Mr. Kurtz's adorers were keeping their uneasy vigil. The monotonous beating of a big drum filled the air with muffled shocks and a lingering vibration. A steady droning sound of many men chanting each to himself some weird incantation came out from the black flat wall of the woods as the humming of bees comes out of a hive, and had a strange narcotic effect upon my half-awake senses. I believe I dozed off leaning over the rail till an abrupt burst of yells, an overwhelming outbreak of a pent-up and mysterious frenzy, woke me up in a bewildered wonder. It was cut short all at once and the low droning went on with an effect of audible and soothing silence. I glanced casually into the little cabin. A light was burning within, but Mr. Kurtz was not there.

"I think I would have raised an outcry if I had believed my eyes. But I didn't believe them at first—the thing seemed so impossible. The fact is, I was completely unnerved by a sheer blank fright, pure abstract terror, unconnected with any distinct shape of physical danger. What made this emotion so overpowering was—how shall I define it—the moral shock I received, as if something altogether monstrous, intolerable to thought and odious to the soul had been thrust upon me unexpectedly. This lasted of course the merest fraction of a second and then the usual sense of commonplace deadly danger, the possibility of a sudden onslaught and massacre, or something of the kind, which I saw impending was positively welcome and composing. It pacified me, in fact, so much that I did not raise an alarm.

"There was an agent buttoned up inside an ulster and sleeping on a chair on deck within three feet of me. The yells had not awakened him; he snored very slightly. I left him to his slumbers and leaped ashore. I did not betray Mr. Kurtz—it was ordered I should never betray him—it was written I should be loyal to the nightmare of my choice. I was anxious to deal with this shadow by myself alone—and to this day I don't know why I was so jealous of sharing with any one the peculiar blackness of that experience.

"As soon as I got on the bank I saw a trail—a broad trail through the grass. I remember the exultation with which I said to myself, 'He can't walk—he is crawling on all-fours—I've got him.' The grass was wet with dew. I strode rapidly with clenched fists. I fancy I had some vague notion of falling upon him and giving him a drubbing. I don't know. I had some imbecile thoughts. The knitting old woman with the cat obtruded herself upon my memory as a most improper person to be sitting at the other end of such an affair. I saw a row of pilgrims squirting lead in the air out of Winchesters held to the hip. I thought I would never get back to the steamer and imagined myself living alone and unarmed in the woods to an advanced age. Such silly things—you know. And I remember I confounded the beat of the drum with the beating of my heart and was pleased at its calm regularity.

"I kept to the track though—then stopped to listen. The night was very clear, a dark blue space sparkling with dew and starlight in which black things stood very still. I thought I could see a kind of motion ahead of me. I was strangely cocksure of everything that night. I actually left the track and ran in a wide semicircle (I verily believe chuckling to myself) so as to get in front of that stir, of that motion I had seen—if indeed I had seen anything. I was circumventing Kurtz as though it had been a boyish game.

"I came upon him and if he had not heard me coming, I would have fallen over him too, but he got up in time. He rose, unsteady, long, pale, indistinct like a vapour exhaled by the earth, and swayed slightly, misty and silent before me while at my back the fires loomed between the trees, and the murmur of many voices issued from the forest. I had cut him off cleverly, but when actually confronting him I seemed to come to my senses; I saw the danger in its right proportion. It was by no means over yet. Suppose he began to shout. Though he could hardly stand there was still plenty of vigour in his voice. 'Go away—hide yourself,' he said in that profound tone. It was very awful. I glanced back. We were within thirty yards from the nearest fire. A black figure stood up, strode on long black legs, waving long black arms across the glow. It had horns—antelope horns, I think—on its head. Some sorcerer, some witch-man, no doubt; it looked fiend-like enough. 'Do you know what you are doing?' I whispered. 'Perfectly,' he answered raising his voice for that single word; it sounded to me far off and yet loud like a hail through a speaking-trumpet. If he makes a row we are lost, I thought to myself. This clearly was not a case for fisticuffs, even apart from the very natural aversion I had to beat that Shadow— this wandering and tormented thing. 'You will be lost,' I said—'utterly lost.' One gets sometimes such a flash of inspiration, you know. I did say the right thing, though indeed he could not have been more irretrievably lost than he was at this very moment when the foundations of our intimacy were being laid—to endure—to endure—even to the end—even beyond.

" 'I had immense plans,' he muttered irresolutely. 'Yes,' said I, 'but if you try to shout I'll smash your head with . . .' There was not a stick or a stone near. 'I will throttle you for good,' I corrected myself. 'I was on the threshold of great things,' he pleaded in a voice of longing with a wistfulness of tone that made my blood run cold. 'And now for this stupid scoundrel . . .' 'Your success in Europe is assured in any case,' I affirmed steadily. I did not want to have the throttling of him, you understand—and indeed it would have been very little use for any practical purpose. I tried to break the spell, the heavy mute spell of the wilderness that seemed to draw him to its pitiless breast by the awakening of forgotten and brutal instincts, by the memory of gratified and monstrous passions. This alone, I was convinced, had driven him out to the edge of the forest, to the bush, towards the gleam of fires, the throb of drums, the drone of weird incantations; this alone had beguiled his unlawful soul beyond the bounds of permitted aspirations. And, don't you see, the terror of the position was not in being knocked on the head—though I had a very lively sense of that danger too—but in this, that I had to deal with a being to whom I could not appeal in the name of anything high or low. I had, even like the niggers, to invoke him—himself—his own exalted and incredible degradation. There was nothing either above or below him—and I knew it. He had kicked himself loose of the earth. Confound the man! he had kicked the very earth to pieces. He was alone—and I before him did not know whether I stood on the ground or floated in the air. I've been telling you what we said—repeating the phrases we pronounced—but what's the good. They were common everyday words—the familiar vague sounds exchanged on every waking day of life. But what of that? They had behind them, to my mind, the terrific suggestiveness of words heard in dreams, of phrases spoken in nightmares. Soul! If anybody had ever struggled with a soul I am the man. And I wasn't arguing with a lunatic either. Believe me or not, his intelligence was perfectly clear—concentrated, it is true, upon himself with horrible intensity, yet clear, and therein was my only chance—barring, of course, the killing him there and then, which wasn't so good on account of unavoidable noise. But his soul was mad. Being alone in the wilderness, it had looked within itself and, by Heavens I tell you, it had gone mad. I had—for my sins, I suppose—to go through the ordeal of looking into it myself. No eloquence could have been so withering to one's belief in mankind as his final burst of sincerity. He struggled with himself too. I saw it—I heard it. I saw the inconceivable mystery of a soul that knew no restraint, no faith, and no fear, yet struggling blindly with itself. I kept my head pretty well, but when I had him at last stretched on the couch, I wiped my forehead while my legs shook under me as though I had carried half a ton on my back down that hill. And yet I had only supported him, his bony arm clasped round my neck—and he was not much heavier than a child.

"When next day we left at noon, the crowd, of whose presence behind the curtain of trees I had been acutely conscious all the time, flowed out of the woods again, filled the clearing, covered the slope with a mass of naked, breathing, quivering, bronze bodies. I steamed up a bit, then swung down-stream, and two thousand eyes followed the evolutions of the splashing, thumping, fierce river-demon beating the water with its terrible tail and breathing black smoke into the air. In front of the first rank along the river three men plastered with bright red earth from head to foot strutted to and fro restlessly. When we came abreast again they faced the river, stamped their feet, nodded their horned heads, swayed their scarlet bodies; they shook towards the fierce river-demon a bunch of black feathers, a mangy skin with a pendent tail—something that looked like a dried gourd; they shouted periodically together strings of amazing words that resembled no sounds of human language; and the deep murmurs of the crowd, interrupted suddenly, were like the responses of some satanic litany.

"We had carried Kurtz into the pilot-house. There was more air there. Lying on the couch he stared through the open shutter. There was an eddy in the mass of human bodies and the woman with helmeted head and tawny cheeks rushed out to the very brink of the stream. She put out her hands, shouted something, and all that wild mob took up the shout in a roaring chorus of articulated, rapid, breathless utterance.

" 'Do you understand this?' I asked.

"He kept on looking out past me with fiery, longing eyes, with a mingled expression of wistfulness and hate. He made no answer, but I saw a smile, a smile of indefinable meaning, appear on his colourless lips that a moment after twitched convulsively. 'Do I not?' he said slowly, gasping, as if the words had been torn out of him by a supernatural power.

"I pulled the string of the whistle, and I did this because I saw the pilgrims on deck getting out their rifles with an air of anticipating a jolly lark. At the sudden screech there was a movement of abject terror through that wedged mass of bodies. 'Don't! don't you frighten them away,' cried some one on deck disconsolately. I pulled the string time after time. They broke and ran, they leaped, they crouched, they swerved, they dodged the flying terror of the sound. The three red chaps had fallen flat, face down on the shore as though they had been shot dead. Only the barbarous and superb woman did not so much as flinch and stretched tragically her bare arms after us over the sombre and glittering river.

"And then that imbecile crowd down on the deck started their little fun and I could see nothing more for smoke.

"The brown current ran swiftly out of the heart of darkness bearing us down towards the sea with twice the speed of our upward progress. And Kurtz's life was running swiftly too, ebbing, ebbing out of his heart into the sea of inexorable time. The Manager was very placid, he had no vital anxieties now, he took us both in with a comprehensive and satisfied glance: the 'affair' had come off as well as could be wished. I saw the time approaching when I would be left alone of the party of 'unsound method.' The pilgrims looked upon me with disfavour. I was, so to speak, numbered with the dead. It is strange how I accepted this unforeseen partnership, this choice of nightmares forced upon me in the tenebrous land invaded by these mean and greedy phantoms.

"Kurtz discoursed. A voice! a voice! It rang deep to the very last.

It survived his strength to hide in the magnificent folds of eloquence the barren darkness of his heart. Oh, he struggled, he
struggled. The wastes of his weary brain were haunted by shadowy
images now—images of wealth and fame revolving obsequiously
around his unextinguishable gift of noble and lofty expression. My
Intended, my station, my career, my ideas—these were the subjects
for the occasional utterances of elevated sentiments. The shade of
the original Kurtz frequented the bedside of the hollow sham
whose fate it was to be buried presently in the mould of primeval
earth. But both the diabolic love and the unearthly hate of the
mysteries it had penetrated fought for the possession of that soul
satiated with primitive emotions, avid of lying fame, of sham distinction, of all the appearances of success and power.

"Sometimes he was contemptibly childish. He desired to have
kings meet him at railway stations on his return from some ghastly
Nowhere, where he intended to accomplish great things. 'You show
them you have in you something that is really profitable, and then
there will be no limits to the recognition of your ability,' he would
say. 'Of course you must take care of the motives—right motives—
always.' The long reaches that were like one and the same reach,
monotonous bends that were exactly alike, slipped past the steamer
with their multitude of secular[9] trees looking patiently after this
grimy fragment of another world, the forerunner of change, of conquest, of trade, of massacres, of blessings. I looked ahead—
piloting. 'Close the shutter,' said Kurtz suddenly one day; 'I can't
bear to look at this.' I did so. There was a silence. 'Oh, but I will
wring your heart yet!' he cried at the invisible wilderness.

"We broke down—as I had expected—and had to lie up for repairs at the head of an island. This delay was the first thing that
shook Kurtz's confidence. One morning he gave me a packet of papers and a photograph—the lot tied together with a shoe-string.
'Keep this for me,' he said. 'This noxious fool' (meaning the Manager) 'is capable of prying into my boxes when I am not looking.' In
the afternoon I saw him. He was lying on his back with closed eyes,
and I withdrew quietly, but I heard him mutter, 'Live rightly, die,
die. . . .' I listened. There was nothing more. Was he rehearsing
some speech in his sleep, or was it a fragment of a phrase from
some newspaper article. He had been writing for the papers and
meant to do so again, 'for the furthering of my ideas. It's a duty.'

"His was an impenetrable darkness. I looked at him as you peer
down at a man who is lying at the bottom of a precipice where the
sun never shines. But I had not much time to give him because I
was helping the engine-driver to take to pieces the leaky cylinders,

9. Ancient.

to straighten a bent connecting-rod, and in other such matters. I lived in an infernal mess of rust, filings, nuts, bolts, spanners, hammers, ratchet-drills—things I abominate because I don't get on with them. I tended the little forge we fortunately had aboard; I toiled wearily in a wretched scrap-heap—unless I had the shakes too bad to stand.

"One evening coming in with a candle I was startled to hear him say a little tremulously, 'I am lying here in the dark waiting for death.' The light was within a foot of his eyes. I forced myself to murmur, 'Oh, nonsense!' and stood over him as if transfixed.

"Anything approaching the change that came over his features I have never seen before and hope never to see again. Oh, I wasn't touched. I was fascinated. It was as though a veil had been rent. I saw on that ivory face the expression of sombre pride, of ruthless power, of craven terror—of an intense and hopeless despair. Did he live his life again in every detail of desire, temptation, and surrender during that supreme moment of complete knowledge? He cried in a whisper at some image, at some vision—he cried out twice, a cry that was no more than a breath:

" 'The horror! The horror!'

"I blew the candle out and left the cabin. The pilgrims were dining in the mess-room and I took my place opposite the Manager, who lifted his eyes to give me a questioning glance which I successfully ignored. He leaned back, serene, with that peculiar smile of his sealing the unexpressed depths of his meanness. A continuous shower of small flies streamed upon the lamp, upon the cloth, upon our hands and faces. Suddenly the Manager's boy put his insolent black head in the doorway and said in a tone of scathing contempt:

" 'Mistah Kurtz—he dead.'

"All the pilgrims rushed out to see. I remained and went on with my dinner. I believe I was considered brutally callous. However, I did not eat much. There was a lamp in there—light—don't you know—and outside it was so beastly, beastly dark. I went no more near the remarkable man who had pronounced judgment upon the adventures of his soul on this earth. The voice was gone. What else had been there? But I am of course aware that next day the pilgrims buried something in a muddy hole.

"And then they very nearly buried me.

"However, as you see, I did not go to join Kurtz there and then. I did not. I remained to dream the nightmare out to the end and to show my loyalty to Kurtz once more. Destiny. My destiny! Droll thing life is—that mysterious arrangement of merciless logic for a futile purpose. The most you can hope from it is some knowledge of yourself—that comes too late—a crop of unextinguishable regrets. I have wrestled with death. It is the most unexciting contest you can imagine. It takes place in an impalpable greyness with nothing underfoot, with nothing around, without spectators, without clamour, without glory, without the great desire of victory, without the great fear of defeat, in a sickly atmosphere of tepid scepticism, without much belief in your own right, and still less in that of your adversary. If such is the form of ultimate wisdom then life is a greater riddle than some of us think it to be. I was within a hair's-breadth of the last opportunity for pronouncement, and I found with humiliation that probably I would have nothing to say. This is the reason why I affirm that Kurtz was a remarkable man. He had something to say. He said it. Since I had peeped over the edge myself, I understand better the meaning of his stare that could not see the flame of the candle but was wide enough to embrace the whole universe, piercing enough to penetrate all the hearts that beat in the darkness. He had summed up—he had judged. 'The horror!' He was a remarkable man. After all, this was the expression of some sort of belief; it had candour, it had conviction, it had a vibrating note of revolt in its whisper, it had the appalling face of a glimpsed truth—the strange commingling of desire and hate. And it is not my own extremity I remember best—a vision of greyness without form filled with physical pain and a careless contempt for the evanescence of all things—even of this pain itself. No. It is his extremity that I seem to have lived through. True, he had made that last stride, he had stepped over the edge, while I had been permitted to draw back my hesitating foot. And perhaps in this is the whole difference; perhaps all the wisdom, and all truth, and all sincerity, are just compressed into that inappreciable moment of time in which we step over the threshold of the invisible. Perhaps. I like to think my summing-up would not have been a word of careless contempt. Better his cry—much better. It was an affirmation, a moral victory paid for by innumerable defeats, by abominable terrors, by abominable satisfactions. But it was a victory. That is why I have remained loyal to Kurtz to the last, and even beyond, when a long time after I heard once more not his own voice but the echo of his magnificent eloquence thrown to me from a soul as translucently pure as a cliff of crystal.

"No, they did not bury me, though there is a period of time which I remember mistily, with a shuddering wonder, like a passage through some inconceivable world that had no hope in it and no desire. I found myself back in the sepulchral city resenting the sight of people hurrying through the streets to filch a little money from each other, to devour their infamous cookery, to gulp their unwholesome beer, to dream their insignificant and silly dreams. They trespassed upon my thoughts. They were intruders whose knowledge of life was to me an irritating pretence because I felt so sure they could not possibly know the things I knew. Their bearing, which was simply the bearing of commonplace individuals going about their business in the assurance of perfect safety, was offensive to me like the outrageous flauntings of folly in the face of a danger it is unable to comprehend. I had no particular desire to enlighten them, but I had some difficulty in restraining myself from laughing in their faces so full of stupid importance. I daresay I was not very well at that time. I tottered about the streets—there were various affairs to settle—grinning bitterly at perfectly respectable persons. I admit my behaviour was inexcusable, but then my temperature was seldom normal in these days. My dear aunt's endeavours to 'nurse up my strength' seemed altogether beside the mark. It was not my strength that wanted nursing, it was my imagination that wanted soothing. I kept the bundle of papers given me by Kurtz not knowing exactly what to do with it. His mother had died lately, watched over, as I was told, by his Intended. A clean-shaved man with an official manner and wearing gold-rimmed spectacles called on me one day and made inquiries, at first circuitous, afterwards suavely pressing, about what he was pleased to denominate certain 'documents.' I was not surprised because I had had two rows with the Manager on the subject out there. I had refused to give up the smallest scrap out of that package and I took the same attitude with the spectacled man. He became darkly menacing at last and with much heat argued that the Company had the right to every bit of information about its 'territories.' And, said he, 'Mr. Kurtz's knowledge of unexplored regions must have been necessarily extensive and peculiar—owing to his great abilities and to the deplorable circumstances in which he had been placed; therefore . . .' I assured him Mr. Kurtz's knowledge however extensive did not bear upon the problems of commerce or administration. He invoked then the name of science. 'It would be an incalculable loss if,' etc. etc. I offered him the report on the 'Suppression of Savage Customs' with the postscriptum torn off. He took it up eagerly but ended by sniffing at it with an air of contempt. 'This is not what we had a right to expect,' he remarked. 'Expect nothing else,' I said. 'There are only private letters.' He withdrew upon some threat of legal proceedings and I saw him no more, but another fellow calling himself Kurtz's cousin appeared two days later and was anxious to hear all the details about his dear relative's last moments. Incidentally he gave me to understand that Kurtz had been essentially a great musician. 'There was the making of an immense success,' said the man who was an organist, I believe, with lank grey hair flowing over a greasy coat-collar. I had no reason to doubt his statement, and to this day I am unable to say what was Kurtz's profession,

whether he ever had any—which was the greatest of his talents. I
had taken him for a painter who wrote for the papers, or else for a
journalist who could paint—but even the cousin (who took snuff
during the interview) could not tell me what he had been—exactly.
He was a universal genius—on that point I agreed with the old
chap who thereupon blew his nose noisily into a large cotton hand-
kerchief and withdrew in senile agitation bearing off some family
letters and memoranda without importance. Ultimately a journalist
anxious to know something of the fate of his 'dear colleague' turned
up. This visitor informed me Kurtz's proper sphere ought to have
been politics 'on the popular side.' He had furry straight eyebrows,
bristly hair cropped short, an eyeglass on a broad ribbon, and, becoming expansive, confessed his opinion that Kurtz really couldn't
write a bit—'but Heavens! how that man could talk! He electrified
large meetings. He had the faith—don't you see—he had the faith.
He could get himself to believe anything—anything. He would have
been a splendid leader of an extreme party.' 'What party?' I asked.
'Any party,' answered the other. 'He was an—an—extremist.' Did I
not think so? I assented. Did I know, he asked, with a sudden flash
of curiosity, 'what it was that had induced him to go out there?'
'Yes,' said I and forthwith handed him the famous Report for publication if he thought fit. He glanced through it hurriedly, mumbling
all the time, judged 'it would do,' and took himself off with this
plunder.

"Thus I was left at last with a slim packet of letters and the girl's
portrait. She struck me as beautiful—I mean she had a beautiful
expression. I know that the sunlight can be made to lie too, yet one
felt that no manipulation of light and pose could have conveyed the
delicate shade of truthfulness upon those features. She seemed
ready to listen without mental reservation, without suspicion, without a thought for herself. I concluded I would go and give her back
her portrait and those letters myself. Curiosity. Yes. And also some
other feeling perhaps. All that had been Kurtz's had passed out of
my hands: his soul, his body, his station, his plans, his ivory, his career. There remained only his memory and his Intended—and I
wanted to give that up too to the past, in a way—to surrender personally all that remained of him with me to that oblivion which is
the last word of our common fate. I don't defend myself. I had no
clear perception of what it was I really wanted. Perhaps it was an
impulse of unconscious loyalty or the fulfilment of one of those
ironic necessities that lurk in the facts of human existence. I don't
know. I can't tell. But I went.

"I thought his memory was like the other memories of the dead
that accumulate in every man's life—a vague impress on the brain
of shadows that had fallen on it in their swift and final passage, but

before the high and ponderous door, between the tall houses of a street as still and decorous as a well-kept alley in a cemetery, I had a vision of him on the stretcher opening his mouth voraciously as if to devour all the earth with all its mankind. He lived then before me, he lived as much as he had ever lived—a shadow insatiable of splendid appearances, of frightful realities, a shadow darker than the shadow of the night, and draped nobly in the folds of a gorgeous eloquence. The vision seemed to enter the house with me—the stretcher, the phantom-bearers, the wild crowd of obedient worshippers, the gloom of the forests, the glitter of the reach between the murky bends, the beat of the drum regular and muffled like the beating of a heart, the heart of a conquering darkness. It was a moment of triumph for the wilderness, an invading and vengeful rush which it seemed to me I would have to keep back alone for the salvation of another soul. And the memory of what I had heard him say afar there, with the horned shapes stirring at my back in the glow of fires within the patient woods, those broken phrases came back to me, were heard again in their ominous and terrifying simplicity. I remembered his abject pleading, his abject threats, the colossal scale of his vile desires, the meanness, the torment, the tempestuous anguish of his soul. And later on I seemed to see his collected languid manner when he said one day 'This lot of ivory now is really mine. The Company did not pay for it. I collected it myself at a very great personal risk. I am afraid they will try to claim it as theirs though. H'm. It is a difficult case. What do you think I ought to do—resist? Eh? I want no more than justice.' . . . He wanted no more than justice—no more than justice! I rang the bell before a mahogany door on the first floor and while I waited he seemed to stare at me out of the glassy panel—stare with that wide and immense stare embracing, condemning, loathing all the universe. I seemed to hear the whispered cry, 'The horror! The horror!'

"The dusk was falling. I had to wait in a lofty drawing-room with three long windows from floor to ceiling that were like three luminous and bedraped columns. The bent gilt legs and backs of the furniture shone in indistinct curves. The tall marble fireplace had a cold and monumental whiteness. A grand piano stood massively in a corner with dark gleams on the flat surfaces like a sombre and polished sarcophagus. A high door opened—closed. I rose.

"She came forward all in black with a pale head, floating towards me in the dusk. She was in mourning. It was more than a year since his death, more than a year since the news came; she seemed as though she would remember and mourn for ever. She took both my hands in hers and murmured, 'I had heard you were coming.' I noticed she was not very young—I mean not girlish. She had a mature capacity for fidelity, for belief, for suffering. The room seemed to

have grown darker as if all the sad light of the cloudy evening had
taken refuge on her forehead. This fair hair, this pale visage, this
pure brow, seemed surrounded by an ashy halo from which the
dark eyes looked out at me. Their glance was guileless, profound,
confident, and trustful. She carried her sorrowful head as though
she were proud of that sorrow, as though she would say, I—I alone
know how to mourn for him as he deserves. But while we were still
shaking hands such a look of awful desolation came upon her face
that I perceived she was one of those creatures that are not the
playthings of Time. For her he had died only yesterday. And by Jove,
the impression was so powerful that for me too he seemed to have
died only yesterday—nay, this very minute. I saw her and him in the
same instant of time—his death and her sorrow—I saw her sorrow
in the very moment of his death. Do you understand? I saw them
together—I heard them together. She had said with a deep catch of
the breath, 'I have survived'—while my strained ears seemed to
hear distinctly, mingled with her tone of despairing regret, the
summing-up whisper of his eternal condemnation. I asked myself
what I was doing there, with a sensation of panic in my heart as
though I had blundered into a place of cruel and absurd mysteries
not fit for a human being to behold. She motioned me to a chair.
We sat down. I laid the packet gently on the little table and she put
her hand over it. . . . 'You knew him well,' she murmured after a
moment of mourning silence.

" 'Intimacy grows quickly out there,' I said. 'I knew him as well as
it is possible for one man to know another.'

" 'And you admired him!' she said. 'It was impossible to know him
and not to admire him. Was it?'

" 'He was a remarkable man,' I said unsteadily. Then before the
appealing fixity of her gaze that seemed to watch for more words on
my lips I went on, 'It was impossible not to . . .'

" 'Love him,' she finished eagerly, silencing me into an appalled
dumbness. 'How true! how true! But when you think that no one
knew him so well as I! I had all his noble confidence. I knew him
best.'

" 'You knew him best,' I repeated. And perhaps she did. But with
every word spoken the room was growing darker and only her forehead smooth and white remained illumined by the unextinguishable light of belief and love.

" 'You were his friend,' she went on. 'His friend,' she repeated a
little louder. 'You must have been if he had given you this and sent
you to me! I feel I can speak to you—and oh, I must speak. I want
you—you who have heard his last words—to know I have been worthy of him. . . . It is not pride. . . . Yes! I am proud to know I un-

derstood him better than any one on earth—he told me so himself. And since his mother died I have had no one—no one—to—to . . .'

"I listened. The darkness deepened. I was not even sure whether he had given me the right bundle. I rather suspect he wanted me to take care of another batch of his papers which after his death I saw the Manager examining under the lamp. And the girl talked, easing her pain in the certitude of my sympathy she talked, as thirsty men drank. I had heard that her engagement with Kurtz had been disapproved by her people. He wasn't rich enough or something. And indeed I don't know whether he had not been a pauper all his life. He had given me some reason to infer that it was his impatience of comparative poverty that drove him out there.

" '. . . Who was not his friend who had heard him speak once?' she was saying. 'He drew men towards him by what was best in them.' She looked at me with intensity. 'It is the gift of the great,' she went on and the sound of her low voice seemed to have the accompaniment of all the other sounds full of mystery, desolation, and sorrow I had ever heard—the ripple of the river, the soughing[1] of the trees swayed by the wind, the murmurs of the crowds, the faint ring of incomprehensible words cried from afar, the whisper of a voice speaking from beyond the threshold of an eternal darkness. 'But you have heard him. You know!' she cried.

" 'Yes, I know,' I said with something like despair in my heart, but bowing my head before the faith that was in her, before that great and saving illusion that shone with an unearthly glow in the darkness, in the triumphant darkness from which I could not have defended her—from which I could not even defend myself.

" 'What a loss to me—to us,' she corrected herself with beautiful generosity. Then added in a murmur, 'To the world.' By the last gleams of twilight I could see the glitter of her eyes full of tears—of tears that would not fall.

" 'I have been very happy—very fortunate—very proud,' she went on. 'Too fortunate. Too happy for a little while. And now I am unhappy for—for life.'

"She stood up. Her fair hair seemed to catch all the remaining light in a glimmer of gold. I rose too.

" 'And of all this,' she went on mournfully, 'of all his promise and of all his greatness, of his generous mind, of his noble heart nothing remains—nothing but a memory. You and I . . .'

" 'We shall always remember him,' I said hastily.

" 'No!' she cried. 'It is impossible that all this should be lost—that such a life should be sacrificed to leave nothing—but sorrow.

1. Rustling.

You know what vast plans he had. I knew of them too—I could not perhaps understand—but others knew of them. Something must remain. His words at least have not died.'

" 'His words will remain,' I said.

" 'And his example,' she whispered to herself. 'Men looked up to him—his goodness shone in every act. His example. . . .'

" 'True,' I said, 'his example too. Yes, his example. I forgot that.'

" 'But I do not. I cannot—I cannot believe—not yet. I cannot believe that I shall never see him again, that nobody will see him again, never, never, never!'

"She put out her arms, as if after a retreating figure, stretching them black and with clasped pale hands across the fading and narrow sheen of the window. Never see him! I saw him clearly enough then. I shall see this eloquent phantom as long as I live and I shall see her too, a tragic and familiar Shade resembling in this gesture another one, tragic also and bedecked with powerless charms, stretching bare brown arms over the glitter of the infernal stream, the stream of darkness. She said suddenly very low, 'He died as he lived.'

" 'His end,' said I with dull anger stirring me, 'was in every way worthy of his life.'

" 'And I was not with him,' she murmured. My anger subsided before a feeling of infinite pity.

" 'Everything that could be done . . .' I mumbled.

" 'Ah, but I believed in him more than any one on earth—more than his own mother, more than—himself. He needed me. Me! I would have treasured every sigh, every word, every sign, every glance.'

"I felt like a chill grip on my chest. 'Don't,' I said in a muffled voice.

" 'Forgive me. I—I—have mourned so long in silence—in silence. . . . You were with him to the last? I think of his loneliness. Nobody near to understand him as I would have understood. Perhaps no one to hear . . .'

" 'To the very end,' I said shakily. 'I heard his very last words. . . .' I stopped in a fright.

" 'Repeat them,' she murmured in a heart-broken tone. 'I want—I want—something—something—to—to live with.'

"I was on the point of crying at her, 'Don't you hear them.' The dusk was repeating them in a persistent whisper all around us, in a whisper that seemed to swell menacingly like the first whisper of a rising wind. 'The horror! The horror!'

" 'His last word—to live with,' she insisted. 'Don't you understand I loved him—I loved him—I loved him.'

"I pulled myself together and spoke slowly.

" 'The last word he pronounced was—your name.'

"I heard a light sigh and then my heart stood still, stopped dead short by an exulting and terrible cry, by the cry of inconceivable triumph and of unspeakable pain. 'I knew it—I was sure!' . . . She knew. She was sure. I heard her weeping; she had hidden her face in her hands. It seemed to me that the house would collapse before I could escape, that the heavens would fall upon my head. But nothing happened. The heavens do not fall for such a trifle. Would they have fallen, I wonder, if I had rendered Kurtz that justice which was his due? Hadn't he said he wanted only justice? But I couldn't. I could not tell her. It would have been too dark—too dark altogether. . . ."

Marlow ceased and sat apart, indistinct and silent, in the pose of a meditating Buddha. Nobody moved for a time. "We have lost the first of the ebb," said the Director suddenly. I raised my head. The offing was barred by a black bank of clouds, and the tranquil waterway leading to the uttermost ends of the earth flowed sombre under an overcast sky—seemed to lead into the heart of an immense darkness.

Textual Appendix

Heart of Darkness was written in a little less than two months, from mid-December 1898 to early February 1899, for publication in *Blackwood's Edinburgh Magazine*. As Robert Kimbrough's textual history below explains, the novella first appeared in three installments in consecutive monthly issues of *Blackwood's* from February through April 1899, and it was then collected three years later in the volume *Youth: A Narrative and Two Other Stories* (with "Youth" and "The End of the Tether"). Parts of the manuscript and the typescript on which the magazine version was based still survive and are very useful in clarifying the author's intentions. Conrad made many major revisions and minor alterations between the manuscript, the typescript, and the magazine publication, and he introduced fewer, smaller, but still significant changes in the 1902 *Youth* version. Kimbrough indicated the most important of these variations in footnotes to his earlier Norton Critical Editions of *Heart of Darkness*, and they are collected below in a separate section of "Textual Variants" where they are easily available for study without distracting the general reader.

It is unclear how closely Conrad supervised the republication of his works in collected editions, which began with the English edition published by William Heinemann in 1921. A good account of the history of these editions can be found in J. H. Stape's entry on "collected editions" in the *Oxford Reader's Companion to Conrad*, edited by Owen Knowles and Gene M. Moore (Oxford: Oxford UP, 2000), pp. 64–67. Although Conrad initially promised to revise and correct the proofs of the Heinemann edition, he apparently delegated proofreading to his secretary and allowed the publisher's editors considerable latitude with punctuation, capitalization, and even minor grammatical matters. The American collected edition issued at the same time by Doubleday was originally intended to be based on the same proofs as the Heinemann edition, with close supervision by Conrad, but these plans fell through. The Doubleday (or "Sun-Dial") edition is the basis of many reprintings of Conrad's works and has been the standard reference for Conrad scholars, but at least for *Heart of Darkness* it is probably a less reliable representation of Conrad's intentions than the Heinemann, 1902 *Youth*,

Blackwood's, and typescript versions. Kimbrough established the text for his 1988 Norton Critical Edition of *Heart of Darkness* by revising the too-heavily copyedited Heinemann edition in light of indications from the typescript and earlier editions about the author's intentions and inclinations, especially in matters of punctuation and style. Kimbrough's account below of his editing principles lists the substantive changes he made to the 1921 edition. His decision to follow the patterns of punctuation in the typescript and manuscript restores what he calls "the simple, direct flow" of Conrad's original diction. I have made only two small changes where the Doubleday Sun-Dial text seems indisputably clearer and more grammatical (p. 30, 1. 1: "on the other bank" rather than "of"; p. 47, 1. 43: "you hear" instead of "hear you"). Otherwise I agree with Kimbrough that his edition, "based upon a full study of all extant states of the story, from original draft through collected edition, is the most authoritative one printed since Conrad's death" (1988 Norton Critical Edition, p. xiii), and I have consequently chosen to reprint it.

ROBERT KIMBROUGH

Textual History and Editing Principles†

Heart of Darkness first appeared in 1899 as "The Heart of Darkness" in *Blackwood's Magazine* in three parts (February, March, and April), after which it was revised for inclusion by Blackwood in 1902 in a separate volume, *Youth: A Narrative and Two Other Stories* (the third being *The End of the Tether*). All subsequent publications of *Heart of Darkness*, whether reprints or newly set editions, stem from this version of the story, rather than from the one in manuscript or the one in *Blackwood's*. The next significant appearance was in 1917—the story had been reprinted in America in serial form and in three *Youth* volumes—when Conrad wrote an "Author's Note" for a reprint by Dent in London of the *Youth* volume of 1902. Then, in 1921, Doubleday brought out the first collected works of Conrad in a limited American edition, called the "Sun-Dial." At the same time, William Heinemann in London was preparing a limited English edition of the collected work. The first general collected editions were brought out simultaneously in 1923 in New York by Doubleday and in London by Dent. Because Con-

---

† From Robert Kimbrough, "Introduction," Norton Critical Edition of Joseph Conrad, *Heart of Darkness*, ed. Robert Kimbrough, 3rd ed. (New York: W. W. Norton, 1988), pp. x–xiii.

rad kept publishing, further collected editions were needed after his death in 1924, but an editor of *Heart of Darkness* cannot consider them authoritative because Conrad had no chance to correct, revise, or even approve them.

Conrad's literary executor, Richard Curle, reported that although much of Conrad's work is "extant in at least six different states— the manuscript, the corrected typescript, the serial form, the American book form, the English book form, and the collected edition book form," it was "the last alone that Conrad considered his final text" (Richard Curle, *The Last Twelve Years of Joseph Conrad*, Garden City, NY, 1928). Although we know from letters that Conrad took great interest in the 1923 Doubleday and Dent collected editions, Bruce Harkness in *Heart of Darkness and the Critics* (San Francisco, 1960) has shown (and the present editor has verified) that the *Youth* volumes in these two collections are printed from the same plates that were made in America for the 1921 "Sun-Dial" *Youth* volume, a work that is most unreliable both because there is no evidence that Conrad had a chance to oversee the publication and because it is filled with error. Hence, one must move back to the 1921 Heinemann *Youth* volume as a possible copy-text for *Heart of Darkness*.

The Heinemann *Collected Works* is not a reprint, but a separate edition, the type of which was distributed after 780 sets had been printed. Conrad kept abreast of the production and worked closely with the editors on various of the volumes. Departures from the *Heart of Darkness* of 1902 are few, but do present a clarity of phrase and a consistency of syntax found in no other state of the story. The 1921 edition has been used, then, as the copy-text for the present edition.

Because there are, however, four significant forms of the text behind Conrad's "final" one—the nearly complete manuscript, the partial typescript, the *Blackwood's Magazine* version of 1899, and the Blackwood *Youth* volume of 1902—the present edition carries a selection of variant readings that permits the reader to follow Conrad as he worked toward establishing the final meaning and art of his text. The manuscript is a "clean" one; it moves steadily forward, having no long insertions, taking no false tacks, showing few second thoughts, and containing almost no revisions longer than a sentence. Because it is the most explicit of the extant versions, many passages that were later suppressed help one understand the meaning of the final text of *Heart of Darkness*. The magazine version is less explicit, omitting words, phrases, and one whole scene, but it has only one totally rewritten passage and only one other fully revised. The 1902 version differs from the magazine mainly in matters of style, in smoothness of phrase and syntax, but Conrad did tone down noticeably two descriptions of the native woman who appears toward the end of the story. Although no major changes appear in the 1921 edition, it is the most polished and consistent in style of all previous editions and reprints.

Nevertheless, the present text contains fifteen substantive and some two thousand accidental departures from 1921. Substantive changes are usually taken to refer to matters of wording, and accidentals, to matters of punctuation and capitalization. As the two words imply, a substantive variant is felt to be one that consciously changes meaning, while an accidental variant is felt to be indifferent with regard to meaning. But such a separation is artificial, for the way a sentence is pointed can change its implied meaning just as forcefully as can a change in its wording. The pointing of Marlow's sentences provides a case in point.

When I undertook the first Norton Critical Edition of *Heart of Darkness*, I was absolutely enchanted by Conrad's manuscript: its uninhibited flow, its simple directness. My instinct was to edit the manuscript for printing, but I was dissuaded because orthodox textual bibliography conservatively said: Do not rush to change what the author did not change in the last text approved by that author. * * *

Today, orthodoxy has changed: While the "final" text still claims authority, the manuscript and the copy provided to a publisher's copy editor also have been granted a special kind of authority. Specifically, if a clear rationale of punctuation (and capitalization) within the manuscript and typescript of a work has been ignored by the publishing-house editor who prepared copy for the printer, then the editor of a critical edition of that work is justified in reclaiming the author's intentions through the reestablishment of the original rationale of punctuation. In the present case, Conrad's punctuation of the manuscript and typescript of *Heart of Darkness* is light; Blackwood's (both in *Blackwood's Magazine* and in *Youth*) is heavy—lots of colons and semicolons and exclamation points and question marks and restrictive commas.

For the complete story and for further justification for the adjustment of house-introduced accidentals, see the excellent work of Marion Michael and Wilkes Berry, "The Typescript of 'The Heart of Darkness,'" *Conradiana* 12 (1980): 147–55. But, in short, Conrad's practice was to have his wife, Jessie, type his manuscripts; he would then correct and change the typescript before sending it to the publisher; and when possible he always wanted to read proof before final printing. Once under contract for *Heart of Darkness*, Conrad wrote feeling the pressure of deadlines, but Jessie fell sick after typing fifty-seven pages (and four lines) of manuscript, which came to thirty-five pages of typescript. Conrad corrected and changed these pages but sent the rest of the manuscript, pages 58–90, directly to David Meldrum, Blackwood's London literary agent. Meldrum had this balance of the manuscript typed and returned to Conrad, but sent the first thirty-five typed pages on to Edinburgh. Conrad corrected the typed version of manuscript pages 58–90, marked where he thought the first installment could end, and sent the lot to Edinburgh. Most of the manuscript lying behind the thirty-five pages typed by Jessie is lost; on the other hand, we have no further typed copy or corrected proofs for any part of the rest of the manuscript, which survives almost without interruption or loss. But a rationale of punctuation can be established by studying the hand changes in the typescript and by collating the places where the surviving manuscript and the typescript coincide and by studying the original punctuation in the rest of the manuscript.

By reinstating the simple, direct flow of the manuscript, I have reestablished the speaking voice of Marlow that was originally heard on the *Nellie*. In so doing, I have also returned to him fifteen original words or phrases that never made it into print and whose absence was never later corrected by Conrad. None of the following emendations is purely "editorial"; each is fully substantiated by the manuscript (and in some few cases, the typescript). In the following list, after the page and line number, the new reading is given, followed by the 1921 printed version:

7.14:   on, *for* in
12.30:   appears, *for* appeared
14.13:   drooped, *for* dropped
15.15:   excavations hanging, *for* excavations, or hanging
15.34:   of, *for* or
18.21:   later on, *for* later
18.28:   Caravans. (*omitted by first printer, and thereafter*)
22.6:   Triumphant, *for* Because triumphant
23.42:   later on, *for* later
31.24:   had, *for* has
37.13:   shore, *for* short
49.42:   found time for it., *for* found time for!
58.41:   shadow of the forest, *for* shadows of the forests
72.15:   the faith, *for* faith
76.12:   black, *for* back

Textual Variants

Significant variations from four sources are listed below, keyed by page and line number to this edition, with the following annotations: *Ms* for readings from the manuscript; *Ts* for the typescript;

Maga for *Blackwood's Magazine*, and *1902* for the first book form. The version in the noted source is given to the right of a word or phrase that indicates what replaced it or where it would be inserted in relation to this edition. When there are significant alterations within a passage (deletions and insertions made in the typescript or manuscript entry), deletions are indicated by angle-brackets (like so: "<deletion>") and insertions by slash-marks (like so: "/insertion/"). Insertions within passages that were subsequently deleted are indicated as "<deleted passage /insertion/>" whereas insertions that replace deleted passages are shown thus: "<deleted passage>/inserted current replacement/." These notations are new to this edition. Only those variants have been included that in the current editor's judgment are significant for stylistic or thematic reasons. I have deleted some of Kimbrough's entries but have added others from my own inspection of the typescript and the manuscript.

3.3	it	*Maga*: us
3.17	He resembled . . .	*Ts. passage canceled, revision (current text) made in pen*: The auburn neck, the broad shoulders, the set of the blue clothes, the solid and balanced aspect of the whole figure suggested the idealized type of the pilot, a conductor of ships—in dangerous waters trust personified—the mast men's confidence. It was difficult to realize that his work was lying at his back within the brooding gloom.
3.24	yarns	*Ts*: /—and even convictions/
3.25	many years	*Ts*: <age and his goodness> /many years and many virtues/
5.30	a direct	*Ms* [begins here]: an effective
5.33	outside	*Ms*: outside in the unseen, enveloping the tale which <brought it out only> /could only bring it out/ as a glow brings out a haze, in the likeness of one of these misty halos that now and then are made visible
5.41	nineteen	*Ms, Ts*: eighteen
7.5	for the sake of what	*Ms*: for the sake of what <was to be got, but at any rate they

had no pretty fictions about it. They had no international associations from motives of philanthropy with some third rate king at the head> was to be got. That's all. The best of them is they didn't get up pretty fictions about it. Was there, I wonder, an association on a philanthropic basis to develop Britain, with some third rate king for a president and solemn old senators discoursing about it approvingly and philosophers with uncombed beards praising it, and men in market places crying it up. Not much! And that's what I like! No! No! It was just [*canceled in Ts*]

7.11   sentimental pretence   *Ms*: sentimental mouthing pretence

7.17   river.   *Ms*: river. A big steamer came down all a long blaze of lights like a town viewed from the sea bound to the uttermost ends of the earth and timed to the day, to the very hour, with nothing unknown in her path[,] nothing but a few coaling stations. She went full-speed, noisily, an angry commotion of the waters followed her spreading from bank to bank—passed, vanished all at once—timed from port to port, to the very hour. And the earth suddenly seemed shrunk to the size of a pea spinning in the heart of an immense darkness full of sparks born, scattered, glowing, going out beyond the ken of men. We looked on . . . [*canceled in Ts*]

7.18   nothing else to do   *Ms*: nothing else to do til the <turn of the tide> /flood tide was done/: but it was only when after a long silence he said <in a hesitating, tentative voice—"You know, I had turned fresh water sailor for a time once," that we knew we would hear were fated to hear Marlow relate one of his inconclusive experiences> in a hesitating and if reluctant voice—"I suppose you fellows remember I did once turn fresh water sailor for a bit," that we knew" [*Ms* breaks off and begins again on p. 8 with "he was shabby and careless. . . ."]

7.25   showing   *Ts*: showing himself in this remark curiously like most tellers of tales who seem always so strangely <ignorant> /unaware/ of what their audience would best like to hear, "<only> *yet* to understand the effect of it . . .

8.41   with,' etc. etc.   *Ts*: with etc. etc." <All this fuss> /She was determined to make no end of fuss/ to get me appointed skipper of a river steam-boat, /if such was my fancy/. <It's curious how women are out of touch with the reality of facts. Yes. They are out of it, they are out of it. Yet I verily believe they can carry through anything in the world—up to a certain point.>

9.14   cause   *Ts*: the noble <work> /cause/

9.39   In a very few hours   *Ts*: In a very few hours I arrived in a city <that makes me always think of a whitened sepulchre. Its quiet streets, empty decorum of its boulevards, all these big houses so intensely respectable to look at

		and so extremely tight closed suggest the reserve of discreet turpitudes> /that always makes me think of a whitened sepulchre/.
10.17	some real work	*Ts:* some <decent> /real/ work
10.21	fascinating—deadly—	*Ts:* fascinating—<poisonous> /deadly/—
11.17	a young chap	*Ts:* a <pimple faced> young chap
12.20	triumphant.	*Ts:* triumphant <and more excited than I supposed her capable of being>
12.31	Something like	*Ts:* Something like an <agent> /emissary of light/,
13.19	Come and find out.	*Ts:* Come and <see> /find out/
13.20	monotonous	*Ts:* <monstrous> /monotonous/
13.34	flung	*Ts:* <chucked> /flung/
13.38	back-cloth.	*Ms:* back-cloth. Of all my life this passage is the part the most unreal. [*canceled in Ts*]
14.12	their wars	*Ms:* their heroic wars
14.13	six-inch	*Ms:* ten-inch; *Ts* and *Maga:* eight-inch; *1902:* six-inch
14.16	empty immensity	*Ts:* In the <vast solitude, in the> empty immensity
14.22	somebody on board	*Ms:* somebody <telling me> /on board assuring me earnestly/ there was a camp of <niggers> natives—he called them enemies—. . .
14.39	river.	*Ms* [*canceled in Ts*]: river where my work was waiting for me. We went up some twenty miles and anchored off the seat of the government. I had heard enough in Europe about its advanced state of civilization: the papers, nay the very paper vendors in the sepulchral city were boasting about the steam tramway and the hotel—especially the hotel. I beheld that wonder. It was like a symbol at the gate. It stood

alone, a grey high cube of iron
with two tiers of galleries outside towering above one of
those ruinous-looking fore-
shores you come upon at home
in out-of-the-way places where
refuse is thrown out. To make
the resemblance complete it
wanted only a drooping post
bearing a board with the legend: rubbish shot here, and
the symbol would have had the
clearness of the naked truth.
Not that a man could not be
found even there, just as a
precious stone is sometimes
found in a dustbin.

I had one dinner in the hotel and found out the tramway
ran only twice a day, at meal-
times. It brought I believe the
whole government with the exception of the governor general
down from the hill to be fed by
contract. They filled the dining
room, uniforms and civilian
clothes[,] sallow faces, pur-
poseless expressions. I was astonished at their number. An
air of weary bewilderment at
finding themselves where they
were sat upon all the faces,
and in their demeanour they
pretended to take themselves
seriously just as the greasy and
dingy place that was like one
of those infamous eating shops
you find near the slums of
cities, where everything is suspicious, the linen, the crock-
ery, the food[,] the owner[,]
the patrons, pretended to be a
sign of progress; as the enormous baobab on the barren
top of the hill amongst the

government buildings[,] soldier's huts, wooden shanties,
corrugated iron hovels, soared,
spread out a maze of denuded
boughs as though it had been
a shade giving tree, as ghastly
as a skeleton that posturing in
showy attitudes would pretend
to be a man.

I was glad to think my work
only began two hundred miles
away from there. I could not
be too far away from that comedy of light at the door of
darkness. As soon as I could I
left for a place thirty miles
higher up. From there I would
have to walk on the caravan
road some hundred and seventy miles more to the starting
point of inland navigation.

I had my passage . . .

15.12 perhaps.'

Ms [canceled in Ts]: perhaps.

The little steamer had no
speed to speak of and I was
rather impatient to see the first
establishment, the shore station of my company. We had
left the coast belt of forest and
barren, stony hills came to
view right and left of the
stream, bordering flat strips of
reedy coarse grass. <As we
rounded a point I heard far
ahead a powerful and muffled
detonation as of a big gun. After a time there was another. It
reminded me of the ship
shelling the continent. "What's
that?" I asked. "Railway station," answered the Swede
curtly, preparing to make a
crossing to the south bank.>

At last we <rounded> turned
a bend.

15.27	pieces of	*Ts*: <rusty pieces of> /pieces of decaying/
16.17	of these high	*Ms*: of these <just and mysterious> /high and just/ proceedings
16.27	I foresaw	*Ts*: <it seemed to me there dwelt> /I foresaw that in the blinding sunshine of that land I would become acquainted with/ a flabby, pretending, weak-eyed devil
16.34	the purpose of which	*Ts*: the purpose of which <as of many other things I was to see afterwards I could not devine [*sic*]> /I found it impossible to divine [spelled correctly]/. It wasn't a /quarry or a/ sandpit anyhow.
17.15	legality	*Ms*: pomp
17.15	surroundings	*Ms*: strangeness [*Ts mistypes this as "strangers," which Conrad corrects in pen to "surroundings," apparently without checking the Ms*]
18.5	clean	*Ms*: clear silk; *Maga* and *1902*: clear
18.17	his vast cuffs	*Ts*: his /vast/ cuffs
18.22	to sport such	*Ts*: to <have> /sport/ such linen
18.33	hut	*Ms*: tent
18.44	to guard against	*Ts*: <mistakes> /clerical errors/
19.2	Kurtz	*Ms. canceled*: Klein (*and the next three times; thereafter*: Kurtz)
19.32	buzz	*Ts*: the /steady/ buzz of flies
20.13	suggestive, and	[*The typescript ends here with a note at the bottom in ink: "35 to p. 58 of MS fourth line," followed by an arrow indicating continuation on the next page*]
22.27	insolence.	*Ms*: insolence. <He said when /directly/ he saw me—"You have been a very long time coming up." I explained why, and he went on

as though I had not spoken.—
"So long that I had to start
without you. The stations must
be provisioned and the agents
relieved. We had so many delays, accidents of all sorts. I
don't know who is dead and
who is alive. The death of your
predecessor stopped the relief—The steamer had to return and ever since. . . . The
situation is grave—very grave.
Rumours reached me from up
river that Mr Kurtz is ill—I
trust it is not true.>

23.21	life.	*Ms*: so unreal in my life. <It was a parody of things that may be done.> And outside,
25.8	while.	*Ms* and *Maga*: while. His allusions were Chinese to me. It was
26.7	servile	*Ms* and *Maga*: obsequious
27.33	meaning	*Ms*: its meaning—its <lesson> /subtle and penetrating essence/. It is impossible.
29.9	expended	*Ms*: I had expended enough /hard/ work on her <to make her worth caring for> to make me love her.
31.41	fired	*Ms*: spat
32.40	possible.	*Ms*: possible. <Can I help him being alone?>
34.16	life	*Ms*: bowels
35.20	expected	*Ms*: expected <to get something. It seemed to crawl nowhere. Reach after reach opened and closed /behind of /[illegible] it crawled towards Kurtz—exclusively. Towards the man with /possessed of/ moral ideas holding a torch in the heart of darkness.> get something.
35.43	surroundings.	*Ms*: surroundings. It could only be obtained by con-

quest—or by surrender, but we passed on indifferent, surprising, less than phantoms, wondering

36.10   faces,

Ms: faces. You know how it is when we hear the band of a regiment. A martial noise—and you pacific father, mild guardian of a domestic hearth-stone [*sic*] suddenly find yourself thinking of carnage. The joy of killing—hey? Or did you never, when listening to another kind of music, did you never dream yourself capable of becoming a saint—if—if. Aha! Another noise, another appeal, another response. All true. All there—in you. Not for you tho' the joy of killing—or the felicity of being a saint. Too many things in the way, business, houses, omnibuses, police[,] the man next door. You don't know my respectable friends how much you owe to the man next door. He is a great fact. There[']s very few places on earth where you haven't a man next door to you or something of him, the merest trace, his footprint—that's enough. You heard the yells and saw the dance and there was the man next door to call you names if you felt an impulse to yell and dance yourself. Another kindly appeal too, and, by Jove, if you did not watch yourself, if you had no weak spot in you where you could take refuge, you would perceive a responsive stir. Why not! Especially if you had a brain. There's all the past as

well as all the future in a
man's mind. And no kind
neighbor to hang you promptly.
The discretion of the wilderness, the night, the darkness of
the land that would hide everything. Principles? Principles—
acquisitions, clothes, rags, rags
that fall off if you give yourself
a good shake. There was the
naked truth—dancing, howling, praying, cursing. Rage.
Fear. Joy. Who can tell. It was
an appeal. Who's that grunting? You don't think I went
ashore to dance too. Not I. I
had to mess about with white
lead and strips of blanket
bandaging those leaky steam
pipes—I tell you. And I had to
watch the steering, and I had
to look after the savage who
was fireman. He was being
improved—he was improved.
He could fire up a vertical
boiler

38.41	affair lay	*Ms*: affair, its meaning and its lesson, lay
40.14	murmured	*Ms*: mumbled
43.40	western	*Ms canceled*: east *and* eastern
45.4	heavy	*Ms*: beastly heavy
47.45	exploded!	*Ms*: exploded. <I am amazed I didn't shed tears.> Absurd!
48.18	worse.	*Ms*: worse. That's a monster-truth with many maws to whom we've got to throw every year—or every day—no mat-ter—no sacrifice is too great—a ransom of pretty, shining lies—not very new, perhaps—but spotless, aureoled, tender. Oh, she
49.31	wraith	*Ms*: ghost
50.22	brutes!	*Ms*: brutes! <Kill every single brute of them.> The curious
50.27	upon his career.	*Ms*: upon 'my career.' His

		<pamphlet> Intended, his ivory, his pamphlet, his future, his career!
54.27	astonishment	*Ms*: astonishment <but giving myself up to the incomprehensible seduction of his youth>. There he was
56.39	tale	*Ms* and *Maga*: tale of cruelty and greed
57.19	symbolic; they	*Ms* and *Maga*: symbolic of some cruel and forbidden knowledge. They
57.43	last	*Ms*: last. If so, then justice was done.
58.25	all.	*Ms*: all. And his was a sturdy allegiance, soaring bravely above the facts which it could see with a bewilderment and a sorrow akin to despair.
58.34	broke down	*Ms*: broke down. "I don't <understand," he wailed. Tears welled out of his eyes. He positively wept before> understand," he groaned.
59.22	phantom	*Ms*: phantom who ruled this land had been
60.27	moved	*Ms*: moved <the barbarous apparition> a wild and gorgeous apparition of a woman.
60.42	soul.	*Ms* and *Maga*: soul. And we men looked at her—at any rate I looked at her.
61.4	brooding	*Ms*: implacable brooding
61.7	stopped	*Ms* and *Maga*: and she stopped. Had her heart failed her, or had her eyes veiled with that mournfulness that lies over all the wild things of the earth seen the hopelessness of longing that will find out sometimes even a savage soul in the loneliness [*Maga*: lonely darkness] of its being? Who can tell. Perhaps she did not know herself. The young fellow

61.14	embrace.	*Ms*: embrace. Her sudden gesture <had the desperate eloquence of> /was as startling as/ a cry but not a sound was heard. The <silence remained suspended over our heads more formidable than the wildest uproar> /formidable silence of the scene completed the memorable impression./ *Maga*: embrace. Her sudden gesture seemed to demand a cry, but the unbroken silence that hung over the scene was more formidable than any sound could be. *1902*: embrace. A formidable silence hung over the scene.
62.19	as if I also	*Ms*: as if I also <was already in a grave> /was buried <already> in a vast grave full of unspeakable secrets/.
63.11	three black fellows	*Ms*: three fellows
64.26	peculiar	*Ms* and *Maga*: dismal
65.24	thing.	*Ms* and *Maga*: thing that seemed released from one grave only to sink forever into another.
66.16	lunatic	*Ms* and *Maga*: mad man
67.17	not?' he	*Ms* and *Maga*: not? I will return.' he
67.32	The brown current	*Ms*: The /brown/ current ran swiftly /out of the heart of darkness/ bearing us down <on our return> /towards the sea/ with twice the speed of our upward progress.
68.5	My Intended, my station	*Ms*: My Intended, my ivory, my station
68.26	'Oh, but I will wring your heart yet!'	*Ms*: 'Oh! but I will make you serve my ends.'
69.8	tremulously	*Ms* and *Maga*: querulously
69.13	rent.	*Ms* and *Maga*: rent. I saw on that ivory visage the expression of strange pride, of mental power, of avarice, of blood-

thirstiness, of cunning, of excessive terror, of intense and
hopeless despair. Did he live
his life through in every detail
of desire[,] temptation[,] and
surrender during that short
and supreme moment? *Ms only
continues*: He cried at some
image, at some vision, he cried
with a cry that was no more
than a breath—

"Oh! the horror!"

I blew the candle out and
left the cabin. Never before in
his life had he been such a
master of his magnificent gift
as in his last speech on earth.
<The eloquence of it.>

The pilgrims

69.35	had pronounced	*Ms* and *Maga*: had so unhesi-tatingly pronounced
72.29	features.	*Ms* and *Maga*: features. She looked out trustfully.
73.2	cemetery	*Ms* and *Maga*: well-kept sepul-chre
73.19	simplicity.	*Ms* and *Maga*: simplicity. 'I have lived—supremely! *Maga only*: What do you want here? I have been dead—and damned.' 'Let me go—I want more of it.' More of what? More blood, more heads on stakes, more adoration, rapine, and murder. I remembered
73.31	cry, 'The horror! The horror!'	*Ms*: cry, "Oh! The horror!"
74.3	brow, seemed	*Ms*: brow, this candid brow, seemed
74.14	death.	*Ms*: death. It was too terrible.
74.18	condemnation.	*Ms*: condemnation. I tell you it was terrible.
74.21	behold.	*Ms* and *Maga*: behold. I wanted to get out.
74.28	admire him	*Ms*: admire him, <not to love him>. Was it?
75.6	lamp.	*Ms* and *Maga*: lamp. But in the

		box I brought to his bedside there were several packages [*Maga only*: pretty well alike, all] tied with shoe-strings and probably he had made a mistake. And the girl
76.17	the infernal stream	*Ms*: the infernal stream that flows from the heart of darkness
76.42	wind. 'The horror! The horror!'	*Ms*: wind. 'Oh! The horror!'
77.4	I was sure!' . . . She knew.	*Ms*: I was sure!' She knew! She was sure! It seemed to me the house would collapse, the heavens would fall upon my head. But nothing happened. The heavens do not fall for such a trifle. Would they have fallen, I wonder, if I had rendered Kurtz justice. <He wanted only justice.> Hadn't he said he wanted only justice? But I couldn't. I could not tell her. It would have been too dark—too dark altogether."

<He was silent> /Marlow ceased and sat in the pose of a meditating Buddha/. Nobody moved for a time. "We have lost the first of the ebb," said the Director suddenly. I looked around. The offing was barred by a black bank of clouds and the tranquil waterway <leading>/that leads/ to the uttermost ends of the earth flowing sombre under an overcast sky seemed to lead into the heart of an immense darkness.

BACKGROUNDS AND CONTEXTS

Imperialism and the Congo

1902 *ENCYCLOPÆDIA BRITANNICA*

Congo Free State†

The Congo Free State (*État Indépendant du Congo*) is one of the largest of the political divisions of Equatorial Africa. It occupies a unique position among modern states, as it may be said to owe its existence to the ambition and force of character of a single individual. It dates its formal inclusion among the independent states of the world from 1885, when its founder, Leopold II, king of the Belgians, became its head. But to understand how it came into existence, a brief account is needed of its Sovereign's connexion with the African continent. In 1876 King Leopold summoned a conference at Brussels of the leading geographical experts in Europe, which resulted in the creation of "The International Association for the Exploration and Civilization of Africa." To carry out its objects an International Commission was founded, with Committees in the principal countries of Europe. Committees were in fact so established, but the Belgian Committee at Brussels, where also were the headquarters of the International Commission, displayed from the first greater activity than did any of the other committees. It turned its attention in the first place to East Africa, and several expeditions were sent out, which resulted in the founding of a Belgian station at Karema on Lake Tanganyika. But the return of Mr (afterwards Sir) H. M. Stanley[1] from his great journey of exploration down the Congo, forcibly directed the attention of King Leopold to the possibilities for exploration and civilization offered by the Congo region.

† From *The New Volumes of the Encyclopædia Britannica constituting, in Combination with the Existing Volumes of the Ninth Edition [1875–89], the Tenth Edition of That Work* (London, Edinburgh, and New York: Encyclopædia Britannica Company, 1902), 3:200–207. This encyclopedia article suggests the state of informed public opinion about the Congo in the year *Heart of Darkness* appeared in book form. The Ninth Edition contains no entry on the Congo Free State, and its article on the Congo was apparently written in the late 1870s, before the 1884 Berlin conference that recognized Leopold's domain.
1. Henry M. Stanley (1841–1904), Anglo-American journalist and explorer. His first expedition to Africa (1868–71) was commissioned by the New York *Herald* to find the lost explorer David Livingstone, whom he greeted with the now-famous question. He was the first European to follow the Congo River from its source to the sea (1874–77), and he later helped to organize the Congo Free State and traveled to the Congo on King Leopold's behalf (1879–84). [Editor]

On the invitation of the king, Mr Stanley visited Brussels, and on November 25th 1878 a separate committee of the International Association was organized at Brussels, under the name "Comité d'Études du Haut Congo." Shortly afterwards this committee became the "International Association of the Congo," which in its turn was the forerunner of the Congo Free State. The Association was provided with a nominal capital of £40,000, but from the first its funds were largely supplemented from the private purse of King Leopold; and by a gradual process of evolution the work, which was originally, in name at least, international in character, became a purely Belgian enterprise.

Mr Stanley, as agent of the Association, spent four years on the river, in exploring and concluding treaties with local chiefs. The first station was founded in February 1880 at Vivi, and before returning to Europe in August 1884 Mr Stanley had established twenty-two stations on the Congo and its tributaries. Numerous expeditions were organized by King Leopold in the Congo basin, and the activity of the International Association and its agents began seriously to engage the attention of the European Powers interested in Africa. On behalf of Portugal, claims were advanced to the Congo, based on the discovery of its mouth by Portuguese navigators centuries before. In the interests of France, M. de Brazza was actively exploring on the northern banks of the Congo, and had established various posts, including one where the important station of Brazzaville is now situated.

The fact that the International Association of the Congo had no admitted status as a sovereign power rendered the tenure of its acquisition somewhat precarious, and induced King Leopold to make determined efforts to secure for his enterprise a recognized position. Early in 1884 a series of diplomatic events brought the question to a head. * * * The United States of America was the first Great Power, in a convention signed on the 22nd of April 1884, to recognize the Association as a properly constituted state. Simultaneously, King Leopold had been negotiating with the French Government, the Association's most serious rival, not only to obtain recognition but on various boundary questions. * * * Germany was the next Great Power to recognize the position of the Free State, on the 8th November 1884, and the same recognition was subsequently accorded by Great Britain on 16th December; Italy, 19th December; Austria-Hungary, 24th December; Holland, 27th December; Spain, 7th January, 1885; France and Russia, 5th February; Sweden and Norway, 10th February; Portugal, 14th February; and Denmark and Belgium, 23rd February. While negotiations with Germany for the recognition of the status of the Congo Free State were in progress, Prince Bismarck issued invitations to the Powers to an International Conference at Berlin. The Conference assembled on the 15th of November 1884, and its deliberations ended on the 26th of February of the following year by the signature of a General Act, which dealt with the relations of the European Powers to other regions of Africa as well as the Congo basin.

The provisions affecting the Congo may be briefly stated. A Conventional Basin of the Congo was defined, which comprised all the regions watered by the Congo and its affluents, including Lake Tanganyika, with its eastern tributaries, and in this Conventional Basin it was declared that "the trade of all nations shall enjoy complete freedom." Freedom of navigation of the Congo and all its affluents was also secured, and differential dues on vessels and merchandise were forbidden. Trade monopolies were prohibited, and provisions made for civilizing the natives, the suppression of the slave trade, and the protection of missionaries, scientists, and explorers. Provision was made for the Powers owning territory in the Conventional Basin to proclaim their neutrality. Only such taxes or duties were to be levied as had "the character of an equivalent for services rendered to navigation itself"; and it was further provided that (Article 16) "The roads, railways, or lateral canals which may be constructed with the special object of obviating the innavigability or correcting the imperfection of the river route on certain sections of the course of the Congo, its affluents, and other waterways, placed under a similar system as laid down in Article 15, shall be considered, in their quality of means of communication, as dependencies of this river and as equally open to the traffic of all nations. And as on the river itself, so there shall be collected on these roads, railways, and canals only tolls calculated on the cost of construction, maintenance, and management, and on the profits due to the promoters"; while as regards the tariff of these tolls, strangers and natives of the respective territories were to be treated "on a footing of perfect equality." The International Association not having possessed, at the date of the assembling of the Conference, any recognized status, was not formally represented at Berlin, but the flag of the Association having, before the close of the Conference, been recognized as that of a sovereign state by all the Powers, with the exception of Turkey, the Association formally adhered to the General Act.

Thus early in 1885 King Leopold had secured the recognition of the Association as an independent state. * * * In April 1885 the Belgian Chamber authorized King Leopold "to be the chief of the state founded in Africa by the International Association of the Congo," and declared that "the union between Belgium and the new State of the Congo shall be exclusively personal." This act of the Belgian Legislature regularized the position of King Leopold, who at once began the work of organizing an administration for the new state. In a circular-letter addressed to the Powers on the 1st of August 1885, His Majesty declared the neutrality of the "Independent State of the Congo," and set out the boundaries which were then claimed for the new state, but it was not until fifteen years later that the frontiers of the Free State were finally settled. * * * The net result of [various treaties] is to leave the Congo Free State with France, Portugal, and Great Britain as her neighbours on the north, with Great Britain and Germany as her neighbours on the east, and with Great Britain and Portugal on her southern frontier. * * *

The international position of the Free State is a somewhat anomalous one. It is an independent state administered as if it were a colony. By his will dated the 2nd August 1889, King Leopold bequeathed to Belgium "all our sovereign rights over the Independent State of the Congo, as they are recognized by the declarations, conventions, and treaties concluded since 1884 between the foreign Powers on the one side, the International Association of the Congo and the Independent State of the Congo on the other, as well as all the benefits, rights, and advantages attached to that sovereignty." It was subsequent to the execution of this will that the Belgian State in July 1890 acquired the right * * * of annexing the Free State in ten years and six months from that date. In the year 1895, owing to its financial difficulties, the Free State was obliged to ask the consent of the Belgian Government to a project for raising a further loan. The Belgian Ministry of that time believed the occasion opportune for advancing the date of the annexation of the Free State as a Belgian colony. A Bill was introduced with this object into the Belgian Legislature, but after long delays and a violent Press campaign the Ministry fell, the Bill was withdrawn, and the Chambers voted a further loan to the Free State to enable it to tide over its immediate difficulties. However, either on the decease of the sovereign, or at some earlier date, the Belgians must come to a decision whether or not they will accept the responsibility for King Leopold's African kingdom.

* * *

Physical Features

Except for its short coast-line on the Atlantic, and for a small area on its north-eastern frontier, the Free State lies wholly within the geographical basin of the Congo. It may roughly be divided into three zones—(1) the small coast zone west of the Crystal Mountains, through which the Congo breaks in a succession of rapids to the Atlantic; (2) the great central zone bounded on the north by the Congo and the Mobangi river, on the east by the Mitumba range of mountains, and on the south by the Congo-Zambezi watershed and the Portuguese frontier; and (3) the smaller zone east of the Mitumba range, including the upper courses of some of the Congo tributaries which have forced their way through the mountains, and west of Lake Mweru and the upper course of the Luapula, as well as a small area which belongs geographically to the Nile valley. * * * The Congo and its tributary streams form, both from the point of view of the physical geography and the commercial development of the Congo Free State, its most important feature; but next in importance are the immense forests which clothe the banks of the rivers, the remains of the great forest which appears at one time to have covered the whole of the centre of the continent. The wooded savannahs, where it is anticipated that in the course of time numerous herds of cattle may be reared, are mostly situated on the higher lands of the Central zone, where the land dips down from the Mitumba Mountains to the Congo.

Climate.—Situated on the Equator, between about 5° N. and 11° S. lat., the Congo Free State shows only a slight variation of temperature all the year round. From July to August the heat increases slightly, with a more rapid rise to November. During December the thermometer remains stationary, and in January begins to rise again, reaching its maximum in February. March is also a month of great heat; in April there is a steady decline into May, with a more rapid decline in June, the minimum being reached again in July. * * * Storms of extreme violence, accompanied by torrential rain, and in rare instances by hailstones, are of not uncommon occurrence. On the coast and along the course of the lower river fogs are very rare, but in the interior early morning fogs are far from uncommon. Europeans are subject to the usual tropical diseases, and the country is not suited for European colonization.

Area and Population

The area is roughly estimated at 900,000 square miles, and the native population is variously estimated at from 30,000,000 (Stanley) to 14,000,000 (Saint Martin). The estimated area is probably above rather than below the proper figure. The vast bulk of the population belongs to the Bantu stock, but there are found, in the great forests along the river banks, sparsely distributed bands of the pigmy people, who probably represent the aboriginal inhabitants of Central Africa. In the north-eastern corner of the State, in the upper basin of the Welle and the Mbomu, the Azandé, a race of warriors and hunters with a social, political, and military organization superior to that of the Bantu tribes of the Congo basin, had intruded from the north, and were forcing their way southwards towards the Congo when the agents of the State appeared in that region and arrested their farther progress. Traces of Arab blood are still found in the districts where the slave traders from the east coast had established stations. The European population at the end of 1886 numbered 254, of whom 46 were Belgians. In 1890 there were 744 Europeans, of whom 338 were Belgians; in 1895, 1076, of whom 691 were Belgians. In January 1900 the European population was as follows:—Belgians, 1187; Italians, 176; British, 99; Dutch, 95; Swedes, 81; Portuguese, 72; French, 53; Germans, 42; Danish, 39; Americans, 33; Norwegians, 25; Swiss, 13; Austrians, 7; Spaniards, 6; and other nationalities, 30,—a total of 1958.

Stations

There are no large towns in the European sense, but a number of stations have been established, some of which have acquired a certain importance and have become the centre of a comparatively large European population. Of these, *Boma* is the headquarters of the local administration, and the residence of a British vice-consul. It is situated on the right bank of the Lower Congo, about 60 miles from its mouth, is one of the principal ports of call for steamers, and the centre of a considerable trade. In 1899 the number of steamers entering the port of Boma was 84, of 164,035 tons, and the number of coasting vessels 196, of 6484 tons. *Banana*, close to the mouth of the Congo and Banana Point, possesses one of the best natural harbours on the west coast of Africa, and is capable of sheltering vessels of the largest tonnage. There are a number of European factories, some of them dating from very early days, and the place is still the centre of a considerable commerce. The French consulate is situated at Banana. In 1899 the number of seagoing vessels entering the port was 108, of 205,610 tons, and the number of coasting vessels 244, of 13,353 tons. *Matadi* is situated on the left bank of the Congo, at the highest point of the lower river which can be reached by seagoing vessels. It is the point of departure of the Congo railway. The railway company has constructed two jetties at which steamers can discharge their cargo. Matadi is probably destined to eclipse both Boma and Banana as a port, but at present no statistics are available as to the number or tonnage of the vessels calling there. *Lukunga*, situated on the banks of the river of that name, a southern tributary of the Congo, about half-way between Matadi and Stanley Pool, was formerly the capital of the Falls district, and the chief recruiting station for porters on the Lower Congo. *Tumba*, the present capital of the district, is a station on the Congo railway, the half-way house between Matadi and Stanley Pool, where the trains stop for the night. It is about 117 miles from Matadi and 143 from Ndolo, the terminus of the railway on Stanley Pool. *Ndolo* is situated a short distance from the Pool, and has two channels by which vessels can enter and leave the port. Extensive works have been undertaken, and it is intended to make Ndolo the headquarters of the steamers that ply on the inland waterways. Quays and a slip for launching vessels have been constructed. *Leopoldville* is the capital of the Stanley Pool district, and was one of the earliest stations founded by the Association. It is situated about 7 miles from Ndolo on the flanks of Mount Leopold, and it is considered probable that it may some day supplant Boma as the headquarters of the administration when the increased importance of the middle and upper river regions makes it necessary to move the centre of administration from the lower river. * * *

Constitution

The Free State is an absolute monarchy, but the Sovereign has never set foot in his African territory, which is administered from Brussels. There is no "constitution," but King Leopold's power is circumscribed in certain directions by the General Act of Berlin, to which the Free State adhered in 1885, by which freedom of trade and free navigation of the Congo and its affluents are secured. Civil and criminal codes have been promulgated by decrees, and in both cases the laws of Belgium have been adopted as the basis of legislation, and modified to suit the special requirements of the Free State. In addition to the decrees, which are signed by the Sovereign and countersigned by the Secretary of State, provision is made for the issue of Regulations and Ordinances by the Governor-General. The Governor-General may, in case of urgency, issue an Ordinance suspending for a limited period a Decree issued by the Sovereign. Ordinances issued by the Governor-General remain in force for six months, at the termination of which period they expire, unless they have in the meantime been superseded by Decree. All Decrees are published in the *Bulletin Officiel*, which is issued monthly at Brussels. The Sovereign is assisted in the task of government by a Secretary of State, whose duty it is not only to countersign all Decrees, but to superintend their execution. There are three Departments of State, each presided over by a Secretary-General in subordination to the Secretary of State. These departments are:—(1) Foreign Affairs, (2) Finance, (3) Interior. There is also a Treasurer-General, and a chief of the Cabinet of the Secretary of State. All these officials have their headquarters at Brussels. The headquarters of the local administration are at Boma, on the lower river, the King being represented by a Governor-General, who is the head both of the naval and military authorities. He is assisted by a Deputy Governor-General, by a number of Inspectors, a Secretary-General, and several Directors. A Consultative Committee or Council of the heads of the various departments and higher officials advises the Governor-General on all matters which he may lay before it. There are seven departments of the administration:—(1) Justice, (2) Transports, Marine and Public Works, (3) Superintendence of State Lands, (4) Agriculture and Industry, (5) Defence, (6) Force Publique, and (7) Finance. For administrative purposes the Free State is divided into 14 districts, each of which is governed by a Commissary, with a staff of Assistant Commissaries, Sub-Commissaries, and clerks.

*   *   *

Judicial Machinery

Until May 1897 the Upper Congo was under military law, but from that date civil law has been administered throughout the State, wherever the authority of the State extended. Courts of First Instance have been instituted in the various districts, and there is a Court of Appeal at Boma which revises the decisions of the inferior tribunals. There is a further appeal, in all cases where the sum in dispute exceeds a thousand pounds, to a Superior Council at Brussels composed of a number of jurisconsults, who sit as a Cour de Cassation. In consequence of repeated charges of the ill-treatment of natives being made against officers of the Administration, King Leopold instituted a Commission for the Protection of Natives, and nominated several missionaries of different denominations to serve on it. It is the duty of the Commission to report to the judicial authorities, or to the Governor-General, any cases of the ill-treatment of the natives which may come to the knowledge of its members.

Religion and Instruction

The native population are pagans, fetish worshippers, and on a very low plane of civilization. The State makes no provision for their religious teaching, but by the Berlin Act missionaries of all denominations are secured perfect freedom of action. The State has established three agricultural and technical colonies for lads up to the age of fourteen. Each of these colonies, which are situated at Boma, Leopoldville, and New Antwerp, makes provision for the training of five hundred boys, who are recruited from those rescued from slavery, from orphans, and from children abandoned or neglected by their parents. Practical instruction is given in various subjects, but the main object is to provide recruits for the armed force of the State, and only such lads as are unfitted to be soldiers are drafted into other occupations. A few native children are sent to

Belgium to be educated. Missionaries have displayed great activity on the Congo, and are encouraged by the Administration. In 1900 there were 300 missionaries, of whom 180 were Roman Catholics and 120 Protestants, scattered among 76 mission stations. The missionaries do not confine themselves to religious instruction, but seek to raise the general level of the native population. In many districts cannibalism is rife, and degrading ceremonies are practised. There are two Roman Catholic bishops, one of whom resides at Leopoldville, the other at Baudouinville, and Roman Catholic churches for the European population are maintained at Boma and Matadi.

Finance

In the years that preceded the founding of the Congo Free State the funds for carrying on the work of the International Association of the Congo were provided by King Leopold out of His Majesty's privy purse, and for some time after the recognition of the Free State this system was continued. Mr Demetrius Boulger states that, in the first ten years of his work on the Congo, King Leopold spent £1,200,000 from his private fortune. The first five years of the existence of the new State were greatly hampered by the provision of the Berlin Act prohibiting the imposition of any duties on goods imported into the Congo region, but at the Brussels Conference, in the summer of 1890, a declaration was signed by the Powers signatory to the Berlin Act authorizing the imposition of import duties not exceeding 10 per cent. [of their value], except in the case of spirits, which were to be subject to a higher duty. * * * The Free State is in fact a great commercial undertaking as well as a governing body. It has established plantations in various parts of the State domains, or Crown lands, but these are mainly in the experimental stage, and the bulk of the revenue from the State domains is derived from the collection of caoutchoue, or rubber, from the forest, and the trade in ivory. In 1886 the total revenue of the State only amounted to 74,261 francs. * * * The following table shows the rapid advance made in the revenue derived from the State domains:—

Year	From State Domains
	Francs
1886	74,261
1891	1,319,145
1896	5,887,404
1900	11,200,000

* * *

Defence

The Administration was at first compelled to recruit soldiers among races outside the State territories, but in 1886 a small beginning was made in recruiting among the local tribes. The greater part of the army consisted in 1901 of locally-raised levies, recruited partly by voluntary enlistment and partly by the enforced enlistment of a certain number of men in each district, who are selected by the Commissary in conjunction with the local chiefs. In 1899 the effective force was fixed at 11,850 men, divided into 23 companies, and commanded by 200 European commissioned officers and 241 sergeants. The term of service for volunteers does not exceed seven years, while the militiamen raised by enforced enlistment serve for five years on active service, and for two years in the reserve. The men are armed with the Albani, the officers with the Mauser rifle. There are seven camps of instruction, and the artillery includes Krupps, Maxims, and Nordenfeldts. A fort has been erected at Chinkakassa near Boma, commanding the river below the Falls, and there is another fort at Kinshassa on Stanley Pool to protect Leopoldville and the railway terminus. * * *

Land and Production

On the 1st of July 1885 it was decreed that "unoccupied lands are considered as belonging to the State." There are three forms of ownership recognized in the Free State—(1) the right of the natives to land in their actual occupation; (2) private ownership by Europeans of land which they have acquired, and of which they are the registered owners; and (3) State ownership of all the land not included in either of the two former categories. * * * There is a separate department for the management of the Domain or Crown lands. Plots for factories and blocks of agricultural land are sold at certain fixed rates, but the main contribution to the State revenue from the Domain lands is obtained * * * from the collection of rubber and ivory. In 1891 and 1892 the State endeavoured to obtain a monopoly of the rubber trade, and circulars were issued to the Commissaries in certain districts instructing them that not only was the collection of rubber by the natives to be regulated, but that in future the natives were to be compelled to sell their rubber to the State. Vigorous protests by the private trading companies were made against this attempted violation of the freedom of trade secured by the Berlin Act, and eventually the circulars were withdrawn and an arrangement made by which certain areas were reserved to the State and certain areas to private traders. * * *

Minerals

Comparatively little is known of the mineral wealth of the country. Iron is widely distributed, and worked in a primitive fashion. It has been found in the Manyanga country, the Manyema country, on the Upper Congo, in the Urua country, in the basins of the Kasai and the Lualaba, and in Katanga. Immense ironstone hills, estimated to contain millions of tons of ironstone of superior quality, have been reported in the southeastern region. The wealth of Katanga in copper has been described by several travellers, and the expedition sent out in 1891 reported that the richest deposits are to be found in the southern districts on the bank of the Lufira river. Copper is also reported in other districts, such as Mpala and Ulvira on Lake Tanganyika. Gold has been discovered in Katanga, but before the advent of Europeans was held in less repute than copper. Lead, tin (Mobangi basin), sulphur, and mercury are also reported to exist, but until the introduction of European methods it is impossible to say what are the mineral resources of the Congo region, and whether they can be worked at a profit.

Animal and Vegetable Products

Elephant and hippopotamus ivory formed for some years the most important article of export. When Europeans first entered the Congo basin the natives were found to have large stores of "dead ivory" in their possession. These stores are still being drawn on for export, supplemented by the "live ivory" obtained by the killing of elephants in the present day. In July 1889, as a precaution against the extermination of the elephant, the King issued a decree prohibiting the killing of elephants without special permission. Large herds still exist in the Congo forests, especially in the eastern and northeastern districts. A reference to the commercial statistics will show that ivory is still the second most important export from the Free State. It is, however, a bad second to caoutchouc, the rubber of commerce, which is obtained from the rubber-bearing liana— *Landolphia florida*—which exists in practically inexhaustible quantities. In 1886 the value of the rubber exports only amounted to 159,000 francs. In 1900 the value had risen to 28,973,505 francs. Palm oil, palm nuts, gum copal, and timber are other natural products which swell the volume of exports, though not at present to any considerable extent. Timber is as yet only exported to the value of between £3000 and £4000, but the vast forests contain many trees, the wood of which is sufficiently valuable to pay the cost of transport to Europe. Ebony, teak, African cedar, mahogany are a few only of the woods that abound on the Congo. Coffee and tobacco are found in a wild state, and there is an immense number of fruit-bearing trees, and of plants yielding spices and essences which may in time be turned to profitable account.

Agriculture

Until the advent of Europeans the natives, except in the immediate neighbourhood of some of the Arab settlements, did little more than cultivate small patches of land close to their villages. They grew bananas, manioc, the Spanish potato, the sugar cane, maize, sorghum, rice, millet, eleusine, and other fruits and vegetables, as well as tobacco, but the constant state of fear in which they lived, both from their neighbours and from the Arabs, offered small inducement to industry. Future agricultural development will depend on the success which attends the efforts to turn the native into a regular labourer. Plantations have been established both by the State and by private companies, and already small quantities of coffee, cocoa, tobacco, and maize have been exported. There are no statistics of the number of domestic animals in the country, but there is a number of horses, mules, donkeys, cattle, and pigs, and it is believed that cattle-rearing may be profitably undertaken in the eastern portions where the country rises towards the Mitumba Range, when the political conditions and improved transport arrangements make such an experiment possible.

Industries

In some districts the natives possess considerable skill in working in wood, ivory, and metals, but the Congo industries are at present purely local. Iron and copper are extracted by certain tribes, which enjoy a practical monopoly of this kind of work. The knives, spears, and shields of native workmanship frequently show both ingenuity and skill, alike in design and in execution. European fabrics have, among the tribes nearest the coast, already affected the weaving of cloths by the natives, but over a great part of the State territory the natives still manufacture cloth from vegetable fibres. They employ four different colours; yellow, the natural colour, black, red, and brown, which are obtained by dyeing, and these colours they combine into effective designs. In some tribes a rude form of printing designs on cloth is practised, and on the Sankuru and Lukenye a special kind of cloth, with a heavy pile resembling velvet, is made by the Basongo-Meno and other tribes.

Commerce

The following table shows the total exports under the headings—
(1) Special Commerce, which includes only such articles as
orginate from the Congo Free State; and (2) General Commerce,
which includes exports of all kinds from the Free State, whatever
their place of origin:—

Year	Special	General
1887	1,980,441	7,667,949
1890	8,242,199	14,109,781
1895	10,943,019	12,135,656
1898	22,163,482	25,396,706
1899	36,067,959	39,138,283

The following table shows the value of the principal products exported from the Free State (Special Commerce) at three periods:—

Articles	1887	1895	1899
	Francs.	Francs.	Francs.
Caoutchoue .	116,768	2,882,585	28,100,917
Ivory . . .	795,700	5,844,640	5,834,620
Palm nuts . .	590,781	1,242,898	1,293,413
Palm oil . .	462,609	935,658	734,511
Timber . .	. . .	12,200	91,312
Miscellaneous .	14,583	25,038	13,186
	1,980,441	10,943,019	36,067,959

The increasing importance of the trade with Belgium is shown in
the following table, in which will be found the value of the general
exports to Belgium, Holland, and Great Britain at three periods:—

Country	1890	1895	1899
	Francs.	Francs.	Francs.
Belgium . .	2,217,599	8,999,660	32,367,828
Holland . .	8,073,208	885,405	1,656,561
Great Britain .	833,941	592,496	281,593

*   *   *

Shipping and Navigation

There is a fortnightly service of steamers between Antwerp and Boma and Banana. There is also frequent steam communication with Liverpool, Hamburg, Rotterdam, and Lisbon. In 1899 there entered at Boma and Banana 192 seagoing vessels of 369,645 tons, and cleared 197 vessels of 375,715 tons. Of the tonnage entered, 191,843 was Belgian; 79,037, British; and 65,682, German. Of the tonnage cleared 189,933 was Belgian; 85,588 was British; and 67,113, German. During the same year 440 coasting vessels of 19,838 tons entered, and 451 vessels of 20,557 tons cleared from the same ports.

Internal Communications

From the mouth of the Congo to the beginning of the rapids, which render the river unnavigable—a distance of about a hundred miles—the State maintains a fleet of seven steamers, in which passengers and goods are transported from the larger ocean-going steamers to Matadi, the point of departure of the railway. Matadi can, however, be approached by ships of considerable burden. Before the railway, all merchandise and goods for the interior had to be carried by porters from the coast to Stanley Pool. This method was both costly and inconvenient. The journey took three weeks. In 1887 the King granted to the Congo Industrial and Commercial Company a concession to construct a railway from the lower river to Stanley Pool, and, after a survey had been made, a Congo Railway Company was founded in Brussels in July 1889, with a capital of 25 million francs, of which the Belgian Government subscribed 10 millions. The moving spirit in this great enterprise was Colonel Thys. The work was begun almost immediately, but nearly insuperable difficulties were encountered, both engineering and financial. The line was finally completed in March 1898, and formally opened to traffic in the following July—nine years after its practical inception. The length of the line is 260 miles, and its inland terminus is at Ndolo on Stanley Pool, a short distance from Leopoldville. There is a weekly service of three passenger trains in each direction, two days being occupied on the journey. The trains do not run during the night. The single through fare for Europeans is £20, and the freight charges are proportionately high, judged by European standards, though considerably below the charges which had to be paid before the railway was built. The cost of constructing and equipping the railway was 68 millions of francs. Other railways which are projected are a short line from Boma to the Lukulu river, for the purpose of opening up the Mayumbe province; a line or lines of railway between the navigable waters of the Upper Congo and Lake Tanganyika, with subsidiary lines which would develop the rich provinces of Manyema, Urua, and Katanga; and a railway in the Upper Welle district, for the purpose of opening up the north-eastern provinces and affording rapid access to the leased territories on the Upper Nile.

Waterways

It is, however, in the splendid navigable waterways of the main Congo stream and its tributaries that the Free State has found, and will continue to find, its most powerful instrument in the development of its resources. * * * The State maintains on these waterways a fleet of steamers which in 1900 numbered 26 vessels, for the purpose of preserving authority, provisioning the stations, promoting trade, and operating the postal service. Private trading companies, French, Belgian, and Dutch, and several Missionary Societies also maintain steamers on the inland waters, and the number is being rapidly increased since the docks have been built at Ndolo and the railway offers increased facilities for transport. Away from the railway and the waterways, transport is still mainly effected by porters.

* * *

1910 *ENCYCLOPÆDIA BRITANNICA*

[European Reaction to Leopold's Abuses]†

* * *

The discussions which from time to time took place in the Belgian parliament on the affairs of the Congo State were greatly embittered by the charges brought against the state administration. The administration of the state had indeed undergone a complete change since the early years of its existence. A decree of the 1st of July 1885 had, it is true, declared all "vacant lands" the property of the state (*Domaine privé de l'état*),[1] but it was not for some time

† The Encyclopædia Britannica: A Dictionary of Arts, Sciences, Literature and General Information, 11th ed. (New York: The Encyclopædia Britannica Co., 1910), 6:920–22. After recounting the history of the formation of the Congo Free State for several pages, following word-for-word the account of the 10th edition (see above), this entry then discusses the abuses of Leopold's administration of the Congo and the increasing European clamor for a change of regime. See the selection by Alan Simmons in this Norton Critical Edition for an analysis of the influence *Heart of Darkness* may have had on the Congo reform movement. Notes are the Editor's.
1. Private domain of the state (French).

that this decree was so interpreted as to confine the lands of the natives to those they lived upon or "effectively" cultivated. Their rights in the forest were not at first disputed, and the trade of the natives and of Europeans was not interfered with. But in 1891— when the wealth in rubber and ivory of vast regions had been demonstrated—a secret decree was issued (Sept. 21) reserving to the state the monopoly of ivory and rubber in the "vacant lands" constituted by the decree of 1885, and circulars were issued making the monopoly effective in the Aruwimi-Welle, Equator and Ubangi districts. The agents of the state were enjoined to supervise their collection, and in future natives were to be obliged to sell their produce to the state. By other decrees and circulars (October 30 and December 5, 1892, and August 9, 1893) the rights of the natives and of white traders were further restricted. No definition had been given by the decree of 1885 as to what constituted the "vacant lands" which became the property of the state, but the effect of the later decrees was to assign to the government an absolute proprietary right over nearly the whole country; a native could not even leave his village without a special permit. The oppressive nature of these measures drew forth a weighty remonstrance from the leading officials, and Monsieur C. Janssen, the governor, resigned. Vigorous protests by the private trading companies were also made against this violation of the freedom of trade secured by the Berlin Act, and eventually an arrangement was made by which certain areas were reserved to the state and certain areas to private traders, but the restrictions imposed on the natives were maintained. Large areas of the state domain were leased to companies invested with very extensive powers, including the exclusive right to exploit the produce of the soil. In other cases, *e.g.* in the district of Katanga, the state entered into partnership with private companies for the exploitation of the resources of the regions concerned. The "concession" companies were first formed in 1891 under Belgian law; in 1898 some of them were reconstituted under Congo law. In all of them the state had a financial interest either as shareholder or as entitled to part profits.

This system of exploitation of the country was fruitful of evil, and was mainly responsible for the bad treatment of the natives. Only in the lower Congo and a narrow strip of land on either side of the river above Stanley Pool was there any freedom of trade. The situation was aggravated by the creation in 1896, by a secret decree, of the *Domaine de la couronne*,[2] a vast territory between the Kasai and Ruki rivers, covering about 112,000 sq. m. To administer this domain, carved out of the state lands and treated as the private

2. Domain of the crown (French).

property of Leopold II, a *Fondation*[3] was organized and given a civil personality. It was not until 1902 that the existence of the *Domaine de la couronne* was officially acknowledged. The *Fondation* controlled the most valuable rubber region in the Congo, and in that region the natives appeared to be treated with the utmost severity. In the closing years of the 19th century and the early years of the 20th the charges brought against the state assumed a more and more definite character. As indicated, they fell under two main heads. In the first place the native policy of the Congo government was denounced as at variance with the humanitarian spirit which had been regarded by the powers as one of the chief motives inspiring the foundation of the Congo State. In the second place it was contended that the method of exploitation of the state lands and the concessions system nullified the free trade provisions of the Berlin Act. Reports which gave colour to these charges steadily accumulated, and gave rise to a strong agitation against the Congo State system of government. This agitation was particularly vigorous in Great Britain, and the movement entered on a new era when on the 20th of May 1903 the House of Commons agreed without a division to the following motion:—

> "That the government of the Congo Free State having, at its inception, guaranteed to the powers that its native subjects should be governed with humanity, and that no trading monopoly or privilege should be permitted within its dominions, this House request His Majesty's Government to confer with the other powers, signatories of the Berlin General Act, by virtue of which the Congo Free State exists, in order that measures may be adopted to abate the evils prevalent in that state."

In accordance with this request the 5th marquess of Lansdowne, then secretary of state for foreign affairs, issued a despatch on the 8th of August 1903 to the British representatives at the courts of the powers which signed the Berlin Act, drawing attention to the alleged cases of ill-treatment of natives and to the existence of trade monopolies in the Congo Free State, and in conclusion stating that His Majesty's government would "be glad to receive any suggestions which the governments of the signatory powers might be disposed to make in reference to this important question, which might perhaps constitute, wholly or in part, the subject of a reference to the tribunal at the Hague." This despatch failed to evoke any response from the powers, with the single exception of Turkey, but the public agitation against the Congo State régime continued

3. Foundation (French).

to grow in force, being greatly strengthened by the publication in February 1904 of a report by Mr Roger Casement,[4] then British consul at Boma, on a journey which he had made through the middle Congo region in 1903 (described as the "Upper" Congo in the report). The action on the part of the British government resulted in considerable correspondence with the Congo government, which denied the charges of systematic ill-treatment of the natives and controverted the contention that its policy constituted an infringement of the Berlin Act. In July 1904, however, King Leopold issued a decree appointing a commission of inquiry to visit the Congo State, investigate the condition of the natives, and if necessary recommend reforms.* * *

*   *   *

The report of the commission of inquiry was published, minus the minutes of the evidence submitted to the commissioners in November 1905. While expressing admiration for the signs which had come under its notice of the advance of civilization in the Congo State, the commission confirmed the reports of the existence of grave abuses in the upper Congo, and recommended a series of measures which would in its opinion suffice to ameliorate the evil. It approved the concessions system in principle and regarded forced labour as the only possible means of turning to account the natural riches of the country, but recognized that though freedom of trade was formally guaranteed there was virtually no trade, properly so called, among the natives in the greater portion of the Congo State, and particularly emphasized the need for a liberal interpretation of the land laws, effective application of the law limiting the amount of labour exacted from the natives to forty hours per month, the suppression of the "sentry" system, the withdrawal from the concession companies of the right to employ compulsory measures, the regulation of military expeditions, and the freedom of the courts from administrative tutelage. Simultaneously with the report of the commission of inquiry there was published a decree appointing a commission to study the recommendations contained in the report, and to formulate detailed proposals.

*   *   *

The report of the reforms commission was not made public, but as the fruit of its deliberations King Leopold signed on the 3rd of June 1906 a number of decrees embodying various changes in the administration of the Congo State. By the advocates of radical reforms these measures were regarded as utterly inadequate, and even in Belgium, among those friendly to the Congo State system of administration, some uneasiness was excited by a letter which

4. See the selection by Roger Casement in this Norton Critical Edition.

was published along with the decrees, wherein King Leopold inti-
mated that certain conditions would attach to the inheritance he
had designed for Belgium. Among the obligations which he enu-
merated as necessarily and justly resting on his legatee was the duty
of respecting the arrangements by which he had provided for the
establishment of the *Domaine de la couronne* and the *Domaine
privé de l'état*. It was further declared that the territories bequeathed would be inalienable.

The fears excited by this letter that King Leopold desired to re-
strict Belgium's liberty of action in the Congo State when the latter
should become a Belgian colony were not diminished by the announcement in November 1906 of four new concessions, confer-
ring very extensive rights on railway, mining and rubber companies
in which foreign capital was largely interested. This was immediately before the opening in the Belgian chamber of a fresh debate
in which the history of the Congo question entered on a new stage
of critical importance not only from the national but the international point of view. It had become evident, indeed, that things
could not continue as they were. In reply to an influential deputa-
tion which waited upon him on the 20th of November, Sir Edward
Grey, speaking as the representative of the British government in
his capacity as secretary of state for foreign affairs, expressed the
desire "that Belgium should feel that her freedom of action is un-
fettered and unimpaired and her choice unembarrassed by anything which we have done or are likely to do"; but he added that if
Belgium should fail to take action "it will be impossible for us to
continue to recognize indefinitely the present state of things without a very close examination of our treaty rights and the treaty obligations of the Congo State."

*   *   *

While [legislation was drafted to replace the absolutism of the
king with parliamentary control], further evidence was forthcoming
that the system complained of on the Congo remained unaltered,
and that the "reforms" of June 1906 were illusory. Various revolts of
the natives also occurred, and in some parts of the state complete
anarchy prevailed. Not only in Great Britain and America did the
agitation against the administration of the Congo State gain
ground, but in Belgium and France reform associations enlightened
public opinion. The government of Great Britain let it be known
that its patience was not inexhaustible, while the senate of the
United States declared that it would support President Roosevelt in
his efforts for the amelioration of the condition of the inhabitants
of the Congo. The attitude of the powers was at the same time perfectly friendly towards Belgium. In this manner the movement in
favour of ending the baneful régime of Leopold II was strength-

ened. On the 10th of July 1907 the Belgian premier announced that negotiations with the Congo State would be renewed, and on the 28th of November following a treaty was signed for the cession of the Congo State to Belgium. This treaty stipulated for the maintenance of the *Fondation de la couronne*. This "government within a government" was secured in all its privileges, its profits as heretofore being appropriated to allowances to members of the royal family and the maintenance and development of "works of public utility" in Belgium and the Congo, those works including schemes for the embellishment of the royal palaces and estates in Belgium and others for making Ostend "a bathing city unique in the world." The state was to have the right of redemption on terms which, had the rubber and ivory produce alone been redeemed, would have cost Belgium about £8,500,000.

Even those politicians least disposed to criticize the actions of the king protested vigorously against the provisions concerning the *Fondation*. It was recognized that the chamber would not vote the treaty of cession unless those provisions were modified. Negotiations between Leopold II and the Belgian premier followed. While they were in progress the British government again expressed its views, and in very monitory language. They were conveyed in a passage in the king's speech at the opening of parliament on the 29th of January, and in a statement by Sir Edward Grey in the House of Commons on the 26th of February. Sir Edward Grey affirmed that the Congo State had "morally forfeited every right to international recognition," and quoted with approval Lord Cromer's statement that the Congo system was the worst he had ever seen. The foreign secretary declared, in reference to the negotiations for the transfer of the Congo to Belgium, that any semi-transfer which left the controlling power in the hands of "the present authorities" would not be considered by Great Britain as a guarantee of treaty rights. On the same day that Sir Edward Grey spoke a parliamentary paper was issued (*Africa No. 1*, 1908) containing consular reports on the state of affairs in the Congo. The most significant of these reports was from Mr. W. G. Thesiger, consul at Boma, who in a memorandum on the application of the labour tax, after detailing various abuses, added, "The system which gave rise to these abuses still continues unchanged, and so long as it is unaltered the condition of the natives must remain one of veiled slavery." Eight days later (on the 5th of March) an additional act was signed in Brussels annulling the clauses in the treaty of cession concerning the *Fondation*, which was to cease to exist on the day Belgium assumed the sovereignty of the Congo and its property to be absorbed in the state domains. Leopold II, however, was able to obtain generous compensation for the surrender of the *Fondation*. Certain fragments of the domain, including an estate of 155 sq. m. in Africa, a villa at Ostend, and some land at Laeken, were kept by the king, who further retained a life interest in property on the Riviera and elsewhere. Belgium undertook at her own charges and at an estimated cost of £2,000,000 to complete "the works of embellishment" begun in Belgium with funds derived from the *Fondation* and to create a debt of £2,000,000 chargeable on the funds of the colony, which sum was to be paid to the king in fifteen annual instalments—the money, however, to be expended on objects "connected with and beneficial to the Congo." The annuities to members of the royal family were to be continued, and other subsidies were promised. But the most important provision was the agreement of Belgium to respect the concessions granted in the lands of the *Fondation* in November 1906 to the American Congo Company and the *Compagnie forestière et minière*, companies in which the Congo State had large holdings.

* * *

* * * Public opinion in Belgium was disturbed and anxious at the prospect of assuming responsibility for a vast, distant, and badly administered country, likely for years to be a severe financial drain upon the resources of the state. But, though those who opposed annexation formed a numerous body, all political parties were agreed that in case of annexation the excesses which had stained the record of the Free State should cease.[5]

KING LEOPOLD II

[The Sacred Mission of Civilization]†

Our refined society attaches to human life (and with reason) a value unknown to barbarous communities. When our directing will is implanted among them its aim is to triumph over all obstacles, and results which could not be attained by lengthy speeches may follow philanthropic influence. But if, in view of this desirable spread of civilisation, we count upon the means of action which confer upon us dominion and the sanction of right, it is not less true that our ultimate end is a work of peace. Wars do not necessarily mean the ruin of the regions in which they rage; our agents do not ignore this fact, so from the day when their effective superiority is affirmed, they feel profoundly reluctant to use force. The

---

5. On 14 November 1908, the Belgian legislature approved legislation to assume administrative control of the Congo, and the Congo Free State ceased to exist.
† From Guy Burrows, *The Land of the Pigmies* (London, 1898), p. 286.

wretched negroes, however, who are still under the sole sway of their traditions, have that horrible belief that victory is only decisive when the enemy, fallen beneath their blows, is annihilated. The soldiers of the State, who are recruited necessarily from among the natives, do not immediately forsake those sanguinary habits that have been transmitted from generation to generation. The example of the white officer and wholesome military discipline gradually inspire in them a horror of human trophies of which they previously had made their boast. It is in their leaders that they must see living evidence of these higher principles, taught that the exercise of authority is not at all to be confounded with cruelty, but is, indeed, destroyed by it. I am pleased to think that our agents, nearly all of whom are volunteers drawn from the ranks of the Belgian army, have always present in their minds a strong sense of the career of honour in which they are engaged, and are animated with a pure feeling of patriotism; not sparing their own blood, they will the more spare the blood of the natives, who will see in them the all-powerful protectors of their lives and their property, benevolent teachers of whom they have so great a need.

GEORGE WASHINGTON WILLIAMS

An Open Letter to His Serene Majesty Leopold II, King of the Belgians and Sovereign of the Independent State of Congo†

Good and Great Friend,

I have the honour to submit for your Majesty's consideration some reflections respecting the Independent State of Congo, based upon a careful study and inspection of the country and character of the personal Government you have established upon the African Continent.

In order that you may know the truth, the whole truth, and nothing but the truth, I implore your most gracious permission to address you without restraint, and with the frankness of a man who

† From John Hope Franklin, *George Washington Williams: A Biography* (Chicago: U of Chicago P, 1985), pp. 243–54. Williams (1849–91) was an African American minister, journalist, lawyer, legislator, historian, and Civil War veteran. In 1890, the same year that Conrad traveled up the Congo River, Williams journeyed to the Congo Free State under the sponsorship of an American railroad magnate and, after two months of travel, reached Stanley Falls. There he wrote his "Open Letter" to Leopold II, with whom he had spoken in Belgium before beginning his expedition. Williams reports that he had "been interested in the success of the Congo State" because he felt it would advance "the overthrow of the African Slave-Power and the spread of civilization," but he informed his patron that what he found there convinced him of the "deceit, obtusiveness, ignorance and cruelty of the State of the Congo" (quoted in Franklin, pp. 266, 195).

feels that he has a duty to perform to *History, Humanity, Civilization* and to the *Supreme Being*, who is himself the "King of Kings."

Your Majesty will testify to my affection for your person and friendship for your African State, of which you have had ample practical proofs for nearly six years. My friendship and service for the State of Congo were inspired by and based upon your publicly declared motives and aims, and your personal statement to your humble subscriber:—humane sentiments and work of Christian civilization for Africa. Thus I was led to regard your enterprise as the rising of the Star of Hope for the Dark Continent, so long the habitation of cruelties; and I journeyed in its light and laboured in its hope. All the praiseful things I have spoken and written of the Congo country, State and Sovereign, were inspired by the firm belief that your Government was built upon the enduring foundation of *Truth, Liberty, Humanity* and *Justice*.

It afforded me great pleasure to avail myself of the opportunity afforded me last year, of visiting your State in Africa; and how thoroughly I have been disenchanted, disappointed and disheartened, it is now my painful duty to make known to your Majesty in plain but respectful language. Every charge which I am about to bring against your Majesty's personal Government in the Congo has been carefully investigated; a list of competent and veracious witnesses, documents, letters, official records and data has been faithfully prepared, which will be deposited with Her Britannic Majesty's Secretary of State for Foreign Affairs, until such time as an International Commission can be created with power to send for persons and papers, to administer oaths, and attest the truth or falsity of these charges.

I crave your Majesty's indulgence while I make a few preliminary remarks before entering upon the specifications and charges.

Your Majesty's title to the territory of the State of Congo is badly clouded, while many of the treaties made with the natives by the "Association Internationale du Congo," of which you were Director and Banker, were tainted by frauds of the grossest character. The world may not be surprised to learn that your flag floats over territory to which your Majesty has no legal or just claim, since other European Powers have doubtful claims to the territory which they occupy upon the African Continent; but all honest people will be shocked to know by what grovelling means this fraud was consummated.

There were instances in which Mr. Henry M. Stanley sent one white man, with four or five Zanzibar soldiers, to make treaties with native chiefs. The staple argument was that the white man's heart had grown sick of the wars and rumours of war between one chief and another, between one village and another; that the white man was at peace with his black brother, and desired to "confederate all

African tribes" for the general defense and public welfare. All the sleight-of-hand tricks had been carefully rehearsed, and he was now ready for his work. A number of electric batteries had been purchased in London, and when attached to the arm under the coat, communicated with a band of ribbon which passed over the palm of the white brother's hand, and when he gave the black brother a cordial grasp of the hand the black brother was greatly surprised to find his white brother so strong, that he nearly knocked him off his feet in giving him the hand of fellowship. When the native inquired about the disparity of strength between himself and his white brother, he was told that the white man could pull up trees and perform the most prodigious feats of strength. Next came the lens act. The white brother took from his pocket a cigar, carelessly bit off the end, held up his glass to the sun and complaisantly smoked his cigar to the great amazement and terror of his black brother. The white man explained his intimate relation to the sun, and declared that if he were to request him to burn up his black brother's village it would be done. The third act was the gun trick. The white man took a percussion cap gun, tore the end of the paper which held the powder to the bullet, and poured the powder and paper into the gun, at the same time slipping the bullet into the sleeve of the left arm. A cap was placed upon the nipple of the gun, and the black brother was implored to step off ten yards and shoot at his white brother to demonstrate his statements that he was a spirit, and, therefore, could not be killed. After much begging the black brother aims the gun at his white brother, pulls the trigger, the gun is discharged, the white man stoops . . . and takes the bullet from his shoe!

By such means as these, too silly and disgusting to mention, and a few boxes of gin, whole villages have been signed away to your Majesty.

In your personal letter to the President of the Republic of the United States of America, bearing date of August 1st, 1885, you said that the possessions of the International Association of the Congo will hereafter form the Independent State of the Congo. "I have at the same time the honour to inform you and the Government of the Republic of the United States of America that, authorised by the Belgian Legislative Chambers to become the Chief of the new State, I have taken, in accord with the Association, the title of Sovereign of the Independent State of Congo." Thus you assumed the headship of the State of Congo, and at once organised a personal Government. You have named its officers, created its laws, furnished its finances, and every act of the Government has been clothed with the majesty of your authority.

On the 25th of February 1884, a gentleman, who has sustained an intimate relation to your Majesty for many years, and who then wrote as expressing your sentiments, addressed a letter to the United States in which the following language occurs:—"It may be safely asserted that no barbarous people have ever so readily adopted the fostering care of benevolent enterprise, as have the tribes of the Congo, and never was there a more honest and practical effort made to increase their knowledge and secure their welfare." The letter, from which the above is an excerpt, was written for the purpose of securing the friendly action of the Committee on Foreign Relations, which had under consideration a Senate Resolution in which the United States recognized the flag of the "Association Internationale du Congo" as the flag of a friendly Government. The letter was influential, because it was supposed to contain the truth respecting the natives, and the programme, not only of the Association, but of the new State, its legitimate successor, and of your Majesty.

When I arrived in the Congo, I naturally sought for the results of the brilliant programme:—"*fostering care*," "*benevolent enterprise*," an "*honest and practical effort*" to increase the knowledge of the natives "*and secure their welfare.*" I had never been able to conceive of Europeans, establishing a government in a tropical country, without building a hospital; and yet from the mouth of the Congo River to its head-waters, here at the seventh cataract, a distance of 1,448 miles, there is not a solitary hospital for Europeans, and only three sheds for sick Africans in the service of the State, not fit to be occupied by a horse. Sick sailors frequently die on board their vessels at Banana Point; and if it were not for the humanity of the Dutch Trading Company at that place—who have often opened their private hospital to the sick of other countries—many more might die. There is not a single chaplain in the employ of your Majesty's Government to console the sick or bury the dead. Your white men sicken and die in their quarters or on the caravan road, and seldom have christian burial. With few exceptions, the surgeons of your Majesty's government have been gentlemen of professional ability, devoted to duty, but usually left with few medical stores and no quarters in which to treat their patients. The African soldiers and labourers of your Majesty's Government fare worse than the whites, because they have poorer quarters, quite as bad as those of the natives; and in the sheds, called hospitals, they languish upon a bed of bamboo poles without blankets, pillows or any food different from that served to them when well, rice and fish.

I was anxious to see to what extent the natives had "*adopted the fostering care*" of your Majesty's "benevolent enterprise" (?), and I was doomed to bitter disappointment. Instead of the natives of the Congo "adopting the fostering care" of your Majesty's Government, they everywhere complain that their land has been taken from them by force; that the Government is cruel and arbitrary, and declare that they neither love nor respect the Government and its flag. Your Majesty's Government has sequestered their land, burned their towns, stolen their property, enslaved their women and children, and committed other crimes too numerous to mention in detail. It is natural that they everywhere shrink from "*the fostering care*" your Majesty's Government so eagerly proffers them.

There has been, to my absolute knowledge, no "*honest and practical effort made to increase their knowledge and secure their welfare.*" Your Majesty's Government has never spent one franc for educational purposes, nor instituted any practical system of industrialism. Indeed the most unpractical measures have been adopted *against* the natives in nearly every respect; and in the capital of your Majesty's Government at Boma there is not a native employed. The labour system is radically unpractical; the soldiers and labourers of your Majesty's Government are very largely imported from Zanzibar at a cost of £10 *per capita*, and from Sierre Leone, Liberia, Accra and Lagos at from £1 to £1/10. *per capita*. These recruits are transported under circumstances more cruel than cattle in European countries. They eat their rice twice a day by the use of their fingers; they often thirst for water when the season is dry; they are exposed to the heat and rain, and sleep upon the damp and filthy decks of the vessels often so closely crowded as to lie in human ordure. And, of course, many die.

Upon the arrival of the survivors in the Congo they are set to work as labourers at one shilling a day; as soldiers they are promised sixteen shillings per month, in English money, but are usually paid off in cheap handkerchiefs and poisonous gin. The cruel and unjust treatment to which these people are subjected breaks the spirits of many of them, makes them distrust and despise your Majesty's Government. They are enemies, not patriots.

There are from sixty to seventy officers of the Belgian army in the service of your Majesty's Government in the Congo of whom only about thirty are at their post; the other half are in Belgium on furlough. These officers draw double pay,—as soldiers and as civilians. It is not my duty to criticise the unlawful and unconstitutional use of these officers coming into the service of this African State. Such criticism will come with more grace from some Belgian statesman, who may remember that there is no constitutional or organic relation subsisting between his Government and the purely personal and absolute monarchy your Majesty has established in Africa. But I take the liberty to say that many of these officers are too young and inexperienced to be entrusted with the difficult work of dealing with native races. They are ignorant of native character, lack wis-

dom, justice, fortitude and patience. They have estranged the natives from your Majesty's Government, have sown the seed of dis-
cord between tribes and villages, and some of them have stained
the uniform of the Belgian officer with murder, arson and robbery.
Other officers have served the State faithfully, and deserve well of
their Royal Master.

Of the unwise, complicated and stupid dual Government of the
State of Congo I cannot say much in this letter, reserving space for
a careful examination of it in another place. I may say that the use-
fulness of many a Congo official is neutralised by having to keep a
useless set of books. For example: an officer is in command of a station and he wishes to buy two eggs. He makes this entry in a ruled
and printed book: "For nourishment bought two eggs for two
Ntaka." In another book he must make this entry: "Two Ntaka gone
out of the store." And in another book he must enter this purchase
seven times! Comment upon such supreme folly is unnecessary. We
need only feel compassion for the mental condition of the man in
Brussels who invented this system, and deep sympathy with its victims in the Congo.

From these general observations I wish now to pass to specific
charges against your Majesty's Government.

FIRST.—Your Majesty's Government is deficient in the moral,
military and financial strength, necessary to govern a territory of
1,508,000 square miles, 7,251 miles of navigation, and 31,694
square miles of lake surface. In the Lower Congo River there is but
one post, in the cataract region one. From Leopoldville to
N'Gombe, a distance of more than 300 miles, there is not a single
soldier or civilian. Not one out of every twenty State-officials know
the language of the natives, although they are constantly issuing
laws, difficult even for Europeans, and expect the natives to comprehend and obey them. Cruelties of the most astounding character
are practised by the natives, such as burying slaves alive in the grave
of a dead chief, cutting off the heads of captured warriors in native
combats, and no effort is put forth by your Majesty's Government to
prevent them. Between 800 and 1,000 slaves are sold to be eaten by
the natives of the Congo State annually; and slave raids, accomplished by the most cruel and murderous agencies, are carried on
within the territorial limits of your Majesty's Government which is
impotent. There are only 2,300 soldiers in the Congo.

SECOND.—Your Majesty's Government has established nearly fifty
posts, consisting of from two to eight mercenary slave-soldiers from
the East Coast. There is no white commissioned officer at these
posts; they are in charge of the black Zanzibar soldiers, and the
State expects them not only to sustain themselves, but to raid
enough to feed the garrisons where the white men are stationed.

These piratical, buccaneering posts compel the natives to furnish them with fish, goats, fowls, and vegetables at the mouths of their muskets; and whenever the natives refuse to feed these vampires, they report to the main station and white officers come with an expeditionary force and burn away the homes of the natives. These black soldiers, many of whom are slaves, exercise the power of life and death. They are ignorant and cruel, *because* they do not comprehend the natives; they are imposed upon them by the State. They make no report as to the number of robberies they commit, or the number of lives they take; they are only required to subsist upon the natives and thus relieve your Majesty's Government of the cost of feeding them. They are the greatest curse the country suffers now.

THIRD.—Your Majesty's Government is guilty of violating its contracts made with its soldiers, mechanics and workmen, many of whom are subjects of other Governments. Their letters never reach home.

FOURTH.—The Courts of your Majesty's Government are abortive, unjust, partial and delinquent. I have personally witnessed and examined their clumsy operations. The laws printed and circulated in Europe "for the protection of the blacks" in the Congo, are a dead letter and a fraud. I have heard an officer of the Belgian Army pleading the cause of a white man of low degree who had been guilty of beating and stabbing a black man, and urging race distinctions and prejudices as good and sufficient reasons why his client should be adjudged innocent. I know of prisoners remaining in custody for six and ten months because they were not judged. I saw the white servant of the Governor-General, CAMILLE JANSSEN, detected in stealing a bottle of wine from a hotel table. A few hours later the Procurer-General searched his room and found many more stolen bottles of wine and other things, not the property of servants. No one can be prosecuted in the State of Congo without an order of the Governor-General, and as he refused to allow his servant to be arrested, nothing could be done. The black servants in the hotel, where the wine had been stolen, had been often accused and beaten for these thefts, and now they were glad to be vindicated. But to the surprise of every honest man, the thief was sheltered by the Governor-General of your Majesty's Government.

FIFTH.—Your Majesty's Government is excessively cruel to its prisoners, condemning them, for the slightest offences, to the chain gang, the like of which cannot be seen in any other Government in the civilised or uncivilised world. Often these ox-chains eat into the necks of the prisoners and produce sores about which the flies circle, aggravating the running wound; so the prisoner is constantly worried. These poor creatures are frequently beaten with a dried piece of hippopotamus skin, called a "chicote," and usually the blood flows at every stroke when well laid on. But the cruelties visited upon soldiers and workmen are not to be compared with the sufferings of the poor natives who, upon the slightest pretext, are thrust into the wretched prisons here in the Upper River. I cannot deal with the dimensions of these prisons in this letter, but will do so in my report to my Government.

SIXTH.—Women are imported into your Majesty's Government for immoral purposes. They are introduced by two methods, viz., black men are dispatched to the Portuguese coast where they engage these women as mistresses of white men, who pay to the procurer a monthly sum. The other method is by capturing native women and condemning them to seven years' servitude for some imaginary crime against the State with which the villages of these women are charged. The State then hires these women out to the highest bidder, the officers having the first choice and then the men. Whenever children are born of such relations, the State maintains that the woman being its property the child belongs to it also. Not long ago a Belgian trader had a child by a slave-woman of the State, and he tried to secure possession of it that he might educate it, but the Chief of the Station where he resided, refused to be moved by his entreaties. At length he appealed to the Governor-General, and he gave him the woman and thus the trader obtained the child also. This was, however, an unusual case of generosity and clemency; and there is only one post that I know of where there is not to be found children of the civil and military officers of your Majesty's Government abandoned to degradation; white men bringing their own flesh and blood under the lash of a most cruel master, the State of Congo.

SEVENTH.—Your Majesty's Government is engaged in trade and commerce, competing with the organised trade companies of Belgium, England, France, Portugal and Holland. It taxes all trading companies and exempts its own goods from export-duty, and makes many of its officers ivory-traders, with the promise of a liberal commission upon all they can buy or get for the State. State soldiers patrol many villages forbidding the natives to trade with any person but a State official, and when the natives refuse to accept the price of the State, their goods are seized by the Government that promised them "protection." When natives have persisted in trading with the trade-companies, the State has punished their independence by burning the villages in the vicinity of the trading houses and driving the natives away.

EIGHTH.—Your Majesty's Government has violated the General Act of the Conference of Berlin by firing upon native canoes; by confiscating the property of natives; by intimidating native traders, and preventing them from trading with white trading companies; by

quartering troops in native villages when there is no war; by causing vessels bound from "Stanley-Pool" to "Stanley-Falls," to break
their journey and leave the Congo, ascend the Aruhwimi river to
Basoko, to be visited and show their papers; by forbidding a mission
steamer to fly its national flag without permission from a local Government; by permitting the natives to carry on the slave-trade, and
by engaging in the wholesale and retail slave-trade itself.

NINTH.—Your Majesty's Government has been, and is now, guilty
of waging unjust and cruel wars against natives, with the hope of
securing slaves and women, to minister to the behests of the officers of your Government. In such slave-hunting raids one village is
armed by the State against the other, and the force thus secured is
incorporated with the regular troops. I have no adequate terms with
which to depict to your Majesty the brutal acts of your soldiers
upon such raids as these. The soldiers who open the combat are
usually the bloodthirsty cannibalistic Bangalas, who give no quarter
to the aged grandmother or nursing child at the breast of its
mother. There are instances in which they have brought the heads
of their victims to their white officers on the expeditionary steamers, and afterwards eaten the bodies of slain children. In one war
two Belgian Army officers saw, from the deck of their steamer, a native in a canoe some distance away. He was not a combatant and
was ignorant of the conflict in progress upon the shore, some distance away. The officers made a wager of £5 that they could hit the
native with their rifles. Three shots were fired and the native fell
dead, pierced through the head, and the trade canoe was transformed into a funeral barge and floated silently down the river.

In another war, waged without just cause, the Belgian Army officer in command of your Majesty's forces placed the men in two or
three lines on the steamers and instructed them to commence firing when the whistles blew. The steamers approached the fated
town, and, as was usual with them, the people came to the shore to
look at the boats and sell different articles of food. There was a
large crowd of men, women and children, laughing, talking and exposing their goods for sale. At once the shrill whistles of the steamers were heard, the soldiers levelled their guns and fired, and the
people fell dead, and wounded, and groaning, and pleading for
mercy. Many prisoners were made, and among them four comely
looking young women. And now ensued a most revolting scheme:
your Majesty's officers quarreling over the selection of these
women. The commander of this murderous expedition, with his
garments stained with innocent blood, declared, that his rank entitled him to the first choice! Under the direction of this same officer
the prisoners were reduced to servitude, and I saw them working
upon the plantation of one of the stations of the State.

TENTH.—Your Majesty's Government is engaged in the slave-trade, wholesale and retail. It buys and sells and steals slaves. Your Majesty's Government gives £3 per head for able-bodied slaves for military service. Officers at the chief stations get the men and receive the money when they are transferred to the State; but there are some middle-men who only get from twenty to twenty-five francs per head. Three hundred and sixteen slaves were sent down the river recently, and others are to follow. These poor natives are sent hundreds of miles away from their villages, to serve among other natives whose language they do not know. When these men run away a reward of 1,000 N'taka is offered. Not long ago such a re-captured slave was given one hundred "chikote" each day until he died. Three hundred N'taka-brassrod is the price the State pays for a slave, when bought from a native. The labour force at the stations of your Majesty's Government in the Upper River is composed of slaves of all ages and both sexes.

ELEVENTH.—Your Majesty's Government has concluded a contract with the Arab Governor at this place for the establishment of a line of military posts from the Seventh Cataract to Lake Tanganyika, territory to which your Majesty has no more legal claim, than I have to be Commander-in-Chief of the Belgian army. For this work the Arab Governor is to receive five hundred stands of arms, five thousand kegs of powder, and £20,000 sterling, to be paid in several instalments. As I write, the news reaches me that these much-treasured and long-looked-for materials of war are to be discharged at Basoko, and the Resident here is to be given the discretion as to the distribution of them. There is a feeling of deep discontent among the Arabs here, and they seem to feel that they are being trifled with. As to the significance of this move Europe and America can judge without any comment from me, especially England.

TWELFTH.—The agents of your Majesty's Government have misrepresented the Congo country and the Congo railway. Mr. H. M. STANLEY, the man who was your chief agent in setting up your authority in this country, has grossly misrepresented the character of the country. Instead of it being fertile and productive it is sterile and unproductive. The natives can scarcely subsist upon the vegetable life produced in some parts of the country. Nor will this condition of affairs change until the native shall have been taught by the European the dignity, utility and blessing of labour. There is no improvement among the natives, because there is an impassable gulf between them and your Majesty's Government, a gulf which can never be bridged. HENRY M. STANLEY's name produces a shudder among this simple folk when mentioned; they remember his broken promises, his copious profanity, his hot temper, his heavy blows, his severe and rigorous measures, by which they were

mulcted of their lands. His last appearance in the Congo produced
a profound sensation among them, when he led 500 Zanzibar soldiers with 300 campfollowers on his way to relieve EMIN PASHA.
They thought it meant complete subjugation, and they fled in confusion, but the only thing they found in the wake of his march was
misery. No white man commanded his rear column, and his troops
were allowed to straggle, sicken and die; and their bones were scattered over more than two hundred miles of territory.

Emigration cannot be invited to this country for many years. The
trade of the Upper Congo consists only of ivory and rubber. The
first is very old and the latter very poor. If the railway were completed now, it would not be able to earn a dividend for ten or twelve
years; and as I have carefully inspected the line of the proposed
road, I give it as my honest judgment that it cannot be completed
for eight years. This is due to the stock-holders; they should be un-
deceived. I am writing a report on the Congo Railway, and will not
present any data in this letter upon that subject.

Conclusions

Against the deceit, fraud, robberies, arson, murder, slave-raiding,
and general policy of cruelty of your Majesty's Government to the
natives, stands their record of unexampled patience, long-suffering
and forgiving spirit, which put the boasted civilisation and pro-
fessed religion of your Majesty's Government to the blush. During
thirteen years only one white man has lost his life by the hands of
the natives, and only two white men have been killed in the Congo.
Major BARTTELOT was shot by a Zanzibar soldier, and the captain of
a Belgian trading-boat was the victim of his own rash and unjust
treatment of a native chief.

All the crimes perpetrated in the Congo have been done in *your*
name, and *you* must answer at the bar of Public Sentiment for the
misgovernment of a people, whose lives and fortunes were entrusted to you by the august Conference of Berlin, 1884–1885. I
now appeal to the Powers, which committed this infant State to
your Majesty's charge, and to the great States which gave it international being; and whose majestic law you have scorned and tram-
pled upon, to call and create an International Commission to
investigate the charges herein preferred in the name of Humanity,
Commerce, Constitutional Government and Christian Civilisation.

I base this appeal upon the terms of Article 36 of Chapter VII of the
General Act of the Conference of Berlin, in which that august assem-
bly of Sovereign States reserved to themselves the right "to introduce
into it later and by common accord the modifications or ameliora-
tions, the utility of which may be demonstrated [by] experience."

I appeal to the Belgian people and to their Constitutional Government, so proud of its traditions, replete with the song and story of its champions of human liberty, and so jealous of its present position in the sisterhood of European States,—to cleanse itself from the imputation of the crimes with which your Majesty's personal State of Congo is polluted.

I appeal to Anti-Slavery Societies in all parts of Christendom, to Philanthropists, Christians, Statesmen, and to the great mass of people everywhere, to call upon the Governments of Europe; to hasten the close of the tragedy your Majesty's unlimited Monarchy is enacting in the Congo.

I appeal to our Heavenly Father, whose service is perfect love, in witness of the purity of my motives and the integrity of my aims; and to history and mankind I appeal for the demonstration and vindication of the truthfulness of the charges I have herein briefly outlined.

And all this upon the word of honour of a gentleman, I subscribe myself your Majesty's humble and obedient servant.

GEO W. WILLIAMS.

Stanley Falls, Central Africa,
    July 18th, 1890.

ROGER CASEMENT

The Congo Report†

Mr. Casement to the Marquess of Lansdowne[1]

London, December 11, 1903.
My Lord,
I have the honour to submit my Report on my recent journey on the Upper Congo.

† Roger Casement, "The Congo Report" (1904), from Peter Singleton-Gates and Maurice Girodias, *The Black Diaries: An Account of Roger Casement's Life and Times with a Collection of His Diaries and Public Writings* (New York: Grove Press, 1959), pp. 98–190.

A veteran of the Congo, with twenty years of experience in the country, Casement was the recently appointed British consul to the Congo when the House of Commons passed a resolution in 1903 instructing the government to investigate and take action to stop the abuses there. Casement's report caused an outcry in Britain and brought him into contact with E. D. Morel, leader of the Congo Reform Association. Conrad met and liked Casement during his 1890 trip to the Congo, and they later renewed their friendship in London. On their relationship, see the selection by Alan Simmons in this Norton Critical Edition below. Also see Hunt Hawkins, "Joseph Conrad, Roger Casement and the Congo Reform Movement," *Journal of Modern Literature* 9:1 (1981–82): 65–80, and Adam Hochschild, *King Leopold's Ghost: A Story of Greed, Terror, and Heroism in Colonial Africa* (Boston: Houghton Mifflin, 1998), pp: 195–208. Notes are the Editor's.
1. Secretary of the British Foreign Office (equivalent to the American Secretary of State).

I left Matadi on the 5th of June, and arriving at Leopoldville on the 6th, remained in the neighbourhood of Stanley Pool until the 2nd of July, when I set out for the Upper Congo. My return to Leopoldville was on the 15th of September, so that the period spent in the Upper River was one of only two and a half months, during which time I visited several points on the Congo River itself, up to the junction of the Lolongo River, ascended that river and its principal feeder, the Lopori, as far as Bongandanga, and went round Lake Mantumba.

Although my visit was of such short duration, and the points touched at nowhere lay far off the beaten tracks of communication, the region visited was one of the most central in the Congo State, and the district in which most of my time was spent, that of the Equator, is probably the most productive. Moreover, I was enabled, by visiting this district, to contrast its present day state with the condition in which I had known it some sixteen years ago. Then (in 1887) I had visited most of the places I now revisited, and I was thus able to institute a comparison between a state of affairs I had myself seen when the natives lived their own savage lives in anarchic and disorderly communities, uncontrolled by Europeans, and that created by more than a decade of very energetic European intervention. That very much of this intervention has been called for no one who formerly knew the Upper Congo could doubt, and there are today widespread proofs of the great energy displayed by Belgian officials in introducing their methods of rule over one of the most savage regions of Africa.

Admirably built and admirably kept stations greet the traveller at many points; a fleet of river steamers, numbering, I believe, forty-eight, the property of the Congo Government, navigate the main river and its principal affluents at fixed intervals. Regular means of communication are thus afforded to some of the most inaccessible parts of Central Africa.

A railway, excellently constructed in view of the difficulties to be encountered, now connects the ocean ports with Stanley Pool, over a tract of difficult country, which formerly offered to the weary traveller on foot many obstacles to be overcome and many days of great bodily fatigue. The cataract region, through which the railway passes, is a generally unproductive and even sterile tract of some 220 miles in breadth. This region is, I believe, the home, or birthplace of the sleeping sickness—a terrible disease, which is, all too rapidly, eating its way into the heart of Africa, and has even traversed the entire continent to well-nigh the shores of the Indian Ocean. The population of the Lower Congo has been gradually reduced by the unchecked ravages of this, as yet, undiagnosed and incurable disease, and as one cause of the seemingly wholesale diminution of human life which I everywhere observed in the regions revisited, a prominent place must be assigned to this malady. The natives certainly attribute their alarming death rate to this as one of the inducing causes, although they attribute, and I think principally, their rapid decrease in numbers to other causes as well. Perhaps the most striking change observed during my journey into the interior was the great reduction observable everywhere in native life. Communities I had formerly known as large and flourishing centres of population are today entirely gone, or now exist in such diminished numbers as to be no longer recognizable. The southern shores of Stanley Pool had formerly a population of fully 5,000 Batekes, distributed through the three towns of Ngaliema's (Leopoldville), Kinchasa and Ndolo, lying within a few miles of each other. These people, some two years ago, decided to abandon their homes, and in one night the great majority of them crossed over into the French territory on the north shores of Stanley Pool. Where formerly had stretched these populous native African villages, I saw today a few scattered European houses, belonging either to Government officials or local traders. In Leopoldville today there are not, I should estimate, 100 of the original natives or their descendants now residing.

A hospital for Europeans and an establishment designed as a native hospital are in charge of a European doctor. Another doctor also resides in the Government station whose bacteriological studies are unremitting and worthy of much praise. When I visited the three mud huts which serve the purpose of the native hospital, all of them dilapidated, and two with the thatched roofs almost gone, I found seventeen sleeping sickness patients, male and female, lying about in the utmost dirt. Most of them were lying on the bare ground—several out on the pathway in front of the houses, and one, a woman, had fallen into the fire just prior to my arrival (while in the final, insensible stage of the disease) and had burned herself very badly. She had since been well bandaged, but was still lying out on the ground with her head almost in the fire, and while I sought to speak to her, in turning she upset a pot of scalding water over her shoulder. All the seventeen people I saw were near their end, and on my second visit two days later, the 19th June, I found one of them lying dead in the open.

In somewhat striking contrast to the neglected state of these people, I found, within a couple of hundred yards of them, the Government workshop for repairing and fitting the steamers. Here all was brightness, care, order, and activity, and it was impossible not to admire and commend the industry which had created and maintained in constant working order this useful establishment. In conjunction with a local missionary, some effort was made during my stay at Leopoldville to obtain an amelioration of the condition of the sleeping sickness people in the native hospital, but it was stated, in answer to my friend's representations, that nothing could be done in the way of building a proper hospital until plans now under consideration had been matured elsewhere. The structures I had visited, which the local medical staff greatly deplored, had endured for several years as the only form of hospital accommodation provided for the numerous native staff of the district.

The Government stores at Leopoldville are large and well built, and contain not only the goods the Government itself sends up river in its fleet of steamers, but also the goods of the various Concession Companies. As a rule, the produce brought down river by the Government steamers is transshipped direct into the railway trucks which run alongside the wharf, and is carried by train to Matadi for shipment to Europe. The various Companies carrying on operations on the Upper Congo, and who hold concessions from the Congo Government, are bound, I was told, by Conventions to abstain from carrying, save within the limits of their Concessions, either goods or passengers. This interdiction extends to their own merchandise and their own agents. Should they carry, by reason of imperative need outside these limits any of their own goods or their own people, they are bound to pay to the Congo Government either the freight or passage money according to the Government tariff, just as though the goods or passengers had been conveyed on one of the Government vessels. The tariff upon goods and passengers carried along the interior waterways is a fairly high one, not perhaps excessive under the circumstances, but still one that, by reason of this virtual monopoly, can produce a yearly revenue which must go far towards maintaining the Government flotilla. * * * That this restriction of public conveyance by Government vessel alone is not altogether a public gain my own experience demonstrated. I had wished to leave Stanley Pool for the Upper Congo at an early date after my arrival in Leopoldville, but as the Government vessels were mostly crowded, I could not proceed with any comfort by one of these. The steamship 'Flandre', one of the largest of these vessels, which left Leopoldville for Stanley Falls on the 22nd of June, and by which I had, at first, intended to proceed, quitted port with more than twenty European passengers over her complement, all of whom, I was informed, would have to sleep on deck.

I accordingly was forced to seek other means of travelling, and through the kindness of the Director of one of the largest commercial companies (the Société Anonyme Belge du Haut-Congo) I found excellent accommodation, as a guest, on one of his steamers. Although thus an invited guest and not paying any passage money, special permission had to be sought from the Congo Government before this act of courtesy could be shown to me, and I saw the telegram from the local authority, authorizing my conveyance to Chumbiri.

At F. . .[2] I spent four days. I had visited this place in August 1887 when the line of villages comprising the settlement contained from 4,000 to 5,000 people. Most of these villages today are completely deserted, the forest having grown over the abandoned sites, and the entire community at the present date cannot number more than 500 souls. There is no Government station at F . . . but the Government telegraph line which connects Leopoldville with Coquilhatville, the headquarters of the Equator district, runs through the once townlands of the F . . . villages close to the river bank. The people of the riverside towns, and from 20 miles inland, have to keep the line clear of undergrowth, and in many places the telegraph road serves as a useful public path between neighbouring villages. Some of the natives of the neighbourhood complained that for this compulsory utilitarian service they had received no remuneration of any kind; and those at a distance that they found it hard to feed themselves when far from their homes they were engaged upon this task. Inquiry in the neighbourhood established that no payment for this work had seemingly been made for fully a year.

Men are also required to work at the neighbouring wood-cutting post for the Government steamers, which is in charge of a native Headman or Kapita, who is under the surveillance of a European 'Chef de Poste' at Bolobo, the nearest Government station, which lies about forty miles upstream. These wood-cutters, though required compulsorily to serve and sometimes irregularly detained, are adequately paid for their services.

* * *

The reasons for the decrease of population at F . . . given me, both by the natives and others, point to sleeping-sickness as probably one of the principal factors. There has also been emigration to the opposite side of the river, to the French shore, but this course, has never, I gather, been popular. The people have not easily accommodated themselves to the altered conditions of life brought about by European Government in their midst. Where formerly they were accustomed to take long voyages down to Stanley Pool to sell slaves, ivory, dried fish, or other local products against such European merchandise as the Bateke middlemen around the Pool had to offer in exchange, they find themselves today debarred from all such forms of activity.

2. In response to complaints from Leopold's defenders, the Foreign Office attempted to dilute the impact of Casement's report by replacing the names of locations and individuals with initials. This also made it more difficult to verify his claims. See Hochschild, p. 204.

The open selling of slaves and the canoe convoys, which once navigated the Upper Congo, have everywhere disappeared. No act of the Congo State Government has perhaps produced more laudable results than the vigorous suppression of this widespread evil. In the 160 miles journey from Leopoldville to F . . . I did not see one large native canoe in midstream, and only a few small canoes creeping along the shore near to native villages. While the suppression of an open form of slave dealing has been an undoubted gain, much that was not reprehensible in native life has disappeared along with it. The trade in ivory today has entirely passed from the hands of the natives of the Upper Congo, and neither fish nor any other outcome of local industry now changes hands on an extensive scale or at any distance from home.

So far as I could observe in the limited time at my disposal the people at F . . . rarely leave their homes save when required by the local Government official at Bolobo to serve as soldiers, or woodcutters at one of the Government posts, or to convey the weekly supplies of food required of them to the nearest Government station. These demands for foodstuffs comprise fowls and goats for the consumption of the European members of the Government staff at Leopoldville, or for passengers on the Government steamers. They emanate from the Chief of the Staff at Bolobo, who, I understand, is required in so far as he can to keep up this supply. In order to obtain this provision he is forced to exercise continuous pressure on the local population, and within recent times that pressure has not always taken the form of mere requisition. Armed expeditions have been necessary and a more forcible method of levying supplies has been adopted than the law either contemplated or justifies. Very specific statements as to the harm one of these recent expeditions worked in the country around F . . . were made to me during my stay there. The officer in command of G . . . district, at the head of a band of soldiers, passed through a portion of the district wherein the natives, unaccustomed to the duties expected of them, had been backward in sending both goats and fowls.

The results of this expedition, which took place towards the end of 1900, was that in fourteen small villages traversed seventeen persons disappeared. Sixteen of these whose names were given to me were killed by the soldiers, and their bodies recovered by their friends, and one was reported as missing. Of those killed, eleven were men, three women and one a boy child of five years. Ten persons were tied up and taken away as prisoners, but were released on payment of sixteen goats by their friends, except one, a child, who died at Bolobo. In addition 48 goats were taken away and 225 fowls; several houses were burned and a quantity of their owner's property either pillaged or destroyed. Representations on behalf of the injured villagers were made to the Inspecteur d'Etat at Leopoldville, who greatly deplored the excesses of his subordinates, and for the livestock or goods destroyed or taken away. The local estimate of the damage done amounted to 71,730 brass rods (3,586 Fr)[3] which included 20,500 brass rods (1,025 Fr) assessed as compensation for the seventeen people. Three of these were Chiefs, and the amount asked for would have worked out at about 1,000 brass rods (50 Fr) per head, not probably an extravagant estimate for human life, seeing that the goats were valued at 400 rods each (20 Fr). A total sum, I was told, of 18,000 brass rods (950 Fr) was actually paid to the injured villagers by the Government Commissioner who came from Stanley Pool; and this sum, it was said, was levied as a fine for his misconduct on the officer responsible for the raid. I could not learn what other form of punishment, if any, was inflicted on this officer. He remained as the Government representative for some time afterwards, was then transferred to another post in the immediate neighbourhood, and finally went home at the expiration of his service.

At Bolobo, where I spent ten days waiting for a steamer to continue my journey, a similar state of affairs prevails to that existing at F . . . Bolobo used to be one of the most important native settlements along the south bank of the Upper Congo, and the population in the early days of civilised rule numbered fully 40,000 people, chiefly of the Bobangi tribe. Today the population is believed to be not more than 7,000 to 8,000 souls. The Bolobo tribes were famous in their former days for their voyages to Stanley Pool and their keen trading ability. All of their large canoes have today disappeared, and while some of them still hunt hippopotami—which are still numerous in the adjacent waters—I did not observe anything like industry among them.

Indeed, it would be hard to say how the people now live or how they occupy their own time. They did not complain so much of the weekly enforced food supplies required of them, which would, indeed, seem to be an unavoidable necessity of the situation, as to the unexpected calls frequently made upon them. Neither ivory nor rubber is obtained in this neighbourhood. The food supply and a certain amount of local labour is all that is enforced. As woodcutters, station hands in the Government post, canoe paddlers, workers on the telegraph route or in some other public capacity, they are liable to frequent requisition.

The labour required did not seem to be excessive, but it would seem to be irregularly called for, unequally distributed, or only poorly remunerated, or sometimes not remunerated at all.

Complaints as to the manner of exacting service are much more

3. Eight- to nine-inch brass rods, each equivalent to one-twentieth of a Belgian franc, were the local currency in the Congo Free State.

frequent than complaints as to the fact of service being required. If
the local official has to go on a sudden journey men are summoned
on the instant to paddle his canoe, and a refusal entails imprison-
ment or a beating. If the Government plantation or the kitchen garden require weeding, a soldier will be sent to call in the women
from some of the neighbouring towns. To the official this is a necessary public duty which he cannot but impose, but to the women
suddenly forced to leave their household tasks and to tramp off,
hoe in hand, baby on back, with possibly a hungry and angry husband at home, the task is not a welcome one.

I learned at Bolobo that a large influx from the I . . . district
which comprises the 'Domaine de la Couronne' had lately taken
place into the country behind G . . . The nearest settlement of
these emigrants was said to be about 20 to 25 miles from G . . . and
I determined to visit the place. I spent three days on this journey,
visited two large villages in the interior belonging to the K . . . tribe,
wherein I found that fully half the population now consisted of
refugees belonging to the L . . . tribe who had formerly dwelt near
I . . . I saw and questioned several groups of these people, whom I
found to be industrial blacksmiths and brass-workers. These people
consisted of old and young men, women and children. They had
fled from their country and sought asylum with their friends the K
. . . during the last four years. The distance they had travelled in
their flight they put at about six or seven days' march—which I
should estimate at from 120 to 150 miles of walking. They went on
to declare, when asked why they had fled, that they had endured
such ill-treatment at the hands of the Government officials and the
Government soldiers in their own country that life had become intolerable, that nothing had remained for them at home but to be
killed for failure to bring in a certain amount of rubber or to die
from starvation or exposure in their attempts to satisfy the demands
made upon them. The statements made to me by these people were
of such a nature that I could not believe them to be true. The fact
remained, however, that they had certainly abandoned their homes
and all that they possessed, had travelled a long distance and now
preferred a species of mild servitude among the K . . . to remaining
in their own country. I took careful notes of the statements made to
me by these people.

*   *   *

The town of N . . . consists approximately of seventy-one K . . .
houses and seventy-three occupied by L . . . These latter seemed industrious, simple folk, many weaving palm fibre into mats or native
cloth; others had smithies, working brass wire into bracelets,
chains and anklets; some iron workers making knives. Sitting down
in one of these blacksmith's sheds, the five men at work ceased and

came over to talk to us. I counted ten women, six grown up men and eight lads and women in this shed of L . . . I then asked them to tell me why they had left their homes. Three of the men sat down in front of me, and told a tale which I cannot think can be true, but it seemed to come straight from their hearts. I repeatedly asked certain parts to be gone over again while I wrote in my notebook. The fact of my writing down and asking for names, etc., seemed to impress them, and they spoke with what certainly impressed me as being great sincerity.

I asked, first, why they had left their homes, and had come to live in a strange, far-off country among the K . . . where they owned nothing, and were little better than servitors. All, when this was put, women as well, shouted out: 'On account of the rubber tax levied by the Government posts.'

I asked, then, how this tax was imposed. One of them, who had been hammering out an iron collar on my arrival, spoke first:

'I am N.N. These two beside me are O.O. and P.P. all of us Y. . . . From our country each village had to take twenty loads of rubber. These loads were big; they were as big as this . . .' (producing an empty basket which came nearly up to the handle of my walking stick). 'That was the first size. We had to fill that up, but as rubber got scarcer the white man reduced the amount. We had to take these loads in four times a month.'

Question: 'How much pay do you get for this?'

Answer (entire audience): 'We got no pay We got nothing.'

And then, N.N., whom I asked again, said:

'Our village got cloth and a little salt, but not the people who did the work. Our Chief ate up the cloth; the workers got nothing. The pay was a fathom of cloth and a little salt for every basket full, but it was given to the Chief, never to the men. It used to take ten days to get the twenty baskets of rubber—we were always in the forest to find the rubber vines, to go without food, and our women had to give up cultivating the fields and gardens. Then we starved. Wild beasts—the leopards killed some of us while we were working away in the forest and others got lost or died from exposure and starvation and we begged the white men to leave us alone, saying we could get no more rubber, but the white men and their soldiers said: "Go. You are only beasts yourselves, you are only nyama (meat)." We tried, always going further into the forest, and when we failed and our rubber was short, the soldiers came to our towns and killed us. Many were shot, some had their ears cut off; others were tied up with ropes round their necks and bodies and taken away. The white men sometimes at the post did not know of the bad things the soldiers did to us, but it was the white men who sent the soldiers to punish us for not bringing in enough rubber.'

Another native took up the story:

'We said to the white man: "We are not enough people now to do what you want of us. Our country has not many people in it and we are dying fast. We are killed by the work you make us do, by the stoppage of our plantations, and the breaking up of our homes." The white man looked at us and said: "There are lots of people in Mputu" (Europe, the white man's country). "If there are many people in the white man's country there must be many people in the black man's country." The white man who said this was the chief white man at F.F . . . His name was A.B. He was a very bad man. Other white men at Bula Matadi had been bad and wicked. These had killed us often and killed us by their own hands as well as by their soldiers. Some white men were good. These ones told them to stay in their homes and did not hunt and chase them as the others had done, but after what they had suffered they did not trust more anyone's word and they had fled from their country and were now going to stay here, far from their homes, in this country where there was no rubber.'

Question: 'How long is it since you left your homes, since the big trouble you speak of?'

Answer: 'It lasted three full seasons, and it is now four seasons since we fled and came into this country.'

Question: 'How many days is it to your own country?'

Answer: 'Six days of quick marching. We fled because we could not endure the things done to us. Our Chiefs were hanged and we were killed and starved and worked beyond endurance to get rubber.'

Question: 'How do you know it was the white men themselves who ordered these cruel things to be done to you? These things must have been done without the white men's knowledge by the black soldiers.'

Answer: 'The white men told their soldiers: "You kill only women; you cannot kill men." So then the soldiers when they killed us' (here P.P. who was answering stopped and hesitated, and then pointing to the private parts of my bulldog—it was lying asleep at my feet) 'then they cut off those things and took them to the white men, who said: "It is true, you have killed men." '

Question: 'You mean to tell me that any white man ordered your bodies to be mutilated like that and those parts of you carried to him?'

Answer (all shouting out): 'Yes, any white man. D.E. did it.'

There is no doubt that these people were not inventing. Their vehemence, their flashing eyes, their excitement was not simulated. Doubtless they exaggerated the numbers, but they were clearly telling me what they knew and loathed.

Went on about fifteen minutes to another L . . . group of houses in the midst of the K . . . town. Found here an old Chief sitting in the open village Council house with two lads. An old woman soon came and joined, and another man. The woman began talking with much earnestness. She said the Government had worked them so hard that they had no time to tend their fields and gardens and they had starved to death. Her children had died; her two sons had been killed. The old Chief said:

'We used to hunt elephants long ago and there were plenty in our forests, and we got much meat; but Bula Matadi killed the elephant hunters because they could not get rubber, and so we starved. We were sent out to get rubber, and when we came back with little rubber we were shot.'

Question: 'Who shot you?'

Answer: 'The white men sent their soldiers out to kill us.'

Question: 'How do you know it was the white men sent the soldiers? It might be only these savage soldiers themselves?'

Answer: 'No, no, sometimes we brought rubber into the white men's stations. We took rubber to D.E . . .'s station, E.E . . . and to F.F . . . When it was not enough rubber the white men would put some of us in lines, one behind the other and would shoot through all our bodies. Sometimes he would shoot us like that with his own hand; sometimes his soldiers would do it.'

Question: 'You mean to say that you were killed in the Government posts by the Government white men themselves or under their very eyes?'

Answer (emphatically): 'We were killed in the stations of the white men themselves. We were killed by the white man himself. We were shot before his eyes.'

The foregoing entries made at the time in my notebook seemed to me, if not false, greatly exaggerated, although the statements were made with every air of conviction and sincerity. A few days afterwards when I was at Stanley Pool, I received further evidence in a letter of which the following is an extract:

'I was sorry not to see you as you passed down and so missed the opportunity of conveying to you personally a lot of evidence as to the terrible maladministration practised in the past in this district. I saw the official at the post of E.E . . . He is the successor of the infamous wretch D.E. of whom you heard so much yourself from the refugees at N . . . This D.E. was in this district and he it was that depopulated the country. His successor M.N. is very vehement in his denunciation of him and declares that he will leave nothing undone that he can do to bring him to justice. M.N. told me that when he took over the station at E.E . . . from D.E., he visited the prison and almost fainted, so horrible was the condition of the place and the poor wretches in it. He told me of many things he had heard from the soldiers. Of D.E. shooting with his own hand man after man who had come in with an insufficient quantity of rubber. Of his putting one behind the other and shooting them all with one cartridge. Those who accompanied me also heard from the soldiers many frightful stories and abundant confirmation of what was told us at N . . . about the taking to D.E. of the organs of the men slain by the sentries of the various posts. I saw a letter from the present officer at R.F . . . to M.N. in which he upbraids him for not using more vigorous means, telling him to talk less and shoot more, and reprimanding him for not killing more than one in a district under his care where there was a little trouble.'

From a separate communication I extract the following:

'After a few hours we came to a State rubber post. In nearly every instance these posts are most imposing, some of them giving rise to the supposition that several white men were residing in them. But in only one did we find a white man—the successor of D.E. At one place I saw lying about in the grass surrounding the post, which is built on the site of several large towns, human bones, skulls and in some cases complete skeletons. On enquiring the reason for this unusual sight: "Oh," said my informant, "when the bambote (soldiers) were sent to make us cut rubber there were so many killed we got tired of burying, and sometimes when we wanted to bury we were not allowed to."

' "But why did they kill you so?"

' "Oh, sometimes we were ordered to go and the sentry would find us preparing food to eat while in the forest, and he would shoot two or three to hurry us along. Sometimes we would try and do a little work on our plantations, so that when the harvest time came we should have something to eat, and the sentry would shoot some of us to teach us that our business was not to plant but to get rubber. Sometimes we were driven off to live for a fortnight in the forest without any food and without anything to make a fire with, and many died of cold and hunger. Sometimes the quantity brought was not sufficient, and then several would be killed to frighten us to bring more. Some tried to run away, and died of hunger and privation in the forest in trying to avoid the State posts."

' "But," said I, "if the sentries killed you like that, what was the use? You could not bring more rubber when there were fewer people."

' "Oh, as to that, we do not understand it. These are the facts."

'And looking around on the scene of desolation, on the untended farms and neglected palms, one could not but believe that in the main the story was true. From State sentries came confirmation and particulars even more horrifying, and the evidence of a white

man as to the state of the country—the unspeakable condition of
the prisons at the State posts—all combined to convince me over
and over again that, during the last seven years, this "Domaine
Privé" of King Leopold has been a veritable hell on earth.'

Leaving Bolobo on the 23rd July, I passed on up river in a small
steam launch I had been fortunate enough to secure for my own
private use. We touched at several points on the French shore, and
on the 25th July reached Lukolela, where I spent two days. This
district had, when I visited it in 1887, numbered fully 5,000 people; today the population is given, after a careful enumeration, at
less than 600. The reasons given me for their decline in numbers
were similar to those furnished elsewhere, viz., sleeping sickness,
general ill-health, insufficiency of food and the methods employed
to obtain labour from them by local officials and the exactions
levied upon them . . .

*   *   *

From Lukolela I proceeded to O . . ., which I purposed visiting.
O . . . with its two adjoining villages, when I had last seen them in
the autumn of 1887, had presented a scene of the greatest anima-
tion. The population of the three towns then numbered some 4,000
to 5,000 people. Scores of men had put off in canoes to greet us
with invitations that we should spend the night in their village. On
steaming into O . . . I found that this village had entirely disappeared, and that its place was occupied by a large 'camp d'instruction,' where some 800 native recruits, brought from various parts of
the Congo State, are drilled into soldierhood by a Commandant
and a staff of seven or eight European officers and noncommissioned officers . . . From the Commandant and his officers
a cordial welcome was received. The camp as a military centre is
excellently chosen, the situation of Irebu commanding not only the
Lake Mantumba waterway, but one of the chief navigable channels
of the Congo; and it is, moreover, situated opposite the estuary of
the great Ubangi river, which is probably the most important Congo
affluent. The Commandant informed me that a very large supply of
native food, amply sufficient for the soldiers under his command,
was supplied weekly by the natives of the surrounding district.

From Irebu I proceeded some 25 miles to Ikoko, once a large village on the north shore of Lake Mantumba. I remained in Lake
Mantumba seventeen days, visiting during that time, the Government post at Bikoro on the east shore of the lake and many native
towns scattered round the lake side. Lake Mantumba is a fine sheet
of water about 25 or 30 miles long and some 12 or 15 miles broad
at the broadest part, surrounded by a dense forest. The inhabitants
of the district are of the Ntomba tribe and are still rude savages, using very fine bows and arrows and ill-made spears as their weapons.

There are also in the forest country many families or clans of a dwarf race called Batwas, who are of much more savage and untameable disposition than the Ntombas, who form the bulk of the population. Both Batwas and Ntombas are still cannibals and cannibalism, although repressed and not so openly indulged in as formerly, is still prevalent in the district.

I have dwelt upon the condition of P . . . and the towns I visited around Lake Mantumba in my notes taken at the time, and these are appended hereto.

Statement

IN REGARD TO THE CONDITION OF THE NATIVES IN LAKE MANTUMBA REGION DURING THE PERIOD OF THE RUBBER WARS WHICH BEGAN IN 1893.

The disturbance consequent on the attempt to levy a rubber tax in this district, a tax which has since been discontinued, appears to have been endured up to 1900.

The population during the continuance of these wars diminished, I estimate, by some 60 per cent, and the remnant of the inhabitants are only now, in many cases, returning to their destroyed or abandoned villages.

During the period 1893–1901, the Congo State commenced the system of compelling the natives to collect rubber, and insisted that the inhabitants of the district should not go out of it to sell their produce to traders.

This great decrease in population has been, to a very great extent, caused by the extreme measures resorted to by officers of the State, and the freedom enjoyed by the soldiers to do just as they pleased. There are more people in the district near the villages, but they are hidden away in the bush like hunted animals with only a few branches thrown together for shelter, for they have no trust that the present quiet state of things will continue, and they have no heart to build houses or make good gardens.

The decrease has several causes:

1.) O . . . was deserted because of the demands for rubber made by M. N . . . , O . . . and several others were similar cases. The natives went to the French territory.

2.) 'War', in which women and children were killed as well as men. Women and children were killed not in all cases by stray bullets, but were taken as prisoners and killed. Sad to say, these horrible cases were not always the acts of some black soldier. Proof was laid against one officer, who 'shot' one woman and one man, while they were before him as prisoners with their hands tied, and no attempt was made by the accused to deny the truth of the statement. To those killed in the so-called 'war' must be added large numbers of those who died while kept as prisoners of war. Others were carried to far distant camps and have never returned. Many of the young were sent to Missions, and the death rate was enormous. Here is one example: Ten children were sent from a State Steamer to a mission, and in spite of comfortable surroundings, there were only three alive at the end of a month. The others had died of dysentery and bowel troubles contracted during the voyage. Two struggled on for about fifteen months, but never recovered strength and at last died. In less than two years only one of the ten was alive.

3.) Another cause of the decrease is that the natives are weakened in body through insufficient and irregular food supply. They cannot resist disease as of old. In spite of assurance that the old state of things will not come again, the native refuses to build good houses, make large gardens, and make the best of the new surroundings—he is without ambition because without hope, and when sickness comes he does not seem to care.

4.) Again a lower percentage of births lessen the population. Weakened bodies is one cause of this. Another reason is that women refuse to bear children, and take means to save themselves from motherhood. They give as the reason that if 'war' should come to a woman 'big with child' or with a baby to carry, 'she' cannot well run away and hide from the soldiers.

There are [three] points in connection with the war (so-called):

(1) The cause;

(2) The manner in which it was conducted;

(3) The Natives never had obeyed any other man than their own Chiefs. When Leopold II became their King they were not aware of the fact, nor had they any hand in the making of the new arrangement. Demands were made upon them, and they did not understand why they should obey the stranger. Some of the demands were not excessive, but others were simply impossible. There was not much within their reach, and it was a dangerous thing to be a stranger in a strange part of the forests . . . Another fertile source of war lay in the actions of the native soldiers. Generally speaking their statements against other natives were received as truth that needed no support. Take the following as an example: one morning it was reported that State soldiers had shot several people near the channel leading from H.K. . . to the Congo. Several canoes full of manioc had been also seized, and the friends of the dead and owners of the two canoes asked that they might have the canoes and food, and that they might take the bodies and bury them. But this was refused. It was alleged that the people were shot in the act of deserting from the State into French territory. The Chief who was

shot was actually returning from having gone from M.O.P. to a village and was killed east of his home, while 'France' lay to the west.
The soldiers said that the people had been challenged to stop and
that they refused, and that they had been shot as they paddled
away. But really they had landed when called by the soldiers; they
had been tied hand and foot, and then shot. One woman had struggled when shot, and had broken the vines with which her feet were
tied, and she, though wounded, had tried to escape. A second bullet made her fall, but yet she rose and ran a few steps when a third
bullet laid her low. Their hands had all been taken off—i.e., the
right hand of each—for evidence of the faithfulness of the soldiers.
M.O.P. shot two of the soldiers, but the leader of the party was not
shot, though the whole matter was carried through by him and he
it was that gave M.O.P. the false report . . .

In most of the fights then the natives were merely trying to defend themselves and their homes from attacks made by black soldiers sent to punish them for some failure to do their duty to the
State: and if the cause for war was weak, the way in which it was
carried out was often revolting. It was stated that these soldiers
were often sent out to make war on a village without a white officer
accompanying them, so that there was nothing to keep them from
awful excesses.

It is averred that canoes have been seen returning from distant
expeditions with no white man in charge, and with human hands
dangling from a stick in the bow of the canoe, or in small baskets—
being carried to the white man as proofs of their courage and devotion to duty. If one in fifty of native reports are true, there has been
great lack on the part of some white men. Statements made to me
by certain natives are appended. Many similar statements were
made to me during the time I spent at Lake Mantumba, some of
those made by native men being unfit for repetition.

Q.Q.'s statement:
I was born at K.K. . . After my father died my mother and I went
to L.L. . . When we returned to K.K . . . soon after P.Q. came to
fight with us because of rubber. K.K. did not want to take rubber to
the white man. We and our mothers ran away far into the bush.
The Bula Matadi soldiers are very strong and they fought hard. One
soldier was killed and they killed one K.K. . . man. Then the white
men let us go home and they went home, and then, we too came
out of the bush. This was the first fight. After that another fighting
took place. I, my mother, grandmother and my sister, we ran into
the bush. When the soldiers came into the bush near us they were
calling my mother by name and I was going to answer, but my
mother put her hand to my mouth to stop me. When they called my

mother, if she had not stopped me from answering, we would all have been killed then. A great number of our people were killed by the soldiers. The friends who were left buried the dead bodies and there was much weeping. Then the soldiers came again to fight with us and we ran into the bush, but they really came to fight with M.M. . . They killed a lot of M.M. . . people and then one soldier came out to K.K. . . and the K.K. . . people killed him with a spear. And when the other soldiers heard that their friend was killed they came in a large number and followed us into the bush. Then the soldiers fired a gun and some people were killed. After that they saw a little bit of my mother's head, and the soldiers ran quickly towards the place where we were and caught my grandmother, my mother, my sister and another little one, younger than us. Several of the soldiers argued about my mother, because each wanted her for a wife, so they finally decided to kill her. They killed her with a gun—they shot her through the stomach—she fell and when I saw that I cried very much, because they killed my mother and my grandmother and I was left alone. My mother was near to the time of her confinement at the time. And they killed my grandmother and I saw it all done. They took hold of my sister and asked where her older sister was and she said: 'She has just run away.' They said, 'Call her.' She called me, but I was too frightened and would not answer and I ran and went away and came out at another place and I could not speak because my throat was so sore. I saw a little bit of 'kwanga' lying on the ground and I picked it up to eat. At that place there used to be a lot of people, but when I got there, there were none. My sister was taken to P . . . and I was at this place alone. One day I saw a man coming from the back country. He was going to kill me but afterwards he took me to a place where there were people, and there I saw my stepfather. He asked to buy me from this man, but the man would not let him. He said, 'She is my slave now; I found her.' One day the men went out fishing and when I looked I saw the soldiers coming, so I ran away, but a string caught my foot and I fell, and a soldier named N.N.N. caught me. He handed me over to another soldier and as we went away we saw some Q . . . people fishing, and the soldiers took a lot of fish from them and a Q . . . woman and we went to P . . . and they took me to the white man.

Signed: Q.Q.

*   *   *

S.S.'s *statement:*

S.S. came from the far back, R.R. . . . One day the soldiers went to her town to fight; she did not know that the soldiers had come to fight them until she saw the people from the other side of the town running towards their end, then they, too, began to run away. Her father, mother, three brothers, and sister were with her. About four men were killed at this scare. It was at this fight that one of the station girls, D.P.P., was taken prisoner. After several days, during which time they were staying at other villages, they went back to their own town. They were only a few days in their own town when they heard that the soldiers who had been at the other towns were coming their way too, so the men gathered up all their bows and arrows and went out to the next town to wait for the soldiers to fight them. Some of the men stayed behind with all the women and children. After that S.S. and her mother went out to their garden to work; while there S.S. told her mother that she had dreamed that Bula Matadi was coming to fight with them, but her mother told her she was trying to tell stories. After that S.S. went back to the house and left her mother in the garden. After she had been a little while in the house with her little brother and sister she heard the firing of guns. When she heard that she took up her little sister and a big basket with a lot of native money in it, but she could not manage both, so she left the basket behind and ran away with the youngest child; the little boy ran away by himself. The oldest boys had gone away to wait for the soldiers at the other town. As she went past she heard her mother calling to her, but she told her to run away in another direction, and she would go on with the little sister. She found her little sister rather heavy for her, so she could not run very fast, and a great number of people went past her, and she was left alone with the little one. Then she left the main road and went to hide in the bush. When night came on she tried to find the road again and followed the people who had passed her, but she could not find them, so she had to sleep in the bush alone. She wandered about in the bush for six days, then she came upon a town named S.S. . . . At this town she found that the soldiers were fighting there too. Before entering the town she dug up some sweet manioc to eat, because she was very hungry. She went about looking for a fire to roast the sweet manioc, but she could not find any. Then she heard a noise as of people talking, so she hid her little sister in a deserted house, and went to see those people she had heard talking, thinking they might be those from her own town; but when she got to the house where the noise was coming from she saw one of the soldiers' boys sitting at the door of the house, and then also she could not quite understand their language, so she knew that they were not her people; so she took fright and ran away in another direction from where she had put her sister. After she had reached the outside of the town, she stood still and remembered that she would be scolded by her father and mother for leaving her sister, so she went back at night. She came upon a house where the

white man was sleeping; she saw the sentry on a deck chair outside
in front of the house, apparently asleep, because he did not see her
slip past him. Then she came to the house where her sister was,
and took her and she started to run away again. They slept in a deserted house at the very end of the town. Early in the morning the
white man sent out the soldiers to go and look for people all over
the town and in the houses. S.S. was standing outside in front of
the house, trying to make her sister walk, as she was very tired,
but the little sister could not run away through weakness. While
they were standing outside the soldiers came upon them and took
them both. One of the soldiers said: 'We might keep them both.
The little one is not bad looking,' but the other said: 'No, we are not
going to carry her all the way, we must kill the younger girl,' So they
put a knife through the child's stomach, and left the body lying
there where they had killed it. They took S.S. to the next town,
where the white man had told them to go and fight. They did not go
back to the house where the white man was, but went straight to
the next town. The white man's name was C.D. The soldiers gave
S.S. something to eat on the way. When they came to this next
town they found that all the people had run away.

In the morning the soldiers wanted S.S. to go and look for manioc for them, but she was afraid to go out as they looked to her as if
they wanted to kill her. The soldiers thrashed her very much, and
began to drag her outside, but the Corporal (N.N.M.) came and
took her by the hand and said: 'We must not kill her; we must take
her to the white man.' Then they went back to the town where C.D.
was, and they showed him S.S. C.D. handed her over to the care of
a soldier. At this town she found that they had caught three people,
and among them was a very old woman, and the cannibal soldiers
asked C.D. to give them the old woman to eat and C.D. told them
to take her. Those soldiers took the woman and cut her throat, and
they divided her and ate her. S.S. saw all this done. In the morning
the soldier who was looking after her was sent on some duty by
C.D., and before the soldier went out he had told S.S. to get some
manioc leaves not far from the house and to cook them. After he
left she went to do as he had told her, and these cannibal soldiers
went to C.D. and said that S.S. was trying to run away, so they
wanted to kill her; but he told them to tie her, so the soldiers tied
her to a tree, and she had to stand in the sun nearly all day. When
the soldier who had charge of her came back he found her tied up.
C.D. called to him to ask about S.S., so he explained to C.D. what
he had told S.S. to do, so he was allowed to untie her. They stayed
several days at this place, then C.D. asked S.S. if she knew all the
towns round about, and she said Yes, and then he told her to show
them the way, so that they could go and catch people. They came to

a town and found only one woman, who was dying of sickness, and the soldiers killed her with a knife. At several towns they found no people, but at last they came to a town where several people had run to, as they did not know where else to go, because the soldiers were fighting everywhere. At this town they killed a lot of people— men, women, and children—and took some as prisoners. They cut the hands of those they had killed, and brought them to C.D.; they spread out the hands in a row for C.D. to see. After that they left to return to Bikoro. They took a lot of prisoners with them. The hands they had cut off they left lying, because the white man had seen them, so they did not need to take them to P. . . . Some of the sol- diers were sent to P. . . with the prisoners, but C.D. and the other soldiers went to T.T. . . where there was another white man. S.S. was about two weeks at P . . . and then she ran away into the bush for three days and when she was found she was brought back to S.T., and he asked her why she had run away. She said because the soldiers had thrashed her.

.   .   .   .

S.S.'s mother was killed by soldiers, and her father died of starva- tion, or rather he refused to eat because he was bereaved of his wife and all the children.

Signed: S.S.

U.U.'s statement:

When we began to run away from the fight, we ran away many times. They did not catch me because I was with mother and fa- ther. Afterwards mother died; four days passed, father died also. I and an older sister were left with two younger children and then the fighting came where I had run to. Then my eldest sister called me: 'U.U., come here.' I went. She said: 'Let us run away because we have not anyone to take care of us.' When we were running away we saw a lot of W.W. . . people coming towards us. We told them to run away. War was coming. They said: 'Is it true?' We said: 'It is true; they are coming.' The W. W . . . said: 'We will not run away; we did not see the soldiers.' Only a little while they saw the soldiers, and they were killed. We stayed in a town named X.X . . A male relative called me: 'U.U., let us go;' but I did not want to. The soldiers came there; I ran away by myself; when I ran away I hid in the bush. While I was running I met with an old man who was run- ning from a soldier. He (the soldier) fired a gun. I was not hit, but the old man died. Afterwards they caught me and two men. The soldiers asked: 'Have you a father and mother?' I answered: 'No'. They said to me: 'If you do not tell us we will kill you!' I said:

'Mother and father are dead.' After that my oldest sister was caught, too, in the bush, and they left my little brother and sister alone in the bush to die, because heavy rain came on, and they had not had anything to eat for days and days. At night they tied my hands and feet for fear that I should run away. In the morning they caught three people—two had children—they killed the children. Afterwards I was standing outside, and a soldier asked me: 'Where are you going?' I said: 'I am going home.' He said: 'Come on.' He took his gun, he put me in the house; he wanted to kill me. Then another soldier came and took me. We heard a big noise; they told us the fighting was over but it was not so. When we were going on the way they killed ten children, because they were very small; they killed them in the water. Then they killed a lot of people, and they cut off their hands and put them into baskets and took them to the white man. He counted out the hands—200 in all; they left the hands lying. The white man's name was C.D. After that C.D. sent us prisoners with soldiers to P . . ., to S.T. S.T. told me to weed grass. When I was working outside a soldier came and said: 'Come here,' and when I went he wanted to cut my hand so I went to the white man to tell him, and he thrashed the soldier.

On our way, when we were coming to P. . . , the soldiers saw a little child, and when they went to kill it, the child laughed, so the soldier took the butt of a gun and struck the child with it, and then cut off its head. One day they killed my half sister and cut off her head, hands and feet because she had on rings. Her name was Q.Q.Q. Then they caught another sister, and they sold her to the W.W. . . people, and now she is a slave there. When we came to P. . . , the white man said to send word to the friends of the prisoners to come with goats to buy off some of their relatives. A lot were bought off, but I had no-one to come and buy me off, because father was dead. The white man said to me: 'You shall go to . . .' The white man, S.T., gave me a small boy to care for, but I thought he would be killed, so I helped to get him away. S.T. asked me to bring the boy to him, but I said: 'He has run away.' He said he would kill me, but . . .

Signed: U.U.

A careful investigation of the conditions of native life around the lake confirmed the truth of the statements made to me that the great decrease in population, the dirty and ill-kept towns, and the complete absence of goats, sheep, or fowls—once very plentiful in this country—were to be attributed above all else to the continued effort made during many years to compel the natives to work india-rubber. Large bodies of native troops had formerly been quartered in the district, and the punitive measures undertaken to this end had endured for a considerable period. During the course of these operations there had been much loss of life, accompanied, I fear, by a somewhat general mutilation of the dead, as proof that the soldiers had done their duty. Each village I visited around the lake, save that of Q. . . and one other, had been abandoned by its inhabitants. To some of these villages the people have only just returned: to others they are only now returning. In one I found the bare and burnt poles of what had been dwellings left standing, and at another—that of R . . .—the people had fled at the approach of my steamer, and despite the loud cries of many native guides on board, nothing could induce them to return, and it was impossible to hold any intercourse with them. At the three succeeding villages I visited beyond R . . ., in traversing the lake towards the south, the inhabitants all fled at the approach of the steamer, and it was only when they found whose the vessel was that they could be induced to return.

At one of these villages, S . . ., after confidence had been restored and the fugitives had been induced to come in from the surrounding forest, where they had hidden themselves, I saw women coming back carrying their babies, their household utensils, and even the food they had hastily snatched up, up to a late hour of the evening. Meeting some of these returning women in one of the fields I asked them why they had run away at my approach, and they said, smiling: 'We thought you were Bula Matadi' (i.e., 'Men of the Government'). Fear of this kind was formerly unknown on the Upper Congo; and in much more out-of-the-way places visited many years ago the people flocked from all sides to greet a white stranger. But to-day the apparition of a white man's steamer evidently gave the signal for instant flight.

The Chief of the P . . . post told me that a similar alarm reigned almost everywhere in the country behind his station, and that when he went on the most peaceful missions only a few miles from his house the villages were generally emptied of all human beings when he entered them, and it was impossible in the majority of cases to get into touch with the people in their own homes . . . He gave, as an explanation, when I asked for the reason of this fear of the white man, that as these people were great savages, and knew themselves how many crimes they had committed, they doubtless feared that the white man of the Government was coming to punish their misconduct. He added that they had undoubtedly had 'an awful past' at the hands of some of the officials who had preceded him in the local administration and that it would take some time for confidence to be restored. Men, he said, still came to him whose hands had been cut off by the Government soldiers during those evil days, and he said there were still many victims of this species of mutilation in the surrounding country. Two cases of the kind came to my actual notice while I was at the lake. One, a young man, both of whose hands had been beaten off with the butt ends of rifles against a tree, the other a young lad of 11 or 12 years of age, whose right hand was cut off at the wrist. This boy described the circumstances of his mutilation, and in answer to my enquiry, said that although wounded at the time he was perfectly sensible of the severing of his wrist, but lay still fearing that if he moved he would be killed. In both these cases the Government soldiers had been accompanied by white officers whose names were given to me. Of six natives (one a girl, three little boys, one youth and one old woman) who had been mutilated in this way during the rubber regime, all except one were dead at the date of my visit. The old woman had died at the beginning of this year and her niece described to me how the act of mutilation in her case had been accomplished. The day I left Mantumba five men whose hands had been cut off came to the village of T . . . across the lake to see me, but hearing I had already gone away they returned to their homes. A messenger came in to tell me, and I sent to T . . . to find them, but they had been dispersed. Three of them subsequently returned, but too late for me to see them.

* * *

On my leaving Bongandanga on the 3rd September I returned down the Lopori and Lolongo Rivers, arriving at J . . . The following day, about 9 at night, some natives of the neighbourhood came to see me, bringing with them a lad of about 16 years of age whose right hand was missing. His name was X. and his relatives said they came from K. . . , a village on the opposite side of the river some few miles away. As it was late at night there was some difficulty in obtaining a translation of their statements, but I gathered that X.'s hand had been cut off in K. . . by a sentry of the La Lulanga Company, who was, or had been, quartered there. They said that this sentry, at the time that he had mutilated X., had also shot dead one of the chief men of the town. X., in addition to this mutilation, had been shot in the shoulderblade, and, as a consequence, was deformed. On being shot it was said he had fallen down insensible, and the sentry had then cut off his hand, alleging that he would take it to the Director of the Company at Mampoko. When I asked if this had been done the natives replied that they believed that the hand had only been carried part of the way to Mampoko and then thrown away. They did not think the white man had seen it. They went on to say that they had not hitherto made any complaint of this. They declared they had seen no good object in complaining of a case of this kind since they did not hope any good would result to them. They then went on to say that a younger boy than X. at the beginning of this year (as near as they could fix the date at either the end of January or the beginning of February), had been mutilated in a similar way by a sentry of the same trading Company, who was still quartered in their town, and that when they had wished to bring this latter victim with them the sentry had threatened to kill him and that the boy was now in hiding. They begged that I would myself go back with them to their village and ascertain that they were speaking the truth. I thought it my duty to listen to this appeal, and decided to return with them on the morrow to their town. In the morning, when about to start for K. . . , many people from the surrounding country came in to see me. They brought with them three individuals who had been shockingly wounded by gunfire, two men and a very small boy, not more than 6 years of age, and a fourth—a boy of 6 or 7—whose right hand was cut off at the wrist. One of the men, who had been shot through the arm, declared that he was Y. of L. . . , a village situated some miles away. He declared that he had been shot as I saw under the following circumstances: the soldiers had entered his town, he alleged, to enforce the due fulfilment of the rubber tax due by the community. These men had tied him up and said that unless he paid 1,000 brass rods to them they would shoot him. Having no rods to give them they had shot him through the arm and had left him. The soldiers implicated, he said, were four whose names were given me. They were, he believed, all employees of the La Lulanga Company and had come from Mampoko. At the time when he, Y., was shot through the arm, the Chief of his town came up and begged the soldiers not to hurt him, but one of them, a man called Z., shot the Chief dead. No white man was with these sentries, or soldiers, at the time. Two of them, Y. said, he believed had been sent or taken to Coquilhatville. Two of them—whom he named— he said were still at Mampoko. The people of L. . . had sent to tell the white man at Mampoko of what his soldiers had done. He did not know what punishment, if any, the soldiers had received, for no inquiry had since been made in L. . . , nor had any persons in that town been required to testify against their aggressors. This man was accompanied by four other men of his town. These four men all corroborated Y.'s statement.

These people were at once followed by two men of M. . . , situated, they said, close to K. . . , and only a few miles distant. They brought with them a full-grown man named A.A., whose arm was shattered and greatly swollen through the discharge of a gun, and a small boy named B.B., whose left arm was broken in two places from two separate gun shots—the wrist being shattered and the hand wobbling about loose and quite useless. The two men made the following statement: that their town, like all the others in the neighbourhood, was required to furnish a certain quantity of india-rubber fortnightly to the headquarters of the La Lulanga Company at Mampoko; that at the time these outrages were committed, which they put at less than a year previously, a man named C.C. was a sentry of that Company quartered in their village; that the two now before me had taken the usual fortnight's rubber to Mampoko. On returning to M. . . they found that C.C., the sentry, had shot dead two men of the town named D.D. and E.E. and had tied up this man A.A. and the boy B.B., now before me, to two trees. The sentry said that this was to punish the two men for having taken the rubber to Mampoko without having first shown it to him and paid him a commission on it. The two men asserted that they had at once returned to Mampoko, and had begged the Director of the Company to return with them to M. . . and see what his servants had done. But, they alleged, he had refused to comply with their request. On getting back to their town they then found that the man A.A. and the child B.B. were still tied to the trees, and had been shot in the arms as I now saw. On pleading with the sentry to release these two wounded individuals, he had required a payment of 2,000 brass rods (100 Fr.). One of the two men stayed to collect this money, and another returned to Mampoko to again inform the Director of what had been done. The two men declared that nothing was done to the sentry C.C., but that the white man said that if the people behaved badly again he was to punish them. The sentry C.C., they declared, remained some time longer in M. . . , and they do not now know where he is.

These people were immediately followed by a number of natives who came before me bringing a small boy of not more than 7 years of age, whose right hand was gone at the wrist. This child, whose name was F.F., they had brought from the village of N . . . They stated that some years ago (they could not even approximately fix the date save by indicating that F.F. was only just able to run), N . . . had been attacked by several sentries of the La Lulanga Company. This was owing to their failure in supplying a sufficiency of india-rubber. They did not know whether these sentries had been sent by any European, but they knew all their names, and the Chief of them was one called G.G. G.G. had shot dead the Chief of their town, and the people had run into the forest. The sentries pursued them, and G.G. had knocked down the child F.F. with the butt of his gun and had then cut off his hand. They declared that the hand of the dead man and of this boy F.F. had then been carried away by the sentries. The sentries who did this belonged to the La Lulanga Company's factory at O . . . The man who appeared with F.F. went on to say that they had never complained about it, save to the white man who had then been that Company's agent at O . . . They had not thought of complaining to the Commissaire of the district. Not only was he far away, but they were afraid they would not be believed, and they thought the white men only wished for rubber, and that no good could come of pleading with them.

At the same time a number of men followed, with the request that I would listen to them. W. declared that their town P. . . , which had formerly been on the north bank of the X. . . River (where I had myself seen it), had now been transferred by force to the south bank, close to the factory at Q. . . He said that this act of compulsory transference was the direct act of the Commissaire Général of the . . . district. The Commissaire had visited P. . . on his steamer, and had ordered the people of that town to work daily at Q. . . for the La Lulanga factory. W. had replied that it was too far for the women of P. . . to go daily to Q . . . as was required; but the Commissaire, in reply, had taken fifty women and carried them away with him. The women were taken to Q. . . Two men were taken at the same time. To get these women back, W. went on to say, he and his people had to pay a fine of 10,000 brass rods (500 Fr.). They had paid this money to the Commissaire Général himself. They had then been ordered by the Commissaire to abandon their town, since it lay too far from the factory, and build a fresh town close to Q. . . , so that they might be at hand for the white man's needs. This they had been forced to do—many of them were taken across by force. It was about two years ago, W. thought, that this deportation had been effected, and they now came to beg that I would use my influence with the local authorities to permit their return to their abandoned home. Where they were now situated, close to Q. . . , they were most unhappy, and they only desired to be allowed to return to the former site of P . . .

When I asked the Chief W. why he had not gone to D.F. to complain if the sentries beat him or his people, opening his mouth he pointed to one of the teeth which was just dropping out, and said: 'That is what I got from the D.F. four days ago when I went to tell him what I now say to you.' He added that he was frequently beaten, along with others of his people, by the white man.

One of the men with him, who gave his name as H.H., said that two weeks ago the white man at Q. . . had ordered him to serve as one of the porters of his hammock on a journey he proposed taking inland. H.H. was then just completing the building of a new house, and excused himself on this ground, but offered to fetch a friend as a substitute. The Director of the Company had, in answer to this excuse, burnt down his house, alleging that he was insolent. He had had a box of cloth and some ducks in the house—in fact, all his goods, and they were destroyed in the fire. The white man then caused him to be tied up, and took him with him inland, and loosed him when he had to carry the hammock . . .

Other people were waiting, desirous of speaking with me, but so much time was taken in noting the statements already made that I had to leave, if I hoped to reach K . . . at a reasonable hour. I proceeded in a canoe across the Lulongo and up a tributary to a landing-place which seemed to be about . . . miles from I . . . Here, leaving the canoes, we walked for a couple of miles through a flooded forest to reach the village. I found here a sentry of the La Lulanga Company and a considerable number of natives. After some little delay a boy of about 15 years of age appeared, whose left arm was wrapped up in a dirty rag. Removing this, I found the left hand had been hacked off by the wrist, and that a shot hole appeared in the fleshy part of the forearm. The boy, who gave his name as I.I., in answer to my inquiry, said that a sentry of the La Lulanga Company now in the town had cut off his hand. I proceeded to look for this man, who at first could not be found, the natives to a considerable number gathering behind me as I walked through the town. After some delay the sentry appeared, carrying a cap-gun. The boy, whom I placed before him, then accused him to his face of having mutilated him. The men of the town, who were questioned in succession, corroborated the boy's statement. The sentry, who gave his name as K.K., could make no answer to the charge. He met it by vaguely saying some other sentry of the Company had mutilated I.I.; his predecessor, he said, had cut off several hands, and probably this was one of the victims. The natives around said that there were two other sentries at present in the town, who were not so bad as K.K., but that he was a villain. As the evidence against him was perfectly clear, man after man standing out and declaring he had seen the act committed, I informed him and the people present that I should appeal to the local authorities for his immediate arrest and trial. In the course of my interrogatory several other charges transpired against him. These were of a minor nature, consisting of the usual characteristic acts of blackmailing, only too commonly reported on all sides. One man said that K.K. had tied up his wife and only released her on payment of 1,000 rods. Another man said that K.K. had robbed him of two ducks and a dog. These minor offences K.K. equally demurred to, and again said that I.I. had been mutilated by some other sentry, naming several. I took the boy back with me and later brought him to Coquilhatville, where he formally charged K.K. with the crime, alleging to the Commandant, who took his statement through a special Government interpreter, in my presence, that it had been done 'on account of rubber'. I have since been informed that, acting on my request, the authorities at Coquilhatville had arrested K.K., who presumably will be tried in due course . . .

It was obviously impossible that I should visit all the villages of the natives who came to beg me to do so at J . . . or elsewhere during my journey, or to verify on the spot, as in the case of the boy, the statements they made. In that one case the truth of the charges proferred was amply demonstrated, and their significance was not diminished by the fact that, whereas this act of mutilation had been committed within a few miles of Q. . . , the headquarters of a European civilising agency, and the guilty man was still in their midst, armed with the gun with which he had first shot his victim (for which he could produce no licence when I asked for it, saying it was his employers'), no one of the natives of the terrorized town had attempted to report the occurrence. They had in the interval visited Mampoko each fortnight with the india-rubber from their district. There was also in their midst another mutilated boy, X., whose hand had been cut off either by this or another sentry. The main waterway of the Lulongo River lay at their doors, and on it well-nigh every fortnight a Government steamer had passed up and down stream on its way to bring the india-rubber of the A.B.I.R. Company to Coquilhatville. They possessed, too, some canoes; and, if all other agencies of relief were closed, the territorial tribunal at Coquilhatville lay open to them, and the journey to it downstream from their village could have been accomplished in some twelve hours. It was no greater journey, indeed, than many of the towns I had elsewhere visited were forced to undertake each week or fortnight to deliver supplies to their local tax collectors. The fact that no effort had been made by these people to secure relief from their unhappy situation impelled me to believe that a very real fear of reporting such occurrences actually existed among them. That everything asserted by such a people, under such circumstances, is strictly true I should in no wise assert. That discrepancies must be found in much alleged by such rude savages, to one whose sympathies they sought to awaken, must equally be admitted. But the broad fact remained that their previous silence said more than their present speech. In spite of contradictions, and even seeming misstatements, it was clear that these men were stating either what they had actually seen with their eyes or firmly believed in their hearts. No one viewing their unhappy surroundings or hearing their appeals, no one at all cognizant of African native life or character, could doubt that they were speaking, in the main, truly; and the unhappy conviction was forced upon me that in the many forest towns behind the screen of trees, which I could not visit, these people were entitled to expect that a civilised administration should be represented among them by other agents than what the savages euphemistically termed 'forest guards'.

*   *   *

I decided, owing to pressure of other duties, to return from Con-
quilhatville to Stanley Pool. The last incident of my stay in the Upper Congo occurred the night prior to my departure. Late that
night a man came with some natives of the S. . . district, represented as his friends, who were fleeing from their homes, and
whom he begged me to carry with me to the French territory at
Lukolela. These were L.L. of T. . . and seven others. L.L. stated
that, owing to his inability to meet the impositions of the Commissaire of the S . . . district, he had, with his family, abandoned his
home and was trying to reach Lukolela. He had already come 80
miles downstream by canoe, but was now hiding with friends in
one of the towns near Coquilhatville. Part of the imposition laid on
his town consisted of two goats which had to be supplied each
month for the white man's table at S. . . As all the goats in the
neighbourhood had long since disappeared in meeting these demands, he could now only satisfy this imposition by buying in inland districts such goats as were for sale. For these he had to pay
3,000 rods each (150 Fr.), and as the Government's remuneration
amounted to only 100 rods (5 Fr.) per goat, he had no further
means of maintaining the supply. Having appealed in vain for the
remission of this burden, no other course was left open to him but
to fly. I told this man I regretted I could not help him, that his
proper course was to appeal for relief to the authorities of the district; and, this failing, to seek the higher authorities at Boma. This,
he said, was clearly impossible for him to do. On the last occasion
when he had sought the officials at S . . . , he had been told that if
his next tax were not forthcoming he should go into the 'chain
gang'. He added that a neighbouring Chief who had failed in this
respect had just died in the prison gang, and that such would be his
fate if he were caught. He added that, if I disbelieved him, there
were those who would vouch for his character and the truth of his
statement; and I told him and his friend that I should inquire in
that quarter, but that it was impossible for me to assist a fugitive. I
added, however, that there was no law on the Congo Statute Book
which forbade him or any other man from travelling freely to any
part of the country, and his right to navigate in his own canoe the
Upper Congo was as good as mine in my steamer or anyone else's.
He and his people left me at midnight, saying that unless they
could get away with me they did not think it possible they could
succeed in gaining Lukolela. A person at T . . . to whom I referred
this statement informed me that L.L.'s statement was true. He said:
'What L.L. told you, re price of goats, was perfectly true. At U . . .
they are 3,000; and here they are 2,500 to 3,000 rods . . .' Re 'dying
in the chains' U 13.: he had every reason to fear this for recently

two Chiefs died in the chain; viz.: the Chief of a little town above
U. . .—his crime: because he did not move his houses a few hundred yards to join them to . . . as quickly as the Commissaire
thought he should do; secondly, the Chief of T . . .—his crime: because he did not go up every fortnight with the tax. These two men
were chained together and made to carry heavy loads of bricks and
water, and were frequently beaten by the soldiers in charge of
them. There are witnesses to prove this.

Leaving the township of Coquilhatville on the 11th of September
I reached Stanley Pool on the 15th September.

> I have the honour to be
> Your Lordship's obedient servant,
>
> ROGER CASEMENT.

EDMUND D. MOREL

[Property and Trade versus Forced Production]†

> "I admit that labour is imposed upon the natives (le travail est
> imposé), but it is in the interest of all, and when the work is done,
> the native is paid."
> —M. DE FAVEREAU, Belgian Minister for Foreign Affairs

> "They are not entitled to anything: what is given to them is a
> pure gratuity."   —M. SMET DE NAEYER, Belgian Premier

The twistings and wrigglings of Congo State diplomacy, whatever
attraction they may have for learned gentlemen like Professor
Descamps, who recently devoted a volume to proving "judicially"
and to his entire satisfaction that the Congo State represented the
perfectibility of human foresight and goodness in the treatment of
native races, can only inspire the plain man with contempt and repulsion. Stripped of its trappings, the policy of King Leopold stands

† Edmund D. Morel, *King Leopold's Rule in Africa* (New York: Funk and Wagnalls Company, 1905), pp. 89–101. Morel (1873–1924) was founder of the Congo Reform Association and the leader in Britain of the campaign against the atrocities in the Congo Free
State. He was not an opponent of all forms of imperialism, however, and combined a belief in free trade with a romanticized view of pre-colonial African societies. See
Hochschild, pp. 209–224, for a balanced assessment of Morel's achievement and his
limitations. Morel's book includes excerpts from a letter Conrad wrote to Roger Casement condemning Leopold's atrocities. See Alan Simmons, this edition, on Morel's use
of Conrad in his campaign. The epigraphs to this selection come from the Congo debate
in the Belgian parliament (July 1903). Unless indicated, notes are the Editor's.

naked before the world, a loathsome thing. It is the old, old story: the story of evil and greed and lust perpetrated upon a weaker people, but never before, assuredly, has the hypocrisy with which such deeds have been cloaked, attained to heights so sublime. Never before has hypocrisy been so successful. For nearly twenty years has the Sovereign of the Congo State posed before the world as the embodiment of philanthropic motive, high intent, humanitarian zeal, lofty and stimulating righteousness. No more marvellous piece of acting has been witnessed on the world's stage than this.

And let us remember that if the story in itself is old, it nevertheless contains distinctive features of peculiarity. The *conquistadores* of Peru were, after all, the repositories of the national purpose, and their ruthless cruelties were but the concomitants of the national policy. The over-sea slave-trade, first started by Portugal under the plea of religious zeal, and afterwards continued by her, and adopted by other Powers for frankly material reasons, was acquiesced in by the national conscience of the times, and was put to national ends. But what nation is interested in the perpetuation of the system which has converted the Congo territories into a charnel-house? Not Belgium, whose Congo turn-over * * * amounts after nearly twenty years, to 1 per cent of her total trade! Such a thing has never been known as one man with a few partners controlling, for his benefit and that of his associates, one million square miles of territory, and wielding the power of life and death over many millions of human beings.

And what has rallied to his side the support of a certain class of latter-day colonial politicians and amateurs of all that is bad in the frenzied expansionism of the hour? I do not speak of paid journalistic or legal hacks. How can one explain the fascination which a policy absolutely selfish has nevertheless exercised over the minds of many? To those whose business it has been to follow the evolution of European thought concerning tropical Africa during the last decade, the answer to the question need not be sought for. The Sovereign of the Congo State is the living personation; and the administrative system he has conceived and applied is the working embodiment, of the theory that the Negro will not produce without compulsion; and that if tropical Africa can ever be developed, it must be through a *régime* of forced labour. Thus has the Sovereign of the Congo State become a sort of *point d'appui*[1] for the thoughtless, the inexperienced, the inhumane. He has been the one strong man, resolute in his views, inflexible in carrying them out. His would-be imitators have never been deceived by the "Property" quibble. They have known what his policy meant, although they

1. Point of support, prop (French).

may have conveniently shut out some of its unpleasant details from their mental vision. As Mr. Stephen Gwynne has justly remarked, "This new servitude has in it the worst of all elements, in that the slave-owner no longer sees the slaves at work, but sits at home and receives his dividends." But the success of the Sovereign of the Congo State in maintaining with marvellous ability and resource the New African Slave Trade has enlisted the support and the sympathies of all those who, in their haste to get rich, would to-morrow convert the black man throughout Africa, if they could, into a tenant on his own land, a serf doomed to ceaseless and unremunerated toil, in the interests of cosmopolitan exploitationists in Europe.

The peculiar conditions under which the Congo State was created have greatly intensified the mischief, already considerable, of the existence of such a focus of pernicious influence. Its neighbours in Europe and Africa—for if the arms of the Congo State are in Africa, its brain, it cannot be too often stated, is in Brussels—have seen within the last decade the growth of a great revenue through direct "taxation," so-called: the sudden upspringing of an enormously valuable export of raw material which the unremitting labour of literally millions of men could alone have produced; the acquisition of colossal profits by nominally trading Companies—and this while their own possessions were advancing but slowly. They have seen Belgian colonial securities leap to heights undreamt of; fortunes made in a few hours; huge dividends earned after a year or two's working:—all these striking results accomplished by Belgian tyros[2] at colonisation, by a so-called State run to all intents and purposes by a single man. And so, greatly in ignorance, urged on by designing men who had their own ends to serve, two of the Congo State's neighbours in Africa thought they would try their hands at a system which could yield such magnificent material returns. But being civilised nations, they have found, or are ascertaining, that the system cannot be carried out in practice without unending barbarity and they have but added to their difficulties.

The doctrine of forced production is based upon data deliberately falsified. The whole thing, to put it bluntly, is a lie—a mere excuse to palliate the exploits of the buccaneer. The two essentials of this doctrine are, denial to the native of any rights in his land and in the products of commercial value his land produces; to which is added physical force to compel the native to gather those products for the European.

It is simply untrue that the native of Western Africa will not work unless compelled. Experience, facts, the existence of which cannot

2. Novices.

be disputed because they are there palpably and unmistakably before us, disprove the assertion, which is not believed in by those who make it.

Experience, reason, common sense, and justice tells us that it is as wrong as it is foolish, and as foolish as it is wrong, to treat native rights of land-tenure as non-existent. "In dealing with the natives," says Sir William MacGregor, one of our most experienced West African administrators, "one must never touch their rights in land." Similarly we find Doctor Zimmerman, an eminent German colonial authority, declaring that the "protection of property is the surest means" to develop Africa rationally. No student of African questions needs to be reminded of the passionate insistence with which the late Mary Kingsley[3] urged the conservation of native land-tenure, with a force of conviction and a scientific perception of the needful which has never been equalled. Wherever native law and custom have been studied in tropical Africa, we find the same doctrine preached, "If you want to govern successfully and justly, respect native land-tenure."

Says M. Bohn, one of the ablest Frenchmen who have handled West African affairs:

> "Land laws exist in these countries as they do in Europe, and have not been overthrown by wars of conquest or change of rulers. There is nothing more antagonistic to the native mind, whether in the case of Chiefs or subjects, than to have their rights of land-tenure discussed, let alone taken from them."

Or take another experienced Frenchman, M. Fondère:

> "The right to sell his products to whomsoever he may please cannot be denied to the native, because he has always possessed it. Moreover, all stipulations to the contrary notwithstanding, it would be quite illusory to think of taking this right away from the native. That could only be done by force of arms."

*   *   *

Wherever their forms have been examined, native laws of land-tenure have been found to repose upon just principles, to be thoroughly well understood, recognised, and adhered to by the people of the land, and to be worthy of serious and sympathetic study. Tropical Africa is an immensity, and much of it has never been trodden by the white man's foot, let alone observed by the white man's brain, and consequently native laws of land-tenure in a very small portion of it only have been gone into. The results of such

3. Mary Kingsley (1862–1900), author of the best-selling memoir *Travels in West Africa* (1897).

study as has been made are on record, and not only do they exclude
the idea that native land-tenure is the imaginary product of certain
so-called negrophiles in this country, but they prove that it is part
and parcel of the social organisation of the people, a knowledge of
which, as every competent official knows, is essential to good government in tropical Africa. Such knowledge, however, is not essential to slave-driving, and we need not be surprised that the Congo
State dismisses the idea that such a thing as *native* rights in land
can by any possibility be held to exist at all, and affectedly ignores
any other proprietary rights to land but the ones which it has vested
in itself or in its associates.

A European Government may be justified in evolving theoretical
paper rights of sovereignty over land which—and such land does
exist in many parts of tropical Africa—is, through pestilence, inter-
tribal warfare, emigration, or some such cause, really and truly "vacant." It is the clear duty of the European over-lord in tropical
Africa to draft such laws and regulations affecting land duly held
under native tenure, which shall make it difficult, if not impossible,
for the native owner to be cheated out of his land by adventurers
and swindlers. But to treat native land-tenure as a factor of no account in Afro-European relationship, on the plea that native ownership disappears with the simple enunciation of a theoretical right of
proprietorship in Europe, or by signing a piece of parchment conveying the proprietorship of some thousands of square miles of
African territory and all that therein is to a group of financiers, is
merely an attempt to cover spoliation, robbery, and violence under
legal *formulæ*.

To sweep away native land-tenure is the preliminary step to
forced labour, and forced labour in tropical Africa means the enslavement of the African by the European-armed and European-
directed African; and that, in tropical Africa, spells the coming
destruction of European effort.

And so, from denying the rights of the natives to their land, we
come by natural sequence to the doctrine of forced production.
The Congo State claims that, by its system—

> "it is permissible for the native to find by work the remunera-
> tion which contributes to augment his well-being. Such is, in
> fact, one of the ends of the general policy of the State to pro-
> mote the regeneration of the race, by instilling into him a
> higher idea of the necessity of labour. It can be imagined that
> Governments conscious of their moral responsibility do not
> advocate among inferior races the right to idleness and lazi-
> ness with, as their consequence, the maintenance of an anti-
> civilising social state."

Could hypocrisy reach serener heights? The Congo State's consciousness of "moral responsibility" compels it to keep on a war footing an army of nearly 20,000 men, so that the "regeneration of the race" shall not be hindered by this inbred "idleness and laziness."

The Congo State authorities, however, do not appear to have been particularly impressed with the "laziness and idleness" of the native when, in June, 1896, they attached to their own *Bulletin Officiel* the report of an agricultural tour undertaken by M. Emile Laurent, *before the completion of the Matadi-Stanley Pool Railway*. This gentleman was sent on an extensive survey to report upon the "agricultural" possibilities of the country, the characteristics of the various tribes, etc. His testimony to the "idleness" of the native is emphatic. Referring to the region of the Cataracts (Lower Congo, between Matadi and Stanley-Pool), he says:

> "It is here that the natives often build their villages; they plant the palm tree and the *sofa*, which grows well. In this neighbourhood they cultivate sweet potatoes, manioc, and ground-nuts. . . . There is also sandy ground in the district; they form rather large plains, often utilised for the cultivation of the ground-nut. This plant gives abundant crops. Formerly the natives brought the ground-nuts to Matadi to the Dutch factory, in exchange for salt, which they in turn sold to the people of the interior."

Not much sign of "idleness" there, at the time that particular report was penned, apparently. A little later on there was "idleness"; but it was the inertia of death, for death and depopulation had stalked through the land in the shape of forced labour and forced porterage. * * * The ground-nut trade of the Lower Congo region, it is useful to remember, was a very large one before the Congo State assumed the reins of government in the river. It has now virtually disappeared. The Congo Government has recently inaugurated a system of forced labour in the Cataracts region, in order to revive the cultivation of this nut. * * *

We will follow M. Laurent on his journey. Of the Stanley-Pool and Eastern Kwango region he writes as follows:—

> "From what Messrs. Costermans and Deghilage, two officials who have visited this district, tell me, the ground rubber covers vast extents of sandy soil, and the natives exploit it on a large scale. Not long ago the rubber from this region was exported to Portuguese Angola, and there was a considerable trade in it. M. Deghilage tells me that he has seen on the native markets of Kenghe-Diadia thirty tons of this rubber exposed for sale every four days."

That was before the Congo State was paramount in the land; the days when the native could *sell* his produce on legitimate commercial lines; the days when the native either bartered his rubber with other native traders from Portuguese territory, who afterwards sold it to the Portuguese on the coast, or direct with European merchants established in Portuguese territory. Compare the above passage—which, mind you, is an official report—with the claim of the Congo State put forward to-day, to have taught the native of the Congo territories how to collect rubber! "The policy of the State," says the official reply to the British Note, "has not, as has been asserted, killed trade; it has, on the contrary, created it." It did not create the ground-nut trade of the Lower Congo, or the rubber trade of the Kwango, on the testimony of its own expert! But it has certainly killed the former; and as for the latter, the rubber which used to *belong* to the native, and which the native *sold*, is now the *property* of the Kwango Trust, for which the native is expected to collect it, on the usual regenerating lines. One fails to detect any signs of "idleness" in the Kwango region at the time of M. Laurent's report.

From the Kwango district, M. Laurent takes us to Lake Leopold II. district. Here we learn that:

> "I saw a rubber vine which was ten centimetres in diameter and bore numerous transversal incisions, which is a proof that the natives know and practice the right method of extracting rubber. . . . I also noticed the large quantities of gum-copal which is to be found in the neighbourhood of the lake, and which the natives extract from the ground at the foot of the trees along the river."

Always the same peculiar form of "laziness." The district of Lake Leopold II. is now the centre of the secret revenues department, the *Domaine de la Couronne*, the scene of the horrors and desolation so graphically described by Consul Casement * * *. In the Kasai and Lualaba region the "idleness" of the native becomes still more apparent from this report:

> "The population is comparatively dense, and is distinguished for its truly remarkable trading and labour capacities."

* * * The "idleness" of the native, "from the Sankuru River to Nyangwe," is simply deplorable, for, according to M. Laurent:

> "Around these truly negro towns the bush is cultivated for a distance of an hour and a half's walk, and the plantations are often as carefully cultivated as they are in Flanders. The natives cultivate manioc, maize, millet, rice, *voandzou*, and ground-nuts. The latter yield magnificent crops."

So much for the "idleness" of the Congo native, as observed by a trained "agriculturist" employed by the Congo State and as embodied in an official report. It is always well to confound the Congo State authorities with their own published documents; but men who traded with, or travelled among, the Upper Congo natives in many parts of the territory before the grip of Africa's regenerator tightened upon the land, know well that these unfortunate people are no more idle than any of the tropical African peoples, among whom labour other than the labour required for the supply of foodstuffs is not an economic necessity; that their commercial instincts were very highly developed, that they were eager to trade with the white man, and did trade indirectly with the white man; and that, given a fair chance, a large and legitimate trade would have sprung up there, as it has everywhere else in West Africa, when the native has been given markets and decent treatment.

Is this a general statement easy to make, but difficult to prove, so far as the Congo natives are concerned? Let us see. Well, in the first place, we have the official report of M. Laurent. But, after all, that is one man's statement. One of the earlier pioneers of the Congo was M. Herbert Ward. Here is a passage from his book, which rather bears out M. Laurent:

> "The rocky banks and tree-hidden bays concealed no worse foe than the keen Bateke or Byanzi trader, thirsting, not for the white man's blood, but for his cotton cloths and bright brass rods, and anxious only to get the better of him in bargaining, when his natural timidity and suspicion had been lulled to sleep by the exhibition of such 'inconsidered trifles' of this description as my fast-failing and scanty stock enabled me to display whenever my own wants or the necessities of my men induced us to call at any of the villages we might pass."

There we have the picture of a riverain population of keen trading instincts.

With Mr. R. E. Dennett, whose ethnological studies are well known, and who is probably an unrivalled authority on the commercial capacities of the Congo tribes, among whom he has lived for some twenty years, I have exchanged occasionally a friendly correspondence. Some few weeks ago I wrote to him—he was then in Africa—pointing out the State's claim to have introduced commerce in the Upper Congo, and asking him what he thought of it. His reply is now before me.

> "Certainly most of the trade," he writes, "done in the Lower Congo came from the Upper Congo from beyond the Kasai. In 1879 I assisted —— to trade in Kinsembo, and we bought

quite a lot of ivory and rubber coming in from the Upper Congo. In 1880 I was in Ambrizette, and we bought large quantities of the same produce coming from the same district and passing through 'Moaquita's' town. About 1881 most of the traders on the South-West Coast opened up above Musuku, at Noki, Ango-Ango, Kola-Kola, and Matadi, and as a proof that the Coast trade came, for the most part, from the Upper Congo, it may be stated that as soon as these firms commenced buying at these places great quantities of rubber and ivory, the Coast trade fell off enormously. This can again be proved by the fact that as soon as the Belgian Companies went into the interior (*i.e.* the Upper Congo, above the Cataracts, which divide the Upper from the Lower Congo, now connected by a railway) the factories below Matadi (*i.e.* in the Lower Congo, below the Cataracts) fared very badly, only getting that trade which came from the Portuguese Upper Congo."

So, on this evidence—the competency of which no one acquainted with West African affairs will presume to discuss—we find that long before M. Laurent went on his tour of inspection, long before Mr. Ward recorded his experiences, the natives of the Upper Congo were selling large quantities of African produce to the Ba-Congo peoples—ivory and rubber—who in turn carried that produce to the Lower Congo along the caravan road of 200 odd miles, which their feet had trodden and made. And this testimony, let us bear carefully in mind, is amply corroborated in the Protest drawn up by the Belgian companies alluded to in Mr. Dennett's letter * * * when they declared:

"To forbid the natives from selling the ivory and rubber from their forests and plains, which constitutes their hereditary birthright, and in which they have traded from time immemorial, is a violation of natural rights."

Is any more proof needed to confirm the accuracy of my contention, that the natives of the Upper Congo, if they had been decently treated, would have built up a trade of infinitely greater volume, so far as the export of raw material is concerned, than the quantity wrung from them to-day by massacre and outrage; while that produce, legitimately acquired, bartered for, traded for, would have necessitated an import "the counterpart of its value," bringing prosperity to the producer, progress, and development? Whether the reader considers additional proof to be necessary or not, I propose to adduce it, and from no less an authority than the late Sir Henry M. Stanley. Speaking at the London Chamber of Commerce in 1884, Stanley remarked:

"The fixed and permanent way (he was referring to a rail-way) which would be such a benefit to the Cataract region just described, would be of still greater benefit to the Upper Congo and its plain-like lands, and to the keen, enterprising, high-spirited[4] peoples who occupy them. Even now many a flotilla descends the great river 500 miles down to Stanley-Pool, to wait patiently for months before their goods can be disposed of to the Lower Congo caravans."

That was before a single European merchant had established himself beyond Matadi, and, therefore, long prior to the rubber "taxes" of "Bula Matadi"![5]

I began with a Belgian authority to drive my point home. I will end with another. In an official publication printed in Brussels in 1897 (in connection with the Brussels Exhibition of that year), under the auspices of "M. le Commandant Liebrechts," one of the principal Secretaries of State of the Congo Administration in Brussels, I find the following reference to the trading instincts of the great riverain tribe of the Batekes[6] above Stanley-Pool:—

"To this incessant movement produced for long years is due that, much before the arrival of Europeans, the Congo river tribes as far even as the Aruwimi had European goods which had passed from hand to hand from the Coast, and had acquired extraordinary value."

That is a true statement, and the European merchandise was paid for by the native producer in rubber and ivory. Purchased from the factories in the Lower River by natives, transported by them for 200 weary miles along the Cataracts to the Upper River; sold by them to Upper River natives at the Pool against rubber and ivory, which rubber and ivory was carried down to the factories by the native middlemen who had brought up the goods to buy those articles; while the native middle-men in the Upper River, who, Stanley tells us, sometimes waited "for months," having disposed of their

4. Will any one who was acquainted with those peoples in 1884, and who has seen them recently, apply those adjectives to them now? Mr. Casement's report is peculiarly illuminating on this point. Will the reader bear also carefully in mind the word "occupy," and compare it with that convenient term "vacant" so dear to Congolese jurists? [Morel's note]

5. Native name for the Congo State—Stanley's old name. The origin of this name is not generally known. Stanley was so christened in the year 1883 by the inhabitants of the village of M'Fufu near Vivi. One day a man came rushing into the village with the news that a strange white man was breaking stones. It was Stanley blasting the rocks to make a horizontal road for the transport, in sections, of his boat the *L'en Avant*. In the Ba-Congo language, Ntadi means stone; the plural being formed by prefixes, Ntadi is Matadi in the plural. Thus Bula Matadi, the man who broke the stones; and the place where his blasting operations first took place, has preserved the name Matadi. [Morel's note]

6. These Batekes have now nearly all emigrated to the French Congo, abandoning Congo State territory. [Morel's note]

rubber and ivory, started off with full canoes to their customers along the banks of the mighty river and its branches. Such the trade—viewed in its native aspect—which "Bula Matadi" has wiped out by declaring the rubber and ivory of the Upper Congo to be its property, and by compelling the natives to produce it for nothing; such the natural commercial instincts of a people that it has crushed; such the commerce which the Berlin Act was intended not only to preserve, but even to keep unhampered by vexatious customs dues. What are we to think of the honesty of a Government which can declare in 1903 that it has "created trade" and taught the natives the art of collecting rubber, when it has destroyed trade which European enterprise and native energy had established?

Leaving the Congo, the commercial proclivities of the Negro meet us wherever we care to pursue our inquiry, and his alleged idleness vanishes into the mists of mendaciousness whence it originates. Every year the voluntary labour of the West African Negro supplies Europe with nearly four millions sterling of palm-oil and kernels alone, requiring infinite time, infinite toil, and infinite trouble in their preparation; employing hundreds of thousands of African men and women. The voluntary labour of the natives of the French Colony of Senegal and the British Colony of Gambia supplies Europe every year with ground-nuts to the tune of over one million sterling.

Last year the voluntary labour of the natives of the Gold Coast supplied Europe with £100,000 worth of high-class cocoa, and they and their relatives on the French Ivory Coast sent us £500,000 worth of mahogany. From West Africa the Negro sends us every year thousands of tons of precious cabinet woods, involving the expenditure of an enormous amount of physical labour in felling and squaring the logs, and floating them down the rivers and creeks to the sea. Europe, and especially Great Britain, rely to-day upon the voluntary labour of the Negro to relieve the intolerable strain of the cotton industry, groaning under the dead weight of dependence upon America for the source of the raw material, and the Negro is responding right gallantly to the demand. After only a few months' effort, Lagos is beginning to send us cotton, and Nigeria will do so just as soon as we can give her the light railway that she needs. In the five years ending with 1900 the trade of the British West African Possessions amounted to 43 millions sterling.

These are facts, and they are not got over by calling a man who points them out a "sentimentalist." But the apostles of coercion, and the upholders of the New Slave Trade, do not care for facts; they prefer legal conundrums in which to wrap their selfish creed, and give it an appearance of respectability. Now, as in the days when the conscience of the world awoke to the iniquities of the over-sea slave-trade, we are flooded with hypocritical arguments drawn from false premises, with specious pleadings and judicial compositions designed to confuse the judgment, cloud the understanding, and distort the teachings of history. The Congo State, as I have said before, is the incarnation of all this callous and pernicious humbug. We have fought it, a handful of us, from different standpoints for many a long year, and at last we have dragged the Government and public opinion along with us. We must go on fighting it until the diseases it has introduced into Africa and the virus with which it has temporarily saturated a portion of European thought are utterly destroyed. The one bulwark of the Negro in tropical Africa against the worst excesses of European civilisation is the determination of Europe to conserve his rights in his land and in his property. In helping him to develop his property on scientific lines; in granting him internal peace; in proving to him that he is regarded not as a brute, but as a partner in a great undertaking from which Europe and Africa will derive lasting benefit—Europe will be adopting the only just, right, and practical policy.

That was the policy laid down by the Powers in Berlin in 1885. Any other policy is doomed to ultimate failure and disaster to Europe, and must result in untold misery to the peoples of tropical Africa. Any other policy must be resisted to the uttermost by all those who believe in the great future which is in store for tropical Africa wisely administered by the white man, and who have some regard for the honour of Europe and the just and humane treatment of the races of Africa.

ADAM HOCHSCHILD

Meeting Mr. Kurtz†

At the beginning of August 1890, several weeks after he wrote his furious *Open Letter* to King Leopold II, George Washington Williams finished the long return journey down the Congo River to the station of Kinshasa, on Stanley Pool. Either in the waters of the pool or when docked on the riverbank at Kinshasa, Williams's steamboat crossed paths with a boat that was at the start of its voyage upstream, the *Roi des Belges*, a long, boxy sternwheeler with a funnel and pilot house on its top deck. Had Williams managed to catch a glimpse of the other boat's crew, he would have seen a

† From *King Leopold's Ghost: A Story of Greed, Terror, and Heroism in Colonial Africa* (Boston: Houghton Mifflin, 1998), pp. 140–49. Copyright © 1998 by Adam Hochschild. Reprinted by permission of Houghton Mifflin Company. All rights reserved. Unless indicated, notes are the author's.

stocky, black-bearded officer with eyes that look, in the photographs we have, as if they were permanently narrowed against the
tropical sun. Newly arrived in the Congo, the young officer would
be at the captain's side for the entire trip upstream, learning the
river in preparation for taking command of a steamer himself.

The apprentice officer was in many ways typical of the whites
who came to the Congo at this time: an unmarried young man, in
need of a job, who had a yen for adventure and some troubles in his
past. Konrad Korzeniowski, born in Poland, had grown up with an
image of Africa based on the hazy allure of the unknown: "When
nine years old or thereabouts . . . while looking at a map of Africa
of the time and putting my finger on the blank space then representing the unsolved mystery of that continent, I said to myself . . .
'When I grow up I shall go *there*.' "[1] In his youth, partly spent in
France, he had problems with debts, dabbled, he claimed, in gun-
running, and made a suicide attempt. He then spent more than a
decade as a ship's officer in the British merchant marine, learning
English along the way, although never losing his strong Polish accent. In early 1890, Korzeniowski was looking in vain for a master's
berth at sea. While job-hunting in London, a city filled with talk of
Stanley's just-completed Emin Pasha expedition,[2] he began thinking again of the exotic land of his childhood fantasies. He went to
Brussels, applied for work on the Congo River, and returned to Belgium for his final job interview just as Stanley was finishing his gala
visit to the city.

In conversations before he took up his new job, the thirty-two-
year-old Korzeniowski showed that, like almost everyone in Europe,
he believed Leopold's mission in Africa was a noble and "civilizing"
one. He then said goodbye to his relatives and sailed for the Congo
on the ship that carried the first batch of rails and ties for the new
railway. Like other white men heading for the interior, he first had to
make the long trek from Matadi around the rapids, along with a caravan of black porters. Once he reached the river at last, he filled his
diary with the notes of a businesslike seaman, making long entries
about shoals, refueling points, and other items not included on the
primitive navigational charts available. It would be almost a decade
before the aspiring steamship captain managed to get down on paper the other features of the Congo not shown on the map, and by
that time, of course, the world would know him as Joseph Conrad.

1. Joseph Conrad, *A Personal Record* (London: J. M. Dent, 1912), p. 13. [See the selection
   in this Norton Critical Edition. Editor]
2. The Emin Pasha was the German governor of southern Sudan, Eduard Schnitzer, who
   was cut off from the outside world in the mid-1880s by a rebellion of native Muslim fun-
   damentalists. Sent by Leopold to rescue him, Stanley traveled through the Congo
   (1887–89), wreaking havoc as he went, and later wrote a best-selling book about his adventures. [Editor]

He spent some six months in the Congo altogether, carrying with him the partly written manuscript of his first novel, *Almayer's Folly*. The thousand-mile apprenticeship trip upriver, from Stanley Pool to Stanley Falls, took only four weeks, a fast voyage for the time. Sandbars, rocks, and shallow water made navigation tricky, especially far up the river in the dry season, which it then was. "The subdued thundering mutter of the Stanley Falls hung in the heavy night air of the last navigable reach of the Upper Congo . . ." he later wrote, "and I said to myself with awe, 'This is the very spot of my boyish boast.' . . . What an end to the idealized realities of a boy's daydreams!"[3]

At Stanley Falls, both Conrad and the steamer's captain fell ill. Conrad recovered sooner, and on the first part of the return trip downriver—going with the current, the boat traveled almost twice as fast as earlier—he was in command of the *Roi des Belges*. But a few weeks after the voyage ended, he canceled his contract and began the long journey back to Europe.

Several bitter disappointments punctured Conrad's dreams. At the start, he hit it off badly with an official of the company he was working for, which meant that he would not gain command of a steamer after all. Then, after coming downstream, he got sick again, with malaria and dysentery, and had to convalesce at an American Baptist mission station on Stanley Pool, in the care of a Scotch missionary doctor. He remained so weak that he had to be carried back to the coast and never fully recovered his health. Finally, he was so horrified by the greed and brutality among white men he saw in the Congo that his view of human nature was permanently changed. Until he spent his six months in Africa, he once told his friend the critic Edward Garnett, he had had "not a thought in his head."[4]

After brooding about his Congo experience for eight years, Conrad transformed it into *Heart of Darkness*, probably the most widely reprinted short novel in English. The nautical jottings in his ship's officer's notebook—"Lulonga Passage. . . . NbyE to NNE. On the Port Side: Snags. Soundings in fathoms: 2, 2, 2, 1, 1, 2, 2, 2, 2"[5]— now become prose unsurpassed by any of the other literary travelers to the Congo over the years:

> Going up that river was like travelling back to the earliest beginnings of the world, when vegetation rioted on the earth and

3. Joseph Conrad, "Geography and Some Explorers," in *Last Essays* (London: J. M. Dent, 1926), p. 17. [See the selection in this Norton Critical Edition. Editor]
4. Quoted in Edward Garnett, "Introduction" to *Letters from Conrad 1895–1924* (London: Nonesuch Press, 1928), p. xii.
5. Joseph Conrad, "Up-river Book" in *Congo Diary and Other Uncollected Pieces*, ed. Zdzislaw Najder (New York: Doubleday, 1978), p. 33.

the big trees were kings. An empty stream, a great silence, an impenetrable forest. The air was warm, thick, heavy, sluggish. There was no joy in the brilliance of sunshine. The long stretches of the waterway ran on, deserted, into the gloom of overshadowed distances. On silvery sandbanks hippos and alligators sunned themselves side by side. The broadening waters flowed through a mob of wooded islands. You lost your way on that river as you would in a desert and butted all day long against shoals trying to find the channel till you thought yourself bewitched and cut off for ever from everything you had known.[6]

Marlow, the narrator of *Heart of Darkness* and Conrad's alter ego, is hired by an ivory-trading company to sail a steamboat up an unnamed river whose shape on the map resembles "an immense snake uncoiled, with its head in the sea, its body at rest curving afar over a vast country and its tail lost in the depths of the land" (8). His destination is a post where the company's brilliant, ambitious star agent, Mr. Kurtz, is stationed. Kurtz has collected legendary quantities of ivory, but, Marlow learns along the way, is also rumored to have sunk into unspecified savagery. Marlow's steamer survives an attack by blacks and picks up a load of ivory and the ill Kurtz; Kurtz, talking of his grandiose plans, dies on board as they travel downstream.

Sketched with only a few bold strokes, Kurtz's image has nonetheless remained in the memories of millions of readers: the lone white agent far up the great river, with his dreams of grandeur, his great store of precious ivory, and his fiefdom carved out of the African jungle. Perhaps more than anything, we remember Marlow, on the steamboat, looking through binoculars at what he thinks are ornamental knobs atop the fenceposts in front of Kurtz's house—and then finding that each is "black, dried, sunken, with closed eyelids—a head that seemed to sleep at the top of that pole, and with the shrunken dry lips showing a narrow white line of the teeth" (57).

High school teachers and college professors who have discussed this book in thousands of classrooms over the years tend to do so in terms of Freud, Jung, and Nietzsche; of classical myth, Victorian innocence, and original sin; of postmodernism, postcolonialism, and poststructuralism. European and American readers, not comfortable acknowledging the genocidal scale of the killing in Africa at the turn of the century, have cast *Heart of Darkness* loose from its historical moorings. We read it as a parable for all times and

6. Joseph Conrad, *Heart of Darkness*, pp. 33–34. [Page references are to this Norton Critical Edition. Editor]

places, not as a book about one time and place. Two of the three times the story was filmed, most notably in Francis Ford Coppola's *Apocalypse Now*, it was not even set in Africa. But Conrad himself wrote, "*Heart of Darkness* is experience . . . pushed a little (and only very little) beyond the actual facts of the case."[7] Whatever the rich levels of meaning the book has as literature, for our purposes what is notable is how precise and detailed a description it is of "the actual facts of the case": King Leopold's Congo in 1890, just as the exploitation of the territory was getting under way in earnest.

In the novel Marlow, as Conrad had done, begins his trip with the long walk around the rapids: "A slight clinking behind me made me turn my head. Six black men advanced in a file toiling up the path. They walked erect and slow, balancing small baskets full of earth on their heads, and the clink kept time with their footsteps. . . . I could see every rib, the joints of their limbs were like knots in a rope, each had an iron collar on his neck and all were connected together with a chain whose bights swung between them, rhythmically clinking" (15). These were the laborers starting work on Leopold's railway.

A few pages later, Marlow describes a spot where some starving railway workers had crawled away to die. Farther along the trail, he sees "now and then a carrier dead in harness, at rest in the long grass near the path, with an empty water-gourd and his long staff lying by his side," and notes the mysterious "body of a middle-aged negro, with a bullet-hole in the forehead" (20). This is simply a record of what Conrad himself saw on his walk around the rapids to Stanley Pool. In his diary entry for July 3, 1890, he noted: "Met an off[ic]er of the State inspecting; a few minutes afterwards saw at a camp[in]g place the dead body of a Backongo. Shot? Horrid smell." The following day: "Saw another dead body lying by the path in an attitude of meditative repose." And on July 29: "On the road today passed a skeleton tied up to a post."[8]

During the hike around the rapids, Marlow also describes how people had fled to avoid being conscripted as porters: "The population had cleared out a long time ago. Well if a lot of mysterious niggers armed with all kinds of fearful weapons suddenly took to travelling on the road [in England] between Deal and Gravesend catching the yokels right and left to carry heavy loads for them, I fancy every farm and cottage thereabouts would get empty very soon. . . . I passed through several abandoned villages" (19–20). This, too, was what Conrad himself saw. The porters of the caravan the novelist was with came close to mutiny during the trip. Only

---

7. Joseph Conrad, Preface to *Youth: A Narrative, and Two Other Stories* (New York: Doubleday, 1924), p. xi. [See below in this Norton Critical Edition. Editor]
8. Conrad, *Congo Diary*, pp. 8, 9, 13. [See selection in this Norton Critical Edition. Editor]

three and a half years later a fierce uprising would break out along this very route, as Chief Nzansu and his men fought their long, doomed battle against the Force Publique.

In describing the caravans of porters that walked this trail, Marlow gives a crisp summary of the Leopoldian economy: "a stream of . . . rubbishy cottons, beads, and brass-wire set into the depths of darkness and in return came a precious trickle of ivory" (18). In 1890, this was still the colony's most prized commodity. "The word 'ivory' rang in the air, was whispered, was sighed. You would think they were praying to it," says Marlow. He even mentions Leopold's commission system for agents: "The only real feeling was a desire to get appointed to a trading-post where ivory was to be had, so that they could earn percentages" (23,24).

Conrad stayed true to life when creating the charismatic, murderous figure at the center of his novel, perhaps the twentieth century's most famous literary villain. Mr. Kurtz was clearly inspired by several real people, among them Georges Antoine Klein, a French agent for an ivory-gathering firm at Stanley Falls. Klein, mortally ill, died on shipboard, as Kurtz does in the novel, while Conrad was piloting the *Roi des Belges* down the river. Another model closer to Kurtz in character was Major Edmund Barttelot, the man whom Stanley left in charge of the rear column on the Emin Pasha expedition. It was Barttelot * * * who went mad, began biting, whipping, and killing people, and was finally murdered. Yet another Kurtz prototype was a Belgian, Arthur Hodister, famed for his harem of African women and for gathering huge amounts of ivory. Hodister eventually muscled in too aggressively on the territory of local Afro-Arab warlords and ivory-traders, who captured and beheaded him.

However, Conrad's legion of biographers and critics have almost entirely ignored the man who resembles Kurtz most closely of all, * * * the swashbuckling Captain Léon Rom of the Force Publique.[9] It is from Rom that Conrad may have taken the signal feature of his villain: the collection of African heads surrounding Kurtz's house.

The "Inner Station" of *Heart of Darkness*, the place Marlow looks at through his binoculars only to find Kurtz's collection of the shrunken heads of African "rebels," is loosely based on Stanley Falls. In 1895, five years after Conrad visited this post, Léon Rom was station chief there. A British explorer-journalist who passed through Stanley Falls that year described the aftermath of a punitive military expedition against some African rebels: "Many women and children were taken, and twenty-one heads were brought to the

9. Leopold's private army and police force in the Congo Free State. [Editor]

falls, and have been used by Captain Rom as a decoration round a flower-bed in front of his house!"[1] If Conrad missed this account, which appeared in the widely read *Century Magazine*, he almost certainly noticed when *The Saturday Review*, a magazine he admired and read faithfully, repeated the story in its issue of December 17, 1898. That date was within a few days of when Conrad began writing *Heart of Darkness*.

Furthermore, in the Congo, Rom and Conrad may have met.

On August 2, 1890, Conrad, accompanied by another white man and a caravan of porters, finished his month-long trek inland from the coast. Five miles before his caravan reached the village of Kinshasa on Stanley Pool, where the *Roi des Belges* was waiting, it had to pass through the neighboring post of Leopoldville. These two collections of thatch-roofed buildings were only an hour and a half's walk apart. (They soon grew and merged into one city, called Leopoldville by the Belgians and Kinshasa today.) When Conrad's caravan, trudging along a path near the riverbank, passed through Leopoldville, the station chief there was Léon Rom. Conrad made no entry in his diary on August 2, and Rom's notebook, which in a calligraphic hand faithfully records any raid or campaign that could win him another medal, mentions no expeditions away from Leopoldville at that time. If Rom was on hand, he would certainly have greeted a caravan with European newcomers, for there were only a few dozen white men at Leopoldville and Kinshasa, and new ones did not arrive every day. What, if anything, spoken or unspoken, passed between Rom and Conrad we will never know. Rom's collection of twenty-one African heads lay in a different place and a different time, half a decade in the future, but when Conrad read about Rom in December 1898, it is possible that he made the connection to a young officer he had met in the Congo.

Heart of Darkness is one of the most scathing indictments of imperialism in all literature, but its author, curiously, thought himself an ardent imperialist where England was concerned. Conrad fully recognized Leopold's rape of the Congo for what it was: "The horror! The horror!" his character Kurtz says on his deathbed. And Conrad's stand-in, Marlow, muses on how "the conquest of the earth, which mostly means the taking it away from those who have a different complexion or slightly flatter noses than ourselves, is not a pretty thing when you look into it too much" (7). Yet in almost the same breath, Marlow talks about how the British territories colored red on a world map were "good to see at any time because one knows that some real work is done in there"; British colonialists

1. E. J. Glave in *Century Magazine*, September 1897, p. 706.

were "bearers of a spark from the sacred fire" (10,5). Marlow was speaking for Conrad, whose love of his adoptive country knew no bounds: Conrad felt that "liberty . . . can only be found under the English flag all over the world."[2] And at the very time he was denouncing the European lust for African riches in his novel, he was an investor in a gold mine near Johannesburg.

Conrad was a man of his time and place in other ways as well. He was partly a prisoner of what Mark Twain, in a different context, called "the white man's notion that he is less savage than the other savages."[3] *Heart of Darkness* has come in for some justified pummeling in recent years because of its portrayal of black characters, who say no more than a few words. In fact, they don't speak at all: they grunt; they chant; they produce a "drone of weird incantations" and "a wild and passionate uproar"; they spout "strings of amazing words that resembled no sounds of human language . . . like the responses of some satanic litany" (65,36,67). The true message of the book, the Nigerian novelist Chinua Achebe has argued, is: "Keep away from Africa, or else! Mr. Kurtz . . . should have heeded that warning and the prowling horror in his heart would have kept its place, chained to its lair. But he foolishly exposed himself to the wild irresistible allure of the jungle and lo! the darkness found him out.' "[4]

However laden it is with Victorian racism, *Heart of Darkness* remains the greatest portrait in fiction of Europeans in the Scramble for Africa. When Marlow says goodbye to his aunt before heading to his new job, "she talked about 'weaning those ignorant millions from their horrid ways,' till, upon my word, she made me quite uncomfortable. I ventured to hint that the Company was run for profit" (12).[5] Conrad's white men go about their rape of the continent in the belief that they are uplifting the natives, bringing civilization, serving "the noble cause."

All these illusions are embodied in the character of Kurtz. He is both a murderous head collector and an intellectual, "an emissary of . . . science and progress" (25). He is a painter, the creator of "a

2. Frances B. Singh, "The Colonialistic Bias of *Heart of Darkness*," *Conradiana* 10 (1978): 41–54.
3. Mark Twain, *More Tramps Abroad* (London: Chatto & Windus, 1897), pp. 137–38.
4. Chinua Achebe, "An Image of Africa," *The Massachusetts Review* 18 (1977): 792. [In this Norton Critical Edition. Editor]
5. The biggest profiteer, King Leopold II, does not appear in *Heart of Darkness*, although he does in *The Inheritors*, the lesser novel that Conrad later co-authored with Ford Madox Ford. One of its central characters is the heavily bearded Duc de Mersch, who controls the Greenland Protectorate. The duc's Society for the Regeneration of the Arctic Regions is dedicated to uplifting the benighted Eskimos by bringing them a railway, proper clothes, and other benefits of civilization. The duc has invested in an English newspaper in an attempt to buy favorable press coverage of his "philanthropic" activities. "We have," he says, "protected the natives, have kept their higher interests ever present in our minds." The Greenland of the novel is rich in oil and gold.

small sketch in oils" (25) of a woman carrying a torch that Marlow finds at the Central Station. And he is a poet and journalist, the author of, among other works, a seventeen-page report—"vibrating with eloquence . . . a beautiful piece of writing" (49–50)—to the International Society for the Suppression of Savage Customs. At the end of this report, filled with lofty sentiments, Kurtz scrawls in a shaky hand: "Exterminate all the brutes!" (50).

In Kurtz's intellectual pretensions, Conrad caught one telling feature of the white penetration of the Congo, where conquest by pen and ink so often confirmed the conquest by rifle and machine gun, Ever since Stanley shot his way down the Congo River and then promptly wrote a two-volume best-seller, ivory collectors, soldiers, and explorers had tried to imitate him—in books, and in thousands of articles for the geographical society journals and magazines about colonial exploration that were as popular in the late nineteenth century as the *National Geographic* is in the United States today. It was as if the act of putting Africa on paper were the ultimate proof of the superiority of European civilization. This aspect of Kurtz is yet another reason to suspect that, in creating him, Conrad was partly inspired by Léon Rom. Rom * * * was a budding entomologist. He was also a painter; when not collecting butterflies or human heads, he did portraits and landscapes, of which five survive in a Belgian museum today. Most interesting of all, he was a writer.

In 1899, Rom, by then back in Belgium, published a book of his own. *Le Nègre du Congo* is an odd little volume—jaunty, arrogant, and sweepingly superficial. Short chapters cover "Le Nègre en général," the black woman, food, pets, native medicine, and so on. Rom was an enthusiastic hunter who jubilantly posed for one photo atop a dead elephant, and his chapter on hunting is as long as those on Congolese religious beliefs, death rituals, and chiefly succession combined.

The voice we hear in Rom's book is very much like the voice in which we might imagine Mr. Kurtz writing his report to the International Society for the Suppression of Savage Customs. Of *la race noire*, Rom says, "The product of a mindless state, its feelings are coarse, its passions rough, its instincts brutish, and, in addition, it is proud and vain. The black man's principal occupation, and that to which he dedicates the greatest part of his existence, consists of stretching out on a mat in the warm rays of the sun, like a crocodile on the sand. . . . The black man has no idea of time, and, questioned on that subject by a European, he generally responds with something stupid."

There is much more in this vein. When Rom describes, for example, the Congolese conscripted to work as porters, he says they enjoyed themselves splendidly. As a caravan sets off in the morning, the porters all bustle noisily about, each one eagerly wanting "to succeed in finding a place in line of his choice, for example beside a friend with whom he can trade dreams of the previous night or elaborate the menu, more or less varied and delicious, of the meal they will have at the next stop."

At some point while he was in the Congo, Rom must have begun planning his book. Did Rom, finding that Conrad spoke perfect French, confide in him his literary dreams? Did Conrad see one of Rom's paintings on the wall at Leopoldville, just as Marlow sees one of Kurtz's? Or was it sheer coincidence that the real head-collector Rom and the imaginary head-collector Kurtz were both painters and writers? We will never know.

There are several other tantalizing parallels between Léon Rom and Mr. Kurtz. In the novel, Kurtz succeeds in "getting himself adored" (57) by the Africans of the Inner Station: chiefs crawl on the ground before him, the people obey him with slavish devotion, and a beautiful black woman apparently is his concubine. In 1895, a disapproving Force Publique lieutenant confided to his diary a strikingly similar situation involving a fellow officer:

> He makes his agents *starve* while he gives lots of food to the black women of his harem (for he wants to act like a great Arab chief). . . . Finally, he got into his dress uniform at his house, brought together his women, picked up some piece of paper and pretended to read to them that the king had named him the big chief and that the other whites of the station were only small fry. . . . He gave fifty lashes to a poor little negress because she wouldn't be his mistress, then he *gave* her to a soldier.

What is significant is how the diarist introduces his account of the officer: "This man wants to play the role of a second Rom."[6]

Finally, the murderousness of Kurtz seems to echo one other detail about Rom. When Rom was station chief at Stanley Falls, the governor general sent a report back to Brussels about some agents who "have the reputation of having killed masses of people for petty reasons." He mentions Rom's notorious flower bed ringed with human heads, and then adds: "He kept a gallows permanently erected in front of the station!"[7]

We do not know whether Rom was already acting out any of these dreams of power, murder, and glory when Conrad passed

6. Louis Leclerq, "Les carnets de campagne de Louis Leclerq. Étude de mentalité d'un colonial belge," ed. Pierre Salmon, *Revue de l'Université de Bruxelles* Nouvelle Serié 3 (February–April 1970): 264.
7. Quoted in Jules Marchal, *L'État Libre du Congo: Paradis Perdu. L'Histoire du Congo 1876–1900* (Borgloon, Belgium: Éditions Paula Bellings, 1996), 1: 298.

through Leopoldville in 1890 or whether he only talked of them. Whatever the case, the moral landscape of *Heart of Darkness* and the shadowy figure at its center are the creations not just of a novelist but of an open-eyed observer who caught the spirit of a time and place with piercing accuracy.

ALAN SIMMONS

[Conrad, Casement, and the Congo Atrocities]†

What facts do we know of the Africa experiences of Conrad and Casement? We know a little of the history of their meeting in the Congo. In his "The Congo Diary," Conrad records their meeting at Matadi, in June 1890, thus: "Made the acquaintance of Mr. Roger Casement, which I should consider as a great pleasure under any circumstances and now it becomes a positive piece of luck. Thinks, speaks well, most intelligent and sympathetic."[1]

For his part, Casement, too, recalled Conrad with fondness. In a letter to E. D. Morel, dated 23 October 1903, Casement wrote: "Conrad is a charming man—gentle, kind and sympathetic."[2]

Conrad's diary reveals that he arrived at Matadi, from Boma, on 13th June 1890 and that he left again, for Kinshasa, on 28th June 1890, when, he records, he "Parted with Casement in a very friendly manner." In a letter to Quinn, dated 24 May 1916, Conrad recalls that Casement

> knew the coast languages well. I went with him several times on short expeditions to hold "palavers" with neighbouring village-chiefs. The object of them was procuring porters for the

† From "The Language of Atrocity: Representing the Congo of Conrad and Casement," *Conrad in Africa: New Essays on "Heart of Darkness,"* ed. Attie de Lange and Gail Fincham (New York: Columbia UP, 2002), pp. 85–106. Unless indicated, notes are the author's.

1. Joseph Conrad, *Congo Diary and Other Uncollected Pieces*, ed. Zdzisław Najder (New York: Doubleday, 1978), p. 7. [In this Norton Critical Edition. Editor] It is a fine historical irony that Conrad and Casement, whose work would contribute to the demise of the Congo Free State, should meet in 1890, the year that, according to Barbara Emerson, "marked what was probably the zenith of Leopold II's reputation" (*Leopold II of the Belgians: King of Colonialism* [London: Weidenfeld and Nicholson, 1979], 150): it was the twenty-fifth anniversary of Leopold's accession to the Belgian throne and marked by celebrations in his honour; it was the year of the Brussels Anti-Slavery Conference (November 1889 to July 1890), as a result of which Leopold won the right to levy import duties in the Congo Free State, ostensibly to furnish him with the means to challenge the slave trade; and, in the Spring, Stanley had published his widely-reported encomium proclaiming to the Belgians that "if royal greatness consists in the wisdom and goodness of a sovereign leading his people with the solicitude of a shepherd watching over his flock, then the greatest sovereign is your own" (quoted in Emerson, 149).

2. Letter from Roger Casement to E. D. Morel, dated 23 October 1903 LSE Manuscript Library, "Morel Papers F8/16: Roger Casement 1899–1904."

Company's caravans from Matadi to Leopoldville—or rather to Kinchassa [sic] (on Stanley Pool). Then I went up into the interior to take up my command of the stern-wheeler "Roi des Belges" and he, apparently, remained on the coast.[3]

It is tempting to infer from this that Conrad's bilingual entries in his diary owe something to Casement and that he learnt enough Kikongo words from Casement to cope on the march inland.

Conrad's Congo experience lasted about six months; Casement's experience of Africa, by comparison, spans nearly twenty years, ending in October 1903 when he left his consulate at Boma, from which vantage point he had compiled the evidence to substantiate his Report, which came before the British Parliament in 1904.[4] Both men were profoundly affected by their Congo experiences. In her diary, Lady Ottoline Morrell records that, during her first visit to Conrad, "He spoke of the horrors of the Congo, from the moral and physical shock of which he said he had never recovered."[5] Conrad also told Edward Garnett: "before the Congo I was a mere animal."[6] For his part, Casement records: "In these lonely Congo forests where I found Leopold, I found also myself, an incorrigible Irishman."[7] The separate but comparable views of Africa of the two men found an outlet in their writings: drawing on his Congo experiences, Conrad wrote his Congo Diary; the short story, "An Outpost of Progress"; the novella, "Heart of Darkness"; and the essay, "Geography and Some Explorers." Casement's writings about his experiences are of two sorts: first, there are his official reports to Whitehall, the most famous of which is his Congo Report, written in late 1903 and early 1904, and published in February 1904; and, second, there are his letters publicizing the Congo atrocities and inspiring Edmund Dene Morel, the founder and editor of the *West African Mail*, to set up the Congo Reform Association in March 1904. Casement was eager to enlist Conrad's assistance to the

3. Joseph Conrad, *Collected Letters*, ed. Frederick R. Karl and Laurence Davies (Cambridge: Cambridge UP, 1983–1996), 5:596–97.
4. The report was published on 15 February 1904, having been edited by the Foreign Office against the wishes of Casement, who argued that they had issued "a cooked and garbled report" which "By suppressing evidences of sincerity and altering dates (or suppressing them rather) and omitting names . . . has certainly rendered the task of the Brussels people to confute me easier than it would otherwise have been." (Letter from Roger Casement to Harry Farnhall, dated 20 February 1904. PRO reference FO 10/808.) An unedited copy of the original was used by the commission of enquiry which investigated conditions in the Congo, between October 1904 and February 1905, and which confirmed Casement's findings. It was, effectively, this confirmation that led to the Congo being gradually wrested from Leopold II's grasp by Belgium over the next three years.
5. Ottoline Morrell, *Memoirs: A Study in Friendship, 1873–1915*, ed. R. Gathorne Hardy (New York: Faber and Faber, 1964).
6. Quoted in Jocelyn Baines, *Joseph Conrad: A Critical Biography* (London: Weidenfeld, 1993), p. 119.
7. Quoted in Michael Taussig, *Shamanism, Colonialism, and the Wild Man: A Study in Terror and Healing* (Chicago: Chicago UP, 1987), p. 19.

cause of the Congo Reform Association, writing to Morel from Loanda, on 23 October 1903:

> Another man who might be of help (in [a] literary way) is Joseph Conrad the author of some excellent English—a Pole, a seaman and an ex-Congo traveller. I knew him well—and he knows something of the Congo—indeed one or two of his shorter stories—such as "The Heart of Darkness" deal with his own view of Upper Congo life.[8]

Casement, who was collecting documentary evidence from eye-witnesses of the Belgian cruelty, concludes the letter saying that Conrad "will, I hope, move his pen when I see him at home." For his part, in a letter to Casement, dated 21 December 1903, Conrad writes: "It is an extraordinary thing that the conscience of Europe which seventy years ago has put down the slave trade on humanitarian grounds tolerates the Congo State today. It is as if the moral clock had been put back many hours." This letter concludes: "Once more my best wishes go with you on your crusade. Of course You may make any use you like of what I write to you" (*Collected Letters*, 3:96–97).

At this point it is tempting to identify the two men, via their mutual detestation of the atrocities being carried out in the Congo, with the movement for reform which was steadily gathering momentum. But their accounts suggest that the men saw different things whilst in the Congo, so, we need to ask: *who* saw *what*, and *when*?

Casement's report to Parliament, in 1904, on conditions in the Congo Free State contained accounts of mutilation of the local natives perpetrated by the Colonial administration. According to Ford Madox Ford, Casement was "driven mad by the horrors that he had there witnessed": "I myself have seen in the hands of Sir Roger Casement who had smuggled them out of the country, the hands and feet of Congolese children which had been struck off by Free State officials, the parents having failed to bring in their quota of rubber or ivory."[9]

Such atrocities provided the impetus for the founding of the Congo Reform Association by Edmund Morel in 1904, encouraged by Casement. Casement's crusade led him to solicit eye-witness accounts of conditions in the Congo both to add momentum to the Reform Movement and to counter the mis-information campaign being waged by the Belgian authorities, who were arguing that mutilation was a native, rather than a state, practice.

8. LSE Manuscript Library, "Morel Papers F8/16: Roger Casement 1899–1904." Casement's reference to Conrad's novella as "*The* Heart of Darkness" suggests that he read it in serial form in *Blackwood's Magazine*.
9. Ford Madox Ford, *A History of Our Own Times*, ed. Solon Beinfeld and Sondra Stang (Manchester: Carcanet, 1989), pp. 122n, 126n.

One of the people to whom Casement appealed for a testament was Joseph Conrad, whose reply, in a letter of 17 December 1903, initially confirms that such mutilation was not a native practice: "During my sojourn in the interior, keeping my eyes and ears well open too, I've never heard of the alleged custom of cutting off hands amongst the natives; and I am convinced that no such custom ever existed along the whole course of the main river to which my experience is limited" (*Collected Letters*, 3:95).

But Conrad's letter goes on to deny the practice among the State troops too:

> Neither in the casual talk of the white men nor in the course of definite inquiries as to the tribal customs was ever such a practice hinted at; certainly not among the Bangalas who at that time formed the bulk of the State troops. My informants were numerous, of all sorts—and many of them possessed of abundant knowledge. (95)

The date here is important: Conrad's letter to Casement is written in December 1903. On 20 May 1903, in response to reports of atrocities against the labourers working to collect rubber in the Congo, the British Government sent its consul, Roger Casement, on a fact-finding mission; these findings were recorded in Casement's Congo report, written in late 1903 and published in February 1904. Edmund Morel recalls his first meeting with Roger Casement in December 1903 and being told "the story of a vile conspiracy against civilization."[1] Since the atrocities to which Casement is responding are those he sees in 1903, and Conrad's experience is limited to a period thirteen years previously, it is tempting to argue that this is a relatively recent practice and leave it there. But there are inconsistencies in the responses of both men.

First of all, Casement's letters and reports from his various visits to Africa themselves bear witness to a profound change in his own attitude towards the Africans. Here, for instance, is part of the report he wrote to the Acting Consul-General in 1894, whilst surveying an area of the Niger Coast Protectorate with a view to building a road and securing labour for the purpose:

> My view of these people may be the wrong one, but I believe their dislike to the white man getting into their country is founded far less on their fears of the harm we may do them, than on the dread of the good we may do them.
>
> Our ways are not their ways. They have made evil their good; they cling to their cruelties and superstitions, their *idion* crowns, and symbols of fetish power, to their right to buy and

1. William Roger Louis and Jean Stenger, eds., *E. D. Morel's "History of the Congo Reform Movement"* (Oxford: Oxford UP, 1968), p. 161.

sell man; to the simple emblems as well as to the substantial advantages of a savage life, and claim to practice on another's body, the cruel punishments which, as they themselves say, from the beginning of the world existed, despite the white man or his laws. To all such, the coming of the "consul" means "red ruin and the breaking up of laws," as our roads into their midst, and the good we seek to do them are equally hateful, for both foreshadow the end of their own power to do after the fashion of their fathers.[2]

Not only does this hint at mutilation among the natives, but Casement's colonial attitude here leads one to suspect that there may well have been practices to which he was simply insensitive at this period. * * *

Conrad's reaction to the mutilations is even more ambiguous. Just a week after writing his letter to Casement denying the existence of mutilation, Conrad wrote [a] letter to Cunninghame Graham * * *, in which he says of Casement that "He could tell you things! Things I've tried to forget; things I never did know" (*Collected Letters*, 3:102). The suggestion of events too painful to revisit leads one to wonder whether the "unspeakable rites" in "Heart of Darkness" have their source in the mutilations against which Casement inveighed.

This issue of mutilation—and Conrad's reaction to it—extends to the relationship between the character of Fresleven in "Heart of Darkness" and his real-life counterpart, Johannes Freiesleben. In the novella, Marlow learns that his predecessor was killed over a quarrel with a village chief. When Marlow goes to recover Fresleven's remains, he discovers that these have simply been left where he fell:

> Afterwards nobody seemed to trouble much about Fresleven's remains, till I got out and stepped into his shoes. I couldn't let it rest, though; but when an opportunity offered at last to meet my predecessor, the grass growing through his ribs was tall enough to hide his bones. They were all there. (*Heart of Darkness*, 9).

Fresleven's original, Johannes Freiesleben, was indeed killed over a quarrel with natives in the Congo, aged twenty-nine, on 29 January 1890. Intriguingly, one contemporary report of this incident, the diary entry of the Congo missionary George Grenfell for 4 March 1890, whilst corroborating the unburied month-old corpse also mentions its mutilation: "Lingerji says the murdered man is still unburied—his hands and feet have been cut off—his clothes

2. Report dated 4 July 1894 (Public Record Office reference: FO881/6546).

taken away and his body covered with a native cloth."[3] Given this corroboration, Conrad's reticence about this mutilation (Fresleven's bones "were all there") calls into question his denial to Casement in the letter quoted above.

"Heart of Darkness" contains another reference to mutilation in the heads on stakes which surround Kurtz's hut and which provide evidence of his barbarity. Is this based on fact or fiction? Among the papers of the missionary, Doctor William Holman Bentley (whose letters confirm both Casement's recruitment to the mission, on 29 November 1888, and the end of his term of employment, on 29 April 1889), there is a sketch he made whilst in the Congo of a hut on whose roof is a pile of human skulls.[4]

Reports of how the *Force Publique* officer, Léon Rom, ornamented the flower bed in front of his house with twenty-one human skulls, appeared in *The Century Magazine* in Glave's diary (and were repeated in the *Saturday Review* of 17 December 1898). Glave records:

> The state soldiers are constantly stealing, and sometimes the natives are so persecuted, they resent this by killing and eating their tormentors. Recently the state post on the Lomani lost two men killed and eaten by the natives. Arabs were sent to punish the natives; many women and children were taken and twenty-one heads were brought to the Falls and have been used by Captain Rom as a decoration around the flower bed of his house![5]

Conrad may well have read a version of this "ornamentation" in the *Saturday Review*. Hochschild even speculates that Conrad and Rom might have met when Conrad passed through Leopoldville, as Rom was the station chief there at the time.

The point remains, though, that, if such evidence of mutilation was available at the time of their shared stay in the Congo, why didn't Casement respond some ten years earlier than he did to the plight of the natives? And, if this evidence was not available, is the picture of the Congo that Conrad paints in "Heart of Darkness" painted from life or painted from the reports of atrocities then beginning to circulate? Perhaps the way out of this dilemma can be found in the idea of language itself. Marlow's description of the rites over which Kurtz presides as "unspeakable" suggests that lan-

3. Quoted in Norman Sherry, *Conrad's Western World* (Cambridge: Cambridge UP, 1971), p. 18.
4. Baptist Missionary Archives, William Holman Bentley papers. Reference: Box A34. The Baptist Missionary Archives are housed at the Angus Library, Regent's Park College, Oxford.
5. Quoted in Sven Lindqvist, *Exterminate All the Brutes* (London: Granta, 1997), pp. 28–29.

guage is inadequate to communicate what he witnesses. But Conrad and Casement's differing versions of their Congo experiences are reflected in different kinds of writing for very different audiences: Casement's factual Congo Report is intended for Parliament whilst Conrad's fictional account in "Heart of Darkness" is intended for the marketplace. Their approaches meant that Conrad could sublimate in metaphor the facts that Casement had to confront directly. These different registers raise the question: what is the language of atrocity?

In the macabre ornamentation around Kurtz's hut, "Heart of Darkness" contains an obvious example of mutilation which, I have claimed, appears to have its basis in fact. The novella also contains references to cannibalism. As the literary examples of Juvenal, Montaigne, and others have demonstrated, the imputation of cannibalism is often fuelled by an ethnic agenda: what *they* do is inadmissible among *us*. The very etymology of the word "cannibal," coined by Christopher Columbus from the name of the Carib natives of the Caribbean, reveals its racist origins. In "Heart of Darkness," Marlow is haunted by the call to which Kurtz succumbs. In a much-quoted passage, Marlow refers to the troubling sense of kinship he feels with what he sees as a savage residue of himself—troubling, presumably, because of the threat this identification poses for his civilized self-definition. It is against this backdrop of anxiety that we must read the possible connection between cannibalism and the "unspeakable rites."

The most obvious example of cannibalism is provided by Marlow's crew, "men one could work with" (*Heart of Darkness*, 34). Their supply of rotten hippo-meat thrown overboard by the "pilgrims," the crew are left with "a few lumps of some stuff like half-cooked dough, of a dirty lavender colour" (41). According to Albert Guerard, "Conrad here operates through ambiguous suggestion (are the lumps human flesh?)."[6] The fact that Marlow goes on to comment that the crew "now and then swallowed a piece . . . but so small that it seemed done more for the looks of the thing than for any serious purpose of sustenance" (41) is interpreted by Reynold Humphries as meaning that this food "has a *ritual* function only to fulfil."[7] In terms of social rites, the debasement of the religious rationale for the colonial venture (through the platitudes of Marlow's aunt and the pilgrims themselves) extends naturally to the parody of the Eucharist in the references to cannibalism.

What of the "unspeakable rites" themselves? What is it that

6. Albert J. Guerard, *Conrad the Novelist* (Cambridge: Harvard UP, 1958), p. 35 [See selection in this Norton Critical Edition. Editor]
7. Reynold Humphries, "Restraint, Cannibalism, and the 'Unspeakable Rites' in 'Heart of Darkness,' " *L'Epoque Conradienne* 1990, 52–78.

makes them "unspeakable" and heads on stakes not? The narrative mixture of denial and evasion in the presentation of Kurtz's cannibalism, if this is what it is, may keep these "rites" hidden, but their "unspeakable" nature is of a piece with the expression of cultural anxieties elsewhere in "Heart of Darkness": the African workers on the steamship are defined as cannibals and yet are not allowed to perform any act of cannibalism; by contrast Kurtz may well have done the deed but can't be described as a cannibal. A complicated and evasive semiotics acts here as a kind of resistance to the act which will trouble the European sense of self as civilized.

In its evasiveness, Marlow's narrative enacts the dilemma of representing "atrocity" generally: what *is* the language to communicate that of which we can't speak? Is there a "rhetoric of the unsayable"? Casement's report on the atrocities committed against the Africans in the Congo—like his subsequent report on the atrocities committed against the Putumayo Indians in South America—resulted from his being sent on a spying mission to establish the veracity of reports and rumours which were beginning to circulate, despite the barrage of State-motivated mis-information. As Frederick Karl puts it: "There are . . . really three Congos: Leopold's, which operated behind intricate disguises and deceptions; Casement's which was close to the reality; and Conrad's, which fell midway between the other two, as he attempted to penetrate the veil and yet was anxious to retain the hallucinatory quality."[8]

But why shouldn't the earlier reports of atrocities, whether emanating from the Congo or the Putumayo basin, have been believed in the first place? E. D. Morel writes that "The struggle in England against the misrule of the Congo state really dates from September, 1896, when the Aborigines Protection Society, tired of making representations to the authorities in Brussels, appealed to the British Government. Its appeal fell on deaf ears."[9] But, even so, in the light of, say, Williams's open letter to Leopold II in 1890, why did it take until 1896 for this "struggle . . . against misrule" to emerge?[1] Whilst one accepts the need for eye-witness evidence of the type that Casement painstakingly gathered at the cost of his own peace of mind, and even accepting that the propaganda machine of Leopold II was formidable, I wonder if a part of the reason for disbelieving these reports lies simply in their stark blatancy. How does one communicate horrors of this degree? Isn't any factual account

8. Frederick R. Karl, *Joseph Conrad: The Three Lives* (London: Faber and Faber, 1989), p. 286.
9. Edmund D. Morel, *King Leopold's Rule in Africa* (London: William Heinemann, 1904), p. ix. [See the selection in this Norton Critical Edition. Editor]
1. See Williams's letter to King Leopold in this Norton Critical Edition. [Editor]

of them doomed to be disbelieved because civilized society has no context for it? Michael Taussig's argument about the present day seems helpful here:

> Today, faced with the ubiquity of torture, terror, and the growth of armies, we in the New World are assailed with new urgency. There is the effort to understand terror, in order to make *others* understand. Yet the reality at stake here makes a mockery of understanding and derides rationality. . . . What sort of understanding—what sort of speech, writing, and construction of meaning by any mode—can deal with and subvert that?[2]

The question of what constitutes authenticity and what constitutes authority when trying to understand the Congo and Putumayo atrocities is at issue here. What is involved in the issue of authenticity? Surely not simply factual reporting, as the reports which first circulated, like Hardenburg's findings in Putumayo, were thought too extreme to be believed.[3] In other words, when communicating atrocities, a discourse is required that is capable of conveying the "unspeakable" truth without sounding exaggerated or preposterous. It is not only that which is true but also that which can be believed that concerns us. And I feel that the contribution of "Heart of Darkness" to the reform movement may lie, ultimately, in helping to create the context and the conditions for believing the tales of atrocity coming out of the Congo precisely because the scale of the "horror" to which it alludes cannot be adequately conveyed through facts anyway.

If we learn anything from the factual evidence available to us about conditions in the Congo Free State it is that *everyone* is implicated in the atrocities to some degree. Casement's concern with establishing that the Belgians were solely responsible for the mutilations is limited precisely because it reduces the atrocities to a contrast between us and them. * * * What existed in the Congo Free State was on such a scale that it offers no moral point of fixity, uncontaminated by the atrocities, from which to pass judgement. How can one record the scale of horror if no-one associated with the atrocities—not even the missionary onlookers who know but remain silent—can be said to be innocent? Compounding this problem, in his recent attempt to trace the seeds of the Holocaust to

2. Taussig, p. 9.
3. In response to his experiences in the Amazon basin, Walter Hardenburg, an American engineer, wrote a series of articles entitled "The Devil's Paradise: A British Owned Congo" which were published in *Truth* magazine in 1909. In response to the public outcry these aroused, the British Government sent Casement, then stationed at Rio de Janeiro, to the Putumayo as its consular representative (see Taussig, 21–9).

European colonial policy in the nineteenth century, in *Exterminate All the Brutes*, Sven Lindqvist argues that the supremacist views of the so-called civilized nations induced a kind of tacit "atrocity blindness" to what was happening in the Congo: "Officially, of course, it was denied. But man to man, everyone knew. That is why Marlow can tell his story as he does in Conrad's novel. He has no need to count up the crimes Kurtz committed. He has no need to describe them. He has no need to produce evidence. For no-one doubted it."[4]

* * *

In his letter to Roger Casement of 21 December 1903, Conrad expresses his revulsion against the conditions in the Congo: * * *

> It is an extraordinary thing that the conscience of Europe which seventy years ago has put down the slave trade on humanitarian grounds tolerates the Congo State to day. It is as if the moral clock had been put back many hours . . . in 1903, seventy five years or so after the abolition of the slave trade (because it was cruel) there exists in Africa a Congo State, created by the act of European Powers where ruthless systematic cruelty towards the blacks is the basis of administration, and bad faith towards all other states the basis of commercial policy. (*Collected Letters*, 3:95)

This letter was used by the Congo Reform Movement in its campaign to bring to public awareness what was happening in the Congo. It was published in the "Special Congo Supplement" to the *West African Mail* in November 1904 (p. 208), in the pages devoted to "Opinions and Testimonies of the Month," under the heading "Views of Joseph Conrad." Morel quoted the letter again in his book *King Leopold's Rule in Africa*, as the conclusion to the penultimate section, entitled "The Congo Debate in the Belgian House of Representatives." Here, he introduced the letter with the words:

> I do not think I can more fittingly close this review of the famous Belgian debate than by giving the following quotation—which I am permitted to do—from a letter written a few weeks ago by Mr. Joseph Conrad to a personal friend. In it the well-known author, who has lived in the Upper Congo, expresses in a few admirable sentences the feeling which all who have studied King Leopold's rule in Africa share with him.[5]

An unidentified review of Morel's book in the *Morning Post* of 12 October 1904 claimed: "At present there are many persons who share the sentiments of Mr. Joseph Conrad, the distinguished nov-

4. Lindqvist, pp. 171–72.
5. Morel, p. 351.

elist, whose views on King Leopold's rule in Africa Mr. Morel is enabled to quote. Mr. Conrad has served on the Upper Congo, and his opinions have, therefore, the value which must attach to impressions based on the personal observations of a singularly acute student of human nature." Conrad's importance to the Congo Reform Association extended beyond his "testament" to his physical presence. For instance, its advertisement for a public meeting to be held at the Holborn Town Hall on 7 June 1905 concludes: "Several other members of Parliament, it is anticipated, will be present, and it is hoped that Mr. Joseph Conrad, who has had personal experience of the system of administration in the Congo basin, will also be able to attend." The report of this meeting does not list Conrad's name among those present.[6] We recall that in Conrad's letter to Cunninghame Graham, dated 26 December 1903, he had excused himself saying: "I would help him but it is not in me. I am only a wretched novelist inventing wretched stories and not even up to that miserable game" (*Collected Letters*, 3:102). Even allowing for the fact that, at this time, Conrad was wrestling with *Nostromo*, "the most anxiously meditated of [his] longer novels" ("Author's Note"), this excuse seems rather excessive for, as I have just argued, by his words, his presence, and his contacts, he is helping.

His real contribution, though, is "Heart of Darkness" itself. In his review of the tale, Edward Garnett called it "a page torn from the life of the Dark Continent—a page which has been hitherto carefully blurred and kept away from human eyes."[7] Morel too praises the novel's factual contribution, calling it a "powerful picture of Congo life."[8] In his "Preface" to "Heart of Darkness," written in 1917, Conrad described it as "experience pushed a little (and only very little) beyond the actual facts of the case for the perfectly legitimate, I believe, purpose of bringing it home to the minds and bosoms of the readers."[9] This relationship between the facts of the Congo atrocities and the fictional form in which Conrad presents them seems to me to be the essence of the novel's contribution to the debate. * * *

Conrad's contribution to the movement for reform in the Congo is precisely the provision of [a] (fictionalised) context which enabled the subsequent transmission of uncomfortable facts. As such, I feel that his fictional account and Casement's factual report are continuous, part of the same continuum. Jeremy Harding points to the inter-textual nature of Conrad's and Casement's texts on the

6. See "Special Congo Supplement," *West African Mail* (June 1905), 318–22.
7. Edward Garnett, unsigned review, *Academy and Literature*, 6 December 1902, 606. [See selection in this Norton Critical Edition. Editor]
8. Morel, p. 174.
9. Conrad, Preface to *Youth* in this edition. [Editor]

Congo when he writes: "It is hard to grasp Marlow's tone of sour incredulity without some acquaintance with Casement's Congo, perhaps the best factual account of its day and impossible to know how far the intuitive disgust of 'Heart of Darkness' played its part, in the growth of an effective dissenting position in Britain on European pillage and brutality in the Free State."[1]

Morel is even more convinced about the influence of Conrad. Writing to Conan Doyle on 7 October 1909, he called "Heart of Darkness" simply "the most powerful thing ever written on the subject."

---

1. Jeremy Harding, "The Greater Hero of the Congo," *Times Literary Supplement* 24 (May 1996).

THE CIVILIZING MISSION

Allegorical representation that identifies King Leopold with Europe's colonial mission of bringing civilization to Africa.
Le Congo Illustré 2 (1893): 80

Congo Free State, 1890

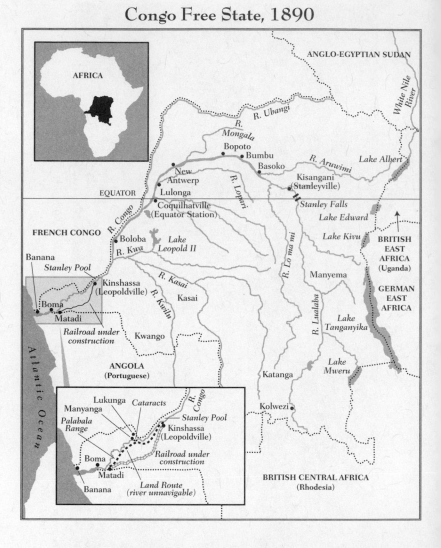

Surrounded by colonies of the major European powers, the so-called Congo Free State was ruled by King Leopold II of Belgium as his private domain. In 1890, Conrad traveled on foot from Matadi to Kinshassa and then by steamer to Stanley Falls, where the Congo River became unnavigable. Illness and a feud with his superiors thwarted his hope to command a steamer on the Kasai River.

YOUNG CONRAD

Photograph of Joseph Conrad before his trip to the Congo in 1890.

196

The steamship *Roi des Belges*, on which Conrad served as second in command and (briefly) captain, photographed on the Sankuru River in the Congo.

Alexandre Delcommune, *Vingt années de Vie africaine* (Brussels: Ferdinand Larcier, 1922). Courtesy of General Research & Reference Division, Schomburg Center for Research in Black Culture. The New York Public Library, Astor, Lenox, and Tilden Foundations.

Conrad's steamer, the *Roi des Belges*, at anchor on the banks of the Upper Congo River in 1889, the year before his journey to Africa.

VILLAGERS VISITING THE STEAMER

Natives from a village on the Kasai River, a tributary of the Congo, visiting the *Roi des Belges* in 1888.

Alexandre Delcommune, *Vingt années de Vie africaine* (Brussels: Ferdinand Larcier, 1922). Courtesy of General Research and Reference Division, Schomburg Center for Research in Black Culture. The New York Public Library, Astor, Lenox, and Tilden Foundations.

FLEENG FROM THE STEAM WHISTLE

A scene reminiscent of Marlow's departure from the Inner Station: "I pulled the string of the whistle. . . . I pulled the string time after time. They broke and ran, they leaped, they crouched, they swerved, they dodged the flying terror of the sound." Marlow's aim is to prevent a massacre, but the intent of the steamer "Peace" depicted here seems to belie its name.

Hermann von Wissman, *My Second Journey through Equatorial Africa from the Congo to the Zambesi in the Years 1886 and 1887*, trans. Minna J. A. Bergmann (London: Chatto and Windus, 1891).

AN ABANDONED STATION

A photograph taken in 1889 of an old, decaying station of the Congo Free State at Coquilhatville (also known as "Equator" because of its location), a village on the Congo River that Conrad passed through a year later on his way to Stanley Falls.

Alexandre Delcommune, *Vingt années de Vie africaine* (Brussels: Ferdinand Larcier, 1922). Courtesy of General Research and Reference Division, Schomburg Center for Research in Black Culture. The New York Public Library, Astor, Lenox, and Tilden Foundations.

GOVERNOR-GENERAL'S INSPECTION

Officials of the Congo Free State conducting an inspection of native militia at Stanley Falls, the "Inner Station" of *Heart of Darkness*. Albert Chapaux, *Le Congo historique, diplomatique, physique, politique, économique, humanitaire et colonial* (Brussels, 1894).

202

CONSTRUCTING THE RAILWAY

A railroad had to be built from Matadi to Kinshassa to circumvent rapids that made the Congo River impassable between its mouth and Stanley Pool, where steamships could begin the journey upriver.

Norman Sherry, *Conrad and His World* (London: Thames & Hudson, 1972). Courtesy of Norman Sherry and Thames & Hudson.

"PRISONERS"

Forced laborers, presumably for constructing the railway, and their Zanzibari guards, in a picture taken at Boma, the port at the confluence of the Congo River with the Atlantic.

Edmund D. Morel, *King Leopold's Rule in Africa* (London: Heinemann, 1904), p. 192.

204

PUNISHMENT

A whip known as the *chicotte*, made of hippopotamus hide, being used by a native guard on a "prisoner."

Regions Beyond [a London missionary periodical]. Courtesy of Anti-Slavery International.

HANDS

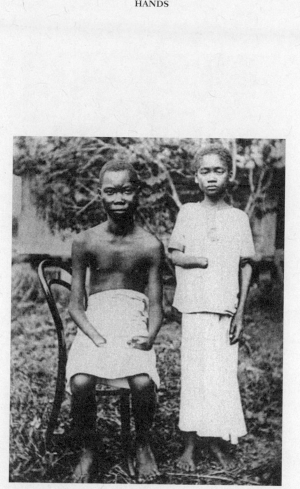

Two youths of the Equator district who have lost their hands through different kinds of colonial brutality. Mola, the boy who is seated had his hands bound so tightly that they were lost to gangrene. Yoka, the boy who is standing had his right hand cut off by soldiers who, in a practice common in Leopold's domain, were required to present a hand for every bullet they used as evidence of an "enemy" killed.

Courtesy of Anti-Slavery International.

AN IVORY CARAVAN

Before the construction of the railway, a caravan gathers at Stanley Pool to take ivory by land to Matadi, where it would be loaded on ships.

Le Congo Illustré 2 (1893): 43.

SPOILS OF EMPIRE

Rubber and ivory, the two most highly prized products of the Congo, collected for transport at a state depot on the Upper Congo.

Sir Harry Johnston, *George Grenfell and the Congo* (London: Hutchinson and Co., 1908), 1:446.

Nineteenth-Century Attitudes toward Race

G. W. F. HEGEL

[The African Character]†

The peculiarly African character is difficult to comprehend, for the very reason that in reference to it, we must quite give up the principle which naturally accompanies all *our* ideas—the category of Universality. In Negro life the characteristic point is the fact that consciousness has not yet attained to the realization of any substantial objective existence—as for example, God, or Law—in which the interest of man's volition is involved and in which he realizes his own being. This distinction between himself as an individual and the universality of his essential being, the African in the uniform, undeveloped oneness of his existence has not yet attained; so that the Knowledge of an absolute Being, an Other and a Higher [Power] than his individual self, is entirely wanting. The Negro, as already observed, exhibits the natural man in his completely wild and untamed state. We must lay aside all thought of reverence and morality—all that we call feeling—if we would rightly comprehend him; there is nothing harmonious with humanity to be found in this type of character. The copious and circumstantial accounts of Missionaries completely confirm this, and Mahommedanism appears to be the only thing which in any way brings the Negroes within the range of culture. The Mahommedans too understand better than the Europeans, how to penetrate into the interior of the country.

The grade of culture which the Negroes occupy may be more nearly appreciated by considering the aspect which *Religion* presents among them. That which forms the basis of religious concep-

† From *Philosophy of History* (1830–31), trans. J. Sibree (New York: Dover, 1956), pp. 93–99. Reprinted with the permission of Dover Publications, Inc. Hegel (1770–1831), German idealist philosopher, author of *The Phenomenology of Mind* (1807), viewed cultures as stages in the historical unfolding of the absolute. Notes are the Editor's.

tions is the consciousness on the part of man of a Higher Power—even though this is conceived only as a *vis naturæ*[1]—in relation to which he feels himself a weaker, humbler being. Religion begins with the consciousness that there is something higher than man. But even Herodotus[2] called the Negroes sorcerers:—now in *Sorcery* we have not the idea of a God, of a moral faith; it exhibits man as the highest power, regarding him as alone occupying a position of command over the power of Nature. We have here therefore nothing to do with a spiritual adoration of God, nor with an empire of Right. God thunders, but is not on that account recognized as God. For the soul of man, God must be more than a thunderer, whereas among the Negroes this is not the case. Although they are necessarily conscious of dependence upon nature—for they need the beneficial influence of storm, rain, cessation of the rainy period, and so on—yet this does not conduct them to the consciousness of a Higher Power: it is they who command the elements, and this they call "magic." The Kings have a class of ministers through whom they command elemental changes, and every place possesses such magicians, who perform special ceremonies, with all sorts of gesticulations, dances, uproar, and shouting, and in the midst of this confusion commence their incantations. * * *

[F]rom the fact that man is regarded as the Highest, it follows that he has no respect for himself; for only with the consciousness of a Higher Being does he reach a point of view which inspires him with real reverence. For if arbitrary choice is the absolute, the only substantial objectivity that is realized, the mind cannot in such be conscious of any Universality. The Negroes indulge, therefore, that perfect *contempt* for humanity, which in its bearing on Justice and Morality is the fundamental characteristic of the race. They have moreover no knowledge of the immortality of the soul, although spectres are supposed to appear. The undervaluing of humanity among them reaches an incredible degree of intensity. Tyranny is regarded as no wrong, and cannibalism is looked upon as quite customary and proper. Among us instinct deters from it, if we can speak of instinct at all as appertaining to man. But with the Negro this is not the case, and the devouring of human flesh is altogether consonant with the general principles of the African race; to the sensual Negro, human flesh is but an object of sense—mere flesh. At the death of a King hundreds are killed and eaten; prisoners are butchered and their flesh sold in the markets; the victor is accustomed to eat the heart of his slain foe. When magical rites are performed, it frequently happens that the sorcerer kills the first that

---

1. Power of nature (Latin).
2. Herodotus (484?–425? B.C.E.), Greek historian.

comes in his way and divides his body among the bystanders. Another characteristic fact in reference to the Negroes is Slavery. Negroes are enslaved by Europeans and sold to America. Bad as this may be, their lot in their own land is even worse, since there a slavery quite as absolute exists; for it is the essential principle of slavery, that man has not yet attained a consciousness of his freedom, and consequently sinks down to a mere Thing—an object of no value. Among the Negroes moral sentiments are quite weak, or more strictly speaking, non-existent. Parents sell their children, and conversely children their parents, as either has the opportunity. Through the pervading influence of slavery all those bonds of moral regard which we cherish towards each other disappear, and it does not occur to the Negro mind to expect from others what we are enabled to claim. The polygamy of the Negroes has frequently for its object the having many children, to be sold, every one of them, into slavery; and very often naïve complaints on this score are heard, as for instance in the case of a Negro in London, who lamented that he was now quite a poor man because he had already sold all his relations. In the contempt of humanity displayed by the Negroes, it is not so much a despising of death as a want of regard for life that forms the characteristic feature. To this want of regard for life must be ascribed the great courage, supported by enormous bodily strength, exhibited by the Negroes, who allow themselves to be shot down by thousands in war with Europeans. Life has a value only when it has something valuable as its object.

Turning our attention in the next place to the category of *political constitution*, we shall see that the entire nature of this race is such as to preclude the existence of any such arrangement. The standpoint of humanity at this grade is mere sensuous volition with energy of will; since universal spiritual laws (for example, that of the morality of the Family) cannot be recognized here. Universality exists only as arbitrary subjective choice. The political bond can therefore not possess such a character as that free laws should unite the community. There is absolutely no bond, no restraint upon that arbitrary volition. Nothing but external force can hold the State together for a moment. A ruler stands at the head, for sensuous barbarism can only be restrained by despotic power. But since the subjects are of equally violent temper with their master, they keep him on the other hand within limits. Under the chief there are many other chiefs with whom the former, whom we will call the King, takes counsel, and whose consent he must seek to gain, if he wishes to undertake a war or impose a tax. In this relation he can exercise more or less authority, and by fraud or force can on occasion put this or that chieftain out of the way. Besides this the Kings have other specified prerogatives. Among the

Ashantees the King inherits all the property left by his subjects at their death. In other places all unmarried women belong to the King, and whoever wishes a wife, must buy her from him. If the Negroes are discontented with their King they depose and kill him. * * * Accompanying the King we constantly find in Negro States, the executioner, whose office is regarded as of the highest consideration, and by whose hands, the King, though he makes use of him for putting suspected persons to death, may himself suffer death, if the grandees desire it.

Fanaticism, which, notwithstanding the yielding disposition of the Negro in other respects, can be excited, surpasses, when roused, all belief. An English traveller states that when a war is determined on in Ashantee, solemn ceremonies precede it: among other things the bones of the King's mother are laved with human blood. As a prelude to the war, the King ordains an onslaught upon his own metropolis, as if to excite the due degree of frenzy. The King sent word to the English Hutchinson: "Christian, take care, and watch well over your family. The messenger of death has drawn his sword and will strike the neck of many Ashantees; when the drum sounds it is the death signal for multitudes. Come to the King, if you can, and fear nothing for yourself." The drum beat, and a terrible carnage was begun; all who came in the way of the frenzied Negroes in the streets were stabbed. On such occasions the King has all whom he suspects killed, and the deed then assumes the character of a sacred act. Every idea thrown into the mind of the Negro is caught up and realized with the whole energy of his will; but this realization involves a wholesale destruction. These people continue long at rest, but suddenly their passions ferment, and then they are quite beside themselves. The destruction which is the consequence of their excitement, is caused by the fact that it is no positive idea, no thought which produces these commotions;—a physical rather than a spiritual enthusiasm. In Dahomey, when the King dies, the bonds of society are loosed; in his palace begins indiscriminate havoc and disorganization. All the wives of the King (in Dahomey their number is exactly 3,333) are massacred, and through the whole town plunder and carnage run riot. The wives of the King regard this their death as a necessity; they go richly attired to meet it. The authorities have to hasten to proclaim the new governor, simply to put a stop to massacre.

From these various traits it is manifest that want of self-control distinguishes the character of the Negroes. This condition is capable of no development or culture, and as we see them at this day, such have they always been. The only essential connection that has existed and continued between the Negroes and the Europeans is that of slavery. In this the Negroes see nothing unbecoming them,

and the English who have done most for abolishing the slave-trade
and slavery, are treated by the Negroes themselves as enemies. For
it is a point of first importance with the Kings to sell their captured
enemies, or even their own subjects; and viewed in the light of such
facts, we may conclude *slavery* to have been the occasion of the increase of human feeling among the Negroes. The doctrine which
we deduce from this condition of slavery among the Negroes, and
which constitutes the only side of the question that has an interest
for our inquiry, is that which we deduce from the Idea: viz. that the
"Natural condition" itself is one of absolute and thorough injustice—contravention of the Right and Just. Every intermediate grade
between this and the realization of a rational State retains—as
might be expected—elements and aspects of injustice; therefore we
find slavery even in the Greek and Roman States, as we do serfdom
down to the latest times. But thus existing in a State, slavery is itself a phase of advance from the merely isolated sensual existence—a phase of education—a mode of becoming participant in a
higher morality and the culture connected with it. Slavery is in and
for itself *injustice*, for the essence of humanity is *Freedom*; but for
this man must be matured. The gradual abolition of slavery is
therefore wiser and more equitable than its sudden removal.

At this point we leave Africa, not to mention it again. For it is no
historical part of the World; it has no movement or development to
exhibit. Historical movements in it—that is in its northern part—belong to the Asiatic or European World. Carthage displayed there an
important transitory phase of civilization; but, as a Phœnician
colony, it belongs to Asia. Egypt will be considered in reference to
the passage of the human mind from its Eastern to its Western
phase, but it does not belong to the African Spirit. What we properly
understand by Africa, is the Unhistorical, Undeveloped Spirit, still
involved in the conditions of mere nature, and which had to be presented here only as on the threshold of the World's History.

*   *   *

CHARLES DARWIN

On the Races of Man†

The question whether mankind consists of one or several species
has of late years been much discussed by anthropologists, who are

† From *The Descent of Man* (1871; rpt. Adelaide, Australia: U of Adelaide Library, 1998
[electronic version]), chapter 7. Darwin (1809–82), English naturalist, laid out the theory of evolution through "natural selection" in *The Origin of Species* (1859). Unless indicated, notes are the author's.

divided into the two schools of monogenists and polygenists.[1]
Those who do not admit the principle of evolution, must look at
species as separate creations, or in some manner as distinct enti-
ties; and they must decide what forms of man they will consider as
species by the analogy of the method commonly pursued in ranking
other organic beings as species. But it is a hopeless endeavour to
decide this point, until some definition of the term "species" is generally accepted; and the definition must not include an indetermi-
nate element such as an act of creation. We might as well attempt
without any definition to decide whether a certain number of
houses should be called a village, town, or city. We have a practical
illustration of the difficulty in the never-ending doubts whether
many closely-allied mammals, birds, insects, and plants, which represent each other respectively in North America and Europe,
should be ranked as species or geographical races; and the like
holds true of the productions of many islands situated at some little
distance from the nearest continent.

Those naturalists, on the other hand, who admit the principle of
evolution, and this is now admitted by the majority of rising men,
will feel no doubt that all the races of man are descended from a
single primitive stock; whether or not they may think fit to desig-
nate the races as distinct species, for the sake of expressing their
amount of difference. With our domestic animals the question
whether the various races have arisen from one or more species is
somewhat different. Although it may be admitted that all the races,
as well as all the natural species within the same genus, have
sprung from the same primitive stock, yet it is a fit subject for discussion, whether all the domestic races of the dog, for instance,
have acquired their present amount of difference since some one
species was first domesticated by man; or whether they owe some
of their characters to inheritance from distinct species, which had
already been differentiated in a state of nature. With man no such
question can arise, for he cannot be said to have been domesticated
at any particular period.

* * *

Although the existing races of man differ in many respects, as in
colour, hair, shape of skull, proportions of the body, &c., yet if their
whole structure be taken into consideration they are found to resemble each other closely in a multitude of points. Many of these
are of so unimportant or of so singular a nature, that it is extremely
improbable that they should have been independently acquired by
aboriginally distinct species or races. The same remark holds good

1. Those who believe that human beings descend from a single origin (Darwin's view that
humans evolved from apes) or from many different species. [Editor]

with equal or greater force with respect to the numerous points of mental similarity between the most distinct races of man. The American aborigines, Negroes and Europeans are as different from each other in mind as any three races that can be named; yet I was incessantly struck, whilst living with the Feugians on board the *Beagle*, with the many little traits of character, shewing how similar their minds were to ours; and so it was with a full-blooded negro with whom I happened once to be intimate.

He who will read Mr. Tylor's and Sir J. Lubbock's interesting works[2] can hardly fail to be deeply impressed with the close similarity between the men of all races in tastes, dispositions and habits. This is shown by the pleasure which they all take in dancing, rude music, acting, painting, tattooing, and otherwise decorating themselves; in their mutual comprehension of gesture-language, by the same expression in their features, and by the same inarticulate cries, when excited by the same emotions. This similarity, or rather identity, is striking, when contrasted with the different expressions and cries made by distinct species of monkeys. There is good evidence that the art of shooting with bows and arrows has not been handed down from any common progenitor of mankind, yet as Westropp and Nilsson have remarked,[3] the stone arrowheads, brought from the most distant parts of the world, and manufactured at the most remote periods, are almost identical; and this fact can only be accounted for by the various races having similar inventive or mental powers. The same observation has been made by archaeologists[4] with respect to certain widely-prevalent ornaments, such as zig-zags, &c.; and with respect to various simple beliefs and customs, such as the burying of the dead under megalithic structures. I remember observing in South America,[5] that there, as in so many other parts of the world, men have generally chosen the summits of lofty hills, to throw up piles of stones, either as a record of some remarkable event, or for burying their dead.

Now when naturalists observe a close agreement in numerous small details of habits, tastes, and dispositions between two or more domestic races, or between nearly-allied natural forms, they use this fact as an argument that they are descended from a common progenitor who was thus endowed; and consequently that all

2. Tylor's *Early History of Mankind*, 1865: with respect to gesture-language, see p. 54. Lubbock's *Prehistoric Times*, 2nd ed., 1869.
3. "On Analogous Forms of Implements," in *Memoirs of Anthropological Society* by H. M. Westropp. *The Primitive Inhabitants of Scandinavia*, Eng. translat., edited by Sir J. Lubbock, 1868, p. 104.
4. Westropp "On Cromlechs," &c., *Journal of Ethnological Soc.*, as given in *Scientific Opinion*, June 2, 1869, p. 3.
5. During his voyage as a naturalist on the *Beagle* (1831–36), during which he made the observations and gathered the evidence on which he based his theory of evolution. [Editor]

should be classed under the same species. The same argument may
be applied with much force to the races of man.

As it is improbable that the numerous and unimportant points of
resemblance between the several races of man in bodily structure
and mental faculties (I do not here refer to similar customs) should
all have been independently acquired, they must have been inherited from progenitors who had these same characters. We thus gain
some insight into the early state of man, before he had spread step
by step over the face of the earth. The spreading of man to regions
widely separated by the sea, no doubt, preceded any great amount
of divergence of character in the several races; for otherwise we
should sometimes meet with the same race in distinct continents;
and this is never the case. Sir J. Lubbock, after comparing the arts
now practised by savages in all parts of the world, specifies those
which man could not have known, when he first wandered from his
original birthplace; for if once learnt they would never have been
forgotten.[6] He thus shews that "the spear, which is but a development of the knife-point, and the club, which is but a long hammer,
are the only things left." He admits, however, that the art of making
fire probably had been already discovered, for it is common to all
the races now existing, and was known to the ancient cave-
inhabitants of Europe. Perhaps the art of making rude canoes or
rafts was likewise known; but as man existed at a remote epoch,
when the land in many places stood at a very different level to what
it does now, he would have been able, without the aid of canoes, to
have spread widely. Sir J. Lubbock further remarks how improbable
it is that our earliest ancestors could have "counted as high as ten,
considering that so many races now in existence cannot get beyond
four." Nevertheless, at this early period, the intellectual and social
faculties of man could hardly have been inferior in any extreme degree to those possessed at present by the lowest savages; otherwise
primeval man could not have been so eminently successful in the
struggle for life, as proved by his early and wide diffusion.

From the fundamental differences between certain languages,
some philologists have inferred that when man first became widely
diffused, he was not a speaking animal; but it may be suspected
that languages, far less perfect than any now spoken, aided by gestures, might have been used, and yet have left no traces on subsequent and more highly-developed tongues. Without the use of
some language, however imperfect, it appears doubtful whether
man's intellect could have risen to the standard implied by his dominant position at an early period. Whether primeval man, when he
possessed but few arts, and those of the rudest kind, and when his

6. *Prehistoric Times*, 1869, p. 574.

power of language was extremely imperfect, would have deserved to be called man, must depend on the definition which we employ. In a series of forms graduating insensibly from some ape-like creature to man as he now exists, it would be impossible to fix on any definite point where the term "man" ought to be used. But this is a matter of very little importance. So again, it is almost a matter of indifference whether the so-called races of man are thus designated, or are ranked as species or sub-species; but the latter term appears the more appropriate. Finally, we may conclude that when the principle of evolution is generally accepted, as it surely will be before long, the dispute between the monogenists and the polygenists will die a silent and unobserved death.

*   *   *

If * * * we look to the races of man as distributed over the world, we must infer that their characteristic differences cannot be accounted for by the direct action of different conditions of life, even after exposure to them for an enormous period of time. The Esquimaux live exclusively on animal food; they are clothed in thick fur, and are exposed to intense cold and to prolonged darkness; yet they do not differ in any extreme degree from the inhabitants of southern China, who live entirely on vegetable food, and are exposed almost naked to a hot, glaring climate. The unclothed Fuegians[7] live on the marine productions of their inhospitable shores; the Botocudos of Brazil wander about the hot forests of the interior and live chiefly on vegetable productions; yet these tribes resemble each other so closely that the Fuegians on board the *Beagle* were mistaken by some Brazilians for Botocudos. The Botocudos again, as well as the other inhabitants of tropical America, are wholly different from the Negroes who inhabit the opposite shores of the Atlantic, are exposed to a nearly similar climate, and follow nearly the same habits of life.

Nor can the differences between the races of man be accounted for by the inherited effects of the increased or decreased use of parts, except to a quite insignificant degree. Men who habitually live in canoes, may have their legs somewhat stunted; those who inhabit lofty regions may have their chests enlarged; and those who constantly use certain sense-organs may have the cavities in which they are lodged somewhat increased in size, and their features consequently a little modified. With civilized nations, the reduced size of the jaws from lessened use—the habitual play of different muscles serving to express different emotions—and the increased size of the brain from greater intellectual activity, have together produced a considerable effect on their general appearance when

7. Inhabitants of Tierra del Fuego, islands off the southern tip of South America. [Editor]

compared with savages.[8] Increased bodily stature, without any corresponding increase in the size of the brain, may (judging from the previously adduced case of rabbits), have given to some races an elongated skull of the dolichocephalic type.

Lastly, the little-understood principle of correlated development has sometimes come into action, as in the case of great muscular development and strongly projecting supra-orbital ridges. The colour of the skin and hair are plainly correlated, as is the texture of the hair with its colour in the Mandans of North America.[9] The colour also of the skin, and the odour emitted by it, are likewise in some manner connected. With the breeds of sheep the number of hairs within a given space and the number of excretory pores are related.[1] If we may judge from the analogy of our domesticated animals, many modifications of structure in man probably come under this principle of correlated development.

We have now seen that the external characteristic differences between the races of man cannot be accounted for in a satisfactory manner by the direct action of the conditions of life, nor by the effects of the continued use of parts, nor through the principle of correlation. We are therefore led to enquire whether slight individual differences, to which man is eminently liable, may not have been preserved and augmented during a long series of generations through natural selection. But here we are at once met by the objection that beneficial variations alone can be thus preserved; and as far as we are enabled to judge, although always liable to err on this head, none of the differences between the races of man are of any direct or special service to him. The intellectual and moral or social faculties must of course be excepted from this remark. The great variability of all the external differences between the races of man, likewise indicates that they cannot be of much importance; for if important, they would long ago have been either fixed and preserved, or eliminated. In this respect man resembles those forms, called by naturalists protean or polymorphic, which have remained extremely variable, owing, as it seems, to such variations being of an indifferent nature, and to their having thus escaped the action of natural selection.

* * *

8. See Prof. Schaaffhausen, translat., in *Anthropological Review*, Oct., 1868, p. 429.
9. Mr. Catlin states (*N. American Indians*, 3rd ed., 1842, vol. i., p. 49) that in the whole tribe of the Mandans, about one in ten or twelve of the members, of all ages and both sexes, have bright silvery grey hair, which is hereditary. Now this hair is as coarse and harsh as that of a horse's mane, whilst the hair of other colours is fine and soft.
1. On the odour of the skin, Godron, *De l'Espece*, tom. ii., p. 217. On the pores of the skin, Dr. Wilckens, *Die Aufgaben der Landwirth. Zootechnik*, 1869, s. 7.

ALFRED RUSSEL WALLACE

[Are Humans One Race or Many?]†

Let us first see what each party has to say for itself. In favour of
the unity of mankind it is argued, that there are no races without
transitions to others; that every race exhibits within itself variations
of colour, of hair, of feature, and of form, to such a degree as to
bridge over, to a large extent, the gap that separates it from other
races. It is asserted that no race is homogeneous; that there is a
tendency to vary; that climate, food, and habits produce, and render permanent, physical peculiarities, which, though slight in the
limited periods allowed to our observation, would, in the long ages
during which the human race has existed, have sufficed to produce
all the differences that now appear. It is further asserted that the
advocates of the opposite theory do not agree among themselves;
that some would make three, some five, some fifty or a hundred
and fifty species of man; some would have had each species created
in pairs, while others require nations to have at once sprung into
existence, and that there is no stability or consistency in any doctrine but that of one primitive stock.

The advocates of the original diversity of man, on the other hand,
have much to say for themselves. They argue that proofs of change
in man have never been brought forward except to the most trifling
amount, while evidence of his permanence meets us everywhere.
The Portuguese and Spaniards, settled for two or three centuries in
South America, retain their chief physical, mental, and moral characteristics; the Dutch boers at the Cape, and the descendants of
the early Dutch settlers in the Moluccas, have not lost the features
or the colour of the Germanic races; the Jews, scattered over the
world in the most diverse climates, retain the same characteristic
lineaments everywhere; the Egyptian sculptures and paintings show
us that, for at least 4000 or 5000 years, the strongly contrasted features of the Negro and the Semitic races have remained altogether
unchanged; while more recent discoveries prove, that the mound-
builders of the Mississippi valley, and the dwellers on Brazilian
mountains, had, even in the very infancy of the human race, some
traces of the same peculiar and characteristic type of cranial formation that now distinguishes them.

If we endeavour to decide impartially on the merits of this difficult controversy, judging solely by the evidence that each party has

---

† From *Natural Selection: A Series of Essays* (London: Macmillan, 1870), pp. 303–31. Wallace (1823–1913), English naturalist, independently developed a theory, similar to Darwin's, of evolution through natural selection.

brought forward, it certainly seems that the best of the argument is on the side of those who maintain the primitive diversity of man. Their opponents have not been able to refute the permanence of existing races as far back as we can trace them, and have failed to show, in a single case, that at any former epoch the well marked varieties of mankind approximated more closely than they do at the present day. At the same time this is but negative evidence. A condition of immobility for four or five thousand years, does not preclude an advance at an earlier epoch, and—if we can show that there are causes in nature which would check any further physical change when certain conditions were fulfilled—does not even render such an advance improbable, if there are any general arguments to be adduced in its favour. Such a cause, I believe, does exist; and I shall now endeavour to point out its nature and its mode of operation.

* * *

In order to answer these questions, we must consider why it is that "natural selection" acts so powerfully upon animals; and we shall, I believe, find, that its effect depends mainly upon their self-dependence and individual isolation. A slight injury, a temporary illness, will often end in death, because it leaves the individual powerless against its enemies. If an herbivorous animal is a little sick and has not fed well for a day or two, and the herd is then pursued by a beast of prey, our poor invalid inevitably falls a victim. So, in a carnivorous animal, the least deficiency of vigour prevents its capturing food, and it soon dies of starvation. There is, as a general rule, no mutual assistance between adults, which enables them to tide over a period of sickness. Neither is there any division of labour; each must fulfil *all* the conditions of its existence, and, therefore, "natural selection" keeps all up to a pretty uniform standard.

But in man, as we now behold him, this is different. He is social and sympathetic. In the rudest tribes the sick are assisted, at least with food; less robust health and vigour than the average does not entail death. Neither does the want of perfect limbs, or other organs, produce the same effects as among animals. Some division of labour takes place; the swiftest hunt, the less active fish, or gather fruits; food is, to some extent, exchanged or divided. The action of natural selection is therefore checked; the weaker, the dwarfish, those of less active limbs, or less piercing eyesight, do not suffer the extreme penalty which falls upon animals so defective.

In proportion as these physical characteristics become of less importance, mental and moral qualities will have increasing influence on the well-being of the race. Capacity for acting in concert for protection, and for the acquisition of food and shelter; sympathy, which leads all in turn to assist each other; the sense of right, which checks depredations upon our fellows; the smaller development of the combative and destructive propensities; self-restraint in present appetites; and that intelligent foresight which prepares for the future, are all qualities, that from their earliest appearance must have been for the benefit of each community, and would, therefore, have become the subjects of "natural selection." For it is evident that such qualities would be for the well-being of man; would guard him against external enemies, against internal dissensions, and against the effects of inclement seasons and impending famine, more surely than could any merely physical modification. Tribes in which such mental and moral qualities were predominant, would therefore have an advantage in the struggle for existence over other tribes in which they were less developed, would live and maintain their numbers, while the others would decrease and finally succumb.

*   *   *

Thus man, by the mere capacity of clothing himself, and making weapons and tools, has taken away from nature that power of slowly but permanently changing the external form and structure, in accordance with changes in the external world, which she exercises over all other animals. As the competing races by which they are surrounded, the climate, the vegetation, or the animals which serve them for food, are slowly changing, they must undergo a corresponding change in their structure, habits, and constitution, to keep them in harmony with the new conditions—to enable them to live and maintain their numbers. But man does this by means of his intellect alone, the variations of which enable him, with an unchanged body, still to keep in harmony with the changing universe.

There is one point, however, in which nature will still act upon him as it does on animals, and, to some extent, modify his external characters. Mr. Darwin has shown, that the colour of the skin is correlated with constitutional peculiarities both in vegetables and animals, so that liability to certain diseases or freedom from them is often accompanied by marked external characters. Now, there is every reason to believe that this has acted, and, to some extent, may still continue to act, on man. In localities where certain diseases are prevalent, those individuals of savage races which were subject to them would rapidly die off; while those who were constitutionally free from the disease would survive, and form the progenitors of a new race. These favoured individuals would probably be distinguished by peculiarities of *colour*, with which again peculiarities in the texture or the abundance of *hair* seem to be correlated, and thus may have been brought about those racial differences of colour, which seem to have no relation to mere temperature or other obvious peculiarities of climate.

From the time, therefore, when the social and sympathetic feelings came into active operation, and the intellectual and moral faculties became fairly developed, man would cease to be influenced by "natural selection" in his physical form and structure. As an animal he would remain almost stationary, the changes of the surrounding universe ceasing to produce in him that powerful modifying effect which they exercise over other parts of the organic world. But from the moment that the form of his body became stationary, his mind would become subject to those very influences from which his body had escaped; every slight variation in his mental and moral nature which should enable him better to guard against adverse circumstances, and combine for mutual comfort and protection, would be preserved and accumulated; the better and higher specimens of our race would therefore increase and spread, the lower and more brutal would give way and successively die out, and that rapid advancement of mental organization would occur, which has raised the very lowest races of man so far above the brutes (although differing so little from some of them in physical structure), and, in conjunction with scarcely perceptible modifications of form, has developed the wonderful intellect of the European races.

*　*　*

When the power that had hitherto modified the body had its action transferred to the mind, then races would advance and become improved, merely by the harsh discipline of a sterile soil and inclement seasons. Under their influence, a hardier, a more provident, and a more social race would be developed, than in those regions where the earth produces a perennial supply of vegetable food, and where neither foresight nor ingenuity are required to prepare for the rigours of winter. And is it not the fact that in all ages, and in every quarter of the globe, the inhabitants of temperate have been superior to those of hotter countries? All the great invasions and displacements of races have been from North to South, rather than the reverse; and we have no record of there ever having existed, anymore than there exists to-day, a solitary instance of an indigenous inter-tropical civilization. The Mexican civilization and government came from the North, and, as well as the Peruvian, was established, not in the rich tropical plains, but on the lofty and sterile plateaux of the Andes. The religion and civilization of Ceylon were introduced from North India; the successive conquerors of the Indian peninsula came from the North-west; the northern Mongols conquered the more Southern Chinese; and it was the bold and adventurous tribes of the North that overran and infused new life into Southern Europe.

It is the same great law of "the preservation of favoured races in the struggle for life," which leads to the inevitable extinction of all those low and mentally undeveloped populations with which Europeans come in contact. The red Indian in North America, and in Brazil; the Tasmanian, Australian, and New Zealander in the southern hemisphere, die out, not from any one special cause, but from the inevitable effects of an unequal mental and physical struggle. The intellectual and moral, as well as the physical, qualities of the European are superior; the same powers and capacities which have made him rise in a few centuries from the condition of the wandering savage with a scanty and stationary population, to his present state of culture and advancement, with a greater average longevity, a greater average strength, and a capacity of more rapid increase,— enable him when in contact with the savage man, to conquer in the struggle for existence, and to increase at his expense, just as the better adapted, increase at the expense of the less adapted varieties in the animal and vegetable kingdoms,—just as the weeds of Europe overrun North America and Australia, extinguishing native productions by the inherent vigour of their organization, and by their greater capacity for existence and multiplication.

If these views are correct; if in proportion as man's social, moral, and intellectual faculties became developed, his physical structure would cease to be affected by the operation of "natural selection," we have a most important clue to the origin of races. For it will follow, that those great modifications of structure and of external form, which resulted in the development of man out of some lower type of animal, must have occurred before his intellect had raised him above the condition of the brutes, at a period when he was gregarious, but scarcely social, with a mind perceptive but not reflective, ere any sense of *right* or feelings of *sympathy* had been developed in him. He would be still subject, like the rest of the organic world, to the action of "natural selection," which would retain his physical form and constitution in harmony with the surrounding universe. He was probably at a very early period a dominant race, spreading widely over the warmer regions of the earth as it then existed, and in agreement with what we see in the case of other dominant species, gradually becoming modified in accordance with local conditions. As he ranged farther from his original home, and became exposed to greater extremes of climate, to greater changes of food, and had to contend with new enemies, organic and inorganic, slight useful variations in his constitution would be selected and rendered permanent, and would, on the

principle of "correlation of growth," be accompanied by corresponding external physical changes. Thus might have arisen those striking characteristics and special modifications which still distinguish
the chief races of mankind. The red, black, yellow, or blushing
white skin; the straight, the curly, the woolly hair; the scanty or
abundant beard; the straight or oblique eyes; the various forms of
the pelvis, the cranium, and other parts of the skeleton.

But while these changes had been going on, his mental development had, from some unknown cause, greatly advanced, and had
now reached that condition in which it began powerfully to influence his whole existence, and would therefore become subject to
the irresistible action of "natural selection." This action would
quickly give the ascendency to mind: speech would probably now
be first developed, leading to a still further advance of the mental
faculties; and from that moment man, as regards the form and
structure of most parts of his body, would remain almost stationary.
The art of making weapons, division of labour, anticipation of the
future, restraint of the appetites, moral, social, and sympathetic
feelings, would now have a preponderating influence on his well
being, and would therefore be that part of his nature on which
"natural selection" would most powerfully act; and we should thus
have explained that wonderful persistence of mere physical characteristics, which is the stumbling-block of those who advocate the
unity of mankind.

We are now, therefore, enabled to harmonise the conflicting
views of anthropologists on this subject. Man may have been, indeed I believe must have been, once a homogeneous race; but it
was at a period of which we have as yet discovered no remains, at a
period so remote in his history, that he had not yet acquired that
wonderfully developed brain, the organ of the mind, which now,
even in his lowest examples, raises him far above the highest
brutes;—at a period when he had the form but hardly the nature of
man, when he neither possessed human speech, nor those sympathetic and moral feelings which in a greater or less degree everywhere now distinguish the race. Just in proportion as these truly
human faculties became developed in him, would his physical features become fixed and permanent, because the latter would be of
less importance to his well being; he would be kept in harmony
with the slowly changing universe around him, by an advance in
mind, rather than by a change in body. If, therefore, we are of opinion that he was not really man till these higher faculties were fully
developed, we may fairly assert that there were many originally distinct races of men; while, if we think that a being closely resembling us in form and structure, but with mental faculties scarcely

raised above the brute, must still be considered to have been human, we are fully entitled to maintain the common origin of all mankind.

* * *

FRANCIS GALTON

The Comparative Worth of Different Races†

I have now completed what I had to say concerning the kinships of individuals, and proceed, in this chapter, to attempt a wider treatment of my subject, through a consideration of nations and races.

Every long-established race has necessarily its peculiar fitness for the conditions under which it has lived owing to the sure operation of Darwin's law of natural selection. However, I am not much concerned, for the present, with the greater part of those aptitudes, but only with such as are available in some form or other of high civilization. We may reckon upon the advent of a time when civilization, which is now sparse and feeble and far more superficial than it is vaunted to be, shall overspread the globe. Ultimately it is sure to do so, because civilization is the necessary fruit of high intelligence when found in a social animal, and there is no plainer lesson to be read off the face of Nature than that the result of the operation of her laws is to evoke intelligence in connexion with sociability. Intelligence is as much an advantage to an animal as physical strength or any other natural gift, and therefore, out of two varieties of any race of animal who are equally endowed in other respects, the most intelligent variety is sure to prevail in the battle of life. Similarly, among intelligent animals, the most social race is sure to prevail, other qualities being equal.

Under even a very moderate form of material civilization a vast number of aptitudes acquired through the "survivorship of the fittest" and the unsparing destruction of the unfit, for hundreds of generations, have become as obsolete as the old mail-coach habits and customs, since the establishment of railroads, and there is not the slightest use in attempting to preserve them; they are hin-

† From *Hereditary Genius: An Inquiry into its Laws and Consequences* (1869; rpt. London: Macmillan and Co., 1914). Galton (1822–1911), cousin of Charles Darwin, founder of "eugenics," the study of genetics to improve inherited characteristics. Eugenics was a dominant movement in European and American medicine until the atrocities of Nazi Germany discredited it, but after the discovery of DNA, the potential of genetic manipulation for improving the human condition has once again become a matter of great interest and controversy. On the history of eugenics and the question of whether it is an elaboration or a misapplication of Darwinian theory, see Joseph L. Graves, Jr., *The Emperor's New Clothes: Biological Theories of Race at the Millennium* (New Brunswick: Rutgers UP, 2001), pp. 86–139. Notes are the Editor's.

drances, and not gains, to civilization. I shall refer to some of these a little further on, but I will first speak of the qualities needed in civilized society. They are, speaking generally, such as will enable a race to supply a large contingent to the various groups of eminent men, of whom I have treated in my several chapters. Without going so far as to say that this very convenient test is perfectly fair, we are at all events justified in making considerable use of it, as I will do, in the estimates I am about to give.

In comparing the worth of different races, I shall make frequent use of the law of deviation from an average to which I have already been much beholden; and, to save the reader's time and patience, I propose to act upon an assumption that would require a good deal of discussion to limit, and to which the reader may at first demur, but which cannot lead to any error of importance in a rough provisional inquiry. I shall assume that the *intervals* between the grades of ability are the *same* in all the races—that is, if the ability of class A of one race be equal to the ability of class C in another, then the ability of class B of the former shall be supposed equal to that of class D of the latter, and so on.[1] I know this cannot be strictly true, for it would be in defiance of analogy if the variability of all races were precisely the same; but, on the other hand, there is good reason to expect that the error introduced by the assumption cannot sensibly affect the offhand results for which alone I propose to employ it; moreover, the rough data I shall adduce, will go far to show the justice of this expectation.

Let us, then, compare the Negro race with the Anglo-Saxon, with respect to those qualities alone which are capable of producing judges, statesmen, commanders, men of literature and science, poets, artists, and divines. If the negro race in America had been affected by no social disabilities, a comparison of their achievements with those of the whites in their several branches of intellectual effort, having regard to the total number of their respective populations, would give the necessary information. As matters stand, we must be content with much rougher data.

First, the negro race has occasionally, but very rarely, produced such men as Toussaint l'Ouverture,[2] who are of our class F; that is

1. Galton ranked the cognitive abilities of different so-called races in sixteen classes: seven grades above the mean (A–G), seven below the mean (a–g), and two extremes (X for a genius, x for an imbecile). He assumed that "the comparative worth of races" could be established by determining the equivalences between these scales. For example, he argued that the most intelligent Englishman (class G or X) would be equal to an intelligent Greek, but not the most intelligent (of class F or G), and that both "races" were superior to Negroes (whose G and X equaled only the E and F ranks of English) and Australians (their G and X equaling the Negro F and G). Incredibly, Galton thought the smartest dogs were as intelligent as the "b–a" class of Australian aborigines or the "c–b" rank of Negroes. See Graves, pp. 92–96.
2. François Dominique Toussaint L'Ouverture (1744–1803), leader of the slave rebellion in Haiti.

to say, its X, or its total classes above G, appear to correspond with our F, showing a difference of not less than two grades between the black and white races, and it may be more.

Secondly, the negro race is by no means wholly deficient in men capable of becoming good factors, thriving merchants, and otherwise considerably raised above the average of whites—that is to say, it cannot unfrequently supply men corresponding to our class C, or even D. It will be recollected that C implies a selection of 1 in 16, or somewhat more than the natural abilities possessed by average foremen of common juries, and that D is as 1 in 64—a degree of ability that is sure to make a man successful in life. In short, classes E and F of the negro may roughly be considered as the equivalent of our C and D—a result which again points to the conclusion, that the average intellectual standard of the negro race is some two grades below our own.

Thirdly, we may compare, but with much caution, the relative position of negroes in their native country with that of the travellers who visit them. The latter, no doubt, bring with them the knowledge current in civilized lands, but that is an advantage of less importance than we are apt to suppose. A native chief has as good an education in the art of ruling men as can be desired; he is continually exercised in personal government, and usually maintains his place by the ascendency of his character, shown every day over his subjects and rivals. A traveller in wild countries also fills, to a certain degree, the position of a commander, and has to confront native chiefs at every inhabited place. The result is familiar enough—the white traveller almost invariably holds his own in their presence. It is seldom that we hear of a white traveller meeting with a black chief whom he feels to be the better man. I have often discussed this subject with competent persons, and can only recall a few cases of the inferiority of the white man,—certainly not more than might be ascribed to an average actual difference of three grades, of which one may be due to the relative demerits of native education, and the remaining two to a difference in natural gifts.

Fourthly, the number among the negroes of those whom we should call half-witted men is very large. Every book alluding to negro servants in America is full of instances. I was myself much impressed by this fact during my travels in Africa. The mistakes the negroes made in their own matters were so childish, stupid, and simpleton-like, as frequently to make me ashamed of my own species. I do not think it any exaggeration to say, that their c is as low as our e, which would be a difference of two grades, as before. I have no information as to actual idiocy among the negroes—I mean, of course, of that class of idiocy which is not due to disease.

The Australian type is at least one grade below the African negro. I possess a few serviceable data about the natural capacity of the Australian, but not sufficient to induce me to invite the reader to consider them.

The average standard of the Lowland Scotch and the English North-country men is decidedly a fraction of a grade superior to that of the ordinary English, because the number of the former who attain to eminence is far greater than the proportionate number of their race would have led us to expect. The same superiority is distinctly shown by a comparison of the well-being of the masses of the population; for the Scotch labourer is much less of a drudge than the Englishman of the Midland counties—he does his work better, and "lives his life" besides. The peasant women of Northumberland work all day in the fields, and are not broken down by the work; on the contrary they take a pride in their effective labour as girls, and, when married, they attend well to the comfort of their homes. It is perfectly distressing to me to witness the draggled, drudged, mean look of the mass of individuals, especially of the women, that one meets in the streets of London and other purely English towns. The conditions of their life seem too hard for their constitutions, and to be crushing them into degeneracy.

The ablest race of whom history bears record is unquestionably the ancient Greek, partly because their master-pieces in the principal departments of intellectual activity are still unsurpassed, and in many respects unequalled, and partly because the population that gave birth to the creators of those master-pieces was very small. Of the various Greek sub-races, that of Attica was the ablest, and she was no doubt largely indebted to the following cause for her superiority. Athens opened her arms to immigrants, but not indiscriminately, for her social life was such that none but very able men could take any pleasure in it; on the other hand, she offered attractions such as men of the highest ability and culture could find in no other city. Thus, by a system of partly unconscious selection, she built up a magnificent breed of human animals, which, in the space of one century—viz. between 530 and 430 B.C.—produced the following illustrious persons, fourteen in number:—

Statesmen and Commanders.—Themistocles (mother an alien), Miltiades, Aristeides, Cimon (son of Miltiades), Pericles (son of Xanthippus, the victor at Mycale).

Literary and Scientific Men.—Thucydides, Socrates, Xenophon, Plato.

Poets.—Æschylus, Sophocles, Euripides, Aristophanes.

Sculptor.—Phidias.

*   *   *

It seems to me most essential to the well-being of future generations, that the average standard of ability of the present time should
be raised. Civilization is a new condition imposed upon man by the
course of events, just as in the history of geological changes new
conditions have continually been imposed on different races of animals. They have had the effect either of modifying the nature of the
races through the process of natural selection whenever the changes
were sufficiently slow and the race sufficiently pliant, or of destroying them altogether when the changes were too abrupt or the race
unyielding. The number of the races of mankind that have been entirely destroyed under the pressure of the requirements of an incoming civilization, reads us a terrible lesson. Probably in no former
period of the world has the destruction of the races of any animal
whatever been effected over such wide areas and with such startling
rapidity as in the case of savage man. In the North American Continent, in the West Indian Islands, in the Cape of Good Hope, in Australia, New Zealand, and Van Diemen's Land, the human denizens
of vast regions have been entirely swept away in the short space of
three centuries, less by the pressure of a stronger race than through
the influence of a civilization they were incapable of supporting.
And we too, the foremost labourers in creating this civilization, are
beginning to show ourselves incapable of keeping pace with our own
work. The needs of centralization, communication, and culture, call
for more brains and mental stamina than the average of our race
possess. We are in crying want for a greater fund of ability in all stations of life; for neither the classes of statesmen, philosophers, artisans, nor labourers are up to the modern complexity of their several
professions. An extended civilization like ours comprises more interests than the ordinary statesmen or philosophers of our present race
are capable of dealing with, and it exacts more intelligent work than
our ordinary artisans and labourers are capable of performing. Our
race is over-weighted, and appears likely to be drudged into degeneracy by demands that exceed its powers. If its average ability were
raised a grade or two, our new classes F and G would conduct the
complex affairs of the state at home and abroad as easily as our present F and G, when in the position of country squires, are able to
manage the affairs of their establishments and tenantry. All other
classes of the community would be similarly promoted to the level of
the work required by the nineteenth century, if the average standard
of the race were raised.

When the severity of the struggle for existence is not too great
for the powers of the race, its action is healthy and conservative,
otherwise it is deadly, just as we may see exemplified in the scanty,
wretched vegetation that leads a precarious existence near the sum-

mer snow line of the Alps, and disappears altogether a little higher
up. We want as much backbone as we can get, to bear the racket to
which we are henceforth to be exposed, and as good brains as possible to contrive machinery, for modern life to work more smoothly
than at present. We can, in some degree, raise the nature of a man
to a level with the new conditions imposed upon his existence, and
we can also, in some degree, modify the conditions to suit his nature. It is clearly right that both these powers should be exerted,
with the view of bringing his nature and the conditions of his existence into as close harmony as possible.

* * *

BENJAMIN KIDD

[Social Progress and the Rivalry of the Races]†

* * * Progress is a necessity from which there is simply no escape, and from which there has never been any escape since the
beginning of life. Looking back through the history of life anterior
to man, we find it to be a record of ceaseless progress on the one
hand, and ceaseless stress and competition on the other. This orderly and beautiful world which we see around us is now, and always has been, the scene of incessant rivalry between all the forms
of life inhabiting it—rivalry, too, not chiefly conducted between different species but between members of the same species. The
plants in the green sward beneath our feet are engaged in silent rivalry with each other, a rivalry which if allowed to proceed without
outside interference would know no pause until the weaker were
exterminated. Every part, organ, or quality of these plants which
calls forth admiration for its beauty or perfection, has its place and
meaning in this struggle, and has been acquired to ensure success
therein. The trees of the forest which clothe and beautify the landscape are in a state of nature engaged in the same rivalry with each
other. Left to themselves they fight out, as unmistakable records
have shown, a stubborn struggle extending over centuries in which
at last only those forms most suitable to the conditions of the locality retain their places. But so far we view the rivalry under simple

† From *Social Evolution* (1894; rpt. New York: G. P. Putnam's Sons, 1920), pp. 31–62.
  Kidd (1858–1916), English social thinker associated with Social Darwinism, the attempt to apply the theory of evolution to social change. Social Darwinism owes more to
  Herbert Spencer (1820–1903) than to Darwin, however, who did not view evolution as
  necessarily progressive. For Darwin, evolution is determined by the relative advantages
  of inheritable variants for reproduction or survival, and these say nothing about the relative superiority or inferiority of a species (whatever that may mean). On race and Social
  Darwinism, see Graves, pp. 74–85.

conditions; it is amongst the forms of animal life as we begin to watch the gradual progress upwards to higher types that it becomes many-sided and complex.

* * *

With whatever feelings we may regard the conflict, it is, however, necessary to remember that it is the first condition of progress. It leads continually onwards and upwards. From this stress of nature has followed the highest result we are capable of conceiving, namely, continual advance towards higher and more perfect forms of life. Out of it has arisen every attribute of form, colour, instinct, strength, courage, nobility, and beauty in the teeming and wonderful world of life around us. To it we owe all that is best and most perfect in life at the present day, as well as all its highest promise for the future. The law of life has been always the same from the beginning,—ceaseless and inevitable struggle and competition, ceaseless and inevitable selection and rejection, ceaseless and inevitable progress.

* * *

We watch the Anglo-Saxon overflowing his boundaries, going forth to take possession of new territories, and establishing himself like his ancestors in many lands. A peculiar interest attaches to the sight. He has been deeply affected, more deeply than many others, by the altruistic influences of the ethical system upon which our Western civilisation is founded. He had seen races like the ancient Peruvians, the Aztecs, and the Caribs, in large part exterminated by others, ruthlessly driven out of existence by the more vigorous invader, and he has at least the wish to do better. In the North American Continent, in the plains of Australia, in New Zealand, and South Africa, the representatives of this vigorous and virile race are at last in full possession,—that same race which, with all its faults, has for the most part honestly endeavoured to carry humanitarian principles into its dealings with inferior peoples, and which not improbably deserves the tribute paid to it on this account by Mr. Lecky who counts its "unwearied, unostentatious, and inglorious crusade against slavery" amongst "the three or four perfectly virtuous acts recorded in the history of nations."

Yet neither wish nor intention has power apparently to arrest a destiny which works itself out irresistibly. The Anglo-Saxon has exterminated the less developed peoples with which he has come into competition even more effectively than other races have done in like case; not necessarily indeed by fierce and cruel wars of extermination, but through the operation of laws not less deadly and even more certain in their result. The weaker races disappear before the stronger through the effects of mere contact. The Australian Aboriginal retires before the invader, his tribes dispersed, his hunting-grounds taken from him to be utilised for other purposes. In New Zealand a similar fate is overtaking the Maoris. This people were estimated to number in 1820, 100,000; in 1840 they were 80,000; they are now estimated at 40,000. The Anglo-Saxon, driven by forces inherent in his own civilisation, comes to develop the natural resources of the land, and the consequences appear to be inevitable. The same history is repeating itself in South Africa. In the words used recently by a leading colonist of that country, "the natives must go; or they must work as laboriously to develop the land as we are prepared to do"; the issue in such a case being already determined. In North America we have but a later stage of a similar history. Here two centuries of conflict have left the red men worsted at every point, rapidly dwindling in numbers, the surviving tribes hemmed in and surrounded by forces which they have no power to resist, standing like the isolated patches of grass which have not yet fallen before the knives of the machine-mower in the harvest field.

No motives appear to be able to stay the progress of such movements, humanise them how we may. We often in a self-accusing spirit attribute the gradual disappearance of aboriginal peoples to the effects of our vices upon them; but the truth is that what may be called the virtues of our civilisation are scarcely less fatal than its vices. Those features of Western civilisation which are most distinctive and characteristic, and of which we are most proud, are almost as disastrous in their effects as the evils of which complaint is so often made. There is a certain grim pathos in the remark of the author of a paper on the New Zealand natives, which appeared in the *Journal of the Anthropological Institute* a few years ago, who, amongst the causes to which the decay of the natives might be attributed, mentioned, indiscriminately, drink, disease, European clothing, peace, and wealth. In whatever part of the world we look, amongst civilised or uncivilised peoples, history seems to have taken the same course. Of the Australian natives "only a few remanents of the powerful tribes linger on. . . . All the Tasmanians are gone, and the Maoris will soon be following. The Pacific Islanders are departing childless. The Australian natives as surely are descending to the grave. Old races everywhere give place to the new." There are probably, says Mr. F. Galton, "hardly any spots on the earth that have not within the last few thousand years been tenanted by very different races." Wherever a superior race comes into close contact and competition with an inferior race, the result seems to be much the same, whether it is arrived at by the rude method of wars of conquest, or by the silent process which we see at work in Australia, New Zealand, and the North American Continent, or by the subtle, though no less efficient, method with which science makes us acquainted, and which is in operation in many parts of our civilisation, where extinction works slowly and unnoticed through the earlier marriages, the greater vitality, and the better chance of livelihood of the members of the superior race.

*   *   *

All this, the conflict of races before referred to, the worsting of the weaker, none the less effective even when it is silent and painless, the subordination or else the slow extinction of the inferior, is not a page from the past or the distant [future]; it is all taking place to-day beneath our eyes in different parts of the world, and more particularly and characteristically within the pale of that vigorous Anglo-Saxon cilvilisation of which we are so proud, and which to many of us is associated with all the most worthy ideals of liberty, religion, and government that the race has evolved.

But it is not until we come to draw aside the veil from our civilisation, and watch what is taking place within our borders between the individuals and classes comprising it, that we begin to realise, with some degree of clearness, the nature of this rivalry which compels us to make progress whether we will or not, its tendency to develop in intensity rather than to disappear, and our own powerlessness either to stay its course or to escape its influence. We had, in the conception of the ancient state, as a condition of society in which the struggle for existence was waged, mainly between organised groups rather than between the individuals comprising them, the key to history before the modern period. In the later type of civilisation, the conditions of the rivalry have greatly changed; but if we look closely at what is taking place, we may see that there has been no cessation or diminution of the rivalry itself. On the contrary, the significance of the change has consisted in the tendency to raise it to a higher level, to greatly enlarge its scope and its efficiency as a cause of progress, by bringing all the members of the community into it on more equal terms, and to render it freer and fairer, but, therefore, none the less strenuous.

*   *   *

Looking round at the nations of to-day and noticing the direction in which they are travelling, it seems impossible to escape the conclusion that the progressive peoples have everywhere the same distinctive features. Energetic, vigorous, virile life amongst them is maintained at the highest pitch of which nature is capable. They offer the highest motives to emulation; amongst them the individual is freest, the selection fullest, the rivalry fairest. But so also is the conflict sternest, the nervous friction greatest, and the stress severest. Looking back by the way these nations have come, we find an equally unmistakable absence of these qualities and conditions amongst the competitors they have left behind. From the nations who have dropped out of the race within recent times backwards through history, we follow a gradually descending series. The contrast already to be distinguished between the advancing and the unprogressive peoples of European race is more noticeable when the former are compared with non-European peoples. The difference becomes still more marked when the existence of the careless, shiftless, easily satisfied negro of the United States or West Indies is contrasted with that of the dominant race amongst whom he lives, whose restless, aggressive, high-pitched life he has neither the desire to live nor the capacity to endure.

* * *

These are the first stern facts of human life and progress which we have to take into account. They have their origin not in any accidental feature of our history, nor in any innate depravity existing in man. They result, as we have seen, from deep-seated physiological causes, the operation of which we must always remain powerless to escape. It is worse than useless to obscure them or to ignore them, as is done in a great part of the social literature of the time. The first step towards obtaining any true grasp of the social problems of our day must be to look fairly and bravely in the face these facts which lie behind them.

PETER EDGERLY FIRCHOW

Race, Ethnicity, Nationality, Empire†

Because its alleged endorsement of racism has been the principal charge leveled against *Heart of Darkness* in the heated postcolonial critical debate of the last two decades—followed by the more attenuated charge of really supporting imperialism while seeming to subvert it—it seems advisable and even necessary to first clear the terminological ground before starting off on any discussion as to whether or how or to what degree *Heart of Darkness* is or is not racist and imperialist. This is all the more necessary and advisable because defining terms has not been the practice of all critics who have sought to come to grips with these profoundly controversial aspects of the story. Chinua Achebe, for example, simply assumes that his readers will understand what he means when he refers to *racism* both in the title and elsewhere in his justly celebrated essay "An Image of Africa: Racism in Conrad's *Heart of Darkness*" (1977),

† From *Envisioning Africa: Racism and Imperialism in Conrad's* Heart of Darkness (Lexington: U of Kentucky P, 2000), pp. 1–17. Copyright © 1999 by the University of Kentucky Press. Reprinted with the permission of the publisher. Unless indicated, notes are the author's.

for otherwise he would surely have taken the trouble to tell them what he meant.[1] But his meaning, and that of other critics of the novel, is by no means self-evident, either in terms of our time or in terms of Conrad's. It is after all important to know, as he along with virtually all other critics of Conrad's story apparently does not, that at the time Conrad was writing his novel, the word *racism* did not exist. The nonexistence of the word does not mean, of course, that the phenomenon itself did not exist; it unquestionably did. But it does mean that people then—even specialized and highly trained people in fields like sociology and anthropology—were accustomed to think very differently about the subject of race than we do at the end of the twentieth century. * * *

One reason the word did not exist when Conrad was writing his story is that thinking in terms of race ("race-thinking," as Hannah Arendt calls it in *The Origins of Totalitarianism*) was so widespread and so "normal" in developed countries like England during the late Victorian period that a word like *racism*, which suggests a negative view of thinking about race, was simply not needed and hence not thought of. The first word with these negative connotations is *racialism*, listed in the 1987 Supplement to the *Oxford English Dictionary* as occurring for the first time in 1907; it is defined as the "belief in the superiority of a particular race leading to prejudice and antagonism towards people of other races, esp. those in close proximity who may be felt as a threat to one's cultural and racial integrity or economic well-being." (The first use of "racism" in this sense, according to the same source, does not occur in English until 1936, twelve years after Conrad's death.) Suggestively, the definition of *racialism* given by the *OED* Supplement—particularly the latter part of the definition—is obviously designed to fit encounters among differing racial groups in Western countries, such as Nazi Germany or Fascist Italy, or the interracial conflicts in Britain in the post–World War II period (as the reference to "economic well-being" suggests), and in fact those are the sources of most of the supporting examples. This definition, however, would certainly not have satisfactorily described the "racist" attitudes toward Africans on the part of the very small group of Europeans in the Congo Free State during the 1880s and 1890s (including Conrad), since on the whole they neither felt their culture threatened nor (with a very few exceptions like Tippo Tib, who in any case was usually held to be Arab rather than African) believed that African rivals could seriously or negatively affect their economic status.

Significant, too, is that this definition implicitly (and explicitly in the example cited for 1938) accepts Jews as belonging to a distinct

---

1. See selection in this Norton Critical Edition. [Editor]

race. Here we encounter one of the most important differences between the "race-thinking" of Conrad's time and that of most of the
intervening period, including our own. This difference is profoundly significant, both in itself and for its relevance to any discussion of possible racism in *Heart of Darkness*. In the late
nineteenth century, the word *race* was thought not to refer primarily, as the original *Oxford English Dictionary* (1884–1928) puts it,
to "one of the great divisions of mankind, having certain physical
peculiarities in common." That sense of the word was indeed one
of the possibilities and was made clear by the last of the supporting
examples: "Blumenbach proposed to establish five races: 1st, the
Caucasian; 2cd, the Mongolian; 3rd, the Ethiopian; 4th, the American; 5th, the Malay." Nowadays, with various terminological modi-
fications/modernizations, that is the generally accepted primary
sense of the word *race*. But in the *OED* it ranks only fourth, preceded by the following earlier and evidently more important definitions: (a) "A limited group of persons descended from a common
ancestor; a house, family, kindred"; (b) "A tribe, nation, or people,
regarded as of common stock": and (c) "A group of several tribes or
peoples, forming a distinct ethnical stock." The last of these meanings is especially relevant here, for in the supporting examples reference is made to a "great Hellen [Hellenic] race" and to the
"whole German race." These last senses of the word *race* are no
longer current; by now they have been wholly replaced by terms
like *nation* and *ethnic group*, but for Conrad and his contemporaries they constituted the first and foremost accepted meaning of
race when refering to another ethnic or national group.[2]

In this earlier sense of the word, Conrad is undoubtedly a "racial-
ist," for his fiction deals from the very outset with the complex in-
terrelations, confrontations, and conflicts between and among
representatives (often explicitly seen as *representatives*) of various
national and ethnic (in the old sense of *racial*) groups. In his first
novel, *Almayer's Folly* (1895), for example, which is set in what today is Indonesia, there are several characters of Dutch or mixed
Dutch-Malay ancestry, an Englishman, and a Chinese, as well as
several Moslem and non-Moslem Malays. Other stories and novels
feature prominently Malay, Arab, African (normally seen as belonging to various distinct tribal groups), English, Scottish, Irish,
Dutch, German, French, Belgian, Swedish, Spanish, Italian, Pol-

2. The definitive substitution of the word (and concept) of *race* with that of *ethnic groups*
came relatively late, with the first draft of the UNESCO Statement on Race in 1950.
There, the principal author, Ashley Montagu, denied the biological validity of the concept of race, using instead a phrase first proposed by Julian Huxley in 1935, "ethnic
groups." Montagu did, however, accept that there were three major "subdivisions" within
the species of *homo sapiens*, "the Mongoloid, the Negroid, and the Caucasoid" (quoted
in Pat Shipman, *The Evolution of Racisim* [New York: Simon and Schuster, 1994],
p. 163).

ish, Russian, South American (both creole and indigenous), and North American characters. These figures are not described in an ethnically or nationally unbiased manner. To any careful reader of Conrad's fiction, it must soon become clear that, with certain notable exceptions, Conrad is consistently less well disposed toward German, Russian, Dutch, Belgian, Arab, North American, or Irish characters than he is toward English, Scottish, Malay, or French ones. Such relative (though not always identical) rankings of ethnic collectives were not unusual at this time; the multicolored map that Marlow sees and comments on in *Heart of Darkness* provides a good example of one. In Arthur Conan Doyle's 1913 story "The Poison Belt," a more elaborate as well as ominous scale is worked out whereby the survival of the fittest is described in terms of which ethnic or racial groups are most likely to die of the effects of a mysterious poison; African and Australian aborigines were hypothetically expected to succumb first, Indians would precede Persians, and then would follow Slavs and Teutons, the southern French, and the French from the North. On a more ironic note, Hilaire Belloc, who was of half-French and half-English parentage, put forward in "The Three Races" (1907) a poetic version of the commonly accepted "scientific" division of Europe into three distinct "racial" groupings, usually ranked in the following order: first, the Germanic or Nordic; second, the Celtic or Alpine; and last, the Iberian or Mediterranean:

I

Behold, my child, the Nordic Man
And be as like him as you can.
His legs are long; his mind is slow;
His hair is lank and made of tow.

II

And here we have the Alpine Race.
Oh! What a broad and foolish face!
His skin is of a dirty yellow.
He is a most unpleasant fellow.

III

The most degraded of them all
Mediterranean we call.
His hair is crisp, and even curls,
And he is saucy with the girls.[3]

3. Hilaire Belloc, *Cautionary Tales* (London: Duckworth, 1939), p. 127. English poet, essayist, and historian, Belloc (1870–1953) was a member of Parliament for the Liberal Party when this poem was written. [Editor]

As the popular examples of Doyle and Belloc suggest, Conrad was by no means alone in thinking in stereotypical ways about other national or ethnic groups, though it should be noted that Conrad's fiction tended in this respect to be subtler and more balanced than that of most other writers of the period. (For example, the vile German captain in *Lord Jim* is more than offset by the saintly German merchant, Stein, in the same novel.) Given the many years—half a lifetime, practically—that Conrad had spent wandering the world in ships or being stranded for weeks in remote places in the Pacific, often sharing close quarters with people from a wide variety of national and ethnic backgrounds, it is not surprising that he should seek to reflect this multinational, multiethnic experience in his work. But although Conrad is clearly a special case, much the same can be said of other, rather more sedentary writers who were roughly his contemporaries: Henry James wrote novels that are populated with a congeries of American, British, French, and Italian characters. The same is true of E.M. Forster, whose novels can be, have been, and probably should be read as a series of attempts to break down the absurdities of "race-thinking" (or "ethnic"-thinking) among the British middle class during the early years of this century. Also, viewed from a larger, sociocultural perspective, the phenomenon of the influx of a wide variety of foreigners into English fiction during this period is closely linked not only to the vast expansion of the Empire (of which more later), but also to the beginnings of the tourist industry. Thomas Cook and Son began its immensely successful international travel business in the 1860s with tours to Switzerland and Italy and a decade later had extended its reach to Palestine, Egypt, and points East. In *Lord Jim* Conrad describes a scene in an unnamed Eastern port where a group of tourists is alarmed by a sudden outburst of loud laughter on the part of one of the main characters. Never before had so many people of middle-class origins and middle-class prejudice traveled to such distant places for pleasure or instruction.

Ironically, race-thinking reached a peak in Britain at precisely the moment when large groups of people involved in the military services, colonial administration, the merchant navy, and tourism were encountering other races and ethnic groups in real life for the first time. Their reactions, as documented in the fiction, journalism, travel books, and memoirs of the period, often reflect a hardening rather than an abatement of prejudice, but even when they did result in increased tolerance, it was almost invariably in the context of continued race-thinking. E.M. Forster, for example, depicts with profound sympathy the psychological and emotional conflicts between Germans and English in *Howards End* (1910) and between the English, the Hindus, and the Moslems in *A Passage to India* (1924), but he never abandons his conviction that there are and should continue to be various differing national groups and identities. Race-thinking could be good, as it was in Forster's case, or it could be bad, as in some of Kipling's writing, but it still remained race-thinking.

*   *   *

It should be clear by now that it is formidably difficult to provide a satisfactory definition for either *race* or *racism*—of the former the 1987 *OED* Supplement remarks that it is "often used imprecisely; even among anthropologists there is no generally accepted classification or terminology," an observation that, if true, leads one to wonder what can possibly be meant by "imprecisely" here—but still it is possible to conclude that, whatever racism may be, there are certainly varying degrees of it; furthermore, even the least tinge of it can lead to fatal contamination. In view of all this difficulty, it is perhaps simplest and best to adopt Frank Reeves's suggestion of separating *racism* into three distinct categories: * * * weak racism, medium racism, and strong racism. Weak racism, in this conception, is the belief that races (however defined, including ethnic and national groups) do exist and that they help to account for social phenomena. Medium racism is identical with weak racism, except that added to it is the belief that some races are superior and others are inferior. Strong racism goes beyond medium racism to prescribe a course of action based on alleged racial superiority, such as the suppression or elimination of other "races."[4] Applying Reeves's categories to *Heart of Darkness*, one is led to conclude that the novel is no more than weakly racist with respect to its attitude toward Africans, for it recognizes their difference from Europeans as a separate race but does not suggest an essential superiority to them (it does, however, imply a temporary cultural superiority). With regard to the Belgians, though, the story seems to endorse a medium racist attitude: the British characters in it, to wit Marlow and his audience aboard the *Nellie*, are consistently viewed as superior in intelligence, ability, and honesty to their purely Belgian equivalents. This comparison on Conrad's part seems to have been quite deliberate, since the position of the Director of Companies is roughly equivalent to that of the "great man" in his Brussels sanctuary; that of the Accountant in the Thames estuary corresponds to the Accountant at the Outer Station; and even the Lawyer is later evoked by the Mephistophelean Brickmaker. The essential superiority of the British is also suggested in characters who possess less-well-defined associations with Britain, such as the Russian

4. Frank Reeves, *British Racial Discourse* (Cambridge: Cambridge UP, 1983), pp. 12–14.

who speaks English and reads British books or Kurtz, who had a partly English mother and was educated in Britain. How strongly Marlow at least, if not Conrad, feels contemptuous of Belgians is apparent from his resentment against all of those inhabitants of Brussels who are "hurrying through the streets to filch a little money from each other, to devour their infamous cookery, to gulp their unwholesome beer, to dream their insignificant and silly dreams" (70).

*   *   *

Conrad himself does not use the word *imperialism* in *Heart of Darkness*, not even when Marlow glances at the map of Africa "marked with all the colours of a rainbow" (10), a political rainbow, which shone forth as the direct result of the most infamous imperialist scramble for territory and prestige in history. The closest he comes is the word *colonists*, which he uses by way of contrast with the word *conquerors* when referring to the Roman subjugation of Britain: "They were no *colonists*, their administration was merely a squeeze, and nothing more, I suspect. They were *conquerors*, and for that you want only brute force" (6–7, my italics). Here "colonists" is clearly meant to be thought of favorably and "conquerors" unfavorably. Ironically, of course, the very word *colonist* is of Roman derivation, pointing directly to the fact that Britain was, as the relevant entry in the *OED* observes, divided into nine *coloniae*, of which London was one—"the biggest, and the greatest, town on earth," according to some of the first words in the novel (3). It is difficult to tell here whether Conrad was himself aware of this irony, though his view of the Roman occupation of Britain is in some ways badly skewed. * * * Nevertheless, in general Avrom Fleishman is no doubt right when he observes that Conrad is anticipating the distinction made a few years later in J.A. Hobson's *Imperialism* (1902) "between 'colonialism,' or emigration to relatively unpopulated areas and the establishment of a culture attempting to reproduce that of the home country (e.g. Australia, New Zealand, Canada), and 'imperialism,' in which the settlers form a ruling caste among an overwhelmingly native population."[5] Hobson himself, who consciously avoids using the word in a negative sense, was skeptical about being able to determine the precise meaning of *imperialism* and any related terms. "A certain broad consistency in its relations to other kindred terms," he writes in the introductory chapter of his celebrated work, "is the nearest approach to definition which such a term as Imperialism admits. Nationalism, internationalism, colonialism, are equally elusive, equally shifty, and the

<hr/>

5. Avrom Fleishman, *Conrad's Politics: Community and Anarchy in the Fiction of Joseph Conrad* (Baltimore: Johns Hopkins UP, 1967), p. 98.

changeful overlapping of all four demands the closest vigilance of students of modern politics."[6]

The word *colonialism* is not listed in the original *OED*; and the 1987 Supplement, which does contain an entry for it, provides no definition that even remotely approximates Fleishman's or Hobson's. Instead, it defines the word as "now freq. used in the derogatory sense of an alleged policy of exploitation of backward or weak peoples by a large power." *Imperialism*, on the other hand, is defined in the original *OED* in quite different terms, as either (1) "an imperial system of government; the rule of an emperor, esp. when despotic or arbitrary"—a definition that, unlike the one for *colonialism*, omits any necessity for a foreign presence and focuses entirely on a "system of government," which, logically, cannot be "systematic" if it is at the same time also "arbitrary"; or (2) as "the principle or spirit of empire; advocacy of what are held to be imperial interests. In recent British politics, the principle or policy (1) of seeking, or at least not refusing, an extension of the British Empire in directions where trading interests and investments require the protection of the flag; and (2) of so uniting the different parts of the Empire having separate governments, as to secure that for certain purposes, such as warlike defence, internal commerce, copyright, and postal communication, they shall be practically a single state." The second of these two definitions consists practically by itself of a little essay in British propaganda, omitting all reference to subject peoples and describing the whole phenomenon not only in lofty abstractions but also entirely from the point of view of the rulers. In this respect it differs radically from the definition of *colonialism*. It also fails to account for at least one of the meanings cited among the supporting examples, where the *Daily Chronicle* is quoted as saying in 1898 (the year when Conrad began writing his story) that imperialism was "that odious system of bluster and swagger and might on which Lord Beaconsfield [Disraeli] and his colleagues bestowed the tawdry nickname of Imperialism." This, in fact, is a meaning that comes far closer to Conrad's description of imperialist activities in *Heart of Darkness* than does the official one provided by the *OED*.

More recently, in the entry "Imperialism/Nationalism" written by Seamus Deane for the well-known handbook *Critical Terms for Literary Study*, Conrad is unambiguously described as revealing "the criminal nature of imperialism," though at the same time Deane cites and agrees with Edward Said's verdict that Conrad simultaneously "subverts *and* reproduces imperialism."[7] Deane also makes a

6. John Atkinson Hobson, *Imperialism: A Study*, 3d ed. (1902; London: Unwin Hyman, 1988), p. 3.
7. Seamus Deane, "Imperialism/Nationalism" in *Critical Terms for Literary Study*, 2nd ed., ed. Frank Lentricchia and Thomas McLaughlin (Chicago: U of Chicago P, 1995), pp. 355–56.

distinction between imperialism and colonialism that differs profoundly from Conrad's or Hobson's. "As a system," Deane argues, "imperialism is distinct from colonialism by virtue of its more coherent organizational form and its more fully articulated characterization of itself as a missionary project to the world at large" (354). Imperialism, in other words, is nothing more than a coherently organized and ideologically committed colonialism. This is surely not a distinction that helps us understand Conrad's (or at least Marlow's) preference for colonists over conquerors, nor does it much clarify how Conrad might be reproducing imperialism's missionary project while at the same time subverting it. Rather, Conrad seems to be claiming that there are two kinds of imperialism: one is British and good; another is non-British and, to varying degrees, not good. * * *

* * * At any rate, * * * critics of *Heart of Darkness* should keep in mind that for Conrad all of these words (and where there were as yet no words, the corresponding concepts) did not convey the same meaning(s) to him as they do to us. As far as he was concerned, *race* included *ethnicity* and *nationality*; it was an inclusive word, with none or only a very few of the ominous connotations it was later to assume for a generation living after the Holocaust. And we should bear in mind as well that *imperialism* was not a universal bogeyman but could be both good and bad, depending on what nation was practicing it.

*   *   *

Conrad in the Congo

JOSEPH CONRAD

[Imagining Africa]†

It was in 1868, when nine years old or thereabouts, that while looking at a map of Africa of the time and putting my finger on the blank space then representing the unsolved mystery of that continent, I said to myself with absolute assurance and an amazing audacity which are no longer in my character now:

"When I grow up I shall go *there*."

And of course I thought no more about it till after a quarter of a century or so an opportunity offered to go there—as if the sin of childish audacity was to be visited on my mature head. Yes. I did go there: *there* being the region of Stanley Falls which in '68 was the blankest of blank spaces on the earth's figured surface.

Selected Letters En Route to the Congo

To Aleksander Poradowski‡

> 16th January, 1890
> [letterhead: The British and
> Foreign Transit Agency. Barr,
> Moering & Co., Shipping and
> Custom House Agents, 36,
> Camomile Street, London, E.C.]

My Dear Uncle.

I have just had a letter from Kazimierówka,[1] in which, in reply to my inquiry, Uncle Tadeusz tells me that you are living in Brussels

---

† From Joseph Conrad, *A Personal Record* (London: J. M. Dent & Sons, 1912), p. 13.
‡ From *The Collected Letters of Joseph Conrad*, ed. Frederick R. Karl and Laurence Davies (Cambridge: Cambridge UP, 1983), 1:33–34. Reprinted by permission of Cambridge University Press. First cousin of Conrad's maternal grandmother, exiled from Poland after the failed 1863 revolution in which Conrad's father also fought. Residing in Brussels, he founded a charitable organization for Polish refugees. Here and elsewhere in this section, annotations are by the editor of this Norton Critical Edition.
1. Family estate in the Ukraine of Tadeusz Bobrowski, Conrad's uncle and guardian, whom he visited for two months in early 1890 before departing for the Congo.

and gives me your address. I am terribly sorry that I did not know this earlier, as I was in Brussels in October last year.[2] It is possible, however, that before long I shall have to visit Brussels again. The object of this scrawl to you is to remember myself to the relation whose great kindness to me in Cracow[3] I have certainly not forgotten. I do not ask whether you will permit me to visit you—for I permit myself not to doubt it; but I would very much like to be certain that you are in Brussels and that I shall be able to find you there in the course of the next month.

I returned to London six months ago after a three years' absence. Of these three years I spent one among the islands of the Malay Archipelago, after which I spent two years as master of an Australian vessel in the Pacific and Indian Oceans.[4] I am now more or less under contract to the 'Société Belge pour le Commerce du Haut Congo' to be master of one of its river steamers. I have not signed any agreement, but Mr. A. Thys, the director of that Company, has promised me the post. Whether he will keep his promise and when he will send me to Africa, I do not yet know; it will probably be in May.

I intend to visit Uncle Tadeusz soon; that is to say I want to, and he also wants me to; but he says that it is difficult during the winter. I am expecting a letter from him in a few days' time, which will decide the matter. If I do go home it will be via Hamburg—returning via Brussels. If, however, my visit is postponed I shall nevertheless be going to Brussels in March in connection with the post in the Congo. Therefore in any case I shall have to pleasure of seeing you, my dear Uncle, and of making myself known to Aunt Poradowska whom I only know from that portrait of her which you had with you in Cracow.

In the meantime, my dear Uncle, a most cordial embrace from your affectionate relation and servant,

                                                  Konrad Korzeniowski.
A letter care of Messrs. Barr Moering will always find me.

2. To be interviewed by Albert Thys (1832–1913), a founder of Leopold's Congo trading company, for the position of captain of a river steamer.
3. Medieval city in south-central Poland where Conrad spent his teenage years after the death of his father, who was a hero in the long struggle for Polish independence.
4. Conrad was master of the *Otago* from January 1888 through March 1889 during a twenty-eight-month stay in the Far East.

To Marguerite Poradowska†

Tuesday, 4 February 1890
[London]

My dear Aunt,

Many thanks for your card, I am leaving London tomorrow, Friday, at 9 a.m. and should arrive in Brussels at 5.30 p.m. I shall therefore be with you at about six. Believe me, with the liveliest gratitude, your very affectionate nephew and very devoted servant.

Conrad Korzeniowski

10 March 1890
Kazimierówka

My dear Aunt,

Only yesterday I received your letter of 15 February, through the agency of our good Aunt Gabrielle. The delay is explained by our absence from Kazimierówka, to which we returned yesterday after an excursion in the immediate area that lasted ten days.

Many thanks for the kind memory you carry of me. My admiration and friendship for you are increased by a feeling of deep gratitude for the goodness you show me. The thought of seeing you again in Brussels will console me when the time to part from my uncle arrives. I leave him on 15 April, and I will have the happiness of seeing you on the 23rd of the same month, if all goes well.

*   *   *

I ask your pardon for such a short letter. The post leaves today and I have received a pile of letters which must be answered promptly. I believe that my recommendation to the Company of the Congo was not strong enough and that the matter will not succeed at all. That vexes me a little.

To our next meeting, dear Aunt—soon, for time goes quickly. I kiss your hands, and I embrace you warmly. Your affectionate nephew

C. Korzeniowski

14 April 1890
Kazimierówka

My dear Aunt,

I have received your kind and charming letter, and this proof of friendship you give me in concerning yourself with my African

† From *The Collected Letters of Joseph Conrad*, 1:36, 41, 48. Wife of Alexander, a novelist, whose connections with the Belgian royal family may have helped Conrad in his quest for a position in the Congo. The model for Marlow's aunt in *Heart of Darkness*.

plans touches me more than I can express. Many thanks for your kind attention. With impatience I await the moment when I shall be able to kiss your hands while thanking you in person.

I am leaving my uncle's in four days. I have some visits to make on the way (among others, one of forty-eight hours to Lublin) so that I shall not be in Brussels until the 29th of this month.—Then we shall talk of your plans to visit Poland and your future projects, which interest me a good deal—as you can well believe.[1]

Have you received my last letter? I wonder. I have some doubts now. Did I understand you correctly? Has my reply offended you? In reading it, please think of the deep attachment I feel for you and also for the memory of my poor dear Uncle Alexander. So be indulgent, my dear and kind aunt.

Au revoir, then, for the time being. We have visitors and I have just escaped for a moment to write these few words. They are calling for me!

> I kiss your hands. Your very devoted friend and nephew
> J. C. Korzeniowski

To Maryleczka Bobrowska†

> London, 2nd May, 1890.

My dear Maryleczka.

I could not write any sooner. I have been extremely busy and in fact still am so. In four days' time I am sailing to the Congo, and I have to prepare myself for a three years' stay in Central Africa. You can, therefore, imagine how precious each minute is to me. I hope that your Mother is better now and that you, my dear, will soon be writing to me. Probably your letter will be too late to find me in Europe, but it is certain to be forwarded to me. Do not be surprised by the delay in getting a reply; no one can tell where your letter will eventually catch up with me.

* * *

> Your loving,
> K. N. Korzeniowski.

---

1. Marguerite's husband, Alexander, died while Conrad was in Brussels. She planned to visit relatives during the summer of 1890 in Lublin, a Polish city on the Ukrainian border not far from the Bobrowski estate.
† From *The Collected Letters of Joseph Conrad*, 1:48, 49. A cousin in Lublin.

London, 6th May, 1890

Maryleczka dear,

I am sailing in an hour. As soon as the photographs are ready I shall send a letter.

*   *   *

Your loving,
K. N. Korzeniowski.

To Marguerite Poradowska†

15 May 1890
Teneriffe[1]

My dear little Aunt,

What if I were to begin by telling you I have so far avoided the fever! What if I could assure you all my letters will start with this good news! Well, we shall see! In the meanwhile I am comparatively happy, which is all one can hope for in this wicked world. We left Bordeaux on a rainy day. Dismal day, a not very cheerful departure, some haunting memories, some vague regrets, some still vaguer hopes. One doubts the future. For indeed—I ask myself—why should anyone believe in it? And, consequently, why be sad about it? A little illusion, many dreams, a rare flash of happiness followed by disillusionment, a little anger and much suffering, and then the end. Peace! That is the programme, and we must see this tragi-comedy to the end. One must play one's part in it.

The screw turns and carries me off to the unknown. Happily, there is another me who prowls through Europe, who is with you at this moment. Who will get to Poland ahead of you. Another me who moves about with great ease; who can even be in two places at once. Don't laugh! I believe it has happened. I am very serious. So don't laugh. I allow you, however, to say: 'What a fool he is!' This is a concession. Life is composed of concessions and compromises.

*   *   *

I kiss your hands and commend myself to your heart.

Your very devoted
Conrad

---

† From *The Collected Letters*, 1:50–51.
1. Capital of the Canary Islands off the northwest coast of Africa, the first port of call after Conrad's departure from France on 6 May.

To Karol Zagórski†

Freetown, Sierre Leone,
22nd May, 1890.

My dearest Karol!

It is just a month today since you were scandalized by my hurried departure from Lublin. From the date and address of this letter you will see that I have had to be pretty quick, and I am only just beginning to breathe a little more calmly. If you only knew the devilish haste I had to make! From London to Brussels, and back again to London! And then again I dashed full tilt to Brussels! If you had only seen all the tin boxes and revolvers, the high boots and the tender farewells; just another handshake and just another pair of trousers!—and if you knew all the bottles of medicine and all the affectionate wishes I took away with me, you would understand in what a typhoon, cyclone, hurricane, earthquake—no!—in what a universal cataclysm, in what a fantastic atmosphere of mixed shopping, business, and affecting scenes, I passed two whole weeks. But the fortnight spent at sea has allowed me to rest and I am impatiently waiting for the end of this trip. I am due to reach Boma on the 7th of next month and then leave with my caravan to go to Léopoldville.[1] As far as I can make out from my 'lettre d'instruction' I am destined to the command of a steamboat, belonging to M. Delcommune's[2] exploring party, which is being got ready. I like this prospect very much, but I know nothing for certain as everything is supposed to be kept secret. What makes me rather uneasy is the information that 60 per cent. of our Company's employees return to Europe before they have completed even six months' service. Fever and dysentery! There are others who are sent home in a hurry at the end of a year, so that they shouldn't die in the Congo. God forbid! It would spoil the statistics which are excellent, you see! In a word, there are only 7 per cent. who can do their three years' service. It's a fact! To tell the truth, they are French! Des nevrosés! (C'est très chic d'être nevrosé[3]—one winks and speaks through the nose.) Yes! But a Polish nobleman, cased in British tar! What a concoction! Nous verrons![4] In any case I shall console my-

† From *The Collected Letters of Joseph Conrad*, 1:51–53. Cousin in Lublin whom Conrad had recently visited.

1. Conrad arrived in Boma at the mouth of the Congo River on 12 June, traveled by steamer to Matadi, and on 28 June left on foot for Leopoldville (or Kinshassa), where the river once again becomes navigable (a journey of 200 miles that took until 1 August).

2. Alexandre Delcommune (1855–1922), explorer on an expedition up the Kasai river; brother of Camille Delcommune, Congo company manager at Kinshassa who formed an intense dislike of Conrad that was reciprocated.

3. Neurotics! (It's very fashionable to be neurotic) (French). Ill and demoralized, Conrad in fact left the Congo six months later.

4. We shall see! (French).

self by remembering—faithful to our national traditions—that I looked for this trouble myself.

When you see—with the help of a microscope, no doubt—the hieroglyphics of my handwriting you will, I expect, wonder why I am writting to you? First, because it is a pleasure to talk to you; next, because, considering the distinguished personage who is penning this autograph, it ought to be a pleasure to you too. You can bequeath it to your children. Future generations will read it with admiration (and I hope with profit). In the meantime, trêve de bêtises![5]

I kiss my dear uncle's and aunt's hands, and your wife's too. I forget none of you, but can't write the whole list because this abominable lamp is going out.

> Yours very affectionately
> K. N. Korzeniowski.

To Marguerite Poradowska†

> 10 June 1890
> Libreville, Gabon

Dear little Aunt,

This being the last port of call before Boma, where my sea-voyage ends, I am beginning this letter here at the moment of leaving so as to continue it during the passage and end it the day of my arrival in Boma, where of course I am going to post it.

No new events. As to feelings, also nothing new, and there is the trouble. For, if one could unburden oneself of one's heart, one's memory (and also—one's brain) and obtain a whole new set of these things, life would become perfectly diverting. As this is impossible, life is not perfectly diverting. It is abominably sad! For example: among other things I should like to forget but cannot—I should like to forget the memory of my charming Aunt. Naturally, it is impossible. Consequently, I remember and am sad. Where are you? How are you? Have you forgotten me? Have you been left undisturbed? Are you working? That above all! Have you found the forgetfulness and peace of work that is creative and absorbing? So, you see! I ask myself all these questions. You have endowed my life with new interest, new affection; I am very grateful to you for this. Grateful for all the sweetness, for all the bitterness of this priceless gift. I now look down two avenues cut through the thick and chaotic jungle of noxious weeds. Where do they go? You follow one, I the other. They diverge. Do you find a ray of sunlight, however pale, at the end of yours? I hope so! I wish it for you! For a long

5. Enough of this foolishness! (French).
† From *The Collected Letters of Joseph Conrad*, 1:55–56, 57.

time I have no longer been interested in the goal to which my road leads. I was going along it with my head lowered, cursing the stones. Now I am interested in another traveller; this makes me forget the petty miseries of my own path.

While awaiting the inevitable fever, I am very well. In order to make my existence even slightly bearable, I need letters, many letters. From you, among others. Do not forget what I am telling you, dear and kind little Aunt.

After my departure from Boma, there may be an extended silence. I shall be unable to write until Léopoldville. It takes twenty days to go there, on foot too! How horrible!

You will probably write to my uncle; it was your intention, I believe. It would be kind if you would give him news of me. For example, that you saw me in Brussels, that I was well in body and spirit. This will give him pleasure and make him easier about my fate. He is very fond of me, and I grow as tender as an old fool when I think of him. Forgive this weakness. When do you return to Brussels? What are your future plans? Tell me all about it in your letter and sit at your desk only when you have a strong inclination to chat with 'the absent one'. 'The absent one' will be my official name in future. I shall be very happy to know that nobody is worrying you; that you work with an untroubled free spirit. I await your new work with curiosity and impatience. You must send it to me. Agreed? I have learned that my company has a sea-going ship and probably will build others. If I could obtain the command of one, that would be much better than the river. Not only is it healthier; there is always the chance of returning to Europe at least every year. When you return to Brussels, I beg you to let me know if any ships of this sort are being built so that I can enter my request. You can learn this through M. Wauters,[1] whereas I, in the depths of Africa, will have no news. I am sure you will do that for me.

Au revoir, dear Aunt. I love and embrace you.
C. Korzeniowski

18 June 1890
Matadi

Thank you! Many thanks, dear Aunt, for your kind and charming letter, which met me at Boma. Only my dear little Aunt could think up such splendid surprises. Has it given me pleasure?! I have a good mind to say No in order to punish you for having asked, for having seemed to doubt it!

---

1. A. J. Wauters, prominent geographer and general secretary for the Belgian companies operating in the Congo Free State.

I leave tomorrow on foot. Not an ass here except your very humble servant. Twenty days of safari. Temperature very bearable here and health very good. I shall write as soon as possible. Now I embrace you very heartily and kiss the hand that wrote the words which made me very happy the day before yesterday. Your very loving nephew and devoted servant

Conrad

ZDZISŁAW NAJDER

[Introduction to "The Congo Diary" and the "Up-river Book"]†

Conrad's stay in the Congo (12 June–4 December 1890) is one of the most important periods of his life. Even if we question as excessive the claim of his first biographer, G. Jean-Aubry, that the journey to the Congo shaped Conrad's philosophical outlook, we must recognize the enormous physical and moral impact of these six months. Conrad signed in Brussels a contract to serve for three years as an officer on river steamboats belonging to the Société Anonyme pour le Commerce du Haut-Congo. He left Europe full of energy and thrilling expectations, with ideas about a "civilizing mission."[1] He returned gravely ill, never to regain fully his good health, disillusioned, with memories to be used later in his most famous story, "Heart of Darkness," and in another bitter denunciation of colonialism, "An Outpost of Progress."

From this period there survive a few letters and also a unique document, the so-called "Congo Diary." The manuscript consists of two notebooks. The first, untitled, is an actual diary, kept by Conrad during his trek from Matadi to Kinshasa between [28] June and 1 August. This part was published (with errors and rather spotty annotation) by Richard Curle in 1926 and included in the volume *Last Essays*. The second, entitled by Conrad "Up-river Book" and commenced on board the steamer *Roi des Belges* on 3 August 1890, does not preserve the form of a diary—there are only four dates, although it spans sixteen days—and contains almost exclusively notes,

† From *Congo Diary and Other Uncollected Pieces*, ed. Zdzisław Najder (New York: Doubleday, 1978), pp. 1–4. Notes are Najder's.
1. Tadeusz Bobrowski to Conrad, 24 June 1890; in *Conrad's Polish Background*, ed. Zdzisław Najder (Oxford: Oxford UP, 1964), p. 129.

instructions and sketches concerning navigation up the Congo, at that time a not-too-frequented and only recently explored river. The second notebook was not published by Curle because, according to him, "it has no personal or literary interest."[2] This I believe is an exaggerated statement; still, since Curle's verdict, no Conrad scholar seems to have looked into the "Up-river Book."

The Congo notes constitute one of Conrad's earliest writings in English and reflect, if not his command of the language (his third), then at least his characteristic difficulties with it. These would come from two sides at once: from the Polish, which was his native language, the only one he used daily for his first seventeen years, and the one in which in 1890 he wrote most of his letters; and from the French, which he learned as a child, mastered during his stay in France in 1874–78 and, of course, used in the Congo. And his difficulties were threefold: choice of words, spelling, and grammar, particularly syntax.

Spelling mistakes are, of course, both most obvious and most trivial. Usually, not only in the notebooks, but in Conrad manuscripts in general, they stemmed from a similarity between an English and a French (differently spelled) word; and so he would write "ressemble" for "resemble," "mentionned" for "mentioned," and so on. Some, like the persistent "lays" and "laying" for "lies" and "lying" (found also, for instance, in a letter to Garnett of 15 March 1895), arise from the intricacies of English conjugation. The really exotic ones, like "andulating" for "undulating," can be explained only by reference to the rules of Polish spelling and pronunciation.

In his choice of words, Conrad would sometimes fail to realize the difference of meaning between similar-looking French and English words: hence "accidented" in the sense of "uneven." In grammar, the pressure of Polish seems to have been stronger throughout his writing career.[3] "There is 3 islands" is, of course, a Gallicism; but "much more trees" is a mistake Poles habitually tend to commit. Syntactically flabby sentences, like the one beginning "The looks of the whole establishment . . ." (27 June) sound perfectly normal in Polish, which is a much more inflected and therefore cohesive language.

* * *

The origins of the two notebooks are different. The "Up-river Book" is written for an obvious and practical purpose: Conrad was expecting to command a steamboat on the Congo and therefore put down data and instructions concerning the best passages, danger-

2. Richard Curle, "Introduction" to Joseph Conrad, "The Congo Diary," *Last Essays* (Garden City, NY: Doubleday, 1926), p. 159.
3. See Arthur P. Coleman, "Polonisms in the English of Conrad's *Chance*," *Modern Language Notes* (November 1931), 46:463–68.

ous shallows and snags, wooded places where fuel could be collected, visibility, orientation points, etc. These notes are made from
a precise location—the bridge; for a specific purpose—to be used
when navigating the boat on the next up-river trip; and for private
use—they are in English, although everybody around spoke French.
(Conrad served on French ships only as a young apprentice and
certainly felt more at ease using English nautical terminology.)

The reasons for keeping the first notebook, the diary proper, are
less evident. The practical importance of these jottings is limited:
only information concerning distances and directions, and perhaps
a few names of people and places, could conceivably be of any future use; these account for only 5 per cent of the text. Most of the
remarks have either descriptive or strictly personal content:
"Kinzilu rushing in. A short distance from the mouth fine waterfall.
Sun rose red—from 9h a.m. infernally hot day. Harou very little
better. Self rather seedy. Bathed."

I believe Conrad made these notes with the intention of using
them later to refresh his memory. He had by that time written a few
chapters of *Almayer's Folly* and was beginning to learn that his
imagination must be firmly supported by his own reminiscences—
or by studying the reminiscences of others. There are indications
that, while on board the *Vidar* (August 1887–January 1888), he
also took notes, later used in his Malayan novels. Contrary to
Curle's opinion, I think it is highly probable that the Congo diary
was not the only one Conrad ever kept: after all, we know for certain that he used to make extensive notes when preparing for and
writing his books. As a beginning author and realizing well the thematic possibilities offered by his African journey, he apparently
wished to put down some distinct and concrete impressions—in order to be able later to bolster his memories with hard data. After arriving at Kinshasa he was, by turn, either too busy or too sick to
continue.

Such a purpose in writing the diary would explain the limitations
of its content. Some critics have noted that Conrad's remarks do
not contain any condemnation, any expression of resentment
against atrocities which he must have observed—if we are to believe "Heart of Darkness"—during his stay in Matadi and on his
walk to Kinshasa. We do not have to assume that the sequence of
events in "Heart of Darkness" follows precisely the sequence of
Conrad's own experiences. But anyway, a closer look at the notes
shows that—apart from the first two entries, covering fifteen days
and rather bitter in tone—there are no general statements there,
only specific, detailed remarks. For the purpose of future remembering they were sufficient, and the only pertinent, material.

*   *   *

JOSEPH CONRAD

The Congo Diary†

Arrived at Matadi on the 13th of June, 1890.[1]

Mr. Gosse, chief of the station (O.K.) retaining us for some reason of his own.

Made the acquaintance of Mr. Roger Casement,[2] which I should consider as a great pleasure under any circumstances and now it becomes a positive piece of luck.

Thinks, speaks well, most intelligent and very sympathetic.

Feel considerably in doubt about the future. Think just now that my life amongst the people (white) around here cannot be very comfortable. Intend avoid acquaintances as much as possible.

Through Mr. R.C. have made the acquain[tan]ce of Mr. Underwood, the Manager of the English Factory (Hatton & Cookson) in Kalla Kalla. Av[era]ge com[merci]al hearty and kind. Lunched there on the 21st.

24th. Gosse and R.C. gone with a large lot of ivory down to Boma. On G.['s] return intend to start to up the river. Have been myself busy packing ivory in casks. Idiotic employment. Health good up to now.

Wrote to Simpson, to Gov. B., to Purd., to Hope, to Capt. Froud, and to Mar.[3] Prominent characteristic of the social life here: people speaking ill of each other.

Saturday, 28th June. Left Matadi with Mr. Harou[4] and a caravan of 31 men. Parted with Casement in a very friendly manner. Mr. Gosse saw us off as far as the State station.

First halt, M'poso. 2 Danes in Comp[a]ny.

---

† From *Congo Diary and Other Uncollected Pieces*, ed. Zdzisław Najder (New York: Doubleday, 1978), pp. 7–15. Minor corrections have been made based on the manuscript. Unless indicated, annotations are by the editor of this Norton Critical Edition.

1. The last station town on the Congo River reachable by boat, about forty miles upriver from the port of Boma. From here Conrad undertook a 200-mile overland trek to Leopoldville (Kinshassa), where he then traveled by steamer to Stanley Falls.

2. When he and Conrad first met, Casement was engaged in recruiting native labor for caravans along the route of the planned railway between Matadi and Leopoldville. He was later British consul to the Congo Free State and author of an influential report (1903) to the British Parliament about atrocities under King Leopold's stewardship. See above in this Norton Critical Edition, pp. 131–60.

3. Najder identifies James H. Simpson as the Australian shipowner for whom Conrad commanded the *Otago*; "Gov. B" as his guardian Tadeusz Bobrowski; "Purd." as the former shipmate William Purdu of Glasgow; George Fountaine Weare Hope, London friend and ex-seaman; Froud, secretary of the London Ship-Master Society, and "Mar." as Marguerite Poradowska [see letter dated 18 June 1890 in this Norton Critical Edition, p. 249].

4. Prosper Harou, an agent of the Société, who arrived from Europe on the same boat as Conrad [Najder].

Sund[ay], 29th. Ascent of Pataballa sufficiently fatiguing. Camped at 11h a.m. at Nsoke River. Mosquitos.

Monday, 30th. To Congo da Lemba after passing black rocks long ascent. Harou giving up. Bother. Camp bad. Water far. Dirty. At night Harou better.

Tuesday, 1st. Left early in a heavy mist, marching towards Lufu River. Part route through forest on the sharp slope of a high mountain. Very long descent. Then market place from where short walk to the bridge (good) and camp. V.[ery] G.[ood] Bath. Clear river. Feel well. Harou all right. 1st chicken, 2 p.[m.]. No sunshine today.

Wednesday, 2nd July.

Started at 5:30 after a sleepless night. Country more open. Gently andulating[5] hills. Road good in perfect order. (District of Lukungu.) Great market at 9:30, bought eggs and chickens[!].

Feel not well today. Heavy cold in the head. Arrived at 11 at Banza Manteka. Camped on the market place. Not well enough to call on the missionary. Water scarce and bad. Camp[in]g place dirty. 2 Danes still in Company.

Thursday, 3rd July.

Left at 6 a.m. after a good night's rest. Crossed a low range of hills and entered a broad valley or rather plain with a break in the middle. Met an off[ic]er of the State inspecting; a few minutes afterwards saw at a camp[in]g place the dead body of a Backongo. Shot? Horrid smell. Crossed a range of mountains, running NW-SE by a low pass. Another broad flat valley with a deep ravine through the centre. Clay and gravel. Another range parallel to the first mentioned, with a chain of low foot-hills running close to it. Between the two came to camp on the banks of the Luinzono River. Camp[in]g place clean. River clear Gov[ernmen]t Zanzibari[6] with register. Canoe. 2 danes camp[in]g on the other bank. Health good.

General tone of landscape gray-yellowish (dry grass), with reddish patches (soil) and clumps of dark green vegetation scattered sparsely about, mostly in steep gorges between the high mountains or in ravines cutting the plain. Noticed Palma Christi—Oil palm. Very straight, tall and thick trees in some places. Name not known to me. Villages quite invisible. Infer their existence from cal[a]bashes suspended to palm trees for the "malafu." Good many caravans and travellers. No women unless on the market place.

---

5. According to Najder, "the beginning 'u' in 'undulating' is pronounced like the Polish 'a.' "
6. Mercenaries from Zanzibar employed as soldiers or policemen by the Congo Free State.

Bird notes charming. One especially, a flute-like note. Another kind of "boom" ressembling[7] the very distant baying of a hound. Saw only pigeons and a few green parroquets; very small and not many. No birds of prey seen by me. Up to 9 a.m. sky clouded and calm. Afterwards gentle breeze from the N[or]th generally and sky clearing. Nights damp and cool. White mists on the hills up about halfway. Water effects, very beautiful this morning. Mists generally raising before sky clears.

Section of today's road.
[a drawing: section of the day's march]
Distance—15 miles.
General direction NNE-SSW

Friday, 4th July.
Left camp at 6h a.m. after a very unpleasant night. Marching across a chain of hills and then in a maze of hills. At 8:15 opened out into an andulating plain. Took bearings of a break in the chain of mountains on the other side. Bearing NNE. Road passes through that. Sharp ascents up very steep hills not very high. The higher mountains recede sharply and show a low hilly country.

At 9:30 market place.
At 10h passed R. Lukanga and at 10:30 camped on the Mpwe R.
Today's march. Direction NNE½N. Dist[an]ce 13 miles.
[section of the day's march]
Saw another dead body lying by the path in an attitude of meditative repose.

In the evening three women of whom one albino passed our camp. Horrid chalky white with pink blotches. Red eyes. Red hair. Features very negroid and ugly. Mosquitos. At night when the moon rose heard shouts and drumming in distant villages. Passed a bad night.

Saturday, 5th July.
Left at 6:15. Morning cool, even cold and very damp. Sky densely overcast. Gentle breeze from NE. Road through a narrow plain up to R. Kwilu. Swift flowing and deep, 50 yds. wide. Passed in canoes. After[war]ds up and down very steep hills intersected by deep ravines. Main chain of heights running mostly NW-SE or W and E at times. Stopped at Manyamba. Camp[in]g place bad—in a hollow—water very indifferent. Tent set at 10:15.

Section of today's road. NNE Dist[an]ce 12 m.
[a drawing]
Today fell into a muddy puddle. Beastly. The fault of the man

---

7. After the French *ressemblant* [Najder].

that carried me. After camp[in]g went to a small stream, bathed and washed clothes. Getting jolly well sick of this fun.

Tomorrow expect a long march to get to Nsona, 2 days from Manyanga. No sunshine today.

Sunday, 6th July.
Started at 5:40. The route at first hilly, then after a sharp descent traversing a broad plain. At the end of it a large market place. At 10h sun came out.

After leaving the market, passed another plain, then walking on the crest of a chain of hills passed 2 villages and at 11h arrived at Nsona. Village invisible.

Section of day's march.
[a drawing]
Direction about NNE.
Distance—18 miles.

In this camp (Nsona) there is a good camp[in]g place. Shady. Water far and not very good. This night no mosquitos owing to large fires lit all round our tent.

Afternoon very close. Night clear and starry.

Monday, 7th July.
Left at 6h after a good night's rest on the road to Inkandu, which is some distance past Lukungu Gov[ernmen]t station.

Route very accidented.[8] Succession of round steep hills. At times walking along the crest of a chain of hills.

Just before Lukunga our carriers took a wide sweep to the southward till the station bore N[or]th. Walking through long grass for 1½ hours. Crossed a broad river about 100 feet wide and 4 deep. After another ½ hours walk through manioc plantations in good order, rejoined our route to the [East] of the Lukunga Sta[ti]on. Walking along an andulating plain towards the Inkandu market on a hill. Hot, thirsty and tired. At 11h arrived on the M[ar]ket place. About 200 people. Business brisk. No water. No camp[in]g place. After remaining for one hour, left in search of a resting place.

Row with carriers. No water. At last, about 1½ p.m., camped on an exposed hillside near a muddy creek. No shade. Tent on a slope. Sun heavy. Wretched.
[section of the day's march]
Direction NE by N.
Distance—22 miles.
Night miserably cold. No sleep. Mosquitos.

8. From the French *accidente*—uneven, rough, hilly [Najder].

Tuesday, 8th July.

Left at 6h a.m.

About ten minutes from camp left main gov[ernmen]t path for the Manyanga track. Sky overcast. Road up and down all the time. Passing a couple of villages.

The country presents a confused wilderness of hills, land slips on their sides showing red. Fine effect of red hill covered in places by dark green vegetation.

½ hour before beginning the descent got a glimpse of the Congo. Sky clouded.

Today's march—3h.

[section of the day's march]

General direction N by E.

Dist[an]ce 9½ miles.

Arrived at Manyanga at 9h a.m.

Received most kindly by Messrs. Heyn & Jaeger. Most comfortable and pleasant halt.

Stayed here till the 25th. Both have been sick. Most kindly care taken of us. Leave with sincere regret.

			(Mafiesa)
Frid[y] 25th	Nkenghe		LEFT
Sat. 26	Nsona		Nkendo
Sund. 27	Nkandu		LUASI
Mond. 28	Nkonzo		(Nkoma)
Tue. 29	Nkenghe		Nzungi
Wedn. 30	Nsona		Inkissi
Thur. 31	Nkandu	mercredi	Stream
Frid[y] 1 Aug.	Nkonzo		Luila
Sat[y]. 2d	Nkenghe		Nselenba
Sund. 3d	Nsona		
Mond. 4th	Nkandu		
Tue. 5th	Nkonzo		
Wedn[y]. 6th	Nkenghe[9]		

Friday, the 25th July 1890.

Left Manyanga at 2½ p.m. with plenty of hammock carriers. H. lame and not in very good form. Myself ditto but not lame. Walked as far as Mafiela and camped—2h.

Saturday, 26th.

Left very early. Road ascending all the time. Passed villages. Country seems thickly inhabited. At 11h arrived at large market place. Left at noon and camped at 1h p.m.

9. Local names of the days of the "week," designated according to marketplaces. [Najder]

[section of the day's march with notes]
a camp—a white man died here—market—govt. post—mount—crocodile pond—Mafiesa

    Gen. direction E 1/2N—W1/2S.

    Sun visible at 8 am. Very hot. Distance—18 miles.

Sunday, 27th.

    Left at 8h am. Sent luggage carriers straight on to Luasi and went ourselves round by the Mission of Sutili.

    Hospitable reception by Mrs. Comber. All the missio[naries] absent.

    The looks of the whole establishment eminently civilized and very refreshing to see after the lots of tumble down hovels in which the State and Company agents are content to live—fine buildings. Position on a hill. Rather breezy.

    Left at 3h pm. At the first heavy ascent met Mr. Davis, miss-[ionary] returning from a preaching trip. Rev. Bentley away in the South with his wife.

    This being off the road, no section given. Distance traversed about 15 miles. General direction ENE.

    At Luasi we get on again on to the Gov[ernmen]t road.

    Camped at 4½ pm. With Mr. Heche in company.

    Today no sunshine.

    Wind remarkably cold. Gloomy day.

Monday, 28th.

    Left camp at 6:30 after breakfasting with Heche.

    Road at first hilly. Then walking along the ridges of hill chains with valleys on both sides. The country more open and there is much more trees[1] growing in large clumps in the ravines.

    Passed Nzungi and camped 11h on the right bank of Ngoma, a rapid little river with rocky bed. Village on a hill to the right.
[section of the day's march]

    General direction ENE.

    Distance—14 miles.

    No sunshine. Gloomy cold day. Squalls.

Tuesday, 29th.

    Left camp at 7h after a good night's rest. Continuous ascent; rather easy at first. Crossed wooded ravines and the river Lunzadi by a very decent bridge.

    At 9h met Mr. Louette escorting a sick agent of the Comp[an]y back to Matadi. Looking very well. Bad news from up the river. All

---

1. From the Polish *wiele więcej drzew*. [Najder]

the steamers disabled. One wrecked.[2] Country wooded. At 10:30
camped at Inkissi.
[section of the day's march]
   General direction ENE.
   Dist[an]ce—15 miles.
   Sun visible at 6:30. Very warm day.
   Inkissi River very rapid, is about 100 yards broad. Passage in ca-
noes. Banks wooded very densely and valley of the river rather deep
but very narrow.
   Today did not set the tent but put up in Gov[ernmen]t shimbek.[3]
Zanzibari in charge—very obliging. Met ripe pineapple for the first
time. On the road today passed a skeleton tied-up to a post. Also
white man's grave—no name. Heap of stones in the form of a cross.
   Health good now.

Wednesday, 30th.
   Left at 6 a.m. intending to camp at Kinfumu. Two hours' sharp
walk brought me to Nsona na Nsefe. Market. ½ hour after, Harou
arrived very ill with billious [*sic*] attack and fever. Laid him down in
Gov[ernmen]t shimbek. Dose of Ipeca.[4] Vomiting bile in enormous
quantities. At 11h gave him 1 gramme of quinine and lots of hot
tea. Hot fit ending in heavy perspiration. At 2 p.m. put him in hammock and started for Kinfumu. Row with carriers all the way.
Harou suffering much through the jerks of the hammock. Camped
at a small stream.
   At 4h Harou better. Fever gone.
[section of the day's march with notes]
wooded—camp—grass—Nsona a Nsefe—wood stream—open—
wood—Lulufu River—a remarkable conical mountain bearing NE
visible from here—Inkissi.
   General direction NE by E.
   Distance—13 miles.
   Up till noon, sky clouded and strong NW wind very chilling.
From 1h pm to 4h pm sky clear and very hot day. Expect lots of
bother with carriers tomorrow. Had them all called and made a
speech which they did not understand. They promise good behaviour.

Thursday, 31st.
   Left at 6h. Sent Harou ahead and followed in ½ an hour. Road
presents several sharp ascents and a few others easier but rather

2. The steamship *Florida* that Conrad was to have commanded.
3. Hut.
4. Drug that induces vomiting, from the herb Ipecacuanha, sometimes used to treat amoe-
   bic (or tropical) dysentery.

long. Notice in places sandy surface soil instead of hard clay as heretofore; think however that the layer of sand is not very thick and that the clay would be found under it. Great difficulty in carrying Harou. Too heavy. Bother! Made two long halts to rest the carriers. Country wooded in valleys and on many of the ridges.

Section of today's road.

[a drawing]

At 2:30 pm reached Luila at last and camped on right bank. Breeze from SW.

General direction of march about NE½E.

Distance est[imated]—16 miles.

Congo very narrow and rapid. Kinzilu rushing in. A short distance up from the mouth fine waterfall.

Sun rose red—from 9h a.m. Infernally hot day.

Harou very little better.

Self rather seedy. Bathed. Luila about 60 feet wide. Shallow.

Friday, 1st of August 1890.

Left at 6:30 am after a very indifferently passed night. Cold, heavy mists. Road in long ascents and sharp dips all the way to Mfumu Mbé.

After leaving there, a long and painful climb up a very steep hill; then a long descent to Mfumu Kono where a long halt was made. Left at 12:30 p.m. towards Nselemba. Many ascents. The aspect of the country entirely changed. Wooded hills with openings. Path almost all the afternoon thro' a forest of light trees with dense undergrowth.

After a halt on a wooded hillside reached Nselemba at 4h 10m p.m. [section of the day's march]

Put up at Gov[ernmen]t shanty.

Row between the carriers and a man stating himself in Gov[ernmen]t employ, about a mat. Blows with sticks raining hard. Stopped it. Chief came with a youth 13 suffering from gunshot wound in the head. Bullet entered about an inch above the right eyebrow and came out a little inside. The roots of the hair, fairly in the middle of the brow in a line with the bridge of the nose. Bone not damaged apparently. Gave him a little glycerine to put on the wound made by the bullet on coming out. Harou not very well. Mosquitos. Frogs. Beastly. Glad to see the end of this stupid tramp. Feel rather seedy. Sun rose red. Very hot day. Wind S[ou]th.

General direction of march—NE by N.

Distance—about 17 miles.

JOSEPH CONRAD

Up-river Book†

Commenced 3. Aug[u]st 1890
S.S. "Roi des Belges"[1]

On leaving—from A after passing the two islands steer for clump—high tree, two isl[and] points. Sandy beach. [Two sketches with contours of land and islands, marked; N°I, A, trees, sandy, point, bay, foul, and stones] N°II Steer for inside sandy point, then keep out (about East by the sun). As you approach coast breaks out into islands—B Steer for end marked B. *From position C. a further point visible.* C. Steer for sandbank II, behind hazy clumps of trees visible on a point of land. No islands visible. Left bank island presents appearance of mainland. Bank II covered at H[igh] W[ater]. Come up right to the bank I. Pass near islet y. Leave bank II on on port side. Steer for sandy path on S[ou]th shore.

N°III.IV.

Position D. Point *a* looks low now. S[ou]th side sandbank cov[ered] at H[igh] W[ater].

The opening narrows. Point *a* advancing.

Position E.

Low land and outlying sandbanks a little to port. Steering for a little square white patch. Stick on it. Pass close to the sands—*Cautiously!*

N°V. (and also IV)

Position F. ENE. Patch about ESE—Pass along sand shore not far from point ⚠ steering well in. Island X on the starboard side and generally kept ahead. On the port side (left bank) extensive and dangerous sand bank. 1½ foot *(Capt. Coch)* As you proceed in point ☉ seems closed in with island X and apparently no passage. Further on it opens again. A small grassy patch marks the end of point ☉ High hills right ahead looming behind island X.

Come right up to the island, then steer along shore to

---

† From *Congo Diary and Other Uncollected Pieces*, ed. Zdzisław Najder (New York: Doubleday, 1978), pp. 17–19. Annotations are by the editor of this Norton Critical Edition.
1. Under the command of the Dane Ludwig Rasmus Koch (1865–1906), the steamer *Roi des Belges* ("King of the Belgians") traveled upstream to Stanley Falls to bring back Georges Antoine Klein, chief agent of the inner station, who was ill and near death. Conrad took notes as an observer on the bridge and assumed command for part of the return trip when Koch fell ill.

the point ⊙ a little on the port bow as from *position F.a.* Coming up to a white patch after opening a small channel cutting X in two. A small island app[arent]ly closes the passage. When nearing the end of X *must* keep close and steer into the bay 8 getting the clump of trees on the port side. Going out the highest mountain will be right ahead—always keep the high mountain ahead crossing over to the left bank. To port of highest mount a low black point. Opposite a long island stretching across. The shore is wooded.

V. Va.

As you approach the shore the black point and the island close in together—No danger. Steering close to the mainland between the island and the grassy sandbank, towards the high mount[ain]s steering close to the left bank *of the river all the time. Entered.*

VI. On left bank wooded point.

Right valley. 1st Reach nearly north.

2nd Reach about NNE.

Left bank. Wooded point.

3d Reach the same and wooded point.

4th Reach NbyE.

Point III. Stones off.

IV. Before getting abreast there is a rocky shoal ⅓ out. 9 hours after entering the river sighted "2 sago-trees point" not at all remarkable. Low flat at the foot of the hills. The appearance of point VI is bushy. Rather low. Round slope behind as per sketch.

Just before coming up to p[oin]t VI got bottom at 6 feet stones. Hauled out. Point VII called "Sandstone Pt." with a small ledge of rock outside of it.

Before closing with it cross over to the right bank.

Moored to—grassy Beach backed by trees. 25 Miles from the entrance—5ʰ30.

4th Aug. VII This reach is about E. Shortly after leaving, point A opens out double in peculiar shape. Off point VIII long stone ridge. Point A has a small sandspit covered at full river. Right below the point there is a small sandbank along the shore. Wooding place. May get in between sandbank and the shore. After passing A point in the middle of the river there is a rocky ledge now above water. Covered at F[ull] W[ater]. River rather narrow. Steering well off the right bank.

Snake tree point has a ledge of rock lying well off. To give a wide berth.

Here begins a reach about NE (by the sun). On the left bank many palms visible.

After passing Sn[ake] Tree point on the left bank entrance to Black River—A remark[ab]le clump little further on R. *bank—Point C.*

Off point C. *cross over.* On the left bank on point XI one palm rather conspicuous when coming up. After turning point C. you open up a remarkable point running from high mountains called point Licha. Wooding place. (6h am.) On the right bank past point C. sandy beaches to be met often. On left bank a little past XI point there is a market place. Rocky shoals near in shore.

From Licha point up. VIII

From Licha—crossing over to right bank where there is outcrop of rock. Small sandy beach near.[2]

* * *

Selected Letters from Africa and After

To Maria Tyszkowa†

Kinshasa,
Stanley Pool,
Congo.
24th September, 1890.

My dear Maryleczka,

Your letter and the photograph reached me today and I hasten to write and explain to you the long interruption in our correspondence.

I have been on the river Congo, some 2,000 versts[1] from the coast where the post office is, so I could neither send nor get news from Europe. I was pleased to get your letter although at the same time it saddened me slightly. I have lived long enough to realize that life is full of griefs and sorrows which no one can escape, nevertheless I cannot help feeling sad at the thought that people whom I love must suffer, and are suffering. It is nonetheless pleasing to get a proof of the trust you place in me by writing openly about

2. The "Up-river Book" continues with similar observations for another twenty pages. See *The Congo Diary*, pp. 19–38.

† From *The Collected Letters of Joseph Conrad*, ed. Frederick R. Karl and Laurence Davies (Cambridge: Cambridge UP, 1983), 1:57–58. Reprinted by permission of Cambridge University Press. Here and elsewhere in this section, annotations are by the editor of this Norton Critical Edition. Although Conrad refers to her affectionately as "sister," Maria Tyszkowa was a cousin, and he was an only child.

1. A Russian *verst* is slightly longer than a kilometer and about two-thirds of an English mile.

your worries. Indeed, I do not deserve to have a place in your hearts—for I am practically a stranger to you—nevertheless the affectionate words you have written are most precious to me. I shall carefully preserve them in my heart, and the photograph will be in my album so that I can glance each day at my dear little sister.

Now that you are married and your desires fulfilled my wish for you both is that your lives will be nothing but sunshine with no clouds in the sky.[2] Please, assure your husband of my deep esteem, and of the very friendly feelings I have for him. I accept your invitation with gratitude and I promise to devote as much time as possible to my good lady sister. I trust that Aunt's health will improve steadily now that all the unpleasant contacts are left behind. I have a letter from Uncle Tadeusz, who intended to visit you in August. He is probably back home by now.

I am very busy with all the preparations for a new expedition to the River Kassai.[3] In a few days I shall probably be leaving Kinshasa again for a few months, possibly even for a year or longer. Thus you must not be surprised if you get no sign of life from me for a long time.

My love to dear Zuzia and my apologies for not having written to her. Please send me her exact address—and your new one as well. I kiss dear Aunt's hands. I commend myself to your thoughts and especially to your heart, dear Maryleczka.

Do not forget about me amidst all the new events in your life. I embrace you most warmly.

Your always loving brother,
K. N. Korzeniowski.

To Marguerite Poradowska†

26 September 1890
Kinshasa

Dearest and best of Aunts!

I received your three letters together on my return from Stanley Falls, where I went as a supernumerary on board the vessel *Roi des Belges* in order to learn about the river. I learn with joy of your success at the Academy, which, of course, I never doubted. I cannot find words sufficiently strong to make you understand the pleasure your charming (and above all kind) letters have given me. They

2. Maria Bobrowska (Conrad's mother's family name) married Teodor Tyszka on 15 July.
3. This expedition under Alexander Delcommune, to which Conrad had been assigned in Belgium, left without him in October because Alexander's brother Camille, the station manager, turned against him. Conrad returned to Europe shortly thereafter without receiving his own command.
† From *The Collected Letters of Joseph Conrad*, 1:61–63. By the tone and content of this letter, it is apparent that Conrad's hopes of a command on the Kassai expedition had been dashed sometime in the previous forty-eight hours.

were as a ray of sunshine piercing through the grey clouds of a
dreary winter day; for my days here are dreary. No use deluding
oneself! Decidedly I regret having come here. I even regret it bitterly. With all of a man's egoism, I am going to speak of myself. I
cannot stop myself. Before whom can I ease my heart if not before
you?! In speaking to you, I am certain of being understood down to
the merest hint. Your heart will divine my thoughts more quickly
than I can express them.

Everything here is repellent to me. Men and things, but men
above all. And I am repellent to them, also. From the manager in
Africa[1] who has taken the trouble to tell one and all that I offend
him supremely, down to the lowest mechanic, they all have the gift
of irritating my nerves—so that I am not as agreeable to them perhaps as I should be. The manager is a common ivory dealer with
base instincts who considers himself a merchant although he is
only a kind of African shop-keeper. His name is Delcommune. He
detests the English, and out here I am naturally regarded as such. I
cannot hope for either promotion or salary increases while he is
here. Besides, he has said that promises made in Europe carry no
weight here if they are not in the contract. Those made to me by
M. Wauters are not. In addition, I cannot look forward to anything
because I don't have a ship to command. The new boat will not be
completed until June of next year, perhaps. Meanwhile, my position
here is unclear and I am troubled by that. So there you are! As
crowning joy, my health is far from good. *Keep it a secret for me*—
but the truth is that in going up the river I suffered from fever four
times in two months, and then at the Falls (which is its home territory), I suffered an attack of dysentery lasting five days. I feel somewhat weak physically and not a little demoralized; and then, really,
I believe that I feel homesick for the sea, the desire to look again on
the level expanse of salt water which has so often lulled me, which
has smiled at me so frequently under the sparkling sunshine of a
lovely day, which many times too has hurled the threat of death in
my face with a swirl of white foam whipped by the wind under the
dark December sky. I regret all that. But what I regret even more is
having tied myself down for three years. The truth is that it is
scarcely probable I shall see them through. Either someone in authority will pick a groundless quarrel in order to send me back
(and, really, I sometimes find myself wishing for it), or I shall be
sent back to Europe by a new attack of dysentery, unless it consigns
me to the other world, which would be a final solution to all my distress! And for four pages I have been speaking of myself! I have not
told you with what pleasure I have read your descriptions of men

1. Camille Delcommune.

and things at home.[2] Indeed, while reading your dear letters I have forgotten Africa, the Congo, the black savages and the white slaves (of whom I am one) who inhabit it. For one hour I have been happy. Know that it is not a small thing (nor an easy thing) to make a human being happy for an *entire hour*. You can be proud of having succeeded. And so my heart goes out to you with a burst of gratitude and the most sincere and most profound affection. When will we meet again? Alas, meeting leads to parting—and the more one meets, the more painful the separations become. Such is Fate.

Seeking a practical remedy to the disagreeable situation which I have made for myself, I conceived of a little plan—still up in the air—in which you could perhaps help me. It appears that this company, or another affiliated with it, will have some ocean-going vessels (or even has one already). Probably that great (or fat?) banker who rules the roost where we are concerned will have a large interest in the other company. If someone could submit my name for the command of one of their ships (whose home port will be Antwerp) I would be able to get away for a day or two in Brussels when you are there. That would be ideal! If they wanted to call me home to take command, I would naturally pay the cost of coming back myself. This is perhaps not a very practicable idea, but if you return to Brussels in the winter, you could learn through M. Wauters what the chances are. Isn't that so, dear little Aunt?

* * *

I urge you by all the gods to keep secret from *everybody* the state of my health, or else my uncle will certainly hear of it. I must finish. I leave within an hour for Bamou, by canoe, to select trees and have them felled for building operations at the station here. I shall remain encamped in the forest for two or three weeks, unless ill. I like the prospect well enough. I can doubtless have a shot or two at some buffaloes or elephants. I embrace you most warmly. I shall write a long letter by the next mail.

Your affectionate nephew
J.C.K.

2. Marguerite was visiting family in Lublin.

From Marguerite Poradowska to Albert Thys†

[29 November 1890
Lublin, Poland]

. . . I received a letter from Mr. Conrad Korzeniowski himself, who has just returned from Stanley Falls after two months' navigation on the up-river. . . . He tells me that his health is greatly affected, and he feels utterly demoralized. Further, the steamer of which he is to take command will not be ready before June, perhaps, and the Director, M. Delcommune, told him plainly that he was not to expect either promotion, or an increase in his salary, as long as he will be in the Congo. He also added that the promises made in the contract, and the promises which you were kind enough to make him are indeed not stated in the contract.

Mr. Korzeniowski's position, therefore, is as false as it can be, which is aggravated by these fevers and dysentery, which have greatly weakened him. Mr. Korzeniowski's family is naturally worried to hear this news; we all hoped that he would be able to stand the climate, but another voyage might destroy his health for always. You can understand that we are all very anxious, and that is why the family has asked me to write to you for advice so that we may know how to get this poor young man out of this dreadful position.

There is some means, which Mr. Conrad submitted himself in his letter, asking me to speak to you about it (as he thinks I am already back in Brussels). It appears that the Cie. Commerciale du Congo (or another affiliated firm) owns a steamer which makes the trip between Banana and Antwerp. It is even said that this society owns several other steamers.

If Mr. Conrad could obtain the command of one of these steamers it would mean that the solution of the problem is ready found, as at sea there will be no more fever nor dysentery. He has asked me, therefore, to beg you to kindly submit his name for the command of one of these steamers which starts from Antwerp. He adds that if he were called back for this purpose he would be prepared to bear himself the expenses of the return voyage. . . . It is sad to think that a capable man such as Mr. Conrad Korzeniowski, who has been used to commanding steamers for fifteen years, should be reduced to this subordinate position, and should be exposed to such fatal disease.

You seemed to have taken an interest in Mr. C. Korzeniowski, and during my stay in Brussels I was able to form an opinion of your kindness, and I hope that you will not withdraw your support,

† From G. Jean-Aubry, *Joseph Conrad in the Congo* (London: William Heinemann, 1926), pp. 70–72. Responding to Conrad's plea for help, Marguerite once again sought to use her Belgian connections by writing to the Director of the Société du Haut-Congo.

but that, on the contrary, you will advise him as to the steps he should take.

From Tadeusz Bobrowski†

[27 December 1890
Kazimierówka, Ukraine]

On the 24th I received your letter dated October 19th, from Kinchassa, which informs me of the unfortunate end of your expedition to the Congo and your return to Europe. Mme. Marguerite (Poradowska) informed me also of it from Lublin, where she heard it through the Director of the Company, to whom she had written for news of you.

. . . Although you assure me that the first sea breeze will give you back your health, I found your writing so changed—which I attribute to fever and dysentery—that since then my thoughts are not at all happy. I never hid from you that I was not partisan to your African project. I remained faithful to my principle to leave everybody to be happy in their own way.

See a specialist on tropical diseases immediately, for our doctors here know nothing on the subject, and I have not even the possibility of telling you to come and rest here.

Tell me also the state of your finances, so that perhaps I may help you to the extent of my means.

To Marguerite Poradowska‡

London, Sunday
[1? February 1891]

My dear Aunt,

Having arrived here safely, I could hardly wait to run to the doctor, who, to begin with, sent me to bed—because of my legs. He has completely reassured me about the general state of my health. I am somewhat anaemic, but all my organs are in good condition.

I got up today expressly to write. I have just finished the letter to my uncle. I feel much stronger, and I don't doubt that within a few weeks I shall be perfectly recovered.

I am ashamed to confess this to your sister-in-law, but I have lost the address she gave me for the package entrusted to my care. I hope she will be kind enough to forgive me and will send the necessary address.

† From Jean-Aubry, *Conrad in the Congo*, p. 72. Bobrowski was Conrad's uncle and guardian.
‡ From *The Collected Letters of Joseph Conrad*, 1:68–69. Despite his assurances about his health, Conrad suffered from malaria, heart palpitations, swollen legs, neuralgia, and various other ailments. He was hospitalized in March and then traveled to Switzerland for treatment later in the spring.

Nothing interesting to tell you. The older I get, the more stupid I become. I would not even know how to make up any news. I am not very cheerful, shut in as I am. I have some books, but the books are stupid too.

I think I shall be able to return to work in six weeks—if I can find any!

If you believe Péchet[1] approachable, I inform you that I am thirty-two years old, have English master's certificate for my service in sail and steam, commanded both—but principally sail—can furnish good references from shipowners and also from London merchants. With all these assets, I burn with the desire to have the honour of commanding one of M. Péchet's steamers. You can also add that, judging from the appearance of my nose, I get drunk only once a year, that I don't seem to have any leanings towards piracy, and that—according to what you know of me—you do not believe me capable of committing embezzlement. I have never come within the jurisdiction of the police, and I am capable of looking discreetly upon a pretty face without leering. It is true I limp, but I am in distinguished company. Timoleon was lame, and there is even a devil in the same condition, according to my information.[2] If, after having understood all that, he refuses to entrust me with a ship, well then, we shall abandon him to his sad fate—and look elsewhere.

My regards to your mother and to the younger Mme Gachet.[3] I hug the children.

I kiss both your hands and, while waiting to hear from you, I am still—and for always—your very devoted nephew and very humble servant

K.N. Korzeniowski

To Roger Casement†

[letterhead: Pent Farm]
1903
17th Dec^er

My dear Casement
During my sojourn in the interior, keeping my eyes and ears well open too, I've never heard of the alleged custom of cutting off

1. Antwerp shipping agents. Nothing came of this suggestion. After recuperating, Conrad worked in a London warehouse during the summer and then sailed to Australia in November as first mate on the *Torrens*.
2. Conrad confuses Timoleon, the Greek statesman, with Tamerlaine, the lame conqueror. The other allusion is to Lesage's satirical novel *Le Diable boiteux* (1707) [Karl and Davies].
3. Marguerite's sister-in-law, mother of two children.
† From *The Collected Letters of Joseph Conrad*, ed. Karl and Davies (Cambridge: Cambridge UP, 1988), 3:95.

hands amongst the natives; and I am convinced that no such custom ever existed along the whole course of the main river to which
my experience is limited.[1] Neither in the casual talk of white men
nor in the course of definite inquiries as to the tribal customs was
ever such a practice hinted at; certainly not amongst the Bangalas
who at that time formed the bulk of the State troops. My inform-
ants were numerous, of all sorts—and many of them possessed of
abundant knowledge.

I have to thank you for Morel's pamphlet[2] which reached me
from L'pool a few days ago. There can be no doubt that his presentation of the commercial policy and the administrative methods of
the Congo State is absolutely true. It is a most brazen breach of
faith as to Europe.[3] It is in every aspect an enormous and atrocious
lie in action. If it were not rather appalling the cool completeness
of it would be amusing.

My best wishes and cordial regards

Yours

Jph. Conrad.

To Roger Casement†

[letterhead: Pent Farm]
21st Dec 1903

My dear Casement

You cannot doubt that I form the warmest wishes for your success. A King, wealthy and unscrupulous, is certainly no mean adversary; for if the personality in this case be a rather discredited
one, the wealth, alas, has never a bad odour—or this wealth in particular would tell its own suffocating tale.

It is an extraordinary thing that the conscience of Europe which
seventy years ago has put down the slave trade on humanitarian
grounds tolerates the Congo State to day. It is as if the moral clock
had been put back many hours. And yet nowadays if I were to over-
work my horse so as to destroy its happiness of physical wellbeing I
should be hauled before a magistrate. It seems to me that the black
man—say, of Upoto—is deserving of as much humanitarian regard
as any animal since he has nerves, feels pain, can be made physically miserable. But as a matter of fact his happiness and misery
are much more complex than the misery or happiness of animals
and deserving of greater regard. He shares with us the conscious-

---

1. See Casement's "Congo Report" in this edition; he had submitted the report to Parliament a few days previously.
2. *The Congo Free State* (Liverpool, 1903). See the selection in this edition by Morel.
3. Because Leopold's exploitation of the Congo Free State violated the agreements at the
   Conference of Berlin (1885).
† From *The Collected Letters of Joseph Conrad*, 3:95–97.

ness of the universe in which we live—no small burden. Barbarism per se is no crime deserving of a heavy visitation; and the Belgians are worse than the seven plagues of Egypt insomuch that in that case it was a punishment sent for a definite transgression; but in this the Upoto man is not aware of any transgression, and therefore can see no end to the infliction. It must appear to him very awful and mysterious; and I confess that it appears so to me too. The amenities of the 'middle passage' in the old days were as nothing to it. The slave trade has been abolished—and the Congo State exists to-day. This is very remarkable. What makes it more remarkable is this: the slave trade was an old established form of commercial activity; it was not the monopoly of one small country established to the disadvantage of the rest of the civilized world in defiance of international treaties and in brazen disregard of humanitarian declarations. But the Congo State created yesterday is all that and yet it exists. This is very mysterious. One is tempted to exclaim (as poor Thiers did in 1871) "Il n'y a plus d'Europe."[1] But as a matter of fact in the old days England had in her keeping the conscience of Europe. The initiative came from here. But now I suppose we are busy with other things; too much involved in great affairs to take up cudgels for humanity, decency and justice. But what about our commercial interests? These suffer greatly as Morel has very clearly demonstrated in his book. There can be no serious attempt to controvert his facts. Or [it] is impossible to controvert them for the hardest of lying won't do it. That precious pair of African witchmen seem to have cast a spell upon the world of whites—I mean Leopold and Thys of course. This is very funny.

And the fact remains that in 1903, seventy five years or so after the abolition of the slave trade (because it was cruel) there exists in Africa a Congo State, created by the act of European Powers where ruthless, systematic cruelty towards the blacks is the basis of administration, and bad faith towards all the other states the basis of commercial policy.

I do hope we shall meet before you leave. Once more my best wishes go with you on your crusade. Of course You may make any use you like of what I write to you.[2] Cordially Yours

Jph Conrad.

1. Adolphe Thiers (1797–1877), French statesman who lamented "There is no more Europe" when Prussia isolated and defeated France in the Franco-Prussian war.
2. Morel read from this letter at rallies against Leopold's abuses.

To R. B. Cunninghame Graham†

Pent Farm.
26ᵗʰ Dec 1903.

Cher Ami.

I snatch this piece of MS paper first of all to thank you for remembering the boy[1] at this festive(?) season. Next to tell you that
H. de Soto[2] is most exquisitely excellent: your very mark and spirit
upon a subject that only *you* can do justice to—with your wonderful English and your sympathetic insight into the souls of the Conquistadores. The glamour, the pathos and the romance of that time
and of those men are only adequately, truthfully, conveyed to us by
your pen; the sadness, the glory and the romance of the endeavour
together with the vanity of vanities of the monstrous achievement
are reflected in your unique style as though you had been writing of
men with whom you had slept by the camp fire after tethering your
horses on the t[h]reshold of the unknown.

*   *   *

One seems to hear the very voice. C'est la verité même![3]It's the
most amazingly natural thing I've ever read; it gives me a furious
desire to learn Spanish and bury myself in the pages of the incom-
parable Garcilasso—if only to forget all about our modern Conquistadores.[4]

Their achievement is monstrous enough in all conscience—but
not as a great human force let loose, but rather like that of a gigantic and obscene beast. Leopold is their Pizarro, Thys their Cortez
and their "lances" are recruited amongst the souteneurs, sous-offs,
maquereaux, fruit-secs[5] of all sorts on the pavements of Brussels
and Antwerp. I send you two letters I had from a man called Casement, premising that I knew him first in the Congo just 12 years
ago. Perhaps you've heard or seen in print his name. He's a protes-
tant Irishman, pious too. But so was Pizarro. For the rest I can assure you that he is a limpid personality. There is a touch of the
Conquistador in him too; for I've seen him start off into an unspeakable wilderness swinging a crookhandled stick for all
weapons, with two bull-dogs: Paddy (white) and Biddy (brindle) at

---

† From *The Collected Letters of Joseph Conrad*, 3:100–102. Graham (1852–1936), Scottish socialist, writer, sometime member of Parliament, one of Conrad's closest friends
and confidants.
1. Conrad's elder son Borys had just turned five.
2. Graham's recently published book *Hernando de Soto*, a narrative of exploration and conquest in Peru and the Gulf of Mexico.
3. It's the truth itself! (French)
4. Garcilaso de le Vega, el Inca (1539?–1616), son of a conquistador and an Inca princess,
whose writings on Peruvian history were one of Graham's sources. Graham argued that
contemporary imperialists (the "modern conquistadors") were just as brutal and deceptive as the Spanish, if not worse.
5. Bullies, noncommissioned officers, pimps, failures (French).

his heels and a Loanda boy carrying a bundle for all company. A few months afterwards it so happened that I saw him come out again, a little leaner a little browner, with his stick, dogs, and Loanda boy, and quietly serene as though he had been for a stroll in a park. Then we lost sight of each other. He was I believe Bsh Consul in Beira,[6] and lately seems to have been sent to the Congo again, on some sort of mission, by the Br Gov^t. I have always thought that some particle of Las Casas'[7] soul had found refuge in his indefatigable body. The letters will tell you the rest. I would help him but it is not in me. I am only a wretched novelist inventing wretched stories and not even up to that miserable game; but your good pen, keen, flexible and straight, and sure, like a good Toledo blade would tell in the fray if you felt disposed to give a slash or two. He could tell you things! Things I've tried to forget; things I never did know. He has had as many years of Africa as I had months—almost.—

* * *

JOSEPH CONRAD

Geography and Some Explorers†

It is safe to say that for the majority of mankind the superiority of geography over geometry lies in the appeal of its figures. It may be an effect of the incorrigible frivolity inherent in human nature, but most of us will agree that a map is more fascinating to look at than a figure in a treatise on conic sections—at any rate for the simple minds which are all the equipment of the majority of the dwellers on this earth.

No doubt a trigonometrical survey may be a romantic undertaking, striding over deserts and leaping over valleys never before trodden by the foot of civilized man; but its accurate operations can never have for us the fascination of the first hazardous steps of a venturesome, often lonely, explorer jotting down by the light of his camp fire the thoughts, the impressions, and the toil of his day.

For a long time yet a few suggestive words grappling with things seen will have the advantage over a long array of precise, no doubt interesting, and even profitable figures. The earth is a stage, and though it may be an advantage, even to the right comprehension of

6. During a twenty-year career in the British consular service, Casement was posted to various sites in Africa and South America.
7. Bartolomé de Las Casas (1474–1566), Spanish missionary and acquaintance of Columbus who fought against the enslavement of Indians in South America.
† From *Last Essays* (Garden City, NY: Doubleday, 1926), pp. 1–4, 13–17. Copyright © 1926 by Doubleday, a division of Bantam Doubleday Dell Publishing Group, Inc. Permission granted by the Trustees of the Joseph Conrad Estate. Notes are the Editor's.

the play, to know its exact configuration, it is the drama of human endeavour that will be the thing, with a ruling passion expressed by outward action marching perhaps blindly to success or failure, which themselves are often undistinguishable from each other at first.

Of all the sciences, geography finds its origin in action, and what is more, in adventurous action of the kind that appeals to sedentary people who like to dream of arduous adventure in the manner of prisoners dreaming behind bars of all the hardships and hazards of liberty dear to the heart of man.

Descriptive geography, like any other kind of science, has been built on the experience of certain phenomena and on experiments prompted by that unappeasable curiosity of men which their intelligence has elevated into a quite respectable passion for acquiring knowledge. Like other sciences it has fought its way to truth through a long series of errors. It has suffered from the love of the marvellous, from our credulity, from rash and unwarrantable assumptions, from the play of unbridled fancy.

Geography had its phase of circumstantially extravagant speculation which had nothing to do with the pursuit of truth, but has given us a curious glimpse of the mediæval mind playing in its ponderous childish way with the problems of our earth's shape, its size, its character, its products, its inhabitants. Cartography was almost as pictorial then as are some modern newspapers. It crowded its maps with pictures of strange pageants, strange trees, strange beasts, drawn with amazing precision in the midst of theoretically conceived continents. It delineated imaginary kingdoms of Monomotopa and of Prester John, the regions infested by lions or haunted by unicorns, inhabited by men with reversed feet, or eyes in the middle of their breasts.

All this might have been amusing if the mediæval gravity in the absurd had not been in itself a wearisome thing. But what of that! Has not the key science of modern chemistry passed through its dishonest phase of Alchemy (a portentous development of the confidence trick), and our knowledge of the starry sky been arrived at through the superstitious idealism of Astrology looking for men's fate in the depths of the infinite? Mere megalomania on a colossal scale. Yet, solemn fooling for solemn fooling of the scientific order, I prefer the kind that does not lay itself out to thrive on the fears and the cupidities of men.

From that point of view geography is the most blameless of sciences. Its fabulous phase never aimed at cheating simple mortals (who are a multitude) out of their peace of mind or their money. At the most it has enticed some of them away from their homes; to death may be, now and then to a little disputed glory, not seldom to contumely,[1] never to high fortune. The greatest of them all, who has presented modern geography with a new world to work upon, was at one time loaded with chains and thrown into prison. Columbus remains a pathetic figure, not a sufferer in the cause of geography, but a victim of the imperfections of jealous human hearts, accepting his fate with resignation. Among explorers he appears lofty in his troubles and like a man of a kingly nature. His contribution to the knowledge of the earth was certainly royal. And if the discovery of America was the occasion of the greatest outburst of reckless cruelty and greed known to history we may say this at least for it, that the gold of Mexico and Peru, unlike the gold of alchemists, was really there, palpable, yet, as ever, the most elusive of the Fata Morgana[2] that lure men away from their homes, as a moment of reflection will convince any one. For nothing is more certain than that there will never be enough gold to go round, as the Conquistadores found out by experience.

I suppose it is not very charitable of me, but I must say that to this day I feel a malicious pleasure at the many disappointments of those pertinacious searchers for El Dorado who climbed mountains, pushed through forests, swam rivers, floundered in bogs, without giving a single thought to the science of geography. Not for them the serene joys of scientific research, but infinite toil, in hunger, thirst, sickness, battle; with broken heads, unseemly squabbles, and empty pockets in the end. I cannot help thinking it served them right. It is an ugly tale, which has not much to do with the service of geography. The geographical knowledge of our day is of the kind that would have been beyond the conception of the hardy followers of Cortés and Pizarro; and of that most estimable of Conquerors who was called Cabeza de Vaca,[3] who was high-minded and dealt humanely with the heathen nations whose territories he traversed in search of one more El Dorado. It is said they loved him greatly, but now the very memory of those nations is gone from the earth, while their territories, which they could not take with them, are being traversed many times every twenty-four hours by the trains of the Southern Pacific railroad.

*   *   *

I have no doubt that star-gazing is a fine occupation, for it leads you within the borders of the unattainable. But map-gazing, to which I became addicted so early, brings the problems of the great spaces of the earth into stimulating and directing contact with sane

---

1. Contemptuous or humiliating treatment.
2. Mirages.
3. Hernán Cortés (1485–1547), Spanish conqueror of Mexico; Francisco Pizarro (ca. 1476–1541), Spanish conqueror of Peru; Álvar Núñez Cabeza de Vaca (ca. 1490–ca. 1557), Spanish explorer of the American Southwest.

curiosity and gives an honest precision to one's imaginative faculty. And the honest maps of the nineteenth century nourished in me a passionate interest in the truth of geographical facts and a desire for precise knowledge which was extended later to other subjects.

For a change had come over the spirit of cartographers. From the middle of the eighteenth century on the business of map-making had been growing into an honest occupation, registering the hard-won knowledge, but also in a scientific spirit recording the geographical ignorance of its time. And it was Africa, the continent out of which the Romans used to say some new thing was always coming, that got cleared of the dull imaginary wonders of the dark ages, which were replaced by exciting spaces of white paper. Regions unknown! My imagination could depict to itself there worthy, adventurous and devoted men, nibbling at the edges, attacking from north and south and east and west, conquering a bit of truth here and a bit of truth there, and sometimes swallowed up by the mystery their hearts were so persistently set on unveiling.

Among them Mungo Park, of western Sudan, and Bruce, of Abyssinia,[4] were, I believe, the first friends I made when I began to take notice—I mean geographical notice—of the continents of the world into which I was born. The fame of these two had already been for a long time European, and their figures had become historical by then. But their story was a very novel thing to me, for the very latest geographical news that could have been whispered to me in my cradle was that of the expedition of Burton and Speke,[5] the news of the existence of Tanganyika and of Victoria Nyanza.

I stand here confessed as a contemporary of the Great Lakes. Yes, I could have heard of their discovery in my cradle, and it was only right that, grown to a boy's estate, I should have in the later sixties done my first bit of map-drawing and paid my first homage to the prestige of their first explorers. It consisted in entering laboriously in pencil the outline of Tanganyika on my beloved old atlas, which, having been published in 1852, knew nothing, of course, of the Great Lakes. The heart of its Africa was white and big.

Surely it could have been nothing but a romantic impulse which prompted the idea of bringing it up to date with all the accuracy of which I was capable. Thus I could imagine myself stepping in the very footprints of geographical discovery. And it was not all wasted time. As a bit of prophetic practice it was not bad for me. Many years afterwards, as second officer in the Merchant Service, it was

4. Mungo Park (1771–1806), British explorer who was attacked and killed by natives while tracing the course of the Niger River; James Bruce (1730–94), Scottish explorer who sought the source of the Nile in Ethiopia.
5. Sir Richard Francis Burton (1821–90) and John Hanning Speke (1827–64) discovered Lake Tanganyika and Victoria Nyanza, the largest lake in Africa.

my duty to correct and bring up to date the charts of more than one ship, according to the Admiralty notices. I did this work conscientiously and with a sense of responsibility; but it was not in the nature of things that I should ever recapture the excitement of that entry of Tanganyika on the blank of my old atlas.

* * *

Not the least interesting part in the study of geographical discovery lies in the insight it gives one into the characters of that special kind of men who devoted the best part of their lives to the exploration of land and sea. In the world of mentality and imagination which I was entering it was they and not the characters of famous fiction who were my first friends. Of some of them I had soon formed for myself an image indissolubly connected with certain parts of the world. For instance, western Sudan, of which I could draw the rivers and principal features from memory even now, means for me an episode in Mungo Park's life.

It means for me the vision of a young, emaciated, fair-haired man, clad simply in a tattered shirt and worn-out breeches, gasping painfully for breath and lying on the ground in the shade of an enormous African tree (species unknown), while from a neighbouring village of grass huts a charitable black-skinned woman is approaching him with a calabash[6] full of pure cold water, a simple draught which, according to himself, seems to have effected a miraculous cure. The central Sudan, on the other hand, is represented to me by a very different picture, that of a self-confident and keen-eyed person in a long cloak and wearing a turban on his head, riding slowly towards a gate in the mud walls of an African city, from which an excited population is streaming out to behold the wonder—Doctor Barth, the protégé of Lord Palmerston, and subsidized by the British Foreign Office, approaching Kano, which no European eye had seen till then, but where forty years later my friend Sir Hugh Clifford, the Governor of Nigeria, travelled in state in order to open a college.[7]

I must confess that I read that bit of news and inspected the many pictures in the illustrated papers without any particular elation. Education is a great thing, but Doctor Barth gets in the way. Neither will the monuments left by all sorts of empire builders suppress for me the memory of David Livingstone.[8] The words "Cen-

---

6. A gourd.
7. Heinrich Barth (1821–65), German explorer who traveled extensively in northern and central Africa for the British government; Kano, a large city in northern Nigeria; Henry John Temple Palmerston (1784–1865), powerful but controversial foreign minister and later prime minister.
8. Scottish missionary and explorer (1813–73), discovered Victoria Falls during his lifelong quest for the source of the Nile; hoped to abolish the African slave trade through the influence of Christianity.

tral Africa" bring before my eyes an old man with a rugged, kind face and a clipped, gray moustache, pacing wearily at the head of a few black followers along the reed-fringed lakes towards the dark native hut on the Congo headwaters in which he died, clinging in his very last hour to his heart's unappeased desire for the sources of the Nile.

That passion had changed him in his last days from a great explorer into a restless wanderer refusing to go home any more. From his exalted place among the blessed of militant geography and with his memory enshrined in Westminster Abbey, he can well afford to smile without bitterness at the fatal delusion of his exploring days, a notable European figure and the most venerated perhaps of all the objects of my early geographical enthusiasm.

Once only did that enthusiasm expose me to the derision of my schoolboy chums. One day, putting my finger on a spot in the very middle of the then white heart of Africa, I declared that some day I would go there. My chums' chaffing was perfectly justifiable. I myself was ashamed of having been betrayed into mere vapouring. Nothing was further from my wildest hopes. Yet it is a fact that, about eighteen years afterwards, a wretched little stern-wheel steamboat I commanded lay moored to the bank of an African river.

Everything was dark under the stars. Every other white man on board was asleep. I was glad to be alone on deck, smoking the pipe of peace after an anxious day. The subdued thundering mutter of the Stanley Falls hung in the heavy night air of the last navigable reach of the Upper Congo, while no more than ten miles away, in Reshid's camp just above the Falls, the yet unbroken power of the Congo Arabs slumbered uneasily. Their day was over. Away in the middle of the stream, on a little island nestling all black in the foam of the broken water, a solitary little light glimmered feebly, and I said to myself with awe, "This is the very spot of my boyish boast."

A great melancholy descended on me. Yes, this was the very spot. But there was no shadowy friend to stand by my side in the night of the enormous wilderness, no great haunting memory, but only the unholy recollection of a prosaic newspaper "stunt" and the distasteful knowledge of the vilest scramble for loot that ever disfigured the history of human conscience and geographical exploration. What an end to the idealized realities of a boy's daydreams! I wondered what I was doing there, for indeed it was only an unforeseen episode, hard to believe in now, in my seaman's life. Still, the fact remains that I have smoked a pipe of peace at midnight in the very heart of the African continent, and felt very lonely there.

The Author on Art and Literature

JOSEPH CONRAD

Preface to *The Nigger of the "Narcissus"*†

A work that aspires, however humbly, to the condition of art should carry its justification in every line. And art itself may be defined as a single-minded attempt to render the highest kind of justice to the visible universe, by bringing to light the truth, manifold and one, underlying its every aspect. It is an attempt to find in its forms, in its colours, in its light, in its shadows, in the aspects of matter and in the facts of life what of each is fundamental, what is enduring and essential—their one illuminating and convincing quality—the very truth of their existence. The artist, then, like the thinker or the scientist, seeks the truth and makes his appeal. Impressed by the aspect of the world the thinker plunges into ideas, the scientist into facts—whence, presently, emerging they make their appeal to those qualities of our being that fit us best for the hazardous enterprise of living. They speak authoritatively to our common-sense, to our intelligence, to our desire of peace or to our desire of unrest; not seldom to our prejudices, sometimes to our fears, often to our egoism—but always to our credulity. And their words are heard with reverence, for their concern is with weighty matters: with the cultivation of our minds and the proper care of our bodies, with the attainment of our ambitions, with the perfection of the means and the glorification of our precious aims.

It is otherwise with the artist.

Confronted by the same enigmatical spectacle the artist de-

† From *The Nigger of the "Narcissus": A Tale of the Forecastle* (1897; Garden City, NY: Doubleday, Page, and Co., 1926), pp. xi–xvi. Written the year before *Heart of Darkness*, this preface is widely regarded as Conrad's most significant statement of his artistic assumptions and aims. Recent discussions of race have also made this novel an important companion piece to *Heart of Darkness*. When it was published in America, its title was changed to *The Children of the Sea* because of the publisher's concerns about sales. Although not mentioned in the preface, which focuses exclusively on artistic matters, the workings of racial prejudice are a central theme of the story.

scends within himself, and in that lonely region of stress and strife, if he be deserving and fortunate, he finds the terms of his appeal. His appeal is made to our less obvious capacities: to that part of our nature which, because of the warlike conditions of existence, is necessarily kept out of sight within the more resisting and hard qualities—like the vulnerable body within a steel armour. His appeal is less loud, more profound, less distinct, more stirring—and sooner forgotten. Yet its effect endures forever. The changing wisdom of successive generations discards ideas, questions facts; demolishes theories. But the artist appeals to that part of our being which is not dependent on wisdom; to that in us which is a gift and not an acquisition—and, therefore, more permanently enduring. He speaks to our capacity for delight and wonder, to the sense of mystery surrounding our lives; to our sense of pity, and beauty, and pain; to the latent feeling of fellowship with all creation—and to the subtle but invincible conviction of solidarity that knits together the loneliness of innumerable hearts, to the solidarity in dreams, in joy, in sorrow, in aspirations, in illusions, in hope, in fear, which binds men to each other, which binds together all humanity—the dead to the living and the living to the unborn.

It is only some such train of thought, or rather of feeling, that can in a measure explain the aim of the attempt, made in the tale which follows, to present an unrestful episode in the obscure lives of a few individuals out of all the disregarded multitude of the bewildered, the simple and the voiceless. For, if any part of truth dwells in the belief confessed above, it becomes evident that there is not a place of splendour or a dark corner of the earth that does not deserve, if only a passing glance of wonder and pity. The motive, then, may be held to justify the matter of the work; but this preface, which is simply an avowal of endeavour, cannot end here—for the avowal is not yet complete.

Fiction—if it at all aspires to be art—appeals to temperament. And in truth it must be, like painting, like music, like all art, the appeal of one temperament to all the other innumerable temperaments whose subtle and resistless power endows passing events with their true meaning, and creates the moral, the emotional atmosphere of the place and time. Such an appeal to be effective must be an impression conveyed through the senses; and, in fact, it cannot be made in any other way, because temperament, whether individual or collective, is not amenable to persuasion. All art, therefore, appeals primarily to the senses, and the artistic aim when expressing itself in written words must also make its appeal through the senses, if its high desire is to reach the secret spring of responsive emotions. It must strenuously aspire to the plasticity of sculpture, to the colour of painting, and to the magic suggestive-

ness of music—which is the art of arts. And it is only through complete, unswerving devotion to the perfect blending of form and
substance; it is only through an unremitting never-discouraged care
for the shape and ring of sentences that an approach can be made
to plasticity, to colour, and that the light of magic suggestiveness
may be brought to play for an evanescent instant over the commonplace surface of words: of the old, old words, worn thin, de-
faced by ages of careless usage.

The sincere endeavour to accomplish that creative task, to go as
far on that road as his strength will carry him, to go undeterred by
faltering, weariness or reproach, is the only valid justification for
the worker in prose. And if his conscience is clear, his answer to
those who in the fulness of a wisdom which looks for immediate
profit, demand specifically to be edified, consoled, amused; who demand to be promptly improved, or encouraged, or frightened, or
shocked, or charmed, must run thus:—My task which I am trying
to achieve is, by the power of the written word to make you hear, to
make you feel—it is, before all, to make you *see*. That—and no
more, and it is everything. If I succeed, you shall find there according to your deserts: encouragement, consolation, fear, charm—all
you demand—and, perhaps, also that glimpse of truth for which
you have forgotten to ask.

To snatch in a moment of courage, from the remorseless rush of
time, a passing phase of life, is only the beginning of the task. The
task approached in tenderness and faith is to hold up unquestion-
ingly, without choice and without fear, the rescued fragment before
all eyes in the light of a sincere mood. It is to show its vibration, its
colour, its form; and through its movement, its form, and its colour,
reveal the substance of its truth—disclose its inspiring secret: the
stress and passion within the core of each convincing moment. In a
single-minded attempt of that kind, if one be deserving and fortunate, one may perchance attain to such clearness of sincerity that
at last the presented vision of regret or pity, of terror or mirth, shall
awaken in the hearts of the beholders that feeling of unavoidable
solidarity; of the solidarity in mysterious origin, in toil, in joy, in
hope, in uncertain fate, which binds men to each other and all
mankind to the visible world.

It is evident that he who, rightly or wrongly, holds by the convictions expressed above cannot be faithful to any one of the temporary formulas of his craft. The enduring part of them—the truth
which each only imperfectly veils—should abide with him as the
most precious of his possessions, but they all: Realism, Romanti-
cism, Naturalism, even the unofficial sentimentalism (which like
the poor, is exceedingly difficult to get rid of), all these gods must,
after a short period of fellowship, abandon him—even on the very

threshold of the temple—to the stammerings of his conscience and to the outspoken consciousness of the difficulties of his work. In that uneasy solitude the supreme cry of Art for Art itself, loses the exciting ring of its apparent immorality. It sounds far off. It has ceased to be a cry, and is heard only as a whisper, often incomprehensible, but at times and faintly encouraging.

Sometimes, stretched at ease in the shade of a roadside tree, we watch the motions of a labourer in a distant field, and after a time, begin to wonder languidly as to what the fellow may be at. We watch the movements of his body, the waving of his arms, we see him bend down, stand up, hesitate, begin again. It may add to the charm of an idle hour to be told the purpose of his exertions. If we know he is trying to lift a stone, to dig a ditch, to uproot a stump, we look with a more real interest at his efforts; we are disposed to condone the jar of his agitation upon the restfulness of the landscape; and even, if in a brotherly frame of mind, we may bring ourselves to forgive his failure. We understood his object, and, after all, the fellow has tried, and perhaps he had not the strength—and perhaps he had not the knowledge. We forgive, go on our way—and forget.

And so it is with the workman of art. Art is long and life is short, and success is very far off. And thus, doubtful of strength to travel so far, we talk a little about the aim—the aim of art, which, like life itself, is inspiring, difficult—obscured by mists. It is not in the clear logic of a triumphant conclusion; it is not in the unveiling of one of those heartless secrets which are called the Laws of Nature. It is not less great, but only more difficult.

To arrest, for the space of a breath, the hands busy about the work of the earth, and compel men entranced by the sight of distant goals to glance for a moment at the surrounding vision of form and colour, of sunshine and shadows; to make them pause for a look, for a sigh, for a smile—such is the aim, difficult and evanescent, and reserved only for a very few to achieve. But sometimes, by the deserving and the fortunate, even that task is accomplished. And when it is accomplished—behold!—all the truth of life is there: a moment of vision, a sigh, a smile—and the return to an eternal rest.

JOSEPH CONRAD

Books†

I

* * * It has been said a long time ago that books have their fate. They have, and it is very much like the destiny of man. They share with us the great incertitude of ignominy or glory—of severe justice and senseless persecution—of calumny and misunderstanding— the shame of undeserved success. Of all the inanimate objects, of all men's creations, books are the nearest to us, for they contain our very thought, our ambitions, our indignations, our illusions, our fidelity to truth, and our persistent leaning towards error. But most of all they resemble us in their precarious hold on life. A bridge constructed according to the rules of the art of bridge-building is certain of a long, honourable and useful career. But a book as good in its way as the bridge may perish obscurely on the very day of its birth. The art of their creators is not sufficient to give them more than a moment of life. Of the books born from the rest-lessness, the inspiration, and the vanity of human minds those that the Muses would love best lie more than all others under the men-ace of an early death. Sometimes their defects will save them. Sometimes a book fair to see may—to use a lofty expression—have no individual soul. Obviously a book of that sort cannot die. It can only crumble into dust. But the best of books drawing sustenance from the sympathy and memory of men have lived on the brink of destruction, for men's memories are short, and their sympathy is, we must admit, a very fluctuating, unprincipled emotion.

No secret of eternal life for our books can be found amongst the formulas of art, any more than for our bodies in a prescribed com-bination of drugs. This is not because some books are not worthy of enduring life, but because the formulas of art are dependent on things variable, unstable and untrustworthy; on human sympathies, on prejudices, on likes and dislikes, on the sense of virtue and the sense of propriety, on beliefs and theories that, indestructible in themselves, always change their form—often in the lifetime of one fleeting generation.

II

Of all books, novels, which the Muses should love, make a seri-ous claim on our compassion. The art of the novelist is simple. At

† From *Notes on Life and Letters* (Garden City, NY: Doubleday, Page and Company, 1923), pp. 3–10. First published in 1905. Notes are the Editor's.

the same time it is the most elusive of all creative arts, the most liable to be obscured by the scruples of its servants and votaries, the one pre-eminently destined to bring trouble to the mind and the heart of the artist. After all, the creation of a world is not a small undertaking except perhaps to the divinely gifted. In truth every novelist must begin by creating for himself a world, great or little, in which he can honestly believe. This world cannot be made otherwise than in his own image: it is fated to remain individual and a little mysterious, and yet it must resemble something already familiar to the experience, the thoughts and the sensations of his readers. At the heart of fiction, even the least worthy of the name, some sort of truth can be found—if only the truth of a childish theatrical ardour in the game of life, as in the novels of Dumas the father. But the fair truth of human delicacy can be found in Mr. Henry James's novels; and the comical, appalling truth of human rapacity let loose amongst the spoils of existence lives in the monstrous world created by Balzac.[1] The pursuit of happiness by means lawful and unlawful, through resignation or revolt, by the clever manipulation of conventions or by solemn hanging on to the skirts of the latest scientific theory, is the only theme that can be legitimately developed by the novelist who is the chronicler of the adventures of mankind amongst the dangers of the kingdom of the earth. And the kingdom of this earth itself, the ground upon which his individualities stand, stumble, or die, must enter into his scheme of faithful record. To encompass all this in one harmonious conception is a great feat; and even to attempt it deliberately with serious intention, not from the senseless prompting of an ignorant heart, is an honourable ambition. For it requires some courage to step in calmly where fools may be eager to rush. As a distinguished and successful French novelist once observed of fiction, "C'est un art *trop* difficile."[2]

It is natural that the novelist should doubt his ability to cope with his task. He imagines it more gigantic than it is. And yet literary creation being only one of the legitimate forms of human activity has no value but on the condition of not excluding the fullest recognition of all the more distinct forms of action. This condition is sometimes forgotten by the man of letters, who often, especially in his youth, is inclined to lay a claim of exclusive superiority for his own amongst all the other tasks of the human mind. The mass of verse and prose may glimmer here and there with the glow of a divine spark, but in the sum of human effort it has no special im-

1. Alexandre Dumas (1802–70), best known for his stories about the Three Musketeers and the Count of Monte Cristo, his son was also a novelist; Henry James (1843–1916), American novelist whom Conrad called a "historian of fine consciences" (see below); Honoré de Balzac (1799–1850), author of the multivolume "Human Comedy," a panoramic depiction of French society.
2. It is an *excessively* difficult art (French).

portance. There is no justificative formula for its existence any
more than for any other artistic achievement. With the rest of them
it is destined to be forgotten, without, perhaps, leaving the faintest
trace. Where a novelist has an advantage over the workers in other
fields of thought is in his privilege of freedom—the freedom of expression and the freedom of confessing his innermost beliefs—
which should console him for the hard slavery of the pen.

III

Liberty of imagination should be the most precious possession of
a novelist. * * *

It must not be supposed that I claim for the artist in fiction the
freedom of moral Nihilism. I would require from him many acts of
faith of which the first would be the cherishing of an undying hope;
and hope, it will not be contested, implies all the piety of effort and
renunciation. It is the God-sent form of trust in the magic force
and inspiration belonging to the life of this earth. We are inclined
to forget that the way of excellence is in the intellectual, as distinguished from emotional, humility. What one feels so hopelessly
barren in declared pessimism is just its arrogance. It seems as if the
discovery made by many men at various times that there is much
evil in the world were a source of proud and unholy joy unto some
of the modern writers. That frame of mind is not the proper one in
which to approach seriously the art of fiction. It gives an author—
goodness only knows why—an elated sense of his own superiority.
And there is nothing more dangerous than such an elation to that
absolute loyalty towards his feelings and sensations an author
should keep hold of in his most exalted moments of creation.

To be hopeful in an artistic sense it is not necessary to think that
the world is good. It is enough to believe that there is no impossibility of its being made so. If the flight of imaginative thought may
be allowed to rise superior to many moralities current amongst
mankind, a novelist who would think himself of a superior essence
to other men would miss the first condition of his calling. To have
the gift of words is no such great matter. A man furnished with a
long-range weapon does not become a hunter or a warrior by the
mere possession of a fire-arm; many other qualities of character
and temperament are necessary to make him either one or the
other. Of him from whose armoury of phrases one in a hundred
thousand may perhaps hit the far-distant and elusive mark of art I
would ask that in his dealings with mankind he should be capable
of giving a tender recognition to their obscure virtues. I would not
have him impatient with their small failings and scornful of their
errors. I would not have him expect too much gratitude from that

humanity whose fate, as illustrated in individuals, it is open to him to depict as ridiculous or terrible. I would wish him to look with a large forgiveness at men's ideas and prejudices, which are by no means the outcome of malevolence, but depend on their education, their social status, even their professions. The good artist should expect no recognition of his toil and no admiration of his genius, because his toil can with difficulty be appraised and his genius cannot possibly mean anything to the illiterate who, even from the dreadful wisdom of their evoked dead, have, so far, culled nothing but inanities and platitudes. I would wish him to enlarge his sympathies by patient and loving observation while he grows in mental power. It is in the impartial practice of life, if anywhere, that the promise of perfection for his art can be found, rather than in the absurd formulas trying to prescribe this or that particular method of technique or conception. Let him mature the strength of his imagination amongst the things of this earth, which it is his business to cherish and know, and refrain from calling down his inspiration ready-made from some heaven of perfections of which he knows nothing. And I would not grudge him the proud illusion that will come sometimes to a writer: the illusion that his achievement has almost equalled the greatness of his dream. * * *

JOSEPH CONRAD

Henry James: An Appreciation†

* * * In one of his critical studies, published some fifteen years ago, Mr. Henry James claims for the novelist the standing of the historian as the only adequate one, as for himself and before his audience.[1] I think that the claim cannot be contested, and that the position is unassailable. Fiction is history, human history, or it is nothing. But it is also more than that; it stands on firmer ground, being based on the reality of forms and the observation of social phenomena, whereas history is based on documents, and the reading of print and handwriting—on second-hand impression. Thus fiction is nearer truth. But let that pass. A historian may be an artist too, and a novelist is a historian, the preserver, the keeper, the expounder, of human experience. As is meet for a man of his descent

† From *Notes on Life and Letters* (Garden City, NY: Doubleday, Page and Company, 1923), pp. 11–19. First published in 1905. Henry James (1843–1916), American expatriate novelist who made his career in England, dramatized the consciousness of exquisitely sensitive characters in morally ambiguous situations. Notes are the Editor's.
1. James's essay "The Art of Fiction" (1884) calls the novel "a personal, a direct impression of life" and claims that "the novelist is [no] less occupied in looking for the truth . . . than the historian."

and tradition, Mr. Henry James is the historian of fine consciences.[2]

Of course, this is a general statement; but I don't think its truth will be, or can be questioned. Its fault is that it leaves so much out; and, besides, Mr. Henry James is much too considerable to be put into the nutshell of a phrase. The fact remains that he has made his choice, and that his choice is justified up to the hilt by the success of his art. He has taken for himself the greater part. The range 'of a fine conscience covers more good and evil than the range of conscience which may be called, roughly, not fine; a conscience, less troubled by the nice discrimination of shades of conduct. A fine conscience is more concerned with essentials; its triumphs are more perfect, if less profitable, in a worldly sense. There is, in short, more truth in its working for a historian to detect and to show. It is a thing of infinite complication and suggestion. None of these escapes the art of Mr. Henry James. He has mastered the country, his domain, not wild indeed, but full of romantic glimpses, of deep shadows and sunny places. There are no secrets left within his range. He has disclosed them as they should be disclosed—that is, beautifully. And, indeed, ugliness has but little place in this world of his creation. Yet it is always felt in the truthfulness of his art; it is there, it surrounds the scene, it presses close upon it. It is made visible, tangible, in the struggles, in the contacts of the fine consciences, in their perplexities, in the sophism of their mistakes. For a fine conscience is naturally a virtuous one. What is natural about it is just its fineness, and abiding sense of the intangible, ever-present, right. It is most visible in their ultimate triumph, in their emergence from miracle, through an energetic act of renunciation. Energetic, not violent; the distinction is wide, enormous, like that between substance and shadow.

Through it all Mr. Henry James keeps a firm hold of the substance, of what is worth having, of what is worth holding. The contrary opinion has been, if not absolutely affirmed, then at least implied, with some frequency. To most of us, living willingly in a sort of intellectual moonlight, in the faintly reflected light of truth, the shadows so firmly renounced by Mr. Henry James's men and women, stand out endowed with extraordinary value, with a value so extraordinary that their rejection offends, by its uncalled-for scrupulousness, those business-like instincts which a careful Providence has implanted in our breasts. And, apart from that just cause of discontent, it is obvious that a solution by rejection must always present a certain lack of finality, especially startling when contrasted with the usual methods of solution by rewards and punish-

2. The French "conscience" also refers to "consciousness" and "perception."

ments, by crowned love, by fortune, by a broken leg or a sudden death. Why the reading public which, as a body, has never laid upon a story-teller the command to be an artist, should demand from him this sham of Divine Omnipotence, is utterly incomprehensible. But so it is; and these solutions are legitimate inasmuch as they satisfy the desire for finality, for which our hearts yearn, with a longing greater than the longing for the loaves and fishes of this earth. Perhaps the only true desire of mankind, coming thus to light in its hours of leisure, is to be set at rest. One is never set at rest by Mr. Henry James's novels. His books end as an episode in life ends. You remain with the sense of the life still going on; and even the subtle presence of the dead is felt in that silence that comes upon the artist-creation when the last word has been read. It is eminently satisfying, but it is not final. Mr. Henry James, great artist and faithful historian, never attempts the impossible.

JOSEPH CONRAD

Preface to *Youth*†

The three stories in this volume lay no claim to unity of artistic purpose. The only bond between them is that of the time in which they were written. They belong to the period immediately following the publication of *The Nigger of the "Narcissus,"* and preceding the first conception of *Nostromo*, two books which, it seems to me, stand apart and by themselves in the body of my work. It is also the period during which I contributed to *Maga*;[1] a period dominated by *Lord Jim* and associated in my grateful memory with the late Mr. William Blackwood's encouraging and helpful kindness.

Youth was not my first contribution to *Maga*. It was the second. But that story marks the first appearance in the world of the man Marlow, with whom my relations have grown very intimate in the course of years.[2] The origins of that gentleman (nobody as far as I know had ever hinted that he was anything but that)—his origins have been the subject of some literary speculation of, I am glad to say, a friendly nature.

One would think that I am the proper person to throw a light on the matter; but in truth I find that it isn't so easy. It is pleasant to

---

† From *Youth: A Narrative and Two Other Stories* (Garden City, NY: Doubleday, Page and Company, 1923), pp. ix–xii. This volume, originally published in 1902, collected "Youth," *Heart of Darkness*, and "The End of the Tether." The preface was added in 1917. Notes are the Editor's.
1. *Blackwood's Magazine*, a monthly that from 1897 to 1902 published "Karain," "Youth," *Heart of Darkness*, and *Lord Jim*.
2. Marlow is the narrator of "Youth," *Heart of Darkness*, *Lord Jim*, and *Chance*.

remember that nobody had charged him with fraudulent purposes or looked down on him as a charlatan; but apart from that he was supposed to be all sorts of things: a clever screen, a mere device, a 'personator,' a familiar spirit, a whispering 'daemon.' I myself have been suspected of a meditated plan for his capture.

That is not so. I made no plans. The man Marlow and I came together in the casual manner of those health-resort acquaintances which sometimes ripen into friendships. This one has ripened. For all his assertiveness in matters of opinion he is not an intrusive person. He haunts my hours of solitude, when, in silence, we lay our heads together in great comfort and harmony; but as we part at the end of a tale I am never sure that it may not be for the last time. Yet I don't think that either of us would care much to survive the other. In his case, at any rate, his occupation would be gone and he would suffer from that extinction, because I suspect him of some vanity. I don't mean vanity in the Solomonian sense.[3] Of all my people he's the one that has never been a vexation to my spirit. A most discreet, understanding man. . . .

Even before appearing in book-form *Youth* was very well received. It lies on me to confess at last, and this is as good a place for it as another, that I have been all my life—all my two lives—the spoiled adopted child of Great Britain and even of the Empire; for it was Australia that gave me my first command.[4] I break out into this declaration not because of a lurking tendency to megalomania, but, on the contrary, as a man who has no very notable illusions about himself. I follow the instincts of vain-glory and humility natural to all mankind. For it can hardly be denied that it is not their own deserts that men are most proud of, but rather of their prodigious luck of their marvellous fortune: of that in their lives for which thanks and sacrifices must be offered on the altars of the inscrutable gods.

Heart of Darkness also received a certain amount of notice from the first; and of its origins this much may be said: it is well known that curious men go prying into all sorts of places (where they have no business) and come out of them with all kinds of spoil. This story, and one other, not in this volume,[5] are all the spoil I brought out from the centre of Africa, where, really, I had no sort of business. More ambitious in its scope and longer in the telling, *Heart of Darkness* is quite as authentic in fundamentals as *Youth*. It is, obviously, written in another mood. I won't characterize the mood

---

3. In Ecclesiastes 1:14, Solomon declares: "I have seen all the works that are done under the sun; and, behold, all is vanity and vexation of spirit."
4. From January 1888 through March 1889, Conrad was master of the Australian ship *Otago*, his only command other than his brief stint in charge of the *Roi des Belges*.
5. The ironically named "Outpost of Progress" (1896).

precisely, but anybody can see that it is anything but the mood of wistful regret, of reminiscent tenderness.

One more remark may be added. *Youth* is a feat of memory. It is a record of experience; but that experience, in its facts, in its inwardness and in its outward colouring, begins and ends in myself. *Heart of Darkness* is experience too; but it is experience pushed a little (and only very little) beyond the actual facts of the case for the perfectly legitimate, I believe, purpose of bringing it home to the minds and bosoms of the readers. There it was no longer a matter of sincere colouring. It was like another art altogether. That sombre theme had to be given a sinister resonance, a tonality of its own, a continued vibration that, I hoped, would hang in the air and dwell on the ear after the last note had been struck.

*   *   *

JOSEPH CONRAD

Preface to *A Personal Record*†

The re-issue of this book in a new form does not strictly speaking require another Preface. But since this is distinctly a place for personal remarks I take the opportunity to refer in this Author's Note to two points arising from certain statements about myself I have noticed of late in the press.

One of them bears upon the question of language. I have always felt myself looked upon somewhat in the light of a phenomenon, a position which outside the circus world cannot be regarded as desirable. It needs a special temperament for one to derive much gratification from the fact of being able to do freakish things intentionally, and, as it were, from mere vanity.

The fact of my not writing in my native language has been of course commented upon frequently in reviews and notices of my various works and in the more extended critical articles. I suppose that was unavoidable; and indeed these comments were of the most flattering kind to one's vanity. But in that matter I have no vanity that could be flattered. I could not have it. The first object of this note is to disclaim any merit there might have been in an act of deliberate volition.

The impression of my having exercised a choice between the two languages, French and English, both foreign to me, has got abroad somehow. That impression is erroneous. *   *   *

† From *A Personal Record* (1912; Garden City, NY: Doubleday, Page and Company, 1923), pp. v–xii. This preface was first published as an "Author's Note" to the 1919 edition.

This misapprehension, for it is nothing else, was no doubt my fault. I must have expressed myself badly in the course of a friendly and intimate talk when one doesn't watch one's phrases carefully. My recollection of what I meant to say is: that *had I been under the necessity* of making a choice between the two, and though I knew French fairly well and was familiar with it from infancy, I would have been afraid to attempt expression in a language so perfectly "crystallized." This, I believe, was the word I used. * * *

The truth of the matter is that my faculty to write in English is as natural as any other aptitude with which I might have been born. I have a strange and overpowering feeling that it had always been an inherent part of myself. English was for me neither a matter of choice nor adoption. The merest idea of choice had never entered my head. And as to adoption—well, yes, there was adoption; but it was I who was adopted by the genius of the language, which directly I came out of the stammering stage made me its own so completely that its very idioms I truly believe had a direct action on my temperament and fashioned my still plastic character.

It was a very intimate action and for that very reason it is too mysterious to explain. The task would be as impossible as trying to explain love at first sight. There was something in this conjunction of exulting, almost physical recognition, the same sort of emotional surrender and the same pride of possession, all united in the wonder of a great discovery; but there was on it none of that shadow of dreadful doubt that falls on the very flame of our perishable passions. One knew very well that this was for ever.

A matter of discovery and not of inheritance, that very inferiority of the title makes the faculty still more precious, lays the possessor under a lifelong obligation to remain worthy of his great fortune. But it seems to me that all this sounds as if I were trying to explain—a task which I have just pronounced to be impossible. If in action we may admit with awe that the Impossible recedes before men's indomitable spirit, the Impossible in matters of analysis will always make a stand at some point or other. All I can claim after all those years of devoted practice, with the accumulated anguish of its doubts, imperfections and falterings in my heart, is the right to be believed when I say that if I had not written in English I would not have written at all.

The other remark which I wish to make here is also a rectification but of a less direct kind. It has nothing to do with the medium of expression. It bears on the matter of my authorship in another way. It is not for me to criticise my judges, the more so because I always felt that I was receiving more than justice at their hands. But it seems to me that their unfailingly interested sympathy has ascribed to racial and historical influences much, of what, I believe, appertains simply to the individual. Nothing is more foreign than what in the literary world is called Sclavonism,[1] to the Polish temperament with its tradition of self-government, its chivalrous view of moral restraints and an exaggerated respect for individual rights: not to mention the important fact that the whole Polish mentality, Western in complexion, had received its training from Italy and France and, historically, had always remained, even in religious matters, in sympathy with the most liberal currents of European thought. An impartial view of humanity in all its degrees of splendour and misery together with a special regard for the rights of the unprivileged of this earth, not on any mystic ground but on the ground of simple fellowship and honourable reciprocity of services, was the dominant characteristic of the mental and moral atmosphere of the houses which sheltered my hazardous childhood:— matters of calm and deep conviction both lasting and consistent, and removed as far as possible from that humanitarianism that seems to be merely a matter of crazy nerves or a morbid conscience.

*   *   *

Selected Letters

To William Blackwood†

Pent Farm
31/12/98

Dear Mr Blackwood.

Come this moment to hand is your good le[t]ter whose kind wishes, believe me, I reciprocate with all my heart.

Your proposal delights me. As it happens I am (and have been for the last 10 days) working for *Maga*. The thing is far advanced and would have been finished by this only our little boy[1] fell ill, I was disturbed and upset and the work suffered. I expect to be ready in a very few days. It is a narrative after the manner of *youth* told by the same man dealing with his experiences on a river in Central Africa.

---

1. Conrad was sometimes linked with Dostoevsky as a "Slavonic" writer. This infuriated him because he found distasteful the mysticism and irrationality implied by the association. He complained, for example, to Edward Garnett (whose wife Constance was Dostoevksy's translator): "I don't know what D stands for or reveals, but I do know that he is too Russian for me. It sounds to me like some fierce mouthings from prehistoric ages" (*Collected Letters*, v:70). [Editor]

† From *The Collected Letters of Joseph Conrad*, ed. Karl and Davies (Cambridge: Cambridge UP, 1986), 2: 139–40. Reprinted by permission of Cambridge University Press. Blackwood had asked Conrad for a contribution to the February issue of *Blackwood's Magazine*, its thousandth number, in which *Heart of Darkness* eventually appeared. All notes in this section are by the editor of this Norton Critical Edition.

1. His eleven-month-old son, Borys.

The *idea* in it is not as obvious as in *youth*—or at least not so obviously presented. I tell you all this, for tho' I have no doubts as to the *workmanship* I do not know whether the *subject* will commend itself to you for that particular number. Of course I should be very glad to appear in it and shall try to hurry up the copy for that express purpose, but I wish you to understand that I am prepared to leave the ultimate decision as to the date of appearance to your decision after perusal.

The title I am thinking of is *"The Heart of Darkness"* but the narrative is not gloomy. The criminality of inefficiency and pure selfishness when tackling the civilizing work in Africa is a justifiable idea. The subject is of our time distinc[t]ly—though not topically treated. It is a story as much as my *Outpost of Progress* was but, so to speak 'takes in' more—is a little wider—is less concentrated upon individuals. I destine it for the vol: which is to bear Your imprint. Its length will be under 20,000 words as I see it now.[2] If suitable and you wish to curtail it a couple of pars: could be taken out—from the proof, perhaps.

There is also the question of McClure securing copyright in the States. They bungled the *Youth* affair and I am not in a position to despise the almighty dollar—as yet.[3]

All I can do is to hurry up. Meantime many thanks for thinking of me.

Friendly greetings to Your Nephew.[4] I am delighted to be remembered by him.

I am dear Mr Blackwood, most sincerely yours

Jph. Conrad

To R. B. Cunninghame Graham†

Pent Farm
8 Feb[r] 99.

Cherissime ami.[1]

I am simply in the seventh heaven to find you like the *H of D* so far. You bless me indeed. Mind you don't curse me by and bye for the very same thing. There are two more instalments in which the idea is so wrapped up in secondary notions that You—even You!—may miss it. And also You must remember that I don't start with an abstract notion. I start with definite images and as their rendering

---

2. The final version is twice as long.
3. The S. S. McClure Company bought the North American rights to several of Conrad's works, but the American copyright of "Youth" was apparently mishandled and Conrad lost money.
4. George Blackwood, later his uncle's successor.
† From *Collected Letters*, 2:157–61.
1. Dearest friend (a mixture of French and Italian).

is true some little effect is produced. So far the note struck chimes in with your convictions—mais après?² There is an après. But I think that if you look a little into the episodes you will find in them the right intention though I fear nothing that is practically effective. Somme toute c'est une bête d'histoire qui aurait pu être quelque chose de très bien si j'avais su l'écrire.³

The thing in West. Gaz. is excellent, excellent. I am most interested in your plans of work and travel. I don't know in which most. Nous allons causer de tout cela.⁴

As to the peace meeting. If you want me to come I want still more to hear you. But—I am not a peace man, nor a democrat (I don't know what the word means really) and if I come I shall go into the body of the hall. I want to hear you—just as I want always to read you. I can't be an accomplice after or before the fact to any sort of fraternity that includes the westerners whom I so dislike. The platform! I pensez-Vous? Il y aura des Russes.⁵ Impossible! I can not admit the idea of fraternity not so much because I believe it impracticable, but because its propaganda (the only thing really tangible about it) tends to weaken the national sentiment the preservation of which is my concern. When I was in Poland 5 years ago and managed to get in contact with the youth of the university in Warsaw I preached at them and abused them for their social democratic tendencies. L'idée democratique est un très beau phantôme, and to run after it may be fine sport, but I confess I do not see what evils it is destined to remedy.⁶ It confers distinction on Messieurs Jaurès, Liebknecht & Cᵒ and your adhesion confers distinction upon it. International fraternity may be an object to strive for and, in sober truth, since it has Your support I will try to think it serious, but that illusion imposes by its size alone. Franchement what would you think of an attempt to promote fraternity amongst people living in the same street. I don't even mention two neighbouring streets. Two ends of the same street. There is already as much fraternity as there can be—and that[']s very little and that very little is no good. What does fraternity mean. Abnegation—self-sacrifice means something. Fraternity means nothing unless the Cain-Abel business. Thats your true fraternity. Assez.⁷ Man is a vi-

2. But after? (French).
3. In short, it's a stupid story that would have been very good if I had known how to write it (French).
4. We will talk about all of this (French). Graham had published a piece about New Zealand in the *Westminster Gazette*.
5. Conrad attended a peace conference organized by the Social Democratic Federation on 8 March 1898 at which Graham spoke. Russian speakers were also on the platform.
6. The idea of democracy is a very beautiful illusion (French). Jean Jaurès (1859–1914), French socialist and pacifist, and Wilhelm Liebknecht (1826–1900), German social democrat, spoke at the conference.
7. Enough (French). The rest of the letter continues in French (translation by Karl and Davies).

cious animal. His viciousness must be organised. Crime is a necessary condition of organised existence. Society is fundamentally
criminal—or it would not exist. Selfishness preserves everything—
absolutely everything—everything we hate and everything we love.
And everything holds together. That is why I respect the extreme
anarchists.—'I hope for general extermination'. Very well. It's justifiable and, moreover, it is plain. One compromises with words.
There's no end to it. It's like a forest where no one knows the way.
One is lost even as one is calling out 'I am saved!'

No. A definite first principle is needed. If the idea of nationhood
brings suffering and its service brings death, that is always worth
more than service to the ghosts of a dead eloquence—precisely because the eloquence is disembodied. Believe me if I tell you that
these questions are very real to me—much more so than to Messrs
Jaurès, Liebknecht and Co. You—you can do everything. Essentially, you are a *frondeur*.[8] You are allowed to be. The Fronde, moreover, was conducted by the aristocracy. For myself, I look at the
future from the depths of a very dark past, and I find I am allowed
nothing but fidelity to an absolutely lost cause, to an idea without a
future.

And so, I often do not think about it. Everything vanishes. Only
truth remains—a sinister and fleeting ghost whose image is impossible to fix. I regret nothing, I hope for nothing, for I realise that
neither regret nor hope means anything to my own being. Towards
myself, I practice a fierce and rational selfishness. Therein I pause.
Then thinking returns. Life starts again, regrets, memories, and a
hopelessness darker than night.

I don't know why I'm telling you all this today. It's that I don't
want you to believe me indifferent. I'm not indifferent to what concerns you. But my concern is elsewhere, my thinking follows another path, my heart wants something else, my soul suffers from
another kind of impotence. Do you understand? You who devote
your talents and your enthusiasm to the cause of humanity, you will
understand no doubt why I must—I need to—keep my thinking in-
violate as a final act of fidelity to a lost cause. It's all I can do. I've
thrown my life to all the winds of heaven, but I have kept my way of
thinking. It's a little thing—it's everything—it's nothing—it's life itself. This letter is incoherent, like my life, but the highest logic is
there nevertheless—the logic that leads to madness. But everyday
worries make us forget the cruel truth. It's fortunate.

Always yours from the heart
Jph Conrad.

8. A nobleman who participated in rebellions against King Louis XIV, 1648–53.

To Hugh Clifford†

Pent Farm
9th Oct 99

My Dear Mr. Clifford.

* * *

Of course the matter is admirable—the knowledge, the feeling, the sympathy; it is sure to win perfect and full recognition. It is all sterling metal; a thing of absolute value. There can be no question of it not only for those who know but even for those who approach the book with blank minds on the subject of the race you have, in more than one sense, made your own. And as to the manner—well! I know you are not a seeker after mere expression and I beg leave to offer only one remark.

You do not leave enough to the imagination. I do not mean as to facts—the facts can not be too explicitly stated; I am alluding simply to the phrasing. True a man who knows so much (without taking into account the manner in which his knowledge was acquired) may well spare himself the trouble of meditating over the words, only that words, groups of words, words standing alone, are symbols of life, have the power in their sound or their aspect to present the very thing you wish to hold up before the mental vision of your readers. The things "as they are" exist in words; therefore words should be handled with care lest the picture, the image of truth abiding in facts should become distorted—or blurred.

These are the considerations for a mere craftsman—you may say; and you may also conceivably say that I have nothing else to trouble my head about. However the *whole* of the truth lies in the presentation; therefore the expression should be studied in the interest of veracity. This is the only morality of *art* apart from *subject*.

* * *

To the New York Times "Saturday Review"‡

Pent Farm, Kent
Aug. 2, 1901

* * * [T]he business of a work striving to be art is not to teach or to prophesy (as we have been charged, on this side, with attempting,) nor yet to pronounce a definite conclusion.

This, the teaching, the conclusions, even to the prophesying,

---

† From *Collected Letters*, 2:199–202. Clifford (1866–1941), colonial civil servant and author, had just sent Conrad his latest volume of stories, *In a Corner of Asia*.
‡ From *Collected Letters*, 2:346–49. The letter responds to a review of *The Inheritors*, an allegorical novel written in collaboration with Ford Madox Hueffer (later Ford Madox Ford; 1873–1939) that satirizes King Leopold II's abuses in the Congo Free State.

may be safely left to science, which, whatever authority it may claim, is not concerned with truth at all, but with the exact order of such phenomena as fall under the perception of the senses. Its conclusions are quite true enough if they can be made useful to the furtherance of our little schemes to make our earth a little more habitable. The laws it discovers remain certain and immovable for the time of several generations. But in the sphere of an art dealing with a subject matter whose origin and end are alike unknown there is no possible conclusion. The only indisputable truth of life is our ignorance. Besides this there is nothing evident, nothing absolute, nothing uncontradicted; there is no principle, no instinct, no impulse that can stand alone at the beginning of things and look confidently to the end. Egoism, which is the moving force of the world, and altruism, which is its morality, these two contradictory instincts of which one is so plain and the other so mysterious, cannot serve us unless in the incomprehensible alliance of their irreconcilable antagonism. Each alone would be fatal to our ambition. For, in the hour of undivided triumph, one would make our inheritance too arid to be worth having and the other too sorrowful to own.

Fiction, at the point of development at which it has arrived, demands from the writer a spirit of scrupulous abnegation. The only legitimate basis of creative work lies in the courageous recognition of all the irreconcilable antagonisms that make our life so enigmatic, so burdensome, so fascinating, so dangerous—so full of hope. They exist! And this is the only fundamental truth of fiction. Its recognition must be critical in its nature, inasmuch that in its character it may be joyous, it may be sad; it may be angry with revolt, or submissive in resignation. The mood does not matter. It is only the writer's self-forgetful fidelity to his sensations that matters. But, whatever light he flashes on it, the fundamental truth remains, and it is only in its name that the barren struggle of contradictions assumes the dignity of moral strife going on ceaselessly to a mysterious end—with our consciousness powerless but concerned sitting enthroned like a melancholy parody of eternal wisdom above the dust of the contest.

Joseph Conrad

To John Galsworthy†

Pent Farm
11th Nov. 1901

Dearest Jack.

*   *   *

The fact is you want more scepticism at the very foundation of your work. Scepticism the tonic of minds, the tonic of life, the agent of truth—the way of art and salvation. In a book you should love the idea and be scrupulously faithful to your conception of life. There lies the honour of the writer, not in the fidelity to his personages. You must never allow them to decoy you out of yourself. As against your people you must preserve an attitude of perfect indifference— the part of creative power. A creator must be indifferent; because directly the 'Fiat!' had issued from his lips there are the creatures made in his image that'll try to drag him down from his eminence— and belittle him by their worship. Your attitude to them should be purely intellectual, more independent, freer, less rigorous than it is. You seem for their sake to hug your conceptions of right or wrong too closely. There is exquisite atmosphere in your tales. What they want now is more air.

*   *   *

To William Blackwood‡

Pent Farm
31 May 1902

Dear Mr Blackwood.

*   *   *

I know exactly what I am doing. Mr George Blackwood's inciden- tal remark in his last letter that the story is not fairly begun yet[1] is in a measure correct but, on a large view, beside the point. For, the writing is as good as I can make it (first duty), and in the light of the final incident, the whole story in all its descriptive detail shall fall into its place—acquire its value and its significance. This is my

---

† From *Collected Letters*, 2:358–60. Galsworthy (1867–1933), English novelist best known for *The Forsyte Saga* (1922) and its sequels. Galsworthy's first story about the Forsyte family appeared in the collection *A Man of Devon*, which Conrad's letter re- sponds to.

‡ From *Collected Letters*, 2:415–18. Anxious with financial difficulties, Conrad met Black- wood in London earlier in the day and apparently had an awkward conversation in which the publisher voiced reservations about the value of his work. "I admit that after leaving you I remained for some time under the impression of my 'worthlessness,' " Conrad writes at the beginning of this long letter of explanation and self-justification; "I know that it is not necessary to say to You but I may just as well point out that I must not by any means be taken for a gifted loafer intent upon living upon credulous publishers."

1. Referring to "The End of the Tether," which appeared in *Blackwood's* in 1902 and was published in *Youth* with *Heart of Darkness*. The criticism Conrad attempts to rebut is that the story starts too slowly and takes too long to develop.

method based on deliberate conviction. I've never departed from it. I call your own kind self to witness and I beg to instance Karain— Lord Jim (where the method is fully developed)—the last pages of Heart of Darkness where the interview of the man and the girl locks in—as it were—the whole 30000 words of narrative description into one suggestive view of a whole phase of life and makes of that story something quite on another plane than an anecdote of a man who went mad in the Centre of Africa. And *Youth* itself (which I delight to know you like so well) exists only in virtue of my fidelity to the idea and the method. The favourable critics of that story, Q amongst others remarked with a sort of surprise "This after all is a story for boys yet— — — — —"[2]

Exactly. Out of the material of a boys' story I've made *Youth* by the force of the idea expressed in accordance with a strict conception of my method. And however unfavourably it may affect the business in hand I must confess that I shall not depart from my method. I am at need prepared to explain on what grounds I think it a true method. All my endeavours shall be directed to understand it better, to develop its great possibilities, to acquire greater skill in the handling—to mastery in short. You may wonder why I am telling you all this.

* * *

To Elsie Hueffer†

Pent Farm
3 Dec 1902

My dear Señora

I ought to have answered your letter before this; but I have been plunged in a torpor so profound that even your attack on my pet Heart of Darkness could do no more than make me roll my eyes ferociously. Then for another day I remained prone revolving thoughts of scathing reply. At last—I arose and . . .

Seriously—I don't know that you are wrong. I admit that your strictures are intelligible to me; and every criticism that is intelligible (a quality by no means common) must have some truth in it, if not the whole truth. I mean intelligible to the author of course. As I began by saying—yours is to me; therefore I, in a manner, bear witness to its truth, with (I confess) the greatest reluctance. And, of course, I don't admit the whole of your case. What I distinctly ad-

2. A. T. Quiller-Couch (1863–1944), English author and reviewer known by the pseudonym "Q."
† From *Collected Letters*, 2:460–61. Hueffer (née Martindale; 1876–1924), wife of Conrad's sometime collaborator Ford Madox Hueffer (Ford). Both families lived in close proximity to one another in Kent, not far from Canterbury and Rye (where Henry James resided).

mit is the fault of having made Kurtz too symbolic or rather symbolic at all. But the story being mainly a vehicle for conveying a batch of personal impressions I gave the rein to my mental laziness and took the line of the least resistance. This is then the whole Apologia pro Vita Kurtzii[1]—or rather for the tardiness of his vitality.

My indignation having been (at first) fulgurant[2] my gratitude for all the charming things you say so well in commendation of your servant burns with a steady and unalterable glow. Indeed, pray believe me, your letter has given me a very great pleasure; and I thank you for writing it; for to write to an author who sends his book is—generally—an odious task.

I may say then "Au revoir à bientôt."[3] I shall bring the cuttings with me. Most of them are unintelligible to me and consequently contain no truth. Jessie sends her love. Believe me always faithfully yours,

Jph Conrad.

To Barrett H. Clark†

Capel House
May 4th 1918

Dear Mr Clark.

* * *

You are right in thinking that I would be gratified by the appreciation of a mind younger than my own. But in truth I don't consider myself an Ancient. My writing life extends but only over twenty-three years, and I need not point out to an intelligence as alert as yours that all that time has been a time of evolution, in which some critics have detected three marked periods—and that the process is still going on. Some critics have found fault with me for not being constantly myself. But they are wrong. I am always myself. I am a man of formed character. Certain conclusions remain immovably fixed in my mind, but I am no slave to prejudices and formulas, and I shall never be. My attitudes to subjects and expressions, the angles of vision, my methods of composition will, within limits, be always changing—not because I am unstable or unprincipled but because I am free. Or perhaps it may be more exact to say, because I am always trying for freedom—within my limits.

Coming now to the subject of your inquiry I wish at first to put

1. A jocular allusion to Cardinal John Henry Newman's autobiography *Apologia pro vita sua* (1864).
2. Flashing like lightning.
3. Farewell until soon (French).
† From *The Collected Letters of Joseph Conrad*, ed. Laurence Davies, Frederick R. Karl, and Owen Knowles (Cambridge: Cambridge UP, 2002), 6:210–11. Clark (1890–1953), American editor and critic.

before you a general proposition: that a work of art is very seldom limited to one exclusive meaning and not necessarily tending to a definite conclusion. And this for the reason that the nearer it approaches art the more it acquires a symbolic character. This statement may surprise you who may imagine that I am alluding to the Symbolist School of poets and prose writers.[1] Theirs however is only a literary proceeding against which I have nothing to say. I am concerned here with something much larger . . . But no doubt you have meditated on this and kindred questions yourself. So I will only call your attention to the fact that the symbolic conception of a work of art has this advantage that it makes a triple appeal covering the whole field of life. All the great creations of literature have been symbolic, and in that way have gained in complexity, in power, in depth and in beauty.

I don't think you will quarrel with me on the ground of lack of precision; for as to precision of images and analysis my artistic conscience is at rest. I have given there all the truth that is in me; and all that the critics may say can make my honesty neither more nor less. But as to "final effect" my conscience has nothing to do with that. It is the critic's affair to bring to its contemplation his own honesty, his sensibility and intelligence. The matter for his conscience is just his judgment. If his conscience is busy with petty scruples and trammelled by superficial formulas then his judgment will be superficial and petty. But an artist has no right to quarrel with the inspirations, either lofty or base, of another soul.

*   *   *

To Richard Curle†

Oswalds, Bishopsbourne, Kent
April 24th, 1922

My dear Richard,

*   *   *

I have this morning received the article for the *Blue Peter*.[1] I think I have given you already to understand the nature of my feelings. Indeed, I spoke to you very openly, expressing my fundamental objection to the character you wished to give to it. I do not for a moment expect that what I am going to say here will convince you or influence you in the least. And, indeed, I have neither the wish

1. Originated in France but also important in England; rejected the materialism of realism and naturalism in favor of imaginative and spiritual suggestiveness. See Arthur Symons, *The Symbolist Movement in Literature* (1908). Also see the selection by Ian Watt in this Norton Critical Edition.
† From *Conrad to a Friend: 150 Selected Letters from Joseph Conrad to Richard Curle* (1928; New York: Russell & Russell, 1968), pp. 112–15. Curle (1883–1968), writer and editor, was a close friend during Conrad's last years and an executor of his estate.
1. Curle's article "Joseph Conrad in the Far East."

nor the right to assert my position. I will only point out to you that my feelings in that matter are at least as legitimate as your own. It is a strange fate that everything that I have, of set artistic purpose, laboured to leave indefinite, suggestive, in the penumbra of initial inspiration, should have that light turned on to it and its insignificance (as compared with, I might say without megalomania, the ampleness of my conceptions) exposed for any fool to comment upon or even for average minds to be disappointed with. Didn't it ever occur to you, my dear Curle, that I knew what I was doing in leaving the facts of my life and even of my tales in the background? Explicitness, my dear fellow, is fatal to the glamour of all artistic work, robbing it of all suggestiveness, destroying all illusion. You seem to believe in literalness and explicitness, in facts and also in expression. Yet nothing is more clear than the utter insignificance of explicit statement and also its power to call attention away from things that matter in the region of art.

There, however, I am afraid we will never agree. Your praise of my work, allied to your analysis of its origins (which really are not its origins at all, as you know perfectly well), sounds exaggerated by the mere force of contrast. I wouldn't talk like this if I did not attach a very great value to everything you write about me and did not believe in its wide influence. It isn't a matter of literary criticism at all if I venture to point out to you that the dogmatic, ex-cathedra[2] tone that you have adopted in your article positively frightens me. As you tell me that you have a copy of the article by you I'll venture to make a few alterations, more to let you see what is in my mind than with any hope of convincing you. I will only remark to you, my dear, that it is generally known that you are my intimate friend, that the text carries an air of authority and that a lot of dam[n]-fools will ascribe to me the initiative and the sanction of all the views and facts expressed. And one really could not blame them if they thought and said that I must have wanted all those facts disclosed.

All those are my personal feelings. You won't wonder at them if I call your attention to the fact that in "Youth," in which East or West are of no importance whatever, I kept the name of the Port of landing out of the record of "poeticised" sensations. The paragraph you quote of the East meeting the narrator is all right in itself; whereas directly it's connected with . . .[3] it becomes nothing at all . . . is a damned hole without any beach and without any glamour, and in relation to the parag. is not in tone. Therefore the par., when

2. Authoritative.
3. "I have here purposely omitted the name because Conrad was very anxious that no one should know it, for reasons he gives" [Curle].

pinned to a particular spot, must appear diminished—a fake. And yet it is true!

However, those are all private feelings. I think too that the impression of gloom, oppression, and tragedy, is too much emphasised. You know, my dear, I have suffered from such judgments in the early days; but now the point of view, even in America, has swung in another direction; and truly I don't believe myself that my tales are gloomy, or even very tragic, that is not with a pessimistic intention. Anyway, that reputation, whether justified or not, has deprived me of innumerable readers and I can only regret that you have found it necessary to make it, as it were, the ground-tone of your laudatory article.

*   *   *

CRITICISM

Contemporary Responses

EDWARD GARNETT

Unsigned Review from *Academy and Literature*†

The publication in volume form of Mr. Conrad's three stories, 'Youth,' 'Heart of Darkness,' 'The End of the Tether,' is one of the events of the literary year. These stories are an achievement in art which will materially advance his growing reputation. Of the stories, 'Youth' may be styled a modern English epic of the Sea; 'The End of the Tether' is a study of an old sea captain who, at the end of forty years' trade exploration of the Southern seas, finding himself dispossessed by the perfected routine of the British empire overseas he has helped to build, falls on evil times, and faces ruin calmly, fighting to the last. These two will be more popular than the third, 'Heart of Darkness,' a study of 'the white man in Africa' which is most amazing, a consummate piece of artistic *diablerie*.[1] On reading 'Heart of Darkness' on its appearance in *Blackwood's Magazine* our first impression was that Mr. Conrad had, here and there, lost his way. Now that the story can be read, not in parts, but from the first page to the last at a sitting, we retract this opinion and hold 'Heart of Darkness' to be the high-water mark of the author's talent. It may be well to analyse this story a little so that the intelligent reader, reading it very deliberately, may see better for himself why Mr. Conrad's book enriches English literature.

'Heart of Darkness,' to present its theme bluntly, is an impression, taken from life, of the conquest by the European whites of a certain portion of Africa, an impression in particular of the civilising methods of a certain great European Trading Company face to face with the 'nigger.' We say this much because the English reader likes to know where he is going before he takes art seriously, and

† *Academy and Literature* (6 December 1902):606. From *Conrad: The Critical Heritage*, ed. Norman Sherry (London: Routledge & Kegan Paul, 1973), pp. 131–33. Garnett (1868–1937), an early friend and literary adviser, recommended Conrad's first novel for publication and introduced him to his collaborator Ford Madox Hueffer (Ford). Although Garnett published this review anonymously, Conrad knew he was the author and wrote to thank him: "your brave attempt to grapple with the fogginess of H of D, to explain what I myself have tried to shape blindfold, as it were, has touched me profoundly" (*Collected Letters*, 2:467–68). Notes are the Editor's.
1. Devilish magic, sorcery.

we add that he will find the human life, black and white, in 'Heart of Darkness' an uncommonly and uncannily serious affair. If the ordinary reader, however, insists on taking the subject of a tale very seriously, the artist takes his method of presentation more seriously still, and rightly so. For the art of 'Heart of Darkness'—as in every psychological masterpiece—lies in the relation of the things of the spirit to the things of the flesh, of the invisible life to the visible, of the sub-conscious life within us, our obscure motives and instincts, to our conscious actions, feelings and outlook. Just as landscape art implies the artist catching the exact relation of a tree to the earth from which it springs, and of the earth to the sky, so the art of 'Heart of Darkness' implies the catching of infinite shades of the white man's uneasy, disconcerted, and fantastic relations with the exploited barbarism of Africa; it implies the acutest analysis of the deterioration of the white man's *morale*, when he is let loose from European restraint, and planted down in the tropics as an 'emissary of light' armed to the teeth, to make trade profits out of the 'subject races.' The weirdness, the brilliance, the psychological truth of this masterly analysis of two Continents in conflict, of the abysmal gulf between the white man's system and the black man's comprehension of its results, is conveyed in a rapidly rushing narrative which calls for close attention on the reader's part. But the attention once surrendered, the pages of the narrative are as enthralling as the pages of Dostoevsky's *Crime and Punishment*. The stillness of the sombre African forests, the glare of sunshine, the feeling of dawn, of noon, of night on the tropical rivers, the isolation of the unnerved, degenerating whites staring all day and every day at the Heart of Darkness which is alike meaningless and threatening to their own creed and conceptions of life, the helpless bewilderment of the unhappy savages in the grasp of their flabby and rapacious conquerors—all this is a page torn from the life of the Dark Continent—a page which has been hitherto carefully blurred and kept away from European eyes. There is no 'intention' in the story, no *parti pris*,[2] no prejudice one way or the other; it is simply a piece of art, fascinating and remorseless, and the artist is but intent on presenting his sensations in that sequence and arrangement whereby the meaning or the meaninglessness of the white man in uncivilised Africa can be felt in its really significant aspects. If the story is too strong meat for the ordinary reader, let him turn to 'Youth,' wherein the song of every man's youth is indeed sung.

*   *   *

2. Position taken in advance (French).

UNSIGNED REVIEW

From the *Manchester Guardian*†

Mr. Joseph Conrad's latest volume, *Youth*, contains three stories, of which the one that gives the title is the shortest. This and the second one may be regarded as a kind of sequence. The third and longest, 'The End of the Tether,' is admirable, but in comparison with the others the tension is relaxed. It is in a manner more deliberate, less closely packed; this is Conrad, but not Conrad in his fine frenzy; it gives an engaging picture of a noble old man, pathetic, imaginative, deserving a whole array of eulogistic adjectives, but it is not of the amazing quality of Mr. Conrad at his best. The other two, though not of such scope and design, are of the quality of *Lord Jim*—that is to say, they touch the high-water mark of English fiction and continue a great expression of adventure and romance. Both stories follow Mr. Conrad's particular convention; they are the outpourings of Marlow's experiences. It would be useless to pretend that they can be very widely read. Even to those who are most impressed an excitement so sustained and prolonged, in which we are braced to encounter so much that menaces and appals, must be something of a strain. 'Youth,' in this conception of Mr. Conrad's, is not the time of freedom and delight, but 'the test, the trial of life.' No labour is too great, no danger is too close for this great adventure of the spirit.

* * *

'Heart of Darkness' is, again, the adventure of youth, an adventure more significant than the mere knockabout of the world. It is youth in the toils, a struggle with phantoms worse than the elements, 'a weary pilgrimage amongst hints for nightmares,' a destructive experience.

* * *

It must not be supposed that Mr. Conrad makes attack upon colonisation, expansion, even upon Imperialism. In no one is the essence of the adventurous spirit more instinctive. But cheap ideals, platitudes of civilisation are shrivelled up in the heat of such experiences. The end of this story brings us back to the familiar, reassuring region of common emotions, to the grief and constancy of the woman who had loved Kurtz and idealises his memory. It shows us how far we have travelled.

Those who can read these two stories in sympathy with Mr. Conrad's temperament will find in them a great expression of the

† *Manchester Guardian* (10 December 1902): 3. From *Critical Heritage*, pp. 134–35. Conrad called this review "fairly intelligent" (*Collected Letters*, 2:468).

world's mystery and romance. They show the impact upon an un-daunted spirit of what is terrible and obscure; they are adventure in terms of experience; they represent the sapping of life that cannot be lived on easy terms. Mr. Conrad's style is his own—concen-trated, tenacious, thoughtful, crammed with imaginative detail, breathless, yet missing nothing. Its grim earnestness bends to ex-cursions of irony, to a casual humour, dry, subdued to its surround-ings. Phrases strike the mind like lines of verse; we weary under a tension that is never slackened. He is one of the greatest of sea-writers and the most subjective of them. His storms are not the pic-turesque descriptions of gigantic phenomena, we see them in the 'weary, serious faces,' in the dreadful concentration of the actors. Mr. Conrad is intensely human and, we may add with some pride of fellowship, intensely modern. By those who seek for the finest ex-positions of the modern spirit 'Youth' and 'Heart of Darkness' can-not be neglected.

UNSIGNED REVIEW

From the *Times Literary Supplement*†

Telling tales, just spinning yarns, has gone out of fashion since the novel has become an epitome of everything a man has to say about anything. The three stories in *Youth* by Joseph Conrad are in this reference a return to an earlier taste. The yarns are of the sea, told with an astonishing zest; and given with vivid accumulation of de-tail and iterative persistency of emphasis on the quality of character and scenery. The method is exactly the opposite of Mr. Kipling's.[1] It is a little precious; one notes a tasting of the quality of phrases and an occasional indulgence in poetic rhetoric. But the effect is not unlike Mr. Kipling's. In the first story, 'Youth,' the colour, the at-mosphere of the East is brought out as in a picture. The concluding scene of the 'Heart of Darkness' is crisp and brief enough for Flaubert,[2] but the effect—a woman's ecstatic belief in a villain's heroism—is reached by an indulgence in the picturesque horror of the villain, his work and his surroundings, which is pitiless in its in-sistence, and quite extravagant according to the canons of art. But

---

† *Times Literary Supplement* (12 December 1902): 372. From *Critical Heritage*, pp. 136–37. Notes are the Editor's.

1. Rudyard Kipling (1865–1936), nationalistic novelist and poet who celebrated the heroic masculine values of the British Empire. On the two author's contrasting attitudes to-ward imperialism, see John A. McClure, *Kipling and Conrad: The Colonial Fiction* (Cambridge, MA: Harvard UP, 1981).
2. Gustave Flaubert (1821–80), French novelist, author of *Madame Bovary* (1857), an im-portant influence on Conrad.

the power, the success in conveying the impression vividly, without loss of energy is undoubted and is refreshing. 'The End of the Tether,' the last of the three, is the longest and best. Captain Whalley is racy of the sea, and an embodiment of its finest traditions; and the pathos of his long-drawn wrestle with the anger of circumstance is poignant to the end. Mr. Conrad should have put him in the forefront of the book. There are many readers who would not get beyond the barren and not very pretty philosophy of 'Youth'; more who might feel they had had enough horror at the end of 'The Heart of Darkness.' But they would miss a great deal if they did not reach 'The End of the Tether.' It has this further advantage over the other two tales, that it is much less clever, much less precious.

UNSIGNED REVIEW

From the *Athenaeum*†

A critical writer has said that all fiction may roughly be divided into two classes: that dealing with movement and adventure, and the other dealing with characterization, the analysis of the human mind. In the present, as in every one of his previous books, Mr. Conrad has stepped outside these boundaries, and made his own class of work as he has made his own methods. All his stories have movement and incident, most of them have adventure, and the motive in all has apparently been the careful analysis, the philosophic presentation, of phases of human character. His studious and minute drawing of the action of men's minds, passions, and principles forms fascinating reading. But he has another gift of which he himself may be less conscious, by means of which his other more incisive and purely intellectual message is translated for the proper understanding of simpler minds and plainer men. That gift is the power of conveying atmosphere, and in the exercise of this talent Mr. Conrad has few equals among our living writers of fiction. He presents the atmosphere in which his characters move and act with singular fidelity, by means of watchful and careful building in which the craftsman's methods are never obtrusive, and after turning the last page of one of his books we rise saturated by the very air they breathed. This is a great power, but, more or less, it is possessed by other talented writers of fiction. The rarity of it in Mr. Conrad lies in this, that he can surround both his characters and his readers with the distinctive atmosphere of a particular story within the limits of a few pages. This is an exceptional gift, and the

† *Athenaeum* (20 December 1902): 824. From *Critical Heritage*, pp. 137–39.

more to be prized in Mr. Conrad for the reason that he shows some signs of growing over-subtle in his analysis of moods, temperaments, and mental idiosyncrasies. It is an extreme into which all artists whose methods are delicate, minute, and searching are apt to be led. We have at least one other analyst of temperament and mood in fiction whose minute subtlety, scrupulous restraint, and allusive economy of words resemble Mr. Conrad's. And, becoming an obsession, these characteristics tend to weary the most appreciative reader.[1] With Mr. Conrad, however, these rather dangerous intellectual refinements are illumined always by a vivid wealth of atmosphere, and translated simply by action, incident, strong light and shade, and distinctive colouring. * * *

The reviewer deliberately abstains both from quotation and from any attempt at analysis of a story like 'The Heart of Darkness.' Any such attempt in a limited space would be a painful injustice where work of this character is concerned. Further, the reader is warned that this book cannot be read understandingly—as evening newspapers and railway novels are perused—with one mental eye closed and the other roving. Mr. Conrad himself spares no pains, and from his readers he demands thoughtful attention. He demands so much, and, where the intelligent are concerned, we think he will command it.

JOHN MASEFIELD

From the *Speaker*†

Mr. Conrad's stories, excellent though they are, leave always a feeling of disappointment, almost of regret. His is a rare temperament, an exotic, a poetic temperament, and its artistic expression, though tense, nervous, trembling with beauty, is always a little elusive, a little alien, of the quality of fine gum from Persia, or of a precious silk from Ghilan.[1]

In this volume Mr. Conrad gives us three stories, and in each shows a notable advance upon the technique and matter of his former work. His manner, indeed, shows a tendency towards the 'precious,' towards the making of fine phrases and polishing of perfect lines. He has filled his missal-marge[2] with flowerets; he has planted

---

1. An unflattering allusion to Henry James, whom Conrad (by contrast) admired. See his "Henry James: An Appreciation" above. [Editor]
† *Speaker* (31 January 1903): 442. From *Critical Heritage*, pp. 141–42. Masefield (1878–1967), English poet, playwright, and novelist who went to sea as a youth. Notes are the Editor's.
1. Center of trade and textile manufacture in northwestern Iran.
2. Margins of a prayer book.

his forest full of trees; till both prayer and forest are in some danger of being hid. In the story called 'Youth,' and still more in the story called 'Heart of Darkness' (both of them stories written as told by one Marlow to a company of friends), he has set down page after page of stately and brilliant prose, which is fine writing, good literature, and so forth, but most unconvincing narrative. His narrative is not vigorous, direct, effective, like that of Mr. Kipling. It is not clear and fresh like that of Stevenson, nor simple, delicate, and beautiful like that of Mr. Yeats.[3] It reminds one rather of a cobweb abounding in gold threads. It gives one a curious impression of remoteness and aloofness from its subject. Often it smells very palpably of the lamp, losing all spontaneity and becoming somewhat rhetorical.* * *

HENRY JAMES

The New Novel†

* * * We take for granted by the general law of fiction a primary author, take him so much for granted that we forget him in proportion as he works upon us, and that he works upon us most in fact by making us forget him.

Mr. Conrad's first care on the other hand is expressly to posit or set up a reciter, a definite responsible intervening first person singular, possessed of infinite sources of reference, who immediately proceeds to set up another, to the end that this other may conform again to the practice, and that even at that point the bridge over to the creature, or in other words to the situation or the subject, the thing "produced," shall, if the fancy takes it, once more and yet once more glory in a gap. It is easy to see how heroic the undertaking of an effective fusion becomes on these terms, fusion between what we are to know and that prodigy of our knowing which is ever half the very beauty of the atmosphere of authenticity; from the moment the reporters are thus multiplied from pitch to pitch the tone of each, especially as "rendered" by his precursor in the series, becomes for the prime poet of all an immense question—these circumferential tones having not only to be such individually separate notes, but to keep so clear of the others, the central, the numerous

3. Robert Louis Stevenson (1850–94), Scottish novelist and poet, author of *Treasure Island* (1883); William Butler Yeats (1865–1939), Irish poet and playwright.
† From *Notes on Novelists* (New York: Charles Scribner's Sons, 1914), pp. 347–48. James's remarks were occasioned by Conrad's novel *Chance* (1914), the last of his four works to employ Marlow as the primary narrator. James finds Conrad "absolutely alone" among his contemporaries "as a votary of the way to do a thing that shall make it undergo most doing" (345).

and various voices of the agents proper, those expressive of the action itself and in whom the objectivity resides. We usually escape the worst of this difficulty of a tone *about* the tone of our characters, our projected performers, by keeping it single, keeping it "down" and thereby comparatively impersonal or, as we may say, inscrutable; which is what a creative force, in its blest fatuity, likes to be. But the omniscience, remaining indeed nameless, though constantly active, which sets Marlow's omniscience in motion from the very first page, insisting on a reciprocity with it throughout, this original omniscience invites consideration of itself only in a degree less than that in which Marlow's own invites it; and Marlow's own is a prolonged hovering flight of the subjective over the outstretched ground of the case exposed. We make out this ground but through the shadow cast by the flight, clarify it though the real author visibly reminds himself again and again that he must—all the more that, as if by some tremendous forecast of future applied science, the upper aeroplane causes another, as we have said, to depend from it and that one still another; these dropping shadow after shadow, to the no small menace of intrinsic colour and form and whatever, upon the passive expanse. * * *

E. M. FORSTER

Joseph Conrad: A Note†

In his *Notes on Life and Letters*,[1] Mr. Conrad takes the public for the second time into the severe little apartment that must, for want of a better word, be called his confidence. It greeted us, first, in *A Personal Record*,[2] where he was interesting, stimulating, profound, beautiful—but confiding? Scarcely; nor is he in these "Notes." He guards himself by ironies and politenesses; he says, "Here is my little interior, which it is your weakness to see and perhaps mine to show; I will tell you what I think about Poland, and luxury-ships, and Henry James. That will satisfy your curiosity, will it not? Good morning. Do not feel obliged to praise what you have seen; indeed, I should almost prefer it if you didn't." And he bows us out.

A proud and formidable character appears rather more clearly

---

† From *Abinger Harvest* (New York: Harcourt, Brace and Company, 1936), pp. 136–38. First published in *Nation and Athenaeum* in March 1921. Copyright © 1936 and renewed 1964 by Edward M. Forster. Reprinted by permission of Harcourt, Inc. Notes are the Editor's.
1. A collection of essays that Conrad had written on various artistic and topical issues from 1898 to 1920. For example, see the selections above from "Books" and "Henry James: An Appreciation."
2. A volume of autobiographical reflections published in 1912.

here than in the novels; that is all we can say. The character will never be really clear, for one of two reasons. The first reason has already been indicated: the writer's dread of intimacy. He has a rigid conception as to where the rights of the public stop, he has determined we shall not be "all over" him, and has half contemptuously thrown open this vestibule and invited us to mistake it for the private apartments if we choose. We may not see such a character clearly because he does not wish us to see. But we also may not see it clearly because it is essentially unclear. This possibility must be considered. Behind the smoke screen of his reticence there may be another obscurity, connected with the foreground by wisps of vapour, yet proceeding from another source, from the central chasm of his tremendous genius. This isn't an aesthetic criticism, nor a moral one. Just a suggestion that our difficulties with Mr. Conrad may proceed in part from difficulties of his own.

What is so elusive about him is that he is always promising to make some general philosophic statement about the universe, and then refraining with a gruff disclaimer. Dealing, even in the slightest of these essays, with vast and eternal issues, he won't say whether such issues lead or don't lead to a goal. "For which may I put you down, Mr. Conrad, for the One or the None?" At such a question Mr. Conrad roughens into a shrewd sailorman promptly. He implies that the One and the None are highly interesting, but that it is more important to distinguish a bulwark from a bollard.[3] Can the reader do that much? If he cannot, may not the interview cease? "I see, Mr. Conrad. You are a cynic." By no means:

> "From a charge of cynicism I have always shrunk instinctively. It is like a charge of being blind in one eye, a moral disablement, a sort of disgraceful calamity that must be carried off with a jaunty bearing—a sort of thing I am not capable of."

And the disclaimers continue each time a general point is raised. He never gives himself away. Our impertinence is rebuked; sentence after sentence discharges its smoke screen into our abashed eyes, yet the problem isn't settled really. Is there not also a central obscurity, something noble, heroic, beautiful, inspiring half a dozen great books; but obscure, obscure? While reading the half-dozen books one doesn't or shouldn't ask such a question, but it occurs, not improperly, when the author professes to be personal, and to take us into that confidence of his. These essays do suggest that he is misty in the middle as well as at the edges, that the secret casket of his genius contains a vapour rather than a jewel; and that we need not try to write him down philosophically, because there is, in

---

3. A bulwark is a wall protecting the upper deck of a ship, and a bollard is a post on a wharf to which vessels are tied.

this particular direction, nothing to write. No creed, in fact. Only opinions, and the right to throw them overboard when facts make them look absurd. Opinions held under the semblance of eternity, girt with the sea, crowned with the stars, and therefore easily mistaken for a creed.

* * *

FORD MADOX FORD

A Personal Remembrance†

From time to time, particularly whilst writing "Heart of Darkness," Conrad would declaim passionately about the gloomy imbecility and cruelty of the Belgians in the Congo Free State. Still more would he so declaim, now and then, after he had been up to London and had met Casement,[1] who had been British Commissioner on the Congo and was passionately the champion of the natives. * * *

* * *

Mr. Henry James used to call Marlowe,[2] the usual narrator for many years of Conrad's stories, "that preposterous master mariner." He meant precisely that Marlowe was more of a philosopher and had a vocabulary vastly larger and more varied than you could possibly credit to the master mariner as a class. Conrad, however, persisted that Marlowe was little above the average of the ship's officer in either particular, and presumably he knew his former service mates better than did Mr. James—or the rest of us. . . . * * *

* * *

About Conrad there was as little of the moralist as there was of the philosopher. When he had said that every work of art has—must have—a profound moral purpose, and he said that every day and all day long, he had done with the subject. So that the writer[3] has always wished that Conrad had never written his famous message on Fidelity. Truly, those who read him knew his conviction that the world, the temporal world, rests on a very few simple ideas—

† From *Joseph Conrad: A Personal Remembrance* (Boston: Little, Brown, 1924), pp. 128–29, 171, 177–78, 192–96, 198–204, 222–26. Reprinted by permission of David Higham & Associates. Ford (1873–1939; original name Hueffer) was Conrad's close friend and collaborator from 1898 to 1909, when the younger man's erratic personal life led to a falling out. Together they wrote *The Inheritors* (1901), *Romance* (1903), and *The Nature of a Crime* (1909). Notes are the Editor's.
1. Roger Casement (1864–1916), friend from their period in the Congo who wrote an influential report for Parliament on King Leopold's abuses (see "Congo Report" above).
2. An unfortunately common misspelling caused by the similarity in the names of Conrad's narrator and the playwright Christopher Marlowe (1564–93).
3. Ford's way of referring to himself.

and it might have been left at that.[4] For it was the very basis of all Conrad's work that the fable must not have the moral tacked on to its end. If the fable has not driven its message home the fable has failed, must be scrapped and must give place to another one.

But the impulse to moralise, to pontify, is a very strong one, and comes in many treacherous guises. One may so easily do it unawares: and instances of Conrad's pontifications are far enough to seek, considering the temporal eminence to which he attained. He let, otherwise, his light so shine before men that few would be inclined to claim him amongst the preachers.

He was before all things the artist and his chief message to mankind is set at the head of this chapter. . . . "It is above all things to make you *see*. . . ."[5] Seeing is believing for all the doubters of this planet, from Thomas to the end: if you can make humanity see the few very simple things upon which this temporal world rests you will make mankind believe such eternal truths as are universal. . . .

* * *

General Effect

We agreed that the general effect of a novel must be the general effect that life makes on mankind. A novel must therefore not be a narration, a report. Life does not say to you: In 1914 my next-door neighbour, Mr. Slack, erected a greenhouse and painted it with Cox's green aluminum paint. . . . If you think about the matter you will remember, in various unordered pictures, how one day Mr. Slack appeared in his garden and contemplated the wall of his house. You will then try to remember the year of that occurrence and you will fix it as August, 1914, because having had the foresight to bear the municipal stock of the City of Liège you were able to afford a first-class season ticket for the first time in your life. You will remember Mr. Slack—then much thinner because it was before he found out where to buy that cheap Burgundy of which he has since drunk an inordinate quantity, though whisky you think would be much better for him! Mr. Slack again came into his garden, this time with a pale, weasely-faced fellow, who touched his cap from time to time. Mr. Slack will point to his house wall several times at different points, the weasely fellow touching his cap at

4. In "A Familiar Preface" to *A Personal Record* (1912), Conrad wrote: "Those who read me know my conviction that the world, the temporal world, rests on a few very simple ideas; so simple that they must be as old as the hills. It rests notably, among others, on the idea of Fidelity."
5. From Conrad's preface to *The Nigger of the "Narcissus"* (see above in this Norton Critical Edition).

each pointing. Some days after, coming back from business, you will have observed against Mr. Slack's wall. . . . At this point you will remember that you were then the manager of the fresh-fish branch of Messrs. Catlin and Clovis in Fenchurch Street. . . . What a change since then! Millicent had not yet put her hair up. . . . You will remember how Millicent's hair looked, rather pale and burnished in plaits. You will remember how it now looks, henna'd; and you will see in one corner of your mind's eye a little picture of Mr. Mills the vicar talking—oh, very kindly—to Millicent after she has come back from Brighton. . . . But perhaps you had better not risk that. You remember some of the things said by means of which Millicent has made you cringe—and her expression! . . . Cox's Aluminum Paint! . . . You remember the half-empty tin that Mr. Slack showed you—he had a most undignified cold—with the name in a horseshoe over a blue circle that contained a red lion asleep in front of a real-gold sun. . . .

And, if that is how the building of your neighbour's greenhouse comes back to you, just imagine how it will be with your love affairs that are so much more complicated. . . .

Impressionism

We accepted without much protest the stigma "Impressionists" that was thrown at us. In those days Impressionists were still considered to be bad people: Atheists, Reds, wearing red ties with which to frighten householders. But we accepted the name because Life appearing to us much as the building of Mr. Slack's greenhouse comes back to you, we saw that Life did not narrate, but made impressions on our brains. We in turn, if we wished to produce on you an effect of life, must not narrate but render impressions.

Selection

We agreed that the whole of Art consists in selection. To render your remembrance of your career as a fish salesman might enhance the story of Mr. Slack's greenhouse, or it might *not*. A little image of iridescent, blue-striped, black-striped, white fish on a white marble slab with water trickling down to them round a huge mass of orange salmon roe; a vivid description of a horrible smell caused by a cat having stolen and hidden in the thick of your pelargoniums a cod's head that you had brought back as a perquisite, you having subsequently killed the cat with a hammer, but long, long before you had rediscovered her fishy booty. . . . Such little impressions might be useful as contributing to illustrate your character—one

should not kill a cat with a hammer! They might illustrate your
sense of the beautiful—or your fortitude under affliction—or the
disagreeableness of Mr. Slack, who had a delicate sense of smell—
or the point of view of your only daughter, Millicent.

We should then have to consider whether your sense of the beautiful or your fortitude could in our rendering carry the story forward
or interest the reader. If it did we should include it; if in our opinion it was not likely to, we should leave it out. Or the story of the
cat might in itself seem sufficiently amusing to be inserted as a purposed *longueur*,[6] so as to give the idea of the passage of time. . . . It
may be more amusing to read the story of a cat with your missing
dinner than to read, "A fortnight elapsed. . . ." Or it might be better
after all to write boldly, "Mr. Slack, after a fortnight had elapsed, remarked one day very querulously, 'That smell seems to get worse instead of better.' "

Selection (Speeches)

That last would be compromise, for it would be narration instead
of rendering: it would be far *better* to give an idea of the passage of
time by picturing a cat with a cod's head, but the length of the story
must be considered. Sometimes to render anything at all in a given
space will take up too much room—even to render the effect and
delivery of a speech. Then just boldly and remorselessly you must
relate and *risk* the introduction of yourself as author, with the danger that you may destroy all the illusion of the story.

* * *

The rendering in fact of speeches gave Conrad and the writer
more trouble than any other department of the novel whatever. It introduced at once the whole immense subject of under what convention the novel is to be written. For whether you tell it direct and as
author—which is the more difficult way—or whether you put it into
the mouth of a character—which is easier by far but much more
cumbersome—the question of reporting or rendering speeches has
to be faced. To pretend that any character or any author writing directly can remember whole speeches with all their words for a matter of twenty-four hours, let alone twenty-four years, is absurd. The
most that the normal person carries away of a conversation after
even a couple of hours is just a salient or characteristic phrase or
two, and a mannerism of the speaker. Yet, if the reader stops to think
at all, or has any acuteness whatever, to render Mr. Slack's speech
directly, "Thet there odour is enough to do all the porters in Com-

6. Long, boring passage.

mon Gorden in. Lorst week it wouldn' no more 'n 'v sent a ole squad of tinwiskets barmy on the crumpet . . ." and so on through an entire monologue of a page and a half, must set the reader at some point or other wondering how the author or the narrator can possibly, even if they were present, have remembered every word of Mr. Slack's long speech. Yet the object of the novelist is to keep the reader entirely oblivious of the fact that the author exists—even of the fact that he is reading a book. This is of course not possible to the bitter end, but a reader *can* be rendered very engrossed, and the nearer you can come to making him entirely insensitive to his surroundings, the more you will have succeeded.

* * *

Conversations

One unalterable rule that we had for the rendering of conversations—for genuine conversations that are an exchange of thought, not interrogatories or statements of fact—was that no speech of one character should ever answer the speech that goes before it. This is almost invariably the case in real life where few people listen, because they are always preparing their own next speeches. When, of a Saturday evening, you are conversing over the fence with your friend Mr. Slack, you hardly notice that he tells you he has seen an incredibly coloured petunia at a market gardener's, because you are dying to tell him that you have determined to turn author to the extent of writing a letter on local politics to the newspaper of which, against his advice, you have become a large shareholder.

* * *

Surprise

We agreed that the one quality that gave interest to Art was the quality of surprise. That is very well illustrated in the snatch of conversation just given. If you reported a long speech of Mr. Slack's to the effect that he was going to enter some of his petunias for the local flower show and those, with his hydrangeas and ornamental sugar-beet, might well give him the Howard Cup for the third time in which case it would become his property out and out. He would then buy two silver and cut-glass epergnes,[7] one to stand on each side of the Cup on his sideboard. He always did think that a touch of silver and cut glass. . . . If, after that, you gave a long speech of your own—after, naturally, you had added a few commonplaces as a politeness to Mr. Slack—if you gave a long speech in which with modesty you dwelt on the powers of observation and of the pen that

7. Ornamental bowls or vases.

you had always considered yourself to possess, and in which you announced that you certainly meant to write a letter to the paper in which you had shares—on the statuary in the façade of the new town hall which was an offence to public decency. . . . And if in addition to that you added a soliloquy from your daughter Millicent to the effect that she intended to obtain on credit from your bootmakers, charging them to your account, a pair of scarlet morocco shoes with two-inch heels with which to go joy-riding on the Sunday with a young actor who played under the name of Hildebrand Hare and who had had his portrait in your paper. . . . If you gave all these long speeches one after the other you might be aware of a certain dullness when you reread that *compte rendu*.[8] . . . But if you carefully broke up petunias, statuary, and flower-show motives and put them down in little shreds, one contrasting with the other, you would arrive at something much more coloured, animated, lifelike and interesting, and you would convey a profoundly significant lesson as to the self-engrossment of humanity. Into that live scene you could then drop the piece of news that you wanted to convey and so you would carry the chapter a good many stages forward.

Here, again, compromise must necessarily come in: there must come a point in the dramatic working up of every scene in which the characters do directly answer each other, for a speech or for two or three speeches. It was in this department, as has already been pointed out, that Conrad was matchless and the writer very deficient. Or, again, a point may come in which it is necessary—in which at least it is to take the line of least resistance—to report directly a whole tremendous effort of eloquence as ebullient as an oration by Mr. Lloyd George[9] on the hymns of the Welsh nation. For there are times when the paraphernalia of indirect speech, interruptions, and the rest retard your action too much. Then they must go; the sense of reality must stand down before the necessity to get on.

But, on the whole, the indirect, interrupted method of handling interviews is invaluable for giving a sense of the complexity, the tantalisation, the shimmering, the haze, that life is.

* * *

Philosophy, Etc.

We agreed that the novel is absolutely the only vehicle for the thought of our day. With the novel you can do anything: you can inquire into every department of life, you can explore every depart-

8. Report of the proceedings (French).
9. David Lloyd George (1863–1945), British politician of Welsh descent.

ment of the world of thought. The one thing that you can not do is to propagandise, as author, for any cause. You must not, as author, utter any views; above all, you must not fake any events. You must not, however humanitarian you may be, over-elaborate the fear felt by a coursed rabbit.

It is obviously best if you can contrive to be without views at all; your business with the world is rendering, not alteration. You have to render life with such exactitude that more specialised beings than you, learning from you what are the secret needs of humanity, may judge how many white-tiled bathrooms are, or to what extent parliamentary representation is, necessary for the happiness of men and women. If, however, your yearning to amend the human race is so great that you cannot possibly keep your fingers out of the watch-springs there is a device that you can adopt.

Let us suppose that you feel tremendously strong views as to sexual immorality or temperance. You feel that you must express these, yet you know that like, say, M. Anatole France,[1] who is also a propagandist, you are a supreme novelist. You must then invent, justify and set going in your novel a character who can convincingly express your views. If you are a gentleman you will also invent, justify and set going characters to express views opposite to those you hold. . . .

*　　*　　*

Progression d'Effet

There is just one other point. In writing a novel we agreed that every word set on paper—*every* word set on paper—must carry the story forward and that, as the story progressed, the story must be carried forward faster and faster and with more and more intensity. That is called *progression d'effet*, words for which there is no English equivalent.

*　　*　　*

There remains to add once more:

But these two writers were not unaware—were not unaware—that there are other methods of writing novels. They were not rigid even in their own methods. They were sensible to the fact that compromise is at all times necessary to the execution of a work of art.

The lay reader will be astonished at this repetition and at these italics. They are inserted for the benefit of gentlemen and ladies who comment on books in the Press.

*　　*　　*

1. French novelist and political satirist (1844–1924).

VIRGINIA WOOLF

Joseph Conrad†

Suddenly, without giving us time to arrange our thoughts or prepare our phrases, our guest has left us; and his withdrawal without
farewell or ceremony is in keeping with his mysterious arrival, long
years ago, to take up his lodging in this country. For there was always an air of mystery about him. It was partly his Polish birth,
partly his memorable appearance, partly his preference for living in
the depths of the country, out of ear-shot of gossips, beyond reach
of hostesses, so that for news of him one had to depend upon the
evidence of simple visitors with a habit of ringing doorbells who reported of their unknown host that he had the most perfect manners, the brightest eyes, and spoke English with a strong foreign
accent.

Still, though it is the habit of death to quicken and focus our
memories, there clings to the genius of Conrad something essentially, and not accidentally, difficult of approach. His reputation of
later years was, with one obvious exception, undoubtedly the highest in England; yet he was not popular. He was read with passionate delight by some; others he left cold and lustreless. Among his
readers were people of the most opposite ages and sympathies.
Schoolboys of fourteen, driving their way through Marryat, Scott,
Henty, and Dickens,[1] swallowed him down with the rest; while the
seasoned and the fastidious, who in process of time have eaten
their way to the heart of literature and there turn over and over a
few precious crumbs, set Conrad scrupulously upon their banquet-
ing table. One source of difficulty and disagreement is, of course,
to be found, where men have at all times found it, in his beauty.
One opens his pages and feels as Helen must have felt when she
looked in her glass and realised that, do what she would, she could
never in any circumstances pass for a plain woman.[2] So Conrad
had been gifted, so he had schooled himself, and such was his obligation to a strange language wooed characteristically for its Latin
qualities rather than its Saxon that it seemed impossible for him to

† From *The Common Reader* (New York: Harcourt, Brace and Company, 1925), pp.
309–11, 313–15. Copyright © 1925 by Harcourt, Inc. and renewed 1953 by Leonard
Woolf. Reprinted by permission of the publisher. First published as the lead article in
the *Times Literary Supplement* after Conrad's death by a heart attack on 3 August 1924.
Notes are the Editor's.
1. Frederick Marryat (1792–1848), author of adventurous tales of the sea; Sir Walter Scott
   (1771–1832), author of *Rob Roy* (1818), *Ivanhoe* (1820), and other historical romances;
   George Alfred Henty (1832–1902), known for his tales of adventure written for boys;
   Charles Dickens (1812–70), popular Victorian novelist.
2. Legendary beauty of Greek mythology who was abducted to Troy, prompting the Trojan
   War.

make an ugly or insignificant movement of the pen. His mistress, his style, is a little somnolent sometimes in repose. But let somebody speak to her, and then how magnificently she bears down upon us, with what colour, triumph, and majesty! Yet it is arguable that Conrad would have gained both in credit and in popularity if he had written what he had to write without this incessant care for appearances. They block and impede and distract, his critics say, pointing to those famous passages which it is becoming the habit to lift from their context and exhibit among other cut flowers of English prose. He was self-conscious and stiff and ornate, they complain, and the sound of his own voice was dearer to him than the voice of humanity in its anguish. The criticism is familiar, and as difficult to refute as the remarks of deaf people when *Figaro* is played.[3] They see the orchestra; far off they hear a dismal scrape of sound; their own remarks are interrupted, and, very naturally, they conclude that the ends of life would be better served if instead of scraping Mozart those fifty fiddlers broke stones upon the road. That beauty teaches, that beauty is a disciplinarian, how are we to convince them, since her teaching is inseparable from the sound of her voice and to that they are deaf? But read Conrad, not in birthday books but in the bulk, and he must be lost indeed to the meaning of words who does not hear in that rather stiff and sombre music, with its reserve, its pride, its vast and implacable integrity, how it is better to be good than bad, how loyalty is good and honesty and courage, though ostensibly Conrad is concerned merely to show us the beauty of a night at sea. But it is ill work dragging such intimations from their element. Dried in our little saucers, without the magic and mystery of language, they lose their power to excite and goad; they lose the drastic power which is a constant quality of Conrad's prose.

* * *

Conrad was compound of two men; together with the sea captain dwelt that subtle, refined, and fastidious analyst whom he called Marlow. "A most discreet, understanding man", he said of Marlow.

Marlow was one of those born observers who are happiest in retirement. Marlow liked nothing better than to sit on deck, in some obscure creek of the Thames, smoking and recollecting; smoking and speculating; sending after his smoke beautiful rings of words until all the summer's night became a little clouded with tobacco smoke. Marlow, too, had a profound respect for the men with whom he had sailed; but he saw the humour of them. He nosed out and described in masterly fashion those livid creatures who prey

3. *The Marriage of Figaro* (1786), opera composed by Wolfgang Amadeus Mozart (1756–1791).

successfully upon the clumsy veterans. He had a flair for human deformity; his humour was sardonic. Nor did Marlow live entirely wreathed in the smoke of his own cigars. He had a habit of opening his eyes suddenly and looking—at a rubbish heap, at a port, at a shop counter—and then complete in its burning ring of light that thing is flashed bright upon the mysterious background. Introspective and analytical, Marlow was aware of this peculiarity. He said the power came to him suddenly. He might, for instance, overhear a French officer murmur "Mon Dieu, how the time passes!"

> Nothing [he comments] could have been more common-place than this remark; but its utterance coincided for me with a moment of vision. It's extraordinary how we go through life with eyes half shut, with dull ears, with dormant thoughts. . . . Nevertheless, there can be but few of us who had never known one of these rare moments of awakening, when we see, hear, understand, ever so much—everything—in a flash, before we fall back again into our agreeable somnolence. I raised my eyes when he spoke, and I saw him as though I had never seen him before.[4]

Picture after picture he painted thus upon that dark background; ships first and foremost, ships at anchor, ships flying before the storm, ships in harbour; he painted sunsets and dawns; he painted the night; he painted the sea in every aspect; he painted the gaudy brilliancy of Eastern ports, and men and women, their houses and their attitudes. He was an accurate and unflinching observer, schooled to that "absolute loyalty towards his feelings and sensations", which, Conrad wrote, "an author should keep hold of in his most exalted moments of creation". And very quietly and compassionately Marlow sometimes lets fall a few words of epitaph which remind us, with all that beauty and brilliancy before our eyes, of the darkness of the background.

                    *   *   *

---

4. A passage from *Lord Jim* (1900) in which Marlow recounts his conversation with a French lieutenant.

Essays in Criticism

ALBERT J. GUERARD

The Journey Within†

The autobiographical basis of the narrative is well known, and its introspective bias obvious; this is Conrad's longest journey into self. But it is well to remember that "Heart of Darkness" is also other if more superficial things: a sensitive and vivid travelogue, and a comment on "the vilest scramble for loot that ever disfigured the history of human conscience and geographical exploration."[1] The Congo was much in the public mind in 1889, when Henry Stanley's relief expedition found Emin Pasha (who like Kurtz did not want to be rescued), and it is interesting to note that Conrad was in Brussels during or immediately after Stanley's triumphant welcome there in April 1890. This was just before he set out on his own Congo journey. We do not know how much the Georges Antoine Klein who died on board the *Roi des Belges* resembled the fictional Kurtz, but Stanley himself provided no mean example of a man who could gloss over the extermination of savages with pious moralisms which were very possibly "sincere."

"Heart of Darkness" thus has its important public side, as an angry document on absurd and brutal exploitation. Marlow is treated to the spectacle of a French man-of-war shelling an unseen "enemy" village in the bush, and presently he will wander into the

† From Albert J. Guerard, *Conrad the Novelist* (Cambridge, MA: Harvard UP, 1958), pp. 33–36, 37–48. Reprinted by permission of the estate. Unless indicated, notes are the author's.

1. *Last Essays*, p. 17. [See "Geography and Some Explorers" in this Norton Critical Edition.] In "Heart of Darkness" Conrad makes once his usual distinction between British imperialism and the imperialism of other nations. On the map in Brussels there "was a vast amount of red—good to see at any time, because one knows that some real work is done in there." His 1899 letters to E. L. Sanderson and to Mme. Angèle Zagórska on the Boer war express his position clearly. The conspiracy to oust the Briton "is ready to be hatched in other regions. It . . . is everlastingly skulking in the Far East. A war there or anywhere but in S. Africa would have been conclusive,—would have been worth the sacrifices" (Jean-Aubry, *Life and Letters*, I, 286). "That they—the Boers—are struggling in good faith for their independence cannot be doubted; but it is also a fact that they have no idea of liberty, which can only be found under the English flag all over the world" (*ibid.*, I, 288).

grove at the first company station where the starving and sick Negroes withdraw to die. It is one of the greatest of Conrad's many
moments of compassionate rendering. The compassion extends
even to the cannibal crew of the *Roi des Belges*. Deprived of the rotten hippo meat they had brought along for food, and paid three
nine-inch pieces of brass wire a week, they appear to subsist on
"lumps of some stuff like half-cooked dough, of a dirty lavender
color" which they keep wrapped in leaves. Conrad here operates
through ambiguous suggestion (are the lumps human flesh?) but
elsewhere he wants, like Gide after him, to make his complacent
European reader *see*: see, for instance, the drunken unkempt official met on the road and three miles farther on the body of the Negro with a bullet hole in his forehead.[2] "Heart of Darkness" is a
record of things seen and done. But also Conrad was reacting to
the humanitarian pretenses of some of the looters precisely as the
novelist today reacts to the moralisms of cold-war propaganda.
Then it was ivory that poured from the heart of darkness; now it is
uranium.[3] Conrad shrewdly recognized—an intuition amply developed in *Nostromo*—that deception is most sinister when it becomes
self-deception, and the propagandist takes seriously his own fictions. Kurtz "could get himself to believe anything—anything." The
benevolent rhetoric of his seventeen-page report for the International Society for the Suppression of Savage Customs was meant
sincerely enough. But a deeper sincerity spoke through his
scrawled postscript: "Exterminate all the brutes!" The conservative
Conrad (who found Donkin fit to be a labor leader) speaks through
the journalist who says that "Kurtz's proper sphere ought to have
been politics 'on the popular side.' "

Conrad, again like many novelists today, was both drawn to idealism and repelled by its hypocritical abuse. "The conquest of the
earth, which mostly means the taking it away from those who have
a different complexion or slightly flatter noses than ourselves, is not
a pretty thing when you look into it too much. What redeems it is
the idea only. An idea at the back of it; not a sentimental pretence
but an idea; and an unselfish belief in the idea . . ." Marlow commits himself to the yet unseen agent partly because Kurtz "had
come out equipped with moral ideas of some sort." Anything would
seem preferable to the demoralized greed and total cynicism of the
others, "the flabby devil" of the Central Station. Later, when he discovers what has happened to Kurtz's moral ideas, he remains faith-

2. Compare "The Congo Diary" [in this Norton Critical Edition]. Conrad did not use the
   skeleton tied to a post that he saw on Tuesday, 29 July. It might have seemed too blatant
   or too "literary" in a novel depending on mortuary imagery from beginning to end.
3. An allusion to the nuclear arms race between the United States and the former Soviet
   Union that was at its height in the late 1950s when Guerard wrote. [Editor]

ful to the "nightmare of my choice." In *Under Western Eyes* Sophia Antonovna makes a distinction between those who burn and those who rot, and remarks that it is sometimes preferable to burn. The Kurtz who had made himself literally one of the devils of the land, and who in solitude had kicked himself loose of the earth, burns while the others rot. Through violent not flabby evil he exists in the moral universe even before pronouncing judgment on himself with his dying breath. A little too much has been made, I think, of the redemptive value of those two words—"The horror!" But none of the company "pilgrims" could have uttered them.

*   *   *

In any event, it is time to recognize that the story is not primarily about Kurtz or about the brutality of Belgian officials but about Marlow its narrator. To what extent it also expresses the Joseph Conrad a biographer might conceivably recover, who in 1898 still felt a debt must be paid for his Congo journey and who paid it by the writing of this story, is doubtless an insoluble question. I suspect two facts (of a possible several hundred) are important. First, that going to the Congo was the enactment of a childhood wish associated with the disapproved childhood ambition to go to sea, and that this belated enactment was itself profoundly disapproved, in 1890, by the uncle and guardian.[4] It was another gesture of a man bent on throwing his life away. But even more important may be the guilt of complicity, just such a guilt as many novelists of the Second World War have been obliged to work off. What Conrad thought of the expedition of the Katanga Company of 1890–1892 is accurately reflected in his remarks on the "Eldorado Exploring Expedition" of "Heart of Darkness": "It was reckless without hardihood, greedy without audacity, and cruel without courage . . . with no more moral purpose at the back of it than there is in burglars breaking into a safe." Yet Conrad hoped to obtain command of the expedition's ship even after he had returned from the initiatory voyage dramatized in his novel. Thus the adventurous Conrad and Conrad the moralist may have experienced collision. But the collision, again as with so many novelists of the second war, could well have been deferred and retrospective, not felt intensely at the time.

So much for the elusive Conrad of the biographers and of the "Congo Diary." Substantially and in its central emphasis "Heart of Darkness" concerns Marlow (projection to whatever great or small degree of a more irrecoverable Conrad) and his journey toward and through certain facets or potentialities of self. F. R. Leavis seems to regard him as a narrator only, providing a "specific and concretely

---

4. Tadeusz Bobrowski (1829–1894). [See Conrad's letters to him about the Congo journey in this Norton Critical Edition.]

realized point of view."[5] But Marlow reiterates often enough that he is recounting a spiritual voyage of self-discovery. He remarks casually but crucially that he did not know himself before setting out, and that he likes work for the chance it provides to "find yourself . . . what no other man can ever know." The Inner Station "was the farthest point of navigation and the culminating point of my experience." At a material and rather superficial level, the journey is through the temptation of atavism.[6] It is a record of "remote kinship" with the "wild and passionate uproar," of a "trace of a response" to it, of a final rejection of the "fascination of the abomination." And why should there not be the trace of a response? "The mind of man is capable of anything—because everything is in it, all the past as well as all the future." Marlow's temptation is made concrete through his exposure to Kurtz, a white man and sometime idealist who had fully responded to the wilderness: a potential and fallen self. "I had turned to the wilderness really, not to Mr. Kurtz." At the climax Marlow follows Kurtz ashore, confounds the beat of the drum with the beating of his heart, goes through the ordeal of looking into Kurtz's "mad soul," and brings him back to the ship. He returns to Europe a changed and more knowing man. Ordinary people are now "intruders whose knowledge of life was to me an irritating pretence, because I felt so sure they could not possibly know the things I knew."

On this literal plane, and when the events are so abstracted from the dream-sensation conveying them, it is hard to take Marlow's plight very seriously. Will he, the busy captain and moralizing narrator, also revert to savagery, go ashore for a howl and a dance, indulge unspeakable lusts? The late Victorian reader (and possibly Conrad himself) could take this more seriously than we; could literally believe not merely in a Kurtz's deterioration through months of solitude but also in the sudden reversions to the "beast" of naturalistic fiction. Insofar as Conrad does want us to take it seriously and literally, we must admit the nominal triumph of a currently accepted but false psychology over his own truer intuitions. But the triumph is only nominal. For the personal narrative is unmistakably authentic, which means that it explores something truer, more fundamental, and distinctly less material: the night journey into the unconscious, and confrontation of an entity within the self. "I flung one shoe overboard, and became aware that that was exactly what I had been looking forward to—a talk with Kurtz." It little matters what, in terms of psychological symbolism, we call this double or say he represents: whether the Freudian id or the Jungian shadow

5. F. R. Leavis, *The Great Tradition* (London, 1948), p. 183.
6. Regression to a primitive state. [Editor]

or more vaguely the outlaw. And I am afraid it is impossible to say where Conrad's conscious understanding of his story began and ended. The important thing is that the introspective plunge and powerful dream seem true; and are therefore inevitably moving.

Certain circumstances of Marlow's voyage, looked at in these terms, take on a new importance. The true night journey can occur (except during analysis) only in sleep or in the waking dream of a profoundly intuitive mind. Marlow insists more than is necessary on the dreamlike quality of his narrative. "It seems to me I am trying to tell you a dream—making a vain attempt, because no relation of a dream can convey the dream-sensation, that commingling of absurdity, surprise, and bewilderment in a tremor of struggling revolt . . ." Even before leaving Brussels Marlow felt as though he "were about to set off for the center of the earth," not the center of a continent. The introspective voyager leaves his familiar rational world, is "cut off from the comprehension" of his surroundings; his steamer toils "along slowly on the edge of a black and incomprehensible frenzy." As the crisis approaches, the dreamer and his ship move through a silence that "seemed unnatural, like a state of trance"; then enter (a few miles below the Inner Station) a deep fog. "The approach to this Kurtz grubbing for ivory in the wretched bush was beset by as many dangers as though he had been an enchanted princess sleeping in a fabulous castle."[7] Later, Marlow's task is to try "to break the spell" of the wilderness that holds Kurtz entranced.

The approach to the unconscious and primitive may be aided by a savage or half-savage guide, and may require the token removal of civilized trappings or aids; both conceptions are beautifully dramatized in Faulkner's "The Bear." In "Heart of Darkness" the token "relinquishment" and the death of the half-savage guide are connected. The helmsman falling at Marlow's feet casts blood on his shoes, which he is "morbidly anxious" to change and in fact throws overboard.[8] (The rescue of Wait in *The Nigger of the "Narcissus"* shows a similar pattern.) Here we have presumably entered an area of unconscious creation; the dream is true but the teller may have no idea why it is. So too, possibly, a psychic need as well as literary tact compelled Conrad to defer the meeting between Marlow and Kurtz for some three thousand words after announcing that it took

7. The analogy of unspeakable Kurtz and enchanted princess may well be an intended irony. But there may be some significance in the fact that this once the double is imagined as an entranced feminine figure.
8. Like any obscure human act, this one invites several interpretations, beginning with the simple washing away of guilt. The fear of the blood may be, however, a fear of the primitive toward which Marlow is moving. To throw the shoes overboard would then mean a token rejection of the savage, not the civilized-rational. In any event it seems plausible to have blood at this stage of a true initiation story.

place. We think we are about to meet Kurtz at last. But instead Marlow leaps ahead to his meeting with the "Intended"; comments on Kurtz's megalomania and assumption of his place among the devils of the land; reports on the seventeen-page pamphlet; relates his meeting and conversation with Kurtz's harlequin disciple—and only then tells of seeing through his binoculars the heads on the stakes surrounding Kurtz's house. This is the "evasive" Conrad in full play, deferring what we most want to know and see; perhaps compelled to defer climax in this way. The tactic is dramatically effective, though possibly carried to excess: we are told on the authority of completed knowledge certain things we would have found hard to believe had they been presented through a slow consecutive realistic discovery. But also it can be argued that it was psychologically impossible for Marlow to go at once to Kurtz's house with the others. The double must be brought on board the ship, and the first confrontation must occur there. We are reminded of Leggatt in the narrator's cabin, of the trapped Wait on the *Narcissus*.[9] The incorporation and alliance between the two becomes material, and the identification of "selves."

Hence the shock Marlow experiences when he discovers that Kurtz's cabin is empty and his secret sharer gone; a part of himself has vanished. "What made this emotion so over-powering was— how shall I define it?—the moral shock I received, as if something altogether monstrous, intolerable to thought and odious to the soul, had been thrust upon me unexpectedly." And now he must risk the ultimate confrontation in a true solitude and must do so on shore. "I was anxious to deal with this shadow by myself alone— and to this day I don't know why I was so jealous of sharing with anyone the peculiar blackness of that experience." He follows the crawling Kurtz through the grass; comes upon him "long, pale, indistinct, like a vapor exhaled by the earth." ("I had cut him off cleverly . . .") We are told very little of what Kurtz said in the moments that follow; and little of his incoherent discourses after he is brought back to the ship. "His was an impenetrable darkness. I looked at him as you peer down at a man who is lying at the bottom of a precipice where the sun never shines"—a comment less vague and rhetorical, in terms of psychic geography, than it may seem at a first reading. And then Kurtz is dead, taken off the ship, his body buried in a "muddy hole." With the confrontation over, Marlow must still emerge from environing darkness, and does so through that other deep fog of sickness. The identification is not yet completely broken. "And it is not my own extremity I remember best—

9. Two other Conradian "doubles": the stowaway in "The Secret Sharer" (1910), whom the narrator-captain secretly assists, and the malingering James Wait, whom the crew both resents and supports. [Editor]

a vision of grayness without form filled with physical pain, and a careless contempt for the evanescence of all things—even of this pain itself. No! It is his extremity that I seem to have lived through." Only in the atonement of his lie to Kurtz's "Intended," back in the sepulchral city, does the experience come truly to an end. "I laid the ghost of his gifts at last with a lie . . ."

Such seems to be the content of the dream. If my summary has even a partial validity it should explain and to an extent justify some of the "adjectival and worse than supererogatory insistence" to which F. R. Leavis (who sees only the travelogue and the portrait of Kurtz) objects. I am willing to grant that the unspeakable rites and unspeakable secrets become wearisome, but the fact—at once literary and psychological—is that they must remain *unspoken*. A confrontation with such a double and facet of the unconscious cannot be reported through realistic dialogue; the conversations must remain as shadowy as the narrator's conversations with Leggatt. So too when Marlow finds it hard to define the moral shock he received on seeing the empty cabin, or when he says he doesn't know why he was jealous of sharing his experience, I think we can take him literally . . . and in a sense even be thankful for his uncertainty. The greater tautness and economy of "The Secret Sharer" comes from its larger conscious awareness of the psychological process it describes; from its more deliberate use of the double as symbol. And of the two stories I happen to prefer it. But it may be the groping, fumbling "Heart of Darkness" takes us into a deeper region of the mind. If the story is not about this deeper region, and not about Marlow himself, its length is quite indefensible. But even if one were to allow that the final section is about Kurtz (which I think simply absurd), a vivid pictorial record of his unspeakable lusts and gratifications would surely have been ludicrous. I share Mr. Leavis' admiration for the heads on the stakes. But not even Kurtz could have supported many such particulars.

"I listened on the watch for the sentence, for the word, that would give me the clue to the faint uneasiness inspired by this narrative that seemed to shape itself without human lips in the heavy night air of the river." Thus one of Marlow's listeners, the original "I" who frames the story, comments on its initial effect. He has discovered how alert one must be to the ebb and flow of Marlow's narrative, and here warns the reader. But there is no single word; not even the word *trance* will do. For the shifting play of thought and feeling and image and event is very intricate. It is not vivid detail alone, the heads on stakes or the bloody shoes; nor only the dark mass of moralizing abstraction; nor the dramatized psychological intuitions apart from their context that give "Heart of Darkness" its brooding weight. The impressionist method—one cannot leave this story without subscribing to the obvious—finds here one of its great triumphs of tone. The random movement of the nightmare is also the controlled movement of a poem, in which a quality of feeling may be stated or suggested and only much later justified. But it is justified at last.

The method is in important ways different from that of *Lord Jim*, though the short novel was written during an interval in the long one, and though Marlow speaks to us in both. For we do not have here the radical obfuscations and sudden wrenchings and violent chronological ambiguities of *Lord Jim*. Nor are we, as in *Nostromo*, at the mercy of a wayward flashlight moving rapidly in a cluttered room. "Heart of Darkness" is no such true example of spatial form.[1] Instead the narrative advances and withdraws as in a succession of long dark waves borne by an incoming tide. The waves encroach fairly evenly on the shore, and presently a few more feet of sand have been won. But an occasional wave thrusts up unexpectedly, much farther than the others: even as far, say, as Kurtz and his Inner Station. Or, to take the other figure: the flashlight is held firmly; there are no whimsical jerkings from side to side. But now and then it is raised higher, and for a brief moment in a sudden clear light we discern enigmatic matters to be explored much later. Thus the movement of the story is sinuously progressive, with much incremental repetition. The intent is not to subject the reader to multiple strains and ambiguities, but rather to throw over him a brooding gloom, such a warm pall as those two Fates in the home office might knit, back in the sepulchral city.

Yet no figure can convey "Heart of Darkness" in all its resonance and tenebrous atmosphere. The movement is not one of penetration and withdrawal only; it is also the tracing of a large grand circle of awareness. It begins with the friends, on the yacht under the dark above Gravesend and at last returns to them, to the tranquil waterway that "leading to the uttermost ends of the earth flowed sombre under an overcast sky—seemed to lead into the heart of an immense darkness." For this also "has been one of the dark places of the earth," and Marlow employs from the first his methods of reflexive reference and casual foreshadowing. The Romans were men enough to face this darkness of the Thames running between savage shores. "Here and there a military camp lost in a wilderness, like a needle in a bundle of hay—cold, fog, tempests, disease, exile, and death—death skulking in the air, in the water, in the bush." But these Romans were "no colonists," no more than the pilgrims

---

1. See Joseph Frank, "Spatial Form in Modern Literature" in *Critiques and Essays in Criticism*, ed. R. W. Stallman (New York: Ronald Press, 1949), pp. 315–28. Frank argues that the temporal dislocations of modern narratives make space rather than time their organizing principle. [Editor]

of the Congo nineteen hundred years later; "their administration was merely a squeeze." Thus early Marlow establishes certain political values. The French gunboat firing into a continent anticipates the blind firing of the pilgrims into the jungle when the ship has been attacked. And Marlow hears of Kurtz's first attempt to emerge from the wilderness long before he meets Kurtz in the flesh, and wrestles with his reluctance to leave. Marlow returns again and again, with increasing irony, to Kurtz's benevolent pamphlet.

The travelogue as travelogue is not to be ignored; and one of Roger Casement's consular successors in the Congo (to whom I introduced "Heart of Darkness" in 1957) remarked at once that Conrad certainly had a "feel for the country." The demoralization of the first company station is rendered by a boiler "wallowing in the grass," by a railway truck with its wheels in the air. Presently Marlow will discover a scar in the hillside into which drainage pipes for the settlement had been tumbled; then will walk into the grove where the Negroes are free to die in a "greenish gloom." The sharply visualized particulars suddenly intrude on the somber intellectual flow of Marlow's meditation: magnified, arresting. The boilermaker who "had to crawl in the mud under the bottom of the steamboat . . . would tie up that beard of his in a kind of white serviette he brought for the purpose. It had loops to go over his ears." The papier-mâché Mephistopheles is as vivid, with his delicate hooked nose and glittering mica eyes. So too is Kurtz's harlequin companion and admirer, humbly dissociating himself from the master's lusts and gratifications. "I! I! I am a simple man. I have no great thoughts." And even Kurtz, shadow and symbol though he be, the man of eloquence who in this story is almost voiceless, and necessarily so—even Kurtz is sharply visualized, an "animated image of death," a skull and body emerging as from a winding sheet, "the cage of his ribs all astir, the bones of his arm waving."

This is Africa and its flabby inhabitants; Conrad did indeed have a "feel for the country." Yet the dark tonalities and final brooding impression derive as much from rhythm and rhetoric as from such visual details: derive from the high aloof ironies and from a prose that itself advances and recedes in waves. "This initiated wraith from the back of Nowhere honored me with its amazing confidence before it vanished altogether." Or, "It is strange how I accepted this unforeseen partnership, this choice of nightmares forced upon me in the tenebrous land invaded by these mean and greedy phantoms." These are true Conradian rhythms, but they are also rhythms of thought. The immediate present can be rendered with great compactness and drama: the ship staggering within ten feet of the bank at the time of the attack, and Marlow's sudden glimpse of a face amongst the leaves, then of the bush "swarming with human limbs." But still more immediate and personal, it may be, are the meditative passages evoking vast tracts of time, and the "first of men taking possession of an accursed inheritance." The prose is varied, far more so than is usual in the early work, both in rhythm and in the movements from the general to the particular and back. But the shaped sentence collecting and fully expending its breath appears to be the norm. Some of the best passages begin and end with them:

> "Going up that river was like traveling back to the earliest be-ginnings of the world, when vegetation rioted on the earth and the big trees were kings. An empty stream, a great silence, an impenetrable forest. The air was warm, thick, heavy, sluggish. There was no joy in the brilliance of sunshine. The long stretches of the waterway ran on, deserted, into the gloom of overshadowed distances. On silvery sandbanks hippos and alli-gators sunned themselves side by side."

The insistence on darkness, finally, and quite apart from ethical or mythical overtone, seems a right one for this extremely personal statement. There is a darkness of passivity, paralysis, immobiliza-tion; it is from the state of entranced languor rather than from the monstrous desires that the double Kurtz, this shadow, must be saved. In Freudian theory, we are told, such preoccupation may in-dicate fear of the feminine and passive. But may it not also be con-nected, through one of the spirit's multiple disguises, with a radical fear of death, that other darkness? "I had turned to the wilderness really, not to Mr. Kurtz, who, I was ready to admit, was as good as buried. And for a moment it seemed to me as if I also were buried in a vast grave full of unspeakable secrets. I felt an intolerable weight oppressing my breast, the smell of the damp earth, the un-seen presence of victorious corruption, the darkness of an impene-trable night."

It would be folly to try to limit the menace of vegetation in the restless life of Conradian image and symbol. But the passage re-minds us again of the story's reflexive references, and its images of deathly immobilization in grass. Most striking are the black shad-ows dying in the greenish gloom of the grove at the first station. But grass sprouts between the stones of the European city, a "whited sepulcher," and on the same page Marlow anticipates com-ing upon the remains of his predecessor: "the grass growing through his ribs was tall enough to hide his bones." The critical meeting with Kurtz occurs on a trail through the grass. Is there not perhaps an intense horror behind the casualness with which Mar-low reports his discoveries, say of the Negro with the bullet in his forehead? Or: "Now and then a carrier dead in harness, at rest in the long grass near the path, with an empty water gourd and his long staff lying by his side."

All this, one must acknowledge, does not make up an ordinary light travelogue. There is no little irony in the letter of November 9, 1891, Conrad received from his guardian after returning from the Congo, and while physically disabled and seriously depressed: "I am sure that with your melancholy temperament you ought to avoid all meditations which lead to pessimistic conclusions. I advise you to lead a more active life than ever and to cultivate cheerful habits."[2] Uneven in language on certain pages, and lacking "The Secret Sharer"'s economy, "Heart of Darkness" nevertheless remains one of the great dark meditations in literature, and one of the purest expressions of a melancholy temperament.

CHINUA ACHEBE

An Image of Africa: Racism in Conrad's *Heart of Darkness*†

In the fall of 1974 I was walking one day from the English Department at the University of Massachusetts to a parking lot. It was a fine autumn morning such as encouraged friendliness to passing strangers. Brisk youngsters were hurrying in all directions, many of them obviously freshmen in their first flush of enthusiasm. An older man going the same way as I turned and remarked to me how very young they came these days. I agreed. Then he asked me if I was a student too. I said no, I was a teacher. What did I teach? African literature. Now that was funny, he said, because he knew a fellow who taught the same thing, or perhaps it was African *history*, in a certain Community College not far from here. It always surprised him, he went on to say, because he never had thought of Africa as having that kind of stuff, you know.[1] By this time I was walking much faster. "Oh well," I heard him say finally, behind me: "I guess I have to take your course to find out."

A few weeks later I received two very touching letters from high school children in Yonkers, New York, who—bless their teacher—

---

2. G. Jean-Aubry, *Joseph Conrad: Life and Letters* (1927), 1:148.
† Revised version for the 1988 third Norton Critical Edition of *Heart of Darkness*, pp. 251–62. Originally delivered as a Chancellor's Lecture at the University of Massachusetts, Amherst, on 18 February 1975, then published under the title "An Image of Africa" in *The Massachusetts Review*, 18 (1977): 782–94. Used by permission of the author. When Achebe's revisions are significant, the 1977 version is given in the notes. Unless indicated, the other notes are the author's.
1. "Now that was funny, he said, because he had never thought of Africa as having that kind of stuff, you know" [1977].

had just read *Things Fall Apart*.[2] One of them was particularly
happy to learn about the customs and superstitions of an African
tribe.

I propose to draw from these rather trivial encounters rather
heavy conclusions which at first sight might seem somewhat out of
proportion to them. But only, I hope, at first sight.

The young fellow from Yonkers, perhaps partly on account of his
age but I believe also for much deeper and more serious reasons, is
obviously unaware that the life of his own tribesmen in Yonkers,
New York, is full of odd customs and superstitions and, like everybody else in his culture, imagines that he needs a trip to Africa to
encounter those things.

The other person being fully my own age could not be excused
on the grounds of his years. Ignorance might be a more likely reason; but here again I believe that something more willful than a
mere lack of information was at work. For did not that erudite
British historian and Regius Professor at Oxford, Hugh Trevor
Roper, also pronounce that African history did not exist?

If there is something in these utterances more than youthful in-
experience, more than a lack of factual knowledge, what is it?
Quite simply it is the desire—one might indeed say the need—in
Western psychology to set Africa up as a foil to Europe, as a place
of negations at once remote and vaguely familiar, in comparison
with which Europe's own state of spiritual grace will be manifest.

This need is not new; which should relieve us all of considerable
responsibility and perhaps make us even willing to look at this phenomenon dispassionately. I have neither the wish nor the compe-
tence to embark on the exercise with the tools of the social and
biological sciences but more simply in the manner of a novelist responding to one famous book of European fiction: Joseph Conrad's
Heart of Darkness, which better than any other work that I know
displays that Western desire and need which I have just referred to.
Of course there are whole libraries of books devoted to the same
purpose but most of them are so obvious and so crude that few
people worry about them today. Conrad, on the other hand, is undoubtedly one of the great stylists of modern fiction and a good
story-teller into the bargain. His contribution therefore falls auto-
matically into a different class—permanent literature—read and
taught and constantly evaluated by serious academics. *Heart of
Darkness* is indeed so secure today that a leading Conrad scholar
has numbered it "among the half-dozen greatest short novels in the
English language."[3] I will return to this critical opinion in due

2. Achebe's great novel of Africa (1959). [Editor]
3. Albert J. Guerard, Introduction to *Heart of Darkness* (New York: New American Library,
   1950), p. 9.

course because it may seriously modify my earlier suppositions about who may or may not be guilty in some of the matters I will now raise.

Heart of Darkness projects the image of Africa as "the other world," the antithesis of Europe and therefore of civilization, a place where man's vaunted intelligence and refinement are finally mocked by triumphant bestiality. The book opens on the River Thames, tranquil, resting peacefully "at the decline of day after ages of good service done to the race that peopled its banks." But the actual story will take place on the River Congo, the very antithesis of the Thames. The River Congo is quite decidedly not a River Emeritus. It has rendered no service and enjoys no old-age pension. We are told that "Going up that river was like travelling back to the earliest beginnings of the world."

Is Conrad saying then that these two rivers are very different, one good, the other bad? Yes, but that is not the real point. It is not the differentness that worries Conrad but the lurking hint of kinship, of common ancestry. For the Thames too "has been one of the dark places of the earth." It conquered its darkness, of course, and is now in daylight and at peace. But if it were to visit its primordial relative, the Congo, it would run the terrible risk of hearing grotesque echoes of its own forgotten darkness, and falling victim to an avenging recrudescence of the mindless frenzy of the first beginnings.

These suggestive echoes comprise Conrad's famed evocation of the African atmosphere in *Heart of Darkness*. In the final consideration his method amounts to no more than a steady, ponderous, fake-ritualistic repetition of two antithetical sentences, one about silence and the other about frenzy. We can inspect samples of this on pages 34 and 35 of the present edition: a) *It was the stillness of an implacable force brooding over an inscrutable intention* and b) *The steamer toiled along slowly on the edge of a black and incomprehensible frenzy*. Of course there is a judicious change of adjective from time to time, so that instead of *inscrutable*, for example, you might have *unspeakable*, even plain *mysterious*, etc., etc.

The eagle-eyed English critic F. R. Leavis drew attention long ago to Conrad's "adjectival insistence upon inexpressible and incomprehensible mystery." That insistence must not be dismissed lightly, as many Conrad critics have tended to do, as a mere stylistic flaw; for it raises serious questions of artistic good faith. When a writer while pretending to record scenes, incidents and their impact is in reality engaged in inducing hypnotic stupor in his readers through a bombardment of emotive words and other forms of trickery much more has to be at stake than stylistic felicity. Generally normal readers are well armed to detect and resist such underhand activity. But Conrad chose his subject well—one which was guaranteed not to put him in

conflict with the psychological pre-disposition of his readers or raise
the need for him to contend with their resistance. He chose the role
of purveyor of comforting myths.

The most interesting and revealing passages in *Heart of Darkness*
are, however, about people. I must crave the indulgence of my
reader to quote almost a whole page from about the middle of the
story when representatives of Europe in a steamer going down the
Congo encounter the denizens of Africa.

> We were wanderers on a prehistoric earth, on an earth that
> wore the aspect of an unknown planet. We could have fancied
> ourselves the first of men taking possession of an accursed in-
> heritance, to be subdued at the cost of profound anguish and
> of excessive toil. But suddenly as we struggled round a bend
> there would be a glimpse of rush walls, of peaked grass-roofs, a
> burst of yells, a whirl of black limbs, a mass of hands clapping,
> of feet stamping, of bodies swaying, of eyes rolling under the
> droop of heavy and motionless foliage. The steamer toiled
> along slowly on the edge of a black and incomprehensible
> frenzy. The prehistoric man was cursing us, praying to us, wel-
> coming us—who could tell? We were cut off from the compre-
> hension of our surroundings; we glided past like phantoms,
> wondering and secretly appalled, as sane men would be before
> an enthusiastic outbreak in a madhouse. We could not under-
> stand because we were too far and could not remember, be-
> cause we were travelling in the night of first ages, of those ages
> that are gone, leaving hardly a sign—and no memories.
>
> The earth seemed unearthly. We are accustomed to look
> upon the shackled form of a conquered monster, but there—
> there you could look at a thing monstrous and free. It was un-
> earthly and the men were. . . . No they were not inhuman.
> Well, you know that was the worst of it—this suspicion of their
> not being inhuman. It would come slowly to one. They howled
> and leaped and spun and made horrid faces, but what thrilled
> you was just the thought of their humanity—like yours—the
> thought of your remote kinship with this wild and passionate
> uproar. Ugly. Yes, it was ugly enough, but if you were man
> enough you would admit to yourself that there was in you just
> the faintest trace of a response to the terrible frankness of that
> noise, a dim suspicion of there being a meaning in it which
> you—you so remote from the night of first ages—could com-
> prehend.

Herein lies the meaning of *Heart of Darkness* and the fascination it
holds over the Western mind: "What thrilled you was just the
thought of their humanity—like yours. . . . Ugly."

Having shown us Africa in the mass, Conrad then zeros in, half a

page later, on a specific example, giving us one of his rare descriptions of an African who is not just limbs or rolling eyes:

> And between whiles I had to look after the savage who was
> fireman. He was an improved specimen; he could fire up a ver-
> tical boiler. He was there below me and, upon my word, to
> look at him was as edifying as seeing a dog in a parody of
> breeches and a feather hat walking on his hind legs. A few
> months of training had done for that really fine chap. He
> squinted at the steam-gauge and at the water-gauge with an
> evident effort of intrepidity—and he had filed his teeth too, the
> poor devil, and the wool of his pate shaved into queer patterns,
> and three ornamental scars on each of his cheeks. He ought to
> have been clapping his hands and stamping his feet on the
> bank, instead of which he was hard at work, a thrall to strange
> witchcraft, full of improving knowledge.

As everybody knows, Conrad is a romantic on the side. He might
not exactly admire savages clapping their hands and stamping their
feet but they have at least the merit of being in their place, unlike
this dog in a parody of breeches. For Conrad things[4] being in their
place is of the utmost importance.

"Fine fellows—cannibals—in their place," he tells us pointedly.
Tragedy begins when things leave their accustomed place, like Europe leaving its safe stronghold between the policeman and the
baker to take a peep into the heart of darkness.

Before the story takes us into the Congo basin proper we are
given this nice little vignette as an example of things in their place:

> Now and then a boat from the shore gave one a momentary
> contact with reality. It was paddled by black fellows. You could
> see from afar the white of their eyeballs glistening. They
> shouted, sang; their bodies streamed with perspiration; they
> had faces like grotesque masks—these chaps; but they had
> bone, muscle, a wild vitality, an intense energy of movement
> that was as natural and true as the surf along their coast. They
> wanted no excuse for being there. They were a great comfort
> to look at.

Towards the end of the story Conrad lavishes a whole page[5] quite
unexpectedly on an African woman who has obviously been some
kind of mistress to Mr. Kurtz and now presides (if I may be permitted a little liberty)[6] like a formidable mystery over the inexorable
imminence of his departure:

---

4. "(and persons)" [1977]. The next two paragraphs (from "Fine fellows" to "a great comfort to look at") were added in 1988.
5. "great attention" [1977].
6. "a little imitation of Conrad" [1977].

> She was savage and superb, wild-eyed and magnificent. . . .
> She stood looking at us without a stir and like the wilderness
> itself, with an air of brooding over an inscrutable purpose.

This Amazon is drawn in considerable detail, albeit of a pre-
dictable nature, for two reasons. First, she is in her place and so
can win Conrad's special brand of approval and second, she fulfills
a structural requirement of the story: a savage counterpart to the
refined, European woman who will step forth to end the story:

> She came forward all in black with a pale head, floating toward
> me in the dusk. She was in mourning. . . . She took both my
> hands in hers and murmured, "I had heard you were coming."
> . . . She had a mature capacity for fidelity, for belief, for suffer-
> ing.

The difference in the attitude of the novelist to these two women
is conveyed in too many direct and subtle ways to need elaboration.
But perhaps the most significant difference is the one implied in
the author's bestowal of human expression to the one and the withholding of it from the other. It is clearly not part of Conrad's purpose to confer language on the "rudimentary souls" of Africa. In
place of speech they made "a violent babble of uncouth sounds."[7]
They "exchanged short grunting phrases" even among themselves.
But most of the time they were too busy with their frenzy. There are
two occasions in the book, however, when Conrad departs somewhat from his practice and confers speech, even English speech, on
the savages. The first occurs when cannibalism gets the better of
them:

> "Catch 'im," he snapped with a bloodshot widening of his eyes
> and a flash of sharp teeth—"catch 'im. Give 'im to us." "To
> you, eh?" I asked; "what would you do with them?" "Eat 'im!"
> he said curtly. . . .

The other occasion was the famous announcement:

> "Mistah Kurtz—he dead."

At first sight these instances might be mistaken for unexpected
acts of generosity from Conrad. In reality they constitute some of
his best assaults. In the case of the cannibals the incomprehensible
grunts that had thus far served them for speech suddenly proved inadequate for Conrad's purpose of letting the European glimpse the
unspeakable craving in their hearts. Weighing the necessity for
consistency in the portrayal of the dumb brutes against the sensa-
tional advantages of securing their conviction by clear, unambigu-

---

7. Sentence added in 1988.

ous evidence issuing out of their own mouth Conrad chose the latter. As for the announcement of Mr. Kurtz's death by the "insolent black head in the doorway" what better or more appropriate *finis* could be written to the horror story of that wayward child of civilization who willfully had given his soul to the powers of darkness and "taken a high seat amongst the devils of the land" than the proclamation of his physical death by the forces he had joined?

It might be contended, of course, that the attitude to the African in *Heart of Darkness* is not Conrad's but that of his fictional narrator, Marlow, and that far from endorsing it Conrad might indeed be holding it up to irony and criticism. Certainly Conrad appears to go to considerable pains to set up layers of insulation between himself and the moral universe of his history. He has, for example, a narrator behind a narrator. The primary narrator is Marlow but his account is given to us through the filter of a second, shadowy person. But if Conrad's intention is to draw a *cordon sanitaire*[8] between himself and the moral and psychological malaise of his narrator his care seems to me totally wasted because he neglects to hint however subtly or tentatively at an alternative frame of reference by which we may judge the actions and opinions of his characters. It would not have been beyond Conrad's power to make that provision if he had thought it necessary. Marlow seems to me to enjoy Conrad's complete confidence—a feeling reinforced by the close similarities between their two careers.

Marlow comes through to us not only as a witness of truth, but one holding those advanced and humane views appropriate to the English liberal tradition which required all Englishmen of decency to be deeply shocked by atrocities in Bulgaria or the Congo of King Leopold of the Belgians or wherever.

Thus Marlow is able to toss out such bleeding-heart sentiments as these:

> They were dying slowly—it was very clear. They were not enemies, they were not criminals, they were nothing earthly now, nothing but black shadows of disease and starvation lying confusedly in the greenish gloom. Brought from all the recesses of the coast in all the legality of time contracts, lost in uncongenial surroundings, fed on unfamiliar food, they sickened, became inefficient, and were then allowed to crawl away and rest.

The kind of liberalism espoused here by Marlow/Conrad touched all the best minds of the age in England, Europe and America. It took different forms in the minds of different people but almost always managed to sidestep the ultimate question of equality be-

8. Quarantine barrier (French). [Editor]

tween white people and black people. That extraordinary missionary, Albert Schweitzer, who sacrificed brilliant careers in music and theology in Europe for a life of service to Africans in much the same area as Conrad writes about, epitomizes the ambivalence. In a comment which has often been quoted Schweitzer says: "The African is indeed my brother but my junior brother." And so he proceeded to build a hospital appropriate to the needs of junior brothers with standards of hygiene reminiscent of medical practice in the days before the germ theory of disease came into being. Naturally he became a sensation in Europe and America. Pilgrims flocked, and I believe still flock even after he has passed on, to witness the prodigious miracle in Lamberence, on the edge of the primeval forest.

Conrad's liberalism would not take him quite as far as Schweitzer's, though. He would not use the word *brother* however qualified; the farthest he would go was kinship. When Marlow's African helmsman falls down with a spear in his heart he gives his white master one final disquieting look.

> And the intimate profundity of that look he gave me when he received his hurt remains to this day in my memory—like a claim of distant kinship affirmed in a supreme moment.

It is important to note that Conrad, careful as ever with his words, is concerned not so much about *distant kinship* as about someone *laying a claim* on it. The black man lays a claim on the white man which is well-nigh intolerable. It is the laying of this claim which frightens and at the same time fascinates Conrad, ". . . the thought of their humanity—like yours. . . . Ugly."

The point of my observations should be quite clear by now, namely that Joseph Conrad was a thoroughgoing[9] racist. That this simple truth is glossed over in criticisms of his work is due to the fact that white racism against Africa is such a normal way of thinking that its manifestations go completely unremarked. Students of *Heart of Darkness* will often tell you that Conrad is concerned not so much with Africa as with the deterioration of one European mind caused by solitude and sickness. They will point out to you that Conrad is, if anything, less charitable to the Europeans in the story than he is to the natives, that the point of the story is to ridicule Europe's civilizing mission in Africa.[1] A Conrad student informed me in Scotland that Africa is merely a setting for the disintegration of the mind of Mr. Kurtz.

Which is partly the point. Africa as setting and backdrop which eliminates the African as human factor. Africa as a metaphysical

9. "bloody" [1977].
1. The last clause (beginning "that the point of . . .") was added in 1988.

battlefield devoid of all recognizable humanity, into which the wandering European enters at his peril. Can nobody see the preposterous and perverse arrogance in thus reducing Africa to the role of props for the break-up of one petty European mind? But that is not even the point. The real question is the dehumanization of Africa and Africans which this age-long attitude has fostered and continues to foster in the world. And the question is whether a novel which celebrates this dehumanization, which depersonalizes a portion of the human race, can be called a great work of art. My answer is: No, it cannot.[2] I do not doubt Conrad's great talents. Even *Heart of Darkness* has its memorably good passages and moments:

> The reaches opened before us and closed behind, as if the forest had stepped leisurely across the water to bar the way for our return.

Its exploration of the minds of the European characters is often penetrating and full of insight. But all that has been more than fully discussed in the last fifty years. His obvious racism has, however, not been addressed. And it is high time it was!

Conrad was born in 1857, the very year in which the first Anglican missionaries were arriving among my own people in Nigeria. It was certainly not his fault that he lived his life at a time when the reputation of the black man was at a particularly low level. But even after due allowances have been made for all the influences of contemporary prejudice on his sensibility there remains still in Conrad's attitude a residue of antipathy to black people which his peculiar psychology alone can explain. His own account of his first encounter with a black man is very revealing:

> A certain enormous buck nigger encountered in Haiti fixed my conception of blind, furious, unreasoning rage, as manifested in the human animal to the end of my days. Of the nigger I used to dream for years afterwards.[3]

2. The rest of this paragraph was added in 1988, replacing the original version: "I would not call that man an artist, for example, who composes an eloquent instigation to one people to fall upon another and destroy them. No matter how striking his imagery or how beautiful his cadences fall such a man is no more a great artist than another may be called a priest who reads the mass backwards or a physician who poisons his patients. All those men in Nazi Germany who lent their talent to the service of virulent racism whether in science, philosophy or the arts have generally and rightly been condemned for their perversions. The time is long overdue for taking a hard look at the work of creative artists who apply their talents, alas often considerable as in the case of Conrad, to set people against people. This, I take it, is what Yevtushenko is after when he tells us that a poet cannot be a slave trader at the same time, and gives the striking example of Arthur Rimbaud who was fortunately honest enough to give up any pretenses to poetry when he opted for slave trading. For poetry surely can only be on the side of man's deliverance and not his enslavement; for the brotherhood and unity of all mankind and against the doctrines of Hitler's master races or Conrad's 'rudimentary souls.' "
3. Jonah Raskin, *The Mythology of Imperialism* (New York: Random House, 1971), p. 143.

Certainly Conrad had a problem with niggers. His inordinate love of that word itself should be of interest to psychoanalysts. Sometimes his fixation on blackness is equally interesting as when he gives us this brief description:

> A black figure stood up, strode on long black legs, waving long black arms. . . .

as though we might expect a black figure striding along on black legs to wave white arms! But so unrelenting is Conrad's obsession.

As a matter of interest Conrad gives us in *A Personal Record* what amounts to a companion piece to the buck nigger of Haiti. At the age of sixteen Conrad encountered his first Englishman in Europe. He calls him "my unforgettable Englishman" and describes him in the following manner:

> "(his) calves exposed to the public gaze . . . dazzled the be-holder by the splendor of their marble-like condition and their rich tone of young ivory. . . . The light of a headlong, exalted satisfaction with the world of men . . . illumined his face . . . and triumphant eyes. In passing he cast a glance of kindly curiosity and a friendly gleam of big, sound, shiny teeth . . . his white calves twinkled sturdily."[4]

Irrational love and irrational hate jostling together in the heart of that talented, tormented man. But whereas irrational love may at worst engender foolish acts of indiscretion, irrational hate can endanger the life of the community. Naturally Conrad is a dream for psychoanalytic critics. Perhaps the most detailed study of him in this direction is by Bernard C. Meyer, M.D. In his lengthy book Dr. Meyer follows every conceivable lead (and sometimes inconceivable ones) to explain Conrad. As an example he gives us long disquisitions on the significance of hair and hair-cutting in Conrad. And yet not even one word is spared for his attitude to black people. Not even the discussion of Conrad's antisemitism was enough to spark off in Dr. Meyer's mind those other dark and explosive thoughts. Which only leads one to surmise that Western psychoanalysts must regard the kind of racism displayed by Conrad as absolutely normal despite the profoundly important work done by Frantz Fanon in the psychiatric hospitals of French Algeria.

Whatever Conrad's problems were, you might say he is now safely dead. Quite true. Unfortunately his heart of darkness plagues us still. Which is why an offensive and[5] deplorable book can be described by a serious scholar as "among the half dozen greatest short

---

4. Bernard C. Meyer, M.D., *Joseph Conrad: A Psychoanalytic Biography* (Princeton: Princeton UP, 1967), p. 30.
5. "totally" [1977].

novels in the English language." And why it is today perhaps the most commonly prescribed novel in twentieth-century literature courses in English Departments of American universities.[6]

There are two probable grounds on which what I have said so far may be contested. The first is that it is no concern of fiction to please people about whom it is written. I will go along with that. But I am not talking about pleasing people. I am talking about a book which parades in the most vulgar fashion prejudices and insults from which a section of mankind has suffered untold agonies and atrocities in the past and continues to do so in many ways and many places today. I am talking about a story in which the very humanity of black people is called in question.[7]

Secondly, I may be challenged on the grounds of actuality. Conrad, after all, did sail down the Congo in 1890 when my own father was still a babe in arms. How could I stand up more than fifty years after his death and purport to contradict him? My answer is that as a sensible man I will not accept just any traveller's tales solely on the grounds that I have not made the journey myself. I will not trust the evidence even of a man's very eyes when I suspect them to be as jaundiced as Conrad's. And we also happen to know that Conrad was, in the words of his biographer, Bernard C. Meyer, "notoriously inaccurate in the rendering of his own history."[8]

But more important by far is the abundant testimony about Conrad's savages which we could gather if we were so inclined from other sources and which might lead us to think that these people must have had other occupations besides merging into the evil forest or materializing out of it simply to plague Marlow and his dispirited band. For as it happened, soon after Conrad had written his book an event of far greater consequence was taking place in the art world of Europe. This is how Frank Willett, a British art historian, describes it:

> Gaugin had gone to Tahiti, the most extravagant individual act of turning to a non-European culture in the decades immediately before and after 1900, when European artists were avid for new artistic experiences, but it was only about 1904–5 that African art began to make its distinctive impact. One piece is still identifiable; it is a mask that had been given to Maurice Vlaminck in 1905. He records that Derain was 'speechless' and 'stunned' when he saw it, bought it from Vlaminck and in turn showed it to Picasso and Matisse, who were also greatly af-

6. The 1977 version, reprinting the Chancellor's Lecture, limited its reference to "our own English Department here" and ended the paragraph with this sentence: "Indeed the time is long overdue for a hard look at things."
7. "It seems to me totally inconceivable that great art or even good art could possibly reside in such unwholesome surroundings" [1977].
8. Meyer, p. 30.

fected by it. Ambroise Vollard then borrowed it and had it cast in bronze. . . . The revolution of twentieth century art was under way![9]

The mask in question was made by other savages living just north of Conrad's River Congo. They have a name too: the Fang people, and are without a doubt among the world's greatest masters of the sculptured form. The event Frank Willett is referring to marked the beginning of cubism and the infusion of new life into European art, which had run completely out of strength.

The point of all this is to suggest that Conrad's picture of the peoples of the Congo seems grossly inadequate even at the height of their subjection to the ravages of King Leopold's International Association for the Civilization of Central Africa.

Travellers with closed minds can tell us little except about themselves. But even those not blinkered, like Conrad with xenophobia, can be astonishing blind. Let me digress a little here. One of the greatest and most intrepid travellers of all time, Marco Polo, journeyed to the Far East from the Mediterranean in the thirteenth century and spent twenty years in the court of Kublai Khan in China. On his return to Venice he set down in his book entitled *Description of the World* his impressions of the peoples and places and customs he had seen. But there were at least two extraordinary omissions in his account. He said nothing about the art of printing, unknown as yet in Europe but in full flower in China. He either did not notice it at all or if he did, failed to see what use Europe could possibly have for it. Whatever the reason, Europe had to wait another hundred years for Gutenberg. But even more spectacular was Marco Polo's omission of any reference to the Great Wall of China nearly 4,000 miles long and already more than 1,000 years old at the time of his visit. Again, he may not have seen it; but the Great Wall of China is the only structure built by man which is visible from the moon![1] Indeed travellers can be blind.

As I said earlier Conrad did not originate the image of Africa which we find in his book. It was and is the dominant image of Africa in the Western imagination and Conrad merely brought the peculiar gifts of his own mind to bear on it. For reasons which can certainly use close psychological inquiry the West seems to suffer deep anxieties about the precariousness of its civilization and to have a need for constant reassurance by comparison with Africa. If Europe, advancing in civilization, could cast a backward glance periodically at Africa trapped in primordial barbarity it could say with

9. Frank Willet, *African Art* (New York: Praeger, 1971), pp. 35–36.
1. For the omission of the Great Wall of China, I am indebted to *The Journey of Marco Polo* as recreated by artist Michael Foreman, published by *Pegasus Magazine*, 1974.

faith and feeling: There go I but for the grace of God. Africa is to Europe as the picture is to Dorian Gray[2]—a carrier onto whom the master unloads his physical and moral deformities so that he may go forward, erect and immaculate. Consequently Africa is something to be avoided just as the picture has to be hidden away to safeguard the man's jeopardous integrity. Keep away from Africa, or else! Mr. Kurtz of *Heart of Darkness* should have heeded that warning and the prowling horror in his heart would have kept its place, chained to its lair. But he foolishly exposed himself to the wild irresistible allure of the jungle and lo! the darkness found him out.

In my original conception of this essay I had thought to conclude it nicely on an appropriately positive note in which I would suggest from my privileged position in African and Western cultures some advantages the West might derive from Africa once it rid its mind of old prejudices and began to look at Africa not through a haze of distortions and cheap mystifications but quite simply as a continent of people—not angels, but not rudimentary souls either—just people, often highly gifted people and often strikingly successful in their enterprise with life and society. But as I thought more about the stereotype image, about its grip and pervasiveness, about the willful tenacity with which the West holds it to its heart; when I thought of the West's television and cinema and newspapers, about books read in its schools and out of school, of churches preaching to empty pews about the need to send help to the heathen in Africa, I realized that no easy optimism was possible. And there was, in any case, something totally wrong in offering bribes to the West in return for its good opinion of Africa. Ultimately the abandonment of unwholesome thoughts must be its own and only reward. Although I have used the word *willful* a few times here to characterize the West's view of Africa, it may well be that what is happening at this stage is more akin to reflex action than calculated malice. Which does not make the situation more but less hopeful.

The Christian Science Monitor, a paper more enlightened than most, once carried an interesting article written by its Education Editor on the serious psychological and learning problems faced by little children who speak one language at home and then go to school where something else is spoken. It was a wide-ranging article taking in Spanish-speaking children in America, the children of migrant Italian workers in Germany, the quadrilingual phenomenon in Malaysia, and so on. And all this while the article speaks unequivocally about language. But then out of the blue sky comes this:

---

2. The morally degenerate protagonist in Oscar Wilde's story (1891), who remains youthful and beautiful as his portrait turns old and ugly, reflecting the consequences of his licentious behavior. [Editor]

In London there is an enormous immigration of children who speak Indian or Nigerian dialects, or some other native language.

I believe that the introduction of dialects which is technically erroneous in the context is almost a reflex action caused by an instinctive desire of the writer to downgrade the discussion to the level of Africa and India. And this is quite comparable to Conrad's withholding of language from his rudimentary souls. Language is too grand for these chaps; let's give them dialects!

In all this business a lot of violence is inevitably done not only to the image of despised peoples but even to words, the very tools of possible redress.[3] Look at the phrase *native language* in the *Science Monitor* excerpt. Surely the only *native* language possible in London is Cockney English. But our writer means something else—something appropriate to the sounds Indians and Africans make![4]

Although the work of redressing which needs to be done may appear too daunting, I believe it is not one day too soon to begin. Conrad saw and condemned the evil of imperial exploitation but was strangely unaware of the racism on which it sharpened its iron tooth. But the victims of racist slander who for centuries have had to live with the inhumanity it makes them heir to have always known better than any casual visitor even when he comes loaded with the gifts of a Conrad.

IAN WATT

[Impressionism and Symbolism in *Heart of Darkness*]†

In the tradition of what we are still calling modern literature, the classic status of *Heart of Darkness* probably depends less on the

3. "In all this business a lot of violence is inevitably done to words and their meaning" [1977].
4. "something Indians and Africans speak" [1977]. The original version then concludes with the following two paragraphs:

"Perhaps a change will come. Perhaps this is the time when it can begin, when the high optimism engendered by the breathtaking achievements of Western science and industry is giving way to doubt and even confusion. There is just the possibility that Western man may begin to look seriously at the achievements of other people. I read in the papers the other day a suggestion that what America needs at this time is somehow to bring back the extended family. And I saw in my mind's eye future African Peace Corps Volunteers coming to help you set up the system.

"Seriously, although the work which needs to be done may appear too daunting, I believe that it is not one day too soon to begin. And where better than at a University?"

† From Ian Watt, *Conrad in the Nineteenth Century* (Berkeley: U of California P, 1979), pp. 168, 169–75, 176–79, 183–87, 188–89, 198–200. Copyright © 1979 by Ian Watt. Reprinted with the permission of the University of California Press. Extract from *Conrad in the Nineteenth Century*, published by Chatto & Windus. Reprinted by permission of the publisher. Unless indicated, notes are the author's.

prophetic nature of Conrad's ideas than on its new formal elements.

*   *   *

Conrad's most helpful comment on the method of *Heart of Darkness* occurs very early in the story, where the primary narrator explains that the meanings of Marlow's tales are characteristically difficult to encompass:

> The yarns of seamen have a direct simplicity, the whole meaning of which lies within the shell of a cracked nut. But Marlow was not typical (if his propensity to spin yarns be excepted), and to him the meaning of an episode was not inside like a kernel but outside, enveloping the tale which brought it out only as a glow brings out a haze, in the likeness of one of these misty halos that sometimes are made visible by the spectral illumination of moonshine. (5)

The passage suggests at least three of the distinctive elements in *Heart of Darkness*. First of all there is the duplication of narrators; and the first one, who begins and ends the story in his own voice, feels called on to explain that the second one, Marlow, goes in for a very special kind of storytelling, which has two distinctive qualities. These two qualities are suggested metaphorically, and may be roughly categorised as symbolist and impressionist: the abstract geometry of the metaphor is symbolist because the meaning of the story, represented by the shell of the nut or the haze around the glow, is larger than its narrative vehicle, the kernel or the glow; but the sensory quality of the metaphor, the mist and haze, is essentially impressionist.

(a) *Impressionism*

Mist or haze is a very persistent image in Conrad. It appeared as soon as he began to write: there was an "opaline haze" over the Thames on the morning when he had recalled Almayer; and the original Olmeijer had first come into Conrad's view through the morning mists of Borneo. In *Heart of Darkness* the fugitive nature and indefinite contours of haze are given a special significance by the primary narrator; he warns us that Marlow's tale will be not centered on, but surrounded by, its meaning; and this meaning will be only as fitfully and tenuously visible as a hitherto unnoticed presence of dust particles and water vapour in a space that normally looks dark and void. This in turn reminds us that one of the most characteristic objections to Impressionist painting was that the artist's ostensive "subject" was obscured by his representation of the atmospheric conditions through which it was observed.

Claude Monet, for instance, said of the critics who mocked him: "Poor blind idiots. They want to see everything clearly, even through the fog!"[1] For Monet, the fog in a painting, like the narrator's haze, is not an accidental interference which stands between the public and a clear view of the artist's "real" subject: the conditions under which the viewing is done are an essential part of what the pictorial—or the literary—artist sees and therefore tries to convey.

A similar idea, expressed in a similar metaphor, occurs twenty years later in Virginia Woolf's classic characterization of "Modern Fiction" (1919). There she exempts Conrad, together with Hardy, from her objections to traditional novels and those of her Edwardian contemporaries, H. G. Wells, Arnold Bennett, and John Galsworthy.[2] Her basic objection is that if we "look within" ourselves we see "a myriad impressions" quite unrelated to anything that goes on in such fiction; and if we could express "this unknown and uncircumscribed spirit" of life freely, "there would be no plot, no comedy, no tragedy, no love interest or catastrophe in the accepted style, and perhaps not a single button sewn on as the Bond Street tailors would have it." For, Virginia Woolf finally affirms, "Life is not a series of gig lamps symmetrically arranged; life is a luminous halo, a semi-transparent envelope surrounding us from the beginning of consciousness to the end."

The implications of these images of haze and halo for the essential nature of modern fiction are made somewhat clearer by the analogy of French Impressionist painting, and by the history of the word impressionism.

As a specifically aesthetic term, "Impressionism" was apparently put into circulation in 1874 by a journalist, Louis Leroy, to ridicule the affronting formlessness of the pictures exhibited at the Salon des Indépendants, and particularly of Claude Monet's painting entitled "Impression: Sunrise." In one way or another all the main Impressionists made it their aim to give a pictorial equivalent of the visual sensations of a particular individual at a particular time and place. One early critic suggested that "l'école des yeux" would be a more appropriate designation for them than "Impressionists";[3] what was new was not that earlier painters had been blind to the external world, but that painters were now attempting to give their own personal visual perceptions a more complete expressive autonomy; in the words of Jean Leymarie, what distinguished the French Impres-

---

1. Quoted by Jean Renoir in *Renoir, My Father*, trans. Randolph and Dorothy Weaver (Boston and Toronto, 1958), p. 174.
2. *The Common Reader* (London, 1938), pp. 148–49.
3. Jacques Lethève, *Impressionnistes et Symbolistes devant la presse* (Paris, 1959), p. 63. ["L'école des yeux": "The school of the eyes" (French)—Editor]

sionists was an intuitive "response to visual sensations, devoid of any theoretical principle."[4] It was this aim which, as E. H. Gombrich has said, allots the Impressionist movement a decisive role in the process of art's long transition from trying to portray what all men know to trying to portray what the individual actually sees.[5]

The history of the words "impression" and "impressionism" in English embodies a more general aspect of the long process whereby in every domain of human concerns the priority passed from public systems of belief—what all men know—to private views of reality—what the individual sees. Beginning with the root meaning of "impression"—from *premere*, to "press" in a primarily physical sense, as in the "impression" of a printed book—the *Oxford Dictionary* documents a semantic flow towards meanings whose status is primarily psychological. The meaning of impression as "the effect produced by external force or influence on the senses or mind" was apparently established as early as 1632; and afterwards it proceeded to reflect the process whereby, from Descartes onwards, the concentration of philosophical thought upon epistemological problems gradually focussed attention on individual sensation as the only reliable source of ascertainable truth. The most notable single name connected with the process is probably that of David Hume who opened *A Treatise of Human Nature* (1739–1740) with the ringing assertion, "All the perceptions of the human mind resolve themselves into two distinct kinds, which I shall call IMPRESSIONS and IDEAS." He had then attributed greater "force and violence" to impressions, as opposed to ideas, which he defined as merely the "less lively perceptions" which occur when we reflect on our original sense-impressions.[6] It was in protest against this empirical tradition in philosophy that the first English usage of "impressionism" occurred. In 1839 John Rogers, an eccentric word-coiner who entitled his attack on popery *Antipopopriestian*, wrote an ironical panegyric of the two main English prophets of "universal doubt": "All hail to Berkeley who would have no matter, and to Hume who would have no mind; to the Idealism of the former, and to the *Impressionism* of the latter!"[7]

It is appropriate that the word "impressionism" should be connected with Hume, since he played an important part in making the psychology of individual sensation supplant traditional philosophy as the main avenue to truth and value. One incidental result of this in the romantic and post-romantic period was that the religious, imaginative, emotional and aesthetic orders of being became

4. Jean Leymarie, *Impressionism*, trans. J. Emmons, 2 vols. (Lausanne, 1955), vol. 2, p. 28.
5. E. H. Gombrich, *The Story of Art*, 12th ed. (London, 1972), p. 406.
6. Bk I, "Of the Understanding," Pt. I, sect. i.
7. 2nd ed. (New York, 1841), p. 188.

increasingly private, a trend which in the course of the nineteenth century led both to the Aesthetic movement and to Impressionism. The most influential figure here is Walter Pater. In the famous "Conclusion" to *The Renaissance* (1868–1873), for instance, he speaks of how every person enclosed in "the narrow chamber of the individual mind" can directly experience only "the passage and dissolution of impressions, images, sensations"; these are "unstable, flickering, inconsistent," and the individual mind is therefore condemned to keep "as a solitary prisoner its own dream of a world."

This epistemological solipsism became an important part of the cultural atmosphere of the nineties; but by then the main English usage of the term "impressionism" was in reference to the French school of painters, and to their English counterparts who came to the fore with the foundation of the New English Art Club in 1886.[8] As in France, the term was very quickly extended to ways of writing which were thought to possess the qualities popularly attributed to the painters—to works that were spontaneous and rapidly executed, that were vivid sketches rather than detailed, finished, and premeditated compositions.[9] The literary use of the term remained even more casual and descriptive; although Stephen Crane was widely categorised as an "impressionist,"[1] and in 1898 a reviewer of Conrad's first collection of short stories, *Tales of Unrest*, described him as an "impressionistic realist,"[2] there was little talk of impressionism as a literary movement until considerably later.

It was Ford Madox Ford who gave wide currency to the view that he and Conrad, like Flaubert and Maupassant, had been writers of impressionist fiction. This view was expounded in Ford's 1913 essay "On Impressionism," which sees the distinctive trait of "the Impressionist" as giving "the fruits of his own observations alone";[3] but it is Ford's memoir of Conrad which gives his fullest account of literary impressionism. The memoir was published after Conrad's death, and so we do not know whether Ford's statement there that Conrad "avowed himself impressionist" would have been contradicted by Conrad if communication had been possible. Garnett immediately registered an emphatic protest,[4] but later critics such as

8. See Holbrook Jackson, "British Impressionists," in *The Eighteen-Nineties* (London, 1939), pp. 240–50.
9. See *O E D*, and Todd K. Bender, "Literary Impressionism: General Introduction," in *Preliminary Papers for Seminar #8*, distributed for the Modern Language Association Annual Meeting, 1975 (University of Wisconsin, Madison, 1975), 1–21.
1. By Edward Garnett, for instance, in an 1898 essay reprinted in *Friday Nights* (London, 1922).
2. Cited by Bruce E. Teets and Helmut Gerber, eds., *Joseph Conrad: An Annotated Bibliography of Writings About Him* (De Kalb, Ill., 1971), p. 16.
3. Reprinted in *Critical Writings of Ford Madox Ford*, ed. Frank MacShane (Lincoln, 1964), p. 37.
4. Ford, *Conrad: A Personal Remembrance* (London, 1924), p. 6; Edward Garnett, *Nation and Athenaeum* 36 (1924), 366–68.

Joseph Warren Beach[5] and Edward Crankshaw[6] applied the term to Conrad, and he is now ensconced in literary history as an impressionist.

Conrad certainly knew something about pictorial and literary impressionism, but the indications are that his reactions were predominantly unfavourable.[7] Conrad's tastes in painting, as in music, were distinctly old-fashioned; he apparently disliked Van Gogh and Cézanne, and the only painter he ever mentioned as a model for his own writing was the peasant realist Jean-François Millet: in a letter to Quiller-Couch, Conrad wrote "it has been my desire to do for seamen what Millet (if I dare pronounce the name of that great man and good artist in this connection) has done for peasants."[8] As to literary impressionism, at the very least Conrad probably read a mildly derogatory article on "The Philosophy of Impressionism," which appeared in *Blackwood's Magazine* in May 1898,[9] and presumably knew Garnett's view of Stephen Crane as an artist of "the surfaces of life."

Conrad's own references to Crane's impressionism suggest that he shared Garnett's unsympathetic view of it. Thus, speaking of Crane's story, "The Open Boat," Conrad writes: "He is *the only* impressionist and *only* an impressionist."[1] This was in 1897, and Conrad's sense of the limitations of impressionism apparently hardened later; thus in 1900 he praised the "focus" of some Cunninghame Graham sketches, and added: "They are much more of course than mere Crane-like impressionism."[2] Conrad was to pay much more favourable public tributes to Crane later; but his early private comments make it clear that, much like Garnett, he thought of impressionism as primarily concerned with visual appearances. This is confirmed by Conrad's usage of the term in *The Mirror of the Sea* (1906). He writes there of a sailor asking "in impressionistic phrase: 'How does the cable grow?' " (21); here "impressionistic" can only mean describing how things look as opposed to stating what is "really happening."

Perhaps the most distinctive quality of Conrad's own writing, like

---

5. In *The Twentieth-Century Novel* (New York, 1932), Conrad and Lawrence are categorized under Impressionism; Joyce comes under Post-Impressionism, Virginia Woolf under Expressionism.

6. Crankshaw writes: "The label will do as well as any other" (*Joseph Conrad*, p. 9).

7. Conrad visited Marguerite Poradowska in the Paris apartment of her cousin, Dr. Paul Gachet, close friend of Van Gogh and Cézanne, and found his collection "nightmarish" (René Rapin, ed., *Lettres de Joseph Conrad à Marguerite Poradowska* [Geneva: Dioz, 1966] 87).

8. Zdziław Najder, "Joseph Conrad: A Selection of Unknown Letters," *Polish Perspectives* 13 (1970): 32.

9. By C. F. Keary, no. 991, pp. 630–36.

1. *Letters from Conrad, 1895 to 1924* (London: Nonesuch Press, 1928), p. 107.

2. C. T. Watts, ed., *Joseph Conrad's Letters to R. B. Cunninghame Graham* (Cambridge: Cambridge UP, 1969), p. 130.

Crane's and unlike Ford's, is its strong visual sense; and Conrad's insistence in the preface to *The Nigger of the "Narcissus"* that art depends for its success on an "impression conveyed through the senses," is to that extent wholly consistent with impressionist doctrine. So, indeed, is much of the narrative itself, whose technique constitutes an original kind of multiple visual impressionism. This was immediately recognized by Arnold Bennett when he read *The Nigger of the "Narcissus"*; he wrote admiringly to H. G. Wells in 1897 asking: "Where did the man pick up . . . that *synthetic* way of gathering up a general impression and flinging it at you?"[3]

Heart of Darkness is essentially impressionist in one very special and yet general way: it accepts, and indeed in its very form asserts, the bounded and ambiguous nature of individual understanding; and because the understanding sought is of an inward and experiential kind, we can describe the basis of its narrative method as subjective moral impressionism. Marlow's story explores how one individual's knowledge of another can mysteriously change the way in which he sees the world as a whole, and the form of *Heart of Darkness* proposes that so ambitious an enterprise can only be begun through one man trying to express his most inward impressions of how deeply problematic is the quest for—to use Pater's terms— "an outer world, and of other minds." There is a certain kinship between the protagonist of Pater's *Marius the Epicurean* (1885) and Marlow, who comes to believe something fairly close to the "sceptical argument" of Marius; since "we are never to get beyond the walls of this closely shut cell of one's own personality," it follows that "the ideas we are somehow impelled to form of an outer world, and of other minds akin to our own, are, it may be, but a day dream."[4] *Heart of Darkness* embodies more thoroughly than any previous fiction the posture of uncertainty and doubt; one of Marlow's functions is to represent how much a man cannot know; and he assumes that reality is essentially private and individual—work, he comments, gives you "the chance to find yourself. Your own reality—for yourself, not for others—what no other man can ever know. They can only see the mere show, and never can tell what it really means" (29).

The other most distinctively impressionist aspect of Conrad's narrative method concerns his approach to visual description; and this preoccupation with the problematic relation of individual sense impressions to meaning is shown most clearly in one of the minor innovations of his narrative technique.

Long before *Heart of Darkness* Conrad seems to have been trying

3. *Conrad: The Critical Heritage*, ed. Norman Sherry (London: Routledge and Kegan Paul, 1973), p. 82.
4. Pater, *Marius the Epicurean*, pp. 106, 110.

to find ways of giving direct narrative expression to the way in which the consciousness elicits meaning from its perceptions. One of the devices that he hit on was to present a sense impression and to withhold naming it or explaining its meaning until later; as readers we witness every step by which the gap between the individual perception and its cause is belatedly closed within the consciousness of the protagonist.

*   *   *

This narrative device may be termed delayed decoding, since it combines the forward temporal progression of the mind, as it receives messages from the outside world, with the much slower reflexive process of making out their meaning. * * * Conrad presented the protagonist's immediate sensations, and thus made the reader aware of the gap between impression and understanding; the delay in bridging the gap enacts the disjunction between the event and the observer's trailing understanding of it. In *Heart of Darkness* Conrad uses the method for the most dramatic action of the story, when Marlow's boat is attacked, just below Kurtz's station. Marlow, terrified of going aground, is anxiously watching the cannibal sounding in the bows just below him: "I was looking down at the sounding-pole, and feeling much annoyed to see at each try a little more of it stick out of that river, when I saw my poleman give up the business suddenly, and stretch himself flat on the deck, without even taking the trouble to haul his pole in" (44).

* * * Marlow's initially inexplicable visual impression is accompanied by his irritation at an apparently gratuitous change in the normal order of things. Here, however, the effect is duplicated: "At the same time the fireman, whom I could also see below me, sat down abruptly before his furnace and ducked his head. I was amazed." Only now does the cause of these old changes in posture begin to emerge: "Then I had to look at the river mighty quick, because there was a snag in the fairway. Sticks, little sticks, were flying about—thick: they were whizzing before my nose, dropping below me, striking behind me against my pilot-house." But it is only when Marlow has finished attending to his duty as captain, and negotiated the next snag, that his understanding can finally decode the little sticks: "We cleared the snag clumsily. Arrows, by Jove! We were being shot at!"

Meanwhile the pilgrims, and, to Marlow's fury, even his helmsman, have started "squirting lead" into the bush. Marlow is navigating and catching occasional glimpses of "vague forms of men" through the shutterhole of the pilot-house, when his attention is suddenly deflected:

Something big appeared in the air before the shutter, the rifle went overboard, and the man stepped back swiftly, looked at me over his shoulder in an extraordinary, profound, familiar manner, and fell upon my feet. The side of his head hit the wheel twice, and the end of what appeared a long cane clattered round and knocked over a little camp-stool. It looked as though after wrenching that thing from somebody ashore he had lost his balance in the effort. The thin smoke had blown away, we were clear of the snag, and looking ahead I could see that in another hundred yards or so I would be free to sheer off, away from the bank; but my feet felt so warm and wet that I had to look down. The man had rolled on his back and stared straight up at me; both his hands clutched that cane. It was the shaft of a spear . . . He looked at me anxiously, gripping the spear like something precious, with an air of being afraid I would try to take it away from him (45–46).

A third sudden and unfamiliar action is enacted through the protagonist's consciousness, and the delay in his decoding of it makes the reader simultaneously experience horror and sardonic amusement. Amusement, because we feel a certain patronising contempt for those who do not understand things as quickly as we do, and because there is a gruesome comedy in the mere visual impression of the helmsman's "air of being afraid I would try to take [the spear] away from him." This macabre note has already been prepared for: if the poleman lies down, and then the fireman sits down, it is only natural that Marlow should assume that the dead helmsman's recumbent posture must be just a third example of the crew's deserting their duty just for their personal safety.

Still, the passage is obviously not primarily comic. Conrad's main objective is to put us into intense sensory contact with the events; and this objective means that the physical impression must precede the understanding of cause. Literary impressionism implies a field of vision which is not merely limited to the individual observer, but is also controlled by whatever conditions—internal and external—prevail at the moment of observation. In narration the main equivalents to atmospheric interference in painting are the various factors which normally distort human perception, or which delay its recognition of what is most relevant and important. First of all, our minds are usually busy with other things—Marlow has a lot to do just then, and it is only natural that he should be annoyed by being faced with these three new interferences with his task of keeping the boat from disaster. Secondly, our interpretations of impressions are normally distorted by habitual expectations—Marlow perceives the unfamiliar arrows as familiar sticks. Lastly, we always have many more things in our range of vision than we can pay attention to, so that in a crisis we may miss the most important ones—in this case that the helmsman has been killed. Conrad's method reflects all these difficulties in translating perceptions into causal or conceptual terms. This takes us deeply into the connection between delayed decoding and impressionism: it reminds us, as Michael Levenson has said, of the precarious nature of the process of interpretation in general; and since this precariousness is particularly evident when the individual's situation or his state of mind is abnormal, the device of delayed decoding simultaneously enacts the objective and the subjective aspects of moments of crisis. The method also has the more obvious advantage of convincing us of the reality of the experience which is being described; there is nothing suspiciously selective about the way it is narrated; while we read we are, as in life, fully engaged in trying to decipher a meaning out of a random and pell-mell bombardment of sense impressions.

* * *

(b) *Symbolism*

This concern of the Impressionists with the representation of the world as it is actually perceived was not accepted as a primary aim by the Symbolists. They approached their task from the opposite end of the same newly intensified polarity between the individual consciousness and the external world; their overriding objective was to discover the coherent meanings and values for which they inwardly yearned, but which they could not find in external reality. The fundamental intellectual mode of the Symbolists, therefore, was not science and observation but religion and imagination. The world of visible objects was valued only insofar as it offered concrete manifestations which corresponded to spiritual and imaginative meanings. As Jean Moréas wrote, Symbolist poetry "seeks to clothe the Idea in a perceptible form [*forme sensible*], a form, however, which would not be an aim in itself, but which while being used to express the Idea, would remain secondary to it."[5] This implied movement from the verbal sign to its spiritual idea is necessarily centrifugal; and there is, therefore, a general analogy between the Symbolist view of literature, and that which Conrad's narrator ascribes to Marlow in *Heart of Darkness*.

In the nineties, England was very much more receptive to foreign literature and philosophy than it had been earlier in the Victorian period;[6] in many circles Mr. Podsnap's "Not British" had become a

5. Cited by Franco Russoli, "Images et langages du Symbolisme," in *Le Symbolisme en Europe* (Paris, 1976), p. 17.
6. See Christophe Campos, *The View of France: From Arnold to Bloomsbury* (London, 1965), especially pp. 164–73.

term, no longer of anathema, but of acclamation. As a result, Symbolism, like Impressionism, was much in the air; and so, quite apart from his own wide reading in French, there can be no doubt that, by the time he wrote *Heart of Darkness*, Conrad could hardly have avoided knowing something about the French Symbolists. Under Verlaine's preferred term of Decadents, for instance, they had recently been the subject of a series of essays by Arthur Symons, which were soon to be collected in his influential *The Symbolist Movement in Literature* in 1899. On the other hand, Conrad was not in general very receptive to poetry; and although he knew Arthur Symons, who had published "The Idiots" in his magazine, the *Savoy*, Conrad apparently disliked being tarred with the decadent brush.

It is virtually certain, therefore, that whatever similarities may exist between Conrad and the French Symbolists are not the result of any direct literary influence on Conrad or of his doctrinal adhesion. One can imagine Conrad giving guarded approval only to a part of what W. B. Yeats recalled as the general literary outlook of the contributors to the *Savoy*, among whom he mentioned Conrad by name. Their shared attitude, Yeats wrote in "The Trembling of the Veil," was to argue "something after this fashion: 'Science . . . has won its right to explore whatever passes before its corporeal eye, and merely because it passes. . . . Literature now demands the same right of exploration of all that passes before the mind's eye, and merely because it passes.' " "Merely because it passes" might have drawn a protest from Conrad, and Yeats's ensuing justification of his own attitudes certainly would. Yeats argues that, having been "deprived by Huxley and Tyndall" of a religion, and being consequently possessed by a "conviction that the world was now but a bundle of fragments," it was imperative to restore "Unity of Being" through some spiritual or occult order.[7] Conrad would have laughed scornfully, not at the problem but at the esoteric solutions proposed: his mocking attitude is suggested in a comment on the ideas of Sar Peladan, one of the most committed devotees of the occult among the French Symbolists, whom Conrad found "marvellously and deliciously absurd."[8]

There is, however, much in Conrad's letters which suggests that he shared many of the basic attitudes of the French Symbolists. These attitudes may be summarily divided into two categories: the ontological—the kinds of basic reality, knowledge, or vision, which literature seeks beyond the "bundle of fragments" offered by the external world; and the expressive—the characteristic formal methods by which the reader is induced to seek this vision beyond the work's overt statements.

7. *Autobiographies* (London, 1955), pp. 325–26; 115; 189; 90.
8. *Notes on Life and Letters*, p. 70.

Believing, with Rimbaud in "Soleil et Chair," that "notre pâle rai-
son nous cache l'infini,"[9] the Symbolists commonly expressed their
ontological concern by adopting as practices, subjects, or metaphors, those modes of perception which are the most opposed to
rational observation or analysis—notably dreams, drug-induced hal-
lucinations, and occult rituals. These, together with less extreme
forms of intuition or imagination, were used as ways in which the
spiritual order thought to subsist beneath or beyond surface appearances could be apprehended or made manifest. The basic analogy is that of the Platonic search beyond the transient inadequacies
of the phenomenal world for the ultimate changeless ideas; and
this analogy is present in some of Conrad's statements about his
larger artistic aims. Thus in a letter of 27 January 1897, he wrote
that in *The Nigger of the "Narcissus"* he had "tried to get through
the veil of details at the essence of life."[1] The metaphor of the "veil"
here is reminiscent, not only of much esoteric symbolist doctrine
during the period, but also of the thought of one of its main philosophic sources, Schopenhauer. He habitually called the objective
world Maya, the term for the world's "illusion of multiplicity" in
Hinduism, and taught that through detached contemplation the individual could penetrate the veil of Maya and discover that "there is
really *only one being*."[2]

Conrad thought along somewhat similar lines, except that for
him the "essence of life" remained much more irreducibly plural,
public, and contingent than it was for Plato or Schopenhauer.
When an influential critic, W. L. Courtney, reviewed *The Nigger of
the "Narcissus"* somewhat impercipiently, Conrad objected in terms
that combine impressionist and symbolist attitudes. Denying the
influence of "formulas and theories," and specifically disclaiming
"all allegiance to realism, to naturalism," Conrad asserted that he
wrote "straight from the heart," in an attempt "to give a true impression"; but he then went on to confess "that I also wanted to
connect the small world of the ship with that larger world carrying
perplexities, fears, affections, rebellions, in a loneliness greater
than that of the ship at sea."[3]

In this attempt to connect the literal objects of his narrative with
a "larger world" conceived at a rather high level of abstraction,

9. From Arthur Rimbaud's poem "Sun and Flesh" (1870): "our pale reason hides the infinite from us." [Editor]
1. G. Jean-Aubry, *Joseph Conrad: Life and Letters*, 1:200.
2. *World as Will and Representation*, vol. 2, p. 321.
3. Cited from David R. Smith, " 'One Word More' about *The Nigger of the 'Narcissus,' "*
Nineteenth-Century Fiction 23 (1968): 208–9. Smith shows how the general argument
of the letter closely follows the preface to *The Nigger of the "Narcissus,"* but adds to it
"about as clear a statement of his symbolic intent as [Conrad] ever made" (210). Con-

Conrad is in general accord with the symbolist ontology; as regards expressive technique the parallels are somewhat closer. Several have already been noted—the yearning for the "magic suggestiveness of music" for instance, a priority which echoes Verlaine's "De la musique avant toute chose" in his "Art poétique." Conrad also often speaks of the mysteriously evocative power of words with an emphasis somewhat reminiscent of Mallarmé. Thus in November 1898, just before starting *Heart of Darkness*, he wrote "How fine it could be . . . if the idea had a substance and words a magic power, if the invisible could be snared into a shape."[4] It sounds like a Symbolist prayer; and in a letter of 9 October 1899 to Hugh Clifford, Conrad clarified his views on the evocative role of words. "Words," he wrote, "groups of words, words standing alone, are symbols of life, have the power in their sound or their aspect to present the very thing you wish to hold up before the mental vision of your readers."[5] Conrad was to retain this view of the quasi-magical power of words; in 1911 he wrote to an Italian admirer about his "ineradicable conviction that it is in the living word *que l'on saisit le mieux la forme du rêve*" [that one best captures the shape of the dream].[6]

Conrad, then, sometimes spoke about his larger creative aspirations in terms which recall those which Mallarmé used to summarise the poetic aims of the Symbolists: "*Nommer* un objet, c'est supprimer les trois quarts de la jouissance du poëme qui est faite de deviner peu à peu: le *suggérer*, voilà le rêve. C'est le parfait usage de ce mystere qui constitue le symbole."[7] Throughout his career Conrad retained the general aim of making the work suggest much more than it overtly embodies; thus in 1914 he wrote: "It is a strange fate that everything that I have, of set artistic purpose, laboured to leave indefinite, suggestive, in the penumbra of initial inspiration, should have that light turned on to it and its insignificance (as compared with, I might say without megalomania, the

---

rad's letter went on to give his aim a Schopenhauerian note with the comment: "There is joy and sorrow; there is sunshine and darkness—and all are within the same eternal smile of the inscrutable Maya."

4. Jocelyn Baines, *Joseph Conrad: A Critical Biography* (London: Weidenfeld and Nicholson, 1960), p. 223.

5. Aubry, *Life and Letters*, 1:280.

6. Carlo Angeleri, "Joseph Conrad: Una Lettera Inedita a Carlo Placci," *Paragone* 8 (1957): 55–58.

7. Stéphane Mallarmé, *Oeuvres complètes* (Paris, 1945), p. 869. "To *name* the object is to destroy three quarters of the enjoyment of the poem, which comes from guessing at it bit by bit: to *suggest* the object, that is the dream. It is the perfect practice of this mystery which constitutes the symbol." Conrad's relation to the symbolists, and much else, receives full and illuminating treatment in Donald C. Yelton's *Mimesis and Metaphor: An Inquiry into the Genesis and Scope of Conrad's Symbolic Imagery* (The Hague, 1967), especially pp. 28–67.

ampleness of my conceptions) exposed for any fool to comment upon or even for average minds to be disappointed with."[8]

The parallels between Conrad's basic assumptions and those of the French Symbolists could be expanded and qualified; but the great diversity in the works and doctrines of the French Symbolists, and Conrad's own reluctance to theorise, make it unlikely that a fuller analysis could go very much beyond the analogies which have already been advanced. * * *

                              *   *   *

* * * As to his theoretical position on the symbolic nature of the novel, and on the French Symbolists, Conrad expressed himself most directly, though not unambiguously, in a letter of 1918. In answer to a critic who had written to him about the "final effect" of a work of art, Conrad maintained the general position that "All the great creations of literature have been symbolic." "A work of art," he explained, "is very seldom limited to one exclusive meaning and not necessarily tending to a definite conclusion. And this for the reason that the nearer it approaches art, the more it acquires a symbolic character. This statement may surprise you, who may imagine that I am alluding to the Symbolist School of poets or prose writers. Theirs, however, is only a literary proceeding against which I have nothing to say. I am concerned here with something much larger."[9]

Conrad casually dissociates himself from the French Symbolists, not in order to say anything against their "literary proceedings," but to affirm a "much larger" view: that great works of art do not necessarily "tend to definite conclusions"; and that the extent of their "symbolic character" is directly proportional to the quality of their art.

It is possible that Conrad's use of the word symbolic here may mean no more than that in the greatest works of literature the characters and their destinies stand for much more than their particular selves and actions, and are representative of more universal feelings and situations. This would be a variant of the commonest usage of "symbolic" as meaning "widely representative"; and it would then carry the idea that all the components of the novel should have wider and more general implications. But Conrad seems to be implying something more: only a larger meaning for symbolic, surely, would justify his assumption that his statement may be found "surprising"; and the essence of his statement is presumably that the quality of art is proportional to its range of symbolic meanings. Such a view, of course, would be consistent

---

8. Richard Curle, ed., *Conrad to a Friend: Selected Letters* (London: Sampson Low, Marston, 1928), p. 142.
9. Aubry, *Life and Letters*, 2:205.

both with the image of the glow and the haze, and with the general intention of the French Symbolists. But Conrad's letter is sufficiently obscure to allow of some doubt; and so as regards *Heart of Darkness*, the only real test must be that of its actual narrative practice. * * *

* * *

If Conrad belongs to the symbolist tradition it is only in a limited, eclectic, and highly idiosyncratic way; even if one accepts in some very general sense the view that modern literature is mainly a continuation of the symbolist tradition,[1] and waives the until now insuperable difficulties of definition,[2] there seems little to be gained by categorising Conrad, along with Proust, Kafka, Joyce, Mann, and Faulkner, as a symbolist novelist,[3] especially if this is taken to involve dissociating him from the impressionist tradition to which he is more commonly assigned. The particular case of *Heart of Darkness*, however, is somewhat different; its narrative technique in most respects typifies, and indeed anticipates, the general expressive idiom of modern literature; but its plot, its themes, and some of the evidence about its intentions are closer to some of the central features of the French symbolist movement than any of Conrad's other works.

Its plot contains some very untypical elements of adventure and melodrama, but it is nevertheless based on a simple symbolic quest, in which the various forms of "darkness" which Marlow encounters have as many possible meanings as the blue flower in Novalis. The essence of the action is a process of expanded moral awareness; as Marlow says, his journey was significant only because it "seemed somehow to throw a kind of light on everything about me—and into my thoughts" (7).

The structure of *Heart of Darkness* is very largely based on naturally symbolic actions and objects: the plot—a journey, a death, and a return; the characters—Kurtz, or the helmsman; the incidents—Marlow's interview for the job, or the grove of death; the material objects—the rivets, the staves of the pilgrims, the heads on the posts; the scene—the Thames and the Congo; the atmosphere—light and darkness. In all these elements the symbolic meaning of objects and events is established through the expansion of their in-

---

1. Influentially propounded by Edmund Wilson in *Axel's Castle: A Study of the Imaginative Literature of 1870–1930* (New York, 1931).
2. In his *The Symbolist Aesthetic in France: 1885–1895*, 2nd ed. (Oxford, 1968), A. G. Lehmann concludes that "the terms 'literary symbol' and 'symbolist' are terms which, introduced and fortified by a series of mischances, should never have been allowed to remain in usage" (p. 316).
3. These are all, for instance, classified as "romantic symbolists" in William York Tindall's *The Literary Symbol* (New York, 1955), p. 3. Mark Schorer described *Heart of Darkness* as "that early but wonderful piece of symbolist fiction" in his classic essay "Technique as Discovery" (*The World We Imagine* [New York, 1968], p. 19).

herent properties, and they have a structural, rather than a merely illustrative, function.

The analogy is equally close as regards subject matter. *Heart of Darkness* shares many of the characteristic preoccupations and themes of the French Symbolists: the spiritual voyage of discovery, especially through an exotic jungle landscape, which was a common symbolist theme, in Baudelaire's "Le Voyage" and Rimbaud's "Bâteau ivre," for instance; the pervasive atmosphere of dream, nightmare, and hallucination, again typical of Rimbaud; and the very subject of Kurtz also recalls, not only Rimbaud's own spectacular career, but the typical symbolist fondness for the lawless, the depraved, and the extreme modes of experience.

More generally, we surely sense in *Heart of Darkness* Conrad's supreme effort to reveal, in Baudelaire's phrase about Delacroix, "the infinite in the finite."[4] This intention is suggested in Conrad's title. The Symbolist poets often used titles which suggested a much larger and more mysterious range of implication than their work's overt subject apparently justified—one thinks of the expanding effect of T. S. Eliot's *The Waste Land*, for example, or of *The Sacred Wood*. This centrifugal suggestion was sometimes produced by an obtrusive semantic gap—a coupling of incongruous words or images that forced us to look beyond our habitual expectations; there is, for instance, the initial puzzling shock of the titles of two of the great precursive works of symbolism which appeared in 1873, Rimbaud's *Une Saison en enfer*, and Tristan Corbière's "Les Amours jaunes."[5]

Compared with the particularity of Conrad's earlier and more traditional titles, such as *Almayer's Folly* or *The Nigger of the "Narcissus"*, *Heart of Darkness* strikes a very special note; we are somehow impelled to see the title as much more than a combination of two stock metaphors for referring to "the centre of the Dark Continent" and "a diabolically evil person." Both of Conrad's nouns are densely charged with physical and moral suggestions; freed from the restrictions of the article, they combine to generate a sense of puzzlement which prepares us for something beyond our usual expectation: if the words do not name what we know, they must be asking us to know what has, as yet, no name. The more concrete of the two terms, "heart," is attributed a strategic centrality within a formless and infinite abstraction, "darkness"; the combination defies both visualisation and logic: How can something inorganic like darkness have an organic centre of life and feeling? How can a shapeless absence of light compact itself into a shaped and pulsing

4. *Oeuvres complètes*, ed. Ruff (Paris, 1968), p. 404.
5. *A Season in Hell* and "The Yellow Loves" (both French). [Editor]

presence? And what are we to make of a "good" entity like a heart becoming, of all things, a controlling part of a "bad" one like darkness? *Heart of Darkness* was a fateful event in the history of fiction; and to announce it Conrad hit upon as haunting, though not as obstrusive, an oxymoron as Baudelaire had for poetry with *Les Fleurs du Mal*.[6]

* * *

HUNT HAWKINS

Heart of Darkness and Racism†

In 1975 in a speech at the University of Massachusetts titled "An Image of Africa," Chinua Achebe declared Conrad was "a bloody racist." He has repeated this charge in an article in the *Times Literary Supplement* in 1980, a lecture in London in 1990, a speech at the University of Texas in 1998, and in passing references in several interviews. The original speech was published in *The Massachusetts Review* in 1977 and in a revised version in 1988 in Achebe's collection of essays *Hopes and Impediments* as well the third edition of the Norton *Heart of Darkness*. Since then it has been reprinted many times, often in conjunction with Conrad's novella. Achebe's own novel *Things Fall Apart* is also now frequently anthologized next to *Heart of Darkness*. The controversy stirred by Achebe's declaration has gone on for three decades and shows no signs of abating. It has become a standard topic for school assignments and has fostered the impression that racism is the main, or even the only, issue of importance in Conrad's work. Ironically, it has given new life to Conrad studies while tending to narrow them.

In "An Image of Africa," Achebe comes close to saying that *Heart of Darkness* should cease being taught. After noting that it has been classed as "permanent literature—read and taught and constantly evaluated by serious academics," he asks whether a novel "which depersonalizes a portion of the human race, can be called a great work of art. My answer is: No, it cannot." Finally, he objects against its being "today perhaps the most commonly prescribed novel in twentieth-century literature courses." In his later interviews, however, Achebe makes clear he isn't calling for censorship. For example in 2000 he said about *Heart of Darkness*, "I am not Ayatollah Kho-

6. The flowers of evil (French). [Editor]
† Original version published as "The Issue of Racism in *Heart of Darkness*," *Conradiana* 14.3 (1982): 163–71; updated and extensively revised by the author especially for this Norton Critical Edition. Reprinted by permission of Texas Tech University Press. Notes are the author's.

meini. I don't believe in banning books, but they should be read carefully. Far from wanting the novel banned, I teach it."[1] Indeed, censorship proceeds on the assumption that readers are passive receptacles whereas good teaching should stimulate active, critical reading. In the case of *Heart of Darkness* such reading is especially important because it is such a dense, complex text. On many topics, including race, it offers views that are multiple, ambiguous, ambivalent, conflicting, and perhaps even ultimately incoherent.

Achebe is quite right that much of *Heart of Darkness* dehumanizes Africans. Conrad's narrator, Marlow, often uses frankly derogatory language in describing them. At various points in the story he refers to them as "savages," "niggers," and "rudimentary souls." He applies the following adjectives to their appearance or behavior: "grotesque," "horrid," "ugly," "fiendish," and "satanic." Achebe's 1980 article notes that the story "teems with Africans whose humanity is admitted in theory but totally undermined by the mindlessness of its context and the pretty explicit animal imagery surrounding it."[2] Marlow's explicit animal comparisons are with ants, hyenas, horses, and bees. Thus the image Conrad projects of African life can hardly be called flattering.

* * *

In a related point, Achebe observes that Africans are barely present in *Heart of Darkness*. In Conrad's story, none of the African characters has a name. With the exception of Kurtz's mistress, no African appears for more than a full paragraph. We do not go into the minds of any Africans to see the situation from their point of view. In fact, they barely speak, being limited to a total of four pidgin sentences. It might be said that Conrad failed to portray Africans because he knew little of their culture, having spent less than six months in the Congo, mostly in the company of white men, and without knowledge of any African language. In his novels set in the Far East, where he spent some six years, he does give individual portraits. Still, in his 1896 story set in the Congo, "An Outpost of Progress," Conrad does have speaking, named Africans. And he imaginatively creates dozens of such characters in *Nostromo*, his novel set in Latin America where he spent less than a week. So his comparative reduction and neglect of Africans in *Heart of Darkness* must have been deliberate.

Achebe has explicitly said he wrote his *Things Fall Apart* as a reply to Joyce Cary's *Mister Johnson*, but it also answers *Heart of Darkness*. Achebe's novel about the British takeover of an Ibo village at the end of the nineteenth century gives a comprehensive,

1. Quoted in Maya Jaggi, "Storyteller of the Savannah: Profile of Chinua Achebe," *The Guardian* (18 November 2000).
2. Chinua Achebe, "Viewpoint," *Times Literary Supplement*, 1 February 1980, 113.

carefully balanced picture of an African culture. Moreover, it provides a context for, if it does not exactly condone, some practices that Conrad presents as savage and disturbing. The human sacrifice of Ikemefuna is dictated by the Oracle. And Okonkwo has brought home five human heads from war, drinking from one on great occasions. For many years Conrad's *Heart of Darkness* may well have been the only book set in Africa that students were assigned. Thus it is important that they read *Things Fall Apart* and other works to get a fuller, more accurate portrayal.

It would be a mistake, nonetheless, to read Achebe, any more than Conrad, as representing all of the cultures and situations on the continent. Achebe's Ibo live at approximately the same time but more than a thousand miles from the upper Congo depicted by Conrad. Therefore, it would be wrong simply to see *Things Fall Apart* as the truth concealed behind *Heart of Darkness*. When Conrad visited the upper Congo in 1890, it had been devastated by both Belgian exploitation and thirteen years of Arab slaving run by Tippo Tib, a coastal trader whom Henry M. Stanley had transported to Stanley Falls (Conrad's "Inner Station"). Thus the tribes of the region—specifically, the Bangala, the Balolo, the Wangata, the Ngombe, the Bapoto, and the Babango—were a great deal more disordered and violent than tribes in other parts of Africa. When George Washington Williams visited in the same year as Conrad, he was appalled by the Belgians and became the first total opponent of King Leopold's regime. But at the same time he was shocked by the Africans. In an open letter of protest to Leopold, Williams reported that "Cruelties of the most astounding character are practiced by the natives, such as burying the slaves alive in the grave of a dead chief." He also said, "Between 800 and 1,000 slaves are sold to be eaten by the natives of the Congo State annually." Thus, although Williams denounced the cruelty of Leopold's soldiers, one of his complaints against the regime was, ironically, that it was "deficient in the moral, military, and financial strength necessary to govern."[3]

It is uncertain to what extent Conrad may have witnessed any such practices. He made no mention of them in his Congo diaries, but he did later tell Arthur Symons, "I saw all those sacrilegious rites."[4] Unlike most other Europeans, however, Conrad did not view such rites, even conceived at their worst, as a justification for African subjugation. In a protest letter sent to Roger Casement in

3. George Washington Williams, "An Open Letter to His Serene Majesty Leopold II," in John Hope Franklin, *George Washington Williams: A Biography* (Chicago: U of Chicago P, 1985), p. 248 [see the selection in this Norton Critical Edition].
4. Arthur Symons, "A Set of Six" in *A Conrad Memorial Library: The Collection of George T. Keating* (Garden City, NY: Doubleday, Doran, 1929), p. 170.

1903 as a contribution to the fledgling Congo reform movement,
Conrad declared,

> Barbarism per se is no crime deserving of a heavy visitation;
> and the Belgians are worse than the seven plagues of Egypt in-
> somuch that in that case it was punishment sent for a definite
> transgression; but in this the Upoto man is not aware of any
> transgression, and therefore can see no end to the infliction. It
> must appear to him very awful and mysterious; and I confess
> that it appears so to me too.[5]

Conrad became a staunch, if complicated, opponent of European
expansion. *Heart of Darkness* offers a powerful indictment of imperialism, both explicitly for the case of King Leopold and implicitly
(despite Marlow's comments on the patches of red) for all other
European powers. As Marlow says, "All Europe contributed to the
making of Kurtz." He declares, "The conquest of the earth, which
mostly means the taking it away from those who have a different
complexion or slightly flatter noses than ourselves, is not a pretty
thing." His story graphically demonstrates how ugly it could get.

In his 1975 speech Achebe did not mention Conrad's anti-
imperialism, but in his 1988 revised version, he concluded, "Conrad saw and condemned the evil of imperial exploitation." Conrad
criticized imperialism on many grounds, one being the hypocrisy of
the "civilizing mission." In "The White Man's Burden," published
in 1899, the same year as *Heart of Darkness*, Rudyard Kipling
posited that colonizers selflessly and thanklessly better the lives of
their "new-caught, sullen peoples,/Half devil and half child," coax-
ing them from the bondage of their "loved Egyptian night." The
trope here is temporal, conceiving Europeans (and the Americans
Kipling was encouraging to take over the Philippines) as adults and
advanced while non-Europeans were children and primitive. This
trope, which provided the chief ideological support for late nineteenth-century imperialism, derived largely from Charles Darwin's
theory of evolution. Darwin did not take up the question of evolution of human societies in his *Origin of Species* in 1859, but in *The
Descent of Man* in 1871, he concluded, "There can hardly be a
doubt that we are descended from barbarians. The astonishment
which I felt on first seeing a party of Fuegians on a wild and broken
shore will never be forgotten by me, for the reflection at once
rushed into my mind—such were our ancestors."[6] The co-founder
of evolutionary theory, Alfred Russel Wallace, was more explicit. In

5. *The Collected Letters of Joseph Conrad*, eds. Frederick Karl and Laurence Davies (Cambridge: Cambridge UP, 1988), 3:96.
6. Charles Darwin, *The Descent of Man, and Selection in Relation to Sex* (New York: D. Ap-
   pleton, 1896), 618.

his article "The Origin of Human Races and the Antiquity of Man" published in 1864, Wallace argues that owing to the struggle for survival and natural selection, "the better and higher specimens of our race would therefore increase and spread, the lower and brutal would give way and successively die out, and that rapid advancement of mental organization would occur, which has raised the very lowest races of man so far above the brutes . . . and, in conjunction with scarcely perceptible modifications of form, has developed the wonderful intellect of the Germanic races."[7] By the end of the nineteenth century this view of human social and racial evolution had become firmly entrenched.

There is no doubt that Conrad incorporated the temporal evolutionary trope in *Heart of Darkness*. Marlow described his journey upriver as "traveling back to the earliest beginnings of the world" and the Africans as "the prehistoric man." But rather than using this trope to support imperialism, Conrad uses it to do the opposite. First of all, he points out that Europeans don't live up to their own ideals as civilizers. In a letter to his publisher, William Blackwood, Conrad said of his project, "The criminality of inefficiency and pure selfishness when tackling the civilizing work in Africa is a justifiable idea."[8] In the story he suggests the ideals are mere sham. When Marlow's aunt applauds imperialism for "weaning those ignorant millions from their horrid ways," he "ventured to hint that the Company was run for profit." The only "improved specimens" we see, such as the fireman, are parodies. Otherwise, we just see exploitation and violence. Conrad very clearly expresses his condemnation of European cruelty in such memorable scenes as the French ship firing blindly into the continent, the beating of the African assumed to have started the fire at the Central Station, the carriers found dead in harness on the caravan trail, the man with a bullet-hole in his forehead as a part of road "upkeep," the "pilgrims" shooting from their steamer, the crew not being given food, the chain-gang building the railway, and the contract-laborers languishing in the "grove of death."

In addition to pointing out the hypocrisy with which the ideals of the "civilizing mission" were espoused, Conrad may have questioned the validity of those ideals themselves. Marlow says of Kurtz's report, written while Kurtz was still an emissary of progress,

> The opening paragraph, however, in the light of later information, strikes me now as ominous. He began with the argument that we whites, from the point of development we had arrived

7. Alfred Russel Wallace, "The Origin of Human Races and the Antiquity of Man Deduced from the 'Theory of Natural Selection,'" *Journal of Anthropological Society of London* (1864), 2:clxiv.
8. *Letters of Joseph Conrad*, 2:139–40.

at, "must necessarily appear to them [savages] in the nature of supernatural beings—we approach them with the might as of a deity. . . . By the simple exercise of our will we can exert a power for good practically unbounded."

The ideals themselves carried a hubristic arrogance. Edward Said, and before him Wilson Harris, have observed that Conrad's very style with its first-person narrators, framed narratives, time jumps, fractured sentences, and addiction to adjectives upsets the notion of absolute truths assumed by the "civilizing mission."[9] Both fault Conrad, probably correctly, for not showing non-European resistance and not imagining an alternative to imperialism, but both applaud him for attacking European domination. Conrad likely didn't show more of the Africans because he wanted to focus on the Europeans. As Abdul JanMohamed notes, "Despite what writers like Chinua Achebe say about the denigration of Africans in *Heart of Darkness*, Africans are an incidental part, and not the main objects of representation, in the novella."[1]

Conrad also used the trope of evolution in *Heart of Darkness* to attack imperialism by suggesting that Europeans in colonies could slide backwards on the evolutionary scale. Kurtz is the main example. In Africa the wilderness whispers to Kurtz "things about himself that he did not know." His "forgotten and brutal instincts" are awakened. And he passes beyond "the bounds of permitted aspirations," indulging his greed and lust, placing the heads of "rebels" on posts around his house, presiding at "midnight dances ending with unspeakable rites" (probably human sacrifices), and committing the hubris of setting himself up as a god. Marlow himself feels the temptation to go ashore for "a howl and a dance" though he resists it. And while no match for Kurtz, the other Europeans have become animalistic. The uncle of the manager has a "short flipper of an arm" and the members of the Eldorado Exploring Expedition are "less valuable animals" than their donkeys.

Conrad's effective use of the evolutionary trope against imperialism, however, can still be described as racist since it continues to assume Africans are at the low end of the scale. Thus Achebe finishes his sentence, "Conrad saw and condemned the evil of imperialist exploitation but was strangely unaware of the racism on which it sharpened its iron tooth." Similarly, Patrick Brantlinger observes, "*Heart of Darkness* offers a powerful critique of at least some mani-

9. See Edward Said, *Culture and Imperialism* (New York: Knopf, 1993), and Wilson Harris, "The Frontier on Which *Heart of Darkness* Stands," *Research in African Literatures*, 12:1 (Spring 1981), 86–93.
1. Abdul JanMohamed, "The Economy of Manichean Allegory: The Function of Racial Difference in Colonialist Literature" in *Race, Writing, and Difference*, ed. Henry Louis Gates Jr. (Chicago: U of Chicago P, 1986), p. 90.

festations of imperialism and racism as it simultaneously presents that critique in ways that can be characterized only as imperialist and racist."[2] In a number of passages, however, Conrad reaches to get beyond the evolutionary trope and racism, though often uncertainly and ambiguously.

Frances B. Singh has argued that Conrad viewed Africans as evil and their evil is what has corrupted Kurtz. She maintains *Heart of Darkness* "carries suggestions that the evil which the title refers to is to be associated with Africans, their customs, and their rites" and that Conrad would have us believe Africans "have the power to turn the white man's heart black."[3] For the most part, however, Conrad makes clear that Kurtz's corruption comes not from Africans but from Europe and from Kurtz himself. Kurtz no longer has the restraints provided in Europe by policemen and gossiping neighbors. Since he is "hollow at the core," lacking internal restraints, he is susceptible to the whisper of the wilderness. The dark wilderness, as Marlow realizes by the end of the story, is not just in Africa but lurking in the streets of Brussels and hovering over the Thames. Indeed, it is cosmic as shown in a sentence in the manuscript: "The Earth suddenly seemed shrunk to the size of a pea spinning in the heart of an immense darkness." It is Kurtz who has corrupted his lake tribe rather than the other way around. At one point Conrad does suggest the Africans worshipped evil prior to this corruption. He says Kurtz took a seat "amongst the devils of the land." But the only time Conrad applies the word "satanic" to Africans is in connection with their chanting as Kurtz is being taken away. Conrad largely resists the lead of Kipling, who called non-Europeans "half-devil." He takes care to distinguish between what Kurtz does and what the Africans do, and while he finds great fault with the former, he finds little with the latter. As in his letter to Casement when he wrote: "Barbarism per se is no crime," Conrad in *Heart of Darkness* exonerates the Africans by having Marlow say of Kurtz, "I seemed at one bound to have been transported into some lightless region of subtle horrors, where pure, uncomplicated savagery was a positive relief, being something that had a right to exist—obviously—in the sunshine."

Still, while resisting the common contemporary demonization of Africans, Conrad continues to place them in the category of "savage" and "barbarian." He goes slightly further in several places in the text where he praises the Africans for their energy, vitality, and dignity. Kurtz's mistress is "superb . . . magnificent . . . stately." The

2. Patrick Brantlinger, *Rule of Darkness: British Literature and Imperialism, 1830–1914* (Ithaca: Cornell UP, 1988), p. 257.
3. Frances Singh, "The Colonialist Bias of *Heart of Darkness*," *Conradiana* 10 (1978): 43, 44.

black paddlers off the coast have "a wild vitality, an intense energy of movement." And Conrad has Marlow commend the cannibals in his crew as "fine fellows . . . men one could work with." Moreover, the cannibals possess a mysterious inner restraint in not eating the whites on board even though they are starving. Thus, in a novel that is a relentless, skeptical inquiry into the basis of moral behavior, one that questions morality founded on principles or providence, the cannibals with their "inborn strength" provide one of the few signs of hope. All of these examples, however, are undercut by phrases that continue to associate Africans with the uncivilized. The mistress mirrors the wilderness. The paddlers are "natural." The honor of the cannibals is "primitive." Nonetheless, Conrad does accord them a certain respect. In contrast with the hypocrisies of Europe, they are "true" and "wanted no excuse for being there."

Conrad goes even further in a number of passages where he has Marlow recognize, or almost recognize, or struggle to recognize the humanity of the Africans. Unlike Kurtz, Marlow resists the temptation to exploit Africans. Instead he does what little he can to help by giving his biscuit to the man in the "grove of death" and by pulling his whistle so the "pilgrims" cannot slaughter Kurtz's followers. As a result of his experience, Marlow seems to overcome his prejudices enough to acknowledge the "claim of distant kinship" put upon him by his helmsman through their shared work and shared mortality. Getting to Kurtz, he says, was not worth the loss of this life. Marlow urges his audience to recognize "their humanity—like yours." But these examples are also ambiguous. Marlow can't say whether the person he hands the biscuit is a man or boy because "with them it's hard to tell." The sentence after "their humanity—like yours" consists of a single word: "Ugly." And Marlow quickly throws the body of his helmsman overboard because, amongst the cannibals, a "second-rate helmsman" might become a "first-class temptation." This wavering may be a sign of inner struggle or simply indicate ongoing ambivalence.

The most impressive steps Marlow takes toward recognition, ones overlooked by Achebe, are when he turns the tables. He imagines that Englishmen would soon clear out the road between Deal and Gravesend if African colonizers started catching them to carry heavy loads. And he realizes that in Africa drums may have "as profound a meaning as the sound of bells in a Christian country." Elsewhere drums represent savagery, and Marlow's excited response tells him he's kin to Africans because he also contains primal urges, but in this passage he sees they are kin to him because they also have reverence.

Achebe dismisses Conrad's expressions of sympathy for suffering

Africans as "bleeding heart sentiments." Specifically, he describes as "liberalism" Marlow's reaction to the "grove of death." Perhaps Marlow doesn't fully recognize the humanity and equality of the dying Africans, though his statement that he's "horror-struck" and his rage at the waste of the Belgians seem sincere enough. And perhaps one can fault Marlow for thinking of nothing better to do than hand over a biscuit and to tell his story years later to four men on a boat on the Thames. One can also perhaps fault Conrad for not doing more himself when he returned to England after witnessing the horrors of the Congo. Arthur Conan Doyle and Mark Twain both became actively involved in the Congo Reform Association and wrote books condemning Leopold. Apart from his 1903 letter to Casement, which Conrad allowed to be reproduced and widely distributed, he declined to become further involved. Casement, however, forgave him because he was deep in work on *Nostromo* and fighting an almost incapacitating despair. Casement's co-founder of the C.R.A., Edmund Dene Morel, also forgave Conrad and in 1909, after the Congo had been stripped from Leopold, declared that *Heart of Darkness*, which reached a much larger audience than Marlow's, was the "most powerful thing ever written on the subject."[4]

Racism in Conrad's time was endemic. As Peter Firchow notes, it was so assumed that the word did not yet exist.[5] Part of Conrad's sensitivity to racism came from his being subject to it himself. To the end of his life, he spoke English with such a heavy accent that he was difficult to understand. Although in many ways an Anglophile, Conrad's sense of extreme alienation is suggested by his story "Amy Foster" in which an East European is washed ashore in southern England after a shipwreck and presumed insane because of his strange language. English visitors to Conrad in Kent recollected him as "not of our race" (22), "like a Polish Jew" (40), "the conventional stage Hebrew" (67), "simian" (96), "oriental mannerisms" (104), "very Oriental indeed" (109), "spectacularly a foreigner" (113), "an Oriental face" (115), "semi-Mongolian" (126), and "like a monkey" (138).[6] While Conrad may have expressed some racist attitudes himself, he acidly attacked white racism in his works, perhaps most clearly in his Malayan novels where he shows nothing but contempt for white men who claim superiority solely on the basis of their skin color. One striking example is Peter Willems in *An Outcast of the Islands*. When Willems falls in love

4. Edmund Dene Morel, *History of the Congo Reform Movement*, ed. William Roger Louis and Jean Stengers (London: Oxford UP, 1968), p. 205n.
5. Peter Firchow, *Envisioning Africa: Racism and Imperialism in Conrad's "Heart of Darkness"* (Lexington: U of Kentucky P, 2000), p. 4.
6. Quotations taken from *Joseph Conrad: Interviews and Recollections*, ed. Martin Ray (Iowa City: U of Iowa P, 1990).

with Omar's daughter, Aïssa, he feels he is "surrendering to a wild creature the unstained purity of his life, of his race, of his civilization." Later, after the love is gone, Willems cannot stand Aïssa's staring at him. He calls her eyes "the eyes of a savage; of a damned mongrel, half-Arab, half-Malay. They hurt me! I am white! I swear to you I can't stand this! Take me away. I am white! All white!"[7]

When Achebe revised "An Image of Africa," he de-Anglicized "bloody racist" to "thoroughgoing racist." We must ask, though, how thoroughgoing Conrad was. And we must distinguish degrees and kinds of racism. Whatever may be said of Conrad, he certainly did not share the most extreme racism of his time. He did not wish the annihilation of all non-Europeans. But Achebe seems to think so. In his original version Achebe compared Conrad to "All those men in Nazi Germany who lent their talent to the service of virulent racism." Achebe removed this sentence in his 1988 revision, but in his interview in 2000 when again denying the value of Conrad's work, he said, "I've not encountered any good art that promotes genocide."[8]

The almost inevitable trajectory of Social Darwinism was genocide. Darwin himself concluded in *The Descent of Man*: "At some future period, not very distant as measured by centuries, the civilized races of man will almost certainly exterminate and replace the savage races throughout the world" (156). Alfred Russel Wallace ended his 1864 article by saying, "the higher—the more intellectual and moral—must displace the lower and more degraded races" (clxxix). Eduard von Hartmann in his 1869 *Philosophy of the Unconscious*, a book Conrad read, wrote that it wasn't humane to prolong "the death struggles of savages who are on the verge of extinction. . . . The true philanthropist, if he has comprehended the natural law of anthropological evolution, cannot avoid desiring an acceleration of the last convulsion, and labor for that end."[9] And in 1894 in *Social Evolution* Benjamin Kidd observed, "The Anglo-Saxon has exterminated the less developed peoples with which he has come into competition."[1]

The man in *Heart of Darkness* who writes "Exterminate all the brutes!" is of course Kurtz. He may only be referring to his lake tribe, but pretty clearly he's referring, in the spirit of the Social Darwinists, to all Africans. His statement echoes that of Carlier in "An Outpost of Progress," who voiced "the necessity of exterminat-

7. Joseph Conrad, *An Outcast of the Islands* (New York: Doubleday, Page, 1924), pp. 80, 271.
8. Quoted by Jaggi in "Storyteller of the Savannah."
9. Eduard von Hartmann, *Philosophy of the Unconscious* (1869; London: Kegan Paul, 1893), 2:12.
1. Benjamin Kidd, *Social Evolution* (1894; rpt. New York: G. P. Putnam's Sons, 1920), p. 49.

ing all the niggers before the country could be made habitable."[2] Kurtz scrawls his statement at the bottom of his report for the International Society for the Suppression of Savage Customs as if it were the logical outcome of that project, the "exposition of a method." It's unclear how much Conrad was warning against actual genocide. He was certainly familiar with the theories of the Social Darwinists, but they had not yet been put deliberately in practice, although Europeans had already wiped out several native populations through disease and displacement. In the Congo somewhere between two and ten million Africans were killed during the twenty-three years of King Leopold's rule but not through a policy of extermination. They died through the brutality of forced labor, reprisals, and privation. But in October 1904, when the Herero tribe in Southwest Africa resisted German colonization, General Adolf von Trotha gave orders for all eighty thousand of them to be killed. Over the next two years the Germans succeeded nearly completely in doing so and a new word entered their vocabulary: *Konzentrationslager* or concentration camp. In his 1915 essay "Poland Revisited," Conrad observed that the Germans were "with a consciousness of superiority freeing their hands from all moral bonds, anxious to take up, if I may express myself so, the 'perfect man's burden.' "[3] His words now seem prescient, but they weren't really. The "perfect man's burden" was simply an extension of the "white man's burden," and the genocides of the twentieth century had already begun.

The lasting political legacy of *Heart of Darkness*, more than any confirmation of racism, has been its alarm over atrocity. Its title has entered our lexicon as code for extreme human rights abuses, usually those committed by whites in non-Western countries but also those committed by non-whites and those committed in Europe. Take for example the titles of just three recent books: Jacques Pauw's *Into the Heart of Darkness: Confessions of Apartheid's Assassins*, Shari Turitz's *Confronting the Heart of Darkness: An International Symposium on Torture in Guatemala*, and Ferida Durakovic's book of poems titled simply *Heart of Darkness* about the Serbian siege of Sarejevo and ethnic cleansing in Bosnia. Durakovic thanks "Joseph Conrad, who realized long before others that darkness had a heart, and the heart had darkness."[4] Far from condoning genocide, Conrad clearly saw humanity's horrific capacity and gave it a name.

2. Joseph Conrad, "An Outpost of Progress" in *Tales of Unrest* (New York: Doubleday, Page, 1925), p. 108.
3. Joseph Conrad, "Poland Revisited" in *Notes on Life and Letters* (London: John Grant, 1925), p. 147.
4. Ferida Durakovic, *Heart of Darkness* (Fredonia, NY: White Pine Press, 1998), p. 109.

PETER BROOKS

An Unreadable Report: Conrad's *Heart of Darkness*†

* * * Joseph Conrad's *Heart of Darkness*—published in the last year of the nineteenth century—poses in an exemplary way central questions about the shape and epistemology of narrative. It displays an acute self-consciousness about the organizing features of traditional narrative, working with them still, but suspiciously, with constant reference to the inadequacy of the inherited orders of meaning. It suggests affinities to that pre-eminently nineteenth-century genre, the detective story, but a detective story gone modernist: a tale of inconclusive solutions to crimes of problematic status. In its representation of an effort to reach endings that would retrospectively illuminate beginnings and middles, it pursues a reflection on the formal limits of narrative, but within a frame of discourse that appears to subvert finalities of form. Most of all, it engages the very motive of narrative in its tale of a complexly motivated attempt to recover the story of another within one's own, and to retell both in a context that further complicates relations of actors, tellers, and listeners. Ultimately, all these questions, and everything one says about the tale, must be reconceived within the context of Marlow's act of narration aboard the *Nellie* at the moment of the turning of the tide on the Thames, in the relation of this narrator to his narratees and the relation of the narrative situation to the stories enacted within it.

Heart of Darkness is * * * a framed tale, in which a first narrator introduces Marlow and has the last word after Marlow has fallen silent; and embedded within Marlow's tale is apparently another, Kurtz's, which never quite gets told—as perhaps Marlow's does not quite either, for the frame structure here is characterized by notable uncertainties. Referring * * * to Gérard Genette's tripartite distinction of narrative levels, it is evident that in *Heart of Darkness* everything must eventually be recovered on the plane of narrating, in the act of telling which itself attempts to recover the problematic relations of Marlow's narrative plot to his story, and of his plot and story to Kurtz's story, which in turn entertains doubtful relations with Kurtz's narrative plot and its narrating. Marlow's narrative plot will more and more as it proceeds take as its story what Marlow understands to be Kurtz's story. Yet Kurtz's story has other plots, ways

From *Reading for the Plot: Design and Intention in Narrative* (New York: Knopf, 1984), pp. 238–39, 241–42, 244–45, 246–47, 249–53, 259–63. Copyright © 1984 by Peter Brooks. Used by permission of Alfred A. Knopf, a division of Random House, Inc. Unless indicated, notes are the author's.

in which he would like to have it told: for instance, in his *Report to the Society for the Suppression of Savage Customs* (a plot subverted by the scribbled and forgotten footnote "Exterminate all the brutes"); or else the manner in which posthumously he commands Marlow's "loyalty" in retelling it—as lie—to his Intended. Ultimately, we must ask what motivates Marlow's retellings—of his own and Kurtz's mortal adventures—in the gathering dusk on the Thames estuary.

* * *

* * * There is an absurd disproportion between the ordering systems deployed and the triviality of their effect, as if someone had designed a machine to produce work far smaller than the energy put into it. And there are many other examples that conform to such laws of incongruous effect.

The question of orderings comes to be articulated within the very heart of darkness in an exchange between Marlow and the manager on the question of Kurtz's "method" in the acquisition of ivory, which, we have already learned from the Russian—Kurtz's admirer, and the chief teller of his tale—Kurtz mainly obtained by raiding the country. The manager's rhetoric is punctuated by Marlow's dissents:

> "I don't deny there is a remarkable quantity of ivory—mostly fossil. We must save it, at all events—but look how precarious the position is—and why? Because the method is unsound." "Do you," said I, looking at the shore, "call it 'unsound method'?" "Without doubt," he exclaimed hotly. "Don't you?" . . . "No method at all," I murmured after a while. "Exactly," he exulted. "I anticipated this. Shows a complete want of judgment. It is my duty to point it out in the proper quarter." "Oh," said I, "that fellow—what's his name?—the brickmaker, will make a readable report for you." He appeared confounded for a moment. It seemed to me I had never breathed an atmosphere so vile, and I turned mentally to Kurtz for relief—positively for relief. (pp. 61–62)

The result of this exchange is that Marlow finds himself classified with those of "unsound method," which, of course, is a way of moralizing as lapse from order any recognition of the absence of order, using the concept of disorder to conceal the radical condition of orderlessness. The manager's language—"unsound method," "want of judgment," "duty to point it out in the proper quarter"—refers to ordering systems and in so doing finds a way to mask perception of what Kurtz's experience really signifies. The "readable report," which Marlow notes to be the usual order for dealing with such deviations as Kurtz's, would represent the ultimate system of false ordering, ready-made discourse. What we really need, Marlow seems to suggest, is an *unreadable* report—something like Kurtz's *Report*, perhaps, with its utterly contradictory messages, or perhaps Marlow's eventual retelling of the whole affair.

The text, then, appears to speak of a repeated "trying out" of orders, all of which distort what they claim to organize, all of which may indeed cover up a very lack of possibility of order. This may suggest one relationship between story and narrative plot in the text: a relationship of disquieting uncertainty, where story never appears to be quite matched to the narrative plot that is responsible for it. Yet the orders tried out in *Heart of Darkness* may in their very tenuousness be necessary to the process of striving toward meaning: as if to say that the plotting of stories remains necessary even where we have ceased to believe in the plots we use. Certain minimum canons of readability remain necessary if we are to be able to discern the locus of the necessarily unreadable.

*   *   *

It is * * * gradually impressed upon Marlow, and the reader, that Marlow is in a state of belatedness or secondariness in relation to the forerunner; his journey is a repetition, which gains its meaning from its attachment to the prior journey. Marlow's plot (*sjužet*) repeats Kurtz's story (*fabula*), takes this as its motivating force—and then will seek also to know and to incorporate Kurtz's own plot for his story.

So it is that Marlow's inquest, in the manner of the detective's, becomes the retracing of the track of a precursor. * * * The detective story in its classic form is built on the overlay or superimposition of two temporal orders, the time of the crime (events and motives leading up to the crime) and the time of the inquest (events and motives leading away from the crime, but aimed at reconstructing it), the former sequence *in absentia*, lost to representation except insofar as it can be reconstructed in the time of the inquest, the latter *in praesentia* but existing merely to actualize the absent sequence of the crime. Tzvetan Todorov * * * identified the relation of these two orders as the relation of *fabula* to *sjužet* that one finds in any narrative: a story postulated as prior gone over by a narrative plot that claims thereby to realize it.[1] The detective story may in this manner lay bare the structure of any narrative, particularly its claim to be a retracing of events that have already occurred. The detective retracing the trace of his predecessor and thus uncovering and constructing the meaning and the authority of the narrative represents the very process of narrative representa-

---

1. See Tzvetan Todorov, *The Poetics of Prose*, trans. Richard Howard (Ithaca, NY: Cornell UP, 1977).

tion. This couple, the criminal precursor and the latecomer detective, has special relevance to the situation of Marlow and Kurtz. No more than the detective's, Marlow's narrative is not primary: it attaches itself to another's story, seeking there its authority; it retraces another's path, repeats a journey already undertaken.

* * *

The definition of Kurtz through his "gift of expression" and as "a voice," and Marlow's postulation of this definition of Kurtz as the motivating goal of his own journey, serve to conceptualize the narrative end as expression, voice, articulation, or what Walter Benjamin termed simply "wisdom": the goal of all storytelling which, with the decline of traditional oral transmission, has in the "privatized" genre of the novel come to be defined exclusively as the meaning of an individual life.[2] * * * In Benjamin's argument, the meaning of a life cannot be known until the moment of death: it is at death that a life first assumes transmissible form—becomes a completed and significant statement—so that it is death that provides the authority or "sanction" of narrative. The deathbed scene of the nineteenth-century novel eminently represents the moment of summing-up of a life's meaning and a transmission of accumulated wisdom to succeeding generations. Paternal figures within novels write their own obituaries, transmitting to the younger protagonists something of the authority necessary to view the meaning of their own lives retrospectively, in terms of the significance that will be brought by the as yet unwritten end.

To Marlow, Kurtz is doubly such a deathbed figure and writer of obituary. In the first place, he has reached his journey's end, he is lodged in the heart of darkness and it is from that "farthest point of navigation" that he offers his discourse, that "pulsating stream of light" or "deceitful flow." Kurtz has reached further, deeper than anyone else, and his gift for expression means that he should be able to give articulate shape to his terminus. "Kurtz discoursed. A voice! a voice!" (p. 67) Marlow will later report. But by that point Kurtz's report on the meaning of his navigation into the heart of the jungle will be compounded with his journey to his life's end, and his terminal report on his inner descent into darkness. So that Kurtz's discourse stands to make sense of Marlow's voyage and his life, his journey and his inquest: to offer that final articulation that will give a meaning to journey and experience here at what Marlow has doubly identified as "the farthest point of navigation and the culminating point of my experience" (p. 7). Kurtz is he who has already turned experience into Benjamin's "wisdom," turned story

2. See Walter Benjamin, "The Storyteller," *Illuminations*, trans. Harry Zohn (New York: Schocken, 1969), pp. 83–109. [Editor]

into well-formed narrative plot, matter into pure voice, and who
stands ready to narrate life's story in significant form. Marlow's own
narrative can make sense only when his inquest has reached a "solution" that is not a simple detection but the finding of a message
written at and by the death of another. The meaning of his narrative plot has indeed come to depend on Kurtz's articulation of the
meaning of *his* plot: Marlow's structuring of his own *fabula* as
sjužet has attached itself to Kurtz's *fabula*, and can find its significant outcome only in finding Kurtz's *sjužet*.

For Kurtz, in the heart of darkness and at life's end, has "stepped
over the edge" and has "summed up." Since it is a "summing up"
that Marlow has discovered to be what most he has been seeking—
that summary illumination that retrospectively makes sense of
all that has gone before—his insistence that Kurtz has summed up
is vitally important. At the end of the journey lies, not ivory, gold, or
a fountain of youth, but the capacity to turn experience into language: a voice. * * *

* * *

Marlow's discourse seems to shape itself in opposition to the anticipated objections of an imagined interlocutor. By protesting too
much, he builds those putative objections dialogically into his own
discourse, making it (in Mikhaïl Bakhtin's terms) "double voiced."[3]
Double voicing indeed is suggested by the evocation of the "echo"
of Kurtz's voice. This "echo of his magnificent eloquence" becomes
* * * highly problematic * * * when, later, we understand that the
"soul as translucently pure as a cliff of crystal" is Kurtz's Intended,
and that the "echo" which she hears is a pure fiction in blatant contradiction to that which Marlow hears in the same room with her: a
lie which Marlow is obliged to confirm as conscious cover-up of the
continuing reverberation of Kurtz's last words: "The horror! The
horror!"

This is no doubt the point at issue: that Kurtz's final words
answer so poorly to all of Marlow's insistence on summing-up as
a moment of final articulation of wisdom, truth, and sincerity, as
affirmation and as moral victory. Marlow affirms that it is Kurtz's
ultimate capacity to judge, to use human language in its commu-
nicative and its normative dimensions to transmit an evaluation of
his soul's adventures on this earth, that constitutes his victory: the
victory of articulation itself. And yet, "The horror! The horror!" is
more accurately characterized when Marlow calls it a "cry." It
comes about as close as articulated speech can come to the primal

---

3. On the "dialogic" and "double-voicedness," see in particular Mikhaïl Bakhtin, "Discourse in the Novel," in *The Dialogic Imagination*, ed. Michael Holquist, trans. Holquist
and Caryl Emerson (Austin: U of Texas P, 1981), pp. 259–422, and *Problems of Dostoevsky's Poetics*, trans. R. W. Rotsel (Ann Arbor, MI: Ardis, 1973).

cry, to a blurted emotional reaction of uncertain reference and context. To present "the horror!" as articulation of that wisdom lying in wait at the end of the tale, at journey's end and life's end, is to make a mockery of storytelling and ethics, or to gull one's listeners—as Marlow himself seems to realize when he finds that he cannot repeat Kurtz's last words to the Intended, but must rather cover them up by a conventional ending: "The last word he pronounced was—your name" (p. 76). The contrast of this fictive act of naming—"proper" naming—with Kurtz's actual cry may suggest how poorly Kurtz's summing-up fits Marlow's description of it. Indeed, his cry so resembles the "word of careless contempt" that when we find this phrase in Marlow's account, we tend to take it as applying to Kurtz's last utterance, only to find that it is given as the very contrary thereof. Something is amiss.

We can concede to Marlow his reading of the ethical signified of Kurtz's last words, his "judgment upon the adventures of his soul on this earth" (p. 69)—though we may find the reference of this signified somewhat ambiguous: is the horror within Kurtz or without? Is it experience or reaction to experience? But we have a problem conceiving the signifier as fulfilling the conditions of the wisdom-and-truth-articulating function of the end. More than a masterful, summary, victorious articulation, "The horror!" appears as minimal language, language on the verge of reversion to savagery, on the verge of a fall from language. That Kurtz's experience in the heart of darkness should represent and be represented by a fall from language does not surprise us: this belongs to the very logic of the heart of darkness, which is consistently characterized as "unspeakable." There are the "unspeakable rites" at which Kurtz presides (p. 50), the "unspeakable secrets" of his "method" (p. 62), and, at the very heart of the darkness—at the moment when Marlow pursues Kurtz into the jungle at night, to struggle with his soul and carry him back to the steamer—we have only this characterization of the dark ceremony unfolding by the campfire: "It was very awful" (p. 65). Critics have most often been content to point to the moral signified of such phrases—or to criticize them, and Conrad, for a lack of referential and ethical specificity—but we should feel obliged to read them in their literal statement. What stands at the heart of darkness—at the journey's end and at the core of this tale—is unsayable, extralinguistic.

It cannot be otherwise, for the heart of darkness—and Kurtz himself in the heart—is beyond the system of human social structures which makes language possible and is itself made possible by language: which is unthinkable except through and as language, as that which demarcates culture from nature. The issue is most directly addressed by Marlow when he contrasts Kurtz's position

within the unspeakable and unimaginable darkness to that of his
solidly "moored" listeners aboard the *Nellie*:

> It was impossible—it was not good for one either—trying to
> imagine. He had taken a high seat amongst the devils of the
> land—I mean literally. You can't understand. How could
> you?—with solid pavement under your feet, surrounded by
> kind neighbours ready to cheer you or to fall on you, stepping
> delicately between the butcher and the policeman, in the holy
> terror of scandal and gallows and lunatic asylums—how can
> you imagine what particular region of the first ages a man's un-
> trammelled feet may take him into by the way of solitude—ut-
> ter solitude without a policeman—by the way of silence—utter
> silence, where no warning voice of a kind neighbour can be
> heard whispering of public opinion? These little things make
> all the great difference. (p. 49)

Language is here presented, accurately enough, as a system of police. Incorporate with the *polis*, language forms the basis of social
organization (which itself functions as a language) as a system of
difference, hence of distinction and restraint, which polices individuality by making it part of a transindividual, intersubjective system: precisely what we call society. To policing is contrasted the
utter silence of utter solitude: the realm beyond interlocution, beyond dialogue, hence beyond language. As Marlow puts it when he
struggles to return Kurtz from the jungle to the steamboat, "I had
to deal with a being to whom I could not appeal in the name of
anything high or low. . . . He had kicked himself loose of the earth"
(p. 66).

If Kurtz's summing-up may represent ethically a return to the
earth and its names (though the ethical reference of his last pronouncement is at least ambiguous), as an act of language "The horror! The horror!" stands on the verge of non-language, of nonsense.
This is not to characterize "The horror!" as the Romantic ineffable:
if Marlow appears to affirm an ineffable behind Kurtz's words, his
whole narrative rather demonstrates the nothingness of that behind. Marlow continually seems to promise a penetration into the
heart of darkness, along with a concurrent recognition that he is
confined to the "surface truth." There is no reconciliation of this
standoff, but there may be the suggestion that language, as inter-
locutionary and thus as social system, simply can have no dealings
with an ineffable. For language, nothing will come of nothing.

Certainly the summing up provided by Kurtz cannot represent
the kind of terminal wisdom that Marlow seeks, to make sense of
both Kurtz's story and his own story and hence to bring his narrative to a coherent and significant end. Kurtz's final articulation

should perhaps be typed as more than anything else anaphoric, pointing to the unsayable dumbness of the heart of darkness and to the impossible end of the perfect narrative plot. In this sense, Kurtz's narrative never fully exists, never fully gets itself told. And for the same reason, Marlow's narrative can never speak the end that it has sought so hard to find, and that it has postulated as the very premise and guarantee of its meaning. Marlow's search for meaning appears ever to be suspended, rather in the manner of his description of his encounter with death: "My destiny! Droll thing life is—that mysterious arrangement of merciless logic for a futile purpose. The most you can hope from it is some knowledge of yourself—that comes too late—a crop of unextinguishable regrets" (pp. 69–70). The logic of life's plot is never vouchsafed knowledge of that end which might make its purpose significant. Such knowledge as there is always is caught in a process of suspension and deferral, so that it comes too late. Marlow as the belated follower of Kurtz the predecessor is too late, as, the tale implies, he who seeks to know the end, rather than simply live it, must always be. Ends are not—are no longer?—available.

* * *

The impossibility of summing-up, the impossibility of designating meaning as within the narrative frame, explains why Marlow must retell his tale on board the *Nellie*, seeking meaning in the "spectral illumination" of narrative transaction. If framed narration in general offers a way to make explicit and to dramatize the motive for storytelling, *Heart of Darkness* shows the motive for retelling. Repetition appears to be a product of failure in the original telling—Kurtz's failure to narrate his own story satisfactorily, Marlow's lying version of Kurtz's story to the Intended—just as, in Freud's terms, repetition and working through come into play when orderly memory of the past—recollection of it *as* past—is blocked. We are fully within the dynamics of the transference. But it does not seem possible to conclude that Marlow's retelling on the *Nellie* is wholly a success: it does not meet the standards of intelligibility sought by the first narrator, and the most that can be said of the other narratees is that they are possibly (though not certainly) absorbed by the tale. We have a feeling at the end of Marlow's act of narration that retelling of his tale will have to continue: that the ambiguous wisdom he has transmitted to his listeners will have to be retransmitted by them as narrative to future listeners. The process is potentially infinite, any closure or termination merely provisional. *Heart of Darkness* does not "end"; it is a potentially interminable analysis that simply breaks off.

Any future retelling of Marlow's tale of Kurtz's story will have to be narrative in nature because there is no way to state its kernel, its wisdom, directly: this can only be approached metonymically, through a trying-out of orders, through plottings. And these will never take you there, they will only indicate where "there" might be located. Meaning will never lie in the summing-up but only in transmission: in the passing-on of the "horror," the taint of knowledge gained. Meaning is hence dialogic in nature, located in the interstices of story and frame, born of the relationship between tellers and listeners. Meaning is indeed the implicit dialogue itself, the "set" of the teller's message toward his listener as much as toward the matter of his tale. Marlow is as fully concerned with the hearing as with the telling of his tale and its truth, equally concerned with the "phatic" as with the "emotive" and "referential" functions of language.[4] If meaning must be conceived as dialogic, dialogue represents a centerless and reversible structure, engendering an interminable process of analysis and interpretation, a dynamics of the transference in which the reader is solicited not only to understand the story, but to complete it: to make it fuller, richer, more powerfully ordered, and therefore more hermeneutic. Summing-up and dialogue are offered as two different modes of understanding, each incompatible with the other, yet neither exclusive. Marlow needs the postulation of Kurtz's summing-up in order to make basic sense of his own narrative. Failing himself to sum up, he must pass on his implication as narratee of Kurtz's story to his listeners, implicating them in turn as narratees, trapping them in the dialogic relationship. Figured here as well is the reader's relationship to the text. The reader's own incapacity to sum up—the frustration promoted by the text—is consubstantial with his dialogic implication in the text. The reader is necessarily part of the process of transmission in this tale that is ultimately most of all about transmission.

I have argued that one finally needs to read *Heart of Darkness* as act of narration even more than as narrative or as story. It shows this act to be far from innocent, indeed as based perhaps most of all on the need and the desire to implicate one's listeners in a taint one can't live with alone. It is not simply, and not so much, that confessing excuses but that properly managed it taints. If the listener has listened, he has assumed the position of "thou" to an "I." Reassuming the first-person pronoun for himself, he makes the former "I" into a "thou."[5] The intersubjective and reversible pattern of dialogue has been created. Why are you telling me this? the inter-

4. On these "functions" of language, see Roman Jakobson, "Closing Statement: Linguistics and Poetics," in *Style in Language*, ed. Thomas Sebeok (Cambridge: MIT P, 1960).
5. On the interdependence of the "I" and "thou" in discourse, see Emile Benveniste, "De la subjectivité dans le langage," in *Problèmes de linguistique générale* (Paris: Gallimard, 1967), pp. 258–66.

locutor may want to ask—but by the time he comes to make such a response, it is already too late: like the Ancient Mariner's Wedding Guest, he has been made to hear. If a number of nineteenth- and twentieth-century narrative texts present sophisticated versions of traditional oral storytelling, it is because this gives them a way to force the reader into transferential relationship with what he may not want to see or hear.

Yet another characteristic peculiar to late nineteenth- and early twentieth-century narrative—that which we characterize as modernist—appears to emerge from our study of *Heart of Darkness*. This is the implication that all stories are in a state of being retold, that there are no more primary narratives. Marlow must repeat Kurtz's story, and presumably his listeners will have to repeat Marlow's story of Kurtz's story. Indeed, the very start of Marlow's narrative suggests an infinite possibility of repetition when he reaches back nineteen hundred years to imagine the Roman commander navigating up the Thames, into a land of savagery: a further level of *fabula*, an ancient historical story that all the modern stories must rehearse. One could demonstrate in a number of texts—James's *The Aspern Papers*, for instance, or Gide's *Les Faux-Monnayeurs*, or Faulkner's *Absalom, Absalom!*, even Proust's *Recherche* insofar as Marcel repeats the story of Swann in love—that there seems to be a need for protagonists and storytellers, and particularly protagonists *as* storytellers, to attach their narratives to someone else's, to be ever the belated followers of the track of another. Do we find here once again the influence of the detective story, that genre invented by the nineteenth century and so highly characteristic of it? Partly, perhaps, but also it may be the implicit conviction that there are no new plots, no primary stories left, only the possibility of repeating others. The sons are not free of the fathers but bound to the retracing of their traces. But yet again, the impossibility of original story, the need to retell, places the primary emphasis of the tale on the plane of narration itself, calls attention to the attempt to repeat, reconstruct, retell. In the act of narration, the narrators often end up telling a different story from that they imagined they were telling: the narrator of *The Aspern Papers*, for instance, tells the story of his own crime while intending to tell that of a detection. Marlow, thinking to tell us of Kurtz's victory wrested from innumerable defeats, himself wrests a kind of defeat from the postulated victory.

But to state the outcome of *Heart of Darkness* as either victory or defeat is to posit for it a finality which its very form subverts. In an essay on Henry James, Conrad talks about conventional novelistic ends, what he calls "the usual methods of solution by rewards and punishments, by crowned love, by fortune, by a broken leg or a sudden death."[6] He goes on to note: "These solutions are legitimate inasmuch as they satisfy the desire for finality, for which our hearts yearn, with a longing greater than the longing for the loaves and the fishes of this earth. Perhaps the only true desire of mankind, coming thus to light in its hours of leisure, is to be set at rest." Thus does Conrad offer his version of *Beyond the Pleasure Principle*.[7] That the challenging storyteller should refuse this "rest," postpone and defer the quiescence of the end, becomes clear as Conrad goes on to characterize James's nonfinal, rest-less endings: "You remain with the sense of the life still going on; and even the subtle presence of the dead is felt in that silence that comes upon the artist-creation when the last word has been read." The presence of the dead: certain ghosts, such as Kurtz's, are never laid to rest. The effort to narrate one's life story as it relates to their numinous and baleful presence is never done. One must tell and tell again, hoping that one's repetition will in turn be repeated, that one's voice will re-echo.

PATRICK BRANTLINGER

[Imperialism, Impressionism, and the Politics of Style]†

The politics of Conrad's story is complicated by the story's ambiguous style. I use "impressionism" as a highly inadequate term to characterize the novella's language and narrative structure, in part because Fredric Jameson uses that term in his diagnosis of the "schizophrenic" nature of *Lord Jim*.[1] Conrad's impressionism is for some critics his most praiseworthy quality; to others it appears instead a means of obfuscation, allowing him to mask his nihilism or to maintain contradictory values, or both. Interpretations of *Heart of Darkness* which read it as only racist (and therefore imperialist), or as only anti-imperialist (and therefore antiracist), inevitably founder on its impressionism. To point to only the most obvious difficulty, the narrative frame filters everything that is said not just through Marlow but also through the anonymous primary narrator. At what point is it safe to assume that Conrad/Marlow expresses a

---

6. "Henry James: An Appreciation," pp. 286–88 in this Norton Critical Edition.
7. Sigmund Freud's analysis of the compulsion to repeat (1920). [Editor]
† From *Rule of Darkness: British Literature and Imperialism, 1830–1914* (Ithaca, NY: Cornell UP, 1988), pp. 256–57, 264–67, 268–74. Reprinted by permission of English Literature in Transition. Notes are the author's.
1. Fredric Jameson, *The Political Unconscious: Narrative as a Socially Symbolic Act* (Ithaca: Cornell UP, 1981), 206–80. See also Ian Watt's discussions of "impressionism" and "symbolism" in *Conrad in the Nineteenth Century* (Berkeley: U of California P, 1979), 168–200 [see selection in this Norton Critical Edition].

single point of view? And even supposing Marlow to speak directly
for Conrad, does Conrad/Marlow agree with the values expressed
by the primary narrator? Whatever our answers, *Heart of Darkness*
offers a powerful critique of at least some manifestations of imperialism and racism as it simultaneously presents that critique in
ways that can be characterized only as imperialist and racist. Impressionism is the fragile skein of discourse which expresses—or
disguises—this schizophrenic contradiction as an apparently harmonious whole. Analysis of that contradiction helps to reveal the
ideological constraints upon a critical understanding of imperialism
in literature before World War I. It also suggests how imperialism
influenced the often reactionary politics of literary modernism.

*   *   *

In the world of *Heart of Darkness*, there are no clear answers. Ambiguity, perhaps the main form of darkness in the story, prevails.
Conrad overlays the political and moral content of his novella with
symbolic and mythic patterns that divert attention from Kurtz and
the Congo to misty halos and moonshine. The anonymous primary
narrator uses these metaphors to describe the difference between
Marlow's stories and those of ordinary sailors: "The yarns of seamen have a direct simplicity, the whole meaning of which lies
within the shell of a cracked nut. But Marlow was not typical . . .
and to him the meaning of an episode was not inside like a kernel
but outside, enveloping the tale which brought it out only as a glow
brings out a haze, in the likeness of one of these misty halos that
sometimes are made visible by the spectral illumination of moonshine" (5). This passage announces that locating the "meaning" of
the story will not be easy, may in fact be impossible. It seems almost a confession of defeat or at least of contradiction. Conrad
here establishes as one of his themes the problem of rendering any
judgment whatsoever—moral, political, metaphysical—about Marlow's narrative. It is precisely this complexity—a theme that might
be labeled the dislocation of meaning or the disorientation of values in the story—which many critics have treated as the novella's
finest feature.

   In *The Political Unconscious*, Jameson argues that Conrad's
stories (*Lord Jim* is his main example) betray a symptomatic split
between a modernist will-to-style, leading to an elaborate but essentially hollow impressionism, and the reified, mass-culture tendencies of romance conventions. In a fairly obvious way, *Heart of
Darkness* betrays the same split, moving in one direction toward the
misty halos of a style that seeks to be its own meaning, apart from
any kernel or embarrassingly clear content, but also that grounds itself in the conventions of Gothic romance with their devalued,
mass-culture status—conventions that were readily adapted to the

heroic adventure themes of imperialist propaganda. This split almost corresponds to the contradiction of an anti-imperialist novel
that is also racist. In the direction of high style the story acquires
several serious purposes, apparently including its critique of empire. In the direction of reified mass culture it falls into the stereotypic patterns of race thinking common to the entire tradition of
the imperialist adventure story or quest romance. This double, contradictory purpose, perhaps characteristic of all of Conrad's fiction,
Jameson calls schizophrenic.[2]

By "the manichaeanism of the imperialist imagination" [Benita]
Parry means dividing the world between "warring moral forces"—
good versus evil, civilization versus savagery, West versus East, light
versus darkness, white versus black.[3] Such polarizations are the
common property of the racism and authoritarianism that inform
imperialist ideology, as they are also of the Gothic romance conventions that numerous writers of imperialist adventure tales appropriated. As Martin Green points out, "Conrad of course offers
us an ironic view of that genre. But he affirms its value."[4] Conrad is
a critic of the imperialist adventure and its romantic fictions and simultaneously one of the greatest writers of such fictions, his greatness deriving partly from his critical irony and partly from the
complexity of his style—his impressionism. But the chief difficulty
with Jameson's argument is that the will-to-style in Conrad's text is
also a will to appropriate and remake Gothic romance conventions
into high art. On some level the impressionism of Conrad's novels
and their romance features are identical—Conrad constructs a sophisticated version of the imperialist romance—and in any case
both threaten to submerge or "derealize" the critique of empire
within their own more strictly aesthetic project. As part of that project, providing much of the substance of impressionism, the romance conventions that Conrad reshapes carry with them the
polarizations of racist thought.

In analyzing Conrad's schizophrenic writing, Jameson notes the
proliferation of often contradictory critical opinions which marks
the history of his reception: "The discontinuities objectively present
in Conrad's narratives have, as with few other modern writers, projected a bewildering variety of competing and incommensurable interpretive options." Jameson lists nine critical approaches, from
"the 'romance' or mass-cultural reading of Conrad as a writer of adventure tales [and] the stylistic analysis of Conrad as a practitioner

2. Jameson, Political Unconscious, 219.
3. Parry, Conrad and Imperialism, 23. See also Abdul R. JanMohamed, Manichean Aesthetics: The Politics of Literature in Colonial Africa (Amherst: U of Massachusetts P, 1983).
4. Martin Green, Dreams of Adventure, Deeds of Empire (New York: Basic Books, 1979),
   313.

of . . . [an] 'impressionistic' will to style," to the "myth-critical," the Freudian, the ethical, the "ego-psychological," the existential, the Nietzschean, and the structuralist readings. Jameson omits from the list his own, Marxist reading; what he wishes to suggest is how often criticism ignores or downplays the contradictory politics of Conrad's fiction. Raymond Williams voices a similar complaint:

> It is . . . astonishing that a whole school of criticism has succeeded in emptying *Heart of Darkness* of its social and historical content. . . . The Congo of Leopold follows the sea that Dombey and Son traded across, follows it into an endless substitution in which no object is itself, no social experience direct, but everything is translated into what can be called a metaphysical language—the river is Evil; the sea is Love or Death. Yet only called metaphysical, because there is not even that much guts in it. No profound and ordinary belief, only a perpetual and sophisticated evasion.[5]

There are wonderfully elaborate readings of Marlow's journey as a descent into hell, playing upon Conrad's allusions to Homer, Virgil, Dante, Milton, Goethe, and devil worship. There are just as many elaborate readings of the story as an inward voyage of self-discovery which treat its geopolitical language as symbolizing psychological states and parts of the mind. Conrad, Albert Guerard reminds us, was Freud's contemporary, and in *Heart of Darkness* he produced the quintessential "night journey into the unconscious."[6] Guerard adds that "it little matters what, in terms of psychological symbolism, we . . . say [Kurtz] represents: whether the Freudian id or the Jungian shadow or more vaguely the outlaw." Perhaps it matters just as little whether we say the story takes place in Leopold's Congo or in some purely imaginary landscape.

My point, however, is not to take issue with Guerard and other critics who concentrate on the impressionism of Conrad's story but rather to restore what their readings neglect. In a great deal of contemporary criticism, words themselves have almost ceased to have external referents. Williams does not follow Jameson in accusing Conrad's will-to-style of emptying *Heart of Darkness* of its social and historical content; rather, he accuses criticism of so emptying it. The will-to-style—or the will to a rarefied critical intelligence— devours literary critics, too, leaving structuralists and deconstructionists, Althusserians and Foucauldians. And yet Conrad has anticipated his critics by writing a story in which the meaning does not lie at the center, not even at the heart of darkness, but else-

---

5. Raymond Williams, *The English Novel from Dickens to Lawrence* (New York: Oxford UP, 1970), 145.
6. Albert Guerard, *Conrad the Novelist* (Oxford: Oxford UP, 1958), 39 [see the selection in this Norton Critical Edition].

where, in misty halos—forever beyond some vertiginous horizon that recedes as the would-be critic-adventurer sails toward it.

* * *

One of the most remarkable perversions of the criticism of *Heart of Darkness* has been to see Kurtz not as an abomination, a hollow man with a lust for blood and domination, but as a "hero of the spirit." That phrase is Lionel Trilling's. In describing the establishment of the first course in modern literature at Columbia University, Trilling explains why he put Conrad's novella on the reading list: "Whether or not . . . Conrad read either Blake or Nietzsche I do not know, but his *Heart of Darkness* follows in their line. This very great work has never lacked for the admiration it deserves, and it has been given a . . . canonical place in the legend of modern literature by [T. S.] Eliot's having it so clearly in mind when he wrote *The Waste Land* and his having taken from it the epigraph to 'The Hollow Men.' "[7] Despite the association between Eliot's poem and Conrad's novella, Trilling claims that "no one, to my knowledge, has ever confronted in an explicit way [the latter's] strange and terrible message of ambivalence toward the life of civilization" (17). In *Sincerity and Authenticity*, Trilling adds that Conrad's story is "the paradigmatic literary expression of the modern concern with authenticity," and continues: "This troubling work has no manifest polemical content but it contains in sum the whole of the radical critique of European civilization that has been made by [modern] literature."[8] Trilling appears to interpret literary modernism in its entirety both as apolitical (lacking manifest polemical content) and as offering a "radical critique" of civilization: *Heart of Darkness* he treats as the quintessence of this apolitical critique. He fails to acknowledge that the form of radical critique practiced by high literary modernists (Yeats, Eliot, Pound, and Lawrence, as well as Conrad) readily aligned itself with imperialism and fascism.

Trilling names the political context of *Heart of Darkness*, but the Congo is less important to him than the larger question of the nature of European civilization. Marlow's quest for Kurtz becomes a quest for the truth about that civilization. Trilling arrives at his view of Kurtz partly the way Marlow does, because Kurtz at the end of his Satanic career seems to confront "the horror." "For Marlow," says Trilling, "Kurtz is a hero of the spirit whom he cherishes as Theseus at Colonus cherished Oedipus: he sinned for all mankind. By his regression to savagery Kurtz has reached as far down beneath the constructs of civilization as it was possible to go, to the irreducible truth

7. Lionel Trilling, "On the Modern Element in Literature," in *Beyond Culture: Essays on Literature and Learning* (New York: Harcourt Brace Jovanovich, 1965), 17–18.
8. Lionel Trilling, *Sincerity and Authenticity* (Cambridge: Harvard UP, 1972), 106.

of man, the innermost core of his nature, his heart of darkness. From that Stygian authenticity comes illumination."[9]

Marlow does paradoxically come to admire Kurtz because he has "summed up" or "judged" in his final moments: "He was a remarkable man" (62). Marlow's admiration for Kurtz, however, carries a terrific burden of irony which Trilling does not recognize. Kurtz has not merely lost faith in civilization and therefore experimented with Stygian authenticity—he is also a murderer, perhaps a cannibal. He has allowed his idolators to make human sacrifices in his honor and, like Captain Rom, has decorated his corner of hell with the skulls of his victims. Perhaps Trilling values Kurtz as a hero of the spirit in part because he himself does not clearly see the horror: the deaths of several million Congolese are a high price to pay for the illumination of Stygian authenticity. Trilling's interpretation of Kurtz's dying words—"The horror! The horror!"—simply does not take account of what transpired in Leopold's Congo. His focus is European civilization, not Africa, and so he reaches this bizarre conclusion: "For me it is still ambiguous whether Kurtz's famous deathbed cry refers to the approach of death or to his experience of savage life."

Either Kurtz thinks death "the horror," according to Trilling's view, or Kurtz thinks African savage life "the horror." There is another possibility, of course, which is that Kurtz's dying words are an outcry against himself—against his betrayal of civilization and his Intended, against the smash-up of his early hopes, and against his bloody domination. No one would ever mistake Conrad's other traitors to civilization (Willems who goes wrong and then goes native in *An Outcast of the Islands*, Jones and Ricardo in *Victory*) as heroes of the spirit. Even Lord Jim is no spiritual hero but a moral cripple who regains a semblance of self-respect only after fleeing to Patusan. But how was it possible for Trilling to look past Kurtz's criminal record and identify the horror either with the fear of death or with African savagery? Achebe gives part of the answer: "White racism against Africa is such a normal way of thinking that its manifestations go completely undetected"—so normal that acts which are condemned as the vilest of crimes when committed in the supposedly civilized West can be linked to a heroism of the spirit and to Stygian authenticity when committed in Africa against Africans.

The other part of the answer, however, is that Trilling is right. Conrad himself identifies with and ironically admires Kurtz. He, too, sees him as a hero of the spirit, although the spirit for Conrad is perhaps not what Trilling thinks it is. For Conrad, Kurtz's heroism consists in staring into an abyss of nihilism so total that the

9. Trilling, "On the Modern Element," 18.

issues of imperialism and racism pale into insignificance. It hardly matters if the abyss is of Kurtz's making. No more than Trilling or perhaps most Western literary critics did Conrad concern himself about unspeakable rites and skulls on posts. These appear in Marlow's account like so many melodrama props—the evidence of Kurtz's decline and fall, certainly, but it is still Kurtz who has center stage, with whom Marlow speaks, who is the goal and farthest point of the journey. Kurtz's black victims and idolators skulking in the bushes are only so many props themselves.

Kurtz is not only the hero of the melodrama but an artist, a "universal genius," and a powerful, eloquent voice as well. The African characters, as Achebe points out, are, in contrast, rendered almost without intelligible language. The headman of Marlow's cannibal crew gets in a few phrases of pidgin-minstrelese, something about eating some fellow-Africans. These are the black Kurtz worshipers, shrieking and groaning incoherently in the foggy shrubbery along the river. Kurtz's "superb and savage" mistress, though described in glowing detail, is given no voice, but I imagine that she, at least, unlike the prim, palefaced knitters of black wool back in Brussels, entertained no illusions about Kurtz or imperialism. "It's queer how out of touch with truth women are," says Marlow, but of course he means *white* women (12). Kurtz's black mistress knows all; it's unfortunate that Marlow did not think to interview her.

The voices that come from the heart of darkness are almost exclusively white and male, as usual in imperialist texts. As a nearly disembodied, pure voice emanating from the very center of the story, Kurtz is a figure for the novelist, as is his double Marlow. True, the voice that speaks out of the heart of darkness is a hollow one, the voice of the abyss; but Marlow still talks of Kurtz's "unextinguishable gift of noble and lofty expression." The voice of Kurtz has "electrified large meetings," and through it Kurtz "could get himself to believe anything—anything" (72). Thus Conrad questions or mocks his own voice, his own talent for fiction making, for lying. He knows that the will-to-style, his own impressionism, points toward the production of novels that are hollow at the core—that can justify any injustice—and contain, perhaps, only an abyss, a Kurtz, the horror. Kurtz's devious, shadowy voice echoes Conrad's. It is just this hollow voice, eloquently egotistical, capable both of high idealism and of lying propaganda, which speaks from the center of the heart of darkness to sum up and to judge.

Besides being a painter, musician, orator, and universal genius, Kurtz is also, like Conrad, a writer.[1] What he writes is both an ana-

---

1. Daniel R. Schwarz calls Kurtz a "demonic artist" but does not elaborate on the comparison between Kurtz and Conrad. See his *Conrad: "Almayer's Folly" to "Under Western Eyes"* (Ithaca: Cornell UP, 1980), 72.

logue for the story and its dead center, the kernel of meaning or nonmeaning within its cracked shell. True, Kurtz has not written much, only seventeen pages, but "it was a beautiful piece of writing." His pamphlet for the International Society for the Suppression of Savage Customs is a summa of imperialist rhetoric, which Marlow describes as "eloquent, vibrating with eloquence, but too high-strung, I think":

> He began with the argument that we whites, from the point of development we had arrived at, "must necessarily appear to [savages] in the nature of supernatural beings—we approach them with the might as of a deity," and so on, and so on. "By the simple exercise of our will we can exert a power for good practically unbounded," etc., etc. From that point he soared and took me with him. The peroration was magnificent, though difficult to remember, you know. It gave me the notion of an exotic Immensity ruled by an august Benevolence. It made me tingle with enthusiasm. This was the unbounded power of eloquence [i.e., the unbounded will-to-style]. There were no practical hints to interrupt the magic current of phrases, unless a kind of note at the foot of the last page, scrawled evidently much later, in an unsteady hand, may be regarded as the exposition of a method. It was very simple, and at the end of that moving appeal to every altruistic sentiment it blazed at you, luminous and terrifying, like a flash of lightning in a serene sky: "Exterminate all the brutes!" (50)

Viewed one way, Conrad's anti-imperialist story clearly condemns Kurtz's murderous, imperialist categorical imperative. Viewed another way, Conrad's racist story voices that very imperative, and Conrad knows it. At the hollow center of *Heart of Darkness*, far from the misty halos and moonshine where the meaning supposedly resides, Conrad inscribes a text that, like the novel itself, cancels out its own best intentions.

Kurtz's pamphlet is not the only text-within-the-text of *Heart of Darkness*. Fifty miles up river, Marlôw comes upon an abandoned hut in which he finds an apparent antithesis to Kurtz's report: "Its title was, *An Inquiry into Some Points of Seamanship*, by a man Towser, Towson—some such name—Master in His Majesty's Navy" (37). Towson's book is obviously also, like Kurtz's pamphlet, a product of European, imperialist civilization, but not a lying or hypocritical one. Although "not a very enthralling book," it has "a singleness of intention, an honest concern for the right way of going to work, which made those humble pages . . . luminous with another than a professional light." Marlow's discovery gives him the "delicious sensation of having come upon something unmistakably real." Conrad makes Towson sound like a second Captain Marryat, as the reference to "*His* Majesty's Navy" suggests; both represent the honorable, unreflecting values of discipline, service, courage, and stalwart innocence which Conrad finds in Marryat's novels. But Towson's text has also been scrawled over in strange characters that Marlow takes for a mysterious "cipher" until he encounters the Russian "harlequin" who had taken some presumably half-crazed notes on Towson's pages. When Marlow returns Towson to the Russian, "he made as though he would kiss me. . . . 'The only book I had left, and I thought I had lost it,' he said, looking at it ecstatically" (54). Between Marlow's discovery of Towson and his returning it to the Russian comes the description of Kurtz's mad, genocidal pamphlet. Just as he idolizes Kurtz, the Russian appears also to idolize Towson, so ultimately there may be little or no difference between the two texts. But this, too, is ambiguous, deliberately left in suspense by Conrad, who likes to judge without judging.

Kurtz's pamphlet, as well as what Marlow reveals about his unspeakable rites, allow us to understand his dying words as something more than an outcry of guilt and certainly more than a mere expression of the fear of death or of loathing for African savagery. Those words can be seen as referring to a lying idealism that can rationalize any behavior, to a complete separation between words and meaning, theory and practice. On this level, *Heart of Darkness* offers a devastating critique of imperialist ideology. On another, more general level, however, it offers a self-critique and an attack upon the impressionistic deviousness of art and language. At this more general level, Conrad stops worrying about the atrocities committed in the Congo and identifies with Kurtz as a fellow-artist, a hero of the spirit of that nihilism which Conrad himself found so attractive, perhaps secretly consoling.

On several occasions Conrad compares the artist with the empire builder in a way obviously counter to his critique of imperialism in *Heart of Darkness*. In *A Personal Record*, Conrad writes of "that interior world where [the novelist's] thought and . . . emotions go seeking for . . . imagined adventures," where "there are no policemen, no law, no pressure of circumstance or dread opinion to keep him within bounds." And in the first manuscript of "The Rescuer," which contains Conrad's most sympathetic treatment of imperialism, empire builders are "one of those unknown guides of civilization, who on the advancing edge of progress are administrators, warriors, creators. . . . They are like great artists a mystery to the masses, appreciated only by the uninfluential few."[2] Kurtz is empire

---

2. I owe this point and the quotations that illustrate it to John A. McClure, *Kipling and Conrad: The Colonial Fiction* (Cambridge: Harvard UP, 1981), 89–90.

builder, artist, universal genius, and voice crying out from the wilderness, all in one. But he has lost the faith—whether vision or illusion—which can alone sustain an empire and produce great art. Nihilism is no basis upon which to found or administer a colony, or to write a novel, and Conrad knows it. In suggesting his affinity to Kurtz, he suggests the moral bankruptcy of his own literary project, but he also insists that once there were empire builders and great artists who kept the faith. Conrad frequently expresses his admiration for the great explorers and adventurers, from Sir Walter Raleigh and Sir Francis Drake through James Brooke, the white rajah of Sarawak, and David Livingstone, the greatest of the many great explorers of the Dark Continent.

Conrad's critique of empire is never strictly anti-imperialist. Instead, in terms that can be construed as both conservative and nihilistic, he mourns the loss of the true faith in modern times, the closing down of frontiers, the narrowing of the possibilities for adventure, the commercialization of the world and of art, the death of chivalry and honor. Here the meaning of his emphasis on the lying propaganda of modern imperialism becomes evident. What was once a true, grand, noble, albeit violent enterprise is now "a gigantic and atrocious fraud"—except maybe, Marlow thinks, in the red parts of the map, where "some real work is done." Staring into the abyss of his life, or at least of Kurtz's life, Conrad sees mirrored in his own disillusionment, his own nihilistic darkness, the type of the whole—the path of disintegration which is modern history. It is not just Africa or even just Kurtz that possesses a heart of darkness; Conrad's story bears that title as well.

But I am not going to end by announcing in "a tone of scathing contempt" the death of Conrad's story as a classic, like the insolent manager's boy announcing "Mistah Kurtz—he dead." I agree with Trilling that authenticity, truth telling, far from being a negligible literary effect is the essence of great literature. That almost no other work of British fiction written before World War I is critical of imperialism (Taylor's *Seeta* is indeed exceptional in this regard) is a measure of Conrad's achievement. Yet the real strength of *Heart of Darkness* does not lie in what it says about atrocities in King Leopold's Congo, though its documentary impulse is an important counter to its will-to-style. As social criticism, its anti-imperialist message is undercut by its racism, by its reactionary political attitudes, by its impressionism. There are few novels, however, which so insistently invoke a moral idealism they do not seem to contain and in which the modernist will-to-style is subjected to such powerful self-scrutiny—in which the voice at the heart of the novel, the voice of modern literature, the voice of imperialist civilization itself may in its purest, freest form yield only "The horror! The horror!"

MARIANNA TORGOVNICK

[Primitivism and the African Woman in *Heart of Darkness*]†

The real problem with existing critiques of Conrad as imperialist is not, as the humanists and formalists think, that they pollute art with politics or debase artistic considerations, but that the notion of politics they employ is entirely too circumscribed. Colonialism and imperialism *are* important political issues, but they are not the only ones involved in narratives like *Heart of Darkness* or *Lord Jim*. Conrad engages in a more broadly political description of certain versions of masculinity and femininity, and of certain related ideals, such as "restraint." For all their differences, both the humanist/formalist approaches and existing critiques of Conrad as imperialist operate from within the same system of gender values and notions of the political as Conrad himself. They thus cannot help but ignore important issues raised by the text that are political in a different sense.

*　*　*

I have read *Heart of Darkness* many times and always been a bit repelled by it. But I have never been so much repelled as on this reading, specifically focused on its version of the primitive and hence on the African woman. My repulsion has something to do with the celebrated vagueness of Marlow's style—usually praised by critics as the essence of Conrad's vision and greatness or, more rarely, in a fashion established by F. R. Leavis, seen as ruining the book. My objection is not Leavis's objection that Marlow makes a virtue out of not knowing what he means. Rather my objection is that this vagueness can be and has been so often linked to terms like "psychological complexity" or the "mystery and enigma of things." The work's language veils not only what Kurtz was doing in Africa, but also what Conrad is doing in *Heart of Darkness*.

To lift the veils, we need to move in and out of the boundaries established by the text, maintaining a balance between the narrative's criticism of imperialism and yet lavish, even loving, repetition of primitivist tropes. We need to talk about what the novella refuses to discuss except in the vaguest terms—"the horror, the horror"—what Kurtz was about in Africa. "I don't want to know anything of the ceremonies used when approaching Mr. Kurtz," shouts Marlow with passion (58). But we need to know about them or, if we can-

† From *Gone Primitive: Savage Intellects, Modern Lives* (Chicago: U of Chicago P, 1990), pp. 143, 145–49, 151–54, 154–55, 156, 157–58. Reprinted by permission of the University of Chicago Press. Unless indicated, notes are the author's.

not know, to speculate about these and other things that the novella will not say.

What, then, has Kurtz done? He has, as is made quite clear in the novella, corrupted the idea of work and carried it to the extreme of enslavement. He has taken the mechanics of imperialism and applied them so relentlessly that even the Belgian managers consider his methods "unsound." Kurtz has allowed himself to be worshiped by his African followers. As fantasy, this idea of the cream always rising to the top is perfectly acceptable, indeed almost invariable in the West; Kurtz's mistake has been only going too far in making the fantasy a lived fact, loosening the "restraint" Marlow finds necessary in all things.

But Kurtz has done more, a "more" that remains less specified than his corruption of imperial policy. It is a curious fact that the novella does not do more than hint, for example, in the most indirect way, at Kurtz's relation to the woman who presides over the Africans' farewell; it is an even more curious fact that no critic I have encountered pays much attention to her either. Kurtz has apparently mated with the magnificent black woman and thus violated the British code against miscegenation, a code backed by the policy of bringing wives and families with colonists and administrators whenever possible. The woman is decked with leggings and jewelry that testify to a high position among the Africans—the position, one assumes, of Kurtz's wife. She gives voice to the ineffable sorrow Marlow hears aboard ship the day before he finds Kurtz, and she alone of the Africans is so devoted to Kurtz that she remains, arms outstretched after her lord, when the other Africans disperse at the sound of Marlow's ship's whistle. Marlow clearly conceives of her as a substitute for, an inversion of, Kurtz's high-minded, white "Intended." Like the Belgian woman, she is an impressive figure, but unlike the Intended, she is not "high-minded": she is presented as all body and inchoate emotion. The novella cuts from the figure of the African woman with outstretched arms to the Intended: one woman an affianced bride, one woman, all body, surely an actual bride. Yet the novella will not say so. As in the Tarzan novels, miscegenation is simply not within the ken of the narrative; it is a "love which dare not speak its name."

Miscegenation challenges a boundary highly charged in the West, the boundary of race. Kurtz's other actions also assaulted Western boundaries of love and hate, life and death, body and spirit. At this point, we might zero in on details that the novella and its critics pass over quickly, noting, for example, those heads that adorn Kurtz's palisade, and provide the first hints of "Kurtz's methods":

You remember I told you I had been struck at the distance by
certain attempts at ornamentation, rather remarkable in the
ruinous aspect of the place. Now I had suddenly a nearer view
and its first result was to make me throw my head back as if
before a blow. Then I went carefully from post to post with my
glass, and I saw my mistake. These round knobs were not ornamental but symbolic, they were expressive and puzzling,
striking and disturbing—food for thought and also for vultures
if there had been any looking down from the sky, but at all
events for such ants as were industrious enough to ascend the
pole. . . . I returned deliberately to the first I had seen—and
there it was black, dried, sunken, with closed eyelids—a head
that seemed to sleep at the top of that pole, and with the
shrunken dry lips showing a narrow white line of the teeth,
was smiling too, smiling continuously at some endless and jocose dream of that eternal slumber. (57)

The heads connect Africa as primitive locale with all primitive societies (like the Scotland of *Macbeth* and the English prehistory at
which Marlow begins his narration) in which the spoliation of the
enemy's dead body was a common ritual. Neither the novella nor its
critics seem able to say more about the heads on the posts, which
seem nonetheless to convey a world of information about Kurtz.
What can they mean? We can find some answers by looking at documented instances of head-hunting, and at texts nearly contemporary with *Heart of Darkness* which have an explicit fascination with
headlessness.

Documented accounts of head-hunting and cannibalism suggest
that the practices had very specific, communal goals in primitive
societies: a sense of renewal or "lightening," for example, or the
provision of souls for boys at initiation, or the absorption of a slain
enemy's courage and power.[1] These are, at least, the motivations
most frequently found in the Philippines and New Guinea, where
the practices survived into the 1960s or 1970s among certain
groups and have been studied; the existence of similar practices in
Africa is far less reliably documented and remains largely conjec-
tural.[2] In New Guinea, the practice of collecting heads had a
clearly defined social value, with none of the idiosyncratic, macabre
overtones it acquired in the West. Collected heads were a fact of
life, often a familiar element of decor. The heads collected sometimes belonged not just to slain enemies but to cherished ances-

1. Renato Rosaldo, *Ilongot Headhunting, 1883–1974* (Stanford: Stanford UP, 1980); Alain
   Chenevière, *Vanishing Tribes: Primitive Man on Earth* (New York: Dolphin/Doubleday,
   1988).
2. Peggy Reeves Sanday, *Divine Hunger: Cannibalism as a Cultural System* (London: Cambridge UP, 1986).

tors. The Asmat of New Guinea, for example, traditionally sleep on their fathers' skulls as a means of drawing strength from ancestors.[3]

Kurtz, clearly, viewed the collecting of heads from the point of view of individual, not communal, power. In collecting the heads, he acted out a Western fantasy of savagery, with emotions different from those typically found among primitive peoples. Any account of his motivations must be, of course, hypothetical. But roughly thirty years after Conrad's narrative. Leiris helped found a group called Acéphale, the headless ones.[4] The ideas that cluster around headlessness for this group of Kurtz's near contemporaries can be helpful in illuminating a "dark" portion of the European mind. Acéphale's writings suggest that headlessness was, for Europeans like Kurtz, a means of bypassing routine existence and the mediation of language. Above all, it was a means of getting to the essential.

Acéphale was preoccupied with rituals of slaughter and with headlessness as a metaphor. The group's emblem makes its concern with headlessness and with violence as a form of natural energy quite clear: the emblem shows a naked man brandishing a sword and a torch; the figure has no head, but it does have a death's-head, located where the penis should be. This last detail suggests that the erotic and the violent share a common bodily locus and, sometimes, common motivations. The emblem reveals Acéphale's fascination (akin, as we shall see, to Lawrence's) with "lower" sources of psychic energy and with ways to circumvent the Western emphasis on the mind and rationality. Accordingly, the group unblinkingly entertained the possibility that streams of blood, flooding European streets, would be necessary to overcome the stagnation of modernity.[5] Fantasized scenes of primitive ritual appear in Acéphale as sites of boundary transgression and transcendence—as precursors and stimulants to revolution at home. * * *

*　*　*

Acéphale replaced the penis with the death's-head; its imagery and rhetoric were, as we have seen, fiercely masculinist. To what extent, then, is the nexus of concerns described above specifically

3. Although the Asmat no longer collect the heads of slain enemies, the use of ancestral heads apparently continues and has been assimilated into the group's tenuous form of Christianity. On the Asmat practice of using fathers' skulls as pillows, see Tobias Schneebaum, *Where the Spirits Dwell* (New York: Grove, 1969), and Chenevière, *Vanishing Tribes*.
4. Michel Leiris (1901–1990), French ethnographer of Africa and associate of Parisian surrealists. [Editor]
5. Acéphale was a secret society closely linked to the public forum called the Collège de Sociologie. Its "main goals were the rebirth of myth and the touching off in society of an explosion of the primitive communal drives leading to sacrifice," although its programs did not really address mainstream politics (Alan Stoekl, "Introduction," in Georges Bataille, *Visions of Excess* (Minneapolis: U of Minnesota P, 1985), xix). The images of headlessness derive, no doubt, from the particularities of French revolutionary history, but they tally with Lawrence's images and with a more broadly Euro-American interest.

tied to questions of masculine identity—a hidden sign of masculinity, as the penis is an outer sign? The answer appears to be "to a considerable extent." We saw in Stanley a ruthless censoring of the self based explicitly on what it meant to be an Anglo-Saxon gentleman. We saw in Tarzan's story the suppression of blacks and women as a way to affirm traditional concepts of masculine identity. We saw in Leiris the identification of violence and suffering with the very fact of manhood. Conrad provides additional testimony to the attraction violence exerts for many men in our culture, perhaps as an outlet for the many alternative values conventionally barred to them: free emotional expression, openness to the "feminine" views of mothers and wives, identification with other men on a basis other than competition.[6] Under such conditions, ritualized enactments of violence and death become flirtations with boundary dissolution; they both test and affirm men's need to maintain separation, difference, and control as attributes of masculinity. They become simulacra of, but also charms against, the loss of self inscribed in the fullest erotic experience.[7] Kurtz's rituals of human sacrifice and cannibalism may thus have been motivated by the same Western mixture of thanatophilia and thanatophobia found in other men of his time.

Bringing these perspectives to bear on *Heart of Darkness* helps us say what the novella will not, and maybe cannot, say. Africa and the Africans became Kurtz's grand fantasy-theater for playing out his culture's notions of masculinity and power through the controlled, borrowed rituals attributed to certain groups within Africa, perverted to Western ends. Kurtz has performed experiments, with human subjects, on the boundaries between life and death, things and words. Those experiments profoundly affected his own view of the world, and threaten Marlow's.

When Marlow returns to Brussels after meeting Kurtz, he is at first oppressed by a vision of the emptiness of modern European life. He finds himself "resenting the sight of people hurrying through the streets to filch a little money from each other, to devour their infamous cookery, to gulp their unwholesome beer, to dream their insignificant and silly dreams" (70). Like Kurtz in Africa, he experiences the erosion of conventional European values

6. See Mary Field Belenky et al., *Women's Ways of Knowing* (New York: Basic Books, 1986), and Carol Gilligan, *In a Different Voice* (Cambridge: Harvard UP, 1982) for differing modes of male and female interpersonal relations. See Nancy Chodorow, *The Reproduction of Mothering* (Berkeley: U of California P, 1975), for how males and females react differently to the figure of the mother in our culture.

7. See Georges Bataille's *Erotism* (1957) for some connections between loss of self in erotic experience and in death. See Jessica Benjamin, *Bonds of Love* (New York: Pantheon, 1988), for a discussion of pornography as a form of controlled erotic expression.

and the hollowness of the words that correspond to them. But Marlow is gradually able to exercise "restraint" and to explain his hypercritical view of Brussels as the feverish ravings of a diseased mind: "my temperature was seldom normal in these days," he says (71). And he revises his vision of Belgians scurrying meaninglessly about their city to see instead "commonplace individuals going about their business" (71).

Heart of Darkness thematizes the power of words—words like *work* and *business*—to mask the reality of what is happening in the Congo. Language is a euphemism, a saving lie for all the Europeans. The novella thematizes as well the final impotence of words to mask "the horror" just beyond the boundary of language, the horror Kurtz tries but fails to articulate at the end, a horror alternately identifiable as "the void" or as the brutish potential of human nature. But for all its thematization of the deviousness and limitations of language, the novella ultimately falls into the very traps it exposes—the trap that is sprung when pretty phrases obscure ugly facts, facts like how and why those heads got on the palisade, facts like the African woman's relation to Kurtz, facts like her death at the end, which goes unmentioned, so far as I know, in any commentary on the novella.

Heart of Darkness is narrated by Marlow and shares many of his limitations. The narrative is willing to approach, but finally backs away from, really radical themes—about modern Europe, about the human mind in an indifferent universe, about sacrificial and violent rituals as a charm against death, about the degree to which men are driven to affirm their essentiality and identity. Metaphorically speaking, Conrad too learns to accept Brussels and decides that the thoughts that have come to him in Africa are taboo, to be repressed and banished, except as material for a yarn years later. But we should not lose sight of the loathing for certain Western values that flashes through Marlow's vision of Brussels, a loathing Kurtz may have shared in a locale that would seem the antipodes of Brussels, the center of Africa.

In Conrad, as in Bataille, Lawrence, Eliot, and others of their generation, the creation of specific versions of the primitive often depends on and is conditioned by a sense of disgust or frustration with Western values. The primitive becomes a convenient locale for the exploration of Western dullness or degeneracy, and of ways to transcend it, and thus functions as a symbolic entity. As so often in the West's encounters with the primitive, the primitive responds to Western needs, becoming the faithful or distorted mirror of the Western self.[8] This is one reason why in Conrad (as in Lawrence's

8. Achebe ("Image of Africa") sees the role of Africa as helping to affirm the West's sense of superiority by its availability as an image of the "savage." While this is true, it is only half

visions of the Arctic and the African way, the debased extremes of white and black) the hypercivilized and primitive are collapsed and homologous. Not the same thing, they are nonetheless made to point to the same thing: the dire fate of Western man and culture unless values like "restraint" and "work"—the whole set of values that guides the "us" in "one of us"—can be made to hold. Present as sign and symbol, the primitive lacks authenticity in and of itself. It becomes grist for the Western fantasy-mill.

In *Heart of Darkness*, Conrad approaches fantasy sites like miscegenation, ritual slaughter, and head-hunting. But Conrad never touches down for long or makes the fantasy explicit. Instead of withered heads we remember phrases—"the horror, the horror." Real psychological intensity—or, more radically, a remapping of what *constitutes* psychological intensity—is bypassed in favor of Marlow's vaporish posturings. The novella wants to have it both ways: to criticize language and yet to take refuge in the gorgeousness of Conrad's own language. Like Marlow, it "must make its choice of nightmares," and it chooses, finally, the nightmare of language, that sustainer of civilization. But one feels in *Heart of Darkness* the pressure of other narratives, other dreams and nightmares, that Marlow will not and maybe cannot tell. Marlow interrogates the limits of identity through the words of his narration; but the words only begin to fumble at the realities which have produced the narration.

Conrad's version of the primitive is a cheat. It promises much and seems to offer tolerance and sympathy, balance and wisdom, an unlimited and unconditional exploration of experience extreme in its difference from Western norms. But it leaves out too much and is finally unable to transcend the very Western values it attacks. The "gorgeous virility" of Conrad's style in *Heart of Darkness* and related narratives like *Lord Jim*—its maleness and ability to coin scintillating memorable phrases like "the hollow man," "to the destructive element submit," "one of us," "the horror," and "gorgeous virility" itself—limits, finally, the extent of its vision. The words are so seductive that * * * it is easy to lose sight of the ways in which the words repeat a series of clichés. Something cataclysmic, transcendent appears to be happening; but really the words convey only stale, familiar ideas about Africa and the West's relation to it. The words flirt with a radical critique of certain Western values, but stop short. *Heart of Darkness*, like Marlow, goes only so far.

*   *   *

That African woman is, for me, the crux of *Heart of Darkness*. Like Jewel in *Lord Jim*, she is the representative "native," the only one

---

the story. The West's image of Africa allows Westerners to play out their sense of the *West*'s degenerate condition and to use "Africa" or other sites of "the primitive" as fantasized locales for transcendence and renewal.

fully individualized and described in detail, except for the Helmsman, who also dies in the story. She is, the text insists, the symbol of Africa. Once she enters the narrative, she is made to embody the landscape, rendered throughout in the language of pathetic fallacy:

> the whole sorrowful land, the immense wilderness, the colossal body of the fecund and mysterious life seemed to look at her, pensive, as though it had been looking at the image of its own tenebrous and passionate soul.
>
> She came abreast of the steamer, stood still, and faced us. Her long shadow fell to the water's edge. Her face had a tragic and fierce aspect of wild sorrow and of dumb pain mingled with the fear of some struggling, half-shaped resolve. She stood looking at us without a stir and like the wilderness itself, with an air of brooding over an inscrutable purpose. (60–61)

Why is the woman's sorrow "wild," her pain "dumb," her resolve "half-shaped," her purpose "inscrutable"? Why is she (like the landscape) "fecund and mysterious," "tenebrous and passionate"? Do we not slip here into a prejudiced vocabulary—as Marlow does often when he uses phrases like "fool nigger," "insolent black head," "The man seemed young—almost a boy—but you know with them it's hard to tell" (17). More—why is the woman the embodiment of Africa? What gives Marlow the right (and why does Conrad not challenge his right?) to make this woman so portentous a symbol?

The woman presumably dies when Marlow's ship pulls off and the pilgrims begin their "little fun"—dies because she is unwilling to flinch like the Africans who "broke and ran, they leaped, they crouched, they swerved, they dodged" at the sound of the ship's whistle and hence unknowingly escaped the pilgrims' bullets (67). Her death fulfills her role as emblem of the African landscape and (once recognized) makes explicit the hidden reference of "the feminine" and "the primitive" to death. For the African landscape *is* death in the novella. It is the "white man's grave," "lurking death . . . hidden evil . . . profound darkness." Europeans enter it but leave it either dead or ill or changed and marked forever. Women are uniformly associated with the landscape and with death. Even the eminently white Intended makes Marlow lie, and he "hate[s], detest[s], and can't bear a lie . . . because . . . there is a taint of death, a flavour of mortality in lies" (27).[9]

* * *

The nexus of associations here is one we have seen before in Western conceptions of the primitive—women, sex, death, mortal-

9. Garrett Stewart is interested in the lying/dying connection, but does not pay much attention to the African woman ("Lying as Dying in *Heart of Darkness*," *PMLA* 95 [1980]: 319–31).

ity. As in the work of Picasso, Leiris, and other moderns, the associations are not rational but "intuitive," the underside of the rock of
Western objectivity and aesthetics. Critiques of Conrad and imperialism, helpful as they have been, have not made this crucial connection. They have not focused on the substitution of one value for
another—in this case female for primitive—that is very typical of
Conrad's method, typical indeed of Western thinking about the
primitive. The ease of substitution here and its implications seem
to me the real issues. In some sense, to speak of women in *Heart of
Darkness* and to speak of the primitive are, illogically, one and the
same thing: fantastic, collective ("women are all alike"), seductive,
dangerous, deadly. Until we expose such substitutions, we bypass
the stubborn knot of associations hidden *beneath* the text's superficial attention to them both—a yearning for and yet fear of boundary transgression, violence, and death—which may well be the
text's real interests.

* * *

We are not yet ready and in fact may never be ready to tidily sum
things up, to firmly state the reasons Western primitivism has made
these connections. For they are messy connections, "intuitively"
made and rarely examined. They go back to our earliest sense of
ourselves among others, to the roots of all our actions and reactions, to the ways the conceptions "self" and "other," "male" and
"female," "subject" and "object," "dominant" and "subordinate" first
took shape for us, and how they subsequently developed. They are
more intensely dangerous than the material traditionally addressed
by Freudian psychology, material that has become, over the years,
rather tame. In fact, we have only the most rudimentary tools to
discuss the phenomena I am describing here.

What is clear now is that the West's fascination with the primitive has to do with its own crises in identity, with its own need to
clearly demarcate subject and object even while flirting with other
ways of experiencing the universe. Few periods in history have been
more concerned than modernity with the articulation of the psychological subject and the cultivation of the individualistic self; yet
the fascination with other possibilities, possibilities perhaps embodied in primitive societies, remained acute. "Me Tarzan, you
Jane"; "Dr. Livingstone, I presume"—worlds apart grammatically,
these tag phrases bespeak dramas of identity. In Marlow's narrations (as in Livingstone and Tarzan), masculine identity and the
need to maintain "masculinity" as something separate, apart, "restrained," and in control are hidden motivators and hidden themes.

We have known for some time—how could we not know—that
Conrad's works are about "identity," something achieved through a
devious series of identifications and distinctions, through the di-

alectics of self and other. We have read for some time the structure of *Heart of Darkness* and *Lord Jim* as a series of comparisons and contrasts between one male character and another: Marlow and the Belgians, Marlow and Kurtz; Jim and Marlow and Stein and the French Lieutenant, and the Malay Helmsman, and so on. We have tended to pose those dynamics in traditional psychological terms (Freudian or Jungian) or philosophical terms (the "morally responsible" versus the derelict, the "realistic" versus the "romantic"). I am suggesting here that the texts' treatment of primitive societies and their substitution of the female for the primitive are more explosive than these traditional terms allow. More, I am suggesting that the language of the text is deeply political in ways that the humanists and formalists cannot see and that have not interested the Marxists and anti-imperialists enough. Tracking down what Conrad means by "going primitive" means traveling with and beyond Conrad farther than critics have previously been willing to go.

JEREMY HAWTHORN

The Women of *Heart of Darkness*†

The chain of worship and betrayal that we witness in *Heart of Darkness* is completed by Marlow's own worship of that more perfect world inhabited by women, a worship which leads him to lie to the Intended and thus to perpetuate the cycle of lies that fuels imperialism. Given Conrad's reputation as a very masculine writer, more concerned with the world of male than of female experience, it is salutary to recall that three female characters each play an indispensable role in *Heart of Darkness*—Marlow's aunt, the 'wild and gorgeous apparition of a woman' the reader presumes is Kurtz's African mistress, and Kurtz's Intended. There is additionally Kurtz's portrait of the blindfolded female, and there are the two women knitting black wool met by Marlow in the Company's office in Europe, women whose resemblance to the Fates of classical mythology is clearly intended. Their appearance in the novella suggests that women may have a significant role to play in determining various fates in *Heart of Darkness*. The blindfolded woman suggests that this determining influence may not be a knowing or intended one. * * *

What becomes apparent if we consider the three main female

† From *Narrative Technique and Ideological Commitment* (London: Edward Arnold, 1990), pp. 183–92. Reprinted with the permission of Hodder Education. Notes are the author's.

characters in the novella, is that in *Heart of Darkness* issues of gender are inextricably intertwined with matters of race and culture. To start with, we should note that the following comments made by Marlow about 'women' are clearly aimed at *European women*: they do not apply to the African woman. Nor do they apply to working-class European women; Marlow's statement is both culture- and class-limited.

> 'Girl! What? Did I mention a girl? Oh, she is out of it—completely. They—the women I mean—are out of it—should be out of it. We must help them to stay in that beautiful world of their own, lest ours gets worse. Oh, she had to be out of it.' (48)

The women are 'out of' the man's world just as effectively as Kurtz's ideas and values are out of the horrific world he constructs in Africa. And just as Kurtz's ideas and values become weakened and impoverished by this isolation, so too do the women who are out of it, imprisoned in their 'beautiful world of their own,' end up as debilitated and sterile as the Intended. The remarks quoted above are all of a piece with Marlow's earlier comments about women, comments inspired by his aunt's adoption of the 'rot let loose in print and talk' which leads her to picture him as 'an emissary of light, something like a lower sort of apostle' (12).

> 'It's queer how out of touch with truth women are. They live in a world of their own, and there had never been anything like it, and never can be. It is too beautiful altogether, and if they were to set it up it would go to pieces before the first sunset. Some confounded fact we men have been living contentedly with ever since the day of creation would start up and knock the whole thing over.' (12–13)

What Marlow describes as the 'world of their own' of women in the above passage has much in common with the world of Kurtz's ideals, which he does actually try to set up and which does go to pieces before too many sunsets because some 'confounded fact' starts up and knocks the whole thing over. And indeed, just as Marlow's aunt 'got carried off her feet' (12), so too Kurtz 'had kicked himself loose of the earth' (66).

In a work which * * * explores the fate of an idealism betrayed into a corrupting alliance with imperialism, European women perform an important symbolic function. At the same time as they provide us with a relatively straightforward and realistic depiction of European middle-class women of the time, they also serve a larger representative function, portraying that idealism which the domestic imperialist powers use as apology for their exploitation. This idealism is, paradoxically, nurtured apart from that for which it offers an apology: the activities of the European powers in the subject countries dominated by imperialism. If this argument is accepted, then it must also be accepted that the idealism in question is a weak, emaciated, and unhealthy creature. Neither Marlow's aunt nor Kurtz's Intended could be said to be possessed of any striking features suggestive of energy or practicality. With his aunt Marlow has a last decent cup of tea for many days 'in a room that most soothingly looked just as you would expect a lady's drawing-room to look' (12). It is one of the functions of women and that idealism which they represent to 'soothe' those off to do imperialism's dirty work. Marlow's patronizing tone when talking of his aunt is, however, mild in contrast to the powerful connotations of death and disease to be found in the description of the Intended's home.

> 'The bent gilt legs and back of the furniture shone in indistinct curves. The tall white marble fireplace had a cold and monumental whiteness. A grand piano stood massively in a corner; with dark gleams on the flat surfaces like a sombre and polished sarcophagus.' (73)

The Intended herself is a thing of black and white, of sickliness and death. She has no energy, no living presence.

> 'She came forward, all in black, with a pale head, floating towards me in the dusk. . . .
> This fair hair, this pale visage, this pure brow, seemed surrounded by an ashy halo from which the dark eyes looked out at me.' (73–74)

Note how words connotative of idealism such as 'pure' and 'halo' are made to seem unhealthy and corrupted in this description. This seems to me to support the argument that the way in which European women are portrayed in *Heart of Darkness* serves to strengthen the novella's depiction of idealism as weak, unhealthy and corrupted.

The black-white imagery of *Heart of Darkness*, the effect of which comes to a climax in the meeting between Marlow and the Intended, is complex. An analysis of its function in the passage quoted above would not be easy, and in the novella as a whole it cannot unproblematically be reduced to any schematic system of symbolic meaning. Conrad seems concerned to undercut simple symbolic associations in his use of this imagery, to disabuse the reader of the belief that good and bad can be straightforwardly defined and neatly compartmentalized. Very often in the novella we can observe a process of change from white to black: the centre of Africa is white on the map, but turns out to be a place of darkness;

the Intended is pale and fair, but her dark eyes and the darkness falling in her room suggest that her very purity is productive, however unknowingly, of evil. The complexity of this pattern of imagery also seems to me to have something to say about the marriage of trade and idealism in the work: just as we no longer accept the conventional association of white with purity and virtue by the end of the novella, so too we see that idealism can be corrupted by association with evil forces. The challenge to our conventional views at the level of the novella's imagery duplicates and reinforces the challenge made by the work to other conventional views.

It is apparent from the quoted passage that the Intended's capacity is for devotion, not for living. Existence in a world of their own, then, does not seem to produce any sort of enviable life for European women, but more a sort of living death. And inside the white tomb, black decay and corruption can be found. A disembodied idealism, far from preserving the good, may actually foster the bad. If we accept such an interpretation of aspects of the black-white imagery of the novella, we will have to consider critically Marlow's view that if women are kept confined to that 'world of their own' this may help to make our own (that is, the world of men) better.

The contrast to the Intended offered by Kurtz's African mistress could not be sharper.

> 'She walked with measured steps, draped in striped and fringed cloths, treading the earth proudly, with a slight jingle and flash of barbarous ornaments. She carried her head high; her hair was done in the shape of a helmet; she had brass leggings to the knee, brass wire gauntlets to the elbow, a crimson spot on her tawny cheek, innumerable necklaces of glass beads on her neck; bizarre things, charms, gifts of witch-men, that hung about her, glittered and trembled at every step. She must have had the value of several elephant tusks upon her. She was savage and superb, wild-eyed and magnificent; there was something ominous and stately in her deliberate progress.' (60)

Where the Intended is static and passive, she is active and forceful; where the Intended has the odour of death about her, she is the personification of life; where the Intended is a thing of black and white, she is ablaze with colour; where the Intended is refined to the point of etiolation, she is 'savage and superb'; and where the Intended is clad in mourning, she is clad for war. Moreover, while the Intended has an air of oppressive sterility about her, Marlow says of the African woman that 'the immense wilderness, the colossal body of the fecund and mysterious life seemed to look at her, pensive, as though it had been looking at the image of its own tenebrous and passionate soul'

(60). This aspect of the contrast is particularly important: the Intended and the idealism she represents are sterile; nothing will come of them but death. But the powerful life of the African woman is, like the wilderness reflected in her, passionate and fecund.

The contrast is in tune with others in the novella: between, for instance, the boat 'paddled by black fellows' seen by Marlow on his way to Africa, and the lifeless French man-of-war shelling 'enemies' inland. Marlow sees in that African actuality which is untouched by imperialism an energy, a concentrated life that contrasts with the sterility seen in a European idealism cut off from reality. The life of the African woman is all of a piece: there is no division of ideals and aspirations from actuality, no separation between her and her life activity. This being so, the overwhelmingly positive description which the reader is given of her serves as a critique of the life of the Europeans, divided between sterile ideals and brutal 'horror'. I should add, however, that if we look at the two women together we recognize, I think, a familiar pattern: woman as devoted and chaste spirit, and woman as sensual and sexual flesh. But this reproduction of a well-known stereotypical pattern is not itself restricted to the patriarchal ideology that fosters and benefits from it, for in juxtaposing the two women the narrative of *Heart of Darkness* draws attention to the process whereby women are dehumanized by being divided into spirit and body and are denied the full humanity that requires possession of both.[1]

There are critics who find Marlow's (and Conrad's) account of the African woman melodramatic and unconvincing, just as there are many who find the closing scene between Marlow and the Intended to strain after an effect which it fails to achieve, and it is true that if these scenes are considered in isolation then a convincing case against them can be made along these lines.

> All of these objections [to the final scene with the Intended] seem to have their base on aesthetic grounds, but it could be contended that the problem here too is essentially ideological, since Marlow's response to the Intended is the result of a particular kind of anti-feminism that pervades the novella and may well reflect Conrad's own inadequate response to the feminine. The attitudes of Victorian patriarchy structure the response to women and to savages in the same way, by imposing a sentimental and reductive definition upon the object that removes the necessity of actually looking at it.[2]

1. An article which explores the links between the two women in some detail is Mahmoud K. Kharbutli, "The Treatment of Women in *Heart of Darkness*," *Dutch Quarterly Review* 17(4), 1987, p. 242–3.
2. Peter Hyland, "The Little Woman in the Heart of Darkness," *Conradiana* 20(1), 1988, p. 4.

This is an interesting suggestion, but one which I find mistaken. And the mistake is similar to that which accuses the Conrad of *Heart of Darkness* of racism. For the ideological force of the presentation of the Intended can be tapped only when this presentation is set alongside that of Kurtz's African mistress. It is when the two are seen as two aspects of a patriarchal view of women that the ideological thrust of the work comes into focus, just as Conrad's presentation of Africans in *Heart of Darkness* has to be set against his description of Europeans and of the system they impose upon Africa.

The gender divisions referred to by Marlow are not, of course, just a literary matter, not just a question of the work's symbolic patterns of meaning, nor can they be considered separately from the imperialist brutalities which are recounted in *Heart of Darkness*. The Intended's sterile isolation depicts realistically the separation of those in the domestic culture from full knowledge of what is being done in their name in Africa, while at the same time it is also an accurate portrayal of some of the results of the differential treatment of men and women in the European culture. It is European men who are sent to Africa to further the aims of imperialism; but we see European women—ignorant of what their menfolk are really doing for imperialism—offering powerful ideological support to them. What *Heart of Darkness* suggests to the engaged reader is that the division of ideal and action, of theory and practice, is effected in part by means of the division of genders.

The African woman in *Heart of Darkness* is one of a number of 'native' women in Conrad's fiction who are betrayed through their love for, or involvement with, a white man. Aïssa is betrayed by Willems, Jewel by Jim. And both Hassim and his sister Immada are effectively betrayed by Lingard in *The Rescue*. In Conrad's first published novel *Almayer's Folly*, implicit authorial approval is accorded Nina's decision to reject the possibility of a white husband, to turn her back on the race of her father, and instead to follow Dain. In *Lord Jim* Jewel says to Marlow: 'He has left me. . . . you always leave us—for your own ends', and on the penultimate page of the novel Marlow says of Jim that he 'goes away from a living woman to celebrate his pitiless wedding with a shadowy ideal of conduct.'[3] These two comments are extremely suggestive, and bring to mind a range of significant implications. On the strictly literal level, one is reminded that an aspect of imperialism has always been that of the sexual exploitation of 'native' women by male representatives of the exploiting power, an exploitation which does not typically involve any permanent commitment to the women in-

3. Conrad, *Lord Jim* (1900; Garden City, NY: Doubleday, Page, 1924), pp. 348, 416.

volved, who are always left for the personal 'ends' of the men concerned. But it is striking how Marlow's comment on Jim at the end
of *Lord Jim* can also be applied to Kurtz, who also leaves a 'living
woman' to celebrate a 'pitiless wedding with a shadowy ideal of
conduct'. (Both the African woman and the Intended are abandoned by Kurtz, albeit in different ways.) Kurtz's 'pitiless wedding'
is not a happy one, and he apparently finds in the African woman
qualities which are lacking in the Intended and which he cannot
resist. Kurtz is morally responsible for turning the Intended into a
living corpse, and then unable to resist the attraction of a woman
possessed of precisely that life which European culture has denied
the Intended. (Many of Conrad's contemporary readers would
doubtless have seen Kurtz's relationship with the African woman as
further evidence of his degeneration, and there is some textual evidence that this is how Marlow sees it. But I do not think that the
work as a whole can unproblematically sustain such a reading.)

Kurtz manages to destroy both women. As I have said, in different ways, he abandons both. So positive and forceful is the impression given off by the African woman that it is not hard to forget that
she too has the word 'tragic' applied to her more than once in the
work.

> 'Her face had a tragic and fierce aspect of wild sorrow and of
> dumb pain mingled with the fear of some struggling, half-
> shaped resolve. She stood looking at us without a stir, and like
> the wilderness itself, with an air of brooding over an in-
> scrutable purpose.' (61)

Perhaps Conrad believes that like Taminah in *Almayer's Folly*, she
lacks the language and the self-knowledge to isolate and explore
the source of her pain, which Marlow describes as 'dumb'. But of
course the reader is never allowed to witness her speech or her
thoughts, and this narrative restriction may represent both a limitation of Conrad's experience and of his ideological outlook. (It contrasts strikingly with his ability to make us privy to the speech and
thoughts of his Malays.)

When the steamer leaves, taking Kurtz away from her, we are
told that

> 'Only the barbarous and superb woman did not so much as
> flinch, and stretched tragically her bare arms after us over the
> sombre and glittering river.' (67)

The gesture is recalled by Marlow later on, during his meeting with
Kurtz's Intended.

> 'She put out her arms as if after a retreating figure, stretching
> them back and with clasped pale hands across the fading and

narrow sheen of the window. Never see him! I saw him clearly
enough then. I shall see this eloquent phantom as long as I live,
and I shall see her, too, a tragic and familiar Shade, resembling
in this gesture another one, tragic also, and bedecked with powerless charms, stretching bare brown arms over the glitter of
the infernal stream, the stream of darkness.' (76)

The linking together of the two women at this juncture in the narrative makes an important point. Both women are tragic, both have
been betrayed by Kurtz. Putting women on a pedestal, cutting them
off from reality, and restricting them to a world of sterile ideals and
lifeless illusions is as destructive as treating a woman purely as the
recipient of passion.

The duplicities of imperialism work their way through into human relationships through—among other things—their connection
with gender divisions in the domestic culture. (Another way of
looking at the matter is to say that imperialism involved the projection of divisions and duplicities already existing in Europe on to
the exploited lands. 'Native' women were thus slotted into a role
previously occupied by poor women in the domestic cultures. No
doubt many like Kurtz who never left Europe had their Intendeds
and their mistresses just like Kurtz—even if the mistresses were
white.) * * *

Talking of Jewel in *Lord Jim* Marlow says that her indifference,
'more awful than tears, cries, and reproaches, seemed to defy time
and consolation.'[4] Of the Intended in *Heart of Darkness* Marlow observes that 'I perceived she was one of those creatures that are not
the playthings of Time. For her he had died only yesterday' (74). In
both cases a 'native' woman has been removed from time by association with a European man: has been effectively removed from the
process of living. And in *Heart of Darkness* this separation in some
ways results from a set of disembodied and unreal ideals which are
imposed upon women by men. The Intended's isolation from the
reality of Kurtz is a part of imperialism's nurturing of spurious
ideals, ideals which function more as camouflage than as active
principles or guides to action.

    ' "He was a remarkable man," I said, unsteadily. Then before
the appealing fixity of her gaze, that seemed to watch for more
words on my lips, I went on, "It was impossible not to—"
    ' "Love him," she finished eagerly, silencing me into an ap-
palled dumbness. "How true! How true! But when you think
that no one knew him so well as I! I had all his noble confidence. I knew him best."
    ' "You knew him best," I repeated. And perhaps she did. But

4. *Lord Jim*, p. 348.

with every word spoken the room was growing darker, and only
her forehead, smooth and white, remained illumined by the
unextinguishable light of belief and love.' (74)

The Intended's forehead seems here to symbolize her unshake-
able idealism; unaware of the horror of the world, believing herself
to have known Kurtz better than anyone, she is actually more and
more isolated, and more and more reduced by her isolation. The
whiteness of her forehead parallels Kurtz's own 'ivory' head: unhealthy, unnatural; and illumined by a light which—like the light
held by the painted woman in Kurtz's picture—fails to help its blind
owner to see. The picture is proleptic of Marlow's final scene with
the Intended in a number of ways.

'Then I noticed a small sketch in oils, on a panel, representing
a woman, draped and blindfolded, carrying a lighted torch.
The background was sombre—almost black. The movement of
the woman was stately, and the effect of the torch-light on the
face was sinister.' (25)

The painted woman is as cut off from her surroundings as is the Intended; her torch, like the Intended's idealism, is apparently aimed
at illuminating the darkness, dispelling ignorance, but 'the effect of
the torch-light on the face was sinister'. Ideals held in blind ignorance of reality do not bring good, but its opposite. The picture
helps to support the argument that the novella associates the isolation of European women with the isolation of idealism from that
which it is being used to underwrite.

Why does Marlow remark that perhaps the Intended did know
Kurtz best? Is it that she understood his dreams, his ideals, and
that these were the true centre of Kurtz, that which could explain
both sides of the corrupted idealist? Or is this an indication of Marlow's limitations, of his own desire to maintain a separate world of
imagined ideals, a world in which Kurtz's reality would be measured not by his actions but by his expressed values, his disappointed dreams—'a shadow insatiable of splendid appearances, of
frightful realities; a shadow darker than the shadow of the night,
and draped nobly in the folds of a gorgeous eloquence' (73)?

A brief comparison of the final pages of *Heart of Darkness* with
those of *Under Western Eyes* prompts some relevant observations.
In the later novel, Nathalie Haldin is led to recognize the fact that
her ideals have been cut off from the world, have failed to make
contact with those realities they have claimed to be concerned to
alter. As a result, she travels back to Russia, seeking to renew her
contact with these lost realities at first hand. In contrast, *Heart of
Darkness* ends with Marlow's decision to maintain the ignorance of
the Intended, to keep her in the dark—however much he claims

that it 'would have been too dark—too dark altogether' to tell her the truth about Kurtz.

Does this difference represent a change in Conrad's own views about the need to keep women in that 'world of their own' the existence of which makes 'ours' (i.e. men's[5]) a little better? A case could be made for such a judgement, but it seems to me to ignore the fact that it is Marlow rather than Conrad who argues that women should be kept in that 'world of their own' in *Heart of Darkness*. What the novella gives us is not what Conrad the man thought about women, but Conrad's artistic insight into the way in which gender divisions enter into the duplicities of imperialism. I have suggested that the African woman and Kurtz's Intended can be seen as classic examples of female stereotypes: passive virgin and knowing, active woman. The novella suggests that imperialism was able to inherit these stereotypical female roles and to put them to work for itself, a work that in turn further intensified the domestic oppression of the female sex. (If we wanted an illustration of the distance that separates Conrad from Dickens, his debt to the earlier novelist notwithstanding, we could point to the way in which these familiar female stereotypes are held up to more rigorous criticism in *Heart of Darkness* than ever they are in any of Dickens's works.) And one of the reasons why Conrad's engagement with male-female relationships is so much more satisfactory in *Heart of Darkness* than it is in *Chance* is that in the former work such relationships are seen in a very precisely drawn determining context.

In Conrad's manuscript of *Heart of Darkness*, in the passage in which Marlow says that women must be helped to stay in that beautiful world of theirs, lest ours gets worse, the following words follow the words 'ours gets worse':

> 'That's a monster-truth with many maws to whom we've got to throw every year—or every day—no matter—no sacrifice is too great—a ransom of pretty, shining lies—not very new perhaps—but spotless, aureoled, tender.'[6]

These words make Marlow's position seem far more vulnerable and morally unsound, and they suggest that Marlow's propensity to set up gods or idols to whom ransoms of pretty, shining lies (pretty fictions?) can be paid, and for whom 'no sacrifice is too great', is one which unites him morally with Kurtz. Marlow's choice of the nightmare of Kurtz would thus be seen as a choice of idealism rather than trade or imperialism, but an idealism which is guilty of com-

---

5. And not all men, of course, but those men who needed an idealistic gloss on what they were doing out in the world: not black men, nor white working-class men.
6. Quoted from Conrad's manuscript in Joseph Conrad, *Heart of Darkness* [see the Textual Appendix in this Norton Critical Edition, p. 92].

plicity in imperialism's wrongdoings, an idealism which Marlow should recognize not just as powerless but also as corrupt, which Kurtz himself does in his final outburst.

DAPHNA ERDINAST-VULCAN

The Failure of Metaphysics†

The search for the ultimate foundation is as much an unremovable part of human culture as is the denial of the legitimacy of this search. (L. Kolakowski, *Metaphysical Horror*)

* * *

The quest for the word of authority, the pilgrimage undertaken by Conrad's protagonists, ends in silence. But in the absence of a transcendental, sovereign Word, there emerges the word of the other, and the concept of answerability and responsibility. The response to the other, the perception of the other as a self-other, entails an acceptance of responsibility for him or her as well as for one's own other-created self.

Assuming full and unconditional responsibility for a rejected 'other' who becomes a 'twin', a 'secret sharer' or a 'double'—Kurtz for Marlow, Haldin for Razumov, and the dead mad captain for the narrator of *The Shadow-Line*—Conrad's protagonists deny the modern predicament, the essential alienation of man from man, man from nature, and word from world. Cain, the forefather who sentenced his progeny to exile, had denied the metaphysical-ethical imperative in asking, 'Am I my brother's keeper?' The archetypal denial turns into an affirmation as Conrad's protagonists implicitly declare: 'I am'.

* * *

The failure of metaphysics is nowhere more evident than in *Heart of Darkness*, a novella which hinges on the tension between the strong religious overtones in Marlow's narration and the explicit denial of the metaphysical which his story carries. Marlow himself refuses to explore the question of his initial motive for the journey, dismissing it as a 'notion', an inexplicable urge to get to the heart of Africa. This notion is clearly not an idealized conception of the appointed task which sets Marlow going, for there can be no doubt that he sees through the rhetoric of imperialism even before his discovery of the actual atrocities committed in the name of progress and enlightenment. When the 'excellent aunt' talks of his

† From *Joseph Conrad and the Modern Temper* (Oxford: Clarendon P, 1991), pp. 86, 91–96, 97–98, 99–101, 107–8. Reprinted with the permission of Oxford University Press. Notes are the author's.

role as 'an emissary of light, a lower sort of apostle' or of 'weaning those ignorant millions from their horrid ways' he becomes acutely 'uncomfortable' and reminds her 'that the Company was run for profit', dissociating himself from all that 'rot' and 'humbug' of good intentions which the other so readily accepts (12). Marlow, then, is clearly not an emissary for the 'cause of Progress' even at the outset of his journey, and the theory of his idealistic 'benign' form of imperialism should clearly be ruled out.

However whimsically he chooses to present his venture into the heart of darkness, Marlow's description of his state of mind before setting out on his journey points to a vague but pressing state of *ennui*, a spiritual coma: the city is 'a whited sepulchre', shrouded in 'a dead silence' with 'grass sprouting between the stones' (10), the coast is 'featureless . . . with an aspect of monotonous grimness' (13), and Marlow himself is submerged, even at the beginning of his journey, in a state of numb despair: 'the idleness of a passenger, my isolation among all these men with whom I had no point of contact, the oily and languid sea, the uniform sombreness of the coast, seemed to keep me away from the truth of things, within the toil of a mournful and senseless delusion' (13).

This state of *ennui* and the need to break away from a debilitating stasis and to get at 'the truth of things' are, I believe, fundamentally related to the intellectual unease of the *fin de siècle*, and the cultural pessimism that generated the notion of the decline of the West. Marlow sets out on a journey in search of that lost vitality, the essential wholeness man has lost in the course of his material progress, the distinctly human godlike stature the late Victorians were not certain about any more. Defined in the terms of the present discussion, Marlow's quest is an attempt to reintegrate the 'symbolic' and the 'real,' the sacred and the profane.

Marlow himself may not be fully aware of his motives, but for all his self-deprecating bluffness, he does seem to attach a definite personal significance to his voyage. There is a strong sense of urgency and intense anticipation in his account: 'I . . . could not shake off the idea. . . . The snake had charmed me. . . . I felt somehow I must get there by hook or by crook. . . . Well, you see, the notion drove me' (8). 'I felt as though, instead of going to the centre of a continent, I were about to set off for the centre of the earth' (13).

Marlow's description of his destination is couched in religious terminology which suggests the spiritual nature of his quest. The 'biggest, most blank' space on the map which had so fascinated him when he was 'a little chap', had 'ceased to be a blank space of delightful mystery—a white patch for a boy to dream gloriously over. It had become a place of darkness' (8). The literal meaning of the change is, of course, the on-going European exploration and appropriation of the dark continent, but the very same words might as well have related to the loss of the child's innate and ready faith in a transcendental *locus*, and the onset of the adult's inability to 'see' anything in that space. All that remains of the Eden of childhood is the serpent, 'an immense snake uncoiled, with its head in the sea . . .' (8). Marlow's quest is an attempt to reinstate the 'blank space' as the explorer's destination.

Conrad's use of religious terminology and biblical allusions in *Heart of Darkness* has been noted by critics and effectively summarized by Joan E. Steiner.[1] The allusions to the 'whited sepulchre', the 'apostles', the 'pilgrims' who carry their staves, and the indictment of blindness, hypocrisy, and greed, are used against the colonizing Europeans in an obvious ironic sense. As we shall see, however, Marlow, too, is implicated in the conception of the journey as a pilgrimage, and the irony which is initially directed against the 'false apostles' and the 'faithless pilgrims', ultimately recoils on him.

Marlow's journey is initially presented as a pilgrimage, an escape from the mundane into another dimension of existence. It is a quest which entails the assumption that there exists a metaphysical object, a *locus* of worship to which the pilgrim directs himself. One cannot, however, appreciate the full significance of the journey without taking account of the persistent dissonance between its initial religious context and the unravelling of the metaphysical fabric throughout the text. The dark overtones of religiosity that characterize Marlow's initial account are persistently subverted by a rival discourse, a note of scepticism and despair, and an explicit rejection of the very concept of the pilgrimage. Marlow's pejorative use of the term 'pilgrims' by which he designates the other passengers and the colonialists living in the Congo invalidates his own underlying motivation. One might argue that he refers to the others who idolize the ivory as 'faithless pilgrims' (23), thus implying that he is the only true (i.e. faithful) pilgrim on board. But the incongruous blend of the 'notion' which drives him on a metaphysical quest and the awareness of the cruel farce which is the reality of the journey, the 'merry dance of death and trade' (14) in which he takes part, will remain with Marlow throughout his quest.

In defining Marlow's journey as a pilgrimage, I have so far related only to his state of mind, which is similar to that of a pilgrim, a man in quest of spiritual salvation. But a pilgrimage should rightly be defined by its destination or object as well, and it is at this point that the reader comes up against the elusive, troubling quality of this work, as the object of Marlow's pilgrimage is systematically veiled

1. "Modern Pharisees and False Apostles: Ironic New Testament Parallels in Conrad's 'Heart of Darkness,'" *Nineteenth-Century Fiction* 37.1 (1982):75–96.

under a mist of adjectives. The glitter of the sea is 'blurred by a creeping mist' (13), Marlow feels cut off from 'the world of straightforward facts' (14), as he travels through 'places with farcical names' along a 'formless coast', in a 'weary pilgrimage amongst hints for nightmares' (14). The reader who expects this 'mistiness' to clear as Marlow progresses towards the heart of darkness, and towards the 'revelation' implicitly promised in the concept of the pilgrimage, is faced with a thickening fog in which concrete noun-objects seem to be swallowed by vague and portentous qualifications. The 'merry dance of death and trade' goes on and gathers further momentum, the people become more grotesque and even less comprehensible, and the natural surroundings present a hostile, inscrutable front, in a crescendo of adjectives which culminates in the notorious 'implacable force brooding over an inscrutable intention' (34).

This apparent failure of language, here and elsewhere in the novella, had elicited some exasperated comments, such as E. M. Forster's note that Conrad 'is misty in the middle as well as in the edges, . . . the secret casket of his genius contains a vapour rather than a jewel',[2] and F. R. Leavis's disapproval of Conrad's 'adjectival insistence', and of his attempt "to impose on his readers and on himself . . . a "significance" that is merely an emotional insistence on the presence of what he can't produce'. Leavis concludes that 'the insistence betrays the absence, the willed "intensity", the nullity. He [Conrad] is intent on making a virtue out of not knowing what he means'.[3]

A more recent critical response to that adjectival insistence and mistiness of the narrative regards it as a problematization of the relationship between language and reality, the awareness of language as a factor which constructs—rather than refers to—reality. Ian Watt relates the persistent use of mist or haze imagery to an 'impressionistic' quality in Conrad's work, 'the tendency to focus attention on individual sensation as the only reliable source of ascertainable truth'. This 'epistemological solipsism', which is predominant in the cultural atmosphere of the nineties, is evident in *Heart of Darkness* in its acceptance, as asserted by its very form, of the 'bounded and ambiguous nature of individual understanding' and 'the basis of its narrative method as subjective moral impressionism'. Watt concludes that 'Marlow's emphasis on the difficulty of understanding and communicating his own individual experience aligns *Heart of Darkness* with the subjective relativism of the impressionist attitude'.[4]

2. "Joseph Conrad: A Note," in *Abinger Harvest* (1936; Harmondsworth: Penguin, 1967), pp. 134–5 [see the selection in this Norton Critical Edition].
3. *The Great Tradition* (1948; rpt. London: Chatto & Windus, 1979), p. 180.
4. *Conrad in the Nineteenth Century* (Berkeley: U of California P, 1979), pp. 169, 171, 172–4, 179 [see the selection in this Norton Critical Edition].

My own feeling is that, while the epistemological issues are un-doubtedly present in *Heart of Darkness* and form an integral part of its modernist outlook, they too—like the political and ethical issues of imperialism—are only another dimension of the larger, metaphys-ical theme. I believe that the dialogic dynamics of the novella, the tension between a metaphysical discourse and a hostile, sceptical, anti-metaphysical discourse, operate on the stylistic level as well. Leavis, then, was essentially right in his diagnosis, if not in his dis-approval: the promise of an ultimate significance, of illumination at the heart of darkness (implicit in the metaphysical discourse which sets Marlow's voyage in the context of a pilgrimage), is voided by the conspicuous absence of the object which would carry the meaning. It is belied and subverted by the impressionistic quality which re-flects the utterly subjective, incommunicable, and ultimately unde-cipherable nature of reality. Marlow's language—the adjectives which blur rather than define, the scarcity of concrete noun-objects, and his frequent avowals of the inadequacy of words—is sympto-matic of his predicament. His journey is a metaphysical quest which has no object to project itself onto: the spiritual drive, the 'notion', is there, but the once-blank space on the map, the ultimate destina-tion and object, has now dissolved into the heart of darkness.

* * *

Marlow's pilgrimage, his need to get at the 'ultimate foundation', is perceived as a return to a primary state of wholeness:

> Going up the river was like travelling back to the earliest be-ginnings of the world, when vegetation rioted on the earth. . . . An empty stream, a great silence, an impenetrable forest. . . . There were moments when one's past came back to one . . . but it came in the shape of an unrestful and noisy dream, remem-bered with wonder amongst the overwhelming realities of this strange world of plants, and water, and silence . . . It was the stillness of an implacable force brooding over an inscrutable intention. (33–34)

This description, so blatantly and insistently 'adjectival', harks back to a primordial scene, a Genesis state of undifferentiated vitality, in which Marlow hopes to find his Adam.

* * *

But any anticipation of spiritual comfort—which might be cre-ated by the obvious metaphysical overtones in Marlow's account of his attitude to Kurtz, and by the analogies between his journey and other literary models of metaphysical quests[5]—is brutally dispelled

5. See Lillian Feder, "Marlow's Descent into Hell," *Nineteenth-Century Fiction* 9 (March 1955): 280–92; Robert O. Evans, "Conrad's Underworld," *Modern Fiction Studies* 2 (1956): 56–62.

as Marlow realizes, on the very threshold of his encounter with
Kurtz, that he, too, had been a pilgrim in the worship of a false deity, that the Adam he had hoped to find is, in fact, a Cain.

> We were *wanderers on a prehistoric earth*, on an earth that
> wore the aspect of an unknown planet. We could have fancied
> ourselves the first of men taking possession of *an accursed in-*
> *heritance*, to be subdued at the cost of profound anguish and
> of excessive toil. (35, my emphases)

Marlow realizes that Kurtz is, in fact, a paragon of the blind omniv-
orous greed which motivates the others, that the plenitude he had
hoped to encounter is merely the culmination of the hollowness
which is their essence: the manager with 'nothing within him' (22),
the 'papier-mâché Mephistopheles' who seems to have 'nothing inside him but a little loose dirt' (26), lead up to Kurtz, the superior
agent of the company who is 'hollow at the core' (58). His only distinction is in the intensity and energy with which he had conducted
his business, his 'efficiency', indeed.

Marlow's eventual and explicit condemnation of Kurtz is not only
a moral condemnation of a fellow human being whose lapse into
savagery is a hard blow to Marlow's preconceptions. It is also the
dethroning of a sham idol. Kurtz has attained a deific stature in the
course of Marlow's journey, and his initial exposure carries a reverberating metaphysical significance: 'many powers of darkness
claimed him for their own . . . He had taken a high seat amongst
the devils of the land' (48–49); 'He had the power to charm or
frighten rudimentary souls into an aggravated witch-dance in his
honour' (50).

But the grandeur which seems to be conferred on Kurtz by the
sheer magnitude of his moral degeneration is later deflated as the
metaphysical aura is stripped off, and the Satanic fascination wears
thin. Having met the pathetic, shabby disciple of this sham Satan,
Marlow protests that 'Mr Kurtz was no idol of mine' (58); he now
sees Kurtz as 'an atrocious phantom' (59), a 'pitiful Jupiter' (59); he
realizes that Kurtz's exalted discourse, the voice towards which he
had made his pilgrimage, is 'an immense jabber, silly, atrocious, sordid, savage, or simply mean, without any kind of sense' (48). Marlow's admission that he 'had been robbed of a belief' (47), is not
only a verdict on the civilization of which Kurtz has been the
paragon and the torch-carrier, but also a renunciation of the quest
for a metaphysical source of epistemological and ethical authority.

* * *

Both Kurtz, a quasi-mythical protagonist, and Marlow, the narrator, are perceived as 'voices'. Marlow's anticipation of his meeting
with Kurtz is auditory rather than visual:

I had never imagined him as doing, you know, but as discoursing. . . . The man presented himself as a voice. . . . The point
was in his being a gifted creature, that of all his gifts the one
that stood out preeminently, that carried with it the seal of real
presence, was his ability to talk, his words—the gift of expression, the bewildering, the illuminating, the most exalted and
the most contemptible, the pulsating stream of light, or the deceitful flow from the heart of an impenetrable darkness. (47,
see also 48)

But Marlow, too, is perceived as 'a voice' by the frame narrator: 'For
a long time already [Marlow], sitting apart, had been no more than
a voice. . . . I listened, I listened on the watch for the sentence, for
the word, that would give me the clue . . .' (27).

The difference between these voices is significant: whereas the
Kurtzian voice initially holds the promise of illumination and enlightenment, Marlow professes: 'there was nothing behind me' (28).
He subverts the illusion of authority which is associated with the
teller's voice, and pre-empts the notion of 'a clue' which the frame
narrator anticipates of him, just as he had anticipated the darkness
to be illuminated by Kurtz's voice. The metaphysical vacuum, the
denial of a transcendental authority or 'voice', sets the scene for a
modified view of the artist: no longer a mythical being, an omnipo-
tent creator of a world, he is now seen in the Orphic role, as a hero
who descends into hell, armed with a voice to enchant the furies
for a while, and returns empty-handed to tell his tale.

Marlow's affirmation, 'mine is the speech that cannot be silenced' (36), is a pledge of commitment both to the role of the narrator and to the essential sameness which turns the other into a
'twin', or a 'double'. He has, in fact, assimilated Kurtz's Voice and
Word, but this assimilation is radically different from that of a pilgrim: for Kurtz's voice is no longer the voice of authority, impreg-
nable and immutable, and Marlow is not a ventriloquist. He has
taken on the voice of the other to redeem it through his own.

EDWARD W. SAID

Two Visions in *Heart of Darkness*†

Domination and inequities of power and wealth are perennial facts
of human society. But in today's global setting they are also inter-
pretable as having something to do with imperialism, its history, its
new forms. The nations of contemporary Asia, Latin America, and
Africa are politically independent but in many ways are as dominated and dependent as they were when ruled directly by European
powers. On the one hand, this is the consequence of self-inflicted
wounds, critics like V. S. Naipaul are wont to say: *they* (everyone
knows that "they" means coloreds, wogs, niggers) are to blame for
what "they" are, and it's no use droning on about the legacy of imperialism. On the other hand, blaming the Europeans sweepingly
for the misfortunes of the present is not much of an alternative.
What we need to do is to look at these matters as a network of in-
terdependent histories that it would be inaccurate and senseless to
repress, useful and interesting to understand.

* * *

[I]n the late twentieth century the imperial cycle of the last century in some way replicates itself, although today there are really no
big empty spaces, no expanding frontiers, no exciting new settlements to establish. We live in one global environment with a huge
number of ecological, economic, social, and political pressures
tearing at its only dimly perceived, basically uninterpreted and un-
comprehended fabric. Anyone with even a vague consciousness of
this whole is alarmed at how such remorselessly selfish and narrow
interests—patriotism, chauvinism, ethnic, religious, and racial ha-
treds—can in fact lead to mass destructiveness. The world simply
cannot afford this many more times.

One should not pretend that models for a harmonious world order are ready at hand, and it would be equally disingenuous to suppose that ideas of peace and community have much of a chance
when power is moved to action by aggressive perceptions of "vital
national interests" or unlimited sovereignty. The United States'
clash with Iraq and Iraq's aggression against Kuwait concerning oil
are obvious examples. The wonder of it is that the schooling for
such relatively provincial thought and action is still prevalent,
unchecked, uncritically accepted, recurringly replicated in the education of generation after generation. We are all taught to venerate

† From *Culture and Imperialism* (New York: Knopf, 1993), pp. 19–20, 22–26, 28–31.
Used by permission of Alfred A. Knopf, a division of Random House, Inc. Unless indicated, notes are the author's.

our nations and admire our traditions: we are taught to pursue their interests with toughness and in disregard for other societies. A new and in my opinion appalling tribalism is fracturing societies, separating peoples, promoting greed, bloody conflict, and uninteresting assertions of minor ethnic or group particularity. Little time is spent not so much in "learning about other cultures"—the phrase has an inane vagueness to it—but in studying the map of interactions, the actual and often productive traffic occurring on a day-by-day, and even minute-by-minute basis among states, societies, groups, identities.

No one can hold this entire map in his or her head, which is why the geography of empire and the many-sided imperial experience that created its fundamental texture should be considered first in terms of a few salient configurations. Primarily, as we look back at the nineteenth century, we see that the drive toward empire in effect brought most of the earth under the domination of a handful of powers. To get hold of part of what this means, I propose to look at a specific set of rich cultural documents in which the interaction between Europe or America on the one hand and the imperialized world on the other is animated, informed, made explicit as an experience for both sides of the encounter. * * *

* * *

This imperial attitude is, I believe, beautifully captured in the complicated and rich narrative form of Conrad's great novella *Heart of Darkness*, written between 1898 and 1899. On the one hand, the narrator Marlow acknowledges the tragic predicament of all speech—that "it is impossible to convey the life-sensation of any given epoch of one's existence—that which makes its truth, its meaning—its subtle and penetrating essence. . . . We live, as we dream—alone" (27)—yet still manages to convey the enormous power of Kurtz's African experience through his own overmastering narrative of his voyage into the African interior toward Kurtz. This narrative in turn is connected directly with the redemptive force, as well as the waste and horror, of Europe's mission in the dark world. Whatever is lost or elided or even simply made up in Marlow's immensely compelling recitation is compensated for in the narrative's sheer historical momentum, the temporal forward movement—with digressions, descriptions, exciting encounters, and all. Within the narrative of how he journeyed to Kurtz's Inner Station, whose source and authority he now becomes, Marlow moves backward and forward materially in small and large spirals, very much the way episodes in the course of his journey up-river are then incorporated by the principal forward trajectory into what he renders as "the heart of Africa."

Thus Marlow's encounter with the improbably white-suited

clerk in the middle of the jungle furnishes him with several digres-
sive paragraphs, as does his meeting later with the semi-crazed,
harlequin-like Russian who has been so affected by Kurtz's gifts. Yet
underlying Marlow's inconclusiveness, his evasions, his arabesque
meditations on his feelings and ideas, is the unrelenting course of
the journey itself, which, despite all the many obstacles, is sustained through the jungle, through time, through hardship, to the
heart of it all, Kurtz's ivory-trading empire. Conrad wants us to see
how Kurtz's great looting adventure, Marlow's journey up the river,
and the narrative itself all share a common theme: Europeans performing acts of imperial mastery and will in (or about) Africa.

What makes Conrad different from the other colonial writers
who were his contemporaries is that, for reasons having partly to do
with the colonialism that turned him, a Polish expatriate, into an
employee of the imperial system, he was so self-conscious about
what he did. Like most of his other tales, therefore, *Heart of Darkness* cannot just be a straightforward recital of Marlow's adventures: it is also a dramatization of Marlow himself, the former
wanderer in colonial regions, telling his story to a group of British
listeners at a particular time and in a specific place. That this group
of people is drawn largely from the business world is Conrad's way
of emphasizing the fact that during the 1890s the business of empire, once an adventurous and often individualistic enterprise, had
become the empire of business. (Coincidentally we should note
that at about the same time Halford Mackinder, an explorer, geographer, and Liberal Imperialist, gave a series of lectures on imperialism at the London Institute of Bankers:[1] perhaps Conrad knew
about this.) Although the almost oppressive force of Marlow's narrative leaves us with a quite accurate sense that there is no way out
of the sovereign historical force of imperialism, and that it has the
power of a system representing as well as speaking for everything
within its dominion, Conrad shows us that what Marlow does is
contingent, acted out for a set of like-minded British hearers, and
limited to that situation.

Yet neither Conrad nor Marlow gives us a full view of what is *outside* the world-conquering attitudes embodied by Kurtz, Marlow,
the circle of listeners on the deck of the *Nellie*, and Conrad. By
that I mean that *Heart of Darkness* works so effectively because its
politics and aesthetics are, so to speak, imperialist, which in the
closing years of the nineteenth century seemed to be at the same
time an aesthetic, politics, and even epistemology inevitable and

1. For Mackinder, see Neil Smith, *Uneven Development: Nature, Capital and the Production of Space* (Oxford: Blackwell, 1984), pp. 102–3. Conrad and triumphalist geography
are at the heart of Felix Driver, "Geography's Empire: Histories of Geographical Knowledge," *Society and Space*, 1991.

unavoidable. For if we cannot truly understand someone else's experience and if we must therefore depend upon the assertive authority of the sort of power that Kurtz wields as a white man in the jungle or that Marlow, another white man, wields as narrator, there is no use looking for other, non-imperialist alternatives; the system has simply eliminated them and made them unthinkable. The circularity, the perfect closure of the whole thing is not only aesthetically but also mentally unassailable.

Conrad is so self-conscious about situating Marlow's tale in a narrative moment that he allows us simultaneously to realize after all that imperialism, far from swallowing up its own history, was taking place in and was circumscribed by a larger history, one just outside the tightly inclusive circle of Europeans on the deck of the *Nellie*. As yet, however, no one seemed to inhabit that region, and so Conrad left it empty.

Conrad could probably never have used Marlow to present anything other than an imperialist world-view, given what was available for either Conrad or Marlow to see of the non-European at the time. Independence was for whites and Europeans; the lesser or subject peoples were to be ruled; science, learning, history emanated from the West. True, Conrad scrupulously recorded the differences between the disgraces of Belgian and British colonial attitudes, but he could only imagine the world carved up into one or another Western sphere of dominion. But because Conrad also had an extraordinarily persistent residual sense of his own exilic marginality, he quite carefully (some would say maddeningly) qualified Marlow's narrative with the provisionality that came from standing at the very juncture of this world with another, unspecified but different. Conrad was certainly not a great imperialist entrepreneur like Cecil Rhodes or Frederick Lugard, even though he understood perfectly how for each of them, in Hannah Arendt's words, to enter "the maelstrom of an unending process of expansion, he will, as it were, cease to be what he was and obey the laws of the process, identify himself with anonymous forces that he is supposed to serve in order to keep the whole process in motion, he will think of himself as mere function, and eventually consider such functionality, such an incarnation of the dynamic trend, his highest possible achievement."[2] Conrad's realization is that if, like narrative, imperialism has monopolized the entire system of representation—which in the case of *Heart of Darkness* allowed it to speak for Africans as well as for Kurtz and the other adventurers, including Marlow and his audience—your self-consciousness as an

---

2. Hannah Arendt, *The Origins of Totalitarianism* (1951; new ed. New York: Harcourt Brace Jovanovich, 1973), p. 215. Also see Fredric Jameson, *The Political Unconscious: Narrative as a Socially Symbolic Act* (Ithaca: Cornell UP, 1981), pp. 206–81.

outsider can allow you actively to comprehend how the machine works, given that you and it are fundamentally not in perfect synchrony or correspondence. Never the wholly incorporated and fully acculturated Englishman, Conrad therefore preserved an ironic distance in each of his works.

The form of Conrad's narrative has thus made it possible to derive two possible arguments, two visions, in the post-colonial world that succeeded his. One argument allows the old imperial enterprise full scope to play itself out conventionally, to render the world as official European or Western imperialism saw it, and to consolidate itself after World War Two. Westerners may have physically left their old colonies in Africa and Asia, but they retained them not only as markets but as locales on the ideological map over which they continued to rule morally and intellectually. "Show me the Zulu Tolstoy," as one American intellectual has recently put it.[3] The assertive sovereign inclusiveness of this argument courses through the words of those who speak today for the West and for what the West did, as well as for what the rest of the world is, was, and may be. The assertions of this discourse exclude what has been represented as "lost" by arguing that the colonial world was in some ways ontologically speaking lost to begin with, irredeemable, irrecusably inferior. Moreover, it focusses not on what was shared in the colonial experience, but on what must never be shared, namely the authority and rectitude that come with greater power and development. Rhetorically, its terms are the organization of political passions, to borrow from Julien Benda's critique of modern intellectuals, terms which, he was sensible enough to know, lead inevitably to mass slaughter, and if not to literal mass slaughter then certainly to rhetorical slaughter.

The second argument is considerably less objectionable. It sees itself as Conrad saw his own narratives, local to a time and place, neither unconditionally true nor unqualifiedly certain. As I have said, Conrad does not give us the sense that he could imagine a fully realized alternative to imperialism: the natives he wrote about in Africa, Asia, or America were incapable of independence, and because he seemed to imagine that European tutelage was a given, he could not foresee what would take place when it came to an end. But come to an end it would, if only because—like all human effort, like speech itself—it would have its moment, then it would have to pass. Since Conrad *dates* imperialism, shows its contingency, records its illusions and tremendous violence and waste (as in *Nostromo*), he permits his later readers to imagine something other than an Africa carved up into dozens of European colonies,

---

3. Saul Bellow's controversial challenge to advocates of multiculturalism. [Editor]

even if, for his own part, he had little notion of what that Africa
might be.

*   *   *

Let us return to Conrad and to what I have been referring to as
the second, less imperialistically assertive possibility offered by
Heart of Darkness. Recall once again that Conrad sets the story on
the deck of a boat anchored in the Thames; as Marlow tells his
story the sun sets, and by the end of the narrative the heart of darkness has reappeared in England; outside the group of Marlow's listeners lies an undefined and unclear world. Conrad sometimes
seems to want to fold that world into the imperial metropolitan discourse represented by Marlow, but by virtue of his own dislocated
subjectivity he resists the effort and succeeds in so doing, I have
always believed, largely through formal devices. Conrad's self-
consciously circular narrative forms draw attention to themselves
as artificial constructions, encouraging us to sense the potential of
a reality that seemed inaccessible to imperialism, just beyond its
control, and that only well after Conrad's death in 1924 acquired a
substantial presence.

This needs more explanation. Despite their European names and
mannerisms, Conrad's narrators are not average unreflecting witnesses of European imperialism. They do not simply accept what
goes on in the name of the imperial idea: they think about it a lot,
they worry about it, they are actually quite anxious about whether
they can make it seem like a routine thing. But it never is. Conrad's
way of demonstrating this discrepancy between the orthodox and
his own views of empire is to keep drawing attention to how ideas
and values are constructed (and deconstructed) through dislocations in the narrator's language. In addition, the recitations are
meticulously staged: the narrator is a speaker whose audience and
the reason for their being together, the quality of whose voice, the
effect of what he says—are all important and even insistent aspects
of the story he tells. Marlow, for example, is never straightforward.
He alternates between garrulity and stunning eloquence, and rarely
resists making peculiar things seem more peculiar by surprisingly
misstating them, or rendering them vague and contradictory. Thus,
he says, a French warship fires "into a continent"; Kurtz's eloquence is enlightening as well as fraudulent; and so on—his speech
so full of these odd discrepancies (well discussed by Ian Watt as
"delayed decoding"[4]) that the net effect is to leave his immediate
audience as well as the reader with the acute sense that what he is
presenting is not quite as it should be or appears to be.

---

4. Ian Watt, *Conrad in the Nineteenth Century* (Berkeley: U of California P, 1979), pp.
175–79 [see the selection in this Norton Critical Edition].

Yet the whole point of what Kurtz and Marlow talk about is in fact imperial mastery, white European *over* black Africans, and their ivory, civilization *over* the primitive dark continent. By accentuating the discrepancy between the official "idea" of empire and the remarkably disorienting actuality of Africa, Marlow unsettles the reader's sense not only of the very idea of empire, but of something more basic, reality itself. For if Conrad can show that all human activity depends on controlling a radically unstable reality to which words approximate only by will or convention, the same is true of empire, of venerating the idea, and so forth. With Conrad, then, we are in a world being made and unmade more or less all the time. What appears stable and secure—the policeman at the corner, for instance—is only slightly more secure than the white men in the jungle, and requires the same continuous (but precarious) triumph over an all-pervading darkness, which by the end of the tale is shown to be the same in London and in Africa.

Conrad's genius allowed him to realize that the ever-present darkness could be colonized or illuminated—*Heart of Darkness* is full of references to the *mission civilisatrice*, to benevolent as well as cruel schemes to bring light to the dark places and peoples of this world by acts of will and deployments of power—but that it also had to be acknowledged as independent. Kurtz and Marlow acknowledge the darkness, the former as he is dying, the latter as he reflects retrospectively on the meaning of Kurtz's final words. They (and of course Conrad) are ahead of their time in understanding that what they call "the darkness" has an autonomy of its own, and can reinvade and reclaim what imperialism had taken for *its* own. But Marlow and Kurtz are also creatures of their time and cannot take the next step, which would be to recognize that what they saw, disablingly and disparagingly, as a non-European "darkness" was in fact a non-European world *resisting* imperialism so as one day to regain sovereignty and independence, and not, as Conrad reductively says, to reestablish the darkness. Conrad's tragic limitation is that even though he could see clearly that on one level imperialism was essentially pure dominance and land-grabbing, he could not then conclude that imperialism had to end so that "natives" could lead lives free from European domination. As a creature of his time, Conrad could not grant the natives their freedom, despite his severe critique of the imperialism that enslaved them.

The cultural and ideological evidence that Conrad was wrong in his Eurocentric way is both impressive and rich. A whole movement, literature, and theory of resistance and response to empire exists, * * * and in greatly disparate post-colonial regions one sees tremendously energetic efforts to engage with the metropolitan world in equal debate so as to testify to the diversity and differences of the non-European world and to its own agendas, priorities, and history. The purpose of this testimony is to inscribe, reinterpret, and expand the areas of engagement as well as the terrain contested with Europe. Some of this activity—for example, the work of two important and active Iranian intellectuals, Ali Shariati and Jalal Ali i-Ahmed, who by means of speeches, books, tapes, and pamphlets prepared the way for the Islamic Revolution—interprets colonialism by asserting the absolute opposition of the native culture: the West is an enemy, a disease, an evil. In other instances, novelists like the Kenyan Ngugi and the Sudanese Tayeb Salih appropriate for their fiction such great *topoi* of colonial culture as the quest and the voyage into the unknown, claiming them for their own, post-colonial purposes. Salih's hero in *Season of Migration to the North* does (and is) the reverse of what Kurtz does (and is): the Black man journeys north into white territory.

Between classical nineteenth-century imperialism and what it gave rise to in resistant native cultures, there is thus both a stubborn confrontation and a crossing over in discussion, borrowing back and forth, debate. Many of the most interesting post-colonial writers bear their past within them—as scars of humiliating wounds, as instigation for different practices, as potentially revised visions of the past tending toward a new future, as urgently reinterpretable and redeployable experiences, in which the formerly silent native speaks and acts on territory taken back from the empire. One sees these aspects in Rushdie, Derek Walcott, Aimé Césaire, Chinua Achebe, Pablo Neruda, and Brian Friel. And now these writers can truly read the great colonial masterpieces, which not only misrepresented them but assumed they were unable to read and respond directly to what had been written about them, just as European ethnography presumed the natives' incapacity to intervene in scientific discourse about them. * * *

PAUL B. ARMSTRONG

[Reading, Race, and Representing Others]†

Chinua Achebe's well-known, controversial claim that the depiction of the peoples of the Congo in *Heart of Darkness* is racist and xenophobic stands in striking contrast to James Clifford's praise of Conrad as an exemplary anthropologist. Where Achebe finds prejudice

† From "*Heart of Darkness* and the Epistemology of Cultural Differences" in *Under Postcolonial Eyes: Joseph Conrad After Empire*, ed. Gail Fincham and Myrtle Hooper (Rondebosch: U of Cape Town P, 1996), pp. 21–35, 37–39. Reprinted with the permission of Juta Academic Publishers.

and dismissive reification in the representations of the Other offered by *Heart of Darkness*, Clifford sees in the text a heteroglossic rendering of cultural differences without any attempt to synthesize them. "Joseph Conrad was a bloody racist", Achebe claims, and *Heart of Darkness* is "a story in which the very humanity of black people is called in question"—"a book which parades in the most vulgar fashion prejudices and insults from which a section of mankind has suffered untold agonies and atrocities".[1] By contrast, Clifford holds up the novella as an epistemological model for ethnographers because it "truthfully juxtaposes different truths" and "does not permit a feeling of centeredness, coherent dialogue, or authentic communion" which would give the misleading impression that understanding another culture can be accomplished once and for all: "Anthropology is still waiting for its Conrad".[2] It is curious, to say the least, that the same text can be viewed as an exemplar both of epistemological evil and of virtue—as a model of the worst abuses and the most promising practices in representing other peoples and cultures.

This conflict is only the latest chapter in a long history of disagreement about whether to regard *Heart of Darkness* as a daring attack on imperialism or a reactionary purveyor of colonial stereotypes. The novella has received such divergent responses, I think, because its enactment of the dilemmas entailed in understanding cultural otherness is inherently double and strategically ambiguous. Achebe wrongly assumes that *Heart of Darkness* offers a finished representation of the colonial Other to the metropolitan reader. Instead, the text dramatizes the impossibility of capturing the Other in writing, whether univocal or polysemic, for the very reason that understanding otherness requires an ongoing reciprocity between knower and known through which each comments on, corrects, and replies to the other's representations in a never-ending shifting of positions. Achebe is right to fault the text, however, because it dramatizes a pervasive state of cultural solipsism which it does not itself overcome, and it consequently abounds in representations of the Other which are one-sided and prejudicial. In yet another turn, though, Achebe's very act of writing back to Conrad is already anticipated by the text. Clifford is right that Conrad offers key guidance to anthropological knowing—not, however, because his novel is an ideal ethnography, but because its textual strategies aim to educate the reader about processes which might make possible a dialogue with the Other which is absent from Marlow's monologue.

1. Chinua Achebe, "An Image of Africa," *The Massachusetts Review* 18 (1977): 788, 790; see the selection in this Norton Critical Edition.
2. James Clifford, *The Predicament of Culture: Twentieth-Century Ethnography, Literature, and Art* (Cambridge: Harvard UP, 1988), pp. 92, 102, 96.

Conrad is neither a racist nor an exemplary anthropologist but a skeptical dramatist of epistemological processes. *Heart of Darkness* is a calculated failure to depict achieved cross-cultural understanding. The implication of this failure for the reader is deliberately unclear because Conrad is not certain that hermeneutic education or social change can overcome the solipsism dividing individuals and cultures, even as he is reluctant to give up hope that they might. Truly reciprocal, dialogical understanding of the Other is the unrealized horizon which this text points to but does not reach. *Heart of Darkness* strategically refuses to specify whether this horizon is attainable or will forever recede as we approach it. This ambiguity is an expression of Conrad's unresolved epistemological doubleness—his will-to-believe that our essential solipsism can be overcome coupled with his deep skepticism that (in Marlow's words) "We live, as we dream—alone" (27). Because Conrad cannot resolve this doubleness into a univocal attitude, he stages it for the reader through textual strategies which oscillate between affirming and denying the possibility of understanding otherness.

Heart of Darkness represents dialogical understanding as an unfilled void, an empty set, a lack signified by the dire consequences it leads to. It is important to note how little contact—and even less conversation—Marlow has with Africans. He himself observes early on that "Watching a coast as it slips by the ship is like thinking about an enigma. There it is before you—smiling, frowning, inviting, grand, mean, insipid, or savage, and always mute with an air of whispering—Come and find out" (13). That is his posture for most of the story—observing at a distance people and phenomena with which he has little or no reciprocal engagement and which consequently seem bewildering and mysterious, even frightening or disgusting ("the incomprehensible . . . is also detestable. And it has a fascination too, . . . the fascination of the abomination" (6)). What all of these emotions share is the one-sidedness of their response to alterity, an absence of to-and-fro engagement with it. This lack of reciprocity manifests itself as curiosity, desire, fear, wonder, loathing, or frustration—all one-way attitudes which do not reduce the Other's distance but only confirm and compound its status as alien, whether marvelous or terrible. "We were cut off from the comprehension of our surroundings," Marlow notes as he travels up the river; "we glided past like phantoms, wondering and secretly appalled, as sane men would be before an enthusiastic outbreak in a madhouse" (35). This analogy is apt inasmuch as madness both fascinates and terrifies sanity because it recognizes a kinship which it refuses to accept and explore by making madness an interlocutor.

Marlow explicitly criticizes the blindness and will-to-power of nonreciprocal approaches to alterity—for example: the scientist

who oddly measures only the outside of the skulls of those travelling to Africa, and only on their way out, or the French man-of-war
which shells invisible "enemies" in the forest. The absurd one-
sidedness of these engagements with the unknown suggests that
Marlow would endorse Achebe's complaint that "Travellers with
closed minds can tell us little except about themselves" (791). Marlow indicts the closed-mindedness of non-dialogical encounters
with otherness but then duplicates it, replicating the solipsism he
exposes and laments. Marlow remains for the most part an observer
who does not communicate with the objects of his observation.
Marlow's contacts with Africans are sufficient to reveal his self-
enclosure and to educate him about the dangers of nonreciprocal
impositions of power and knowledge, but insufficient to remove the
alienness of alterity through dialogue, so that he remains a tourist
who sees the passing landscape through a window which separates
him from it, and he consequently commits the crimes of touristic
misappropriation of otherness even as he is aware of and points out
the limitations of that position.

This doubleness is evident in Marlow's complaints about the injustice of naming the Other without allowing revision or response.
After seeing a chain-gang of imprisoned Africans, Marlow remarks:

> these men could by no stretch of the imagination be called en-
> emies. They were called criminals and the outraged law like
> the bursting shells [of the man-of-war] had come to them, an
> insoluble mystery from the sea. All their meagre breasts panted
> together, the violently dilated nostrils quivered, the eyes stared
> stonily uphill. They passed me within six inches, without a
> glance, with that complete, deathlike indifference of unhappy
> savages (16).

The will-to-power in the right-to-name is especially visible when
its labels seem anomalous or arbitrary but remain in force by the
sheer power of the authority behind the definition. But Marlow
challenges this authority by invoking a type—the death-in-life of
the "unhappy savage"—which could be (and has been) seen to be
just as much a stereotype as the labels he unmasks.

Part of his dilemma is that he cannot do without names and
types in opposing the mis-labelling he despises. When he comes
upon the grove where the sick and exhausted prisoners are dying,
he thinks: "They were not enemies, they were not criminals, they
were nothing earthly now, nothing but black shadows of disease
and starvation lying confusedly in the greenish gloom" (17). He can
say what they are not, invoking a type and negating it, but when he
tries to specify what they are, he acknowledges their humanity by
reducing them to objects—"black shapes", "moribund shapes",

"black bones" (17)—images with an inanimate quality which may be appropriate to death but which nonetheless make the dying seem anonymous, impersonal, unhuman. These images render the suffering of the Africans but position Marlow outside it, at a distance his compassion can register but cannot cross. When Marlow recognizes one of the dying individually, he comments: "The man seemed young—almost a boy—but you know with them it's hard to tell" (17). This sort of denial of the Other's differences is classic racism. Curiously, though, it echoes an observation Marlow had just made about the African guard of the chain gang for whom "white men [were] so much alike at a distance that he could not tell who I might be" (16). Although he criticizes the blindness of homogenizing the Other by ironically turning the tables on the white imperialists and doing unto them through African eyes what they do to blacks, Marlow then commits the very mistake he has just mocked. Once again Marlow opposes prejudice only to repeat it.

Marlow tries the tactic of ironic counter-labelling, calling the crimes of imperialism "these high and just proceedings", or referring to the guards as "one of the reclaimed, the product of the new forces at work" (16). But the irony is offered to Marlow's audience—and, across them, to the reader—and is not part of a process of negotiation in which the right-to-name is tested and shared among those directly concerned. Marlow's awareness of the power of language to impose perceptions on the Other is not matched by a sense of language as an instrument of reciprocal exchange to mediate conflicting perceptions. Marlow can only counter the right-to-name with strategies of reverse labelling which fight what they oppose by repeating its lack of dialogue. Marlow thus becomes implicated in what he opposes by his very attempts to unmask it.

Marlow takes the first steps toward a dialogical understanding of Africans by recognizing that their mystery and opacity are a sign of their humanity. Africans are a hermeneutic problem for him because he acknowledges that they have a world which he can only construct by reading signs—filling in gaps in the evidence, imagining hidden sides, and engaging in the other kinds of interpretive activity we invoke when we encounter phenomena which we assume are intelligible because they are evidence of other human life. When he tells the story of his predecessor Fresleven's death, for example, Marlow creates from scant evidence a narrative of mutual misunderstanding which tries to reconstruct how the baffling, terrifying, intimidating European must have appeared to African perceptions (see 9). The very mystery of their thought-processes which makes their world an interpretive challenge presents them as fellow human beings whose lives can be made intelligible by fitting them to narrative patterns which might also apply to one's own life. Rea-

PAUL B. ARMSTRONG

soning similarly from the familiar to the unfamiliar, Marlow transforms the emptiness of the abandoned landscape into a sign of human motivation: "Well if a lot of mysterious niggers armed with all kinds of fearful weapons suddenly took to travelling on the road between Deal and Gravesend catching the yokels right and left to carry heavy loads for them, I fancy every farm and cottage thereabouts would get empty very soon" (19–20). If the hermeneutic circle dictates that we can only make sense of something strange by relating it to what we already understand, Marlow's imaginative reconstruction of other worlds based on the assumption of their resemblance to his own suggests how this circle can be transformed from a trap into a resource for extending our worlds.

His interpretive efforts also demonstrate, however, that the hermeneutic circle becomes vicious and self-enclosing unless it is opened up by making the object of interpretation an interlocutor and a fellow-interpreter. Marlow's attempts at recognition finally end in rejection because he does not move from similarity to reciprocity.

> Well, you know that was the worst of it—this suspicion of their not being inhuman. It would come slowly to one. They howled and leaped and spun and made horrid faces, but what thrilled you was just the thought of their humanity—like yours—the thought of your remote kinship with this wild and passionate uproar. Ugly. Yes, it was ugly enough, but if you were man enough you would admit to yourself that there was just the faintest trace of a response to the terrible frankness of that noise, a dim suspicion of there being a meaning in it which you—you so remote from the night of first ages—could comprehend (36).

The hermeneutic pursuit of self-understanding by understanding others is initiated only to be abandoned here as Marlow acknowledges a relationship with the Other only to devalue it by consigning it to the remote past or subterranean moral regions. The unfamiliar necessarily seems "ugly" to the categories and values of the familiar unless the hermeneutic experience becomes not a one-way encounter but a to-and-fro exchange in which the authority of what we know is called into question and its priority over the unknown is reversed.

Benita Parry oversimplifies, however, when she claims that "both Kurtz and Marlow look upon blacks as another genus."[3] Marlow senses a resemblance with the Other here, and that is why he re-

---

3. Benita Parry, *Conrad and Imperialism: Ideological Boundaries and Visionary Frontiers* (London: Macmillan, 1983), p. 34.

acts defensively. If the Other were not somehow the same as he is, its apparent differences would not be so threatening. Marlow feels shame because an unexpected similarity undermines his sense of self, and his resulting anxiety and embarrassment prevent him from regarding a surprising kinship as a sign of the equal dignity and worth of a potential interlocutor. Because he perceives resemblance as a threat to be warded off by relegating it to lesser aspects of his being, he cuts off the possibility of articulating and exploring it and using it as an instrument of mediation.

Marlow's ambivalence dramatizes the sometimes ambiguous double nature of hermeneutic encounters with other cultures. The experience of alterity can be both frightening and invigorating—a threat to the self and an opportunity for self-recognition and self-expansion. Discovering unexpected similarities with radically different ways of being entails a disorienting and perhaps distressing loss of self-understanding—one turns out not to be exactly who one thought one was—even as it opens up new possibilities of self-knowledge, self-creation, and relationship. Marlow's sense of threat and loss paralyzes him, however, and does not allow him to conceive of the destruction of his previous certainties as a prelude to new constructions of himself and his world.

Marlow tacitly acknowledges the equality of the Other's world by recognizing its power to defamiliarize his own conventions and categories. Abdul JanMohamed argues that "genuine and thorough comprehension of Otherness is possible only if the self can somehow negate or at least severely bracket the values, assumptions, and ideology of his culture."[4] The first step toward engaging in dialogue with another culture is to recognize that one's own is riven with contingency and lacks any essential privilege. Africa has this effect on Marlow by exposing the arbitrariness, the unnaturalness, of his customary ways of being and understanding. Although the African rowers he meets early on seem strange to Marlow ("they had faces like grotesque masks"), he nevertheless finds "they were a great comfort to look at" because "they wanted no excuse for being there" (14). Their naturalness exposes the artificiality of European practices which cannot be universally valid if transplantation robs them of authority. Marlow similarly denaturalizes his own customary ways of seeing when he tries to imagine how his cannibal-crew envisions the white passengers: "just then I perceived—in a new light, as it were—how unwholesome the pilgrims looked, and I hoped, yes I positively hoped, that my aspect was not so—what

4. Abdul R. JanMohamed, "The Economy of Manichean Allegory: The Function of Racial Difference in Colonialist Literature," *Critical Inquiry* 12 (1985): 65.

shall I say?—so—unappetising" (41). Seeing the Europeans as
Africans might challenges the self-evidence of the European perspective and opens up new possibilities of perception.[5]

The loneliness of the jungle continues the process of defamiliar-
ization which Marlow's exposure to Africans begins: "utter solitude
without a policeman— . . . utter silence, where no warning voice of
a kind neighbor can be heard whispering of public opinion" (49).
Without the discipline and coercion of conventional authority
(what everyone thinks polices the thinkable), the contingency of a
society's practices becomes available for thought. Marlow later
finds an "irritating pretence" in "the bearing of commonplace individuals going about their business in the assurance of perfect
safety" and calls them "offensive to me like the outrageous flauntings of folly in the face of a danger it is unable to comprehend. I
had some difficulty in restraining myself from laughing in their
faces so full of stupid importance" (71). They do not share Marlow's sense of the groundlessness and relativity of ways of being
which seem simply natural to them but dangerously lack the foundations they assume they have. But this very sense that his world is
not necessary but only one of many possible worlds is the precondi-
tion for anthropological dialogue between cultures which Marlow
would seem to be more ready for than anyone who has not experienced his metaphysical disorientation.

Marlow's experience suggests the two faces of contingency. Recognizing the arbitrariness of one's practices and values threatens
one's faith in them even as it opens up the possibility of genuinely
reciprocal cross-cultural understanding with other worlds whose
ways of being are no less justified than one's own. If all worlds are
contingent, they are all equal, and a basis for reciprocity has been
established. Marlow's experience in Africa is a tonic blow to the
pride of Europeans whose sense of natural privilege he thinks is a
lie and a sham. But this realization does not transform him into an
anthropological pluralist who is invigorated by the existence of
other worlds. Just as he is angry at his recognition of kinship with
Africans because it threatens his identity, so he is annoyed and
frustrated by his realization that everything he had previously taken
for granted is only an arbitrary convention. Discovering the relativity of worlds is only destructive and not potentially constructive for

5. This is not to say that Marlow gets the African perception of Europeans right. Still, by
reversing perspectives Marlow begins the process R. S. Khare describes: "What we need
is genuine reciprocity in sharing knowledge, which would include reversing the knower-
known relation and ourselves becoming the Other to non-West anthropologists" ("The
Other's Double—The Anthropologist's Bracketed Self: Notes on Cultural Representation
and Privileged Discourse," *New Literary History* 23 [1992]: 7). Marlow does not complete this process, however, because he only imagines African perceptions and does not
elicit them.

Marlow because it robs values of their underpinnings and does not open up the possibility of new kinds of creation or new modes of relationship which would be closed off if our world were the only one there could be. Anything Marlow might do with his knowledge of contingency would simply create more contingency—another groundless construct (like his lie to the Intended)—and his resentment at its ubiquity is proportional to his inability to transform or escape it.

Marlow's sense of the pervasiveness of contingency deprives otherness of its potentially invigorating difference because the same groundlessness is everywhere. Marlow's appreciation of contingency allows him to approach others across cultural barriers with a sympathy and imagination remarkable for his time, but one reason why the encounters never lead to a productive exchange of differences is that Marlow only discovers the same thing at every turn. For example, he says of his cannibal-crew: "I looked at them as you would on any human being with a curiosity of their impulses, motives, capacities, weaknesses, when brought to the test of an inexorable physical necessity", but he cannot fathom their reasons for not satisfying their hunger by eating the white passengers: "these chaps too had no earthly reason for any kind of scruple. Restraint!" (42). He attributes to them a kind of existential heroism in the face of absurdity which corresponds to his own ethic of carrying on with one's duties even when they cannot be justified, but he never checks his interpretation by asking them. If he had, he might have discovered what other commentators have pointed out—namely, that cannibals do not typically eat human flesh to appease hunger but for spiritual reasons as part of specific rituals.[6] Marlow's awareness of the contingency of his customs and beliefs allows him to imagine other worlds, but he always only finds in them further evidence of contingency.

His attitude toward the other African members of his crew is similarly appreciative but ultimately dismissive because Marlow is both open and closed to cultural differences. There is a peculiar combination of mockery and respect in Marlow's description of the native fireman:

> He ought to have been clapping his hands and stamping his feet on the bank, instead of which he was hard at work, a thrall to strange witchcraft, full of improving knowledge. He was useful because he had been instructed; and what he knew was this—that should the water in that transparent thing disappear

6. For a summary of the debates in the anthropological literature about the actual extent of head-hunting and cannibalism and about their social and religious functions, see Marianna Torgovnick, *Gone Primitive: Savage Intellects, Modern Lives* (Chicago: U of Chicago P, 1990), pp. 147–48, 258.

the evil spirit inside the boiler would get angry through the greatness of his thirst and take a terrible vengeance (37).

The oddity of this figure exemplifies the anomalies which result when different cultures meet—what Clifford celebrates as the playful, multivocal effect of "collage" (see 173–77). It is hard to know which looks stranger in the encounter—the "witchcraft" of the boiler or the superstitions of the African, which after all turn out to be an effective way of negotiating his responsibilities. Much is disclosed about both sides which might otherwise not be so visible (how Western instruction demands taking things on faith, for example, and is therefore not as rational as it pretends, and conversely, how effective superstition can be as an instrument for mastering the world and reading signs). The figure of the fireman is a hybrid, heteroglot innovation which creates new possibilities of being not contained in either culture alone but made available as an unexpected consequence of their resources mixing and combining.

Nevertheless, the semantically and existentially productive potential of this figure never fully emerges in the text. The African's dignity as a worker is undermined by Marlow's overriding sense of his representative value as a sign of the absurdity of cultural conventions which seem natural only because we are accustomed to them. His appreciation of the contingency of a culture's habits allows him to be ironic about the native fireman, but it does not lead him to imagine that the fireman might have an ironic view of his situation as well, so that the two of them might play back and forth in exchanging a mutual sense of cultural absurdity instead of the joke all coming from Marlow's side. The fireman remains an object of Marlow's philosophical and cultural contemplation, and his adaptive powers as a creative human subject responding to challenging, bizarre circumstances never receive quite the recognition and respect they deserve. Despite Marlow's appreciation of his efficiency and duty, he is most of all a comic figure of the arbitrariness of cultural practices. Here again the perception of contingency is where Marlow's imagination of cultural differences both starts and stops.

An obvious objection is that Marlow could not be expected to engage in dialogue with his crew because he is their master and a representative of the imperialistic powers. Edward Said points out, for example, "the almost insuperable discrepancy between a political actuality based on force, and a scientific and humane desire to understand the Other hermeneutically and sympathetically in modes not always circumscribed and defined by force", and he argues that "an interlocutor in the colonial situation is . . . by definition either someone who is compliant . . . or someone who . . . simply refuses to talk, deciding that only a radically antagonistic, perhaps violent riposte is the only interlocution that is possible with colonial power."[7] What is remarkable, however, is how close Marlow comes to dialogue which the political structure of his situation would seem to preclude. He repeatedly misses his chances in a way that calls attention to them. Although he occupies a position of authority, his alienation from the local powers and his expectation that his days in Africa are numbered give him an ambiguous position as both an insider and an outsider to the colonial structure. This ambiguity blurs the distinctions which the narrator of "Karain" suggests:

> No man will speak to his master; but to a wanderer and a friend, to him who does not come to teach or to rule, to him who asks for nothing and accepts all things, words are spoken . . . that take no account of race or colour.[8]

Marlow's status as "master" may block him from dialogue with his African crew, but as an outsider to the other Europeans he is also a "wanderer" who is more open to otherness than he would be if he were firmly ensconced in power.

It is perhaps this kind of cross-cultural trust and acceptance which Marlow senses he lost the chance of when he recognizes too late "a kind of partnership" with his African helmsman: "He steered for me—I had to look after him. I worried about his deficiencies, and thus a subtle bond had been created of which I only became aware when it was suddenly broken", when he died and looked at Marlow with an "intimate profundity, . . . like a claim of distant kinship kinship affirmed in a supreme moment" (51). The condescension and inequality of their paternalistic relationship as master and servant prevented Marlow from recognizing until too late that the African was a fellow human being deserving of reciprocal recognition and concern—or even from sensing that such a reciprocity, if in truncated form, was already at work in the exchange of services between them. Their encounter becomes truly dialogical when the African looks back at Marlow, the roles of observer and observed thus reversed, but their exchange of vision is cut short—even as it is made possible—by death. Once again contingency has the double effect of uniting and dividing people. The groundlessness of existence which death reveals allows an uncommon moment of intimacy and exchange which it simultaneously destroys. As before, *Heart of Darkness* opens the possibility of cross-cultural reciprocity only to close it.

7. Edward Said, "Representing the Colonized: Anthropology's Interlocutors," *Critical Inquiry* 15 (1989): 217, 209–10.
8. Joseph Conrad, "Karain: A Memory" (1898), in *Tales of Unrest* (New York: Doubleday, Page and Co., 1924), p. 26.

Prolonging and extending such momentary glimpses of reciprocity would not only require political changes to create conditions of equality which would allow mutual recognition and exchange; building dialogue would also demand that both sides have access to language—if not a common language, at least respect for each other's capacities as language-users. *Heart of Darkness* both denies and affirms that Africans are linguistic beings whose command of language would make communication with them possible. Marlow sometimes refers to African phonemes as "a violent babble of uncouth sounds" (19): "strings of amazing words that resembled no sounds of human language, and the deep murmurs of the crowd, interrupted suddenly, were like the responses of some satanic litany" (67). Dialogue could not occur with beings whose language is regarded as pre-linguistic or as rudimentary and thus not equal to one's own. But Marlow also at times credits African sign-systems with the same value as European languages: "the tremor of far-off drums, sinking, swelling, a tremor vast, faint; a sound weird, appealing, suggestive, and wild—and perhaps with as profound a meaning as the sound of bells in a Christian country" (20). When he hears cries emanating from the shore, he invariably attributes significance to them: "an irresistible impression of sorrow, . . . unrestrained grief, . . . a great human passion let loose" (43). He assumes that these sounds are signs which carry meaning to their users and which could be translated if he knew the code.

When he scares the attacking Africans away by sounding the steam-whistle, his strategy assumes a reciprocal hermeneutic capacity on their part. He bets that they too will read sounds as signs in a translatable language, here construing the whistle as a meaningful indicator of evil intentions and intimidating powers. African hermeneutics imply a capacity to negotiate signs which, as in this case, finds exemplary application in the creation of lies and fictions.

Marlow does not, however, try to cross the linguistic barrier between himself and the Africans. His assumption that they are pre-linguistic or at a rudimentary stage of language—or even that their linguistic capacities are somehow demonic (a "satanic litany")—deprives them of the equality as users of sign-systems without which they cannot be interlocutors. But his intuition that another world—or worlds—which he cannot penetrate can be vaguely and obscurely heard in the sounds of Africa credits Africans with semiotic capacities which could be, but are not, the basis for further reciprocity and exchange. Once again *Heart of Darkness* suggests a possibility of relatedness which it blocks. Although the conditions of imperialistic domination of Africa might have made reciprocity between Europeans and Africans inconceivable, this novella is remarkable for its time (and perhaps for ours) because it makes such dialogue thinkable. One can imagine Marlow talking with Africans because of the semiotic powers he ascribes to them and because of the limitations he recognizes in his own culture's claims to authority. But this dialogue never takes place, and the result is to confirm the different cultures in their solipsistic isolation from one another. Both sides can construe the obscure signs emanating across cultural barriers as indications of other worlds, but neither side is able to parse or translate these signs sufficiently to understand their full relevance and communicate its own meanings in return.

Marlow demonstrates the power of linguistic innovation—especially through metaphor and analogy—to open us up to new worlds at the same time as he dramatizes how the creation of figurative language is necessarily circular and hence potentially self-enclosing. Commenting on the enigma of the figure "heart of darkness", Ian Watt explains: "if the words do not name what we know, they must be asking us to know what has, as yet, no name."[9] This is how metaphor works in general—extending the epistemological limits of language by creating incongruities which we can only make sense of by inventing new interpretive patterns.[1] If something as diffuse as "darkness" seems incapable of having a "heart", or if the typically affirmative values of a "heart" seem inappropriately linked with "dark", then these anomalies disclose limitations in our customary ways of understanding which we must revise and extend. The problem, however, is that these innovations can never be entirely new but are themselves a product of our customary assumptions, previously learned conventions, and past experiences. Hence the complaints of many critics that Marlow's metaphors reveal more about European thought-processes than about Africa. If that is true, it is because of the circularity of metaphor and other forms of semantic innovation which attempt to transcend the limits of a language by invoking and manipulating them. The ambiguity of Marlow's metaphors—do they say more about the Other or about him?—calls attention to the dilemma that existing linguistic and hermeneutic patterns are both the trap he is trying to get out of and his only way out of that trap.

This ambiguity is repeatedly thematized in analogies which insist on how little Marlow knows even as they attempt to use that incapacity to get beyond it. "Going up the river was like travelling back to the earliest beginnings of the world, when vegetation rioted on the earth and the big trees were kings", he reports; "We were wanderers on a prehistoric earth, on an earth that wore the aspect of an

9. Ian Watt, *Conrad in the Nineteenth Century* (Berkeley: U of California P, 1979), pp. 199–200.
1. Paul Ricoeur, *The Rule of Metaphor*, trans. R. Czerny (Toronto: U of Toronto P, 1975).

unknown planet" (33, 35). In a sense, these analogies are hermeneutically useless because neither he nor the reader can know anything about their terms of comparison—about the world's "earliest beginnings" or the characteristics of an unexplored planet. The absurdity of the comparison we are asked to make is useful, however, because it foregrounds the circularity of metaphor—proposing that we imagine what the unknown is like by projecting onto it our sense of the unknown. Because of this redundancy, Marlow's analogies cannot produce new knowledge about the Other; what this very repetitiveness discloses, however, is the circular procedure whereby interpreters attempt to make sense of otherness by projecting onto it what they already know.

This simultaneously enabling and incapacitating circularity characterizes not only Marlow's attempts to know Africa but also his relations with other Europeans, including * * * his audience. * * *

*   *   *

* * * Ian Watt argues that *Heart of Darkness* refutes solipsism because "the fact that Marlow, like Conrad, is speaking to a particular audience . . . enacts the process whereby the solitary individual discovers a way out into the world of others" (212). This is a wishful misreading, however, because such intersubjective exchange is explicitly not dramatized by the text but is instead suggested only to be blocked. The ending of *Heart of Darkness* is instructively different from the nearly contemporary story "Youth" where Marlow addresses the same cast of characters and concludes by asking them to affirm the meaning of his tale: "tell me, wasn't that the best time, that time when we were young at sea. . . . And we all nodded at him: the man of finance, the man of accounts, the man of law, we all nodded at him over the polished table."[2] Such dialogical response is markedly absent at the close of *Heart of Darkness*: "Marlow ceased and sat apart, indistinct and silent, in the pose of a meditating Buddha. Nobody moved for a time. 'We have lost the first of the ebb,' said the Director suddenly" (77). The return to the frame narration elicits the possibility of a response from the audience about the meaning of Marlow's narrative only to swerve away from it.

Dialogue to reach the consensus of "Youth" about the meaning of the tale or to negotiate different readings of it remains an empty set which the text explicitly refuses to fill. The frame narration marks its absence by dramatizing it as an unrealized potentiality. It is what is missing both in Marlow's meditative, solitary silence and in the Director's diversion of the group's attention to practical affairs. The

---

2. Joseph Conrad, "Youth" (1898), in *Youth and Two Other Stories* (1902; New York: Doubleday, Page, and Co., 1924), p. 42.

frame narrator's final comment is addressed to the reader: "I raised my head. The offing was barred by a black bank of clouds, and the tranquil waterway leading to the uttermost ends of the earth flowed sombre under an overcast sky—seemed to lead into the heart of an immense darkness" (77). Instead of elucidating Marlow's enigmatic metaphor, the narrator repeats it and passes it along to us. It is wrong to regard this narrator as an ideal ethnographer or to credit him with a true understanding of the main story, as Clifford does (see 99), because he simply reiterates Marlow's central image without adding to it. That epistemological position is left for the reader to fill. The narrator's repetition calls for an interpretive dialogue between the reader and the text while reenacting Marlow's meditative self-enclosure, both reaching out to us and holding back, both affirming the possibility of exchange and refusing it.

The same double movement of invoking and blocking dialogue characterizes Marlow's entire relation with the frame narration. The pensive self-enclosure of his attitude at the end is suggested at the very beginning when he is introduced as an eccentric figure who "resembled an idol" and "had the pose of a Buddha preaching in European clothes" (3, 6). Although the narrator claims that "the bond of the sea" unites the audience, there are several suggestions that the narrative contract between teller and listener is not freely and fully reciprocal. To begin with, the frame narrator shows an odd if bemused resentment towards Marlow for claiming the right to narrate. When Marlow starts talking, the narrator remarks: "we knew we were fated, before the ebb began to run, to hear about one of Marlow's inconclusive experiences" (7).

Two of the interruptions in Marlow's monologue reinforce the impression of a lack of reciprocity between himself and his listeners. After Marlow credits his audience with the ability to "see more than I could then", he pauses and the narrator notes: "There was not a word from anybody. The others might have been asleep" (27). When someone does speak up, it takes an insult to rouse them: " 'Try to be civil, Marlow,' growled a voice, and I knew there was at least one listener awake besides myself" (34). The social structure of the setting suggests the possibility of dialogue, but the exchange is all one-way, so one-sided that the listeners might as well not be there (or be sleeping), and they are awakened from their passivity only by verbal aggression. The nearest the frame narration comes to reciprocity occurs when Marlow pauses again to ask for tobacco (47) or when he hears a grunt and assumes it signifies a question (and a hostile one at that): "You wonder I didn't go ashore for a howl and a dance?" (36). The narrative contract is grudgingly granted and maintained with almost the bare minimum of exchange necessary to keep Marlow's monologue in motion.

Like Kurtz, Marlow is a voice, to be listened to rather than talked with. His lack of reciprocity with his audience replicates the solipsism he attempts to break through in his story but cannot because of the absence of dialogue which he tells about and repeats in his manner of telling. The breaks in his narration call attention to the one-sidedness of his monologue even as they raise the possibility of changing the one-way passage of meaning from teller to listener by dramatizing the social structure which might convert it into a reciprocal interaction. * * *

The final irony of *Heart of Darkness*, then, is that Marlow may be as opaque to his audience, including the reader, as the Africans are to him because an absence of reciprocity prevents dialogue in both instances. The canonization of *Heart of Darkness* threatens to make this irony deadly by converting the text from a potential interlocutor into an unquestioned cultural icon or (perhaps the same thing) a set of clichés which are too well known to give rise to thought. Just as Oscar Wilde said of *The Old Curiosity Shop* that no one can read about Little Nell's death without laughing, so perhaps no one can any longer make pronouncements about "the horror" or "the darkness" without prompting groans or sly smiles. The value of Achebe's charges is that they break the aura of the text and reestablish reciprocity between it and its interpreters by putting them on equal terms. Venerating *Heart of Darkness* would only confirm Conrad's doubts about the possibility of dialogical understanding and would thus preserve the text under conditions which would distress him. If, however, we recognize how unsettlingly ambiguous this text is about the ideals of reciprocity and mutual understanding which it negatively projects, we can engage in the sort of dialogue with it which Marlow never achieves with Africans or anyone else.

ANTHONY FOTHERGILL

Cannibalising Traditions: Representation and Critique in *Heart of Darkness*†

Conrad's contribution to late Victorian representations of the African "Other" was characteristically complex. He was a writer of his time, but I am not evincing his work simply as an exemplary compendium of the common stereotypes of Victorian Empire. True,

† From Anthony Fothergill, "Cannibalising Traditions: Representation and Critique in *Heart of Darkness*," in *Under Postcolonial Eyes: Joseph Conrad After Empire*, ed. Gail Fincham and Myrtle Hooper (Rondebosch: U of Cape Town P, 1996), pp. 93–94, 98–107. Reprinted with the permission of Juta Academic Publishers. Notes are the author's.

he won early recognition and was published by W. E. Henley in the jingoistic pages of the *New Review*. Henley saw him as one of his regatta, a comrade-in-arms for the literature of imperialist gusto and masculine heroics. But dismissing comparisons with Kipling, Rider Haggard, and R. L. Stevenson, Conrad saw himself using romance genre forms very much for his own ends. He was a writer living culturally at the margins. A foreign sailor coming late to writing (in his third language), a Pole whose nationalism was borne under the yoke of (Russian) imperialism, not in the name of it, Conrad stood both inside and outside Victorian culture. His marginality lent him the capacity to see the culturally familiar with an estranged eye. Thus he did not simply absorb and unproblematically reiterate the ideological predispositions of his time. He represented their forms of representation to "make us see" their hidden terms, to quote his Preface to *The Nigger of the "Narcissus"*.

Heart of Darkness provides us with a representation which demonstrates both the culmination of a profoundly entrenched European literary/political way of seeing the non-European Other *and* a radical critique of it. In that respect, the novel prefigures some of the most significant developments in later twentieth-century analyses of cultural representation. But to recognise the self-critique for what it is, we need first to acknowledge the degree to which Conrad was articulating persistent and widely circulating cultural stereotypes. These crucially influenced Europeans' modes of comprehending their "first" encounter with Africa, for representations of the Other are never original and none are innocent. Conrad shared practices of thought whose roots are buried in much earlier forms of European exploration and colonisation. The power of his writing lies in the contradictions existing between this complicity and his critique of these practices.

*　*　*

Recent studies have done much to uncover the cultural assumptions underpinning anthropological and literary representations of nineteenth- and twentieth-century Africa. Philip Curtin's *The Image of Africa: British Ideas and Action, 1780–1850* (London: Macmillan, 1965), and H. Alan Cairns' *Prelude to Imperialism: British Reactions to Central Africa 1840–1890* (London: Routledge and Kegan Paul, 1965), have sought to establish not so much the history of European contacts with Africa as a history of the images and frames of reference through which the European perceived "the African". This very term—the use of the monolithic, essentialist abstraction, "the African"—is itself, of course, a symptom of the problematics of representation which this essay seeks to address. And if it is validly objected that "the European" is equally false as a category, since it also asserts an ahistorical homogeneity, then

I would say, "Yes, it is false—but not equally false". Binary terms
(European/African, Civilised/Primitive) are never used with impartiality. Only a trick of apparent linguistic symmetry conceals the
fact that the opposition itself is generated by the language of one of
the two sides of the opposition: that which has more powerful interests at stake in the evocation.

Describing pioneers whose religious or trade interests prescribed
their writing, Cairns summarises the mid-Victorian perception of
Africa thus:

> These pioneers saw little of virtue in African cultures. Their
> observations, usually biased, frequently contradictory, and of-
> ten simply wrong, are replete with danger to the uncritical re-
> search worker. In almost all the nineteenth-century books on
> Africa the figure of the white man is writ large on the African
> landscape. In the middle of the dark continent he assumes
> novel and grandiose proportions. In moral, spiritual, and tech-
> nological matters he appears as a giant among pygmies, dwarf-
> ing the Africans among whom his activities are carried out.
> (xii)

A supplementary but crucial argument in the present context is
offered by Curtin, who says that even by the 1850s an imagery of
Africa reproduced in travel and missionary writing was well-
publicised and firmly established in the European mass-circulation
media:

> It was found in children's books, in Sunday School tracts, in
> the popular press. Its major affirmations were the "common
> knowledge" of the educated classes. Thereafter, when new
> generations of explorers or administrators went to Africa, they
> went with a prior impression of what they would find. Most of-
> ten they found it, and in their writings in turn confirmed the
> older image—or at most altered it only slightly. (3:vi)

In other words, anybody going to Africa for the first time had in a
sense already been there; carried, consciously or not, cultural lug-
gage containing well-established assumptions, expectations, and
imaginative constructions of "the African", through which to experience its peoples "at first hand".

The later nineteenth century saw a phenomenal increase in popular and scientific literature dealing with Africa. Learned societies
like the Anthropological Society of London encouraged the devel-
oping study of "primitive" peoples. Stimulus to the enterprise was
added by the perceived cultural implications of Darwin's theory of
evolution and by the archeological discoveries made in the wake of

colonial expansion in the 1870s and 1880s. All this contributed a growing body of "scientific knowledge" about Africa, which reinforced even as it modified the terms of earlier literary representations. Growing commercial and political contact (predating the Scramble for Africa of the mid-1880s but massively increased by it) kindled in the popular imagination an infectious interest in the area and in the currency and potency of the images of Africa and representations of "primitive" man which such literature propagated. Furthermore, World Exhibitions such as the Great Exhibition of 1851 at Crystal Palace and the Paris World Exhibition, and others run by ethnological societies, were enormously popular and influential, reinforcing a heavily mediated, profoundly stereotypic understanding of foreign "races".

Basic structures of understanding Africa and the African Other, premised on Eurocentric fears, desires, and assumed superiority, then, adapted themselves to new colonial impulses. In particular, the view of Africa as "virgin" land ripe for economic exploitation in the last decades of the century affected the way the continent and its peoples were represented. For the material interests of the colonialists, who required adventure capital investment in profitable enterprises, did not always coincide with the interests preoccupying other earlier Europeans in Africa. These had generated images of an exotic, mysterious, and challenging landscape which needed taming (by the intrepid explorer) and of a primitive people who needed converting from heathen beliefs (by missionaries). But the imperialist interest saw the native population less as convertible savage and more as malleable inferior, to be subjugated and controlled as a labour resource.[1]

Given these shifts, let us consider the "common knowledge" propagated by contemporary literary works, in order to locate the tradition which Conrad assimilated. This depiction of the Congolese African by one of the age's "spiritual fathers", P. P. Aurogard, is fairly typical:

> The black race is certainly the race of Ham, the race cursed of God. There is nothing in particular which shows you this, but one can smell it, see it everywhere, and one cannot help feeling both compassion and terror when one sees these poor unfortunates. These black pagans are lazy, greedy, thieves, liars and given over to all kinds of vice [. . .] the scanty clothes

1. For fuller accounts of the representation of Africa, see for example the works of B. V. Street, *The Savage in Literature* (London: Routledge and Kegan Paul, 1982); William Schneider, *An Empire for the Masses: The French Popular Image of Africa, 1870–1900* (London: Greenwood, 1982); and H. Ridley, *Images of Imperial Rule* (London: Croome Helm, 1983).

which these unfortunates wear make them even more savage
and worthy of pity.[2]

In its characteristic self-assurance, its mixed motivation (the savage is both utterly beyond redemption and pitiable enough for
funds to be contributed for spiritual welfare), and its unintentional
self-contradiction (nothing shows you this but it can be seen), this
account manages acrobatics of an almost metaphysical complexity.

Hammond and Jablow emphasise the unequivocally accepted
racial determinism which underlay all such European representations of Africans of the period.[3] Earlier polygenist views of the separate origin and species of Africans, according to which European
races were inherently more developed and hierarchically superior,
eventually gave way before the Darwinian monogenist theory of human evolution. But subsequent popularising versions of Darwin re-
confirmed Europeans' sense of racial and cultural difference and
superiority. Evolutionary theory then became the enabling ground
for perceiving the African as a beastly and time-locked savage, our
"contemporary ancestor". Physical ugliness, non-individuated uni-
formity of appearance, excessive sexual appetite and promiscuity
are the recurrent characteristics of such people and a host of mental and moral failings allegedly reinforced the fact of Africans' social
and cultural backwardness.

It would be inaccurate to say, however, that the eighteenth-
century convention of the Noble Savage was out, and the vision of
the ignoble one was in. The latter overlaid but did not entirely erad-
icate the former. The Noble Savage—quite as unhistoric, of course,
as that of the later "contemporary ancestor"—fed a cultural and
political interest in the "natural" and the "exotic" fostered by the
Romantics and subsequent writers and painters, particularly in
France, in works by Baudelaire, Nerval, Flaubert, and the immensely popular Pierre Loti. The imaginative function of Africa as
exotic Other was twofold. First, it was a space to escape into, one
from which materialistic bourgeois Europe could be criticised. Second, it held out the promise of self-discovery in a confrontation
with the strange and unfamiliar. Stripped of its repressive European
veneer, the authentic self awaited discovery in the landscape of
Africa, where the burdens of "civilisation" could be shed. Thus, the
"savage" Other could embody the freedom that Europeans desired
in order to find their "real" selves.

These uses of the imagined Africa and the "savage", though overlaid and to some extent superceded by later imperial requirements,

---

2. Quoted in R. Slade, *King Leopold's Congo* (Oxford: Oxford UP, 1962), p. 32.
3. D. Hammond and A. Jablow, *The Myth of Africa* (New York: The Library of Social Science, 1977).

were never quite erased. They continued to play an informing part in the discourse of the Other which Conrad assimilated. It was a discourse predicated on a structure of opposites. The "savage" was to be defined by and against what the perceiving Europeans understood themselves to be. The Other was negation, nature, animal, black. *How* these attributes were then evaluated depended on the needs to which the construction was put. In this economy of oppositions, desire and transgression lie in close alliance. But the transgression most to be feared was the transgression of "known" boundaries. Paradoxically, Westernised Africans, like Europeans "gone native", came to be regarded as particularly threatening to an order predicated on absolute difference: they confused and disrupted the natural order.

It is into this contradictory cultural field that we should place Conrad's *Heart of Darkness*, for it embodies a radically ambivalent tendency in representing the Other. At times it endorses stereotypic figures of the "savage" as "uncivilised" and "primitive"—though it does so often with the *aim* of questioning facile oppositions between (superior) Civilised and (inferior) Savage. On such occasions Conrad's implicit assertion—critical enough for Victorian middle-class ears—is, "We are savage primitives, too, beneath the skin". (But note, for this, the "savagery" of the Other has to be assumed.) At other times, his representation of the African offers a self-conscious critique of European *representations*, even to the point of questioning the very basis of such Otherness. In principle, the two tendencies vary according to the proximity or distance of the narrator (Marlow) from the subject of his observation. This is often quite literally a *spatial* proximity or distance. The closer he is to a "savage," the more subtle, less stereotypical, is his regard. The more specific the African's historical or political subjectivity, the more critical Marlow is of typical European representations. When, however, he elides this specificity and regards the African from a distance in time or space, the representation tends to endorse well-established European cultural stereotypes of primitive savages.

Two pivotal episodes in *Heart of Darkness* reveal the tension between endorsement and critique in Conrad: the appearance of the chain-gang soon after Marlow arrives at the Company's station and his subsequent up-river journey when he confronts what he perceives as the threatening mystery of the forest and its inhabitants. The erasure of precise location, of historical and ethnic specificity, gives to the native peoples he represents the appearance of the near-mythic. We are offered "natural man" stripped of the accoutrements of social reality: eternally present, at one with nature, offering some kind of lesson to "us". The translation into "primitive man" becomes all the easier if we are not preoccupied with the specificities of the late nineteenth-century Congo but can let our imaginations freely inscribe the blank page of Otherness. We will need to return presently to the complex erotic component of this "blankness" in the representation of the doubly Other, the "savage" female, Kurtz's "mistress".

Less problematic for the cultural climate in which Conrad wrote is this representation of African natives:

> Going up that river was like travelling back to the earliest beginnings of the world, when vegetation rioted on the earth and the big trees were kings. An empty stream, a great silence, an impenetrable forest. . . . We were wanderers on the prehistoric earth, on an earth that wore the aspect of an unknown planet . . . there would be a glimpse of rush walls, of peaked grass-roofs, a burst of yells, a whirl of black limbs, a mass of hands clapping, of feet stamping, of bodies swaying, of eyes rolling under the droop of heavy and motionless foliage. The steamer toiled along slowly on the edge of a black and incomprehensible frenzy. The prehistoric man was cursing us, praying to us, welcoming us—who could tell? We were cut off from the comprehension of our surroundings. (33–35)

In narrative terms, the journey is one of advance towards Kurtz with echoes of Stanley's search for Livingstone (as a sort of Holy Grail), a narrative with immense resonance in the popular mind. It is a journey of return, through a landscape as primordial as "the night of the first ages". The long forgotten becomes the present; the prehistoric the here and now. The formal qualities of the passage, particularly the use of the iterative past tense suggesting repeated, habitual actions ("we would," "there would be") make time seem to turn back on itself. The iterative tense perfectly mirrors the sense of time suspended. * * * The adoption of this verbal form is at once surreptitious, ideologically potent, and unconsciously poignant. For it asserts a permanence even after death: "they were, are and always will be".

Furthermore, topography and inhabitants merge. The dissolution of boundaries between the "primitive" and the natural world achieves a polymorphous state of threatening and fascinating otherness. The human body is expressed as an unindividuated mass of limbs; human speech is reduced to "incomprehensible frenzy". * * * [T]hese natives are absorbed into the "natural", a virtually de-historicised space. The prehistoric wilderness is given anthropomorphic qualities—the power to look, to have inscrutable purposes—at the moment when the historical, social human being is all but erased. The human primitive, "pre-historic" man, transgresses the border between established categories, such as human/non-human, sane/insane, human/animal, in a way which both horrifies and fascinates Marlow:

> The earth seemed unearthly. We are accustomed to look upon the shackled form of a conquered monster, but there—there you could look at a thing monstrous and free. It was unearthly, and the men were—No, they were not inhuman [. . .] what thrilled you was just the thought of their humanity—like yours—the thought of your remote kinship with this wild and passionate uproar . . . if you were man enough you would admit to yourself that there was in you just the faintest trace of a response to the terrible frankness of that noise. (36)

The thematic thrust of Marlow's narrative radically disturbs the complacent sense of European superiority which his listeners, and Conrad's contemporary readers, would in all likelihood have shared. The thought that "civilised" behaviour may be just a veneer covering aggressive, passionate, incomprehensible energies was a fear too current to be comfortably dismissed. But in order to articulate it, Conrad needed to construct the African as an objectification of what it was they were anxious about. Thus, radical critique and a racist reactionary force combine in this stereotypical representation of the African Other, which simultaneously confirms while undercutting the European cultural myth of the Black as a contemporary ancestor.

The culturally, politically dominant reading of this myth was imperially complacent: we too were once like this, but how developed we are now! But, with a different Darwinian turn, Conrad has also articulated the underlying fear: if we came from this, what secret inheritance may be lurking in our character? (One can almost hear the class anxieties about having come from lowly stock.) But in either case the stereotype of the savage remains intact.

The same contradictory combination of fear and desire can be located in the depiction of the "wild and gorgeous apparition of a woman" (60), Kurtz's native "mistress," as she is almost universally called in Conrad criticism. The appellation "mistress," of course, reveals a different order of stereotyping. Nowhere in the narrative is the black woman referred to as Kurtz's mistress; it is an *inferred* status. But neither for Marlow nor his listeners, nor for Conrad's implied readers, could the "logic" of this inferred stereotype be fully articulated. Nor would it need to be so articulated. As an unspoken "truth", it is always already known that the black native woman in nineteenth-century European narratives means sexual licence. The connotations are activated by a cultural system (with its assumptions about racial difference) which confirms the Black as "passionate" and "sexually active" and the black woman, specifically, as embodying physical temptation and sexual gratification for the white male European. Like the representation of American Indians in the sixteenth century, the comparative nudity of the African woman was read as clear testimony of her transgressive sexuality. The power of the stereotype lies in its self-evidence, as the compliance of most of Conrad's twentieth-century critics testifies. What fascinated and terrified the colonising mind was the thought that the white man might "go native", cross the limits of the permissible and undermine the sexual foundations of the bourgeois world.

The phrase "wild and gorgeous apparition" reinforces Marlow's oxymoronic definition of the wilderness (the unearthly earth): utterly other and incomprehensible, it is nevertheless, indeed therefore, fascinatingly attractive. An incarnation of its seductive and potentially corrupting force, she stands undifferentiated from the wilderness. Its image and soul, in her well-armoured appearance she evokes the familiar Amazonian stereotype, a powerful female threat to the male, even as she is given an emphasis of tragic dignity and sorrow. Victim, like the wilderness, of the European invasion, she also threatens to be its vanquisher. Yet her status in reality is brought into question (as well it might be!): she shares the "unearthliness" of the earth; she occupies a space on the borderline between the real and unreal, human and non-human, material and fantastic—an impossible position to occupy. For all her physicality, she is indeed an "apparition". She functions as an imaginative space onto which Marlow can project the meanings and desires of the European male gaze, while at the same time attributing these as "inherent" qualities to the object gazed at. The European can then "discover" his kinship and fascination for what he has imagined in her. But of course the inscribing is not declared. * * *

There is, moreover, a silencing [of the Other]. We hear *about* her speaking, but we do not hear her words. Like the monstrous natives, she is not allowed to come close enough to speak for herself. If her political space has been colonised, so has her linguistic one. Thus the ideological work of representation can go on unhindered by any entry into the historically specific, into the closer space of contestation and real difference which her talking may reveal. Indeed, were she to come closer she would get shot.

There are two instances in the novel, however, where proximity and contact go some way toward challenging the stereotypes the novel elsewhere depends on: the depictions of the chain-gang and the cannibal crew. The precise, impressionistic description of the former, with its withholding of the term "chain-gang" until the conditions of the natives' bodily presence has been established, shocks the reader into a fresher recognition of events. Indeed, the very process of signification—what is at stake in it—is defamiliarised, held up for scrutiny. No longer can we feel comfortable writing them off as "just" a "chain-gang".

> A slight clinking behind me made me turn my head. Six black men advanced in a file, toiling up the path. They walked erect and slow, balancing small baskets full of earth on their heads, and the clink kept time with their footsteps . . . these men could by no stretch of imagination be called enemies. They were called criminals, and the outraged law, like the bursting shells, had come to them, an insoluble mystery from the sea. (15–16)

Conrad's point here has everything to do with the nature and politics of linguistic representation: "They were called criminals": "They were not enemies, they were not criminals." The "outraged law" (the phrase *and* the institution) is exposed to polemical critique: the real outrage may be the Law's representing the Black as criminal. Calling the Other by certain names legitimises our behaviour towards "it" accordingly: so everything depends on who is doing the looking and representing. However fleetingly, Marlow brings this concern home when, walking close to the chain-gang, he thinks of himself as being looked at:

> They passed me within six inches, without a glance, with that complete, deathlike indifference of unhappy savages. Behind this raw matter one of the reclaimed, the product of the new forces at work, strolled despondently, carrying a rifle by its middle . . . and seeing a white man on the path, hoisted his weapon to his shoulder with alacrity. This was simple prudence, white men being so much alike at a distance that he could not tell who I might be. He was speedily reassured, and with a large, white, rascally grin, and a glance at his charge, seemed to take me into partnership in his exalted trust. After all, I also was a part of the great cause of these high and just proceedings.
> Instead of going up, I turned and descended to the left. My idea was to let that chain-gang get out of sight before I climbed the hill. (16)

Marlow imagines, here, looking from the Other's viewpoint. Of course, he cannot naively adopt the Other's position, and the fact that they do not give him a glance indicates his separation from them as a European master. But the grin of the native guard, and the joke about white men all looking the same (which inverts the cliché and thus again defamiliarises the signifying act) work to explode stereotypic European generalisations about "the Black man". Identified as accomplice to the horror he witnesses, no wonder Marlow wants the chain-gang "out of sight". True, he is still projecting a way of looking on to the Other; that is inescapable. But the stereotyping is signalled and fractured at the point when he locates himself temporarily in the site of the viewed. Marlow thus briefly recognises the dialectics of viewing. In that act, he is forced to acknowledge that his own historical, political position implicates him. Embarrassed when his position is even mildly contested, he is no longer so keen to see or be seen. His (unsuccessful) form of erasure is to walk off into the grove. There, unfortunately for him (Conrad's political honesty here is absolute), he sees more evidence of the results of European well-meaning: cast-off and dying members of the chain-gang. For Marlow—and this is what Conrad is radically, consciously, showing us—the Other has come too close for comfort.

Similar proximity and realignment of perspective occurs with the cannibals on the steamer. In an off-hand sort of way Marlow introduces the reference: "Fine fellows—cannibals—in their place" (34), and it confounds the stereotype he has just encouraged in depicting those natives on shore. The attributes of "frenzied passion" and exotic culinary habits are ones with which our complicit imaginations might willingly toy. Cannibalism has been the stock-in-trade of European inscriptions of the primitive Other since Herodotus, for it epitomises all forms of categorical transgression, all that "we are not". But here the stereotype gets undermined by Marlow's simple praise. "They were men one could work with and I'm grateful to them" (34). The restraint they show under attack and their surprising reticence to eat portly European managerial flesh despite their meagre rations are qualities commented on by Marlow in an approving manner. Conrad knows his audience well enough to evoke the cannibal reference, compulsory in late nineteenth-century "descriptions" of Africa, despite a complete lack of any firm evidence for its widespread existence.[4] But he does so to imply that, with close social and physical contact, under a scrutiny both linguistic and political, the stereotype dissolves.

This sort of proximity does not *deny* the alterity of the Other. What is contested is the complacent idea that "I already know" the Other; that my words can adequately represent the Other; and that it is my place and my right, as if disinterestedly, to do the representing. The recognition of proximity is not a sentimental or self-serving claim to identity. Nor can we claim to get behind our own understanding to adopt an allegedly neutral position of viewing the Other "just as it is". But we *can* be alerted to the degree to which our own projective imaginations, our own contradictions, seek to make of the Other the negative image of ourselves.

4. See William Arens, *The Man-Eating Myth* (Oxford: Oxford UP, 1979) for a critique of the mythic function of, and absence of anthropological evidence "proving," widespread cannibalism.

ANDREW MICHAEL ROBERTS

[Masculinity, Modernity, and Homosexual Desire]†

[T]he epistemology of Conrad's work is explicable in terms of (so-cial) structures of male power and (psychic) structures of male de-sire. A discourse of knowledge, truth and ignorance plays a crucial part in the maintenance of these structures, reinforcing both mas-culine identity and male access to empowering knowledge, while enabling the symbolic, psychic and social exploitation of women. This discourse does not simply attribute knowledge to men and ig-norance to women but variably associates women with particular forms of ignorance and knowledge in such a way as to make them available as symbols of a mysterious truth and objects of a secret knowledge while largely depriving them of the role of knowing sub-ject. Conrad's texts participate in an ideological discourse which both produces 'truths' about women and produces a concept of femininity constructed as the Other of male knowledge. This Other is simultaneously, and paradoxically, the complementary ignorance against which male knowledge defines itself and a symbol of the ul-timate truth which, though unattainable, represents a structurally important horizon of metaphysical knowledge. This discourse, like many discourses which evoke 'woman' as an archetype, is sustained by a willed ignorance concerning particular women. Conrad's work does not always uncritically reproduce such a discourse. In inviting the reader to empathize with women characters and with male characters who temporarily occupy a 'feminized' position, the fic-tion offers some critical purchase on these structures of exploita-tion, without ever fully analysing or stepping outside them.

* * *

The epistemological structure of 'Heart of Darkness' involves a pair of men (Marlow and Kurtz), a group of men (Marlow and his listeners on board the Nellie) and a pair of women (the African woman at the Inner Station and the 'Intended'). The pair of men is the locus of the discovery of a hidden truth; the pair of women rep-resent the complementary exclusion, necessary to maintain the men's belief in the secrecy and power of that truth; the group of men foregrounds the problematics of interpretation but also the possibility of a wider circulation of that truth among men. The two women, in different ways, are excluded by the text from the sub-ject-position of knowledge (that of the knower) and are made into

† From *Conrad and Masculinity* (New York: St. Martin's P, 2000), pp. 121–22, 125–26, 126–28, 130–33, 134–36. Reproduced with permission of Palgrave Macmillan. Notes are the author's.

its object (that which is known). The African woman might, it seems, possess secret knowledge (of Kurtz and his 'unspeakable rites') (50). However, she is allowed no voice, but only the pseudo-eloquence of gestures which allow the narrative voice of Marlow to assimilate her to the jungle. The Intended does speak in the text, but is excluded from this supposedly precious knowledge. At the point where it might be passed to her (and thereby transformed or demystified), a rhetorical move by Marlow bypasses her as the subject of knowledge and utterance and reinstates her as the object of (his own) utterance and (his listeners') knowledge. There is some slippage in the roles occupied by the women, but this slippage is between three roles, each of which is conceived as the antithesis to the powerful, knowing, speaking male subject of knowledge. The knowing subject is opposed to: (1) the ignorant; (2) the known, the object of knowledge; (3) the unknowable.

'Heart of Darkness' is a story about the gaining and passing on (or failure to pass on) of knowledge and about relationships between men. This knowledge is rhetorically structured in terms of the transgression of boundaries; the supposed insight of Kurtz's final words, 'The horror! The horror!' (69), is a result of his having gone beyond various notional boundaries—of 'civilization', of self-restraint, of taboo, finally of death, of his having 'made that last stride . . . stepped over the edge' (70). Marlow's sharing of something of this insight is possible because he too has 'peeped over the edge' (70). Marlow attempts to pass on this (partial) knowledge to his male listeners through the medium of language, but again this is only partly possible. Marlow's confidence that 'you fellows see more' is set against his sense that 'No, it is impossible; it is impossible to convey the life-sensation of any given epoch of one's existence—that which makes its truth, its meaning' (27). Many versions of what this knowledge is are possible: knowledge of the self, * * * of the Other, of the unconscious, of the violence and oppression of colonialism, of the corruption of European civilization, of evil within human nature.

I would suggest that, while at the realist level the story makes, for example, a (limited) critique of colonialism, at the symbolic level the 'truth' which is at its centre is primarily an empty signifier, generated by what Sedgwick terms 'representationally vacant, epistemologically arousing place-markers.'[1] Examples are 'the incomprehensible' (6), 'dark places' (5), 'misty halos' (5), 'subtle and penetrating essence' (27), 'dream' (27), 'The horror!' (82), 'a moral victory paid for by innumerable defeats, by abominable terrors'

---

1. Eve Kosofsky Sedgwick, *Epistemology of the Closet* (Hemel Hempstead, UK: Harvester Wheatsheaf, 1991), p. 95.

(70), 'an immense darkness' (the last words of the story, 77). These terms, in other words, generate a rhetorical and narrative intensity around the idea of something to be known, without ever specifying what that something is. Sedgwick points out the associations of such a technique with a homophobic discourse which treats same-sex desire as something which cannot be spoken of. In 'Heart of Darkness' the technique also produces racist and sexist effects, since Africa, African people and women are drawn into this symbolic black hole. The empty signifier is empty only in terms of the story's symbolic self-understanding; ideologically, it has a history and a meaning.

*   *   *

The much-debated lie to the Intended seems an inevitable point of departure for a discussion of knowledge in 'Heart of Darkness'. The very term 'the Intended' is an example of the way in which the text tempts interpretation into ideological acceptance: it is difficult to refer to the woman whom Marlow meets at the end of the story other than by this term, which involves the critic in replicating her objectification and the subordination of her subjectivity to Kurtz's will. There is another suppression, as well as Marlow's lie to her about Kurtz's last words: the suppression by the text of the name (her name) which he pretends had been those last words. Marlow's lie also associates her (unspoken) name with the idea of horror. In realist terms, the lie needs little explanation. Faced with Kurtz's grieving fiancée, whom he has only just met and who seems to be keeping going psychologically by idealizing her dead lover, is it surprising that Marlow does not risk causing embarrassment and trauma by telling this woman that her lover had become a brutalized mass murderer? What encourages the reader to go beyond such a realist account is the linguistic, symbolic and emotional excess of the passage which includes the lie, the near-hysteria with which Marlow overloads his description of the meeting.

*   *   *

Telling stories about someone is not the usual way of consigning them to oblivion: the Intended is surrendered, less to 'oblivion' than to Marlow's fantasies about her and to his male listeners. This brings us back to the nature of the male bonds in 'Heart of Darkness'. Nina Pelikan Straus argues that "In *Heart of Darkness* women are used to deny, distort, and censor men's passionate love for one another. Projecting his own love on to the form of the Intended, Marlow is able to conceal from himself the dark complexity of his own love—a love that strikes him with horror—for Kurtz."[2] This

2. Nina Pelikan Straus, "The Exclusion of the Intended from Secret Sharing in Conrad's 'Heart of Darkness,'" *Novel* 20 (1987):134.

version of the familiar idea of a 'doubling' between Marlow and
Kurtz in terms of passionate love between men is best understood
via Sedgwick's argument that the visibility of the   homosocial–
homosexual continuum has been 'radically disrupted' in the case of
men in modern Western society.[3] So if we follow Straus in seeing
Marlow's fascination with Kurtz in terms of desire between men
which excludes women from a secret knowledge, this is not necessarily to say that the story is primarily about repressed homosexual
desire. Rather the argument is that the relationship between Marlow and Kurtz takes place within a whole matrix of inter-male relationships involving competitiveness, desire, bonding, the sharing
and appropriation of power and knowledge, and that this matrix of
relations has characteristically functioned in modern Western society through the setting up of powerful barriers between sexual and
other forms of inter-male relationship. Women, by functioning as
objects of exchange (literal or psychic) and of shared desire, have
been used to maintain such a barrier, male desire being channelled
through women. This involves the exclusion of women from the
subject positions of power, knowledge and desire. They are established as that which is desired, that which is the object of knowledge, that which is exchanged or controlled.

However, an interpretation of 'Heart of Darkness' in terms of
male homosexual desire can undoubtedly be made, building on
Straus's article. The secret knowledge which Marlow and Kurtz
come to share (or rather, which Marlow comes to imagine he has
shared with Kurtz), the metaphors of transgressing a boundary with
which Marlow glosses the relationship of this knowledge to death,
the 'unspeakable rites' (50) which Kurtz has practised, all have
distinctively sexual overtones within the discourse of sexuality/
knowledge that Sedgwick identifies in late nineteenth-century Europe. Furthermore, certain of 'Sedgwick's observations on *Billy
Budd* (written in 1891, the year following Conrad's own visit to the
Congo but before his own novella was written) are strikingly relevant to the rhetoric employed by Marlow.[4]

> In the famous passages of *Billy Budd* in which the narrator
> claims to try to illuminate . . . the peculiarly difficult riddle of
> 'the hidden nature of the master-at-arms' Claggart . . . the an-
> swer to the riddle seems to involve not the substitution of se-
> mantically more satisfying alternatives to the epithet 'hidden'
> but merely a series of intensifications of it. Sentence after sen-
> tence is produced in which, as Barbara Johnson points out . . .

3. Sedgwick, *Between Men: English Literature and Male Homosocial Desire* (New York: Columbia UP, 1985), pp. 1–2.
4. *Billy Budd* was not published until 1924, so any links are not a matter of influence but
of comparable social and discursive contexts.

'what we learn about the master-at-arms is that we cannot
learn anything': the adjectives applied to him . . . include 'mysterious,' 'exceptional,' 'peculiar,' 'exceptional' again, 'obscure,'
'phenomenal,' 'notable,' 'phenomenal' again, 'exceptional'
again, 'secretive' . . . [These are combined with] a parallel and
equally abstract chain of damning ethical designations—'the
direct reverse of a saint,' 'depravity,' 'depravity,' 'wantonness of
atrocity,' 'the mania of an evil nature.'[5]

This whole description is remarkably relevant to the way in which
Kurtz, and Marlow's relationship with Kurtz, are defined, or rather
left undefined. Kurtz is described to Marlow as 'a very remarkable
person' (19), as a man who will 'go far, very far' (19) (a richly ironical phrase, with the benefit of hindsight), as 'an exceptional man'
(22), 'a prodigy', 'an emissary of pity, and science, and progress, and
devil knows what else', 'a special being' (25). Marlow comments: 'I
had heard Mr. Kurtz was in there . . . Yet somehow it didn't bring
any image with it—no more than if I had been told an angel or a
fiend was in there' (27). Later we find Kurtz referred to as 'that
man' (31), and, in Marlow's conversation with the 'harlequin' (52),
as one who has 'enlarged my mind' (54). The harlequin tells Marlow that he and Kurtz 'talked of everything . . . Of love, too', although 'It isn't what you think' (what does Marlow think?), but 'It
was in general. He made me see things—things' (55). The harlequin claims that 'you can't judge Mr. Kurtz as you would an ordinary man' (56). Marlow himself describes Kurtz as 'a remarkable
man' (62) and as 'very little more than a voice' (48), a fate which he
shares himself within the narrative frame as it becomes darker on
the *Nellie*—one aspect of the crucial rapprochement or doubling
between Marlow and Kurtz. As well as these 'intensifications' of the
mystery surrounding Kurtz, there are many 'damning ethical designations'; Kurtz, we are told, 'lacked restraint in the gratification of
his various lusts' (57); 'there was something wanting in him' (57);
'he was hollow at the core' (58); he is 'an atrocious phantom' (59),
a 'shadow' (60), 'like a vapour exhaled by the earth' (65), a 'wandering and tormented thing' (65), marked by 'exalted and incredible
degradation' (66), and whose soul 'had gone mad' (66), possessed
by 'diabolic love and . . . unearthly hate' (68) and, of course, in his
own words, 'the horror!' (69).

Faced with this barrage of mystification and condemnation, it is
worth briefly being literal minded as an experiment. What has
Kurtz actually done? He has murdered and brutally exploited
African people, but this he has in common with the others involved
in the imperialist project. What were his 'unspeakable rites' (50),

5. *Epistemology of the Closet*, pp. 94–95.

bearing in mind that they involved 'various lusts' (57) and that Marlow apparently cannot bring himself to be specific about them? Cannibalism? Perhaps, but Marlow seems ready enough to discuss that in relation to the Africans on board the river steamer. Human sacrifice? The heads on stakes might imply this, but, again, Marlow is frank enough about these, and finds them an expression of a 'pure, uncomplicated savagery' (58) which is more tolerable than the imagined details of the ceremonies involving Kurtz. Some form of magic? The witch doctors who appear on the shore are made to appear pathetically powerless. All of these activities might be involved, but none seems adequate to explain the mystique of the unspeakable attributed to Kurtz's practices.

The conclusion, I think, has to be that what Kurtz has done is precisely the non-specified or unspeakable: it is less any set of actual actions than a symbolic location of taboo-breaking. As such, and in the historical context of the turn of the century, it can hardly fail to evoke the homophobic taboo of 'the love that dare not speak its name'. Perhaps the closest that Marlow comes to identifying the unspeakable is when he finds it intolerable to hear about 'the ceremonies used when approaching Mr. Kurtz' (58), which seem to involve crawling. This is one of a number of references to the idea of idol-worship, and suggests the harlequin's adoration and idealization of Kurtz, which Marlow mocks but in some degree comes to share. The focus of horror is thus on Marlow's intense emotional desire to meet Kurtz and identification with him after his death, although this focus is masked by the projection of the 'horror' onto the imagined primitive of Africa. Marlow's own feelings for Kurtz (tinged as they are with idol-worship) are themselves the horror. It is in sexual terms, as well as in terms of imperialist exploitation, that the darkness which Marlow imagines he finds in Africa is reflected back into the heart of the culture inhabited by Marlow and his respectable male listeners.

*   *   *

The case for a reading of 'Heart of Darkness' in terms of homosexual desire may be summarized as follows. It concerns a story told by one man to a group of men with whom he feels a close bond, a bond necessary for them to understand his story, although he nevertheless feels part of it cannot be communicated. His story concerns his growing fascination, disgust and identification for another man, centred on his realization that this man has been involved in taboo practices about which the story-teller (Marlow) will not be specific. This realization creates, at least in the mind of the story-teller, an enduring intimacy with the other man, despite his death, an intimacy involving the sharing of a disgraceful yet exciting knowledge from which the dead man's fiancée must be protected.

I am not, however, arguing that 'Heart of Darkness' is simply a concealed narrative of male homosexual desire. Like many literary texts, it is multiply over-determined. My argument is that the rhetorical and symbolic structures of Conrad's novella constantly evoke discourses of sexual knowledge and ignorance, which, as Sedgwick shows, focused with particular intensity at that period (and since) on a crisis of heterosexual/homosexual definition. The male homosocial relations which are prominent at all levels of 'Heart of Darkness' are structured by this crisis, just as they are structured by the denial of power and utterance to women and by the economics of empire. In terms of the politics of literary inter-pretation, to neglect a reading of the text in terms of homosexual desire would be to repeat the processes of exclusion and denial which have been so prominent in the discourse of male sexuality, just as to read the text's overt marginalization of women as merely social realism is to replicate a sexist discourse, and to defend the text's representation of Africa on the grounds that Africa is used here only as a symbol of the European psyche is to replicate a racist discourse.

The central instance in the story of the structuring of homosocial relations by the problematics of homosexual/heterosexual definition is the doubling between Kurtz and Marlow, which has been exten-sively discussed by critics. Doubles are a recurrent feature of Con-rad's fiction, crucial to the symbolic meaning of this and other stories, most notably 'The Secret Sharer' and *Under Western Eyes*. In the triangular situation which exists in Marlow's mind after Kurtz's death, and especially during the scene with the Intended, there is a notable confusion between identification and desire. His fantasy that he possesses Kurtz, body and soul, is also a fantasy of *being* Kurtz, echoing as it does Kurtz's own obsessional possessiveness:

> All that had been Kurtz's had passed out of my hands: his soul, his body, his station, his plans, his ivory, his career. There re-mained only his memory and his Intended. (72)

> You should have heard him say, 'My ivory' . . . 'My Intended, my ivory, my station, my river, my—' everything belonged to him. It made me hold my breath in expectation of hearing the wilderness burst into a prodigious peal of laughter. . . . Every-thing belonged to him—but that was a trifle. The thing was to know what he belonged to. (48)

This fantasy is enacted in the ambiguity of Marlow's wish to surren-der 'his memory' (50): does this mean Marlow's memory of Kurtz, or Kurtz's own memory? To Marlow they have become almost the same. Does Marlow know what he himself 'belonged to'? Sedgwick refers to Freud's list of the transformations, under a 'homophobic

ANDREW MICHAEL ROBERTS

regime of utterance', of the sentence 'I (a man) *love him* (a man)'
(*Closet*, 161): (1) 'I do not *love* him—I *hate* him'; (2) 'I do not love
him, I love *her*'; (3) '*I* do not love him; *she* loves him'; (4). 'I do not
love him; I do not love anyone'. All of these seem to be in play in
Marlow's scene with the Intended. Number 3 ('*I* do not love him;
she loves him') is readily available as a defence, since it happens to
be true that the Intended loves Kurtz (though Marlow seems keen to
stress the enduring and transcendent power of her love on limited
evidence). Number 2 ('I do not love *him*, I love *her*') is implied in
Marlow's talk of the beauty of the Intended and his hinting at an
undisclosed or unconscious reason for visiting her. Number 1 ('I do
not *love* him—I *hate* him') has always been implicit in Marlow's
mixed attitude of fascination, admiration, fear and disgust towards
Kurtz. Number 4 ('I do not love him; I do not love anyone') would illuminate Marlow's continuing bachelor status, which becomes a
theme and problem only in *Chance*. Most evident of all, however, is
a fifth transformation which Sedgwick adds, observing that it is
characteristic of Nietzsche and underlies Freud's project so inti-
mately that it does not occur to him to make it explicit: 'I do not *love*
him, I *am* him' (*Closet*, 162). Sedgwick's perception that the emergence in the nineteenth century of a definition of the 'homosexual'
in terms of sameness offered a way of concealing and expressing
same-sex desire through images of self-love (*Closet*, 160–1), opens
the possibility of alternative interpretations of many of the pairs of
male doubles that are found in Conrad's work. In the case of 'Heart
of Darkness', Marlow's placing of the Intended as one of Kurtz's possessions, comparable to the ivory in which he traded, is revealed as
part of an economy of repressed same-sex desire, complicit with
both the structures of patriarchy and with the economies of empire.
This link is elucidated by Irigaray:

> The use of and traffic in women subtend and uphold the reign
> of masculine hom(m)o-sexuality, even while they maintain that
> hom(m)o-sexuality in speculations, mirror games, identifica-
> tions, and more or less rivalrous appropriations, which defer
> its real practice. . . . The exchange of women as goods accom-
> panies and stimulates exchanges of other 'wealth' among
> groups of men.[6]

Conrad's text continues this traffic on the level of epistemology,
by offering to male readers a rich series of mirror games and identifications, involving the exchange of women as the objects of
knowledge.

*　　*　　*

6. Luce Irigaray, *This Sex Which Is Not One*, trans. Catherine Porter (Ithaca, NY: Cornell
UP, 1985), p. 172.

J. HILLIS MILLER

Should We Read "Heart of Darkness"?†

> The inaccessible incites from its place of hiding.
> (Jacques Derrida)

Should we read "Heart of Darkness?" May we read it? Must we read it? Or, on the contrary, ought we not to read it or allow our students and the public in general to read it? Should every copy be taken from all the shelves and burned? What or who gives us the authority to make a decision about that? Who is this "we" in whose name I speak? What community forms that "we"? Nothing could be more problematic than the bland appeal to some homogeneous authoritative body, say professors of English literature everywhere, capable of deciding collectively whether "we" should read "Heart of Darkness." By "read" I mean not just run the words passively through the mind's ear, but perform a reading in the strong sense, an active responsible response that renders justice to a book by generating more language in its turn, the language of attestation, even though that language may remain silent or implicit. Such a response testifies to having been changed by the reading.

Part of the problem, as you can see, is that it is impossible to decide authoritatively whether or not we should read "Heart of Darkness" without reading it in that strong sense. By then it is too late. I have already read it, been affected by it, and passed my judgment, perhaps recorded it for others to read. Which of us, however, would or should want to take someone else's word for what is in a book?

Each must read again in his or her turn and bear witness to that reading in his or her turn. In that aphorism about which Jacques Derrida has had so much to say, Paul Celan says, "No one bears witness for the witness." This might be altered to say, "No one can do your reading for you." Each must read for himself or herself and testify anew. This structure is inscribed in "Heart of Darkness" itself. The primary narrator bears witness through exact citation to what he heard Marlow say that night on the deck of cruising yawl *Nellie*, as he and the other men, the Lawyer, the Accountant, the Director of Companies, representatives of advanced capitalism and imperialism, waited for the tide to turn so they could float down the Thames and out to sea, presumably on a pleasure cruise. They have

† From "Should We Read 'Heart of Darkness'?" in *Conrad in Africa: New Essays on "Heart of Darkness,"* ed. Attie de Lange and Gail Fincham with Wiesław Krajka (New York: Columbia UP, 2002), pp. 21–33, 37–39. Reprinted by permission of *East European Quarterly*. Notes are the author's.

enough wealth and leisure to take time off to do as an aesthetic end
in itself what Marlow has done for pay as a professional seaman.
The profession of the primary, framing narrator is never specified.
He cites with what the reader is led to believe is conscientious and
meticulous accuracy just what Marlow said. What Marlow said, put
within quotation marks throughout, is a story, the recounting of
and accounting for what he calls an "experience" that "seemed
somehow to throw a kind of light on everything about me—and
into my thoughts. It was sombre enough, too—and pitiful—not extraordinary in any way—not very clear either. No, not very clear,
and yet it seemed to throw a kind of light" (7). That recounting and
accounting centers on an attempt to "render justice," as Marlow
puts it, to Kurtz, the man he meets at "the farthest point of navigation and the culminating point of my experience." What Marlow
says at the beginning is also an implicit promise to his listeners and
to us as readers. He promises that he will pass on to them and to *us*
the illumination he has received.

   Nor have Conrad's readers failed to respond to this demand for
interpretation. A large secondary literature has sprung up around
"Heart of Darkness." These essays and books of course have a constative dimension. They often provide precious information about
Conrad's life, about his experiences in Africa, about late nineteenth-
century imperialism, especially about that terrible murdering devastation wrought by King Leopold in the Belgian Congo, as it was then
called, about the supposed "originals" of characters in "Heart of
Darkness," and so on. This secondary literature, however, often also
has an explicit performative dimension. Conrad's novella is brought
before the bar of justice, arraigned, tried, and judged. The critic acts
as witness of his or her reading, also as interrogator, prosecuting at-
torney, jury, and presiding judge. The critic passes judgment and
renders justice. "Heart of Darkness" has often received a heavy sentence from its critics. It has been condemned, often in angry terms,
as racist or sexist, sometimes in the same essay as both. Examples
are the influential essay of 1975 by the distinguished Nigerian novelist Chinua Achebe ("Conrad was a bloody racist") or an essay of
1989 by Bette London: "Dependent upon unexamined assumptions,
themselves culturally suspect, the novel, in its representations of sex
and gender, supports dubious cultural claims; it participates in and
promotes a racial as well as gender ideology that the narrative represents as transparent and 'self-evident.' "[1] Edward Said's judgment in
Culture and Imperialism, though giving Conrad his due as a critic of
imperialism and recognizing the complexity of doing justice to

---

1. These citations are from the valuable "Critical History" in Joseph Conrad, *Heart of
Darkness*, ed. Ross C. Murfin, 2nd ed. (Boston–New York: Bedford Books of St. Martin's
Press, 1989), pp. 107, 109.

"Heart of Darkness," is in the end equally severe in his summing up:
"The cultural and ideological evidence that Conrad was wrong in his
Eurocentric way is both impressive and rich."[2]

These are powerful indictments. If what they say renders justice
to "Heart of Darkness," if their witness may be trusted, it might
seem inevitably to follow that the novella should not be read,
taught, or written about, except perhaps as an example of something detestable. Nevertheless, according to the paradox I have already mentioned, *you* could only be sure about this by reading the
novella yourself, thereby putting yourself, if these critics are right,
in danger of becoming sexist, racist, and Eurocentric yourself.

Even so, no one bears witness for the witness, and no one else
can do your reading *for* you. To pass judgment anew it is necessary
to take the risk and read "Heart of Darkness" *for* yourself. I shall
now try to do that. I begin by claiming that "Heart of Darkness" is
a literary work, not history, autobiography, travel writing, journalism, or any other genre.

In just what way does "Heart of Darkness" invite reading as literature rather than, say, as a historical account or as an autobiography? The most obvious way is in the displacement from Conrad to
two imaginary narrators, neither of whom is to be identified with
Conrad, any more than Socrates, in the Platonic dialogues is to be
identified with Plato. The reader who says Conrad speaks directly
for himself either in the words of the frame narrator or in Marlow's
words does so at his or her peril and in defiance of the most ele-
mentary literary conventions. Whatever the frame narrator or Marlow says is ironized or suspended, presented implicitly in parabasis,
by being presented as the speech of an imaginary character.

A second way "Heart of Darkness" presents itself as literature is
in the elaborate tissue of figures and other rhetorical devices that
make up, so to speak, the texture of the text. The simplest and most
obvious of these devices is the use of similes, signalled by "like" or
"as." These similes displace things that are named by one or the
other of the narrators and assert that they are like something else.
This something else forms a consistent subtext or counterpoint
defining everything that can be seen as a veil hiding something
more truthful or essential behind.

The first use of the figure of screens that are lifted to reveal more
screens behind, in a structure that is apocalyptic in the etymologi-
cal sense of "unveiling," as well as in the sense of having to do with
death, judgment, and other last things, comes when the frame narrator, describing the evening scene just before sunset, when the sky
is "a benign immensity of unstained light" (4) as it looks from the

---

2. Edward Said, *Culture and Imperialism* (New York: Vintage Books, 1994), p. 30 [see the
   selection in this Norton Critical Edition].

Nellie at anchor in the Thames estuary, says: "the very mist on the Essex marshes *was like* a gauzy and radiant fabric, hung from the wooded rises inland, and draping the low shores in diaphanous folds" (4—emphasis added). These similes, as they follow in a line punctuating the text at rhythmic intervals, are not casual or fortuitous. They form a system, a powerful undertext beneath the first-level descriptive language. They invite the reader to see whatever either of the narrators sees and names on the first level of narration as a veil or screen hiding something invisible or not yet visible behind it, though when each veil is lifted it uncovers only another veil behind it, according to a paradox essential to the genre of the apocalypse. Apocalypse: the word means "unveiling" in Greek. If one had to name the genre to which "Heart of Darkness" belongs the answer would be that it is a failed apocalypse, or, strictly speaking, since all apocalypses ultimately fail to lift the last veil, it is just that, a member of the genre apocalypse. The film modelled on "Heart of Darkness," *Apocalypse Now* was brilliantly and accurately named, except for that word "now." Apocalypse is never now. It is always to come, a thing of the future, both infinitely distant and immediately imminent.

In "Heart of Darkness," it is, to borrow Conrad's own words, as if each episode were like "some sordid *farce* acted in front of a sinister back-cloth" (13—emphasis added). The novella is structured as a long series of episodes each one of which appears with extreme vividness before the reader's imaginary vision; brought there by Conrad's remarkable descriptive power, only to vanish and be replaced by the next, as though a figured screen had been lifted to reveal yet another figured screen behind it, with the darkness behind all, like that "sinister back-cloth" Marlow names.

A third distinctively literary feature of "Heart of Darkness" has already been named. The novella is ironic through and through. The reader might wish this were not the case and deplore Conrad's radical irony, but there it is, an indubitable fact. "Heart of Darkness" *is* a masterwork of irony, as when the eloquent idealism of Kurtz's pamphlet on "The Suppression of Savage Customs" is undercut by the phrase scrawled at the bottom: "Exterminate all the brutes!" or as the dying Africans in the "grove of death" are called "helpers" in the great "work" of civilizing the continent (19). Marlow's narrative in particular is steeped in irony throughout. The problem is that it is impossible to be certain how to take that irony. Irony is, as Hegel and Kierkegaard said, "infinite absolute negativity," or as Friedrich Schlegel said, a "permanent parabasis," a continuous suspension of clearly identifiable meaning. It is a principle of unintelligibility, or, in Schlegel's words, *"Unverstundlichkeit."* Irony is a constant local feature of Marlow's narrative style—saying one thing and meaning another, as when the Europeans at the Central Station engaged in the terrible work of imperialist conquest, the "merry dance of death and trade," are said to be, in yet another simile, like "pilgrims": "They wandered here and there with their absurd long staves *in* their hands, like a lot of faithless pilgrims bewitched inside a rotten fence" (23—emphasis added). This stylistic undercutting is mimed in that larger structure in which each episode is replaced by the next, so that each is suspended by the reader's knowledge that it is only a contemporary appearance, not some ultimate goal of revelation attained. Each is certain to vanish and be replaced by the next scene to be enacted before that sinister black back-cloth.

A fourth ostentatious literary feature of "Heart of Darkness" is the recurrent *prosopopoeias*, the personifications of the darkness (whatever that word means here). This begins in the title. The darkness has a "heart." *Prosopopoeia* is the ascription of a name, a face, or a voice to the absent, the inanimate, or the dead. By a speech act, a performative utterance, *prosopopoeia* creates the fiction of a personality where in reality there is none. All *prosopopoeias* are also *catachreses*. They move the verbal fiction of a personality over to name something unknown/unknowable, and therefore, strictly speaking, unnamable *in* any literal language, something radically other than human personality: something absent, inanimate, or dead. It is no accident that so many traditional examples of *catachresis* are also personifications: "headland," "face of a mountain," "tongue of land," "table leg." "Heart of Darkness" is another such *catachrestic prosopopoeia*, to give it its barbarous-sounding Greek rhetorical name. We project our own bodies on the landscape and on surrounding artifacts. We give the darkness a heart. In "Heart of Darkness" *prosopopoeias* are a chief means of naming by indirection what Conrad calls, in a misleading and inadequate metaphor, "the darkness," or "the wilderness," or, most simply and perhaps most truthfully, "it." More than a dozen explicit personifications of this something, that *is* not really a person but an "it," asexual or trans-sexual, impersonal, indifferent, though to Marlow it seems like a person, rhythmically punctuate "Heart of Darkness" like a recurring leitmotif. The wilderness surrounding the Central Station, says Marlow, "struck me as something great and invincible, like evil or truth, waiting patiently for the passing away of this fantastic invasion" (23). Of that silent nocturnal wilderness Marlow asserts, "All this was great, expectant, mute, while the man [one of the agents at the station] jabbered about himself. I wondered whether the stillness on the face of the immensity looking at us two were meant as an appeal or as a menace. . . . Could we handle that dumb thing, or would it handle us? I felt

how *big*, how confoundedly big, was that thing that couldn't talk
and perhaps was deaf as well" (26—emphasis added). "It was the
stillness of an implacable force brooding over an inscrutable intention. It looked at you with a vengeful aspect . . . I felt often its mysterious stillness watching me at my monkey tricks, just as it
watches you fellows [his listeners on the *Nellie*] performing on your
respective tight-ropes for—what is it? half a crown a tumble—"
(34).

The wilderness destroys Kurtz by a kind of diabolical seduction:
"The wilderness had patted him on the head, and, behold, it was
like a ball—an ivory ball; it had caressed him, and—lo!—he had
withered; it had taken him, loved him, embraced him, got into his
veins, consumed his flesh, and sealed his soul to its own by the inconceivable ceremonies of some devilish initiation. He was its
spoiled and pampered favourite" (48). The Africans at Kurtz's Inner
Station vanish "without any perceptible movement of retreat, as if
the forest that had ejected these beings so suddenly had drawn
them in again as the breath is drawn in a long aspiration" (59).

This last citation indicates another and not unpredictable feature
of the *prosopopoeias* in "Heart of Darkness." The personification of
the wilderness is matched by a corresponding transformation of the
African people who intervene between Marlow and the "it." Just as
in Thomas Hardy's *The Return of the Native* the extravagant personification of the heath in the night time that opens the novel
leads to the assertion that Eustacia Vye, who rises from a mound in
the heath to stand outlined in the darkness, is, so to speak, the personification of the personification, its crystallization or visible embodiment, so in "Heart of Darkness" all the Africans Marlow meets
are visible representatives and symbols of that "it." Though it may
be racist for Marlow (not necessarily Conrad, the reader should remember) to see the Africans as inscrutably "other," as simple "savages" or "primitives," when their culture is older than any European
one and as complex or sophisticated, if not more so, this otherness
is stressed for the primary purpose of making the Africans visible
embodiments and proofs that the "it," the darkness, is a person.
This is an underlying feature of all Marlow's *prosopopoeias*, but it is
made most explicit in the scene where Kurtz's African mistress appears on the shore:

> She was savage and superb, wild-eyed and magnificent; there
> was something ominous and stately in her deliberate progress.
> And in the hush that had fallen suddenly upon the whole sor-
> rowful land, the immense wilderness, the colossal body of the
> fecund and mysterious life seemed to look at her, pensive, as
> though it had been looking at the image of its own tenebrous
> and passionate soul. . . . She stood looking at us without a stir,

and like the wilderness itself, with an air of brooding over an inscrutable purpose. (60–61)

This passage, like the one describing the way the wilderness has seduced Kurtz, seems to indicate that this "it" is after all gendered, that it is female, a colossal body of fecund and mysterious life. Since the wilderness is supposed to represent a mysterious knowledge, "like evil or truth," this personification does not jibe very well with the "sexist" assertions Marlow makes about the way women in general are, like Kurtz's Intended, "out of it," invincibly innocent and ignorant. At the least one would have to say that two contradictory sexist myths about women are ascribed to Marlow, the European male's tendency to personify the earth as a great mother, full of an immemorial, seductive wisdom, and the European male's tendency to condescend to women as innately incapable of seeing into things as well as men can.

All four of these stylistic features constitute a demand that "Heart of Darkness" be read, read as literature, as opposed to being taken as a straightforwardly mimetic or referential work that would allow the reader to hold Conrad himself directly responsible for what is said as though he were a journalist or a travel writer. Of course any of these features can be used in a non-literary work, but taken all together they invite the reader to declare, "This is literature."

In the name of just what higher responsibility does Conrad justify all this indirection and ironic undercutting, suspending, or redirecting of the straightforwardly mimetic aspect of his novella? In the name of what higher obligation is everything that is referentially named in a pseudo-historical or mimetic way displaced by these ubiquitous rhetorical devices and made into a sign for something else? If "Heart of Darkness" is a literary work rather than history or autobiography, just what kind of literary work is it, just what kind of apocalypse? What lies behind that veil?

The frame narrator, in a passage often cited and commented on, gives the reader a precious clue to an answer to these questions, though it is left to the reader to make use of the clue in his or her reading:

> The yarns of seamen have a direct simplicity, the whole meaning of which lies within the shell of a cracked nut. But Marlow was not typical (if his propensity to spin yarns be excepted), and to him the meaning of an episode was not inside like a kernel but outside [the Ms has "outside in the unseen"], enveloping the tale which brought it out only as a glow brings out a haze, in the likeness of one of those misty halos that sometimes are made visible by the spectral illumination of moonshine. (5)

"To spin yarns" is a cliché for narration. To tell a story is to join many threads together to make a continuous line leading from here to there. Of that yarn cloth may be woven, the whole cloth of the truth as opposed to a lie that, as the proverbial saying has it, is "made up out of whole cloth," a cloth making a web, screen, or veil covering the truth that remains hidden behind or within. This inside/outside opposition governs the narrator's distinction between two kinds of tales. The first is the sort of seaman's yarn it was assumed by many readers and critics Conrad was telling in his stories and novels. Its meaning lies within, like the shell of a cracked nut. I take it this names a realistic, mimetic, referential tale with an obvious point and moral. Marlow's tales, on the other hand, and, by implication at least, this one by Conrad, since so much of it is made up of Marlow's narration, have a different way of making meaning. All the visible, representational elements, all that the tale makes you see, according to that famous claim by Conrad that his goal was "above all to make you *see*," are there not for their own sakes, as mimetically valuable and verifiable, for example for the sake of giving the reader information about imperialism in the Belgian Congo. Those elements have as their function to make something else visible, what the manuscript calls the "unseen," perhaps even the unseeable, as the dark matter of the universe or the putative black holes at the center of galaxies can in principle never be seen, only inferred. Conrad's figure is a different one from those black holes about which he could not have known, though it is still an astronomical trope. It is an example of that peculiar sort of figure that can be called a figure of figure or a figure of figuration.

Just as the mist on a dark night is invisible except when it is made visible as a circular halo around moonlight, light already secondary and reflected from the sun, and just as the mimetic elements of Marlow's tale are secondary to the real things they represent at one remove, so the meaning of Marlow's yarns is invisible in itself and never named in itself. It is not inside the tale but outside, "brought out" indirectly by the things that are named and recounted, thereby made visible, just as, for example, Marlow when he visits the Intended hears Kurtz's last words breathed in a whisper by the dusk: "The dusk was repeating them in a persistent whisper all around us, in a whisper that seemed to swell menacingly like the first whisper of a rising wind. 'The horror! The horror!' " (69). The reader will note the way the whispered sound is onomatopoeically echoed here in the repetition three times of the word "whisper," with its aspirant and sibilant "whuh" and "isp" sounds. The illumination provided by the tale is "spectral." It turns everything into a ghostly phantom, that is, into something that is a revenant, something that has come back from the dead, and that cannot die, that will always, sooner or later, just when we least expect it, come again.

The miniature lesson in aesthetic theory the frame narrator presents here is an admirably succinct distinction between mimetic literature and apocalyptic, parabolic, or allegorical literature. In the latter everything named, with however much verisimilitude, stands for something else that is not named directly, that cannot be named directly, that can only be inferred by those that have eyes to see and ears to hear and understand, as Jesus puts it in the parable of the sower in Matthew 13. All these genres have to do with the promise, with death, with the truly secret, and with last things, "things," as Jesus says, "which have been kept secret from the foundation of the world" (Matthew, 13: 35). It is not so absurd as it might seem to claim that "Heart of Darkness" is a secular version of what are, (originally at least), intertwined religious or sacred genres: apocalypse, parable, allegory. Conrad himself spoke of the "piety" of his approach to writing and of his motive as quasi-religious. "One thing that I am certain of," he wrote in a letter to Arthur Symons, "is that I have approached the object of my task, things human, in a spirit of piety. The earth is a temple where there is going on a mystery play childish and poignant, ridiculous and awful enough in all conscience. Once in I've tried to behave decently. I have not degraded the quasi-religious sentiment by tears and groans; and if I have been amused or indignant, I've neither grinned nor gnashed my teeth."[3]

In the case of "Heart of Darkness" just what is that "something else" for the revelation of which the whole story is written? The clear answer is that the something else is that "it" that Marlow's narration so persistently personifies and that Kurtz passes judgment on when he says "The horror! The horror!" Everything in the whole story, all the mimetic and very similar elements, is for the sake of bringing out a glimpse of that "it," the revelation of which is promised by the frame narrator when he defines the characteristic indirection of meaning in Marlow's yarns.

Many critics, perhaps even most critics, of "Heart of Darkness" have made the fundamental mistake of taking the story as an example of the first kind of seaman's yarn. That is certainly the way Achebe reads it. Those critics, like F. R. Leavis, who have noticed all the language about the "unspeakable" and "inscrutable" "it" have almost universally condemned it as so much moonshine interfering with Conrad's gift for making you see, his gift for descriptive vividness. At least such critics have taken the trouble to read carefully and have noticed that there are important verbal elements in

3. Joseph Conrad, *Collected Letters*, 4:113.

the text that must be accounted for somehow and that do not fit the straightforward mimetic, descriptive paradigm.

Is the "something," the "it," revealed, brought into the open where it may be seen and judged? The clear answer is that it is not. The "it" remains to the end "unnamable," "inscrutable," "unspeakable," falsely, or at any rate unprovably, personified as having consciousness and intention by Marlow's rhetoric, named only indirectly and inadequately by all those similes and figures of veils being lifted. How could something be revealed that can only be revealed to those who have crossed over the threshold of death? The reader is told that "it" is "The horror! The horror!" but just what that means is never explained except in hints and indirections. Nothing definite can be said of the "it" except that it is not nothing, that it is, though even that is not certain, since it may be a projection, not a solicitation, call, or demand from something wholly other. Of the "it" one must say what Wallace Stevens says of the "primitive like an orb," "at the center on the horizon": "It is and it/Is not and, therefore, is." If "it" is wholly other it is wholly other, and nothing more can be said of it except by signs that confess in their proffering to their inadequacy. Each veil lifts to reveal another veil behind.

The structure of "Heart of Darkness" is the structure of the endlessly deferred promise, the implicit promise that Marlow makes at the beginning of his tale when he says that though his meeting with Kurtz, "the farthest point of navigation and the culminating point of my experience," was "not very clear," nevertheless "it seemed to throw a kind of light" (7). Marlow promises to pass this light or illumination on to his hearers. The primary narrator passes it on to us, the readers. The fulfillment of this promise to reveal, however, remains always future, something yet to come, eschatological or messianic rather than teleological. It is an end that can never come within the conditions of the series of episodes that reaches out towards it as life reaches towards death, or as Revelations promises an imminent messianic coming that always remains future, to come, but only beyond the last in the series, across the threshold into another realm and another regime. It is in the name of this unrevealed and unrevealable secret, out of obligation to it, in response to the demand it makes, while still remaining secret and inaccessible, that all "Heart of Darkness" is written. The presence within the novella of this inaccessible secret, a secret that nevertheless incites to narration, is what makes it appropriate to speak of "Heart of Darkness" as literature.

* * *

* * * Since Kurtz embodies the darkness it is logical or inevitable that he himself should become the "god" that the Africans worship and crawl before, in striking anticipation of the fascist or violent authoritarian possibilities within capitalist imperialism. Kurtz's

soul, like the "it," was an "inconceivable mystery" (66). He has "a smile of indefinable meaning" (67). "His was an impenetrable darkness" (68). Marlow's allegiance to Kurtz buries him "in a vast grave full of unspeakable secrets" (62), just as Kurtz's African mistress matches the wilderness in having "an air of brooding over an inscrutable purpose" (61), an "air of hidden knowledge, of patient expectation, of unapproachable silence" (56). It was "the stillness of an implacable force brooding over an inscrutable intention" (34). Kurtz is no more able to remove the last veil in an ultimate revelation than Marlow or Conrad can in their narrations. In all three cases a promise is made whose fulfillment or definitive nonfulfillment always remains yet to come.

What can one say to explain this contradiction, that Kurtz's magnificent idealistic eloquence is at the same time inhabited by an impenetrable darkness? Both Marlow's narration and Kurtz's eloquence, since both are based on that special speech act called a promise, are subject to two ineluctable features of any promise: 1) A promise would not be a promise but rather a constative foreknowledge if it were not possible that it will not be kept. A possible non-fulfillment is an inalienable structural feature of any promise, whether that promise is made in literature or in politics. 2) Any promise is an invocation of an unknown and unknowable future, of a secret other that remains secret and is invited to come into that hollow uncertainty of the promise. In the case of Marlow's narration, which I am taking as an exemplary literary work, what enters the narration is all that talk of the inscrutable, the impenetrable mystery, the unspeakable secret, and so on that has so offended some of Conrad's readers. In Kurtz's case, the millennial promise made by imperialist capitalism, since it is hollow at the core, cannot be separated from the possibility or perhaps even the necessity of invasion by the "it," what Conrad calls the "Heart of Darkness." Kurtz's case is exemplary of that, a parable or allegory of that necessity. No imperialist capitalism without the darkness. They go together. Nor has that spectral accompaniment of capitalism's millennial promise of world-wide peace, prosperity, and universal democracy by any means disappeared today, when the imperialist exploitation of Conrad's day and its accompanying philanthropic idealism has been replaced by the utopian promises made for the new global economy and the new regime of scientifico-bio-medico-techno-mediatic-telecommunications. As Jacques Derrida and Werner Hamacher have recognized,[4] the political left and the polit-

---

4. Jacques Derrida, *Specters of Marx*, trans. Peggy Kamuf (New York: Routledge, 1994), and Werner Hamacher, *"Lingua Amissa*: The Mechanism of Commodity-Language and Derrida's Specters of Marx," *Futures: Of Jacques Derrida*, ed. Richard Rand (Stanford: Stanford UP, 2001), pp. 130–78.

ical right are consonant in the promises they make. The promise of universal prosperity made for the new scientific economy dominated by technology and transformative communications techniques echoes the messianic promise, a messianism without messiah, of classical Marxism. It also echoes the promise made by rightwing ideologies, even the most unspeakably brutal, for example the Nazi promise of a thousand-year Reich.

We are inundated, swamped, engulfed every day by the present form of those promises, in all the media, in newspapers and magazines, on television, in advertising, on the Internet, in political and policy pronouncements—all guaranteeing that everything will get bigger, faster, better, more "user-friendly," and lead to worldwide millennial prosperity. These promises are all made by language or other signs, "the gift of expression, the bewildering, the illuminating, the most exalted and the most contemptible, the pulsating stream of light, or the deceitful flow from the heart of an impenetrable darkness" (47).

I return to my beginning. Should we, ought we to read "Heart of Darkness"? Each reader must decide that for himself or herself. There are certainly ways to read "Heart of Darkness" that might do harm, for example if it is read as straightforwardly endorsing Eurocentric, racist and sexist ideologies. If it is read, however, as I believe it should be read, as a powerful exemplary revelation of the ideology of capitalist imperialism, including its racism and sexism, as that ideology is consonant with a certain definition of literature that is its concomitant, including a non-revelatory revelation or invocation in both of an "exemplary" non-revealable secret, then, I declare, "Heart of Darkness" should be read, ought to be read. There is an obligation to do so.

LISSA SCHNEIDER

Iconography and the Feminine Ideal†

Of the many mythic feminine figures in Conrad's novels and stories, one in particular has elicited fervent reactions: Kurtz's "small sketch in oils," in *Heart of Darkness*, "representing a woman, draped and blindfolded, carrying a lighted torch" (25). As Marlow tells the men aboard the *Nellie*, "The background was somber—almost black. The movement of the woman was stately, and the effect

† From *Conrad's Narratives of Difference: Not Exactly Tales for Boys* (New York: Routledge, 2003), pp. 9–10, 11, 12–18. Reproduced by permission of Routledge/Taylor and Francis Books, Inc. Notes are the author's.

of the torchlight on the face was sinister" (25). The figure in the painting recalls personifications of Liberty and Justice, who are associated with the amazonian ideal. Yet with the paired attributes of torch and blindfold this woman appears both potent and disturbingly powerless. Although Marlow mentions the painting only once in his embedded narrative, critics have been drawn to its paradoxical imagery as perhaps to few other word portraits in Conrad's writings. In their efforts to trace the painting's symbolic resonances, critics variously have seen the blindfolded, torch-bearing figure as a symbol for Kurtz,[1] for Europe "blinded by the light of her civilization,"[2] or even for all "mankind, groping blindly through the darkness of his existence."[3]

These readings hold in common a tendency to naturalize the figure in the painting. However, as Marina Warner explains, "a symbolized female presence both gives and takes value and meaning in relation to actual women."[4] To see the painting's polysemous imagery in terms of a commentary on Kurtz's psychology, on Western imperialist ideology, or, most broadly of all, on the general "despair" of the human condition, is to elide attention to its presentation of a *female* figure. Jeremy Hawthorn, in a notable exception, links "Kurtz's portrait of the blindfolded female" to the European women characters in *Heart of Darkness*, but in a more subtle act of displacement he adds that these female characters are themselves icons who "serve a larger representative function, portraying that idealism which the western imperialist powers use as apology for their exploitation." As he says, "the picture helps to support the argument that the novella associates the isolation of European women with the isolation of idealism from that which it is being used to underwrite."[5] Yet not European women alone are associated with the painting's mythic figure (whose race has always been assumed by critics, but is never actually identified in the text). Although Marlow allies the Intended with the figure in the painting, describing her paradigmatically raised arms as she stands surrounded by "an unearthly glow" (75), Marlow also recalls the up-

1. Frederick Karl, "Introduction to the *Danse Macabre*: Conrad's *Heart of Darkness*" in *Heart of Darkness: A Case Study in Contemporary Criticism*, ed. Ross C. Murfin (New York: St. Martin's P, 1989), p. 132; Mark S. Sexton, "Kurtz's Sketch in Oils: Its Significance to *Heart of Darkness*," *Studies in Short Fiction* 24:4 (Fall 1987): 388; Marianne DeKoven, *Rich and Strange: Gender, History, Modernism* (Princeton: Princeton UP, 1991), p. 113.
2. Brian W. Shaffer, *The Blinding Torch: Modern British Fiction and the Discourse of Civilization* (Amherst: U of Massachusetts P, 1993), p. 2.
3. Wilfred S. Dowden, "The Light and Dark Lie," in *Conrad's Heart of Darkness and the Critics*, ed. Bruce Harkness (Belmont, CA: Wadsworth, 1960), p. 158.
4. Marina Warner, *Monuments and Maidens: The Allegory of the Female Form* (New York: Athenaeum, 1985), p. xx.
5. Jeremy Hawthorn, *Joseph Conrad: Narrative Technique and Ideological Consciousness* (London: Edward Arnold, 1990), pp. 183, 184, 190 [see the selection in this Norton Critical Edition].

stretched arms and amazonian "helmeted head" of Kurtz's African mistress (67), and, in a direct echo of his description of the painting, declares that "there was something *ominous* and *stately* in her deliberate progress" along a lighted embankment by the Congo river (60, emphasis added).

* * *

By force of repetition, Conrad implies that, whether as essence or as social mandate, the relation between blindness and light is somehow bound up with women and femininity. No comparable image in Conrad's writings directly associates men with synchronous blindness and light-bearing. Although indirect associations abound, the effect is always to feminize male characters, who become, at least momentarily, aligned with women. For example, in *Heart of Darkness* Marlow's aunt suggests that he is "something like an emissary of light" (12), but later in the narrative, Marlow compares himself to "a blindfolded man set to drive a van down a bad road" (34). In this moment, Marlow is aligned with the Intended, for he is as "out of it" as she is (48). In other words, the gender of the figure in the painting from *Heart of Darkness* is neither casual nor incidental to its meaning; it maintains a significance that extends beyond an understanding of any one particular Conradian character or text, and certainly extends beyond how European women in Conrad's writings are isolated and exploited by imperialism. * * * Conrad's alliance of a blinded femininity with light informs his representations of English, Italian, Hispanic, Malay, African, French, and Russian women in stories set around the globe. * * * Does the figure of a light-bearing woman who cannot see by the light she casts prescribe woman's passivity and subjection? Does the figure take on the attributes of Liberty and Justice to underwrite an ideal of venerable feminine virtue? Or does the contrast between torch and blindfold on the allegorical body of woman escape traditional, masculine constructions of feminine lack (and impossible virtue) by making manifest the paradox in these mutually exclusive alternatives?

* * *

In *Heart of Darkness*, Marlow discovers the oil sketch of the "draped and blindfolded" woman in the room of the "Manager's spy" at the Central Station, 200 miles from the African coast (24). "Arrested" by the image, he questions his host, who identifies Kurtz as the painter and provides Marlow with his first concrete information about the man whose name has been mentioned all along his journey through the Congo interior (25). Although Kurtz has abandoned his art work, this iconic portrait has also struck a chord with the manager's spy, who has safeguarded it in his room along with his collection of "spears, assegais, shields, knives" and other "trophies" (24). The fascination with the painting exhibited by these two men is striking, particularly in conjunction with the evident critical fascination with its imagery. Why, after all, does the manager's spy—who fears Kurtz and the new "gang of virtue" (25)— keep it? Marlow's interest in the painting precedes his knowledge of the artist's name, so in his case, preoccupation with the enigmatic Kurtz cannot account for the initial attraction. To the contrary, it is in part because of the oil sketch that Marlow aspires to meet Kurtz.

By preserving the painting amid his African "trophies" of tribal weaponry, the manager's spy allies it with classic instruments of male empowerment. Since a trophy usually symbolizes achievement, or commemorates an enemy's defeat, the collection of spears, knives, and other weapons could exemplify dominance over the African natives from whom the manager's spy has usurped them. Although insufficient as a rationale for Marlow's enthrallment, one could argue likewise that possession of the painting provides the manager's spy with access to Kurtz's power, or even that the "trophy" indicates (at least, again, to him) his dominance over Kurtz. As such the image takes on homosocial qualities; the manager's spy attempts to gain access to another man through the body of a woman. Woman becomes a weapon in these "denied erotics of male rivalry" allowing one man to imagine he might stand in for another by virtue of a nearer relation to a painted female figure.[6]

But if in one regard possession of the painting intimates one man's desire to usurp the power and position of its painter and former owner, from another aspect its possession more narrowly implies the subjugation of that which it immortalizes: woman. It is for this reason, in Conrad's "The Return" (written in 1897, nearly two years before *Heart of Darkness*), that Alvan Hervey takes great pride in a remarkably similar "trophy." On his first-floor landing, "a marble woman, decently covered from neck to instep with stone draperies, advanced a row of lifeless toes to the edge of the pedestal, and thrust out blindly a rigid white arm holding a cluster of lights."[7] Hervey's neoclassical statue is an obvious precursor to the figure in the painting. Yet the functional statue in "The Return" is presented as a satiric commentary on Hervey's "artistic tastes"; placed in apposition to a watercolor of "a young lady sprawled with dreamy eyes in a moored boat in company of . . . an enamoured man in a blazer" and a sketch of "a pathetically lean girl" with "expiring eyes" tendering "a flower for sale," it illustrates Hervey's trite notions about femininity and gender roles (116). Indeed, Hervey's painting of the flower vendor ironically recalls the popular Victo-

6. Eve Kosofsky Sedgwick, *Between Men: English Literature and Male Homosocial Desire* (New York: Columbia UP, 1985), p. 181.
7. Joseph Conrad, *Tales of Unrest* (1898; Harmondsworth: Penguin, 1977), pp. 115–16.

rian ideal of woman as innocent flower articulated in John Ruskin's *Sesame and Lilies* (1865). In the context of the rest of his art collection, the statue's significance is inseparable from Hervey's attitudes toward women, for Hervey's takes an equal satisfaction in his "trophy" wife, who had "not a thought of her own in her head" and yet "appeared to him so unquestionably of the right sort that he did not hesitate to declare himself in love" (112).

Still, both the statue and his "well-connected, well educated and intelligent" wife serve to bolster Hervey's sense of position and importance among other men of his class (112). It is interesting how such similar works of art provide both the manager's spy and Alvan Hervey with an inflated perception of their station in life, even though one man finds his society amid the white traders in the African interior, and the other in the culture of haute-bourgeois London businessmen. At the same time, the manager's spy, like Alvan Hervey in "The Return," is a deluded, satiric figure, a "young fool" as Marlow says (27). In other words, it would seem that something of the imagery and symbolism in these art works escapes their limited understanding, and mocks their grasping bids for power.

The painting in *Heart of Darkness* also demands to be understood within the larger context of the other collected "trophies" and artistic portraits in that novel. Associated with weapons and armor, it suggests phallic empowerment; associated with victory, it commemorates symbolic triumph over the feminine. Marlow's interest in the painting parallels his interest in a photograph of the Intended he later discovers among Kurtz's letters and papers. From her picture, which he appropriates for himself, Marlow casts the Intended in terms akin to the mythic figure in the oil sketch. To Marlow, the photographic portrait offers an ideal, iconic image of femininity; as he tells the men aboard the *Nellie*, "She struck me as beautiful—I mean she had a beautiful expression. I know that sunlight can be made to lie too, yet one felt that no manipulation of light and pose could have conveyed the delicate sense of truthfulness upon those features. She seemed ready to listen without mental reservation, without suspicion, without a thought for herself" (72). The association between femininity and the "sunlight" of truthfulness accentuates the process of idealization at work in Marlow's mind and the inspiration he derives from it. As a result, Marlow projects an ideal, phallic woman; endowing her with the capacity to assuage his own feminizing feelings of loss and alienation after his experiences in the Congo, he resolves to seek her out on his return to Brussels. Still, when Marlow finally meets the Intended, the illusion he has created is shattered. Instead of listening to him "without mental reservation, without suspicion, without a thought for herself," she tells him: "I feel I can speak to you—and oh! I must speak" (74). The resulting contrast between woman as iconic object and woman as speaking subject is unbearable for Marlow. Marlow is disappointed not so much because of *what* the Intended says, but rather because she speaks at all. Consequently, in her presence Marlow feels "a sensation of panic" and imagines the surrounding darkness closing in on him (74). Although the Intended's photograph has depicted her in sunlight, she is dressed "all in black" when Marlow actually meets her, and comes "floating towards [him] in the dusk" (73); in Marlow's first view of Kurtz's African Mistress, she stands in brilliant sunlight, "warlike and still in statuesque repose"—and, in her "dumb pain," utterly voiceless "in the hush that had fallen suddenly upon the whole sorrowful land" (60).

Photography differs from most other art forms in that the medium fosters the illusion that it captures reality. In contrast, allegorical art relies for its effect on its ability to place the body under erasure. As Angus Fletcher explains, from its genesis allegory has been interpreted as the "human reconstitution of divinely inspired messages, a revealed transcendental language which tries to preserve the remoteness of a properly veiled godhead."[8] In early modern Europe, however, female figuration eclipsed male forms in almost all new or revitalized allegorical imagery, perhaps because, as Madelyn Gutwirth suggests, "allegory thrives on the multiplicity of meanings men have attached to the female sex."[9] One knows that female allegory presents an image of a woman, yet, at least in theory, one reads the image in terms of its divine "message." Hence in Western allegorical art and iconography, "the female form does not refer to particular women, does not describe women as a group, and often does not even presume to evoke their natures."[1] Voided of its own signifying status, the female body serves as an "abstract dummy" for Western society's most outstanding ideals.[2] Marlow's response to the picture of the Intended shows how images of women, even "realistic" photographic images, are particularly receptive to transference and male fetishistic attachments. Although Marlow's disclaimer acknowledges the possibility of the illusion ("sunlight can be made to lie too"), his subsequent remark denies the prospect of the photographic "lie" in this case. When Marlow sees redemption through "the sunlight of truthfulness" in the Intended's photograph, that framed representation of her living body

8. Angus Fletcher, *Allegory: The Theory of a Symbolic Mode* (Ithaca, NY: Cornell UP, 1964), p. 21.
9. Madelyn Gutwirth, *The Twilight of the Goddesses: Women and Representation in the French Revolution* (New Brunswick, NJ: Rutgers UP, 1992), p. 255.
1. Warner, p. 12.
2. Maurice Agulhon, *Marianne into Battle: Republican Imagery and Symbolism in France, 1789–1880*, trans. Janet Lloyd (Cambridge: Cambridge UP, 1981), p. 1.

480   LISSA SCHNEIDER

becomes an "abstract dummy" for his imagination. *Heart of Darkness* exposes the dichotomy between the photographic "lie" and its female subject; the Intended is not an icon of truth, but a woman whose words reveal her human frailty. Marlow's disappointment when the Intended fails to match his expectations underscores the difficulty, particularly for men, of divorcing female allegorical art from responses to actual women. In Marlow's case, the value and meaning of the former influences his expectations of the latter.

The Intended's photograph covertly manipulates "light and pose" to inspire Marlow, who is already primed to see woman as an icon of redemption. The painting in *Heart of Darkness* and the statue in "The Return," however, blatantly exploit the Eurocentric tropes of allegory. The figure of the blinded torchbearer provides an intrinsic critique of men's tendency to see women in ideal terms. Both the oil sketch in *Heart of Darkness* and the "sightless woman of marble" in "The Return" are overtly ambiguous in their imagery, and prove resistant to the totalizing effects common to female allegory. By juxtaposing essentially different iconographic conventions—Liberty's torch, Justice's blindfold—the two art works draw attention to the confrontation between these conventions as played out on the site of the female body. As a result of this iconographic excess, which closes off the woman from the light, Marlow is both attracted to and disconcerted by the painted figure in *Heart of Darkness*, and finds something "sinister" about the "effect of the torchlight" on her face (25).

As an empowering yet "sinister" trophy, the painting in *Heart of Darkness* embodies the contradictions of Western socio-cultural and psychosexual fantasies about women and the feminine. In Western art and iconography, a torch in the hands of a woman symbolizes wisdom, knowledge, empire, liberty, and Christian virtue; while male blindness is occasionally used to represent insight (Homer, Tiresias, Milton), the blindfolded woman represents ignorance, moral or spiritual blindness, and also—but only since the Renaissance—impartiality.[3] Significantly, the figure of Justice located in front of London's Central Criminal Court at the Old Bailey, the statue of Justice best known to Conrad, is not portrayed blindfolded, but wide-eyed.[4] With her torch and blindfold, the

3. As James Hall explains, "in antiquity, Justice was known for her clear-sightedness"; not until the sixteenth century was she portrayed blindfolded. Hall adds that "elsewhere in the Renaissance, allegory blindfolding implies absence of judgment, as in the case of Cupid, Fortune, Ignorance" (*Dictionary of Subjects and Symbols in Art* [New York: Harper & Row, 1974], p. 183). During the Middle Ages, "Synagogue," Judaism personified, was blindfolded to portray a refusal to see the light of Christian salvation" (Hall, p. 49; Hans Biedermann, *Dictionary of Symbolism: Cultural Icons and the Meanings Behind Them*, trans. James Hulbert [New York: Meridian Books, 1994], p. 42).
4. Conrad regularly passed Old Bailey on his daily promenades while preparing for his Master's license.

robed woman in Kurtz's painting draws upon the dual traditions of woman as pure and virtuous and as tainted by ignorance or a primordial fall from grace.

The torch also belongs to the same paradigm as the spears, knives, and other weapons in the collection of the manager's spy; in psychoanalytic terms, it connotes the phallus (or masculine power). In contrast, the blindfold signifies castration (or disempowerment) and lack. In this sense, to portray woman as blindfolded creates metonymic excess, a negation of a negation, for woman already represents castration and lack within the social order. Thus, in *Memoirs of the Blind*, Jacques Derrida examines European figurations of male blindness or blindfolding as autobiographical metaphors for the artists' disempowerment, and argues that no "great blind women" stand out as historical figures.[5] Mythic images of Marianne and Columbia, the personifications of the French and the American republics, are often portrayed carrying torches; these figures are closely affiliated with the figure of Liberty, first represented as a woman in the third century B.C.[6] But the torch of Liberty was meant to illuminate the paths of men; also to introduce a blindfold—to close her off from its light—creates a visual tautology since the fight for liberty (power), both before and during the birth of Republicanism, was not generally intended to transform the position or status of women. Hence A. L. Janet-Lange's *La France éclairant le Monde* (1848) and Auguste Bartholdi's monumental *Statue of Liberty* (installed [in New York Harbor] in 1877)—both obvious influences for the painting in *Heart of Darkness* and the garish lamp-statue in "The Return"—portray torchbearing matrons to nations in which women were denied citizenship. The confrontation between torch and blindfold on the body of woman exposes the manner in which women come to represent lack, for men, in the social order and draws attention to women's disenfranchisement; it challenges male fantasies of power, the gaze, and the fetishized female body.

It is the totemic, fetishistic aspects of the blinded light bearer (and, likewise, of Marlow's image of the Intended) that both attract and repel Marlow. A fetish is something that is, by definition, quintessentially feminine. Although items like high-heeled shoes or dangling earrings are classic examples of fetishized items, anything can become a fetish; context determines it. For Freud, the fetish or "screen object" is used to obtain sexual gratification; it is both a

5. Jacques Derrida, *Memoirs of the Blind: The Self-Portrait and Other Ruins*, trans. Pascale-Anne Brault and Michael Nass (Chicago: U of Chicago P, 1993), p. 5.
6. Pierre Provoyeur, "Artistic Problems," *Liberty: The French-American Statue in Art and History*, eds. Pierre Provoyeur and June Hargrove (New York: Harper & Row, 1988), p. 78.

substitute for the woman's absent phallus, and a "memorial" to the man's anxious recognition of female anatomical difference.[7] In the Lacanian revision of Freud, however, fetishism is understood more broadly as the means by which men conceal the damaging knowledge of their own disempowerment by displacing it onto women, who are perceived as lacking (although "there is nothing missing in the Real").[8]

For both Freud and Lacan, the dual aspects of denial and recognition of an illusory difference are an integral part of fetishistic attachments. Ironically, Marlow's palpable disappointment with the Intended is fueled by her very complicity with the feminine ideal of purity in which Marlow, with his desire to keep women "out of it," is so invested (48). Selfless in her ministrations to Kurtz's mother, and unshakable in her belief that Kurtz, at the last, thought only of her, the Intended colludes with the Victorian ideal of femininity that would estrange women from knowledge, opportunity, and insight, even as they are upheld as harbingers of a light meant for men. The Intended carries a torch, as it were, not for all men, and certainly not for Marlow, but—as she should in accordance with the Victorian standard of female virtue—only for Kurtz. In her dedication to Kurtz, she reveals the human frailty that Marlow wished to deny in himself by upholding her as an icon of truth.

Conrad's writings are replete with images of women as fetishistic sources of a redeeming light. By continually refiguring this imagery he virtually compels his readers to make intertextual associations. In *Suspense*, Cosmo Latham thinks, "light entered into [Madame de Montevesso's] composition. And it was not the cold light of marble. 'She actually glows,' he said to himself, amazed."[9] In *An Outcast of the Islands*, "The luminous fact" of Aissa's existence plunges Willems, her European lover, into "the sudden darkness of despair" when the Arab woman leaves his presence; Aissa's very body becomes torch-like, for "her moving figure, rippled in a hot wave round [Willems's] body and scorched his face in a burning touch."[1] Conrad's representation of the lighthouse keeper Linda Viola, in the final paragraphs of *Nostromo*, belongs to the same paradigm; fusing torch, lighthouse, and the mythic feminine, Conrad describes how "Linda's black figure detached itself upright on the light of the lantern with her arms raised above her head."[2] Dain

7. Sigmund Freud, "Fetishism," *The Standard Edition of the Complete Psychological Works*, ed. James Strachey and Anna Freud (London: Hogarth P, 1986), 21:154.
8. Jacques Lacan, *Female Sexuality*, trans. Jacqueline Rose, ed. Juliet Mitchell and Jacqueline Rose (New York: W. W. Norton, 1985), p. 115.
9. Joseph Conrad, *Suspense* (Garden City, NY: Doubleday, 1925), p. 129.
1. Joseph Conrad, *An Outcast of the Islands* (1896; Harmondsworth: Penguin, 1975), p. 63.
2. Joseph Conrad, *Nostromo* (1904; Harmondsworth: Penguin, 1990), p. 448.

Maroola, in *Almayer's Folly*, tells Nina Almayer: "When I am not near you, Nina, I am like a man that is blind. What is life to me without light?"[3] His remarks underscore how the fetishized woman covers or compensates for men's own feelings of disempowerment, since blindness is his attribute, not Nina's. In *Under Western Eyes*, Peter Ivanovitch refers in conversation with Razumov to "the inspired penetration" of the "true light of femininity," though he casually exploits his *dame de compagnie*, who is "quite willing to be the blind instrument of higher ends," as she shivers with cold and hunger by his side. Razumov does not understand Ivanovitch's meaning, and replies, "Penetration? Light? This is very mysterious."[4]

Razumov's comic response in *Under Western Eyes* reveals Ivanovitch's gendered metaphor of "penetration" and "light" as masculine fantasy devoid of any material content. By estranging women from his fantasy of the feminine, "the revolutionary feminist" Ivanovitch exposes his wish that, as Marlow had hoped to find in the company of the Intended, this "light" of the feminine shines only for him.[5] Conrad infuses Razumov with Conrad's own ironic awareness of the contradictions at work in men's desire to keep women on pedestals. In an early letter to his cousin, the author Marguerite Poradowska, Conrad wrote: "Do not come down from the pedestal where I have placed you, even though that would bring you nearer to me," only wryly to reverse himself: "I am not always an egoist, I embrace you."[6] Icons, while dear to the heart, are essentially untouchable, creating a peculiar double bind in men's relations to actual women. If Conrad does not altogether renounce this fantasy of the feminine in his writings, there is an extent to which he repeatedly attempts to demystify it: to expose the masculine egotism that demands the illusion.

* * *

3. Joseph Conrad, *Almayer's Folly* (1895; Harmondsworth: Penguin, 1976), p. 61.
4. Joseph Conrad, *Under Western Eyes* (1911; Harmondsworth: Penguin, 1989), pp. 219, 169, 219.
5. *Under Western Eyes*, p. 155.
6. Dated 22 October 1891, in *Collected Letters* 1:100.

Heart of Darkness and Apocalypse Now

LOUIS K. GREIFF

Conrad's Ethics and the Margins of *Apocalypse Now*†

I. *The Doors*

Joseph Conrad receives no screen credits in Francis Ford Coppola's *Apocalypse Now*. Many viewers of the film close to *Heart of Darkness* take this as a kind of confirmation that *Apocalypse Now* insults its literary predecessor by repeatedly violating the novel's original shape and substance. A more complex truth is that amid many real slights and distortions, Coppola also pays meaningful homage to Conrad by preserving the essentials of *Heart of Darkness* on screen in striking and unexpected ways. A model for this involves Conrad's much-discussed frame in *Heart of Darkness*—the Thames River scene on board the cruising yawl *Nellie* which opens and closes the tale. One critic of *Apocalypse Now*, John Pym, states that it would have been impossible for Coppola to reproduce Conrad's frame on film, but that without it the ethical relevance of Kurtz to the lives of "normal" men like Marlow's listeners (or ourselves) is lost.[1] It is hard to imagine Martin Sheen, as Captain Willard, dispensing wisdom on the Hudson, or in San Francisco Bay, to a group of amateur sailors who also represent Western culture in general. Such a comic parody of Conrad is mercifully omitted. Yet in its place *Apocalypse Now* does provide a creative imitation of the Conradian frame—a disembodied voice, as was Marlow's own on the darkened Thames, to begin and end the film. Off-key and compelling, this

† From "Soldier, Sailor, Surfer, Chef: Conrad's Ethics and the Margins of *Apocalypse Now*," *Literature/Film Quarterly* 20:3 (1992): 188–91, 193–94, 194–95, 195–97. Reprinted with permission of *Literature/Film Quarterly*, Copyright © Salisbury University, Salisbury, MD 21801.

1. John Pym, "*Apocalypse Now*: An Errand Boy's Journey," *Sight and Sound* 49 (1979–80): 9–10.

voice belongs to Jim Morrison, lead singer of The Doors—the rock group that quite literally provides entrance and exit to *Apocalypse Now*. Thus, the film's very first line is Jim Morrison's "This is the end, beautiful friend." The beginning announces itself as the ending, just as in *Heart of Darkness* the initial scene on board the *Nellie* occurs, chronologically, long after the events recounted in Marlow's yarn. Also as in *Heart of Darkness*, Coppola's musical frame creates an appropriate bridge between the bizarre tale about to unfold and the wider context of modern cultural experience. With rock music as frame, and particularly with The Doors, Coppola has found an image to conflate nightmare with normalcy—the worst extremes of Vietnam with the givens of American life. Wild, destructive, and self-destructive as it can become, rock music is also inseparable from our daily lives as Americans—as common and accessible to all of us as the portable radio beside the desk at which I write.

II. *Soldier and Errand Boy*

As with structure in *Apocalypse Now*, so too with ethical foundation and meaning. The film, in fact, retains much of Conrad's artistic and philosophic achievement in *Heart of Darkness*, but never predictably and always with surprising transformations. Possibly the most pervasive moral issue in the original text involves Conrad's (and Marlow's) belief in a proportion between man's endeavor and the quality of his being. In the world of Conradian and Marlovian ethics, to work well at one meaningful task—perhaps ideally as a craftsman or an artist works—is to create self along with visible accomplishment. To work badly, erratically, or at conflicting endeavors, on the other hand, is to erode human substance toward hollowness—the extreme condition of moral vulnerability in "Heart of Darkness." Although stated simply here, this two-sided premise provides a key principle of discrimination between Marlow and Kurtz—a determinant of spiritual and physical preservation in one life, and of absolute loss in the other.

For Conrad, Marlow is the consummate salt-water sailor who has crafted his own identity in the very act of perfecting his trade. The fullness of character which results from such a lifelong process affords Marlow the necessary integrity and strength to resist evil and, ultimately, to survive the African ordeal reasonably intact. As Conrad's solid and internally unified hero, Marlow is likened to an artist in at least two separate ways. First, he approaches his seamanship (and even fresh-water sailing when necessary) as part craftsman and part lover—the way an artist would approach his medium. Secondly, in deepening and completing his humanity along with his craft, Marlow has come to be blessed or cursed with the skill of storytelling. Like Coleridge's Ancient Mariner, he spins yarns which are unique among seamen, and which have the power to convey to all men the truth, but not the pain, of his experience.

With artistic inclinations of his own, Kurtz might resemble Marlow if it were not for the multiplicity, or ultimately the chaos, of his accomplishments. Both painter and musician, Kurtz also practices ivory trade, journalism, public speaking, and, for a time, the work of imposing white civilization upon Africa. ". . . to this day [Marlow admits near the end of *Heart of Darkness*] I am unable to say what was Kurtz's profession, whether he ever had any—which was the greatest of his talents. I had taken him for a painter who wrote for the papers, or else for a journalist who could paint—but even . . . [his] cousin . . . could not tell me what he had been—exactly" (71–72). Everything and nothing, what Kurtz emerges as, exactly, is Conrad's hollow man. He is deprived of Marlow's stable substance and ignorant of the focused and yet passionate labor which creates it. In such a condition of emptiness, Kurtz or any man is at extreme risk of moral and, finally, total destruction—open and available to the darkest opportunities around him and to the even darker suggestions within.

To turn from this clear contrast of character and value in *Heart of Darkness* to *Apocalypse Now* is, initially, to encounter confusion—at least if one limits the inquiry to the film's portrayal of Marlow and Kurtz. In the first place, the opposed professional lives of these two men—so carefully established in the text—become precisely reversed in Coppola's hands. It is now Kurtz, Colonel Kurtz, who appears as the solid and dedicated one—a man, according to his dossier, who has concentrated all his life's energy on becoming the absolute officer and soldier. By contrast, Captain Willard, the film's version of Marlow, emerges as fragmented and corrupt in professional terms. Is he a combat soldier, a CIA operative within the military, or simply a hit man? The film audience is never certain, nor, for that matter, is Kurtz. The Colonel, in fact, seems to grasp and to identify Willard's professional emptiness, just as, in the novel, Marlow had discovered a similar problem in Kurtz. "Are you an assassin?" Colonel Kurtz asks Willard soon after their first meeting. When Willard replies "I'm a soldier," Kurtz bluntly corrects him. "You're neither. You're an errand boy sent by grocery clerks to collect a bill."

If the film's two major characters trade professional stance, in relation to *Heart of Darkness*, they do not neatly exchange moral position along with it. More confusing, any ethical significance in their endeavors is blurred and finally lost on screen, so that regardless of how differently Kurtz and Willard go about their business, both seem morally tainted by the film's end and hardly acceptable as a source of wisdom or human value. Kurtz, the pure soldier, delivers a monologue during the film's last sequence which aims to justify any atrocity as acceptable in war. Even with the forgiving assumption that his words articulate a soldier's formula for winning—and thus ending—a war as quickly as possible, the Colonel is not saved from appearing as empty and dangerous as his Conradian namesake. All speeches aside, Colonel Kurtz presides over a Cambodian fortress where chaos has replaced military professionalism as the order of the day. Torture and bloody execution are the main activities at Kurtz's camp. They seem to occur to no specific purpose, almost randomly, and attest, at the very least, to the insanity of the man in charge.

Captain Willard offers little improvement over Kurtz as potential moral center of the film. The audience first sees him on leave, holed up in Saigon in a condition of physical and spiritual depravity. He recovers when given a mission, but then enters a long passive period during the river journey on the PBR. This state is broken only once by significant action, when Willard dispassionately executes a sampan girl—wounded by the boat-crew—so as not to be diverted from his mission. In the film's climactic sequences, at Kurtz's camp, Willard again performs a single major act—another killing, this time of Kurtz himself. In truth, throughout the entire film Willard accomplishes just one thing which can be regarded as unambiguously decent. This is to rescue Lance, a member of the PBR crew, from a feral merger with the Cambodian tribe. Other reflections of morality in Willard's actions can only be described negatively, in terms of what harm he could but doesn't do. He rejects the option, for example, of replacing Kurtz as savage king. Likewise, he does not call in a prearranged airstrike on the fortress or, in Conrad's language, choose to "Exterminate all the brutes" (50). Despite Willard's questionable mix of passivity and violence, Coppola does suggest that he has developed inwardly as a result of his journey and encounter with Kurtz. Yet the nature of such development remains clouded, in any moral or spiritual sense, because Willard simply and silently fades from view. By the film's close, then, neither major character emerges as spokesman or example of anything resembling the Conradian ethic in *Heart of Darkness*. If the focus is limited to Captain Willard and Colonel Kurtz, viewers of *Apocalypse Now* are left—again in Conrad's terms—only with a choice of nightmares or, at best, with unresolved and frustrating ambiguities on either side.

III. Sailor and Saucier

As with the artist's frame for *Heart of Darkness*, however, so too with the philosopher's ethic of human accomplishment. It isn't lost or forgotten at all in *Apocalypse Now* so much as it is transformed to challenge, surprise, and finally enlarge conventional expectation. In fact, the moral conflict of good craftsman and hollow man takes place with full intensity in the film, but not between its major adversaries, Willard and Kurtz. Rather, this critical drama is enacted at the margins of *Apocalypse Now*—among a grouping of lesser figures with decidedly un-Conradian names like Chief and Kilgore, Lance and Chef. Three of these characters are crew members on the River Patrol Boat which transports Willard to Kurtz's Cambodian camp. The fourth man, Colonel Kilgore, does not make this journey with the others, yet—in relation to Conrad's ideas on craftsmanship and its absence—completes the thematic quartet. Coppola's reconstruction of this issue, among the film's minor characters, is accomplished with striking symmetry. The four men in question divide precisely into two pairs, one to depict Marlow's ideal of decency and passionate work—the other to depict Kurtz's emptiness and the embrace of evil which follows from it.

Chief and Chef—as their nearly identical nicknames might suggest—are one such pair of characters and constitute the bright face of Conrad's Janus. This is true although, at first meeting, they seem so unlike one another, even incompatible. One is black, while the other is a white Southerner. The black man, Chief Phillips, is presented as a model of discipline and self-control, to the point of seeming cold and unfeeling at times. By contrast, the white man, a would-be New Orleans saucier, overreacts to everything that happens on the PBR and is never far from hysteria. At one point in Willard's internal monologue, he comments that Chef is "wrapped too tight for Vietnam" and probably "wrapped too tight for New Orleans" as well. Regardless of such differences Coppola has discovered, in Chief and Chef, an effective means to reestablish the Marlow persona in contemporary American terms—also to demonstrate, through these two men, the exact ingredients of Marlow's ethical craftsmanship: a combination of hard discipline, on one hand, and imaginative artistry on the other.

* * *

Like Chief, the sailor in *Apocalypse Now*, Chef the artist reveals Conrad's full ethical principle by combining professional substance with moral sense. Where Chief's morality is essentially humanistic, however—as demonstrated in his parental concern for the crew— Chef's is essentially religious. In fact, Chef's spiritual faith, along with his bitter hatred of the war, makes him unique among the other characters in *Apocalypse Now*. Chef alone, for example, expresses the belief that human beings possess souls and that—rather than all things being relative—good and evil do exist, tangibly and absolutely. From this spiritual perspective, Chef regards Colonel Kurtz as purely evil and, despite his fear, volunteers to be Willard's final partner in the fight against him. Such an odd alliance at the film's conclusion proves grimly ironic since the errand boy assumes command and since the artist—despite imagination, sensitivity, and moral depth—is utterly destroyed in consequence.

IV. Surfers

The boat-crew in *Apocalypse Now* is completed by a second grouping of black and white sailors—Clean and Lance—two youthful figures to balance the more mature presence of Chief and Chef Had Coppola chosen to oppose these light and dark pairs against one another morally, as Kurtz and Marlow are opposed, his rendering of Conrad's ethical drama would have been exactly symmetrical. Clean and Lance do not form such a thematic unit, however, because Clean—unlike the rest of his boatmates—is in truth only a child, innocent as his name implies and not yet old enough, at seventeen, for valid moral choice. Clean's special role in the film, then, is as every war's victimized infant—victimized in his pathetic death and even victimized in his pathetic killing of others. Clean initiates a needless and ugly massacre of civilians on board a sampan, yet he does so out of pure wide-eyed terror, to the point that it would be very difficult to hold him responsible for the event.

To create his composite of Conradian hollowness, Coppola does single out Lance but, in place of Clean, pairs him with an Army Colonel named Kilgore, a figure otherwise unconnected with the PBR crew. Colonel Kilgore at first seems an unlikely counterpart to Lance because, viewed externally, they reflect the opposite ends of the American military spectrum. Lance's early appearance in the film suggests the draftee ill-suited for service life—the beach boy forced into uniform. Kilgore, by contrast, enters *Apocalypse Now* as a caricature of the military persona—all swagger, spit, and polish. Lance and Kilgore are moral (or amoral) brothers nonetheless, different only in the outward images they project, yet alike within. The first hint of this bond is given in the revelation that Lance and Kilgore are Southern Californians who share an identical passion for surfing.

The scene of their first encounter provides useful insight into the moral significance of both characters. Lance and Kilgore meet in the aftermath of a battle just won by the air cavalry unit which Colonel Kilgore commands. An enemy soldier lies gravely wounded, begging his indifferent American and South Vietnamese captors for water. Discovering this, Kilgore becomes enraged. He drives his own men away and, reaching for his canteen, mouths a cliché made familiar by many generations of war movies and westerns: the enemy brave enough to fight me is worthy enough to drink from my canteen. Almost before Kilgore can get the words out, however, he learns that Lance, a famous surfer, is present. All thoughts of life-giving water are replaced, in Kilgore's mind, by visions of the perfect wave. The canteen is cast aside, the soldier left to die, as Kilgore turns away to find his idol and his counterpart. With this scene, Kilgore reveals not just his own emptiness but, along with it, the film's major and enduring image for such a spiritual condition. The surfer of *Apocalypse Now*, in short, is identical to the hollow man of *Heart of Darkness*.

* * *

V. Of Everything that Stands, the End

Based on the present analysis of *Apocalypse Now*, it could be argued that Coppola violates rather than preserves Conrad by banishing a centrally important issue in *Heart of Darkness* to the edges of his film. Four marginal figures reenact Conrad's ethical drama in a subplot, while the major characters, Willard and Kurtz, generate moral uncertainty and an ambiguous resolution at best. Such a reversal, without question, distorts the original text, yet at the same time maintains a unique fidelity to it. In relation to Conrad's cultural preoccupation in *Heart of Darkness*, specifically, the margin of *Apocalypse Now* turns out to be its true center. Within the novel, Conrad puts Marlow and Kurtz forward as discrete individuals yet also as reflections of Western culture as a whole. Through Kurtz he surely wishes to condemn, or at least expose, all Europe's capacity for savagery disguised as enlightenment. To this symbolic purpose, Kurtz—despite his German name—emerges as a truly pan-European figure. "His mother was half-English [Marlow informs us], his father was half-French. All Europe contributed to the making of Kurtz . . ." (49). All Europe, in a certain sense, also contributed to the making of Conrad, the Pole turned Englishman, so that his cultural perspective is by no means narrow or one-sided. Through Marlow and Kurtz together, and really through all the characters in *Heart of Darkness*, Conrad wishes to establish a complete image of Western man—a revelation of his capacity for every possible human attitude and act. The full spectrum in the text seems to run from Marlow's crafted and balanced vision, all the way to Kurtz's concealed emptiness, then finally to Kurtz's moment of honest self-awareness—assurance for Marlow and Conrad alike

that even in complete darkness something of value can be redeemed.

Had Coppola attempted, through Captain Willard and Colonel
Kurtz, to create a similar image for modern America, he would have
failed. These figures are simply too abnormal to be representative—
too distorted and strange to carry Marlow's and Kurtz's kind of cultural weight. In addition, both men belong purely to the military,
thereby remaining somewhat exempt from American norms.
Willard, in fact, as assassin and errand boy, may even be a freak
within this special world. By contrast, Lance, Chef, Chief, Clean,
and even Kilgore—the surfer/soldier—tell a separate and far more
familiar story. It is through these seemingly minor characters that
Coppola projects the film's typically American images and creates
its cultural spectrum. Geographically, the spectrum takes in Southern California, New Orleans, and the south Bronx. Ethically, it
proves broad enough to include Kilgore's and Lance's emptiness—
malignant and benign—Clean's innocence, Chef's imagination and
belief, finally Chief's decent humanity—disciplined yet ultimately
compassionate. By placing the film's critical values and counter values among these characters. Coppola has ingeniously centered the
ethical issue by appearing to marginalize it. Like Jim Morrison and
The Doors, it is the characters at the edges of *Apocalypse Now* who
give us back ourselves as Americans. In them, as in the rock songs
which frame the film, we can detect the strong and creative
rhythms of our own culture and, inseparable from them, its darkest
overtones as well.

* * *

MARGOT NORRIS

Modernism and Vietnam†

Among its many surprises, Francis Ford Coppola's film of the Vietnam War, *Apocalypse Now*, shows the images of two key intertexts
of high modernism "prominently displayed" in Kurtz's compound:
Jessie Weston's *From Ritual to Romance* and Sir James Frazer's *The
Golden Bough*.[1] These two texts on comparative mythology and
religion—associated with the agnostic work of the Cambridge anthropologists of the early twentieth century—undergird the mytho-

---

† From "Modernism and Vietnam: Francis Ford Coppola's *Apocalypse Now*," *Modern Fiction Studies* 44.3 (1998): 730–41. Reprinted with permission of The Johns Hopkins
University Press. Unless indicated, notes are the author's.
1. Joel Zuker, *Francis Ford Coppola: A Guide to References and Sources* (Boston: G. K. Hall,
1984), pp. 77–78.

logical framework of the premier poem of high modernism, T. S. Eliot's *The Waste Land*, that is also considered the most significant poetic expression of World War I. Why did Coppola make a film about the Vietnam War that eschews historical verisimilitude and reference in favor of what T. S. Eliot called "the mythical method"? Coppola's choice—to construct his film upon Joseph Conrad's novella, *Heart of Darkness*, Eliot's *The Waste Land* and other poetry, and the mythic quests and poetic pilgrimages they embody—seems especially eccentric for the treatment of the Vietnam War, which was not, like World War I, a "literary war."[2] Culturally, the Vietnam War was a video war and, aesthetically, a psychedelic war. Indeed, Coppola called *Apocalypse Now* "the first $30 million surrealist movie" ever made.[3] His comment recalls another strange anachronism in the recrudescence of early-twentieth-century art forms to address mid- and late-twentieth-century wars. However effectively modernism may have articulated World War I, it failed to serve as an expressive medium for representing World War II. Yet Surrealism, its avant-garde contemporary, did belatedly serve to depict World War II in Volker Schlöndorff's cinematic translation of Günter Grass's *The Tin Drum*—which shared the Palme d'Or award for best film with *Apocalypse Now* at the 1979 Cannes Film Festival. The clue to the conundrum of Coppola's choice of modernism's mythical method may lie precisely in the problematic power of the surreal to express irrationality, absurdity, incoherence, fragmentation, and futility. *Apocalypse Now*'s many surrealistic scenes and moments forcefully convey the war's incomprehensibility. But by themselves they do not produce an insight or recognition of Vietnam's significance for the American public, or a calculus for its damage to America's moral life. Like Eliot facing the modern world after World War I, Coppola in the aftermath of Vietnam required "a way of controlling, of ordering, of giving significance to the immense panorama of futility and anarchy which is contemporary history."[4] The "mythical method" served them both.

But the "mythical method" incurs the risk and cost of dehistoricizing—and thereby depoliticizing—its historical subject. An even greater danger lies in its use (or abuse) to idealize, apotheosize, occlude, or occult problematic ideologies embedded in the art. However subversive of Victorian pieties and hypocrisies, the work of Conrad, Eliot, Pound, Yeats, and Wyndham Lewis (among others) may be suspected of harboring its own moral darkness in compromised and sometimes incriminating relationships to colonialism,

2. Paul Fussell, *The Great War and Modern Memory* (New York: Oxford UP, 1975), p. 155.
3. Quoted in Michael Goodwin and Naomi Wise, *On Edge: The Life and Times of Francis Coppola* (New York: William Morrow, 1989), p. 262.
4. T. S. Eliot, *Selected Prose*, ed. Frank Kermode (New York: Harcourt, 1975), p. 177.

nationalism, class hatred, misogyny, and racism. We may ask, then, what ideological freight the experimentalism of modernism carried into its afterlife in late-twentieth-century art. In the case of Coppola's use of Conrad and Eliot, there would seem to be cause for worry. Although the impetus for framing a story incorporating the tales of returning Vietnam veterans with Conrad's novella came from Coppola ("he made the crucial suggestion that [John] Milius and [George] Lucas write up the stories with Conrad's *Heart of Darkness* as the underlying structural agent," the screenwriter John Milius initially interpreted Conrad through his own warmongering filter.[5] According to Jeffrey Chown's detailed analysis of Milius's original screenplay, the writer at first cast Conrad's Kurtz as the war's hypothetical savior—the man who "embraces the horror, and more specifically advocates it as the final solution for winning the Vietnam War" (Chown 130). Milius's Kurtz served as model and hero, rather than as nemesis or dark double, for the Army Captain whose name somewhat anagramatically and palindromically deforms that of Conrad's Marlow: Willard. Milius's own 1982 explanation for the film's title confirms that the violent and rightwing sentiments infusing his scripts for *Magnum Force* and *Red Dawn* were fully engaged in his original conceptualization of Coppola's project:

> George Lucas and I were great connoisseurs of the Vietnam War. . . . George and I would talk about the battles all the time and what a great movie it would make. I had the title to call it, *Apocalypse Now*, because all these hippies at the time had these buttons that said "Nirvana Now," and I loved the idea of a guy having a button with a mushroom cloud on it that said "Apocalypse Now," you know, let's bring it on, full nuke. Ever hear that Randy Newman song, "Let's Drop the Big One Now"? That's the spirit that it started in right there. (qtd. in Chown 123)

Coppola actually considered changing the title of the film back to *Heart of Darkness* at one time (Chown 130), and through the narration later added by Michael Herr, he restored the darkly critical vision of Conrad's Marlow to Willard. I will argue that Coppola restored as well Conrad's genius for using both narration and narrative structure to create a textual performance of self-incrimination and moral implication that ultimately extends to the reader and the viewer.

The film's viewer is forced, like Conrad's Marlow and Conrad's reader, to choose between nightmares (" 'Ah! but it was something to have at least a choice of nightmares' " [62]). The nightmares rep-

5. Jeffrey Chown, *Hollywood Auteur: Francis Coppola* (New York: Praeger, 1988), p. 123.

resent forms of violence: the corporate, instrumentalized, ideologically rationalized and morally deceptive violence of the military machine, or the blatant, undisguised, ideologically stripped and frank barbarism that the renegade madman turns on the Vietnam War as the military's unvarnished mirror. In his 1979 interview with Greil Marcus for *Rolling Stone*, Coppola confirms this sense of his film— "I felt that in the end, the movie was always about choice" (qtd. in Chown 143). If Coppola grasped Conrad's strategy for criticizing colonial adventurism through a demonized double—then the continuities of *Apocalypse Now* and Coppola's *Godfather* films become instantly apparent. The *Godfather* series sets forth the same structure of immoral doubles: the overt brutality of the Mafia as product and humanized mirror of the more invisible but pervasive brutality of political institutions whose corrupted legislative, judicial, and police systems fail to protect and deliver justice to their most vulnerable citizens. *Apocalypse Now* illustrates precisely the same point in what Jeffrey Chown calls the film's "puppy-sampan scene" (138). The PBR boat's routine search of a peaceful sampan turns into a massacre less by inadvertence than from the pressure of the irrepressible violence built into the Army's sense of its mission. When Willard dispatches the wounded woman with a shot—as though euthanizing an animal—the military machine's brutality loses all hypocritical ideological cover and becomes narrativizable and visualizable as pure murder, a shadow of the historical My Lai massacre. The sentimental figure of the puppy allows Coppola to avoid a trivializing allusion to the heart-searing images of slain infants at My Lai. Instead, the falsity of the sentimental appeal of such public relations gambits as the Pacification program to "win hearts and minds" in Vietnam is glossed. "It was a way we had over here of living with ourselves," Willard's voice-over narration comments upon his cold killing of the wounded Vietnamese woman, "We'd cut them in half with a machine gun and give 'em a bandaid. It was a lie, and the more I saw of them, the more I hated lies." There has been wide contention that Coppola is not a political auteur ("He is more interested in the politics of family life and interpersonal relationships than in larger political issues"),[6] and an improbable political critic of the Vietnam War ("In pre-1974 interviews and film work, Coppola had never shown even a passing interest in the Vietnam War").[7] However, cinematographer Vittorio Storaro contended that Coppola "wanted to express the main idea of Joseph Conrad, which is the imposition of one culture on top of another culture."[8] By tracing how Coppola translated the philo-

6. Zuker, p. 33.
7. Chown, p. 122.
8. Quoted in Peter Cowie, *Coppola* (New York: Scribner's, 1990), p. 133.

sophical modernism of Conrad (and its resonances in Eliot's poetic language) into the cinematic language of *Apocalypse Now*, I intend to dispute Joel Zuker's contention that in the film "the issue of American colonialism in a war we could never win are [*sic*] passed over."[9]

*   *   *

Conrad's critique of colonialism is structured hermeneutically— as an interpretive quest and moral pilgrimage that operates through the telling, and hearing, of a story, twice: an unnamed narrator tells of a story that Marlow once told aboard ship at anchor. Marlow's story thus becomes an education for a multiple audience in different time frames: immediately, for the unnamed narrator and other denizens of the ship, the *Nellie*, and, remotely, for the putative interlocutor or reader to whom the unnamed narrator repeats Marlow's story. The transmissibility of the story is crucial to its ethically educational function, which is to teach the Westerner the horrors that underwrite colonial empire, and to point out that even silent or ignorant assent to, and benefit from, colonialism spells complicity and guilt. Conrad's "frame" narrative in *Heart of Darkness* allows him to position the reader as a moral double to the unnamed narrator aboard the *Nellie* anchored in the Thames, an affable and ingenuous jingoist who opens the story with a paean to the "great knights-errant of the sea"—"the *Golden Hind* returning with her round flanks full of treasure . . . to the *Erebus* and *Terror*, bound on other conquests. . . . What greatness had not floated on the ebb of that river into the mystery of an unknown earth! . . . The dreams of men, the seed of commonwealths, the germs of empires" (4–5). The narrator's peroration is sharply disrupted when Marlow punctures this imperialist romance with grim naturalism—" 'cold, fog, tempests, disease, exile, and death. . . . They must have been dying like flies here' " (6)—and proceeds to narrate his own education in the sordid truth of the colonial enterprise. Besides setting up a dialogue between the glorification of colonial conquest and its exposé as criminal robbery and murder, the "frame" that makes Marlow's story a twice-told tale serves to establish the lesson's historical reapplicability. Marlow's experience with Belgian commercial exploitation of the Congo repeats the Roman conquest of Britain, and by silent implication, Britain's own more recent conquest of India. Colonialism is a movable horror prone to displacement and repetition.

Coppola abandoned the narrative frame that John Milius had originally written into the script of *Apocalypse Now*, and replaced it with an ambiguous layering of nightmares about the various "mis-

9. Zuker, p. 31.

sions" of his protagonist, Captain Willard. Instead of a patriotic
paean to U.S. foreign policy, the film opens with an expression of
frustrated military desire—"Saigon. Shit! I'm still only in Saigon. . . .
I'm here a week now, waiting for a mission"—that is overtaken by a
voice from a later moment in time to announce its fulfillment and
Willard's education—"Everyone gets everything he wants. I wanted
a mission, and for my sins, they gave me one. Brought it up to me
like room service. . . . It was a real choice mission, and when it was
over, I never wanted another." Coppola opens the film in the interior of Willard's spiritual and psychological heart of darkness expressed in visual images and techniques—the exploding jungle of
nightmare or memory; the rhythmic sounds of heartbeat, ceiling
fan, and helicopter blending into one another; Jim Morrison's eerie
wail of "The End" ("Lost in a Roman wilderness of pain, / and all
the chil-dren a-re insane"); Willard's face, upside down, signaling a
reversed perspective on Vietnam, war stories, and war movies; and
his emotional and mental breakdown expressed in the fractured image of his orientalized movements and martial art gesturings, as he
crashes his hand through the mirror. The result is an effect of lay-
ered but productive trauma, of Willard, already agonized by pain
and guilt, obliged to enact his nightmares over again, until, by the
end of the film, we understand that his encounter with Kurtz has
allowed him to see what he is, to confront his acts and guilts.
"There is no way to tell his story without telling my own. And if his
story is really a confession, then so is mine." If Willard's moves before the mirror resemble the movements of T'ai Chi—a form of
what is sometimes called "internal martial arts"—then his internal
journey into self-recognition is, like Kurtz's, an experience of going
native, of orientalizing himself in a problematical but self-
enlightening *anagnorisis*.[1]

The highly charged effect of Willard's expressionism in the opening sequence of the film is his semiotic equivalent to Kurtz's "the
horror! the horror!" But this stunning psychological effect required
Coppola's sacrifice of the fascinating political point John Milius's
original frame might have brought to the film: "Milius framed the
story with Willard on a boat in Washington's Potomac, telling the
story to a female journalist."[2] We can instantly imagine the dark
resonance of Marlow's opening line in such a venue.—" 'And this
also,' said Marlow suddenly, 'has been one of the dark places of the
earth' " (5). The setting of the United States is as mythified as the
narrator's England—glorified as "dreams of men" and "seed of commonwealths." In Milius's Potomac opening, the story of Vietnam

1. Moment of recognition. [Editor]
2. Chown, p. 131.

narrated in the shadow of the U.S. Capitol could have demythified, obliquely, the nation's genesis as a story of native genocide and cultivation by slavery. The removal of this "frame" seems like a colossal lost opportunity for political comment until we recognize Coppola's intriguing displacement of the burden of its message onto the USO Playboy Playmate show in the middle of the film. Staged and hosted by San Francisco rock concert impresario Bill Graham, the USO show, in which three Playboy Bunnies dressed in "Cowboy and Indian" costumes are ferried in by helicopter to entertain the troops, parodies a military institution that is itself already heavily ironized. USO shows, designed to prop up combat troop morale by inspiring patriotism and reminding the boys of what they are fighting for, traditionally display to soldiers conflicting and confused icons of sexual desire fused with patriotic imagery, manufactured according to the conventions of the entertainment industry. In *Apocalypse Now* this fusion is intriguingly verbally and conceptually textured: the "rock" concert signaling the cultural moment of the sixties set against the Cold War symbol of "rockets" as backdrop for the eroticized movements that update the "Rockettes" with a soft-pornographic inflection. More pointedly, "democracy" is signaled by the domestication of America's bloody genesis in its ludic and juvenile version as stylized "play" of "Cowboys and Indians," performed by Playboy Bunnies posing as domesticated and softened versions of pornographic strippers. However, Coppola has the Playmates' ludic and lewd gunplay incite a frenzied violence in the mob of soldiers who storm the stage in an epic gang rape. The women and their manager escape only by a dangerous helicopter airlift that gestures proleptically toward the final closing scenes of the Vietnam War with its images of frenzied, desperate, dangerous airlift escapes from the collapsing country.

* * *

This reference to U.S. cultural imperialism—the importation of Western values and habits into Eastern colonial contexts—glosses a crucial Conradian theme from *Heart of Darkness*. Conrad sets up the Company for trade, which employs Marlow, as a mirror of the renegade Kurtz in order to interrogate European values exposed as absurd and perverse by their altered African context, and to juxtapose them with the more broadly drawn absurdity and perversity of "going native." Conrad's most ludicrous figure of European maladaptation to the African colonial situation is the Company's chief accountant who, in " 'high starched collar, white cuffs . . . snowy trousers, a clean necktie, and varnished boots' " (18), manages to keep his books " 'in apple-pie order' "—though not without some difficulty. When a wounded agent is temporarily housed in his office, he complains. " 'The groans of this sick person . . . distract my

MARGOT NORRIS

attention. And without that it is extremely difficult to guard against clerical errors in this climate' " (18). Coppola's version of the accountant is the flamboyant Lt. Colonel Kilgore, whose U.S. Cavalry hat announces the "Cowboy and Indian" theme of the subsequent USO show. The Cavalry hat also serves to underline the genocidal destructiveness that overlays the U.S. Army's mythic role of chivalric rescue—as Kilgore's helicopters visit napalm and bullets on a compound housing tidy, uniformed Vietnamese schoolchildren. But it is Kilgore's passion for surfing that imports a key figure from American culture into a combat context that renders its aggressive and obsessive hedonism as perverse as the accountant's professional scrupulosity. Coppola intensifies the supererogatory cultural violence of interpolating surfing into war—by terrifying young Lance Johnson, the iconic image of youthful California innocence and affluence popularized by the Beach Boys in the sixties.

Kilgore's allegorical name points to a one dimensionality that itself has philosophical significance, that makes him—in contrast to the brooding, introspective Kurtz—a Conradian and Eliotian "hollow man" with no interiority, no self-consciousness, no conscience, no powers of *anagnorisis*. His insanity is of a different order than that of Kurtz—who sees his own perversity as the interiorization of the perversity of the war—because it is marked by the absence of any humanity, the hollowness of feeling and lack of sympathetic sight that makes him autotelic, driven purely by his own will, a Nietzschean *Übermensch*. His placement in the pantheon of evil that poses the film's nightmare choices is therefore ambiguous and troublesome. Kilgore is curiously exempted from the poetics of cruelty that hovers around Kurtz's prose and actions, and he presides over his own Conradian "grove of death" (Marlow's first sight of criminalized black workers miserably dying from the brutality of their condition) with a casualness that also marks Coppola's decision to eschew the more egregious representations of atrocity that belong to the iconicity of the American presence in Vietnam. Unlike the historical abominations Michael Herr reports in *Dispatches*—soldiers wearing necklaces made of human ears and unspeakably desecrating the heads of the dead[3]—Coppola has Kilgore merely dispense "Death from Above"—playing cards that mark the corpses as his victims, and that signify the pure arbitrariness and chance of his killing. Kilgore's use of the card deck exceeds in nihilism that of Eliot's Madame Sosostris, the *Waste Land* clairvoyant who degrades the sacred mysteries of the Tarot by deploying its symbols for horoscopes. Unlike Kurtz, who steps into the ritualized universe of the primitive—and becomes, as it were, a mystical In-

---

3. Michael Herr, *Dispatches* (New York: Avon, 1980).

dian—Kilgore remains a flying cowboy, a connoisseur of experience and sensation ("I love the smell of napalm in the morning") whose flight—unlike, say, that of James Dickey's World War II bomber pilot in "The Firebombing"—is aptly characterized by the apotheosized barbarism of Wagner's "Flight of the Valkyries."

Coppola attends to the way Joseph Conrad took the great philosophical themes of the modern—the arbitrariness, randomness, chance, and absurdity of the universe—and gave them a precise function and figuration in the critique of colonialism. Conrad's various images of absurd, objectless fighting and unproductive, futile labor are the first landmarks of Marlow's journey. He encounters a French man-of-war firing into an invisible and unresponsive jungle (" 'there she was, incomprehensible, firing into a continent. Pop, would go one of the six-inch guns; a small flame would dart and vanish, a little white smoke would disappear, a tiny projectile would give a feeble screech—and nothing happened. Nothing could happen. There was a touch of insanity in the proceeding' " [14]) and describes the chaos of his first Company station, where all manner of vague dynamiting and construction projects are going on— " 'They were building a railway. The cliff was not in the way or anything; but this objectless blasting was all the work going on. . . . I avoided a vast artificial hole somebody had been digging on the slope, the purpose of which I found it impossible to divine' " (15–16). Coppola transposes Conrad's Sisyphean vision of the futility of Company labor to the scene of chaos at the Do Lung bridge, the last U.S. Army outpost before Cambodia—"Every night the bridge is rebuilt, and the Vietcong blow it up again. Willard attempts to find the commanding officer. When he asks who is in command, a black soldier replies 'Ain't you?' "[4] By choosing a bridge as the site of utter confusion and anarchy, Coppola brilliantly glosses the ironic contrast with the chivalric military fantasy of leadership, courage, discipline, sacrifice, heroic effort, efficiency, and honor in David Lean's 1957 *The Bridge on the River Kwai*. The folly both Conrad and Coppola underline in their criticism of colonial adventurism with these scenes is the senseless brutality, waste, and destructiveness of enterprises with misguided and hypocritical goals and inept and ill-conceived strategies.

*   *   *

4. Zuker, p. 64.

LINDA J. DRYDEN

"To Boldly Go": *Heart of Darkness* and Popular Culture†

Conrad's *Heart of Darkness* (1899) is a text that has consistently resisted analytic closure. That is to say that its relevance to the twentieth century (and now the twenty-first century) is apparent through the allusions to the story in our media and culture. As each new "horror" of the post-modern world emerges, *Heart of Darkness* acquires new meanings that extend its relevance beyond the imperial boundaries of the Belgian Congo of the 1880s and '90s, and bring to Conrad's vision a shockingly contemporary pertinence. Francis Ford Coppola realized the adaptability of what Conrad was trying to convey when he filmed *Apocalypse Now* in the 1970s: innumerable media references to *Heart of Darkness* have ensued, some inspired by Coppola's film, but many also inspired by renewed interest in Conrad's text. In this discussion I will draw attention to the variety of ways that *Heart of Darkness* has been used in our popular culture, and suggest that there is a broader interdependence between popular culture and some of our most valued literary products. I will argue that literature, and Conrad's novella in particular, have a large role to play in the postmodern erasure of the divide between "high culture" and "low culture."

* * *

Conrad's modernist text dealt with the complex issue of European imperialism in Africa and the moral consequences of that incursion. In *Apocalypse Now* it is recontextualized as a film about America's involvement in Vietnam, bringing new meanings to bear upon Conrad's original text. Such has been the success of the movie that it has recently been rereleased with previously discarded footage restored. Its cult status is now undeniable; it is arguably, for some, more important than the book that inspired it. Without the inspiration from *Heart of Darkness*, Coppola would have made a wholly different movie, probably less powerful and less enduring, and thus the film helps to secure the continuing presence of Conrad's novel in our culture because of the film's own enduring relevance. The popular film gains more dimensional complexity; the novel gains currency and a further reference point from which to evaluate it. As "high" culture collapses into "low" culture, in this way, or rather perhaps as "low" culture acquires the terrain and subject matter of

† From " 'To Boldly Go': Conrad's *Heart of Darkness* and Popular Culture," *Conradiana* 34.3 (2002): 149–70. Reprinted by permission of Texas Tech University Press. Unless indicated, notes are the author's.

"high" culture, the terms "high" and "low" become redundant because of the interdependence of each on the other. The case of *Heart of Darkness* and *Apocalypse Now* is a prime example of how modernism is absorbed into postmodernist practice and is celebrated, even reinvented there.

Kurtz in Conrad's text is singularly silent; his words are reported, but he rarely speaks in the narrative. Yet his dying facial expression speaks to Marlow as eloquently as any words: "I saw on that ivory face the expression of somber pride, of ruthless power, of craven terror—of an intense and hopeless despair. Did he live his life again in every detail of desire, temptation, and surrender during that supreme moment of complete knowledge?" (69). Conrad allows Marlow this speculative interpretation of Kurtz's final moments, but his final words "The horror! The horror!" reverberate through the closing pages of the novella, replete with possible meanings that Marlow is unable to fully decipher. Coppola, aware of Conrad's refusal to nail the meaning of this enigmatic moment, goes some way towards emulating Conrad. Marlon Brando's utterance of Colonel Kurtz's last words, "The horror! The horror!" is a notorious film sequence. It has been regarded as laughably inept, even comical; but it is also possible to see this as an example of Coppola (and Brando) attempting to convey the notoriously slippery nature of Conrad's narrative style. These are just about the last words spoken in the film, which leaves the impact of the utterance symbolically reflecting back on the whole filmic action, at one level. At another level, those two repeated words are conjoined with Jim Morrison's refrain "this is the end," as the musical soundtrack to the closing sequence. This dying whisper of horror is coupled with the equally horrific sight of the sacrificially slaughtered buffalo and the hellish scene as Willard (Martin Sheen) leaves Colonel Kurtz's compound, suggesting the inhumane and bloody nature of Kurtz's regime. Conrad, characteristically, leaves the words undeciphered for the reader. The juxtaposition of musical soundtrack and disturbing visual image goes some way towards unraveling meaning, but at the same time this multi-layering applies more potential signification to the words without fixing that meaning exactly. Thus the film is emulating the written text in a further example of postmodern intertextuality.

The possible meanings contained in Conrad's original words are relocated in the image of the murdered Colonel Kurtz, the sacrificial slaughter of a buffalo, and the lyrics of a popular music icon, as signifiers for a multi-layered narrative closure. As with Eliot's poem,[1] some viewers will remember Conrad's text and add more

---

1. T. S. Eliot, "The Hollow Men" (1925), which alludes to *Heart of Darkness* and which Colonel Kurtz recites in Coppola's film. [Editor]

layers of signification by moving between the film and soundtrack and the original novel about imperialism in Africa. Others, who are perhaps unaware of *Heart of Darkness*, will try to decipher Coppola's complex schema and apply this directly to the American experience in Vietnam. In both cases new meanings are being negotiated, and these meanings depend * * * on what is being signified for the individual viewer. Similarly though, in the novel, Kurtz's dying words are reinterpreted by the narrator, Marlow, for Kurtz's fiancée back in Brussels as "your name" (76). Critical analysis of Conrad's meaning in the words "The horror! The horror!" reveals a very Conradian slippage in signification. It seems that, without directly relating back to the specific African narrative of *Heart of Darkness*, Coppola is creating a similarly complex slippage around the words of his dying Colonel Kurtz. It is thus that the film itself is influenced not only by the novel's narrative and themes but by its form and structure, and by its narrative technique.

So much for the visual and textual interplay between text and film: another issue that needs to be addressed is how the reception of the film may have affected the fortunes of the novel. In other words, does Conrad's novel continue to be so influential because of its own inherent power and literary value, or did Coppola revive its fortunes through mass entertainment, hence allowing the passage of a work of high literature into the popular cultural arena? The answer is not obvious, but it is most likely that both things are happening. In this sense, a kind of two-way process is enacted here whereby literature is influencing the more populist media of the cinema, which itself is reflecting that literature back at an audience who subsequently find a new relevance in an "old masterpiece." Added to this is the increased textual terrain available for analysis by the critic: placing *Apocalypse Now* in the same seminar room as *Heart of Darkness* opens up whole new channels of critical investigation, as any university lecturer who has done so will testify. Many viewers of *Apocalypse Now* are unaware of Conrad's original text, or at least unaware of its influence on the film. Yet there are many who do know of the connection, so to ignore the text when discussing the film would be reductive, effectively * * * discussing the film in a vacuum. Certainly in making *Apocalypse Now* Coppola gave us a new perspective from which to analyze *Heart of Darkness*, and it may well be that in doing so he generated new interest in Conrad's text for new generations of readers. * * *

* * *

In the title of the episode of *The Simpsons* * * * "Bart of Darkness," there is a clear reference to Conrad's text. In another episode, "Kamp Krusty," one is aware that Matt Groening, the creator of *The Simpsons*, was actually parodying William Golding's

1954 novel *Lord of the Flies*. And *Lord of the Flies*, as well as being Golding's acute reaction to the Second World War, is also a dark parody of R. M. Ballantyne's popular imperial adventure story *The Coral Island* (1857), with more than a glance at *Heart of Darkness*. Again we have come full circle: postmodern intertextuality infiltrates popular culture at every turn, a fact that *The Simpsons* cartoon series seems actively to exploit. * * * Conrad was indebted to popular nineteenth-century imperial romance, and in particular a debt is owed by *Heart of Darkness* to Rider Haggard's fiction. Early modernism, one of the most elite cultural practices of the early part of the twentieth century, was thus using popular entertainment, in the form of romance literature, for its own purposes of subversion and referentiality. But then literature, and elite culture has always done so. * * *

In an on-line interview, *The Simpsons'* creator, Matt Groening, says:

> Everybody doesn't have to get every joke. People really appreciate not being condescended to. The history of TV has traditionally been not to do anything that would scandalize grandma or upset junior. Our solution on *The Simpsons* is to do jokes that people who have an education and some frame of reference can get. And the ones who don't, it doesn't matter, because we have Homer banging his head and saying, "D'oh!"
>
> I love the idea that we put in jokes the kids don't get. And that later, when they grow up and read a few books and go to college and watch the show again, they can get it on a completely different level.[2]

Groening is thus consciously underpinning his comic creation with references to works from the canon of "high" culture like *Heart of Darkness* and *Lord of the Flies*, and he is making modest claims for the value of this in terms of education and "culture." Essentially then Groening, as a producer of popular culture, is self-consciously manipulating "high" culture for his own comic and satiric purposes. * * * It is clearly not the case here that a conservatively validated form of culture is, so to speak, "seeping" into popular culture * * *: the inclusion of "high" culture is a conscious choice, in this case for comic effect, but with the understanding that the "educated" section of the audience will get greater satisfaction from the intertextual and perhaps irreverent nature of the allusions. The fact that *Heart of Darkness* can be used in this way in a popular cultural product thus signals its impact on our culture in general.

Heart of Darkness has even found its way into popular narratives

2. This quotation was downloaded from the web some time ago, but appears to be no longer available.

about science fiction film production and the spin off "pulp" novels
from television SF. For example, there was a rumour on the web in
1998 that the *Star Trek* movie *Insurrection* (1999) would be based
on *Heart of Darkness*. In the end the trace of Conrad's novel in the
film was the fact that Data, the android character who seeks to become more human, appeared to go mad on some far distant planet
that the United Federation of Planets was trying to colonize. The final story had more in common with John Sturges's *The Magnificent
Seven* (1960) and subsequent "spaghetti westerns" than it did with
Conrad's text. But, as Michèle and Duncan Barrett have pointed
out, *Star Trek* has, from its very inception, been influenced by the
seafaring narratives of both Conrad and Melville, and by Jules
Verne's early science fantasy tales. The seafaring motif of space
travel in *Star Trek*, with its captains and ships officers, and its naval
rankings all the way down to ensign, draws on an older tradition of
sailing ships. Even the physical structure of the ocean-going ship is
relied upon for its futuristic offspring, the starship: we have hulls
and port bows, brigs and bridges, captains' quarters and sick bays,
all terms from the actual maritime vocabulary.

In a further interesting discussion on the potential influences of
Conrad upon *Star Trek*, the Barretts invoke *The Nigger of the "Narcissus"* (1897):

> At various points the question is raised as to what kind of man
> James Wait is. In Conrad there is a continuing exploration of
> the question of what constitutes humanity. Although, as we
> shall see, this takes offensive forms in regard to race, it is an
> important point of comparison with the questions central to
> *Star Trek*. The crucial point of difference can be simply identi-
> fied: *Star Trek* uses alien species, non-humans (albeit organic,
> cybernetic or whatever) to ask questions about how humanity
> is to be defined. Conrad asks questions about the definition of
> humanity, but he does it by comparing humans of different
> races.[3]

These comments could apply equally to *Heart of Darkness*, as the
Barretts recognize. For example, Marlow's famous comment on the
Africans in the jungle, "what thrilled you was just the thought of
their humanity—like yours—the thought of your remote kinship
with this wild and passionate uproar"(36), is a direct challenge to
the reader to acknowledge the humanity they share with the
African. Stories of interstellar exploration, like *Star Trek*, frequently
use issues of cultural and racial difference to interrogate the wider
question of what constitutes humanity. In another instance, Mar-

---

3. Michèle Barrett and Duncan Barrett, *Star Trek: The Human Frontier* (Cambridge: Polity
P, 2001), p. 30.

low encounters an African who, at the sight of a white face, "hoisted his weapon to his shoulder with alacrity. This was simple prudence, white men being so much alike at a distance that he could not tell who I might be" (16). Marlow, and Conrad, are of course turning the white man's prejudice back on himself here, by trying to see the world through African eyes. In *Star Trek: The Next Generation* we find that the android character, Data, is used in a similar way to comment on human behavior aboard the *Enterprise*; and in the episode, "The Measure of a Man," Data himself becomes the focus of a discussion about what constitutes a sentient being. This is not to suggest that Conrad had an overt influence on this science fiction series, but rather to indicate that the serious themes of some our most valued literature do find expression in popular culture.

The Barretts have taken a close look at the cultural "spin-offs" from the *Trek* series and have identified a collection of literary parodies of *Star Trek: The Next Generation* which they argue endorses their claim that *Star Trek* relies heavily on the maritime tales of Conrad and Melville. One collection of stories, *Treks Not Taken: a parody*, by Stephen Boyett, uses self-conscious references to these two authors. In a tribute to *Moby Dick*, Boyett "features Worf (a being from the planet Klingon) as Queequeg, as well as the characters Piker, Email, and Captain Piquod." In one parody in particular, "Trek of Darkness," Boyett pays direct homage to Conrad, as the Barretts explain:

> Space is very black: "The mournful gloom of dark black space lay brooding darkly and blackly"; "we stared placidly at the vast expanse of black that was like death." Via the Coppola Nebula (a glance towards the Director of *Apocalypse Now*) they reach an outpost staffed by "indigenous aliens who were black-skinned and wore black clothing and write only in black ink." Mr Kurtz is revealed as Mr Kirk, suffering "the horror" of decades of enforced guest appearances as Captain Kirk. (Barrett and Barrett 196–97)

Another complex example of cultural referencing is at play here. Those who have not read *Heart of Darkness* will miss the reference, but for those who have, the parody of Conrad's style throughout the novel is unmistakable. From the very beginning of the novel a sombre, ominous note is struck: "The air was dark above Gravesend, and farther back still seemed condensed into a mournful gloom, brooding motionless over the biggest, and the greatest, town on earth" (3). This atmosphere persists to the very last sentence: "The offing was barred by a black bank of clouds, and the tranquil water-way leading to the uttermost ends of the earth flowed sombre under an overcast sky—seemed to lead into the heart of an immense darkness" (77). The author of "Trek of Darkness" is conscious of Conrad's narrative style and, sometimes excessive, use of adjectives, a tendency towards overblown prose that F. R. Leavis has termed Conrad's "adjectival insistence."[4] And this is another example of popular culture's sophisticated use of "high culture." In this instance what we are witnessing is a deliberate mocking of Conrad's narrative style, a parody that could only be appreciated by the "initiated." Conflating Captain Kirk with Kurtz perpetuates the Conrad parody; but what is of note here too is the way in which references to *Apocalypse Now* also creep in, so that again we are involved in intertextual readings and that circular referentiality mentioned earlier.

The Barretts' book, an academic assessment of the various *Trek* programmes, devotes a whole section to Conrad's influence on *Star Trek*.[5] The arrival on academic bookshelves of a scholarly investigation of such a cult programme as *Star Trek* is not unprecedented, but what is of most significance here is the high profile given to such a literary "heavy weight" as *Heart of Darkness*, and the way in which it is seen to be used in the *Star Trek* universe and in the program's spin off merchandising. Again we can see, as with *The Simpsons*, that popular culture is reliant upon "high" culture for much of its imaginative and creative inspiration. It also depends upon "high" culture to supply its parodic material. The point is that without the elite products of our culture, such as literature, popular culture itself would be impoverished, lacking in cultural reference points on which to base its narratives. One of the most frequently quoted texts within popular culture and media is *Heart of Darkness*; and the fact that this is so indicates that Conrad's novella has influences that reach beyond the sphere of English literature and literary academe: it has become part of our cultural heritage.

* * *

4. F. R. Leavis, *The Great Tradition* (London: Chatto and Windus, 1960), p. 177.
5. See Barrett and Barrett, pp. 27–33: "Conrad's Colonial Horror."

Joseph Conrad: A Chronology

1857   Józef Teodor Konrad Nałęcz Korzeniowski born 3 December in Berdyczów in the Ukraine, a part of Poland annexed by Russia, to Apollo and Ewelina (Bobrowska) Korzeniowski, their first and only child.

1861   Conrad's father arrested and imprisoned in Warsaw's Citadel for anti-Russian revolutionary activity.

1862   Conrad's parents sentenced to exile in a remote Russian village for their work on behalf of Polish independence. Mother and son fall ill on journey.

1865   Mother Ewa dies on 18 April.

1868   Father and son permitted to leave Russia, settle in Cracow in 1869.

1869   Father Apollo dies on 23 May. The eleven-year-old Conrad leads a funeral procession of several thousand mourners demonstrating for Polish independence.

1870–73   Various guardians, tutors, schools. Uncle Tadeusz Bobrowski becomes dominant influence over education and upbringing.

1873   Visits Switzerland and Italy; first view of the sea.

1874–78   Based in Marseilles, serves as apprentice on ships sailing to Caribbean.

1878   Depressed, attempts suicide; joins British Merchant Service, moves to London, takes jobs as ordinary seaman.

1880   Passes second-mate's examination, sails as third mate on *Loch Etive* to Australia.

1881–83   Second mate on *Palestine*, source of incidents in "Youth."

1883–86   Second mate on various ships sailing out of Singapore and ports in India.

1885   Berlin Conference gives King Leopold control over Congo Free State.

1886   Becomes British subject, passes master's examination.

1887   First mate on ships in the East Indies.

1888–89   Master of the *Otago*, his only command, sailing between Australia and ports in the Indian Ocean.

1889   On shore leave in London, begins *Almayer's Folly*.

1890   Visits Poland for first time in sixteen years; travels to
              Africa in May; serves in Congo, June–December,
              traveling to Stanley Falls as second-in-command and
              temporarily captain of the *Roi des Belges*; falls seri-
              ously ill and returns to Europe.

1891   Recuperates in London and Switzerland; sails for
              Australia as first mate on the *Torrens*.

1893–94   Second mate on the *Adowa*, a steamer intended to
              carry French immigrants to Canada; company fails
              before departure; Conrad's sea career ends.

1894   Tadeusz Bobrowski dies on 10 February. Conrad
              meets Edward Garnett, an influential publisher's
              reader, who encourages his literary aspirations.

1895   *Almayer's Folly* published.

1896   Marries Jessie George on 24 March.

1897   *Nigger of the "Narcissus"* published; first story ac-
              cepted by *Blackwood's Magazine* ("Karain"); meets
              Henry James, Stephen Crane, R. B. Cunninghame
              Graham.

1898   Son Borys born on 15 January; moves to Pent Farm
              near Canterbury.

1898–1909   Collaboration and friendship with Ford Madox Ford.
              Together they wrote *The Inheritors* (1901), *Romance*
              (1903), and *The Nature of a Crime* (finished 1906,
              published 1924). They break over Ford's adultery
              and divorce.

1899   "Heart of Darkness" published in *Blackwood's*.

1900   *Lord Jim* published. Literary agent J. B. Pinker be-
              gins to manage Conrad's business affairs.

1902   Book publication of *Heart of Darkness* in *Youth*.

1904   Roger Casement's report to Parliament about
              Leopold's atrocities. Jessie Conrad falls, injures both
              legs, permanently disabled.

1904   *Nostromo* published.

1906   Son John born on 2 August.

1907   *The Secret Agent* published.

1908   Belgium takes over Congo from Leopold after
              mounting international outcry.

1909–10   Serious quarrel with Pinker, to whom Conrad is
              deeply in debt, over slowness to produce material.

1911   *Under Western Eyes* published. American collector
              John Quinn begins purchasing Conrad's manu-
              scripts, easing his financial strains.

1914   *Chance* published, Conrad's first best-seller, due largely to publicity campaign by his new American publisher F. N. Doubleday. Family visit to Poland interrupted by outbreak of World War I, circuitous return to England through Austria and Italy.

1915–18   Borys serves in British army, hospitalized for shell shock in France.

1919   Prosperous after years of financial difficulties, moves to Oswalds in Kent.

1923   Declines honorary degree from Cambridge; promotional tour of America arranged by Doubleday.

1924   Declines knighthood; dies on 3 August, buried in Canterbury Cemetery.

Selected Bibliography

CONRAD'S MAJOR WORKS

Almayer's Folly (1895)
An Outcast of the Islands (1896)
The Nigger of the "Narcissus" (1898)
Tales of Unrest (1898)
Lord Jim (1900)
The Inheritors (1901)
Youth (1902)
Typhoon and Other Stories (1903)
Romance (1903)
The Mirror of the Sea (1906)
The Secret Agent (1907)
Under Western Eyes (1911)
A Personal Record (1912)
Chance (1913)
Victory (1915)
The Shadow-Line (1917)
The Arrow of Gold (1919)
The Rescue (1920)
The Rover (1923)
The Nature of a Crime (1924)
Suspense (1925)

BIOGRAPHIES

Batchelor, John. *The Life of Joseph Conrad: A Critical Biography*. Oxford: Blackwell, 1994.
Karl, Frederick R. *Conrad: The Three Lives*. New York: Farrar, Straus and Giroux, 1979.
Knowles, Owen. *A Conrad Chronology*. London and Basingstoke: Macmillan, 1989.
Meyer, Bernard C. *Joseph Conrad: A Psychoanalytic Biography*. Princeton: Princeton UP, 1967.
Meyers, Jeffrey. *Joseph Conrad: A Biography*. New York: Scribner's, 1991.
Watts, Cedric. *Joseph Conrad: A Literary Life*. London: Macmillan, 1989.
Although not strictly speaking a "biography," the *Oxford Reader's Companion to Conrad*, edited by Owen Knowles and Gene M. Moore (Oxford: Oxford UP, 2000), is an invaluable source of information about Conrad's life and works.

SELECTED CRITICISM

• indicates works included or excerpted in this Norton Critical Edition.

• Achebe, Chinua. "An Image of Africa: Racism in Conrad's *Heart of Darkness*." *Massachusetts Review* 18 (1977): 782–94.

Ambrosini, Richard. *Conrad's Fiction as Critical Discourse.* Cambridge, UK: Cambridge UP, 1991.

Armstrong, Paul B. *The Challenge of Bewilderment: Understanding and Representation in James, Conrad, and Ford.* Ithaca, NY: Cornell UP, 1987.

• ———. "*Heart of Darkness* and the Epistemology of Cultural Differences" in Fincham and Hooper, 21–41.

Ash, Beth Sharon. *In Between: Modernity and the Psychosocial Dilemma in the Novels of Joseph Conrad.* New York: St. Martin's, 1999.

• Brantlinger, Patrick. *Rule of Darkness: British Literature and Imperialism, 1830–1914.* Ithaca, NY: Cornell UP, 1988.

• Brooks, Peter. *Reading for the Plot: Design and Intention in Narrative.* New York: Knopf, 1984.

Cahir, Linda Costanzo. "Narratological Parallels in Joseph Conrad's *Heart of Darkness* and Francis Ford Coppola's *Apocalypse Now*." *Literature/Film Quarterly* 20 (1992): 181–87.

Clifford, James. "On Ethnographic Self-Fashioning: Conrad and Malinowski." *The Predicament of Culture: Twentieth-Century Ethnography, Literature, and Art.* Cambridge, MA: Harvard UP, 1988. 92–113.

DeKoven, Marianne. *Rich and Strange: Gender, History, Modernism.* Princeton: Princeton UP, 1991.

de Lange, Attie and Gail Fincham, eds. *Conrad in Africa: New Essays on "Heart of Darkness".* New York: Columbia UP, 2002.

Denby, David. "Jungle Fever." *New Yorker* 6 Nov. 1995: 118–29.

• Dryden, Linda J. " 'To Boldly Go': Conrad's *Heart of Darkness* and Popular Culture," *Conradiana* 34.3 (2002): 149–70.

• Erdinast-Vulcan, Daphna. *Joseph Conrad and the Modern Temper.* Oxford: Clarendon P, 1991.

Fincham, Gail and Myrtle Hooper, eds. *Under Postcolonial Eyes: Joseph Conrad after Empire.* Rondebosch: U of Cape Town P, 1996.

• Firchow, Peter Edgerly. *Envisioning Africa: Racism and Imperialism in Conrad's* Heart of Darkness. Lexington: UP of Kentucky, 2000.

Fleishman, Avrom. *Conrad's Politics: Community and Anarchy in the Fiction of Joseph Conrad.* Baltimore: Johns Hopkins UP, 1967.

Fleming, Bruce. "Brothers under the Skin: Achebe on *Heart of Darkness*." *College Literature* 19–20 (1992–93): 90–100.

Fogel, Aaron. *Coercion to Speak: Conrad's Poetics of Dialogue.* Cambridge, MA: Harvard UP, 1985.

• Ford, Ford Madox. *Joseph Conrad: A Personal Remembrance.* Boston: Little, Brown, 1924.

• Fothergill, Anthony "Cannibalising Traditions: Representation and Critique in *Heart of Darkness*" in Fincham and Hooper, 93–108.

GoGwilt, Christopher. *The Invention of the West: Joseph Conrad and the Double Mapping of Europe and Empire.* Stanford, CA: Stanford UP, 1995.

Griffith, John W. *Joseph Conrad and the Anthropological Dilemma.* Oxford: Clarendon P, 1995.

• Guerard, Albert J. *Conrad the Novelist.* Cambridge, MA: Harvard UP, 1958.

Hamner, Robert. "Colony, Nationhood and Beyond: Third World Writers and Critics Contend with Joseph Conrad." *World Literature Written in English* 23 (1984): 108–66.

———, ed. *Joseph Conrad: Third World Perspectives.* Washington: Three Continents, 1990.

Hampson, Robert. *Joseph Conrad: Betrayal and Identity.* New York: St. Martin's, 1992.

Harpham, Geoffrey Galt. *One of Us: The Mastery of Joseph Conrad.* Chicago: U of Chicago P, 1996.

Harris, Wilson. "The Frontier on Which *Heart of Darkness* Stands." *Research in African Literature* 12.1 (Spring 1981): 86–93.

Hawkins, Hunt. "Conrad's Critique of Imperialism in *Heart of Darkness*." *PMLA* 94 (March 1979): 286–99.

———. "Conrad's *Heart of Darkness*: Politics and History," *Conradiana* 24.3 (1992): 207–17.

• ———. "The Issue of Racism in *Heart of Darkness*," *Conradiana* 14.3 (1982): 163–71.

———. "Joseph Conrad, Roger Casement, and the Congo Reform Movement." *Journal of Modern Literature* 9, no. 1 (1981–82): 65–80.

———, and Brian W. Shaffer, eds. *Approaches to Teaching Conrad's "Heart of Darkness" and "The Secret Sharer."* New York: Modern Language Association, 2002.

• Hawthorn, Jeremy. *Narrative Technique and Ideological Commitment.* London: Edward Arnold, 1990.

Hay, Eloise Knapp. *The Political Novels of Joseph Conrad.* Chicago: U of Chicago P, 1963.

Henricksen, Bruce. *Nomadic Voices: Conrad and the Subject of Narrative.* Chicago: U of Illinois P, 1992.

Jones, Susan. *Conrad and Women.* Oxford: Clarendon P, 1999.

Kaplan, Carola M. "Colonizers, Cannibals, and the Horror of Good Intentions in Joseph Conrad's *Heart of Darkness*." *Studies in Short Fiction* 34 (1997): 323–33.

Karl, Frederick R., and Laurence Davies, eds. *The Collected Letters of Joseph Conrad.* 6 vols. Cambridge: Cambridge UP, 1983–2002.

Kinkead-Weekes, Mark. "*Heart of Darkness* and the Third World Writer." *Sewanee Review* 98 (1990): 31–49.

Kuesgen, Reinhardt. "Conrad and Achebe: Aspects of the Novel." *World Literatures Written in English* 24 (1984): 27–33.

Levenson, Michael. *Modernism and the Fate of Individuality: Character and Novelistic Form from Conrad to Woolf.* Cambridge: Cambridge UP, 1991.

London, Bette. "Reading Race and Gender in Conrad's Dark Continent." *Criticism* 31 (1989): 235–52.

Lothe, Jakob. *Conrad's Narrative Method.* Oxford: Clarendon P, 1989.

McClure, John. *Conrad and Kipling: The Colonial Fiction.* Cambridge, MA: Harvard UP, 1981.

• Miller, J. Hillis. "Should We Read 'Heart of Darkness'?" in de Lange and Fincham, pp. 21–39.

Mongia, Padmini. "The Rescue: Conrad, Achebe, and the Critics." *Conradiana* 33.2 (2001): 153–63.

Moser, Thomas. *Joseph Conrad: Achievement and Decline.* Cambridge, MA: Harvard UP, 1957.

• Najder, Zdzisław, ed. *Congo Diary and Other Uncollected Pieces.* New York: Doubleday, 1978.

Parry, Benita. *Conrad and Imperialism: Ideological Boundaries and Visionary Frontiers.* London: Macmillan, 1983.

• Roberts, Andrew Michael. *Conrad and Masculinity.* New York: St. Martin's P, 2000.

Robertson, P. J. M. "*Things Fall Apart* and *Heart of Darkness*: A Creative Dialogue." *International Fiction Review* 7.2 (Summer 1980): 106–11.

Roussel, Royal. *The Metaphysics of Darkness.* Baltimore: Johns Hopkins UP, 1971.

• Said, Edward. *Culture and Imperialism.* New York: Knopf, 1993.

———. *Joseph Conrad and the Fiction of Autobiography.* Cambridge, MA: Harvard UP, 1966.

Sarvan, C. P. "Racism and the *Heart of Darkness*." *The International Fiction Review* 7 (1980): 6–10.

• Schneider, Lissa. *Conrad's Narratives of Difference: Not Exactly Tales for Boys.* New York: Routledge, 2003.

Shaffer, Brian W. *The Blinding Torch: Modern British Fiction and the Discourse of Civilization.* Amherst: U of Massachusetts P, 1993.

• Simmons, Alan. "The Language of Atrocity: Representing the Congo of Conrad and Casement" in de Lange and Fincham, pp. 85–106.

Singh, Frances B. "The Colonialistic Bias of *Heart of Darkness,*" *Conradiana* 10 (1978): 41–54.

Stape, John H. *The Cambridge Companion to Joseph Conrad.* Cambridge, UK: Cambridge UP, 1996.

Stewart, Garrett. "Lying as Dying in *Heart of Darkness.*" *PMLA* 95 (1980): 319–31.

• Torgnovnick, Marianna. *Gone Primitive: Savage Intellects, Modern Lives.* Chicago: U of Chicago P, 1990.

• Watt, Ian. *Conrad in the Nineteenth Century.* Berkeley: U of California P, 1979.

———. "Conrad's *Heart of Darkness* and the Critics." *North Dakota Quarterly* 57 (Summer 1989): 5–15.

Watts, Cedric. " 'A Bloody Racist': About Achebe's View of Conrad." *Yearbook of English Studies* 13 (1983): 196–209.

White, Andrea. *Joseph Conrad and the Adventure Tradition: Constructing and Deconstructing the Imperial Subject.* Cambridge, UK: Cambridge UP, 1993.

Wollaeger, Mark. *Joseph Conrad and the Fictions of Skepticism.* Stanford, CA: Stanford UP, 1990.